D1488910

CASTRO

CASTRO

A GRAPHIC NOVEL

REINHARD KLEIST

ARSENAL PULP PRESS ✦ VANCOUVER

CASTRO: A GRAPHIC NOVEL
North American English-language edition (including updated foreword)
published 2015 by Arsenal Pulp Press

Copyright text and illustrations © 2010 by CARLSEN Verlarg GmbH, Hamburg, Germany.
First published in Germany under the title *Castro*.

All rights reserved. No part of this book may be reproduced in any part by any means—graphic, electronic, or mechanical—without the prior written permission of the publisher, except by a reviewer, who may use brief excerpts in a review, or in the case of photocopying in Canada, a license from Access Copyright.

ARSENAL PULP PRESS
Suite 202–211 East Georgia St.
Vancouver, BC V6A 1Z6
Canada
arsenalpulp.com

Cover design by Gerilee McBride
English translation and files provided by Selfmade Hero
Translation of updated foreword by Ivanka Hahnenberger
Translation edited by Susan Safyan
Printed and bound in Canada

Library and Archives Canada Cataloguing in Publication

Kleist, Reinhard, 1970–
[Castro. English]
Castro : a graphic novel / Reinhard Kleist.

Translation of: Castro.
Translated from the German.
ISBN 978-1-55152-594-5 (paperback).—ISBN 978-1-55152-595-2 (epub)

1. Castro, Fidel, 1926– —Comic books, strips, etc. 2. Heads of state—Cuba—Biography—Comic books, strips, etc. 3. Cuba—History—1959–1990—Comic books, strips, etc. 4. Cuba—History—1990– —Comic books, strips, etc. 5. Graphic novels. I. Title. II. Title: Castro. English.

F1788.22.C3K5413 2015   972.91064092   C2015-903463-9
                                                     C2015-903464-7

"In taking power, the revolutionary takes on the injustice of power."

Octavio Paz

FOREWORD
IN THE HAMMOCK WITH FIDEL CASTRO

VOLKER SKIERKA

If there is one figure in modern history whose life especially demands to be told—beyond the parameters of the non-fiction book and documentary film—in the form of a graphic novel, it's that of Fidel Castro. His life story seems to have been taken from a Latin American adventure novel—but the story is not invented, it's true. So true that one couldn't invent it without it seeming implausible.

The Cuban revolutionary leader was and is one of the most interesting and controversial figures in history, who has been both revered and reviled; he is considered both a hero and a devil. Even Che Guevara, the eternal pop icon, would have been nothing without Fidel Castro. There's hardly been a politician in modern times who is as intelligent, educated, and well read; as tall and good-looking; as charismatic and charming; and as well-equipped with a compelling and dangerous instinct for machismo and power as he. Through the power of his words, he has been able to keep both friends and foes in line. Only someone with his unique abilities could take up an armed struggle against a brutal dictatorship that collaborated with the Mafia and was supported by the US, instigate a victorious revolution, and be able to remain in power for decades afterwards. All of this in addition to surviving hundreds of murder plots against him. Even after he dies, Castro will be ensured a special place in history, no matter how thwarted and embattled his regime may have been. Throughout the decades, numerous authors have been challenged by this unique character, but now someone has dared to tell the story of this historic leader of the people in the form of a graphic novel.

The origins of this book date back a few years. I met Reinhard Kleist at a café in Berlin-Kreuzberg, not far from Schlesisches Tor. He talked of an idea then; he was planning a trip to Cuba and asked me, as a Castro biographer, how I viewed the political situation there since Fidel Castro had become ill and stepped down as head of state. The result of Kleist's trip was his fine graphic novel entitled *Havana* (yet to be published in English). It shows great empathy in depicting the daily lives and difficult conditions of primarily young Cubans under an outdated model of Caribbean socialism. *Havana* was, in some ways, Kleist's "overture" to this book on Fidel Castro and the Cuban Revolution. Only after he had "warmed up" with *Havana* and developed a feeling for the Cuban way of life did he dare attempt the big picture—with a biographical portrait of the *Líder Máximo* who has ruled his country for more than five decades with a stern hand. The Jesuit student and son of a large landowner drew his strength and power from the fact that he was the first Cuban *caudillo* or ultimate political-military leader. As his country's "David," he freed his nation from its dependence on the American "Goliath," and for the first time in their history, helped his people acquire national identity and dignity. Pushed from its earliest days into the open arms of the Soviet Union by the narrow-minded American government of Republican President Dwight D. Eisenhower and his vice president Richard Nixon—who even then liked to occupy the gray zone of political legitimacy—Castro was, from then on, able to play a leading role in international politics. With an iron will, he managed to survive generations of American presidents, Soviet secretary-generals, heads of state, democrats, potentates, and even God's representatives on Earth, until he became the longest-ruling head of state of the twentieth century. After the triumphant revolution, Castro's government confiscated all American property in Cuba. This was followed by the failed Bay of Pigs invasion by Cuban-exile mercenaries under the auspices of the CIA, and it brought about the stationing of Soviet nuclear missiles in Cuba in 1962, almost provoking World War III. But perhaps worst of all for the US is the fact that Castro's regime has survived for decades despite the US's lengthy and historically unparalleled embargo. It seems apparent that the Great Power of the North will never forgive these numerous, deep-rooted humiliations in the eyes of history and the world—not even after his death.

It was after a presentation of *Havana* at Vattenfall Reading Days 2009 in Hamburg, Germany, that Reinhard Kleist and his editor Michael Groenewald from the German publishing house Carlsen asked me to assist in an advisory capacity on this book. This I naturally did with great pleasure, not only because I'd been studying the Cuban Comandante for many years for my biography of him, but because this was a new, completely different, and very exciting literary form of biography. The narrative form of a comic book creates room for fictitious truths and conclusions forbidden to non-fiction books. Pointedly placed quotes, dramatic pacing, and a condensed depiction of the course of events can contribute to a deeply felt truth with compelling verisimilitude.

The manner in which Reinhard Kleist has managed to artistically and narratively translate his ideas and our conversations and discussions on Castro and the Cuban Revolution is outstanding. The character of Karl Mertens, introduced to guide the reader through events, could come from any developed country—Germany, the US, Spain, England, or France. Anything but politically astute at the start, the protagonist turns from journalist into idealist, quickly giving up the political neutrality of his profession. Meanwhile, a love story unfolds. To illustrate the crimes perpetrated by the Batista regime of the 1950s, which Castro fought against, Kleist employs the device of drawing Karl Mertens's attention to the Cuban Revolution by using an actual Castro interview conducted by Herbert Matthews that appeared in the *New York Times*. Karl then sets off to meet the leader, who also grants him an interview—ranting while lying in a hammock within his jungle stronghold in the Sierra Maestra. This is how Mertens falls under the spell of events, not only succumbing to the charms of the revolution and its leader, but also to those of a young female revolutionary. Such tales of foreigners (among them journalists and even a rogue CIA agent) making the pilgrimage to Cuba and, if only temporarily, signing up for the revolution, are genuine. Thus Kleist is accurate in disconcertingly caricaturing that type of privileged, First World intellectual, someone all too eager to succumb to the social romanticism of a radical movement in a foreign culture.

The depiction of both Castro's physical appearance and his character over half a century are fascinatingly authentic and succeed in being as exciting as they are entertaining. As well, the representation of place, and the atmosphere of the Zeitgeist during the various phases of the revolution's life and survival—and of its players—demonstrate the accuracy and painstaking precision, the sincerity and authenticity of Kleist's story.

One of the last friends to remain by Castro to the end, the writer Gabriel García Márquez, once wrote in an essay about him, "One thing is certain: wherever he may be, however and with whomever, Fidel Castro is there to win. I don't think there's anyone in this world who could be a worse loser. His attitude in the face of defeat, even in the most minimal actions of everyday life, would seem to obey a private logic: He does not even admit it, and does not have a minute's peace until he succeeds in inverting the terms and converting it into victory." Just as García Márquez characterized him, Kleist has made his Castro accessible to us in this book. At the same time, a soft humor emanates from the speech bubbles and stories throughout; an agreeably ironic distance between the author and Fidel Castro resonates in this narrative, thus making Castro involuntarily distance himself from himself, and this increases our own learning and reading pleasure. In the end, it remains open as to how this story will continue.

UPDATE TO THE FORWORD
JULY 2015

It can be left up to the reader's imagination as to how the story plays out after the epilogue—whether from the point of view of the venerable Karl Merten or of one of Castro's many sons or grandsons or as though the reader stands invisibly by the side of the *Líder Máximo* himself as he looks out over the sea and murmurs through his beard, "Now everything's going to be different!" It may continue from the perspective of Fidel's younger brother Raúl Castro, who took office in 2006, assuring Cuba's elders that he would do all he could to preserve Castro's revolutionary work during his term. Since Fidel Castro's complete withdrawal to his retreat in the village of Siboney in the west of Havana—except for the occasional "Look, I'm still alive!" photo-op—Raúl has made modest steps toward opening the country's economy. Democratic reforms are still on hold, even if the opposition is less persecuted than before. There is also a tendency toward filling positions in important party and government organizations, previously held by the old guard, with a younger generation of loyal individuals. This new guard, which has risen from the old, is meant to keep the system more or less on course in its post-Castro era. Whether it succeeds or not is another matter. Since the 1990s, the military, commanded by Raúl Castro from the time of the revolution, has successfully played an important role in government. Active and former military officers have been placed in many key positions in state and state-owned enterprises. They may have swapped their military uniforms for jeans and a *guayabera* [the cotton short-sleeved shirt worn by men], but they have not changed their ethos or their well-developed ability to maintain the benefits and privileges of rank. It can therefore be assumed that, in the transition from the Castro era to a new unknown future, the military will continue to hold tightly to the strings of political change. This may explain why Cuba has, for quite some time, quietly slipped into what is essentially a military dictatorship *sui generis*.

While the aged "Davids" in Havana, exhausted by endless infighting, kept themselves busy with the rules left behind as their legacy and with storm-proofing their life's work for the future, the "Goliath" in the North—in the guise of the comparatively young President Barack Obama—apparently felt fresh and strong enough to press the "reset" button, as they say in this computer age. On December 17, 2014, nearly six years after Obama's inauguration, a new era in American-Cuban relations began with a pre-Christmas bang. The day after a forty-five minute phone call, the US President in Washington and Raúl Castro in Havana simultaneously announced on television that they were in negotiations to re-establish the diplomatic relations broken off in 1961.

In front of an astonished global audience, Obama said that the fifty-year-old US policy "has failed to advance our interests," and that "neither the American nor the Cuban people are well served by a rigid policy that's rooted in events that took place before most of us were born." And then, a few weeks later, Fidel, now aged if still revered, could only watch from home—like millions of other TV viewers—as his brother and the US President not only shook hands in Panama but also sat down to talk, using interpreters, in front of the whole world, as cameras flashed during this carefully staged event. Pope Francis, a "Jesuit brother" of Fidel Castro's, is to thank for the reason and common sense that are finally being applied to this absurd chapter in world politics. Since the first papal visit in January 1998 by John Paul II, the Catholic Church in Cuba has been playing an increasingly influential role behind the scenes. Further bolstered through a visit by Pope Benedict XVI in 2012, it has subtly supported dissidents and has become, next to the Communist Party, one of the country's most important social and political and, often discreetly, economic bodies. This is also evidenced by the fact that when Pope Francis goes to Cuba in September 2015, he will be the third pope to have visited the island in seventeen years.

Since the United States took Cuba off the State Sponsors of Terrorism list at the end of May 2015—on which it had been placed by the Reagan administration in 1982—the road was paved for the first exchange of ambassadors since 1961 (indeed, on July 1, 2015, the US and Cuba announced the re-opening of embassies in Washington and Havana) and the eventual lifting of the more than fifty-year-old embargo. For both sides, this embargo has always been a blessing and a curse. It has been a curse because it seriously affected Cuba's economic development and has prevented the US and other countries from doing business with the Caribbean island. It has been a blessing for the US because it demonstrated their moral fortitude—and who really has held the hammer—and for Castro's Cuba because it was used to cover up its own mismanagement. But in the end, it was just a weathered bulwark, gnawed away by the ravages of time, which had allowed both sides, for far too long, to dig in and make themselves comfortable behind that anachronistic policy.

Maybe these are the thoughts and insights that the readers of Reinhard Kleist's *Castro* or even that the frail former *Líder Máximo* himself would write into the end of the story. How you feel about Fidel Castro determines how you imagine the end of the story: will it be a happy or a sad ending? Kleist's graphic novel is written so that when the reader finishes the book, either type of ending is imaginable. In real life, however, it'll take longer before it is clear which way Cuba will go. And as for Castro himself, like the old protagonists of fairy tales: whether or not he is dead or alive, the legend will live on.

VOLKER SKIERKA is the author of the non-fiction book *Fidel Castro: Eine Biografie* (Rowohlt Taschenbuch) which has been published in several languages including English (*Fidel Castro: A Biography*; Polity Press, Cambridge). He also co-wrote the ARD/WDR documentary *Fidel Castro— Ewiger revolutionär* (*Fidel Castro: Eternal Revolutionary*), which has been sold in more than thirty countries.

HAVANA, 1960

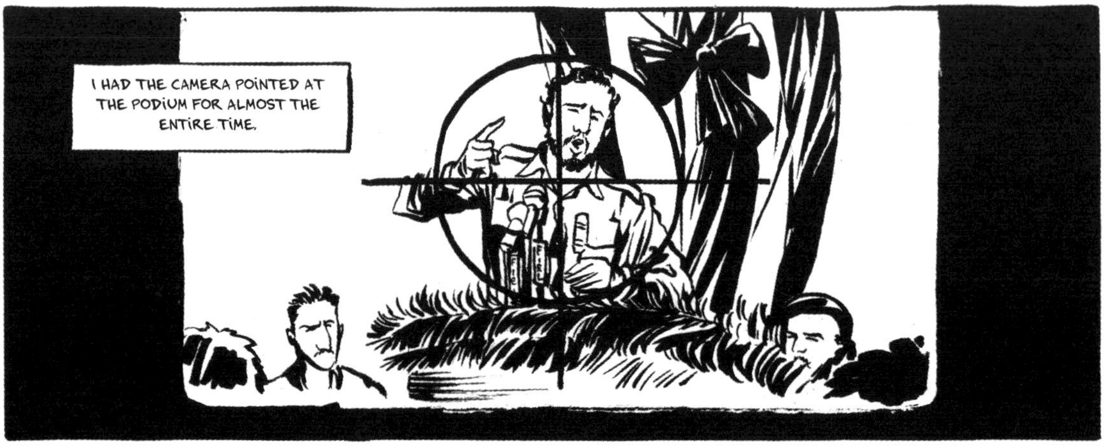
I HAD THE CAMERA POINTED AT THE PODIUM FOR ALMOST THE ENTIRE TIME.

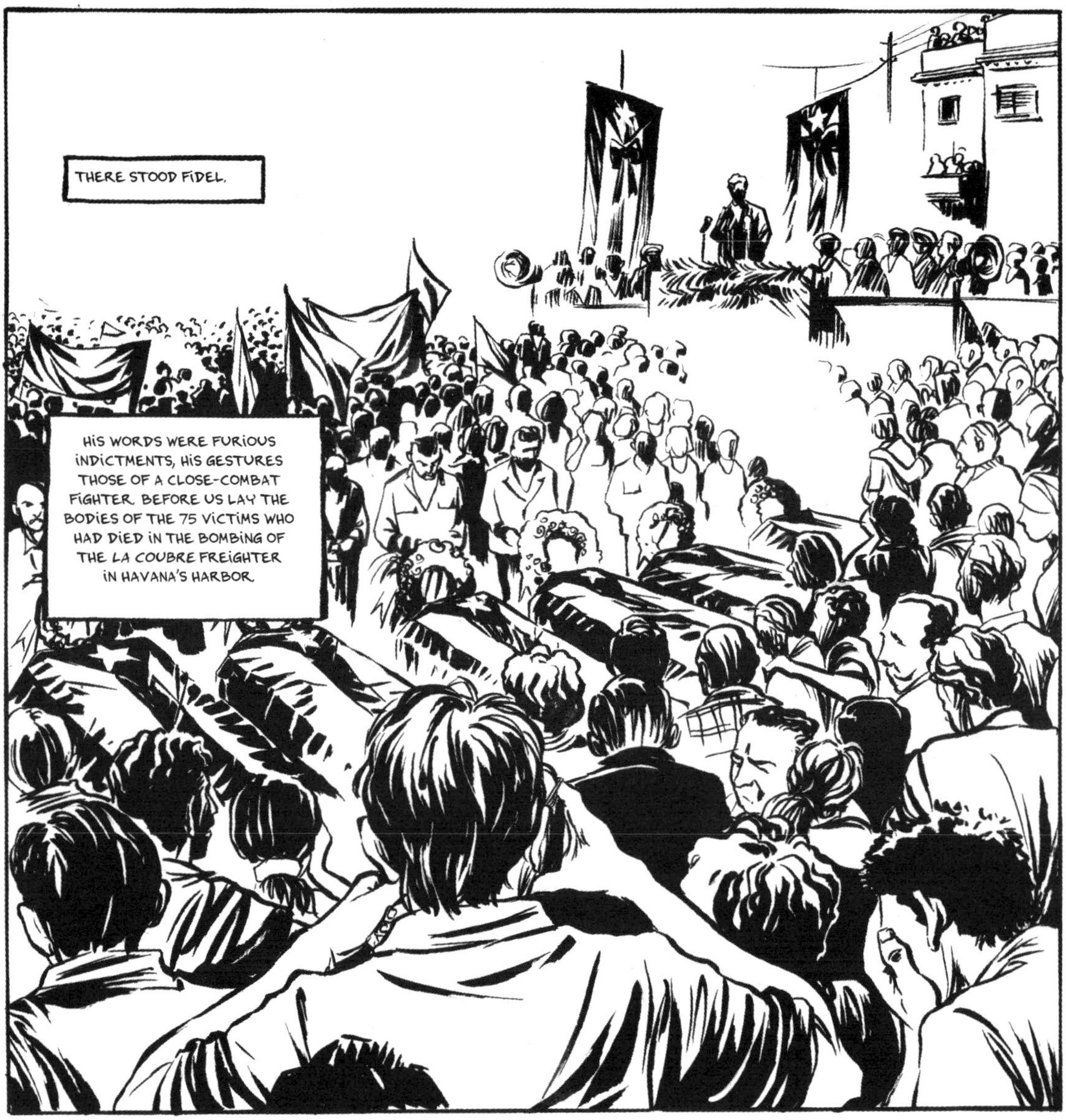
THERE STOOD FIDEL.
HIS WORDS WERE FURIOUS INDICTMENTS, HIS GESTURES THOSE OF A CLOSE-COMBAT FIGHTER. BEFORE US LAY THE BODIES OF THE 75 VICTIMS WHO HAD DIED IN THE BOMBING OF THE *LA COUBRE* FREIGHTER IN HAVANA'S HARBOR.

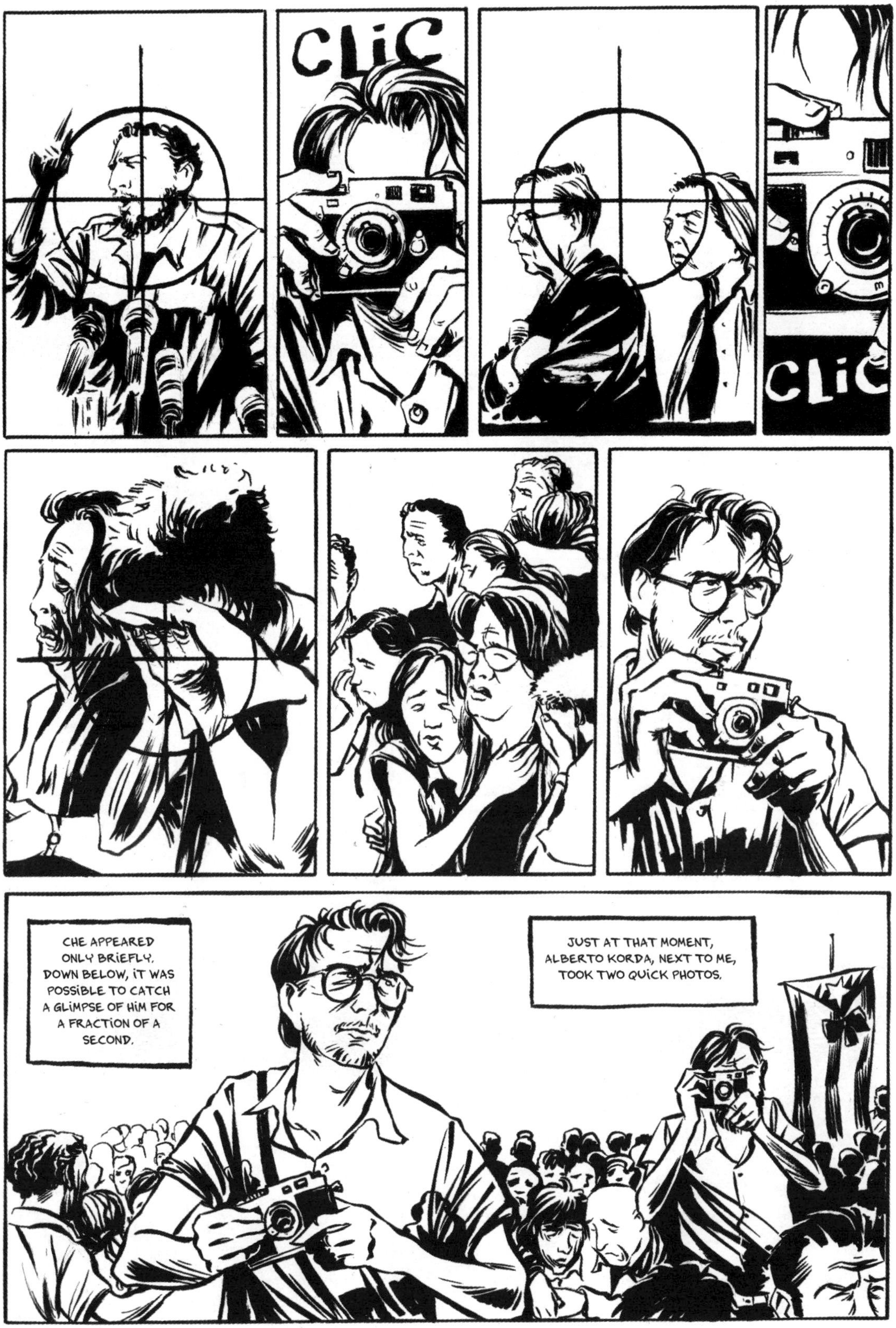
CLIC
CLIC
CHE APPEARED ONLY BRIEFLY. DOWN BELOW, IT WAS POSSIBLE TO CATCH A GLIMPSE OF HIM FOR A FRACTION OF A SECOND.
JUST AT THAT MOMENT, ALBERTO KORDA, NEXT TO ME, TOOK TWO QUICK PHOTOS.

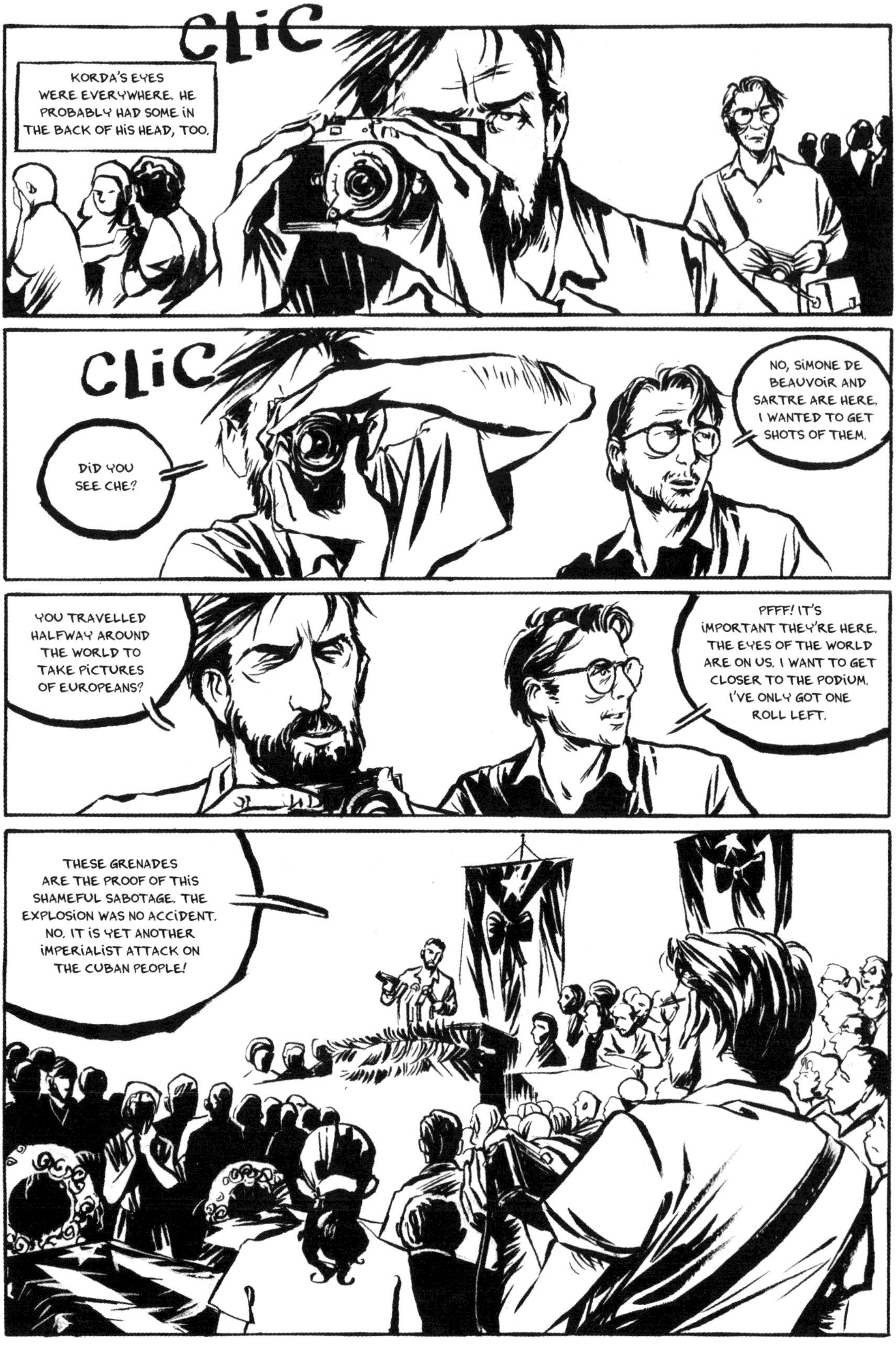
CLIC
KORDA'S EYES WERE EVERYWHERE. HE PROBABLY HAD SOME IN THE BACK OF HIS HEAD, TOO.
CLIC
DID YOU SEE CHE?
NO, SIMONE DE BEAUVOIR AND SARTRE ARE HERE. I WANTED TO GET SHOTS OF THEM.
YOU TRAVELLED HALFWAY AROUND THE WORLD TO TAKE PICTURES OF EUROPEANS?
PFFF! IT'S IMPORTANT THEY'RE HERE. THE EYES OF THE WORLD ARE ON US. I WANT TO GET CLOSER TO THE PODIUM. I'VE ONLY GOT ONE ROLL LEFT.
THESE GRENADES ARE THE PROOF OF THIS SHAMEFUL SABOTAGE. THE EXPLOSION WAS NO ACCIDENT. NO, IT IS YET ANOTHER IMPERIALIST ATTACK ON THE CUBAN PEOPLE!

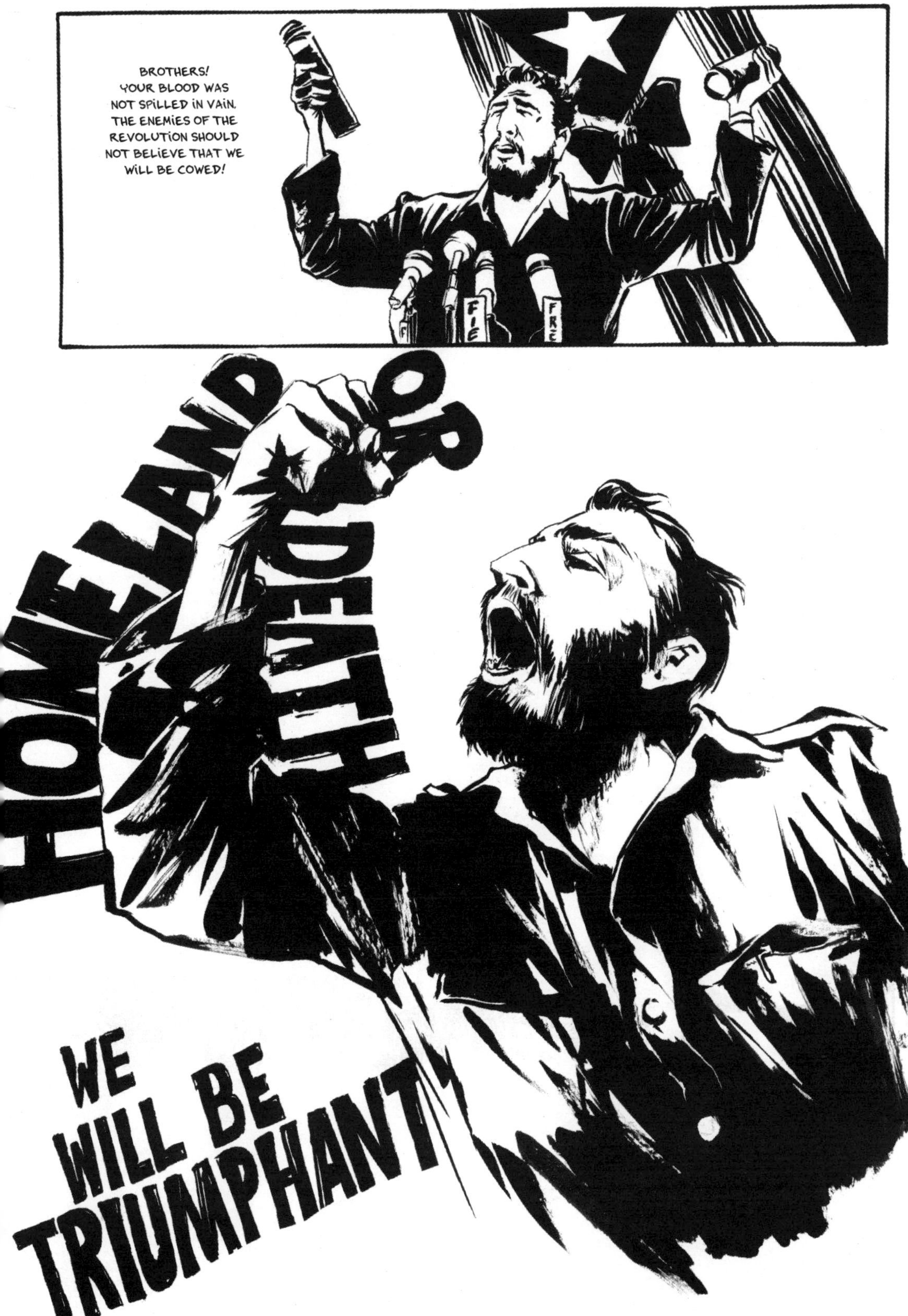
BROTHERS! YOUR BLOOD WAS NOT SPILLED IN VAIN. THE ENEMIES OF THE REVOLUTION SHOULD NOT BELIEVE THAT WE WILL BE COWED!
HOMELAND OR DEATH
WE WILL BE TRIUMPHANT

CHAPTER 1

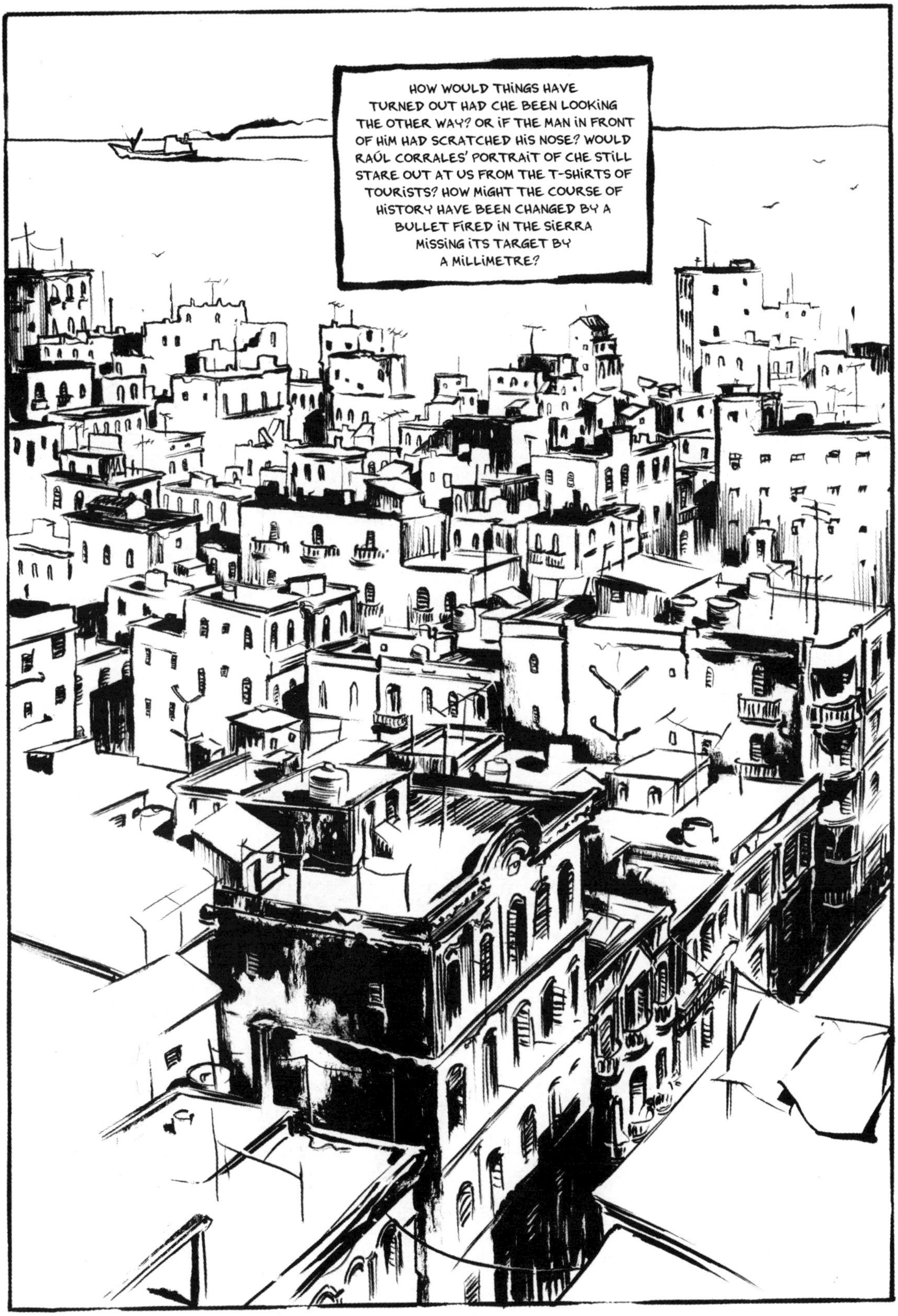
HOW WOULD THINGS HAVE TURNED OUT HAD CHE BEEN LOOKING THE OTHER WAY? OR IF THE MAN IN FRONT OF HIM HAD SCRATCHED HIS NOSE? WOULD RAÚL CORRALES' PORTRAIT OF CHE STILL STARE OUT AT US FROM THE T-SHIRTS OF TOURISTS? HOW MIGHT THE COURSE OF HISTORY HAVE BEEN CHANGED BY A BULLET FIRED IN THE SIERRA MISSING ITS TARGET BY A MILLIMETRE?

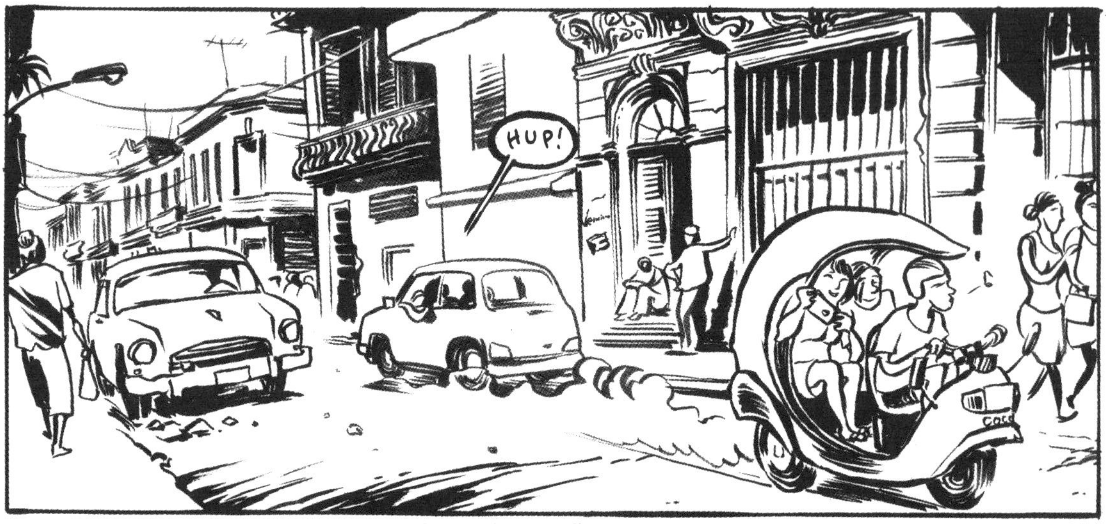
HUP!
COCO

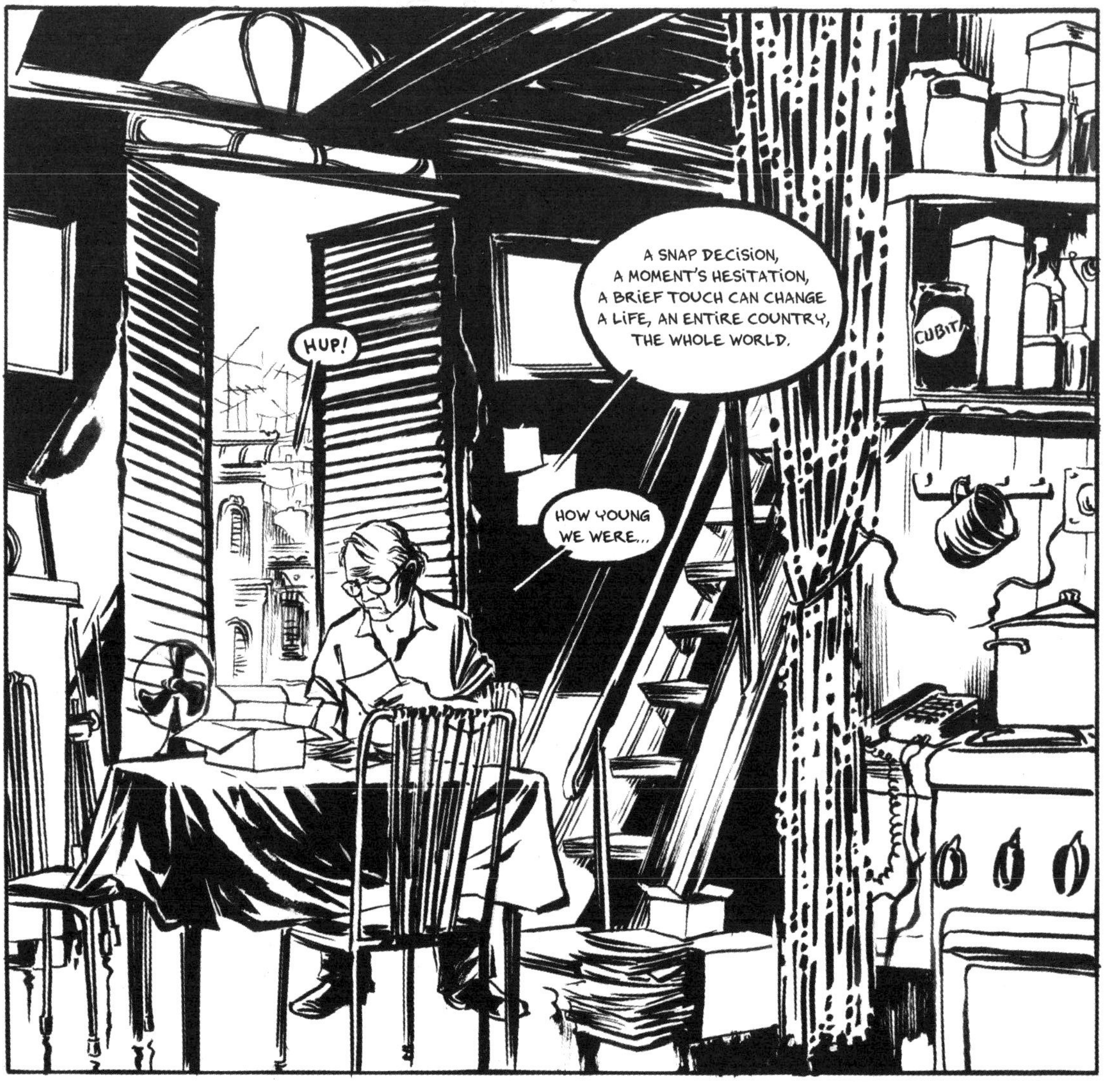
HUP!
A SNAP DECISION, A MOMENT'S HESITATION, A BRIEF TOUCH CAN CHANGE A LIFE, AN ENTIRE COUNTRY, THE WHOLE WORLD.
HOW YOUNG WE WERE...
CUBITA

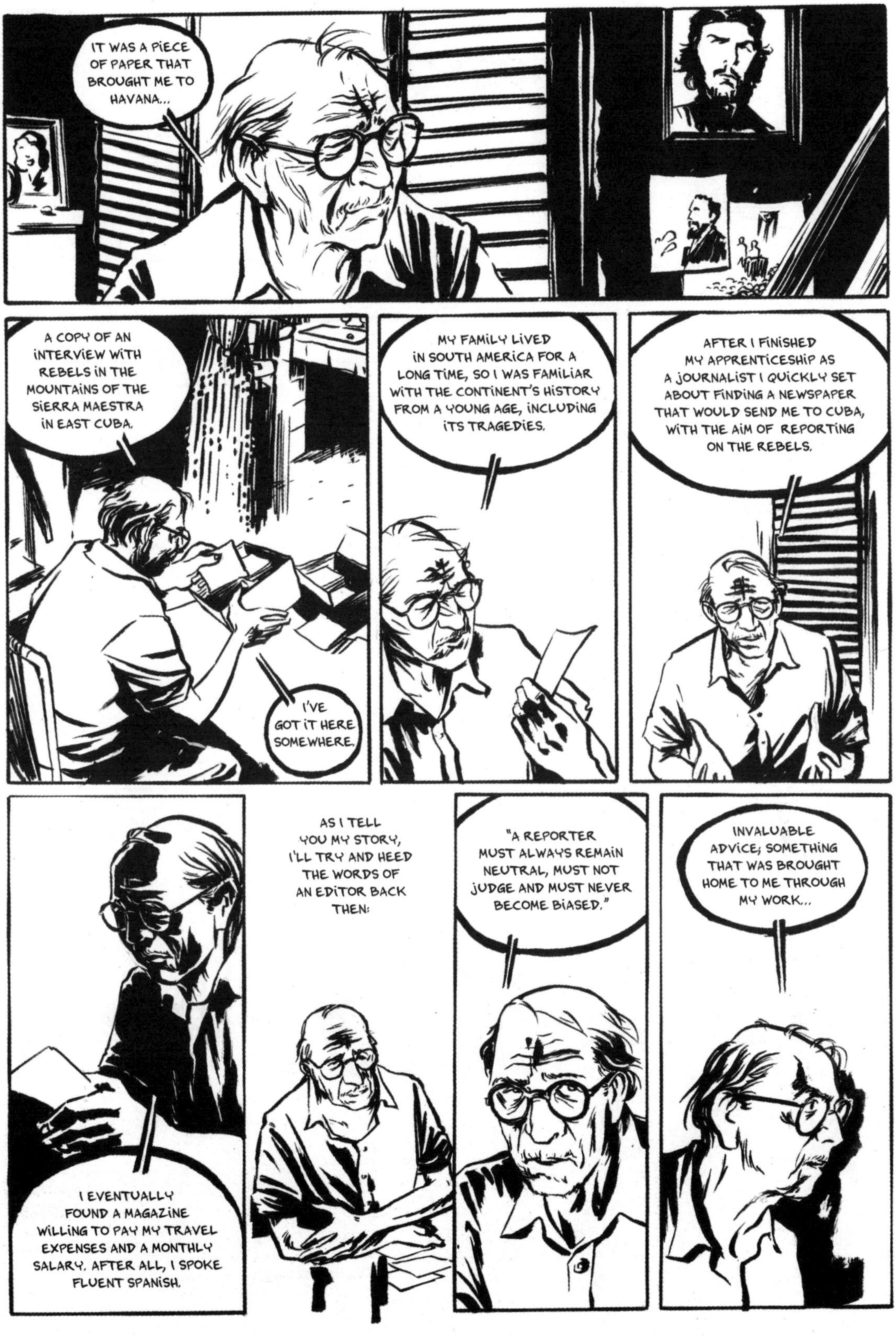

IT WAS A PIECE OF PAPER THAT BROUGHT ME TO HAVANA...
A COPY OF AN INTERVIEW WITH REBELS IN THE MOUNTAINS OF THE SIERRA MAESTRA IN EAST CUBA.
I'VE GOT IT HERE SOMEWHERE.
MY FAMILY LIVED IN SOUTH AMERICA FOR A LONG TIME, SO I WAS FAMILIAR WITH THE CONTINENT'S HISTORY FROM A YOUNG AGE, INCLUDING ITS TRAGEDIES.
AFTER I FINISHED MY APPRENTICESHIP AS A JOURNALIST I QUICKLY SET ABOUT FINDING A NEWSPAPER THAT WOULD SEND ME TO CUBA, WITH THE AIM OF REPORTING ON THE REBELS.
I EVENTUALLY FOUND A MAGAZINE WILLING TO PAY MY TRAVEL EXPENSES AND A MONTHLY SALARY. AFTER ALL, I SPOKE FLUENT SPANISH.
AS I TELL YOU MY STORY, I'LL TRY AND HEED THE WORDS OF AN EDITOR BACK THEN:
"A REPORTER MUST ALWAYS REMAIN NEUTRAL, MUST NOT JUDGE AND MUST NEVER BECOME BIASED."
INVALUABLE ADVICE; SOMETHING THAT WAS BROUGHT HOME TO ME THROUGH MY WORK...

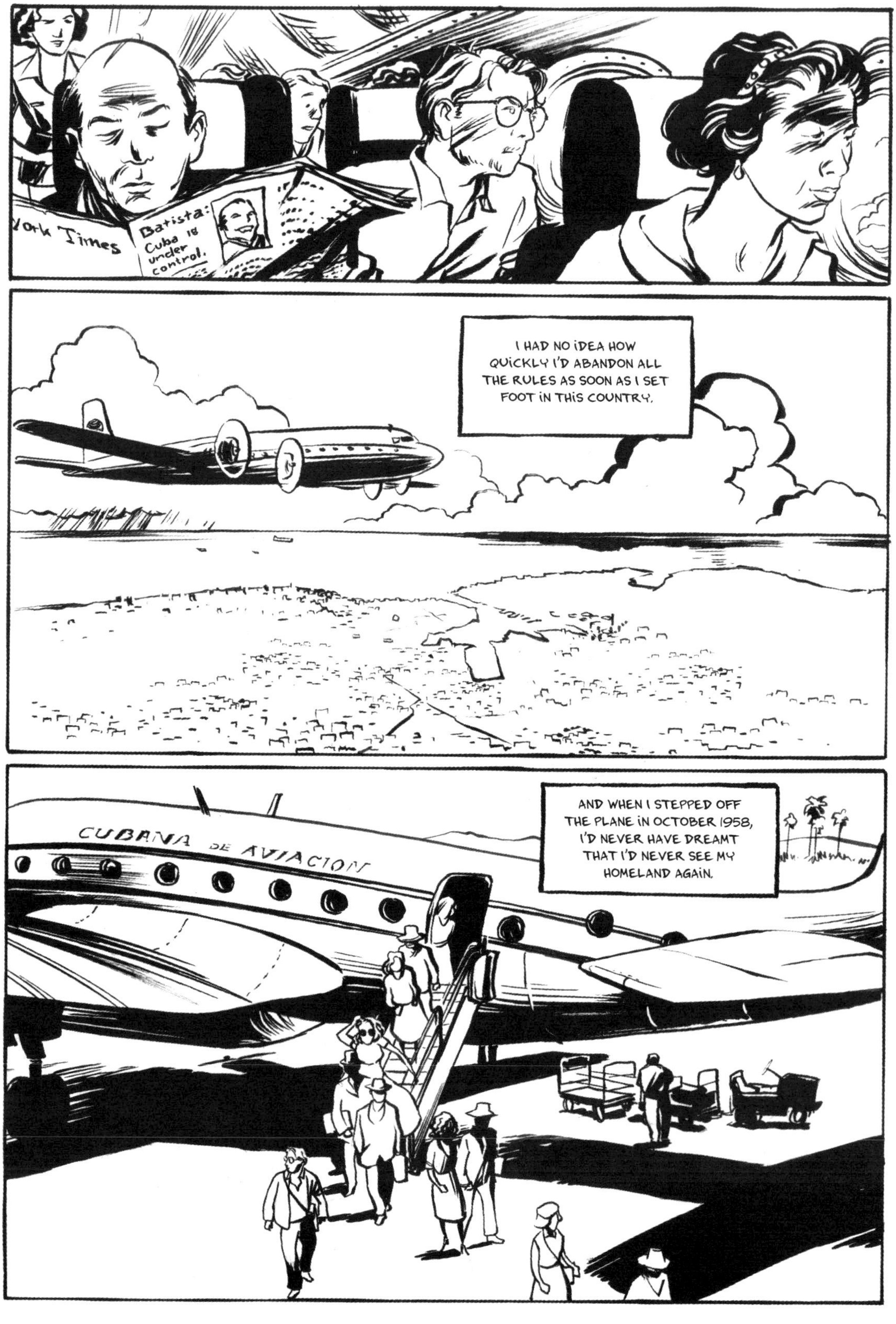
York Times
Batista: Cuba is under control.
I HAD NO IDEA HOW QUICKLY I'D ABANDON ALL THE RULES AS SOON AS I SET FOOT IN THIS COUNTRY.
CUBANA DE AVIACION
AND WHEN I STEPPED OFF THE PLANE IN OCTOBER 1958, I'D NEVER HAVE DREAMT THAT I'D NEVER SEE MY HOMELAND AGAIN.

GET IN, HOM-BRE!

DO YOU KNOW A CHEAP AND CLEAN HOTEL?

50 MINUTOS a MIAMI a vi EL 26 CUBANA

Rivero HOY

A LOT OF SOLDIERS ABOUT.

THE POWERS THAT BE ARE SLOWLY GETTING WORRIED. THE REBELS ALREADY CONTROL THE EAST, WHATEVER THE LIES IN THE PAPERS SAY.

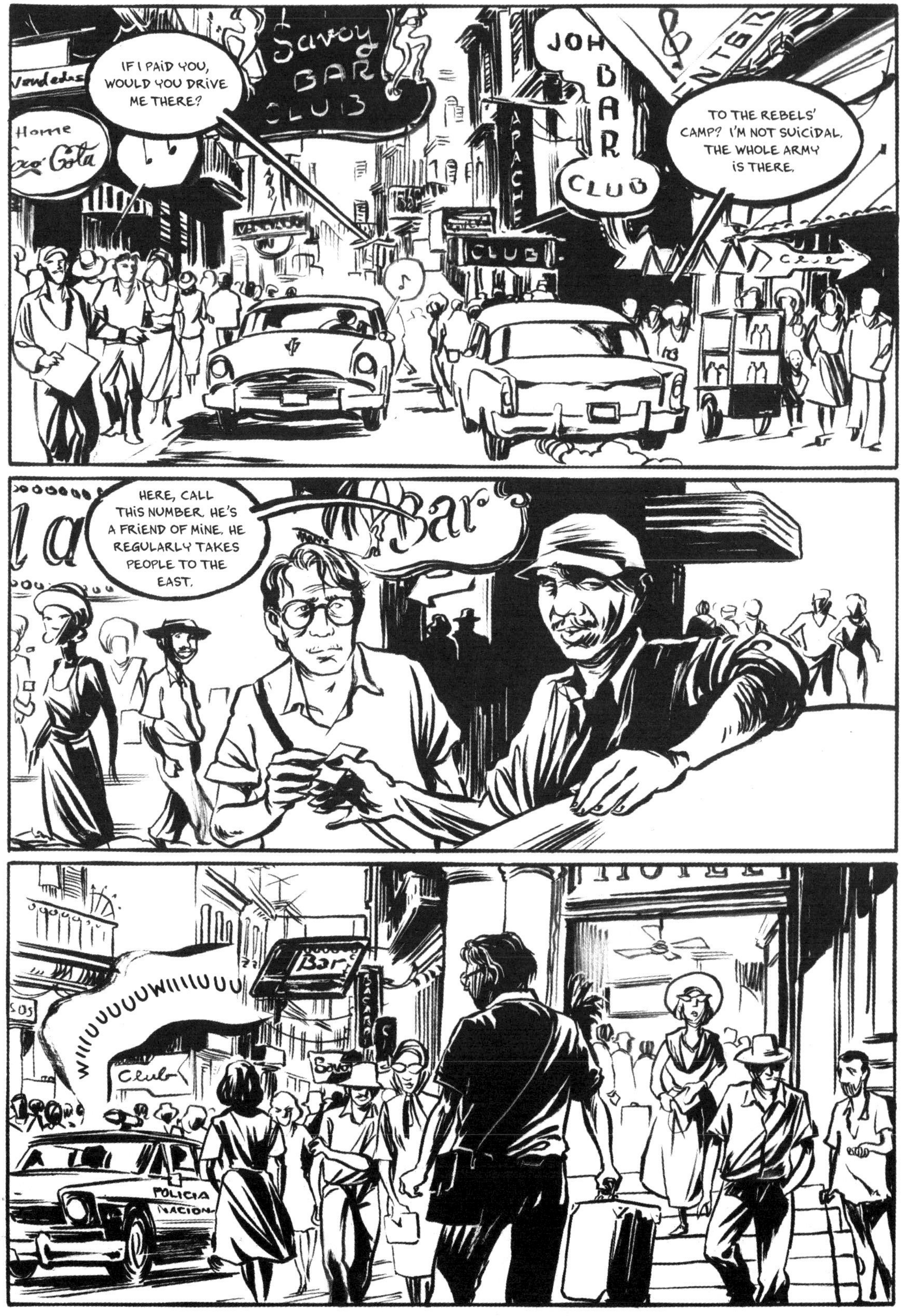
IF I PAID YOU, WOULD YOU DRIVE ME THERE?
TO THE REBELS' CAMP? I'M NOT SUICIDAL. THE WHOLE ARMY IS THERE.
HERE, CALL THIS NUMBER. HE'S A FRIEND OF MINE. HE REGULARLY TAKES PEOPLE TO THE EAST.
WIIIUUUUWIIIUUU
POLICIA
NACION

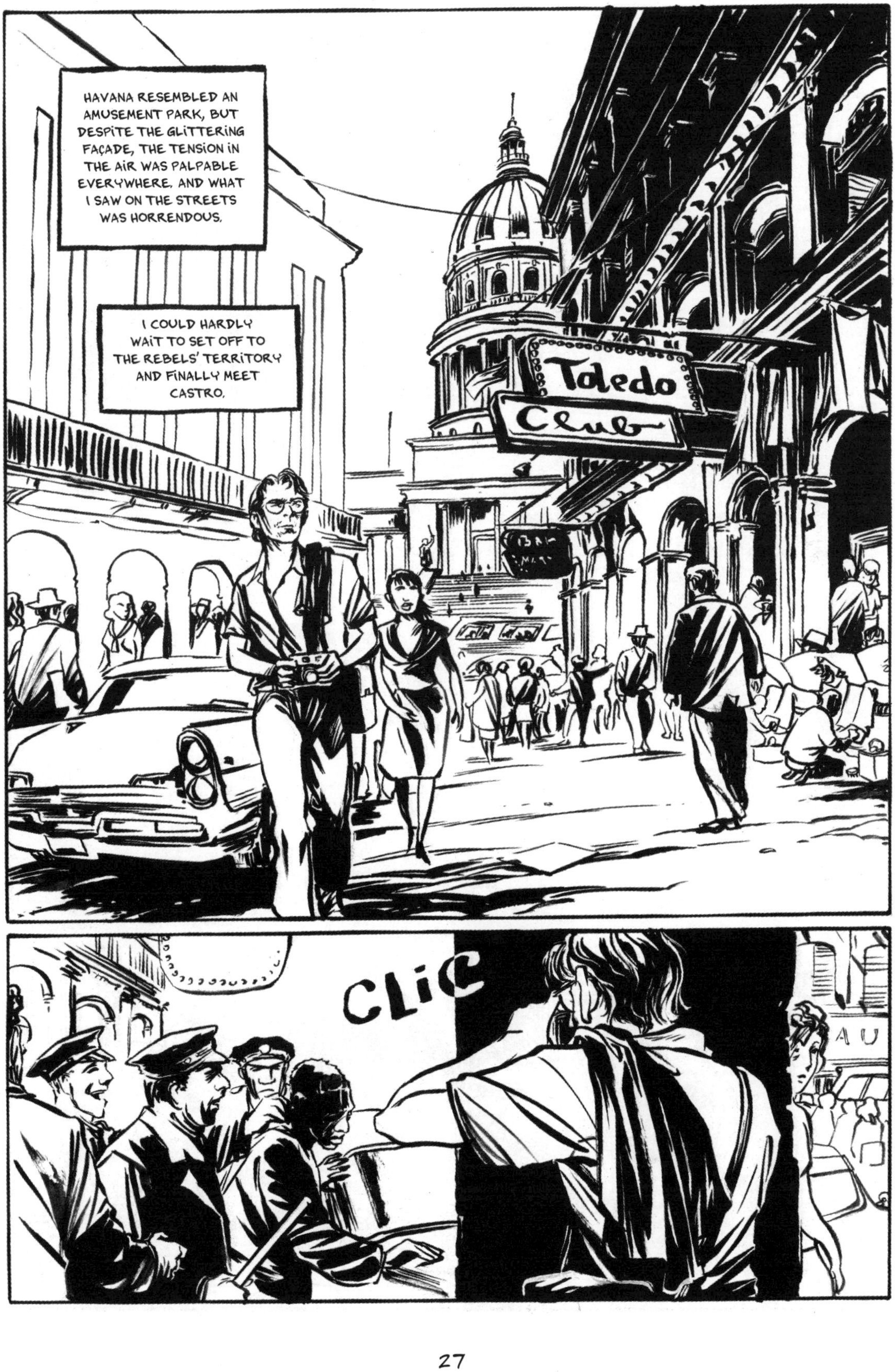
HAVANA RESEMBLED AN AMUSEMENT PARK, BUT DESPITE THE GLITTERING FAÇADE, THE TENSION IN THE AIR WAS PALPABLE EVERYWHERE, AND WHAT I SAW ON THE STREETS WAS HORRENDOUS.
I COULD HARDLY WAIT TO SET OFF TO THE REBELS' TERRITORY AND FINALLY MEET CASTRO.
Toledo
Club
CLIC

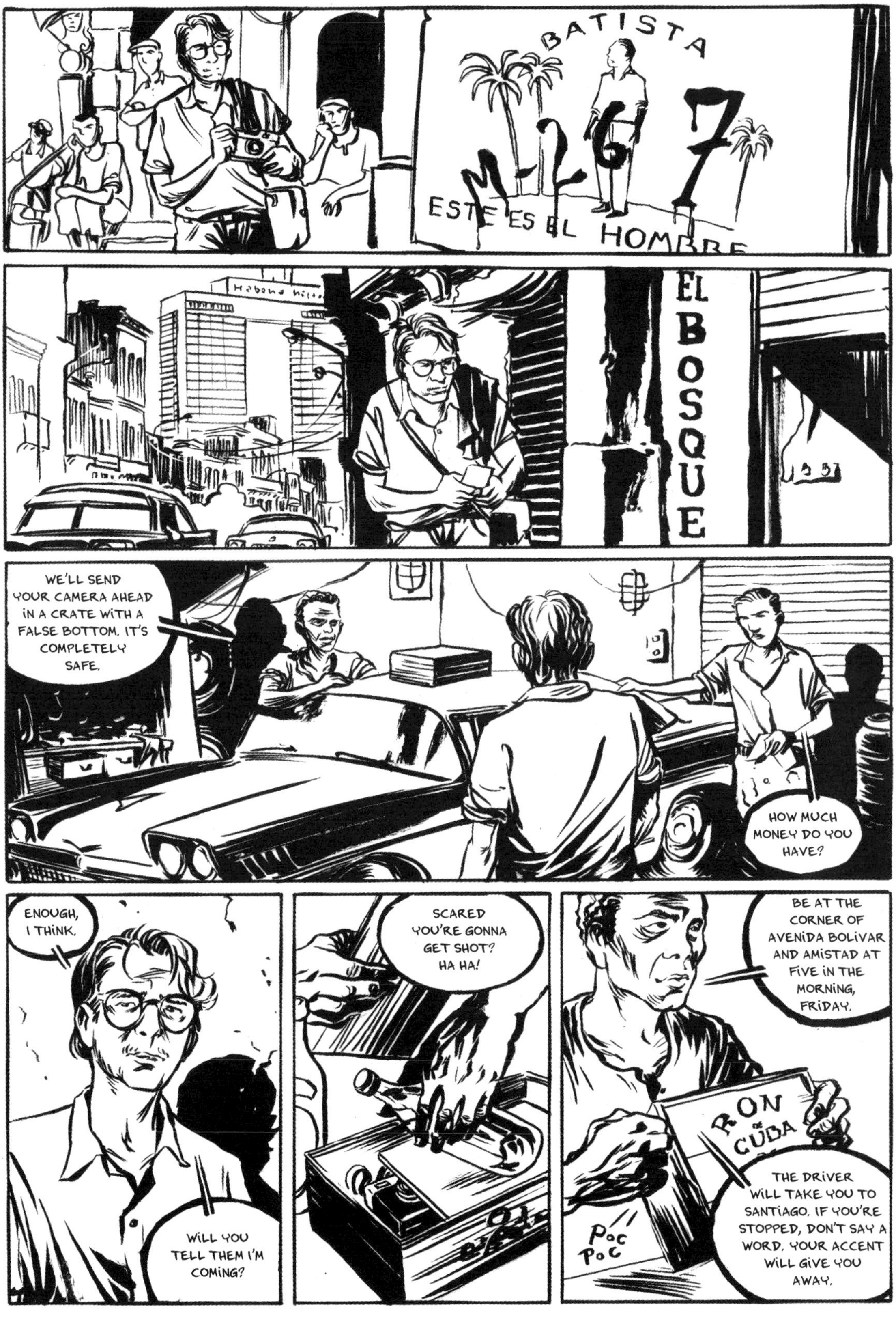
BATISTA
M-26-7
ESTE ES EL HOMBRE
EL BOSQUE
WE'LL SEND YOUR CAMERA AHEAD IN A CRATE WITH A FALSE BOTTOM. IT'S COMPLETELY SAFE.
HOW MUCH MONEY DO YOU HAVE?
ENOUGH, I THINK.
WILL YOU TELL THEM I'M COMING?
SCARED YOU'RE GONNA GET SHOT? HA HA!
BE AT THE CORNER OF AVENIDA BOLIVAR AND AMISTAD AT FIVE IN THE MORNING, FRIDAY.
RON CUBA
POC POC
THE DRIVER WILL TAKE YOU TO SANTIAGO. IF YOU'RE STOPPED, DON'T SAY A WORD. YOUR ACCENT WILL GIVE YOU AWAY.

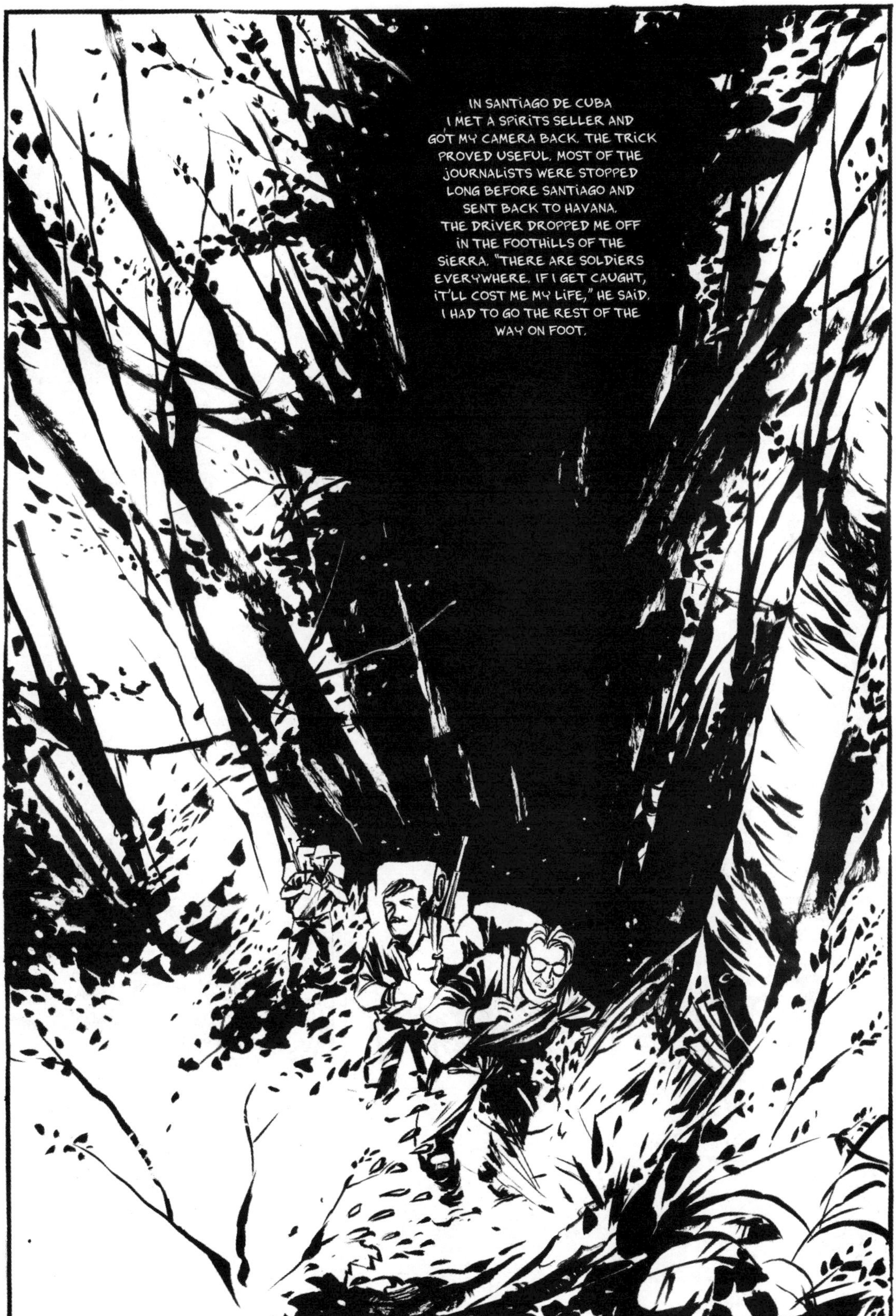
IN SANTIAGO DE CUBA I MET A SPIRITS SELLER AND GOT MY CAMERA BACK. THE TRICK PROVED USEFUL. MOST OF THE JOURNALISTS WERE STOPPED LONG BEFORE SANTIAGO AND SENT BACK TO HAVANA. THE DRIVER DROPPED ME OFF IN THE FOOTHILLS OF THE SIERRA. "THERE ARE SOLDIERS EVERYWHERE. IF I GET CAUGHT, IT'LL COST ME MY LIFE," HE SAID. I HAD TO GO THE REST OF THE WAY ON FOOT.

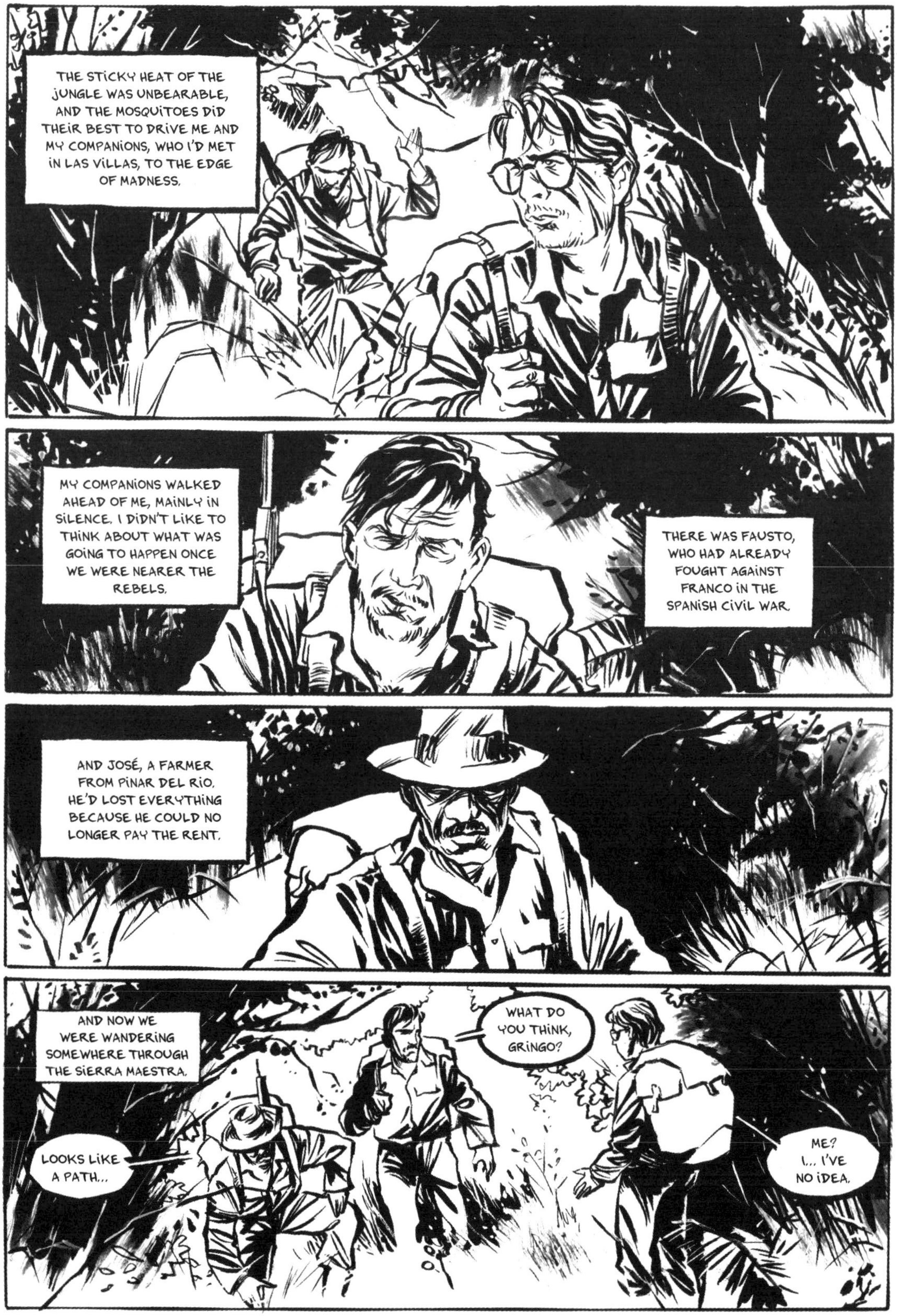
THE STICKY HEAT OF THE JUNGLE WAS UNBEARABLE, AND THE MOSQUITOES DID THEIR BEST TO DRIVE ME AND MY COMPANIONS, WHO I'D MET IN LAS VILLAS, TO THE EDGE OF MADNESS.
MY COMPANIONS WALKED AHEAD OF ME, MAINLY IN SILENCE. I DIDN'T LIKE TO THINK ABOUT WHAT WAS GOING TO HAPPEN ONCE WE WERE NEARER THE REBELS.
THERE WAS FAUSTO, WHO HAD ALREADY FOUGHT AGAINST FRANCO IN THE SPANISH CIVIL WAR.
AND JOSÉ, A FARMER FROM PINAR DEL RIO. HE'D LOST EVERYTHING BECAUSE HE COULD NO LONGER PAY THE RENT.
AND NOW WE WERE WANDERING SOMEWHERE THROUGH THE SIERRA MAESTRA.
WHAT DO YOU THINK, GRINGO?
LOOKS LIKE A PATH...
ME? I... I'VE NO IDEA.

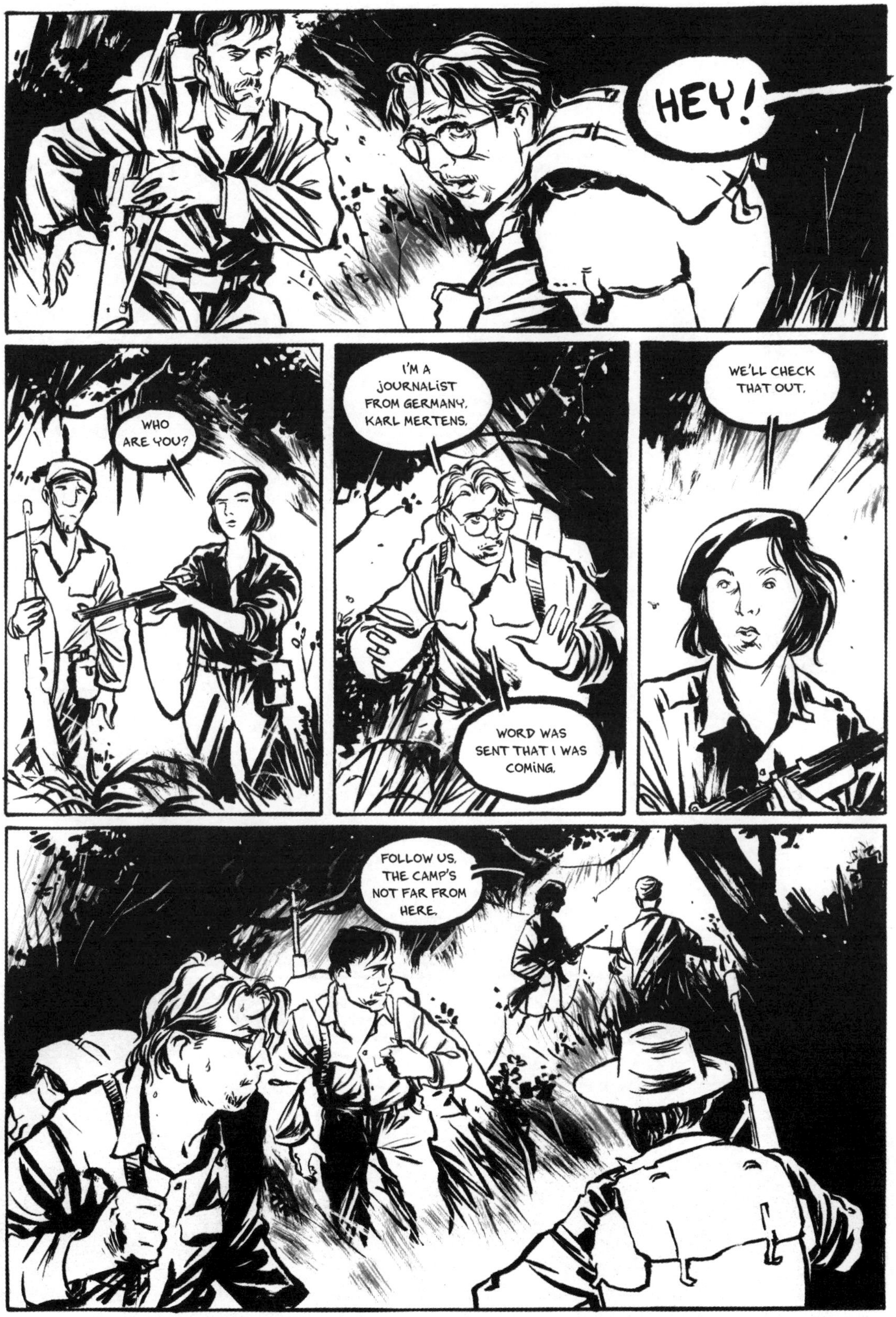
HEY!
WHO ARE YOU?
I'M A JOURNALIST FROM GERMANY, KARL MERTENS.
WORD WAS SENT THAT I WAS COMING.
WE'LL CHECK THAT OUT.
FOLLOW US, THE CAMP'S NOT FAR FROM HERE.

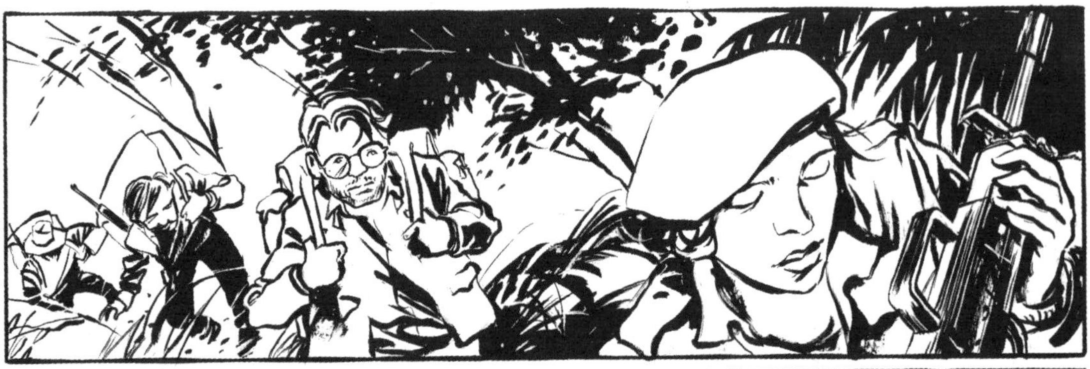

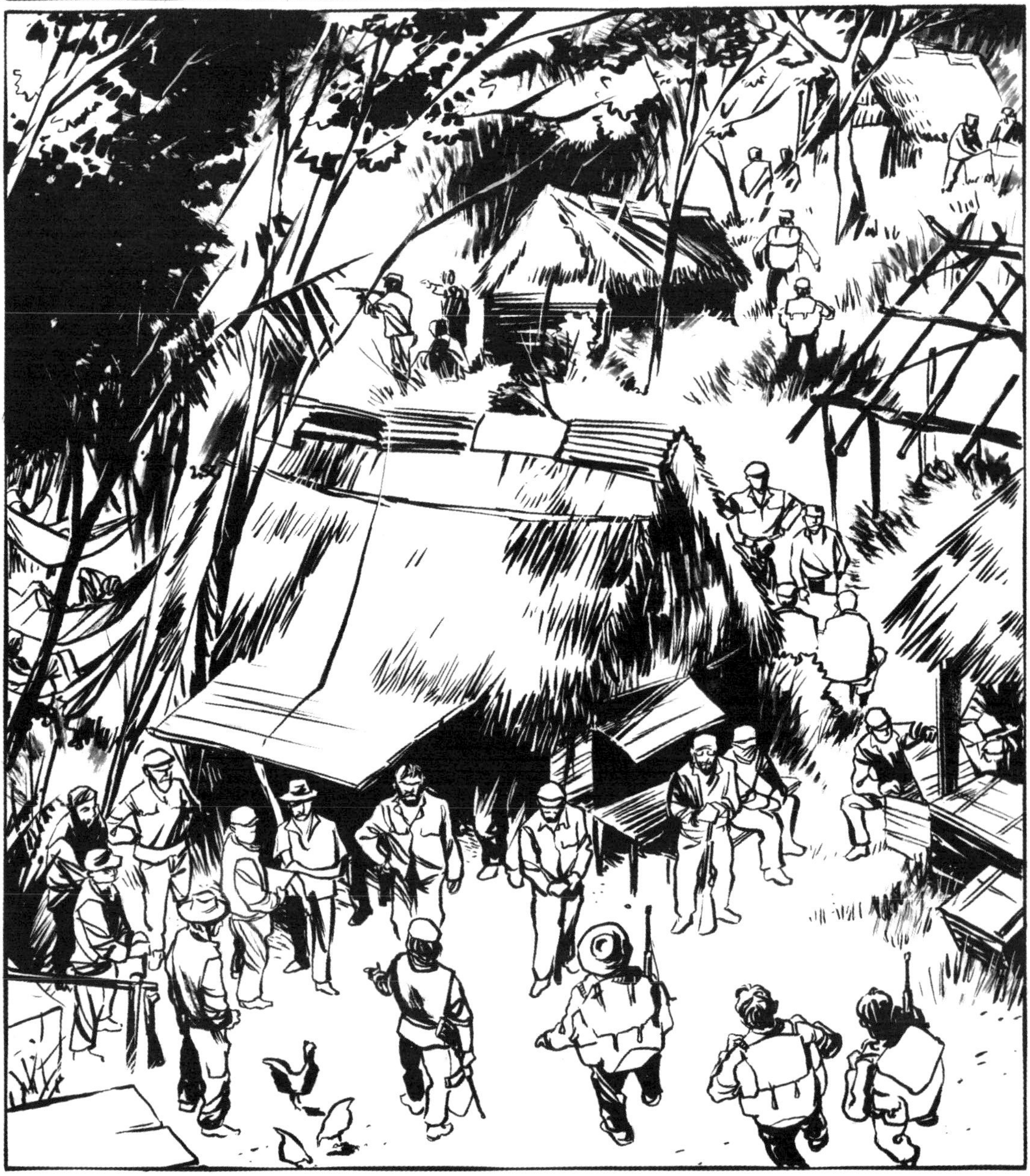

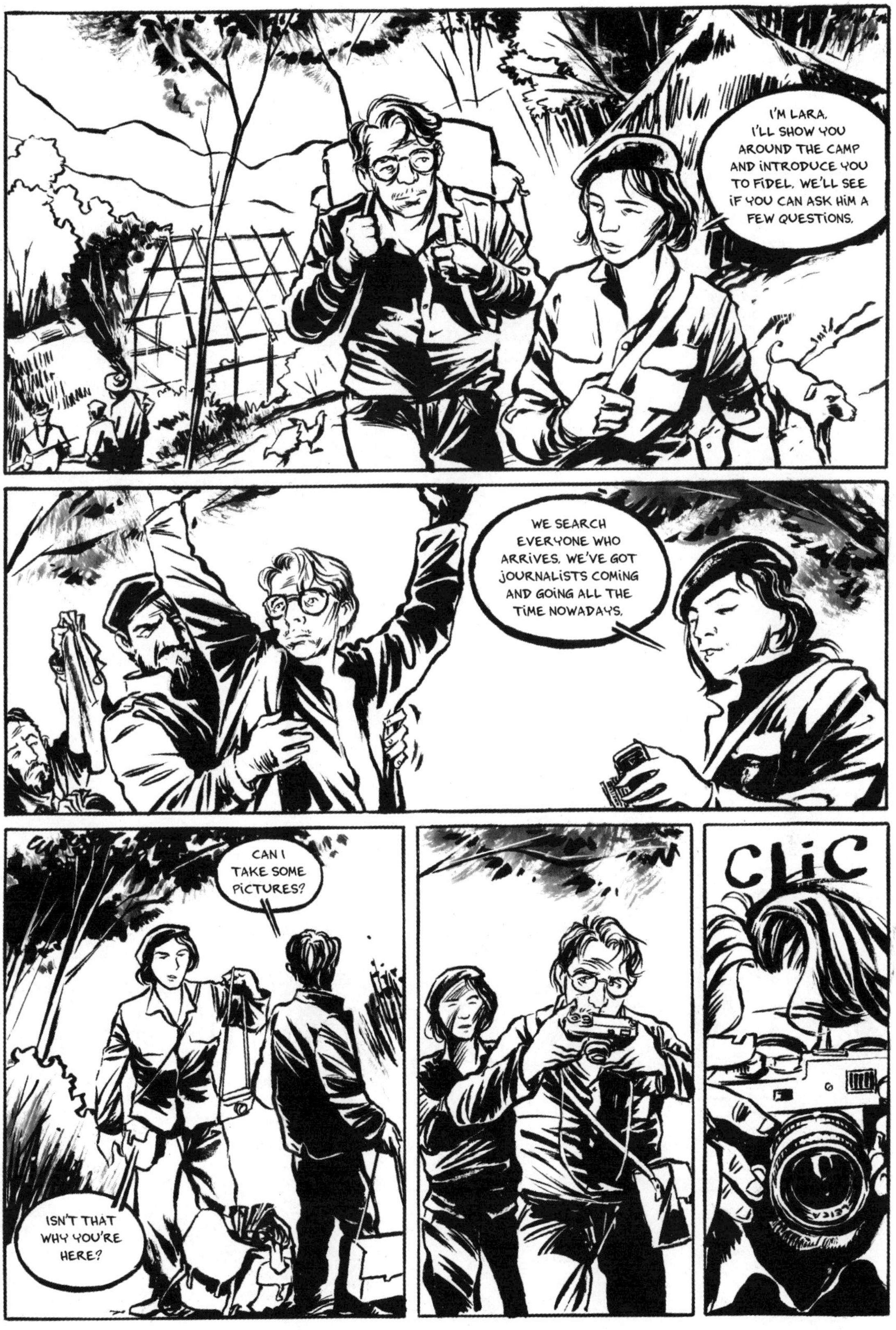
I'M LARA. I'LL SHOW YOU AROUND THE CAMP AND INTRODUCE YOU TO FIDEL. WE'LL SEE IF YOU CAN ASK HIM A FEW QUESTIONS.
WE SEARCH EVERYONE WHO ARRIVES. WE'VE GOT JOURNALISTS COMING AND GOING ALL THE TIME NOWADAYS.
CAN I TAKE SOME PICTURES?
ISN'T THAT WHY YOU'RE HERE?
CLIC

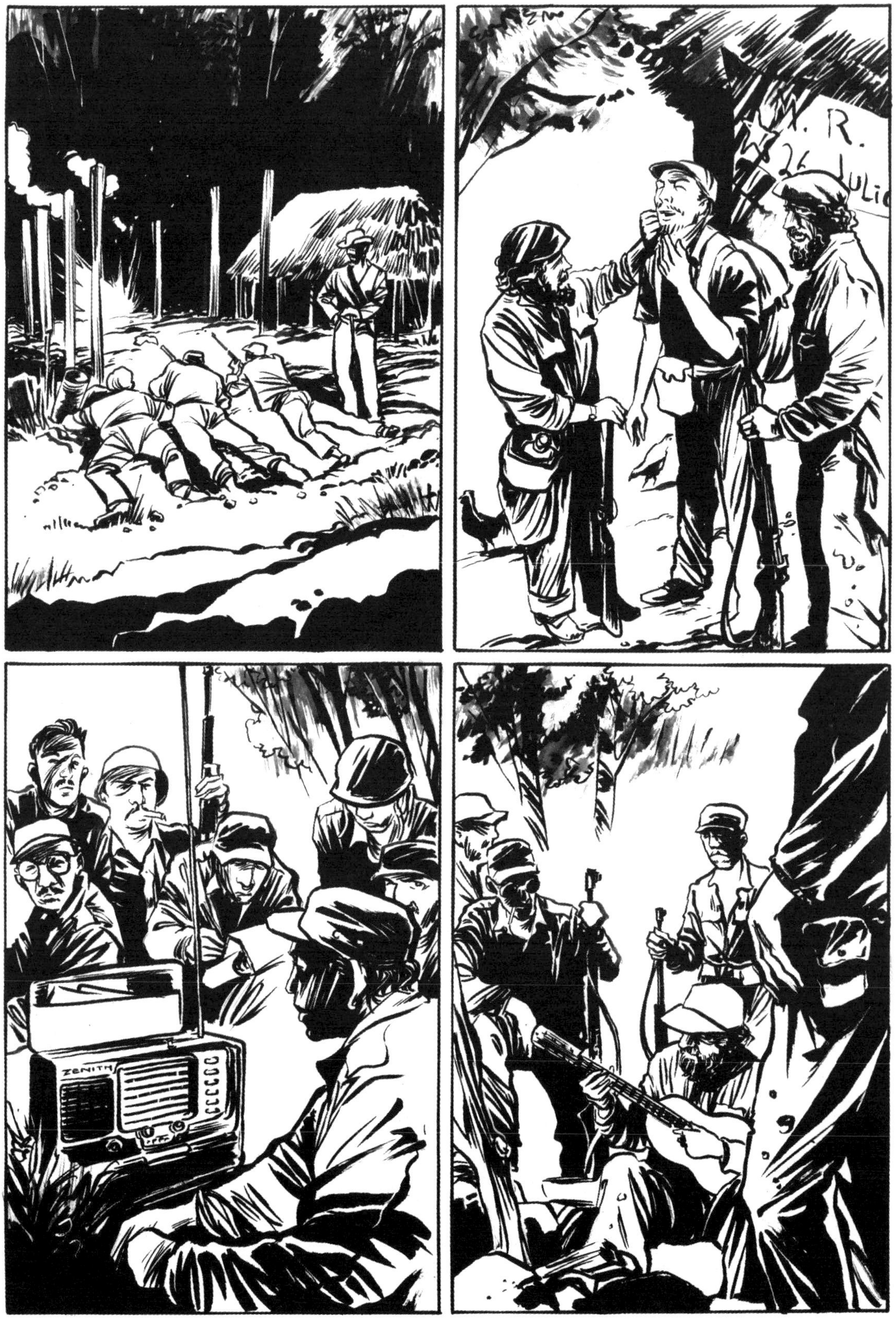
ZENITH

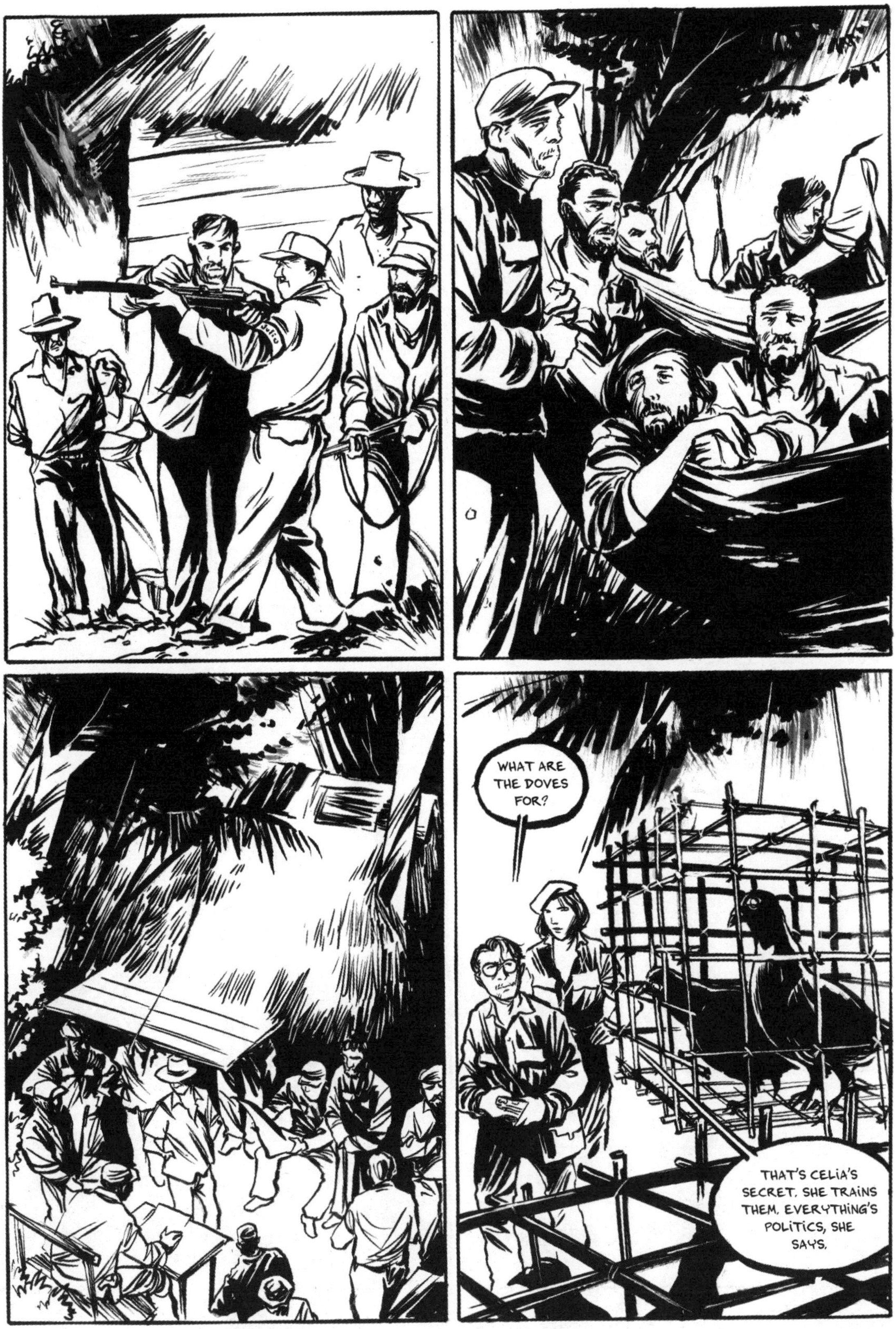
WHAT ARE THE DOVES FOR?
THAT'S CELIA'S SECRET. SHE TRAINS THEM. EVERYTHING'S POLITICS, SHE SAYS.

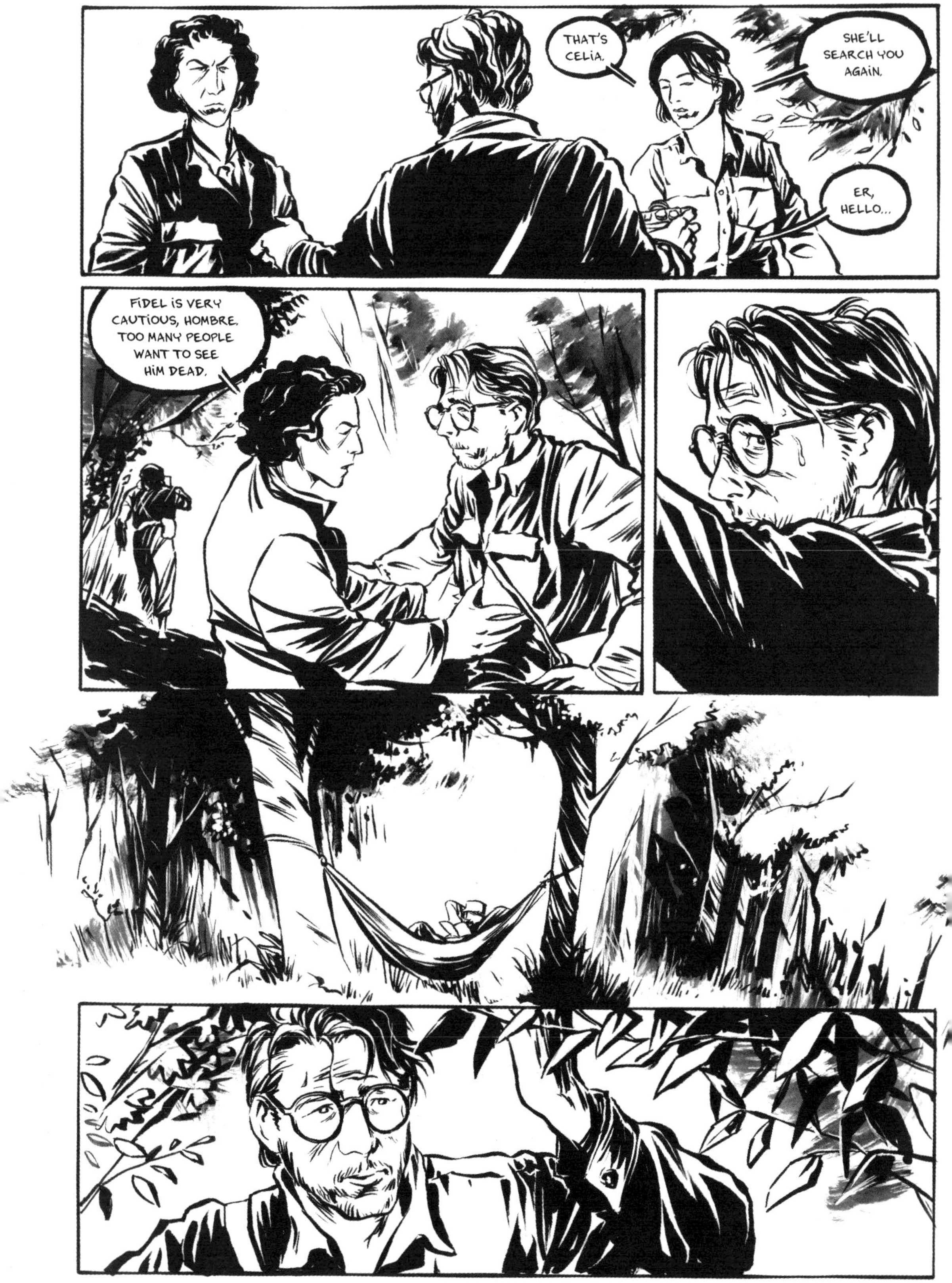
THAT'S CELIA.
SHE'LL SEARCH YOU AGAIN.
ER, HELLO...
FIDEL IS VERY CAUTIOUS, HOMBRE. TOO MANY PEOPLE WANT TO SEE HIM DEAD.

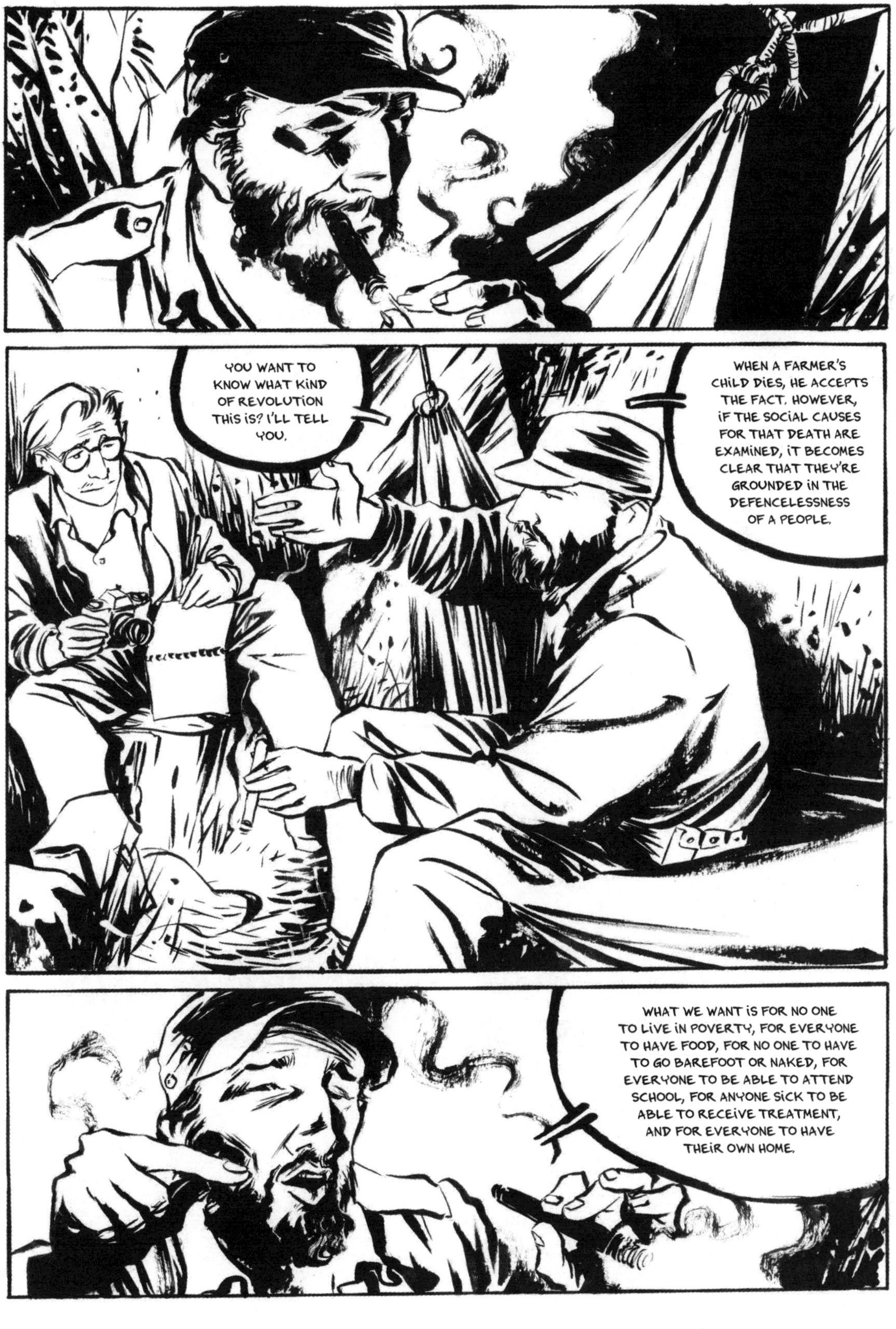
YOU WANT TO KNOW WHAT KIND OF REVOLUTION THIS IS? I'LL TELL YOU.
WHEN A FARMER'S CHILD DIES, HE ACCEPTS THE FACT. HOWEVER, IF THE SOCIAL CAUSES FOR THAT DEATH ARE EXAMINED, IT BECOMES CLEAR THAT THEY'RE GROUNDED IN THE DEFENCELESSNESS OF A PEOPLE.
WHAT WE WANT IS FOR NO ONE TO LIVE IN POVERTY, FOR EVERYONE TO HAVE FOOD, FOR NO ONE TO HAVE TO GO BAREFOOT OR NAKED, FOR EVERYONE TO BE ABLE TO ATTEND SCHOOL, FOR ANYONE SICK TO BE ABLE TO RECEIVE TREATMENT, AND FOR EVERYONE TO HAVE THEIR OWN HOME.

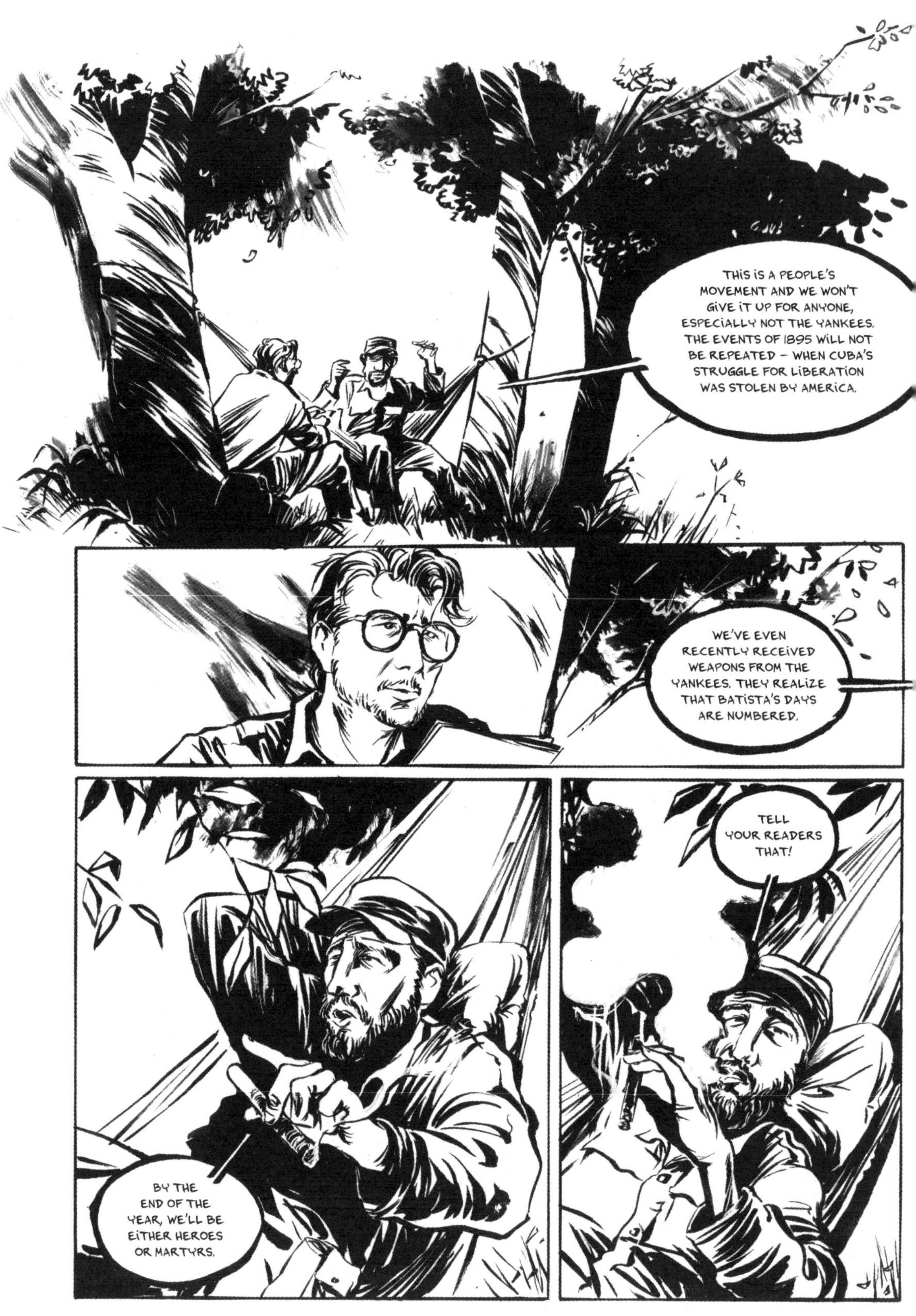
THIS IS A PEOPLE'S MOVEMENT AND WE WON'T GIVE IT UP FOR ANYONE, ESPECIALLY NOT THE YANKEES. THE EVENTS OF 1895 WILL NOT BE REPEATED – WHEN CUBA'S STRUGGLE FOR LIBERATION WAS STOLEN BY AMERICA.
WE'VE EVEN RECENTLY RECEIVED WEAPONS FROM THE YANKEES. THEY REALIZE THAT BATISTA'S DAYS ARE NUMBERED.
BY THE END OF THE YEAR, WE'LL BE EITHER HEROES OR MARTYRS.
TELL YOUR READERS THAT!

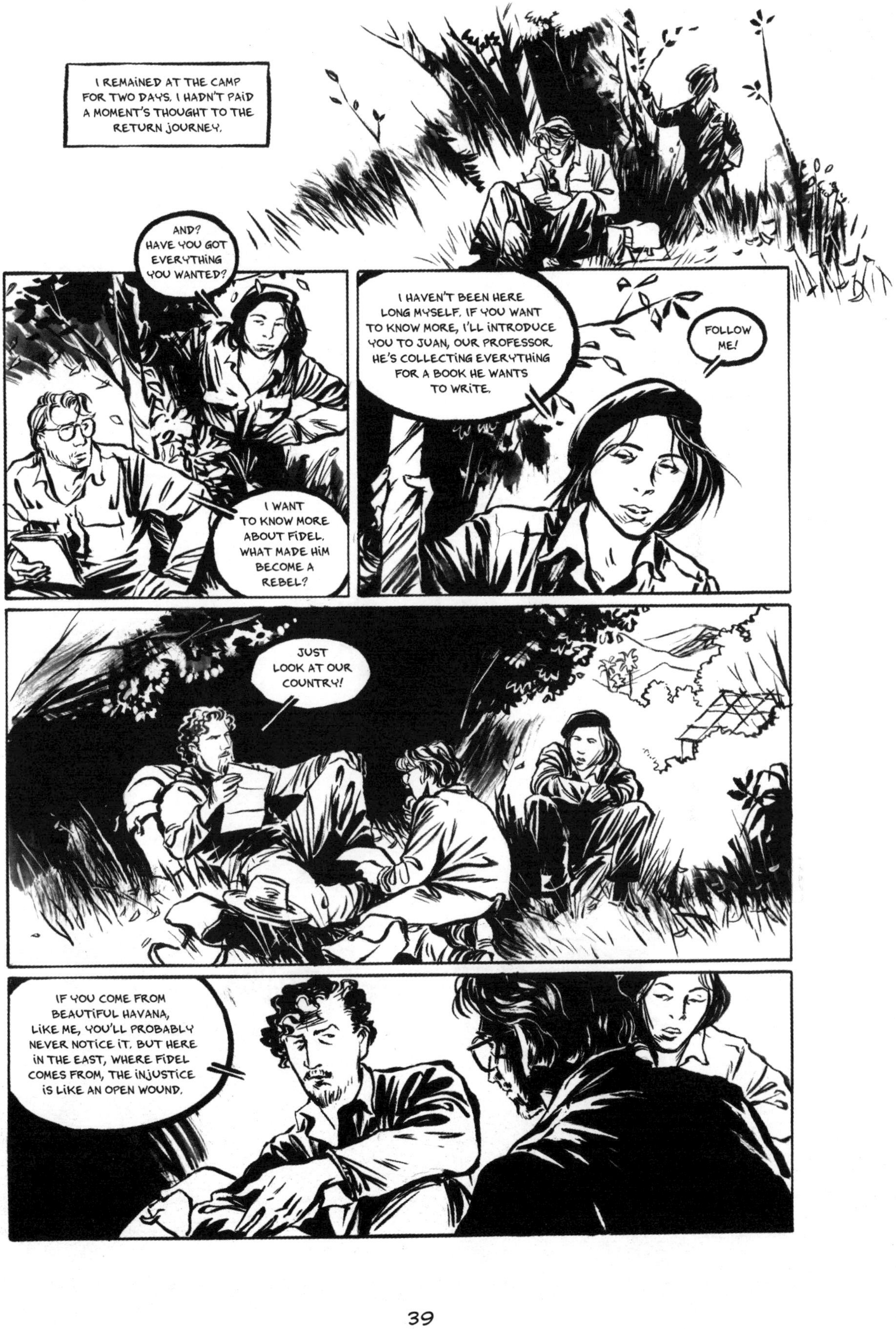

I REMAINED AT THE CAMP FOR TWO DAYS. I HADN'T PAID A MOMENT'S THOUGHT TO THE RETURN JOURNEY.
AND? HAVE YOU GOT EVERYTHING YOU WANTED?
I WANT TO KNOW MORE ABOUT FIDEL. WHAT MADE HIM BECOME A REBEL?
I HAVEN'T BEEN HERE LONG MYSELF. IF YOU WANT TO KNOW MORE, I'LL INTRODUCE YOU TO JUAN, OUR PROFESSOR. HE'S COLLECTING EVERYTHING FOR A BOOK HE WANTS TO WRITE.
FOLLOW ME!
JUST LOOK AT OUR COUNTRY!
IF YOU COME FROM BEAUTIFUL HAVANA, LIKE ME, YOU'LL PROBABLY NEVER NOTICE IT. BUT HERE IN THE EAST, WHERE FIDEL COMES FROM, THE INJUSTICE IS LIKE AN OPEN WOUND.

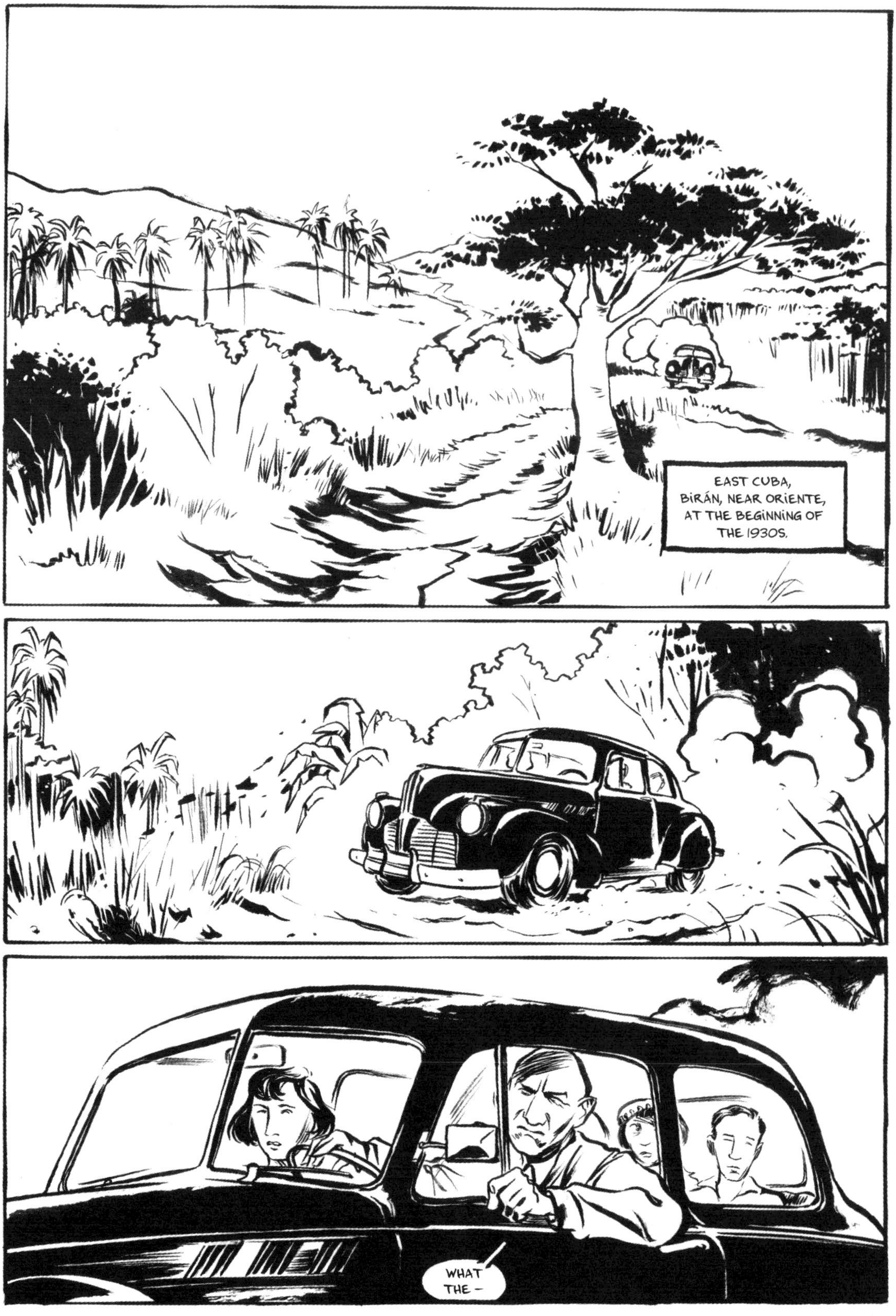
EAST CUBA,
BIRÁN, NEAR ORIENTE,
AT THE BEGINNING OF
THE 1930S.
WHAT
THE -

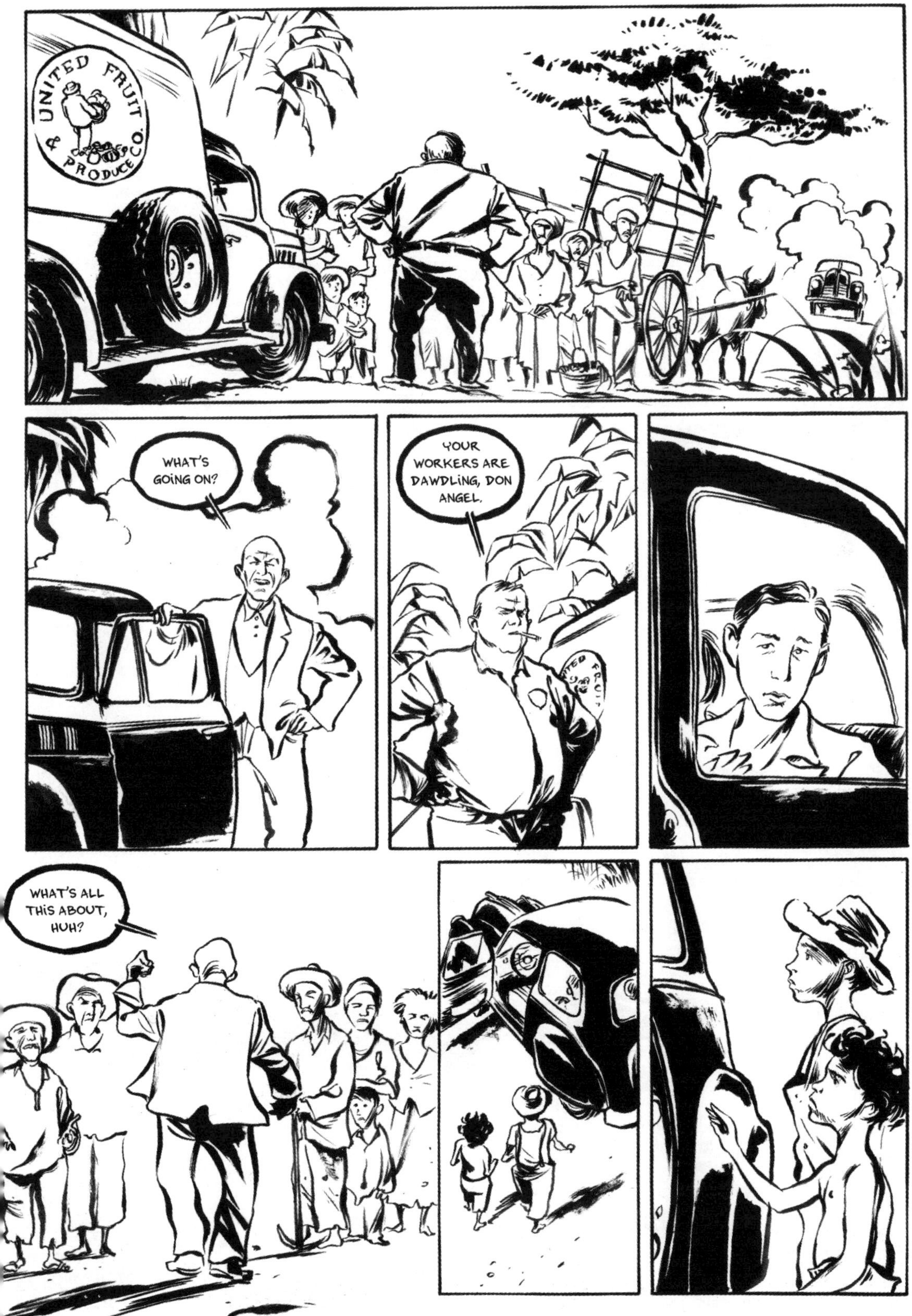
UNITED FRUIT & PRODUCE CO.
WHAT'S GOING ON?
YOUR WORKERS ARE DAWDLING, DON ANGEL.
WHAT'S ALL THIS ABOUT, HUH?

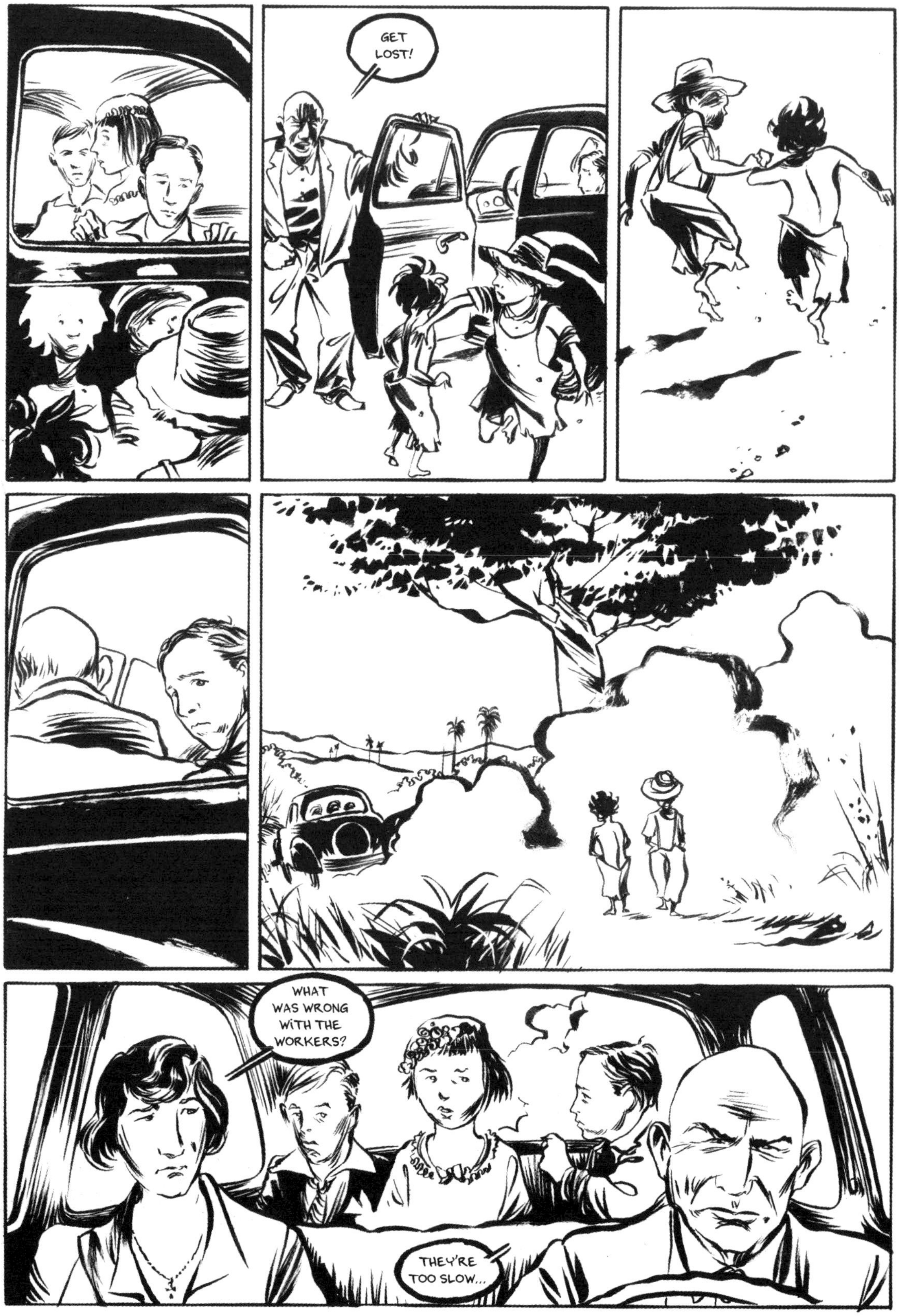
GET LOST!
WHAT WAS WRONG WITH THE WORKERS?
THEY'RE TOO SLOW...

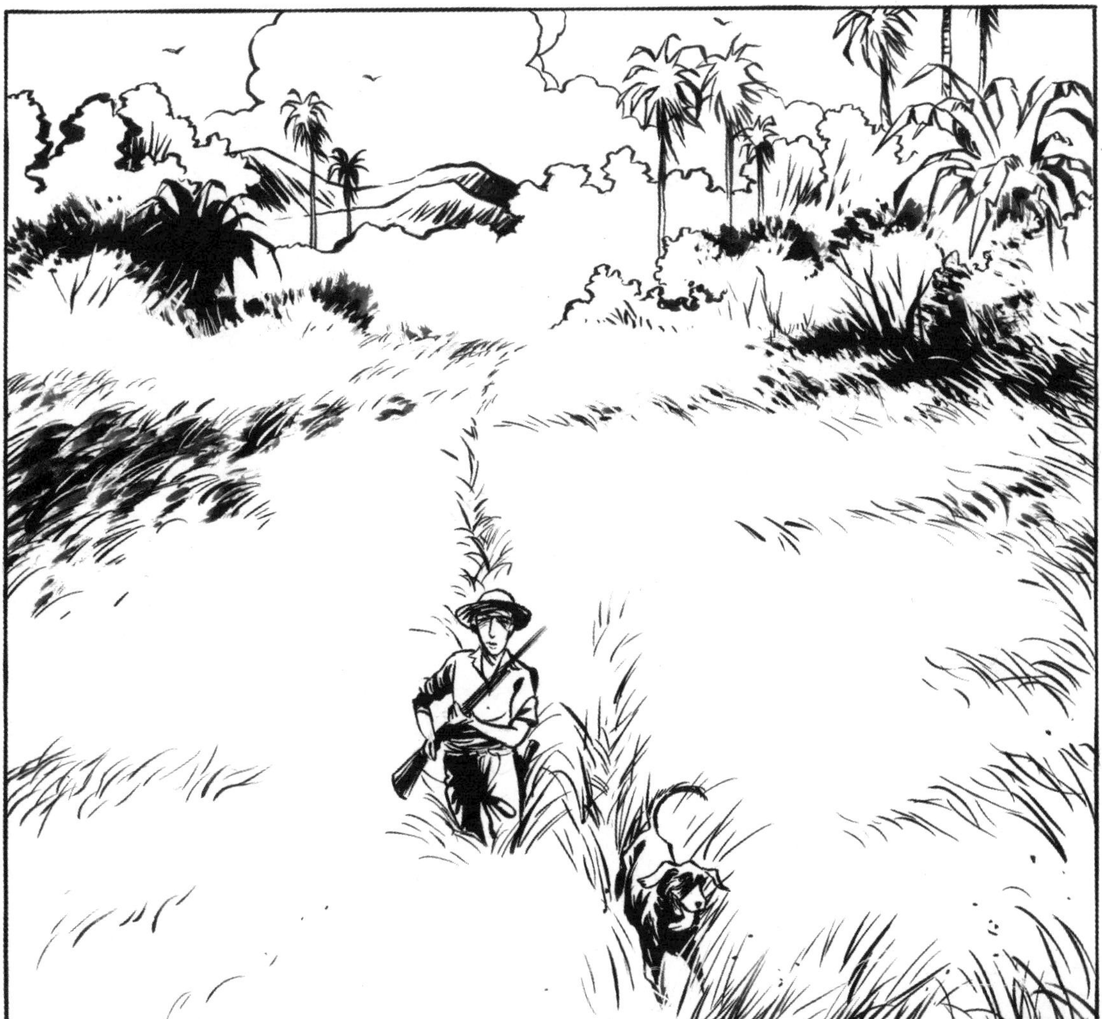

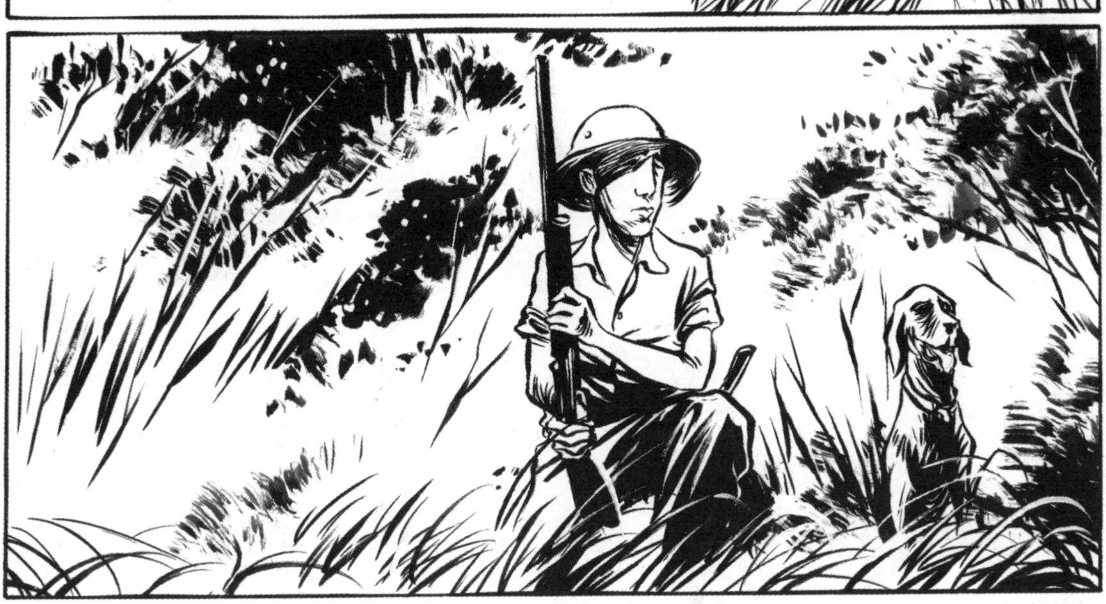

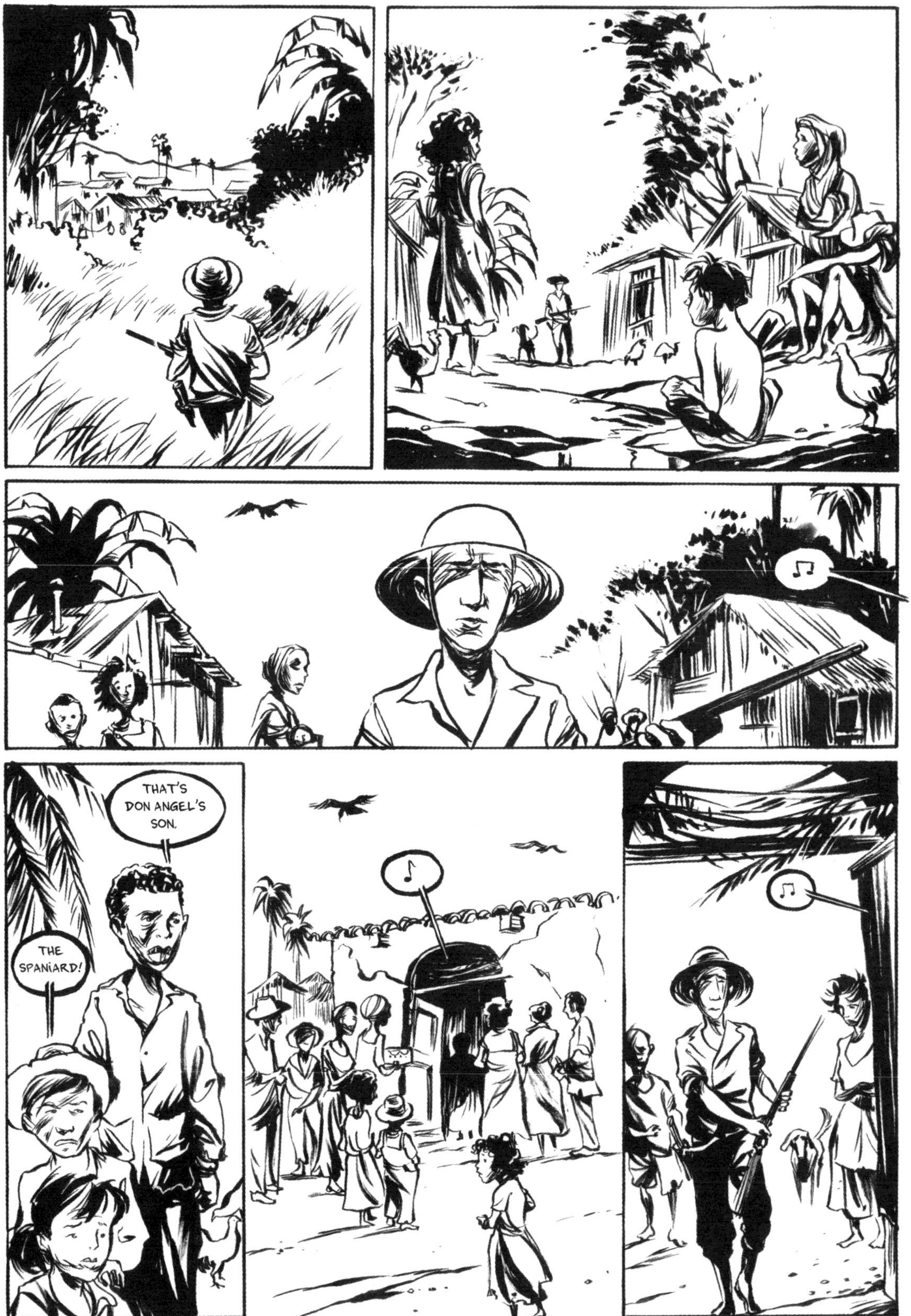
♫
THAT'S DON ANGEL'S SON.
THE SPANIARD!
♪
♫

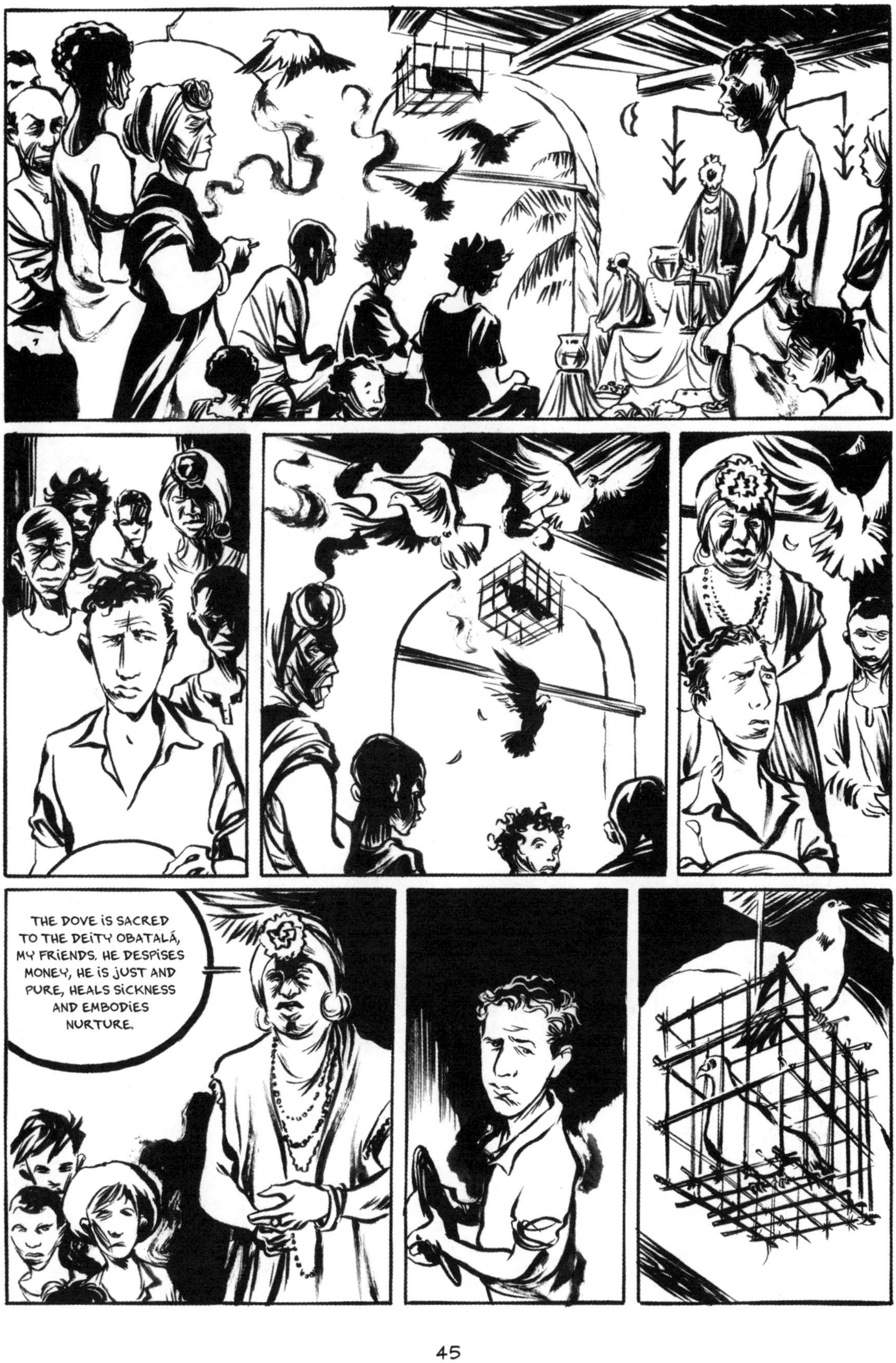
THE DOVE IS SACRED TO THE DEITY OBATALÁ, MY FRIENDS. HE DESPISES MONEY, HE IS JUST AND PURE, HEALS SICKNESS AND EMBODIES NURTURE.

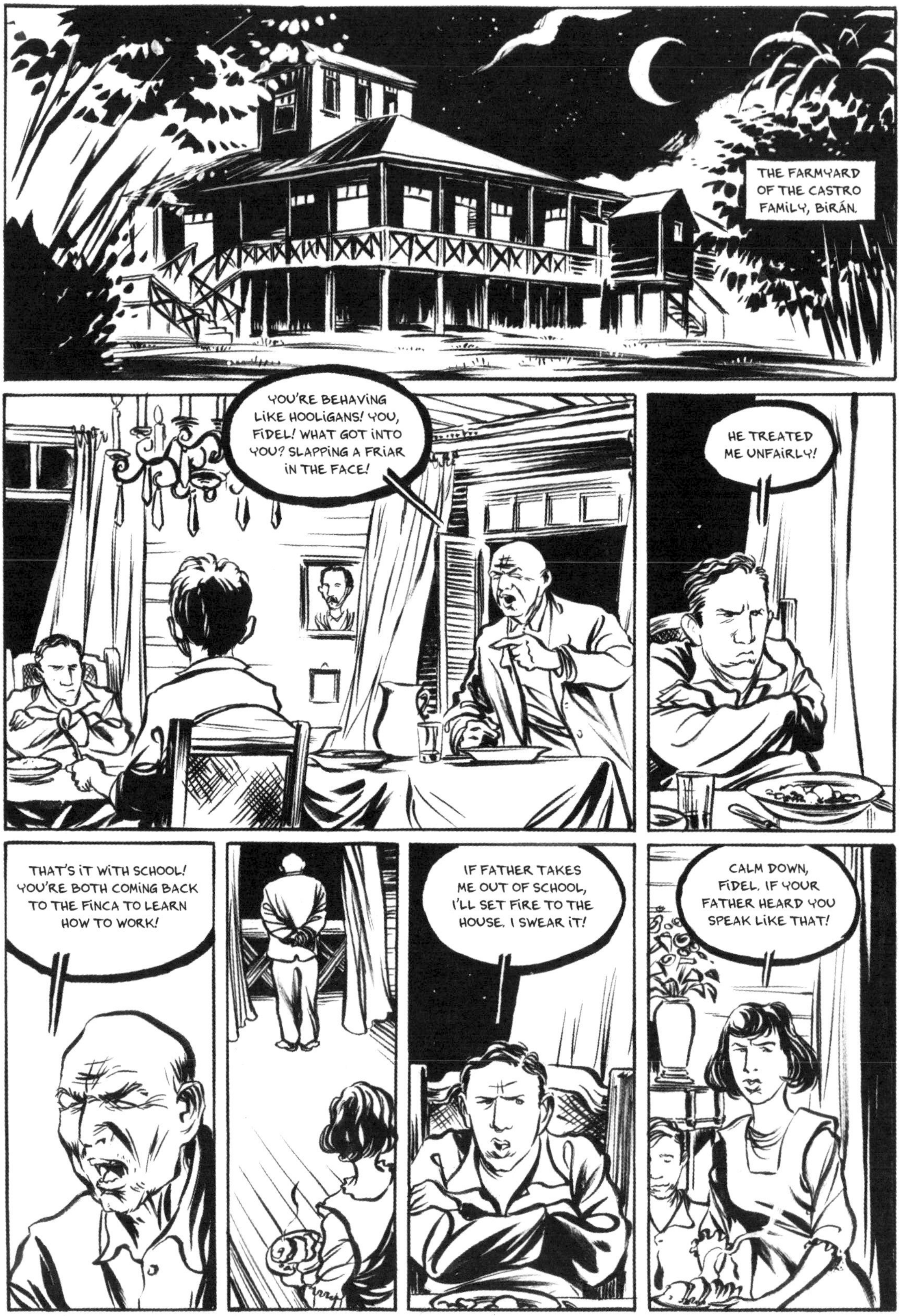
THE FARMYARD OF THE CASTRO FAMILY, BIRÁN.
YOU'RE BEHAVING LIKE HOOLIGANS! YOU, FIDEL! WHAT GOT INTO YOU? SLAPPING A FRIAR IN THE FACE!
HE TREATED ME UNFAIRLY!
THAT'S IT WITH SCHOOL! YOU'RE BOTH COMING BACK TO THE FINCA TO LEARN HOW TO WORK!
IF FATHER TAKES ME OUT OF SCHOOL, I'LL SET FIRE TO THE HOUSE. I SWEAR IT!
CALM DOWN, FIDEL. IF YOUR FATHER HEARD YOU SPEAK LIKE THAT!

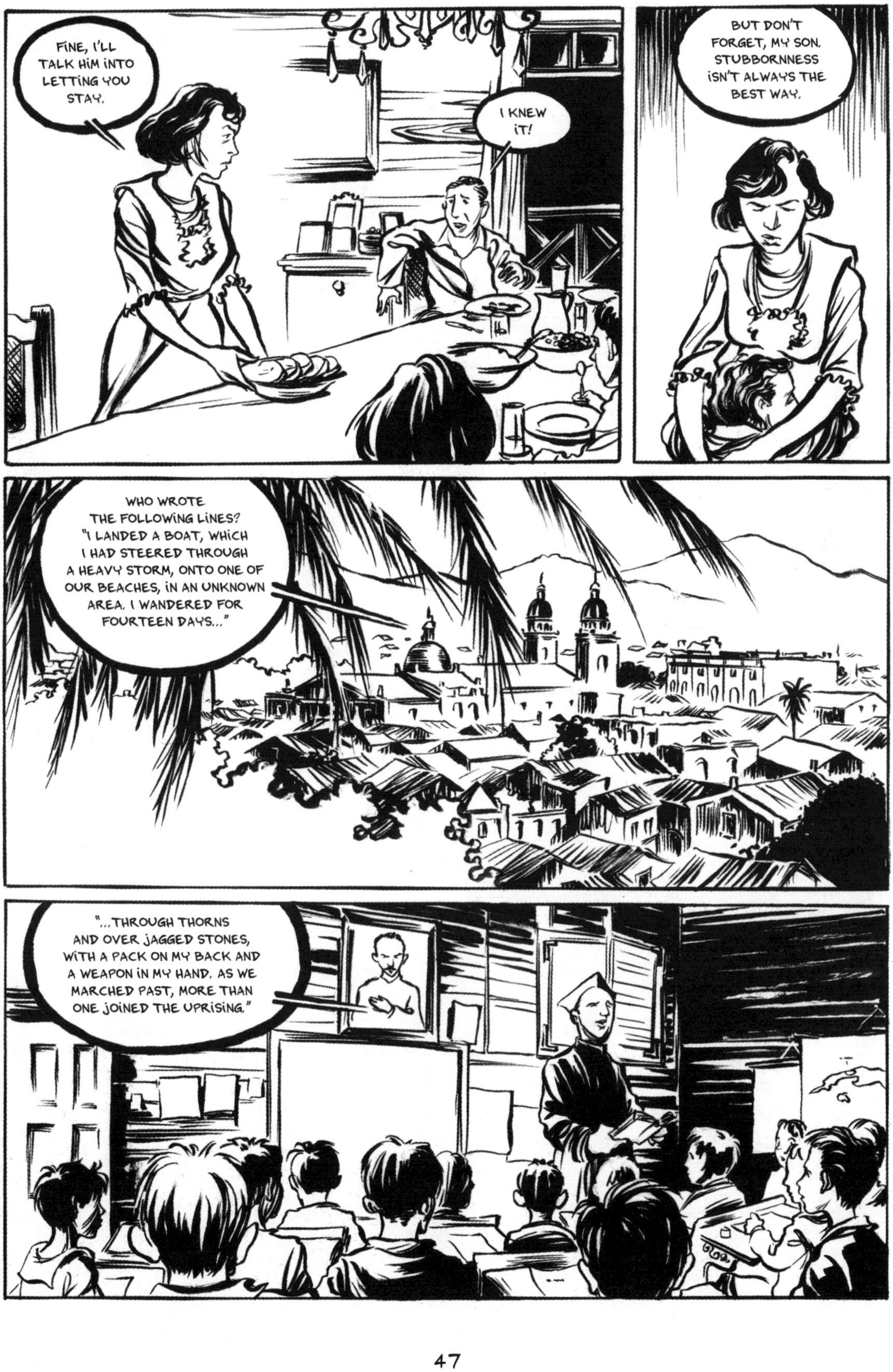
FINE, I'LL TALK HIM INTO LETTING YOU STAY.
I KNEW IT!
BUT DON'T FORGET, MY SON. STUBBORNNESS ISN'T ALWAYS THE BEST WAY.
WHO WROTE THE FOLLOWING LINES? "I LANDED A BOAT, WHICH I HAD STEERED THROUGH A HEAVY STORM, ONTO ONE OF OUR BEACHES, IN AN UNKNOWN AREA. I WANDERED FOR FOURTEEN DAYS..."
"...THROUGH THORNS AND OVER JAGGED STONES, WITH A PACK ON MY BACK AND A WEAPON IN MY HAND. AS WE MARCHED PAST, MORE THAN ONE JOINED THE UPRISING."

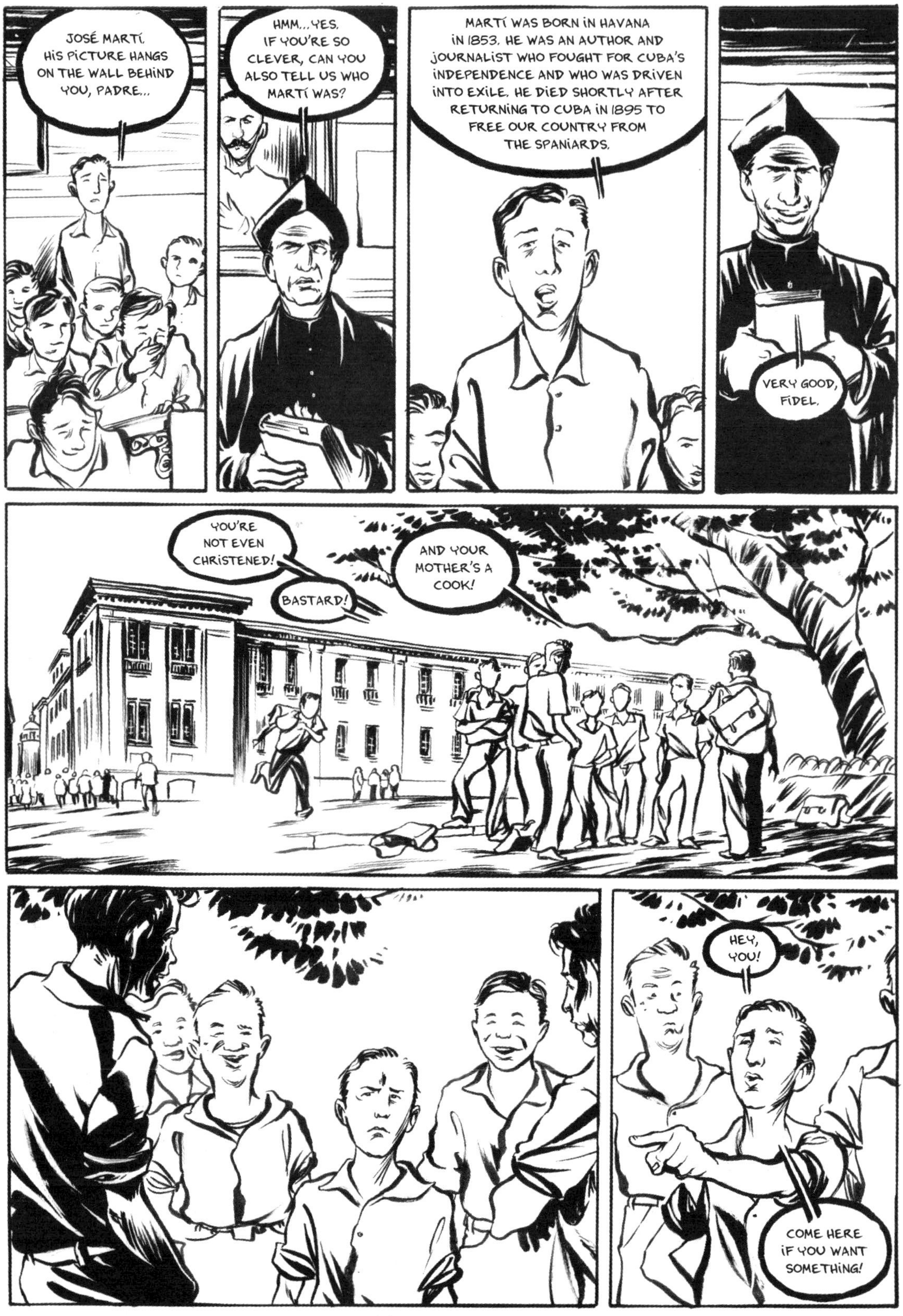
JOSÉ MARTÍ. HIS PICTURE HANGS ON THE WALL BEHIND YOU, PADRE...
HMM... YES. IF YOU'RE SO CLEVER, CAN YOU ALSO TELL US WHO MARTÍ WAS?
MARTÍ WAS BORN IN HAVANA IN 1853. HE WAS AN AUTHOR AND JOURNALIST WHO FOUGHT FOR CUBA'S INDEPENDENCE AND WHO WAS DRIVEN INTO EXILE. HE DIED SHORTLY AFTER RETURNING TO CUBA IN 1895 TO FREE OUR COUNTRY FROM THE SPANIARDS.
VERY GOOD, FIDEL.
YOU'RE NOT EVEN CHRISTENED!
BASTARD!
AND YOUR MOTHER'S A COOK!
HEY, YOU!
COME HERE IF YOU WANT SOMETHING!

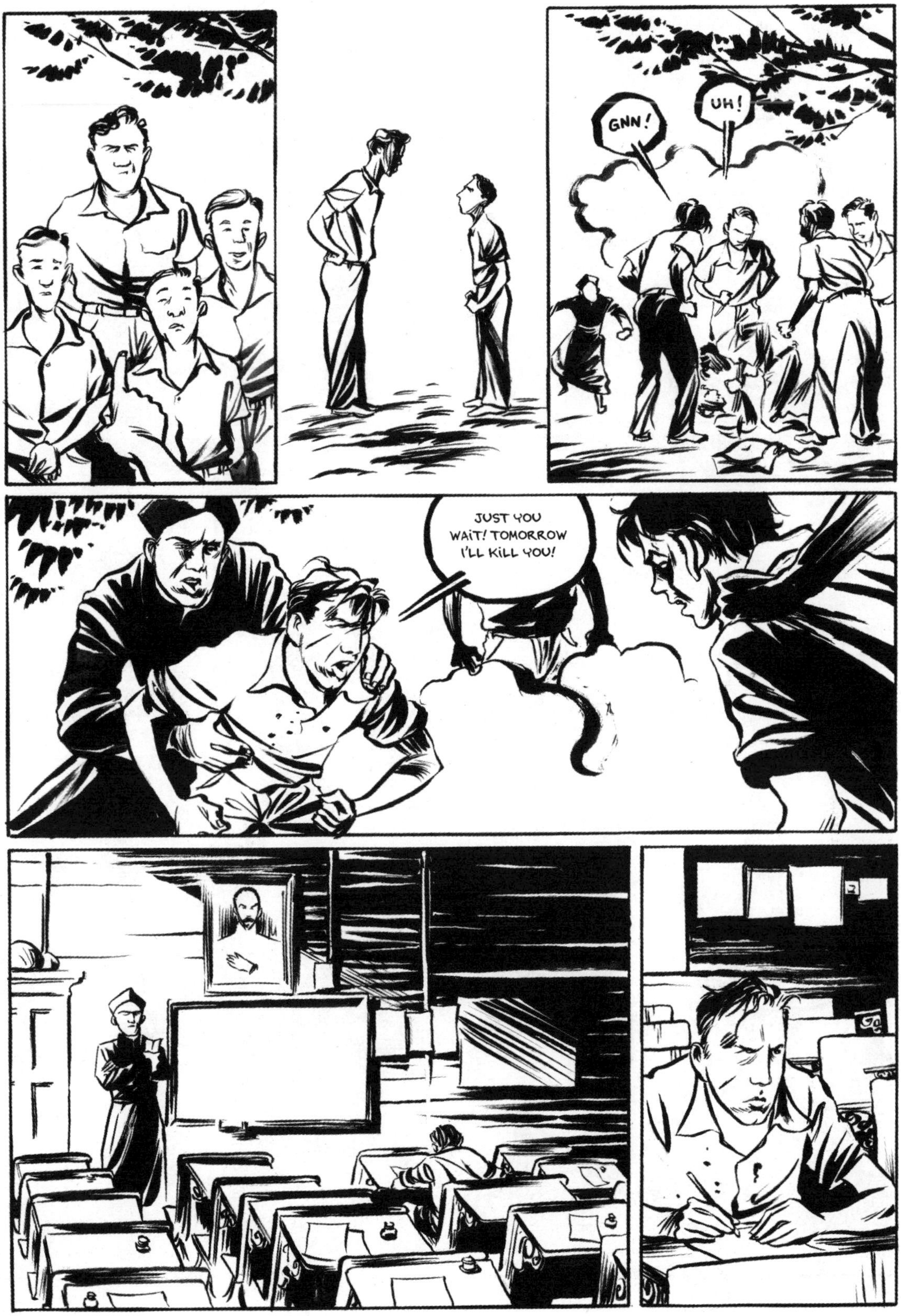
GNN!
UH!
JUST YOU WAIT! TOMORROW I'LL KILL YOU!

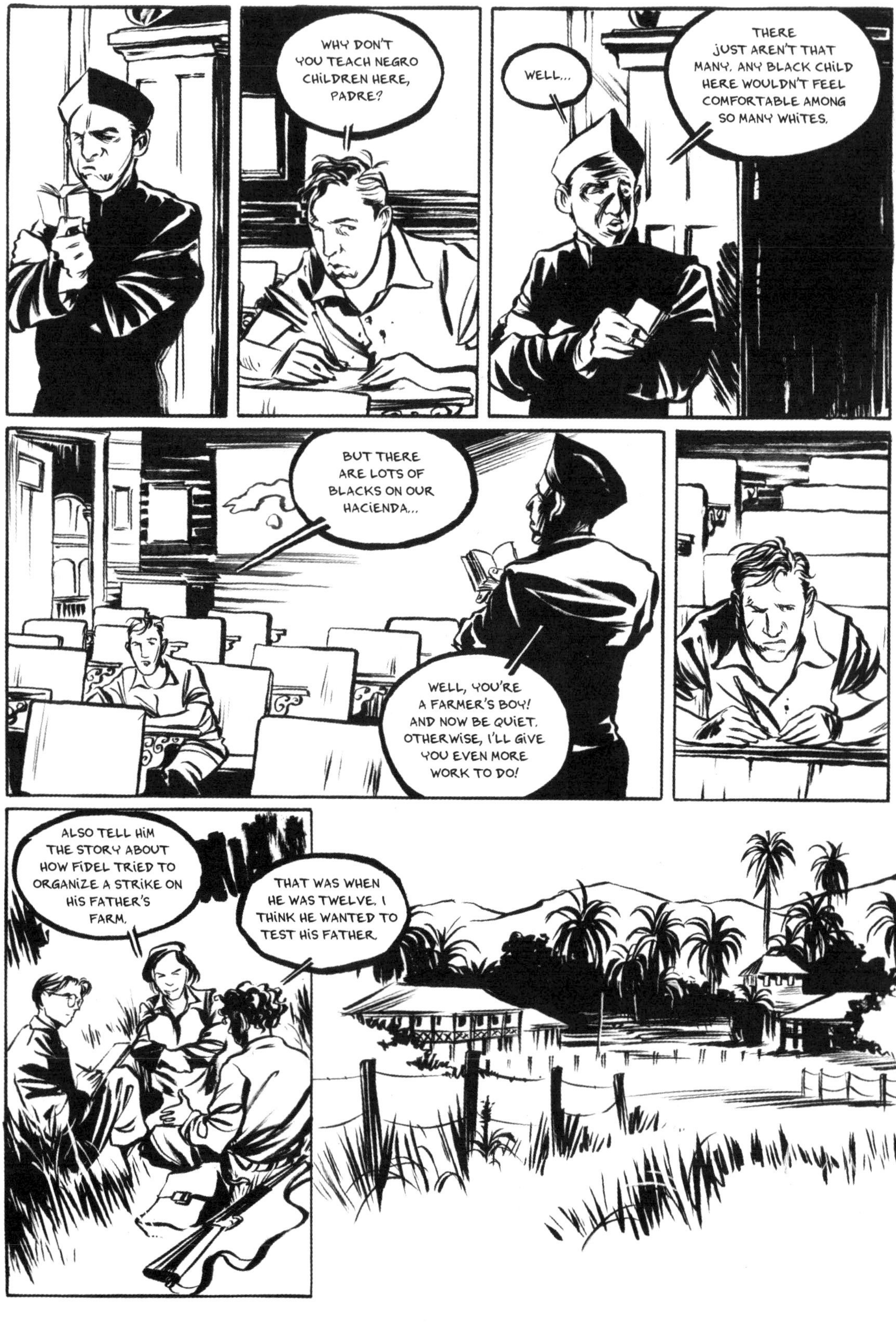
WHY DON'T YOU TEACH NEGRO CHILDREN HERE, PADRE?
WELL...
THERE JUST AREN'T THAT MANY. ANY BLACK CHILD HERE WOULDN'T FEEL COMFORTABLE AMONG SO MANY WHITES.
BUT THERE ARE LOTS OF BLACKS ON OUR HACIENDA...
WELL, YOU'RE A FARMER'S BOY! AND NOW BE QUIET. OTHERWISE, I'LL GIVE YOU EVEN MORE WORK TO DO!
ALSO TELL HIM THE STORY ABOUT HOW FIDEL TRIED TO ORGANIZE A STRIKE ON HIS FATHER'S FARM.
THAT WAS WHEN HE WAS TWELVE. I THINK HE WANTED TO TEST HIS FATHER.

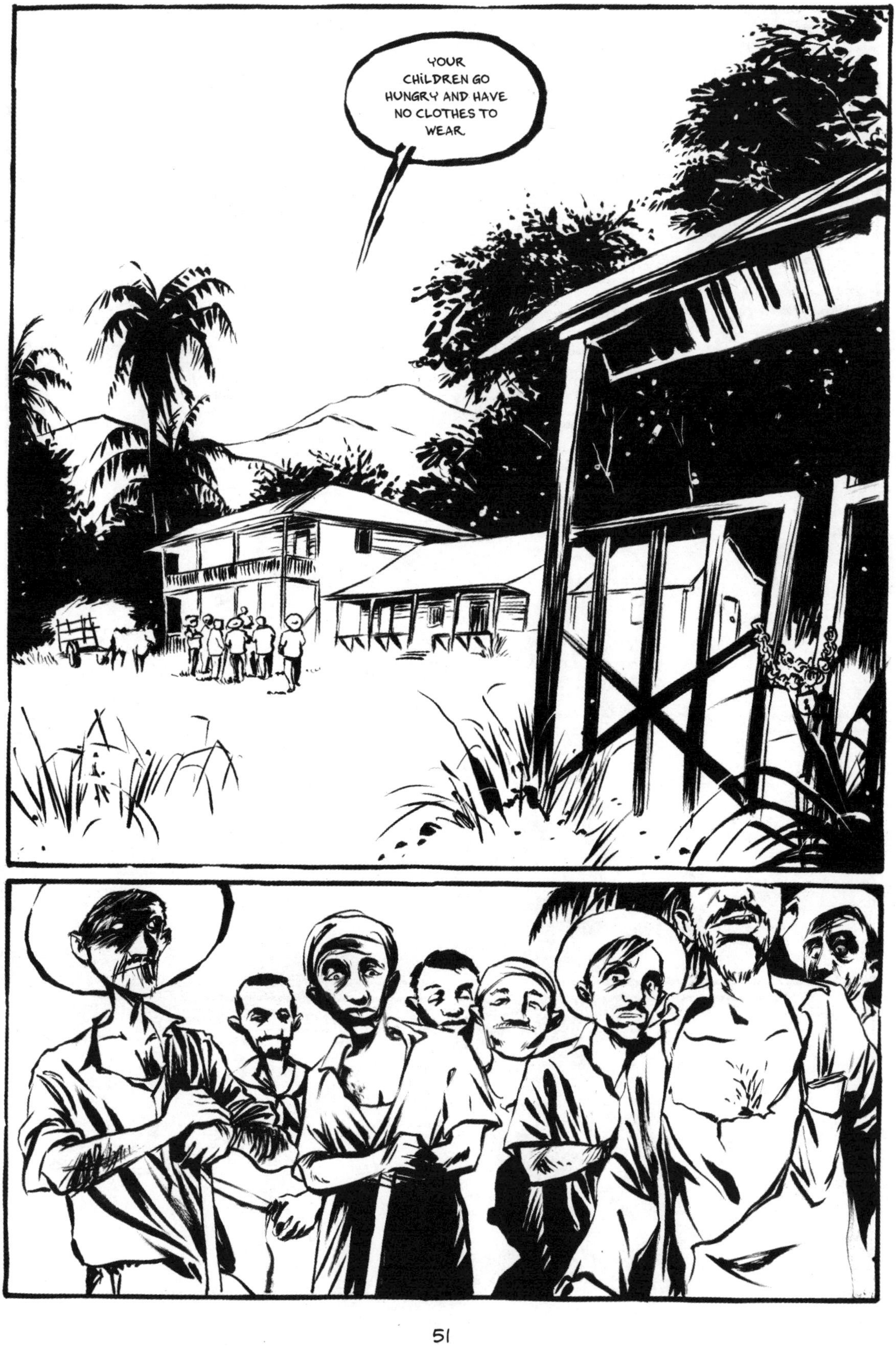
YOUR CHILDREN GO HUNGRY AND HAVE NO CLOTHES TO WEAR.

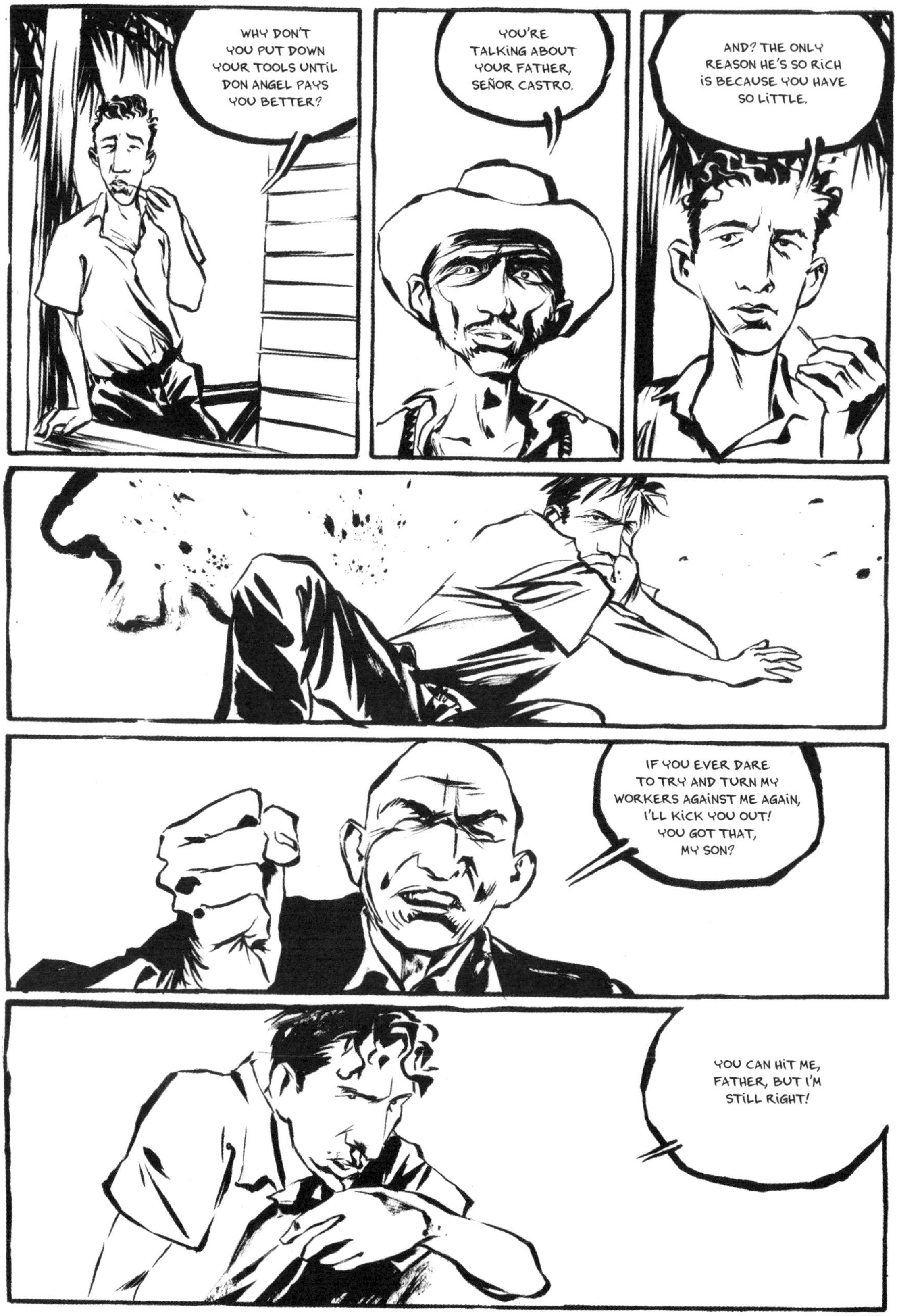
WHY DON'T YOU PUT DOWN YOUR TOOLS UNTIL DON ANGEL PAYS YOU BETTER?
YOU'RE TALKING ABOUT YOUR FATHER, SEÑOR CASTRO.
AND? THE ONLY REASON HE'S SO RICH IS BECAUSE YOU HAVE SO LITTLE.
IF YOU EVER DARE TO TRY AND TURN MY WORKERS AGAINST ME AGAIN, I'LL KICK YOU OUT! YOU GOT THAT, MY SON?
YOU CAN HIT ME, FATHER, BUT I'M STILL RIGHT!

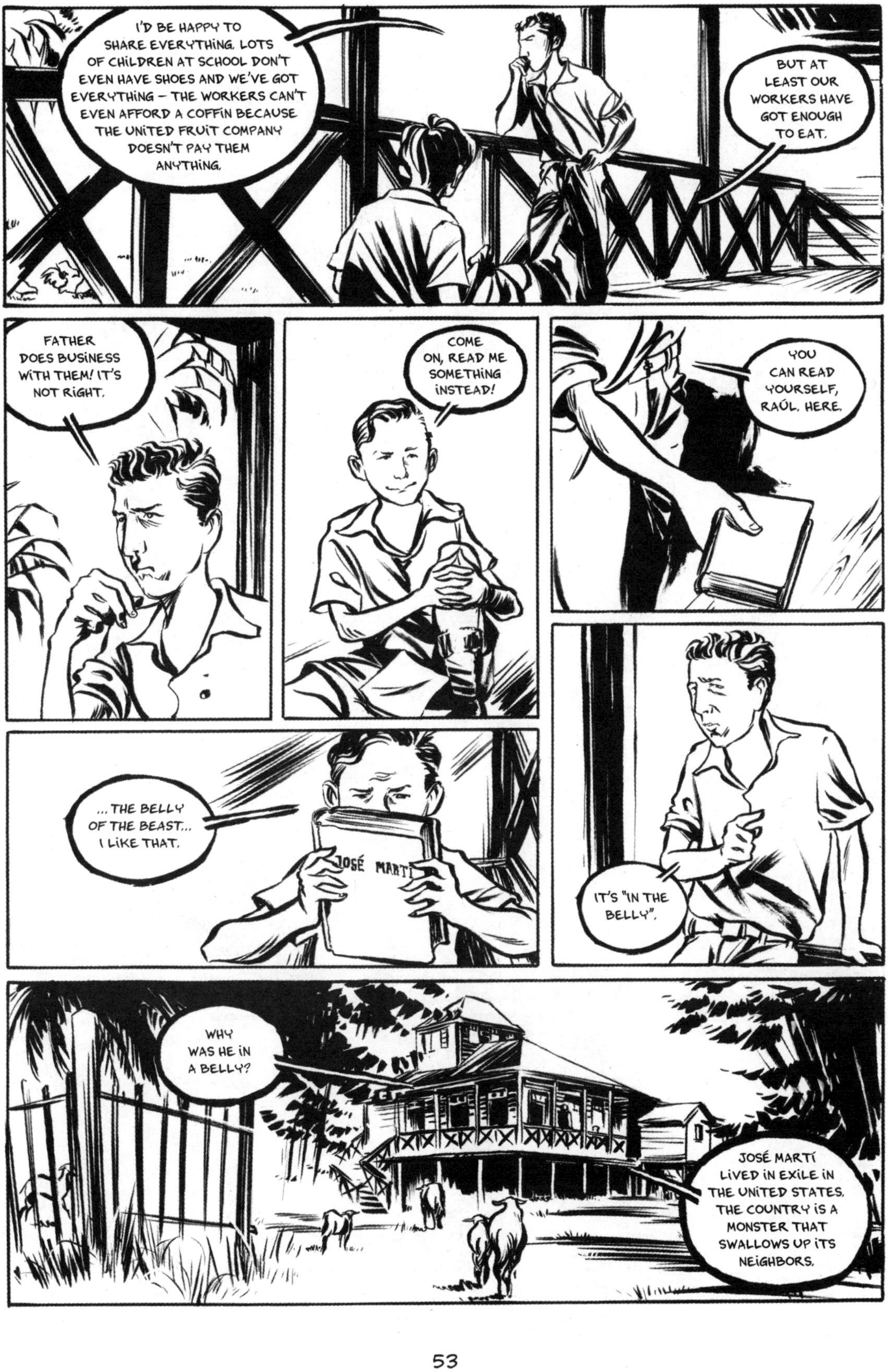

I'D BE HAPPY TO SHARE EVERYTHING. LOTS OF CHILDREN AT SCHOOL DON'T EVEN HAVE SHOES AND WE'VE GOT EVERYTHING – THE WORKERS CAN'T EVEN AFFORD A COFFIN BECAUSE THE UNITED FRUIT COMPANY DOESN'T PAY THEM ANYTHING.
BUT AT LEAST OUR WORKERS HAVE GOT ENOUGH TO EAT.
FATHER DOES BUSINESS WITH THEM! IT'S NOT RIGHT.
COME ON, READ ME SOMETHING INSTEAD!
YOU CAN READ YOURSELF, RAÚL. HERE.
...THE BELLY OF THE BEAST... I LIKE THAT.
JOSÉ MARTÍ
IT'S "IN THE BELLY".
WHY WAS HE IN A BELLY?
JOSÉ MARTÍ LIVED IN EXILE IN THE UNITED STATES. THE COUNTRY IS A MONSTER THAT SWALLOWS UP ITS NEIGHBORS.

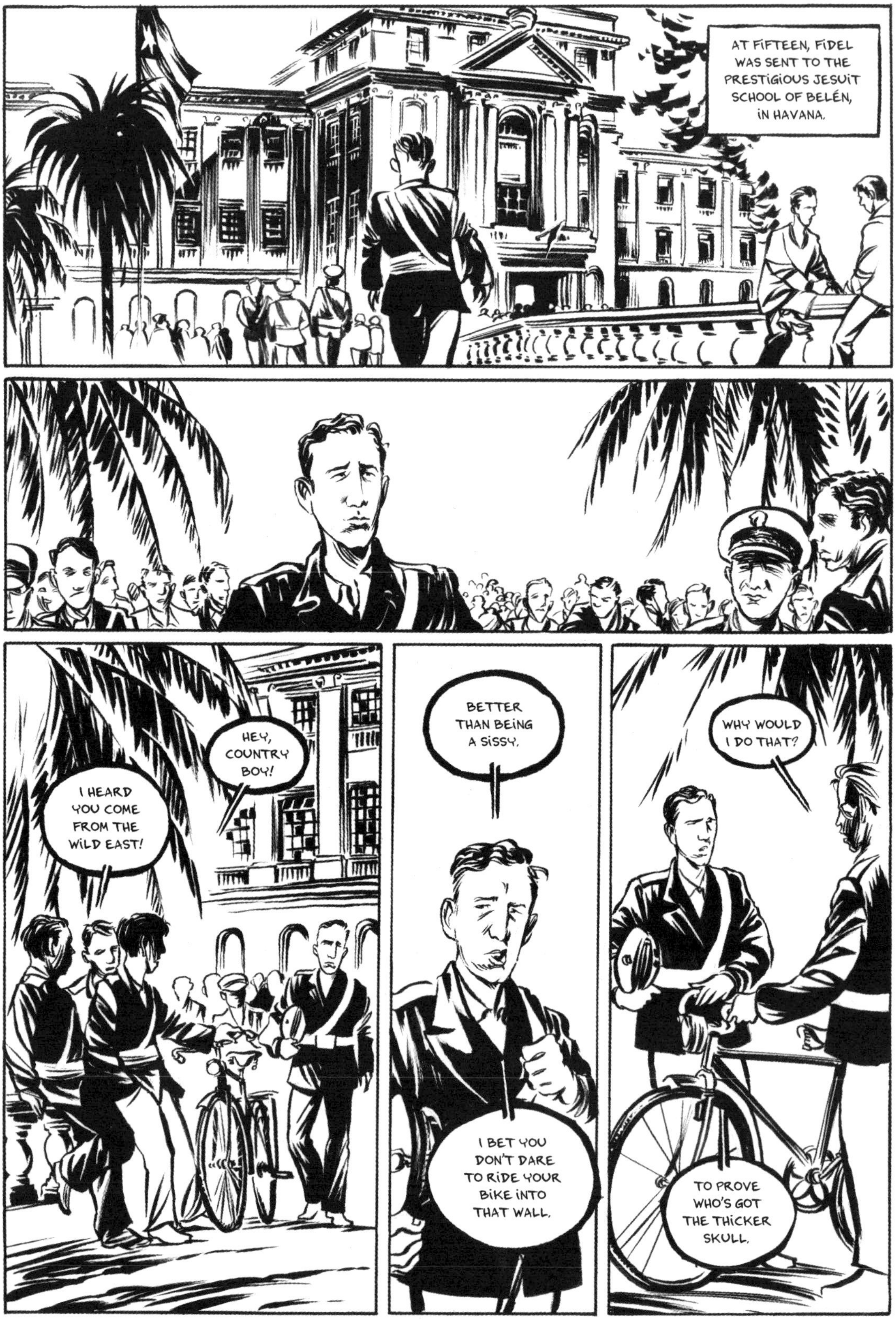
AT FIFTEEN, FIDEL WAS SENT TO THE PRESTIGIOUS JESUIT SCHOOL OF BELÉN, IN HAVANA.
HEY, COUNTRY BOY!
I HEARD YOU COME FROM THE WILD EAST!
BETTER THAN BEING A SISSY.
I BET YOU DON'T DARE TO RIDE YOUR BIKE INTO THAT WALL.
WHY WOULD I DO THAT?
TO PROVE WHO'S GOT THE THICKER SKULL.

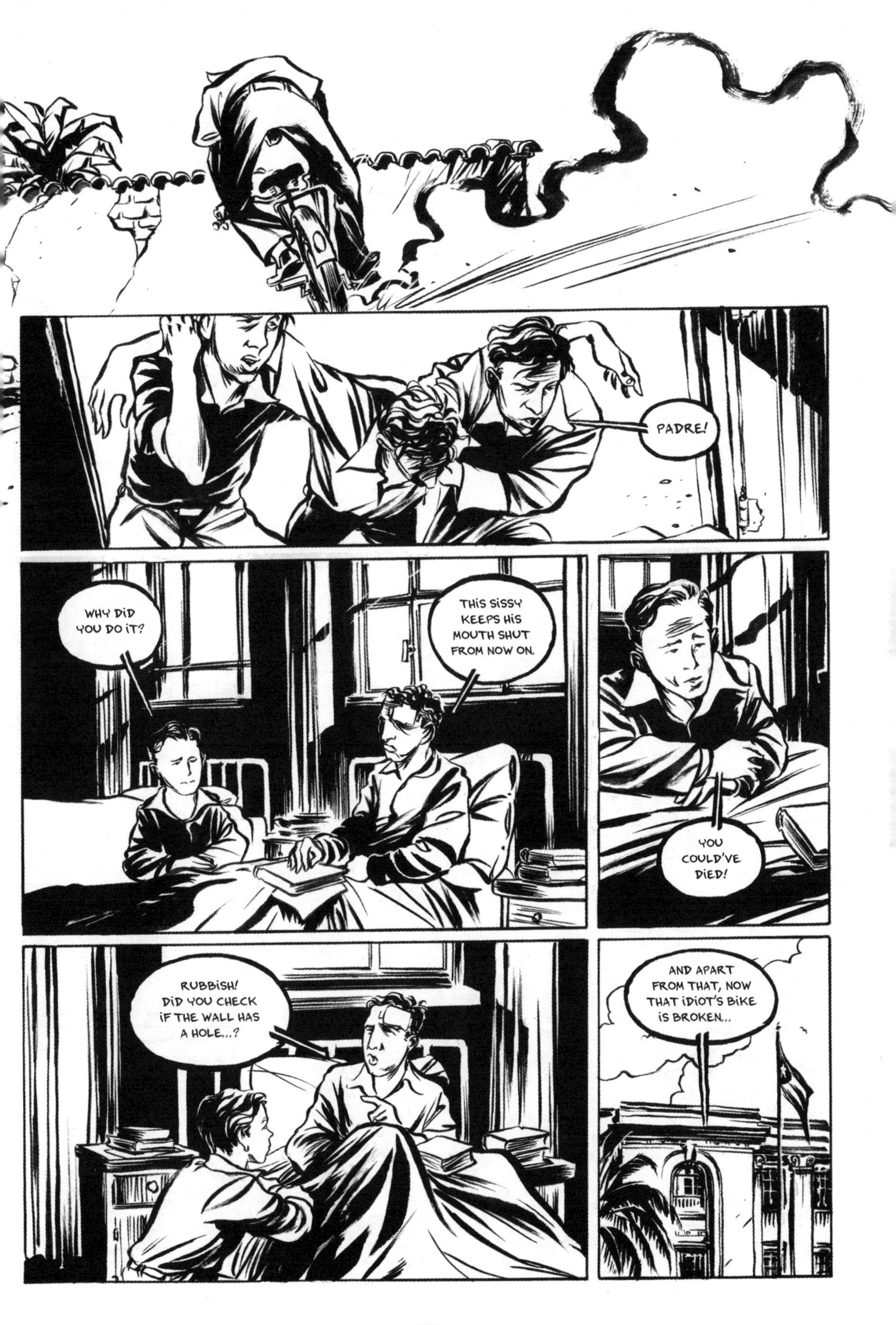
PADRE!
WHY DID YOU DO IT?
THIS SISSY KEEPS HIS MOUTH SHUT FROM NOW ON.
YOU COULD'VE DIED!
RUBBISH! DID YOU CHECK IF THE WALL HAS A HOLE...?
AND APART FROM THAT, NOW THAT IDIOT'S BIKE IS BROKEN...

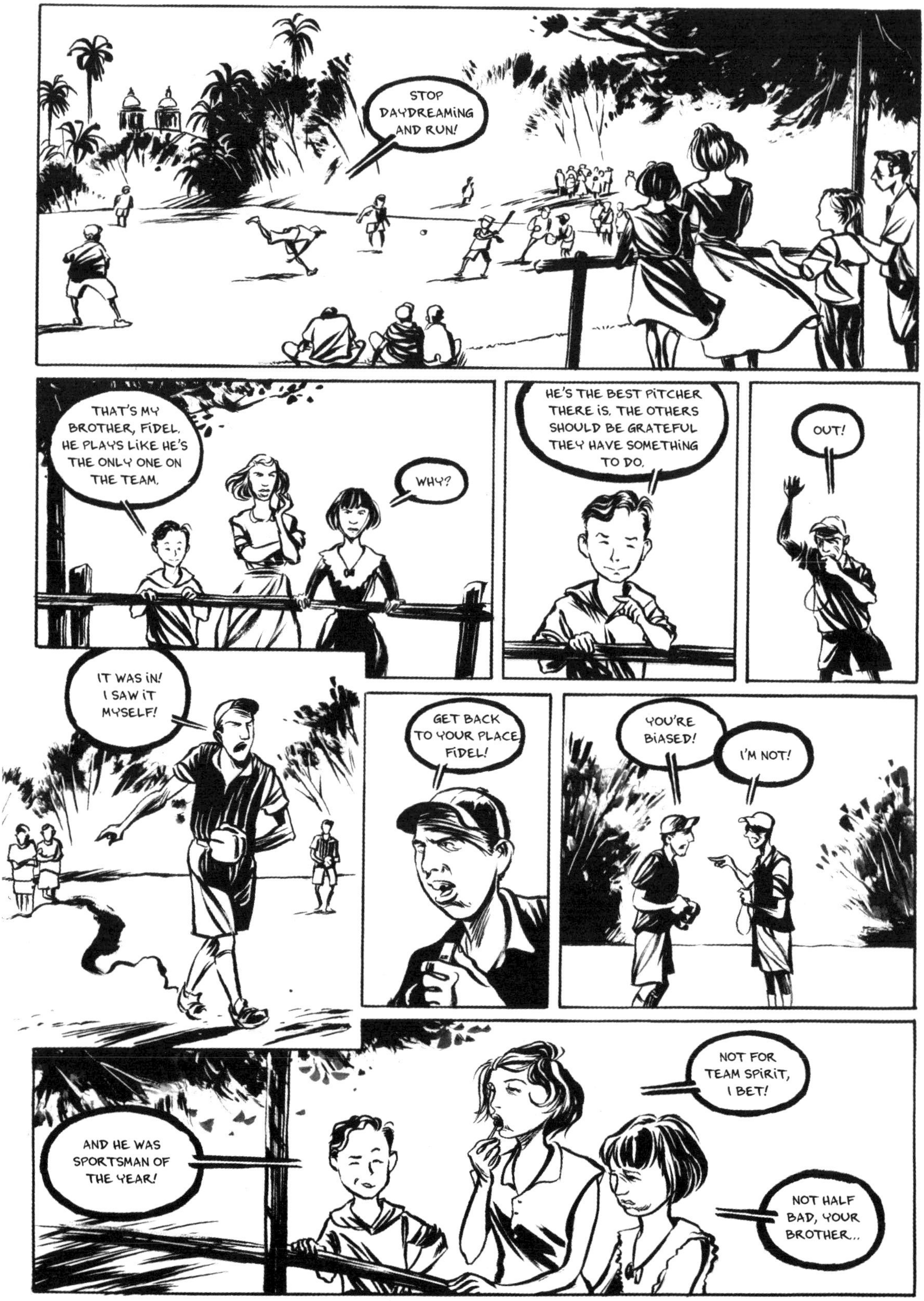
STOP DAYDREAMING AND RUN!
THAT'S MY BROTHER, FIDEL. HE PLAYS LIKE HE'S THE ONLY ONE ON THE TEAM.
WHY?
HE'S THE BEST PITCHER THERE IS. THE OTHERS SHOULD BE GRATEFUL THEY HAVE SOMETHING TO DO.
OUT!
IT WAS IN! I SAW IT MYSELF!
GET BACK TO YOUR PLACE FIDEL!
YOU'RE BIASED!
I'M NOT!
AND HE WAS SPORTSMAN OF THE YEAR!
NOT FOR TEAM SPIRIT, I BET!
NOT HALF BAD, YOUR BROTHER...

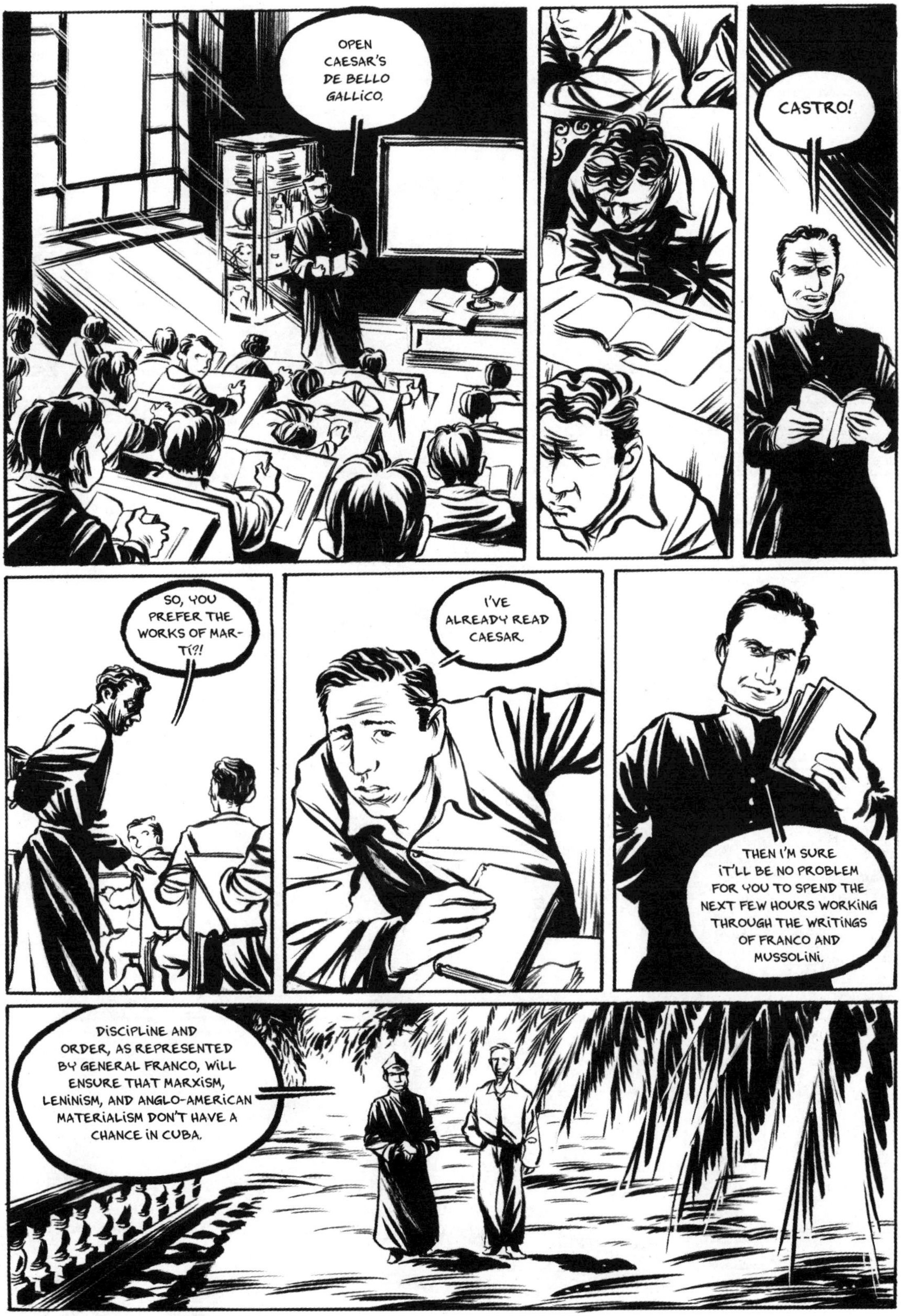
OPEN CAESAR'S DE BELLO GALLICO.
CASTRO!
SO, YOU PREFER THE WORKS OF MAR-TÍ?!
I'VE ALREADY READ CAESAR.
THEN I'M SURE IT'LL BE NO PROBLEM FOR YOU TO SPEND THE NEXT FEW HOURS WORKING THROUGH THE WRITINGS OF FRANCO AND MUSSOLINI.
DISCIPLINE AND ORDER, AS REPRESENTED BY GENERAL FRANCO, WILL ENSURE THAT MARXISM, LENINISM, AND ANGLO-AMERICAN MATERIALISM DON'T HAVE A CHANCE IN CUBA.

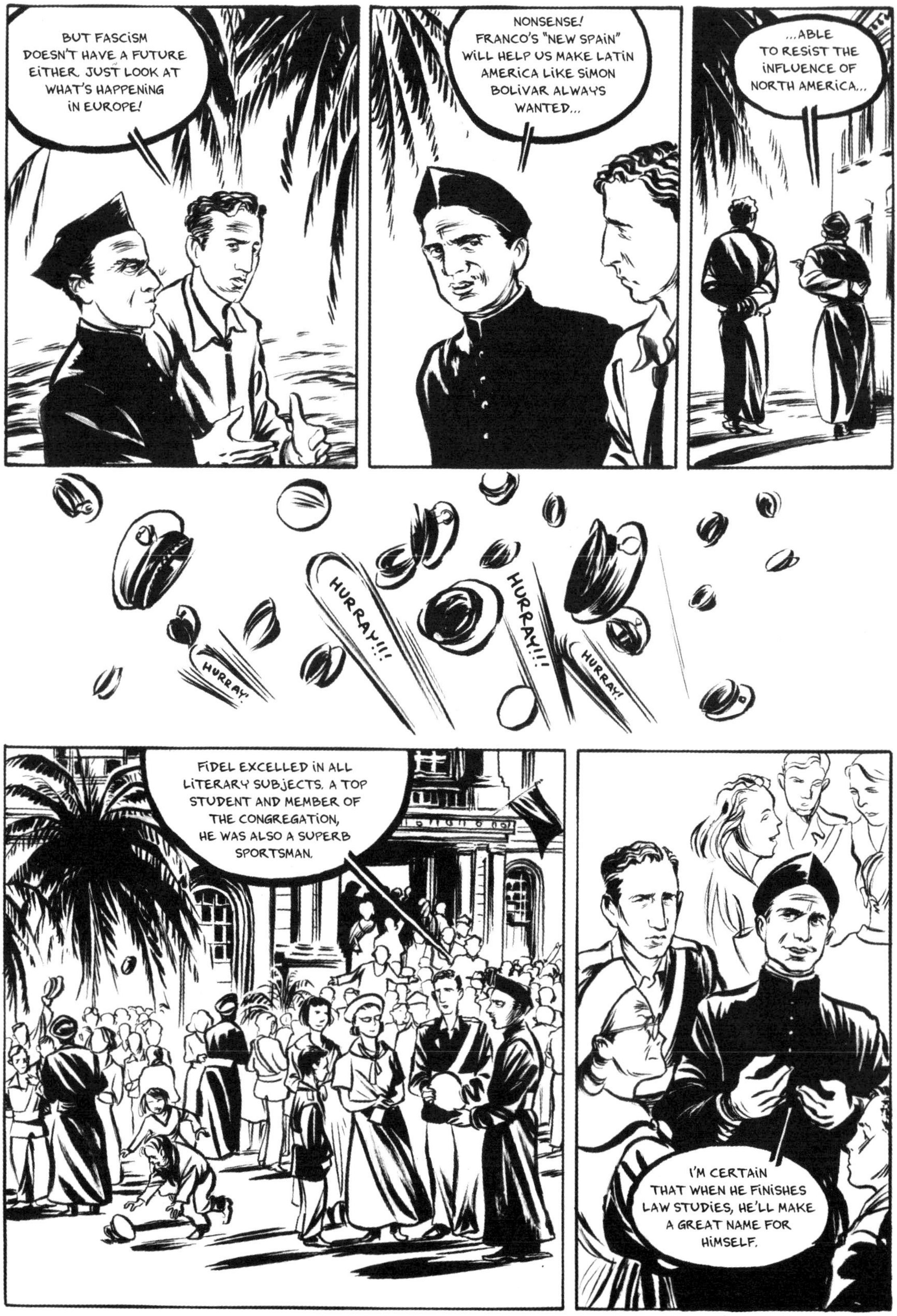
BUT FASCISM DOESN'T HAVE A FUTURE EITHER. JUST LOOK AT WHAT'S HAPPENING IN EUROPE!
NONSENSE! FRANCO'S "NEW SPAIN" WILL HELP US MAKE LATIN AMERICA LIKE SIMON BOLIVAR ALWAYS WANTED...
...ABLE TO RESIST THE INFLUENCE OF NORTH AMERICA...
HURRAY!
HURRAY!!!
HURRAY!!!
HURRAY!
FIDEL EXCELLED IN ALL LITERARY SUBJECTS. A TOP STUDENT AND MEMBER OF THE CONGREGATION, HE WAS ALSO A SUPERB SPORTSMAN.
I'M CERTAIN THAT WHEN HE FINISHES LAW STUDIES, HE'LL MAKE A GREAT NAME FOR HIMSELF.

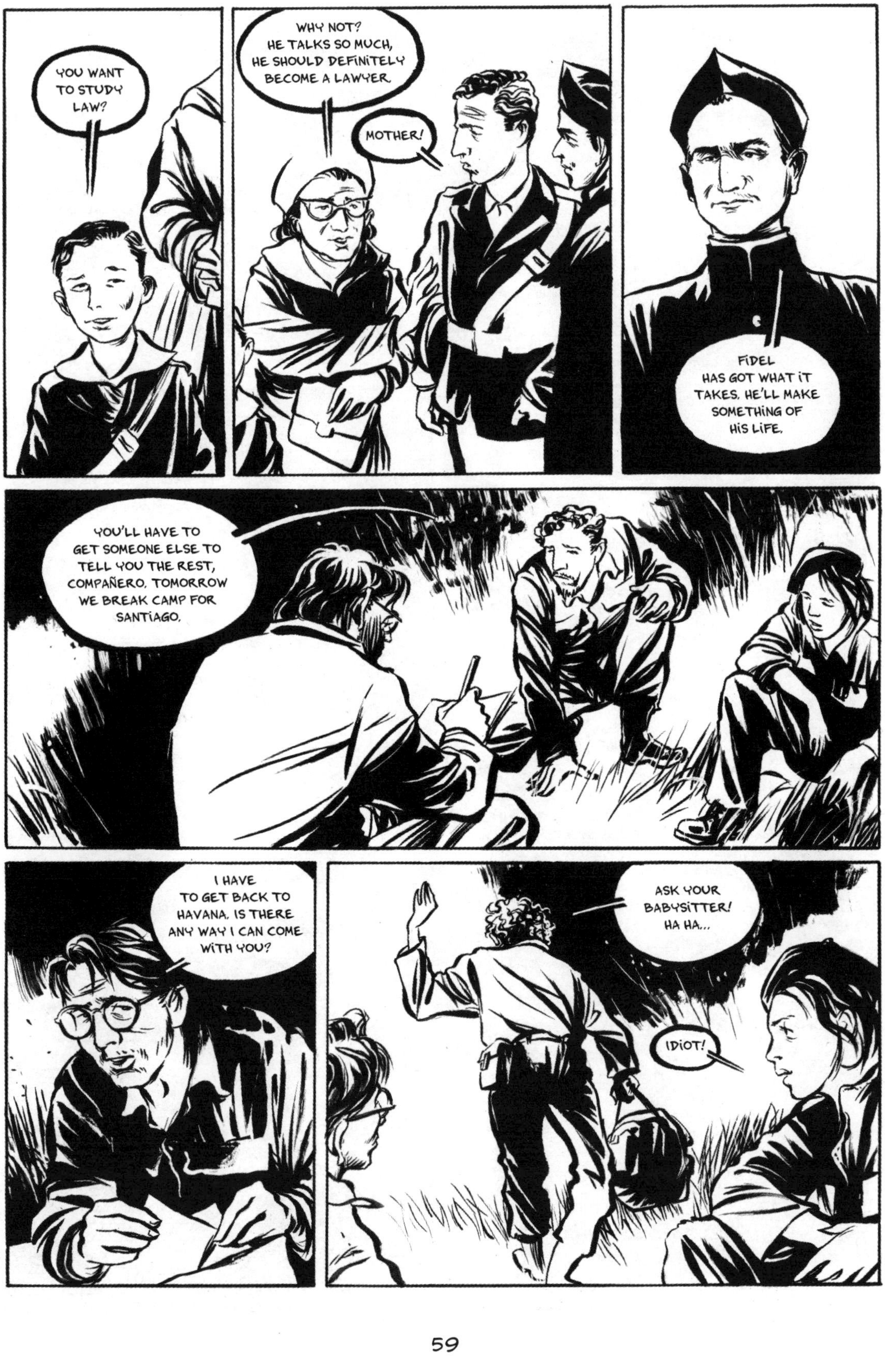
YOU WANT TO STUDY LAW?
WHY NOT? HE TALKS SO MUCH, HE SHOULD DEFINITELY BECOME A LAWYER.
MOTHER!
FIDEL HAS GOT WHAT IT TAKES. HE'LL MAKE SOMETHING OF HIS LIFE.
YOU'LL HAVE TO GET SOMEONE ELSE TO TELL YOU THE REST, COMPAÑERO. TOMORROW WE BREAK CAMP FOR SANTIAGO.
I HAVE TO GET BACK TO HAVANA. IS THERE ANY WAY I CAN COME WITH YOU?
ASK YOUR BABYSITTER! HA HA...
IDIOT!

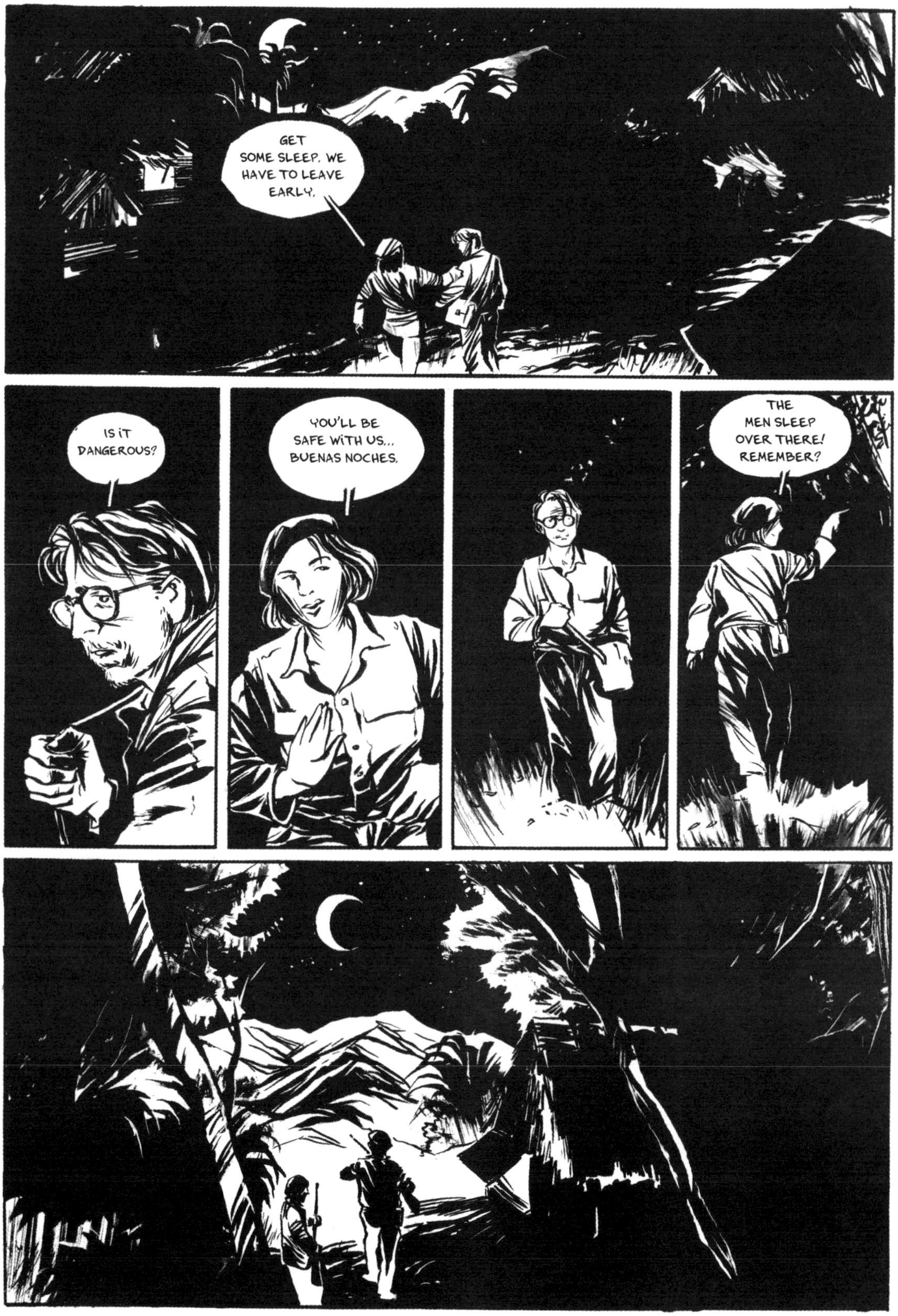
GET SOME SLEEP. WE HAVE TO LEAVE EARLY.
IS iT DANGEROUS?
YOU'LL BE SAFE WiTH US... BUENAS NOCHES.
THE MEN SLEEP OVER THERE! REMEMBER?

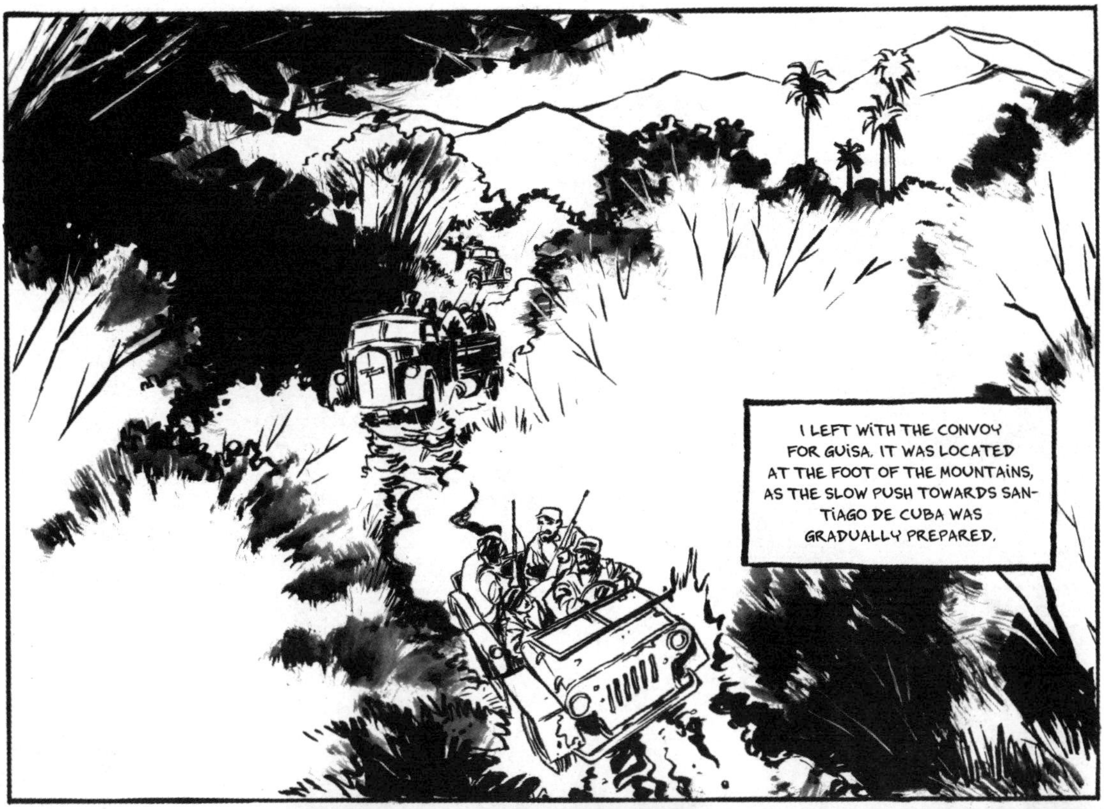
I LEFT WITH THE CONVOY FOR GUISA. IT WAS LOCATED AT THE FOOT OF THE MOUNTAINS, AS THE SLOW PUSH TOWARDS SANTIAGO DE CUBA WAS GRADUALLY PREPARED.

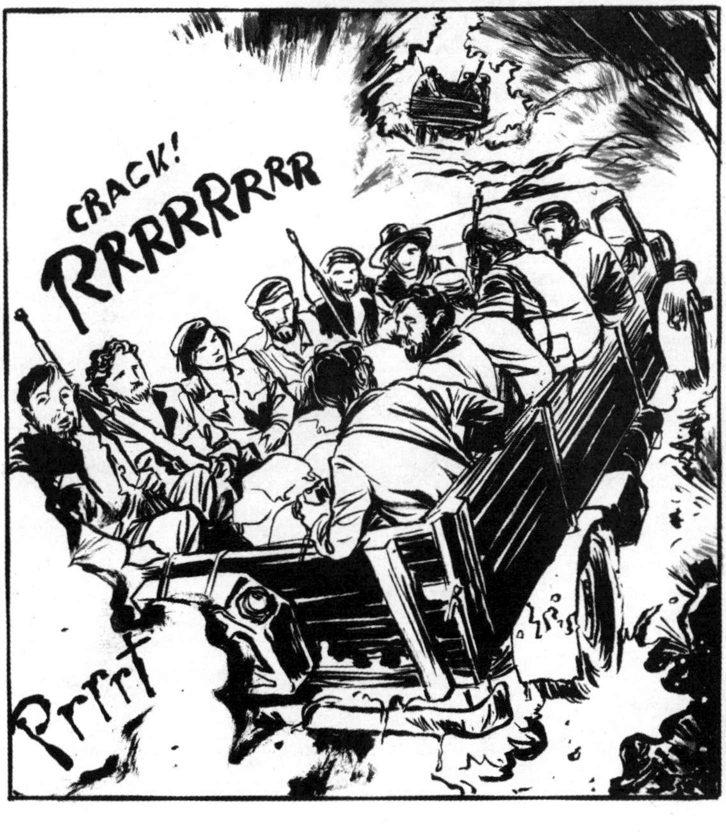
CRACK!
RRRRRRRR
Prrrt

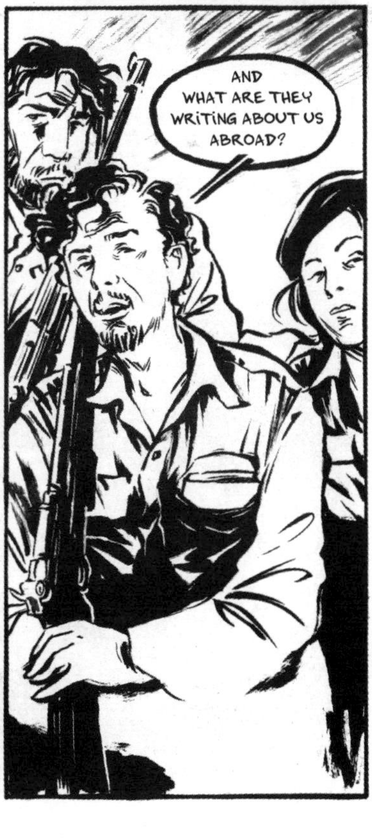
AND WHAT ARE THEY WRITING ABOUT US ABROAD?

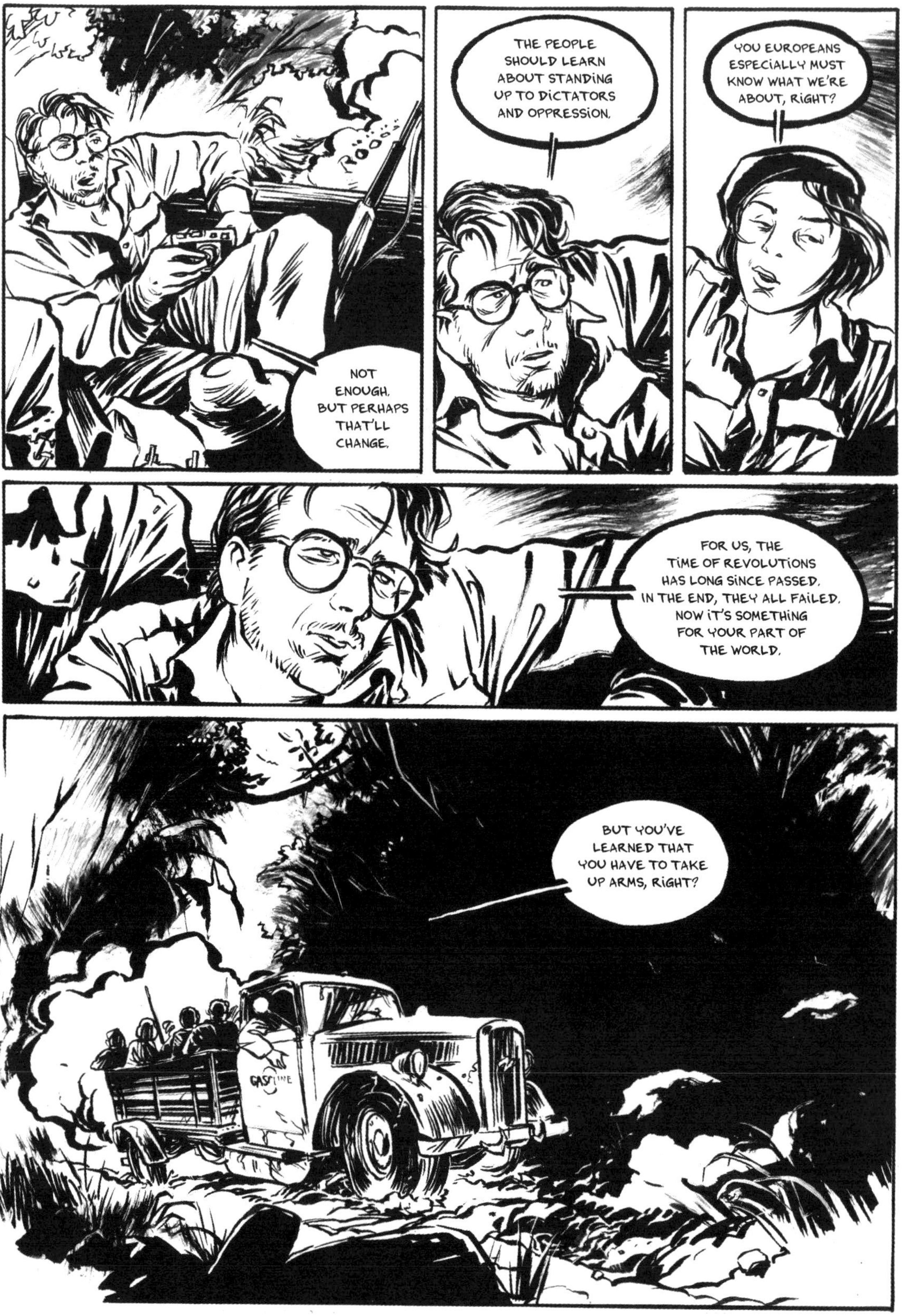
NOT ENOUGH. BUT PERHAPS THAT'LL CHANGE.
THE PEOPLE SHOULD LEARN ABOUT STANDING UP TO DICTATORS AND OPPRESSION.
YOU EUROPEANS ESPECIALLY MUST KNOW WHAT WE'RE ABOUT, RIGHT?
FOR US, THE TIME OF REVOLUTIONS HAS LONG SINCE PASSED. IN THE END, THEY ALL FAILED. NOW IT'S SOMETHING FOR YOUR PART OF THE WORLD.
BUT YOU'VE LEARNED THAT YOU HAVE TO TAKE UP ARMS, RIGHT?
GASOLINE

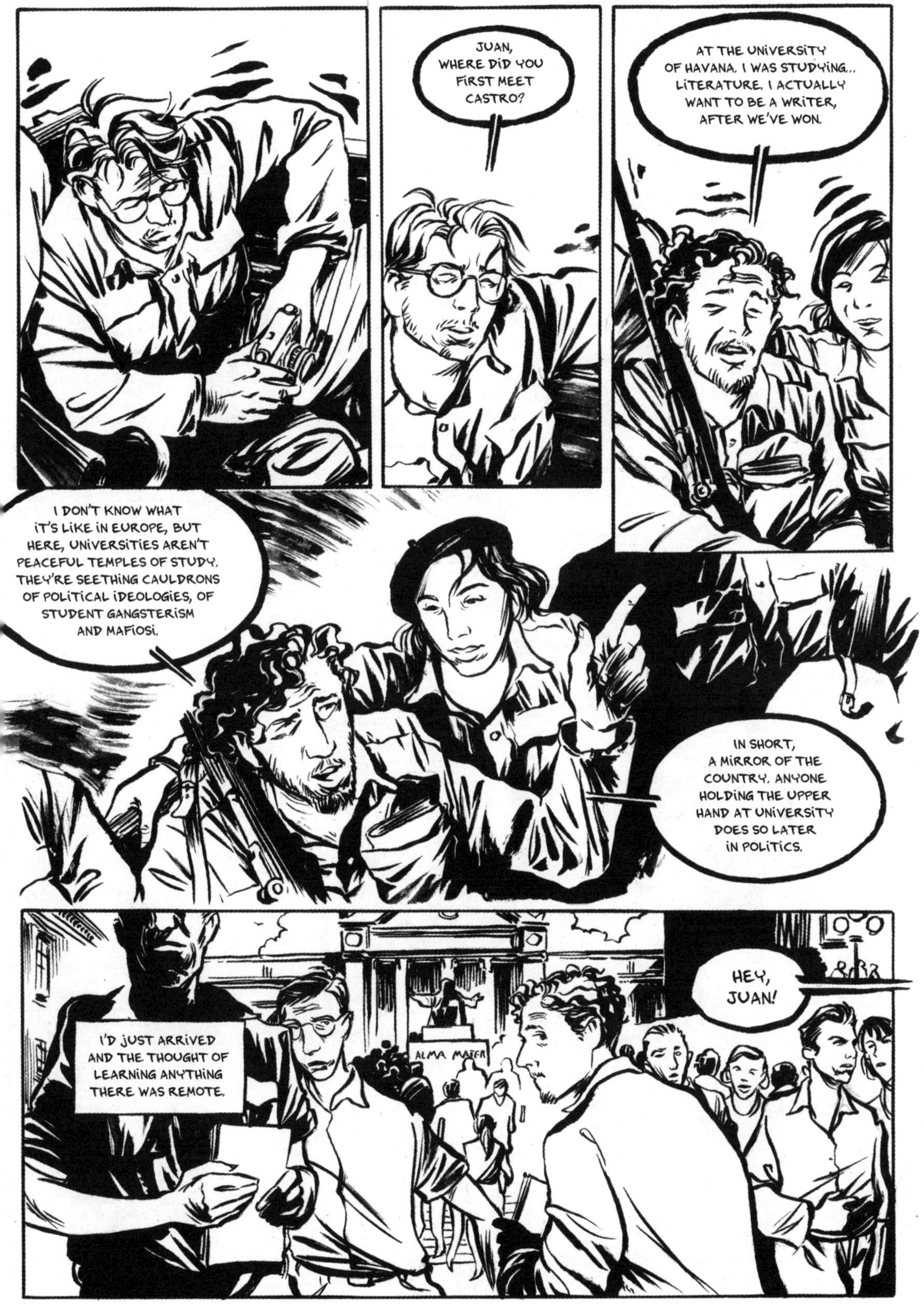
JUAN, WHERE DID YOU FIRST MEET CASTRO?
AT THE UNIVERSITY OF HAVANA. I WAS STUDYING... LITERATURE. I ACTUALLY WANT TO BE A WRITER, AFTER WE'VE WON.
I DON'T KNOW WHAT IT'S LIKE IN EUROPE, BUT HERE, UNIVERSITIES AREN'T PEACEFUL TEMPLES OF STUDY. THEY'RE SEETHING CAULDRONS OF POLITICAL IDEOLOGIES, OF STUDENT GANGSTERISM AND MAFIOSI.
IN SHORT, A MIRROR OF THE COUNTRY. ANYONE HOLDING THE UPPER HAND AT UNIVERSITY DOES SO LATER IN POLITICS.
I'D JUST ARRIVED AND THE THOUGHT OF LEARNING ANYTHING THERE WAS REMOTE.
ALMA MATER
HEY, JUAN!

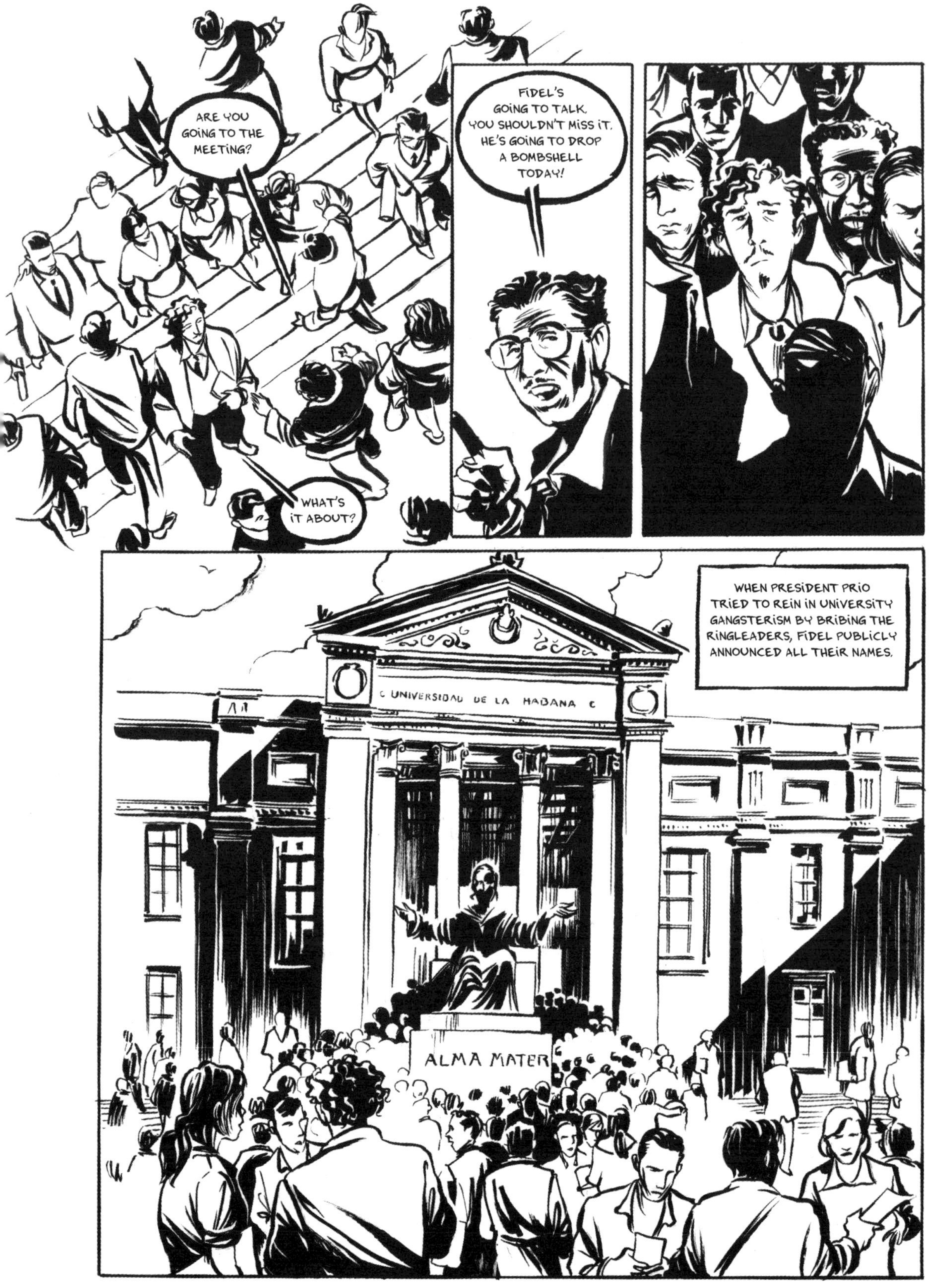
ARE YOU GOING TO THE MEETING?
WHAT'S IT ABOUT?
FIDEL'S GOING TO TALK. YOU SHOULDN'T MISS IT. HE'S GOING TO DROP A BOMBSHELL TODAY!
WHEN PRESIDENT PRIO TRIED TO REIN IN UNIVERSITY GANGSTERISM BY BRIBING THE RINGLEADERS, FIDEL PUBLICLY ANNOUNCED ALL THEIR NAMES.
UNIVERSIDAD DE LA HABANA
ALMA MATER

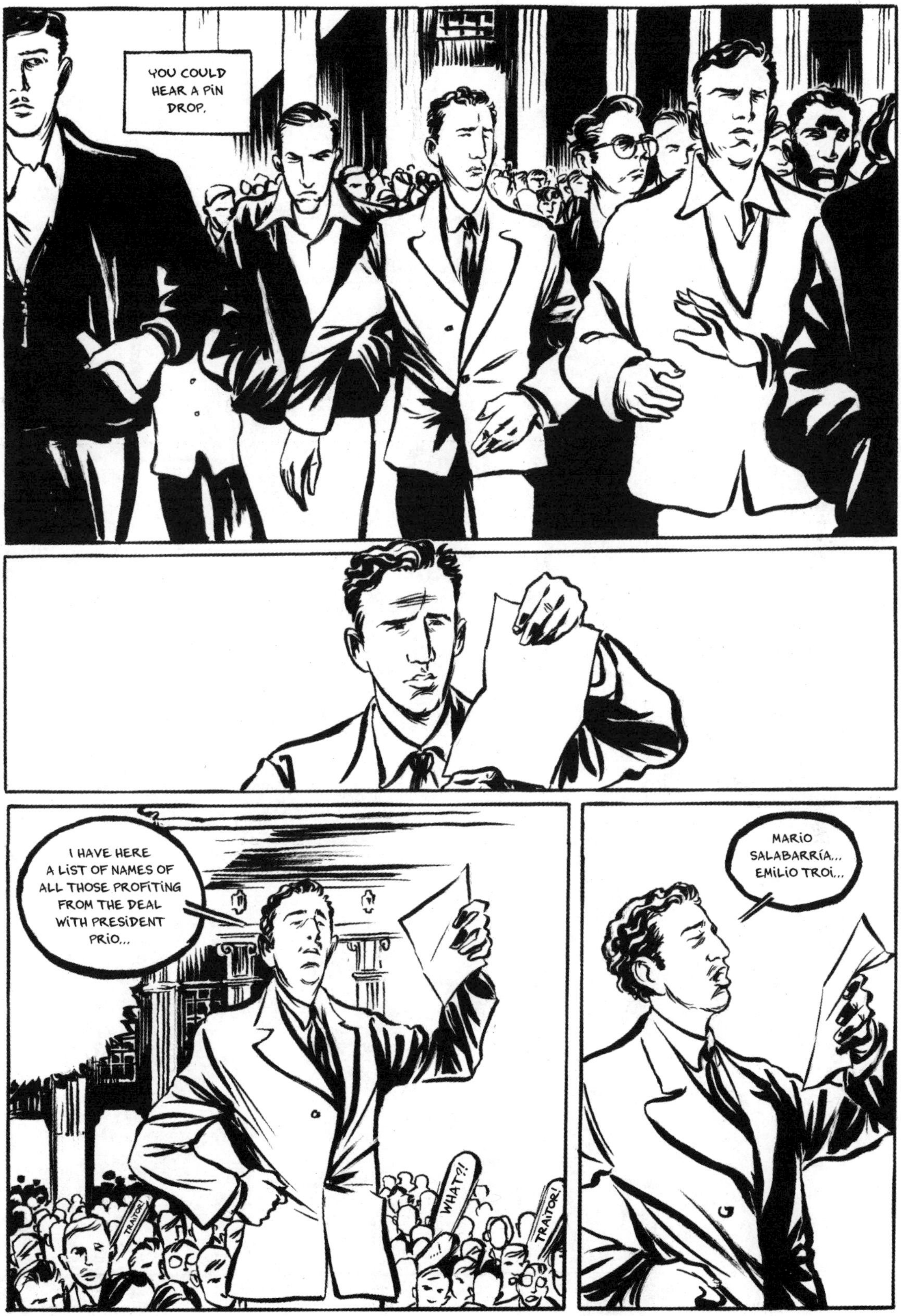
YOU COULD HEAR A PIN DROP.
I HAVE HERE A LIST OF NAMES OF ALL THOSE PROFITING FROM THE DEAL WITH PRESIDENT PRIO...
TRAITOR!
WHAT?!
TRAITOR!
MARIO SALABARRÍA... EMILIO TROI...

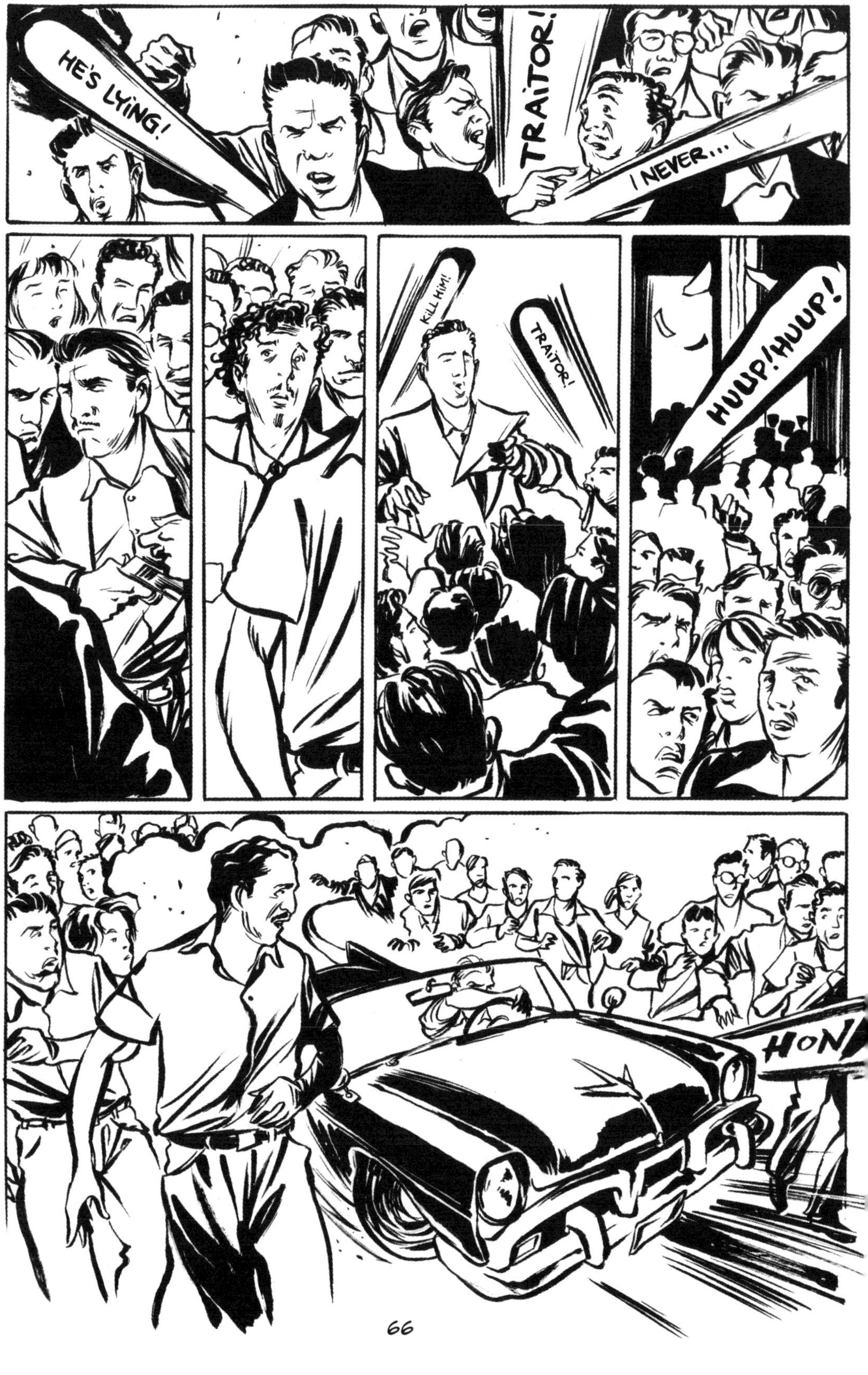
HE'S LYING!
TRAITOR!
I NEVER...
KILL HIM!
TRAITOR!
HUUP! HUUP!
HON

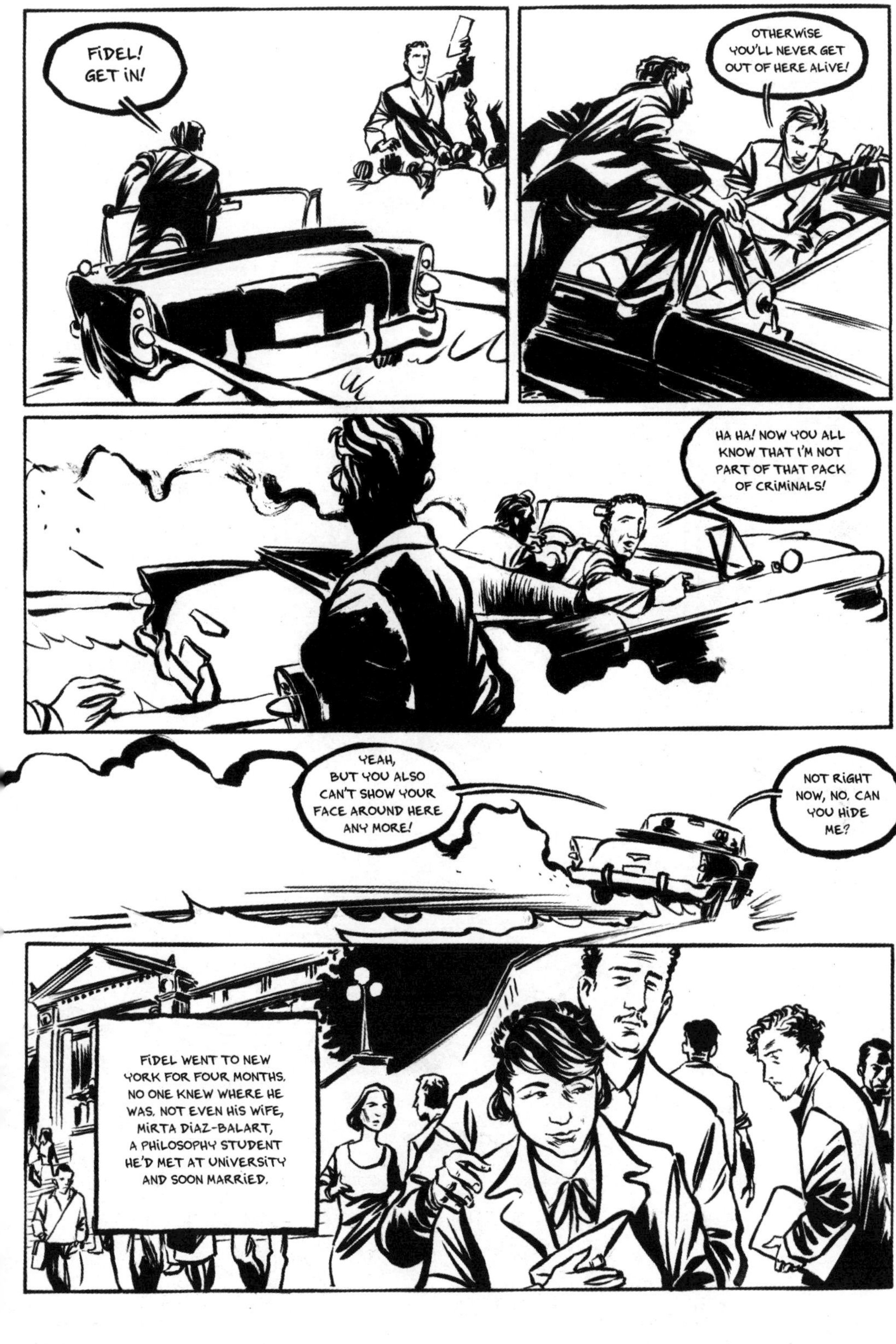
FIDEL! GET IN!
OTHERWISE YOU'LL NEVER GET OUT OF HERE ALIVE!
HA HA! NOW YOU ALL KNOW THAT I'M NOT PART OF THAT PACK OF CRIMINALS!
YEAH, BUT YOU ALSO CAN'T SHOW YOUR FACE AROUND HERE ANY MORE!
NOT RIGHT NOW, NO. CAN YOU HIDE ME?
FIDEL WENT TO NEW YORK FOR FOUR MONTHS. NO ONE KNEW WHERE HE WAS, NOT EVEN HIS WIFE, MIRTA DIAZ-BALART, A PHILOSOPHY STUDENT HE'D MET AT UNIVERSITY AND SOON MARRIED.

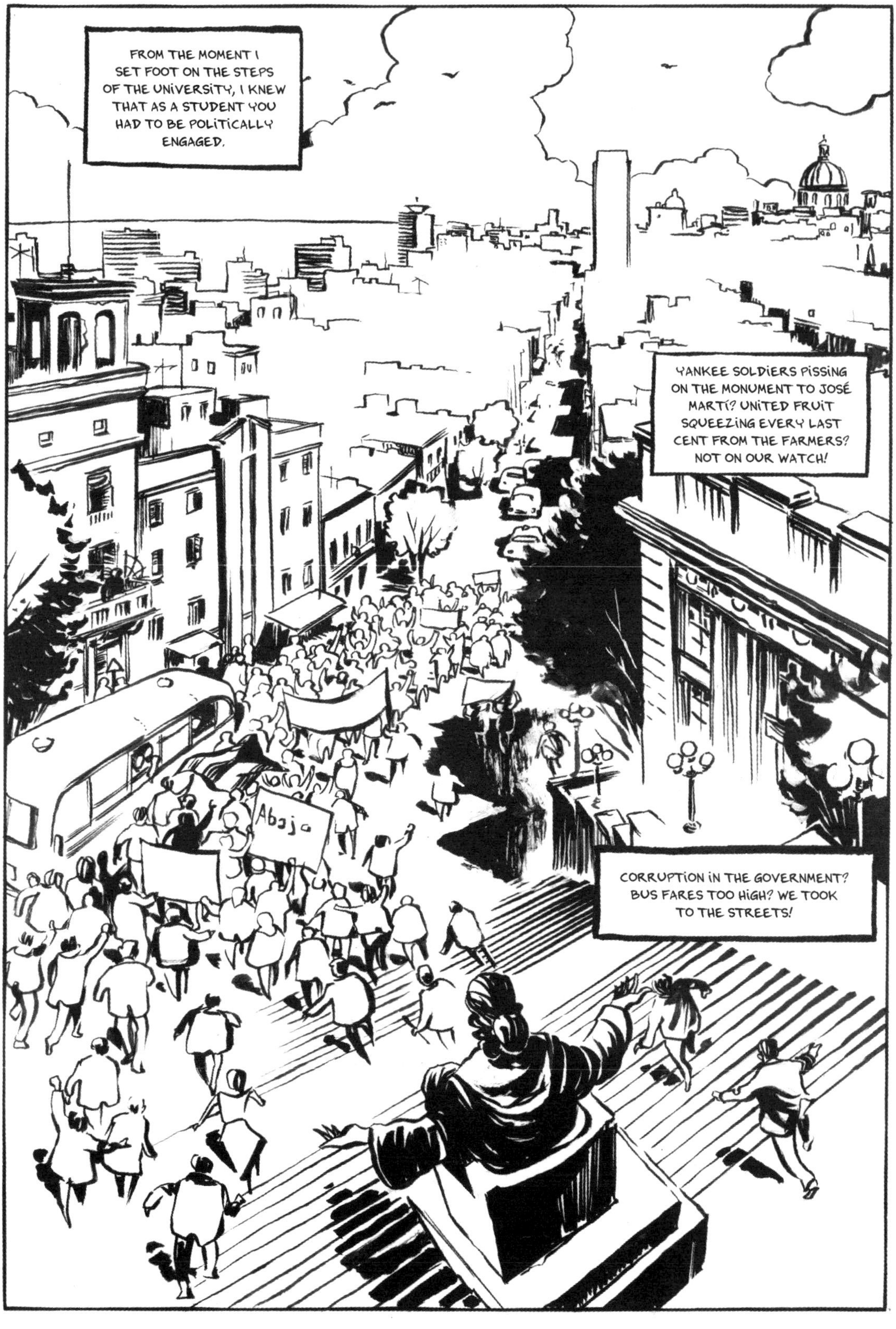
FROM THE MOMENT I SET FOOT ON THE STEPS OF THE UNIVERSITY, I KNEW THAT AS A STUDENT YOU HAD TO BE POLITICALLY ENGAGED.
YANKEE SOLDIERS PISSING ON THE MONUMENT TO JOSÉ MARTÍ? UNITED FRUIT SQUEEZING EVERY LAST CENT FROM THE FARMERS? NOT ON OUR WATCH!
Abajo
CORRUPTION IN THE GOVERNMENT? BUS FARES TOO HIGH? WE TOOK TO THE STREETS!

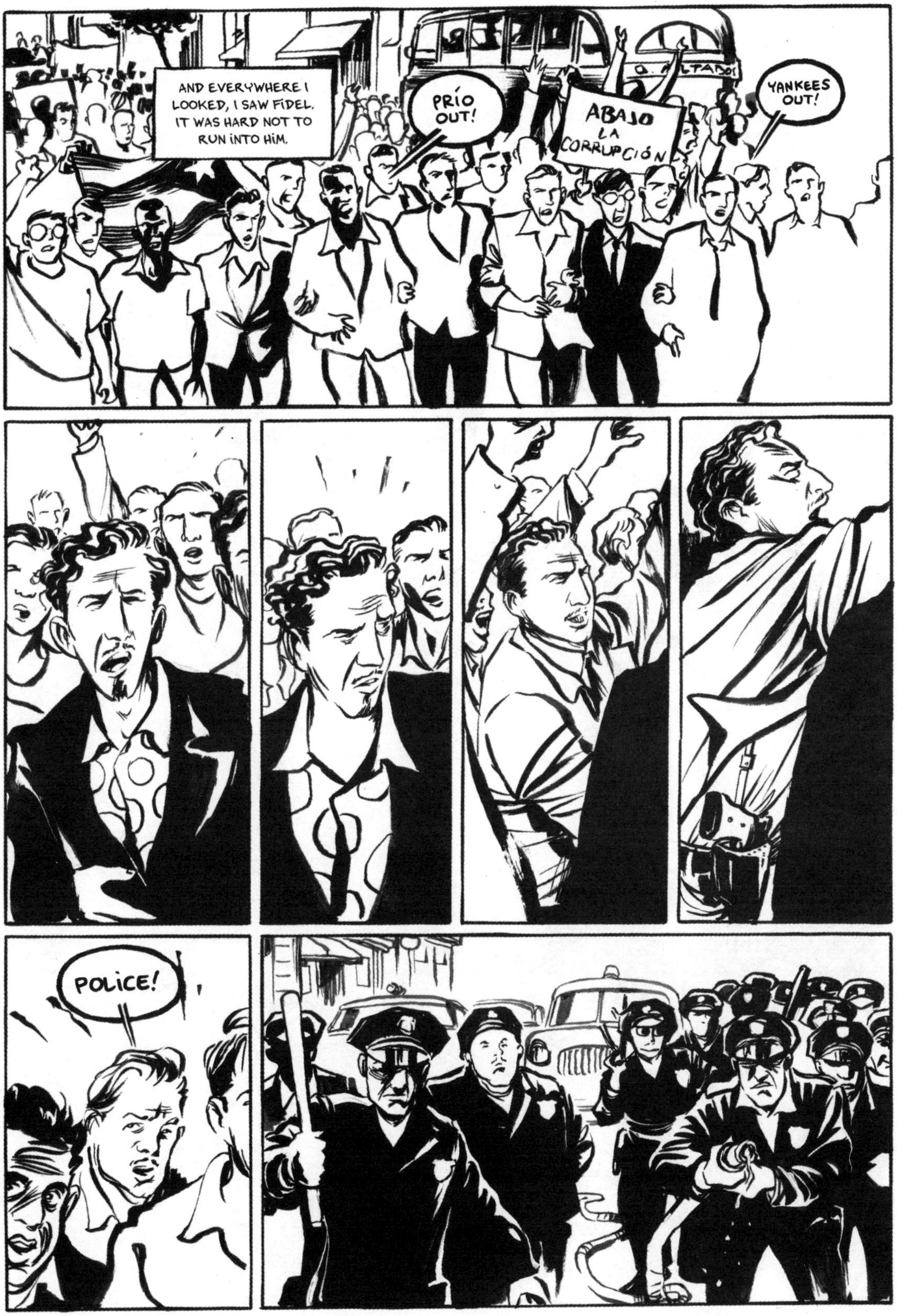
AND EVERYWHERE I LOOKED, I SAW FIDEL. IT WAS HARD NOT TO RUN INTO HIM.
PRÍO OUT!
ABAJO LA CORRUPCIÓN
YANKEES OUT!
POLICE!

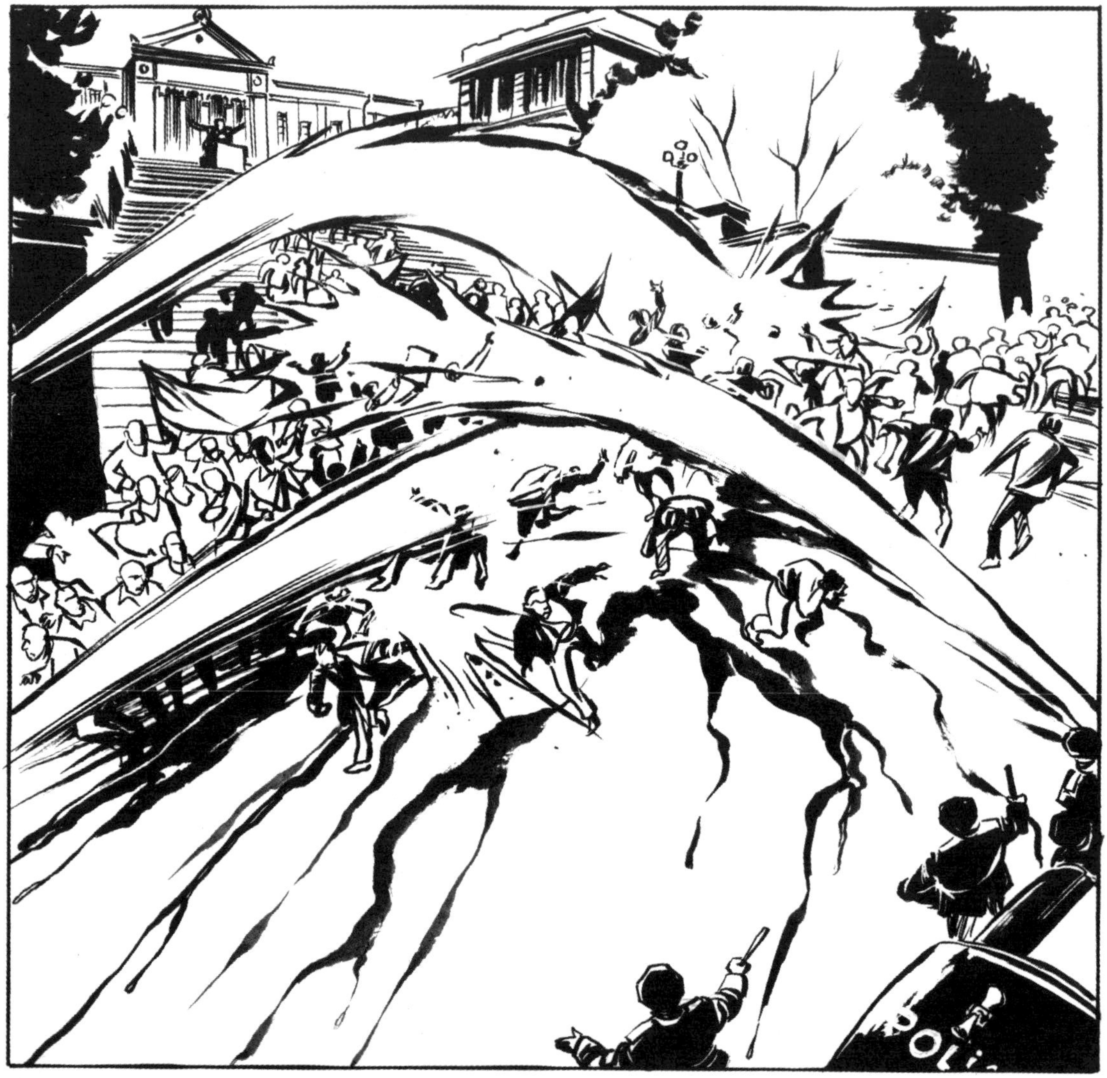
POLI

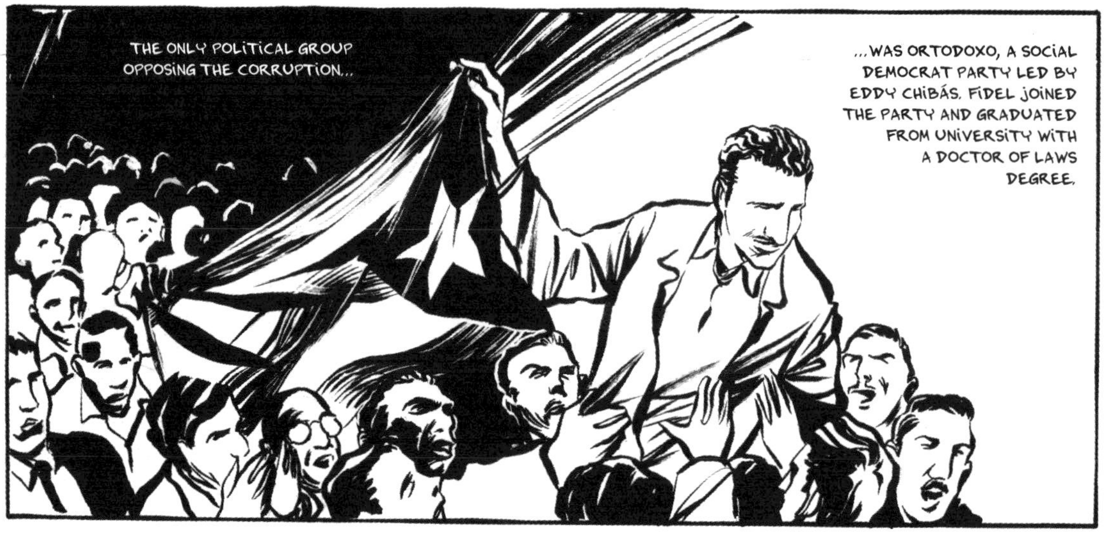
THE ONLY POLITICAL GROUP OPPOSING THE CORRUPTION...
...WAS ORTODOXO, A SOCIAL DEMOCRAT PARTY LED BY EDDY CHIBÁS. FIDEL JOINED THE PARTY AND GRADUATED FROM UNIVERSITY WITH A DOCTOR OF LAWS DEGREE.

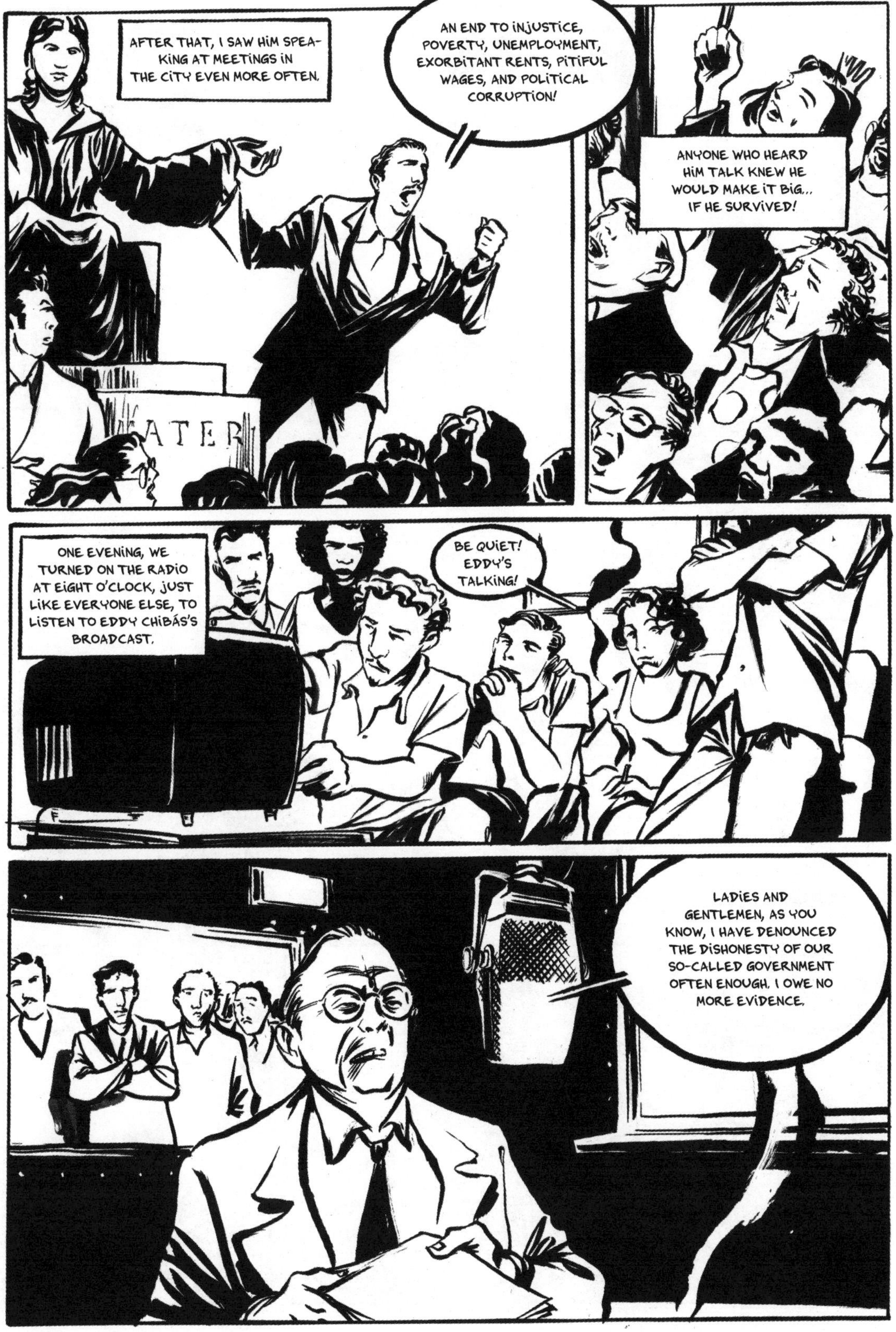
AFTER THAT, I SAW HIM SPEAKING AT MEETINGS IN THE CITY EVEN MORE OFTEN.
AN END TO INJUSTICE, POVERTY, UNEMPLOYMENT, EXORBITANT RENTS, PITIFUL WAGES, AND POLITICAL CORRUPTION!
ATER
ANYONE WHO HEARD HIM TALK KNEW HE WOULD MAKE IT BIG... IF HE SURVIVED!
ONE EVENING, WE TURNED ON THE RADIO AT EIGHT O'CLOCK, JUST LIKE EVERYONE ELSE, TO LISTEN TO EDDY CHIBÁS'S BROADCAST.
BE QUIET! EDDY'S TALKING!
LADIES AND GENTLEMEN, AS YOU KNOW, I HAVE DENOUNCED THE DISHONESTY OF OUR SO-CALLED GOVERNMENT OFTEN ENOUGH. I OWE NO MORE EVIDENCE.

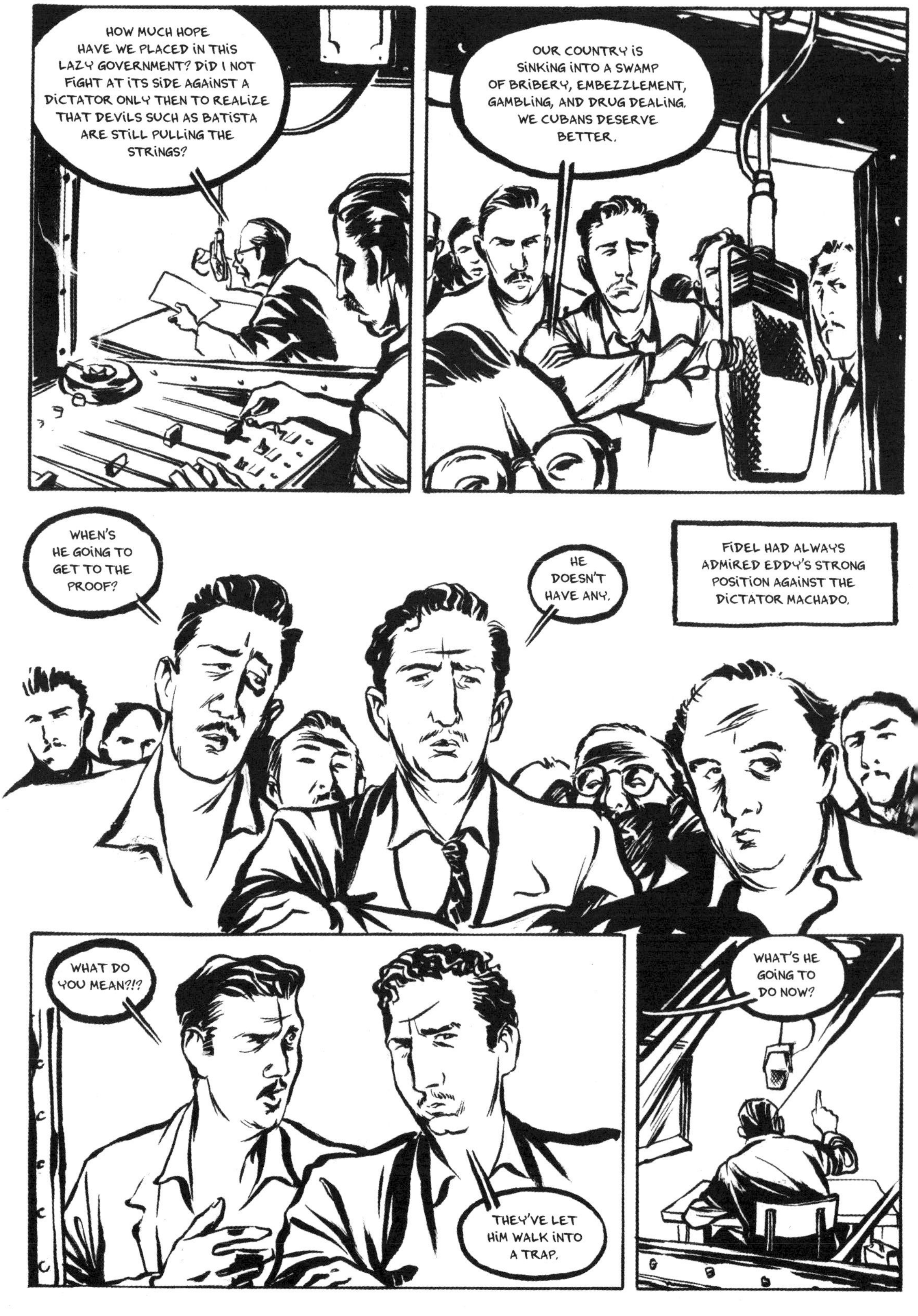
HOW MUCH HOPE HAVE WE PLACED IN THIS LAZY GOVERNMENT? DID I NOT FIGHT AT ITS SIDE AGAINST A DICTATOR ONLY THEN TO REALIZE THAT DEVILS SUCH AS BATISTA ARE STILL PULLING THE STRINGS?
OUR COUNTRY IS SINKING INTO A SWAMP OF BRIBERY, EMBEZZLEMENT, GAMBLING, AND DRUG DEALING. WE CUBANS DESERVE BETTER.
WHEN'S HE GOING TO GET TO THE PROOF?
HE DOESN'T HAVE ANY.
FIDEL HAD ALWAYS ADMIRED EDDY'S STRONG POSITION AGAINST THE DICTATOR MACHADO.
WHAT DO YOU MEAN?!?
THEY'VE LET HIM WALK INTO A TRAP.
WHAT'S HE GOING TO DO NOW?

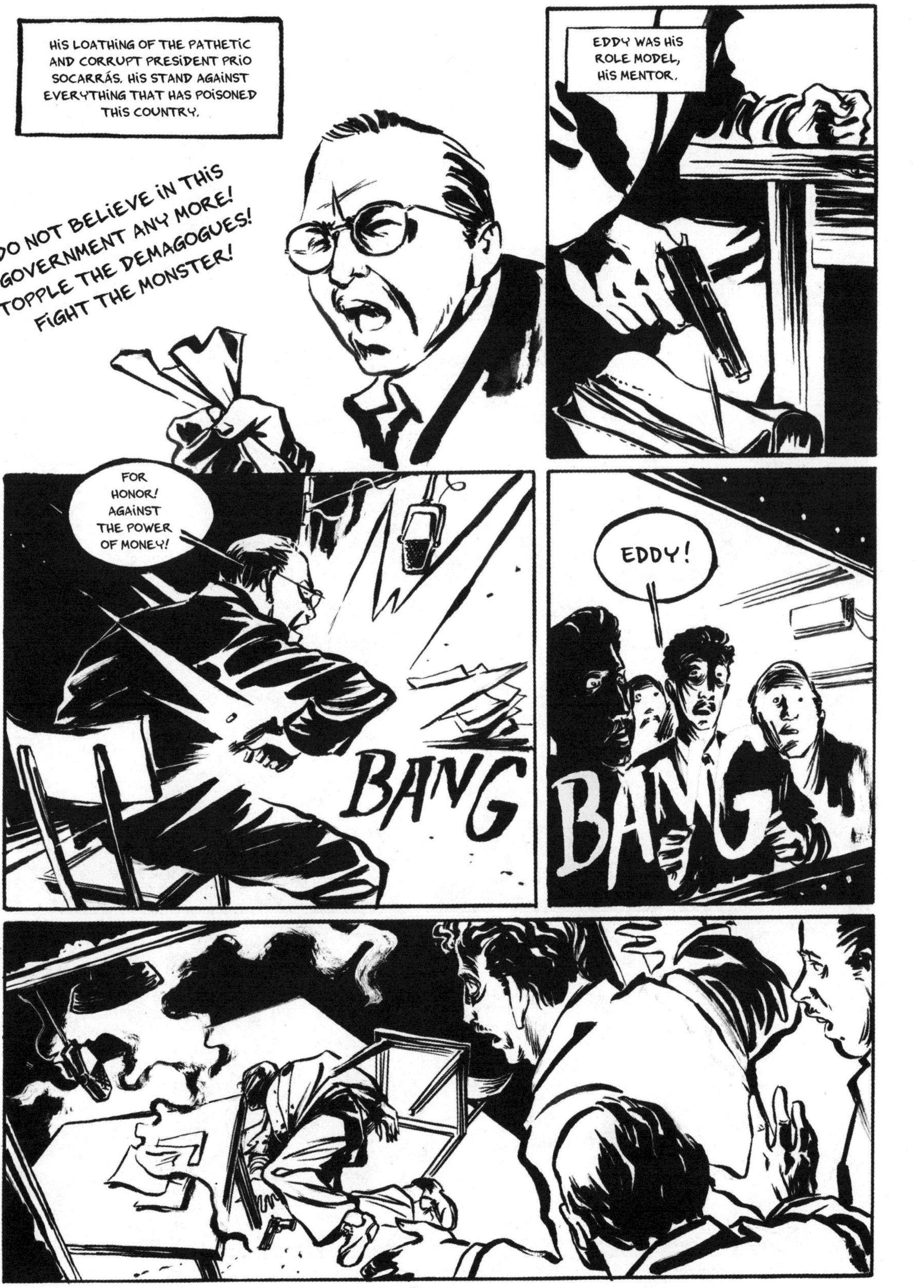
HIS LOATHING OF THE PATHETIC AND CORRUPT PRESIDENT PRIO SOCARRÁS, HIS STAND AGAINST EVERYTHING THAT HAS POISONED THIS COUNTRY.
DO NOT BELIEVE IN THIS GOVERNMENT ANY MORE! TOPPLE THE DEMAGOGUES! FIGHT THE MONSTER!
EDDY WAS HIS ROLE MODEL, HIS MENTOR.
FOR HONOR! AGAINST THE POWER OF MONEY!
BANG
EDDY!
BANG

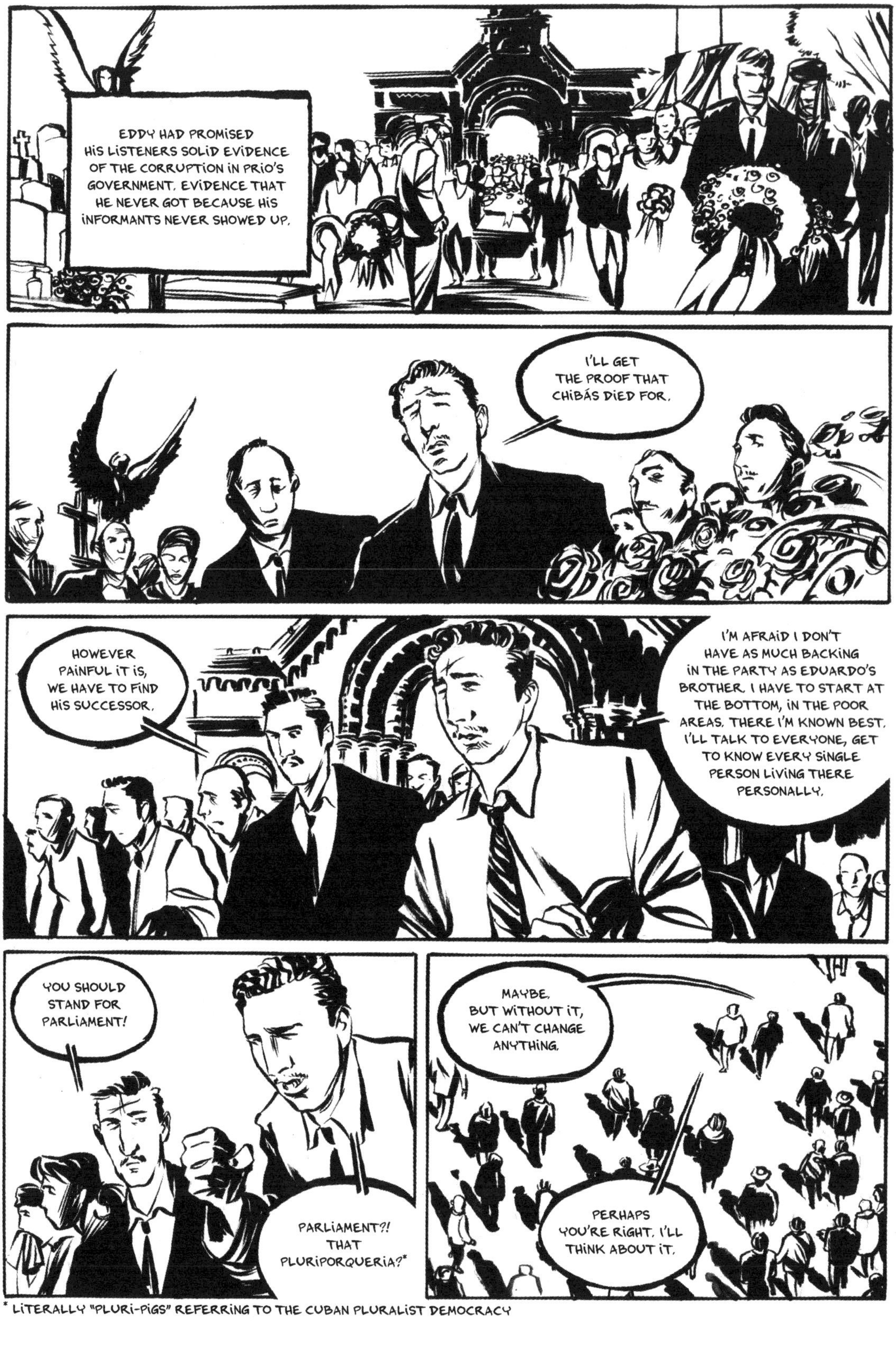
EDDY HAD PROMISED HIS LISTENERS SOLID EVIDENCE OF THE CORRUPTION IN PRIO'S GOVERNMENT. EVIDENCE THAT HE NEVER GOT BECAUSE HIS INFORMANTS NEVER SHOWED UP.
I'LL GET THE PROOF THAT CHIBÁS DIED FOR.
HOWEVER PAINFUL IT IS, WE HAVE TO FIND HIS SUCCESSOR.
I'M AFRAID I DON'T HAVE AS MUCH BACKING IN THE PARTY AS EDUARDO'S BROTHER. I HAVE TO START AT THE BOTTOM, IN THE POOR AREAS. THERE I'M KNOWN BEST. I'LL TALK TO EVERYONE, GET TO KNOW EVERY SINGLE PERSON LIVING THERE PERSONALLY.
YOU SHOULD STAND FOR PARLIAMENT!
PARLIAMENT?! THAT PLURIPORQUERIA?*
MAYBE. BUT WITHOUT IT, WE CAN'T CHANGE ANYTHING.
PERHAPS YOU'RE RIGHT. I'LL THINK ABOUT IT.

* LITERALLY "PLURI-PIGS" REFERRING TO THE CUBAN PLURALIST DEMOCRACY

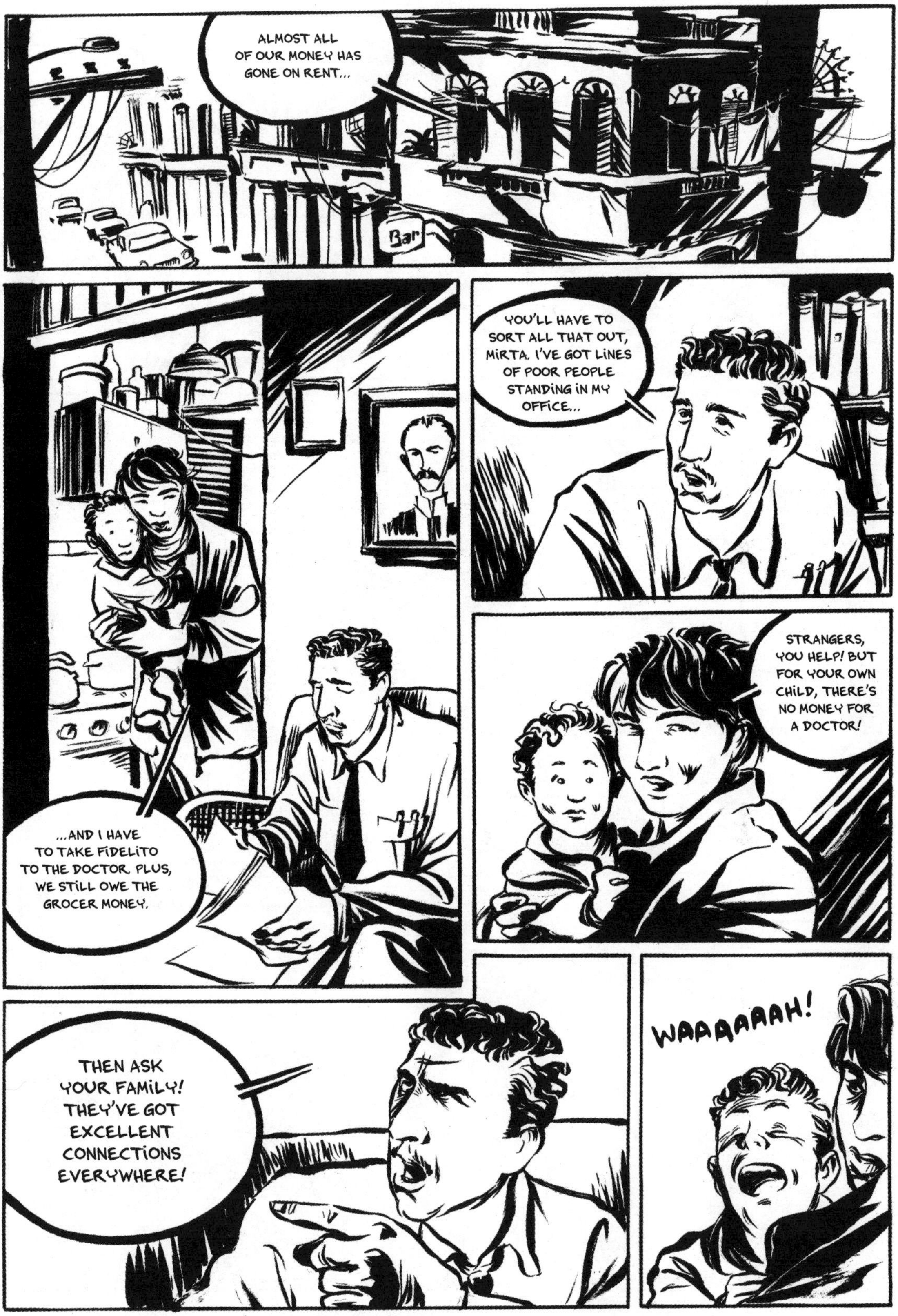
ALMOST ALL OF OUR MONEY HAS GONE ON RENT...
Bar
...AND I HAVE TO TAKE FIDELITO TO THE DOCTOR. PLUS, WE STILL OWE THE GROCER MONEY.
YOU'LL HAVE TO SORT ALL THAT OUT, MIRTA. I'VE GOT LINES OF POOR PEOPLE STANDING IN MY OFFICE...
STRANGERS, YOU HELP! BUT FOR YOUR OWN CHILD, THERE'S NO MONEY FOR A DOCTOR!
THEN ASK YOUR FAMILY! THEY'VE GOT EXCELLENT CONNECTIONS EVERYWHERE!
WAAAAAAH!

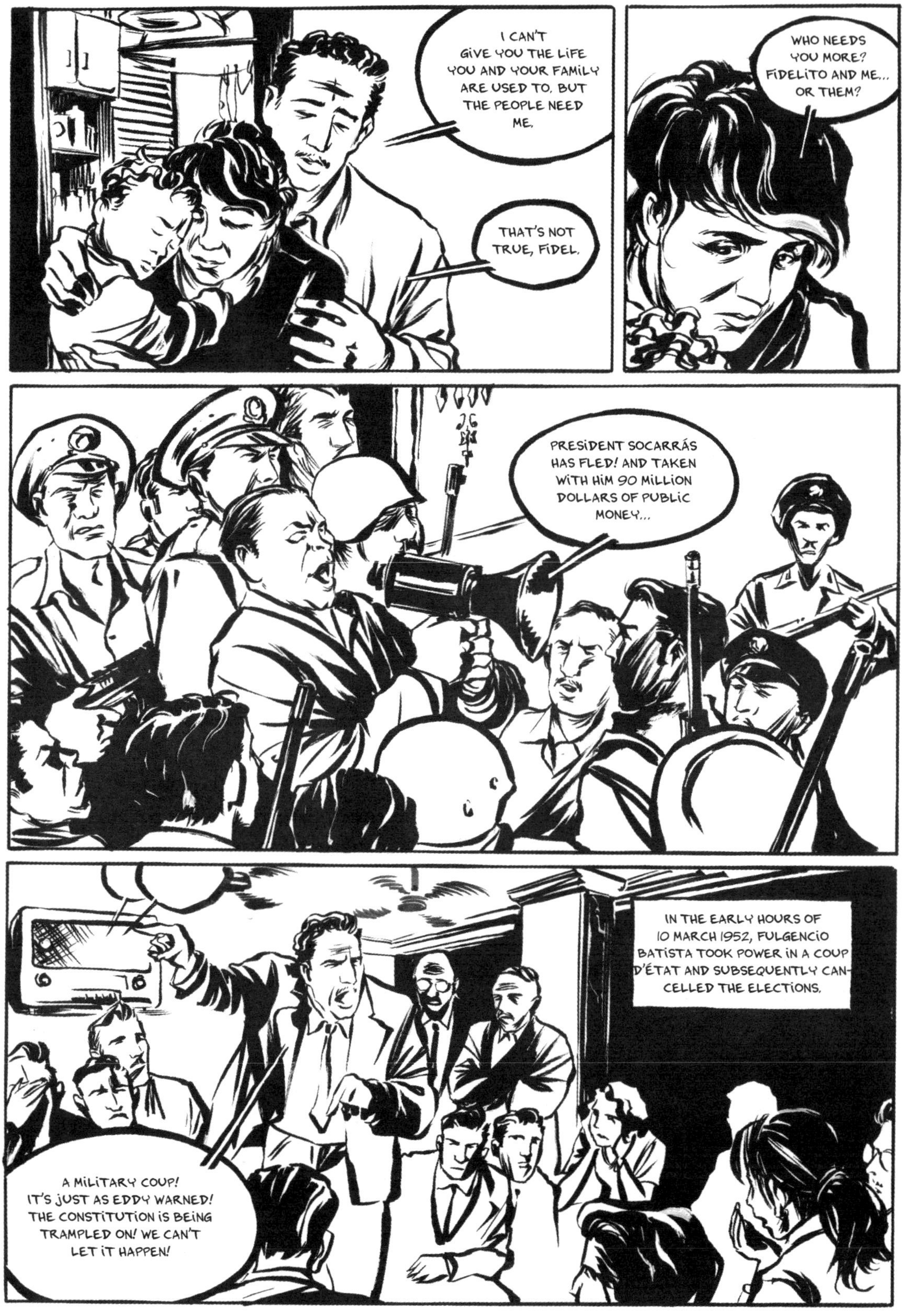
I CAN'T GiVE YOU THE LiFE YOU AND YOUR FAMiLY ARE USED TO, BUT THE PEOPLE NEED ME.
THAT'S NOT TRUE, FiDEL.
WHO NEEDS YOU MORE? FiDELiTO AND ME... OR THEM?
PRESiDENT SOCARRÁS HAS FLED! AND TAKEN WiTH HiM 90 MiLLiON DOLLARS OF PUBLiC MONEY...
IN THE EARLY HOURS OF 10 MARCH 1952, FULGENCiO BATiSTA TOOK POWER iN A COUP D'ÉTAT AND SUBSEQUENTLY CAN-CELLED THE ELECTiONS.
A MiLiTARY COUP! IT'S JUST AS EDDY WARNED! THE CONSTiTUTiON iS BEiNG TRAMPLED ON! WE CAN'T LET iT HAPPEN!

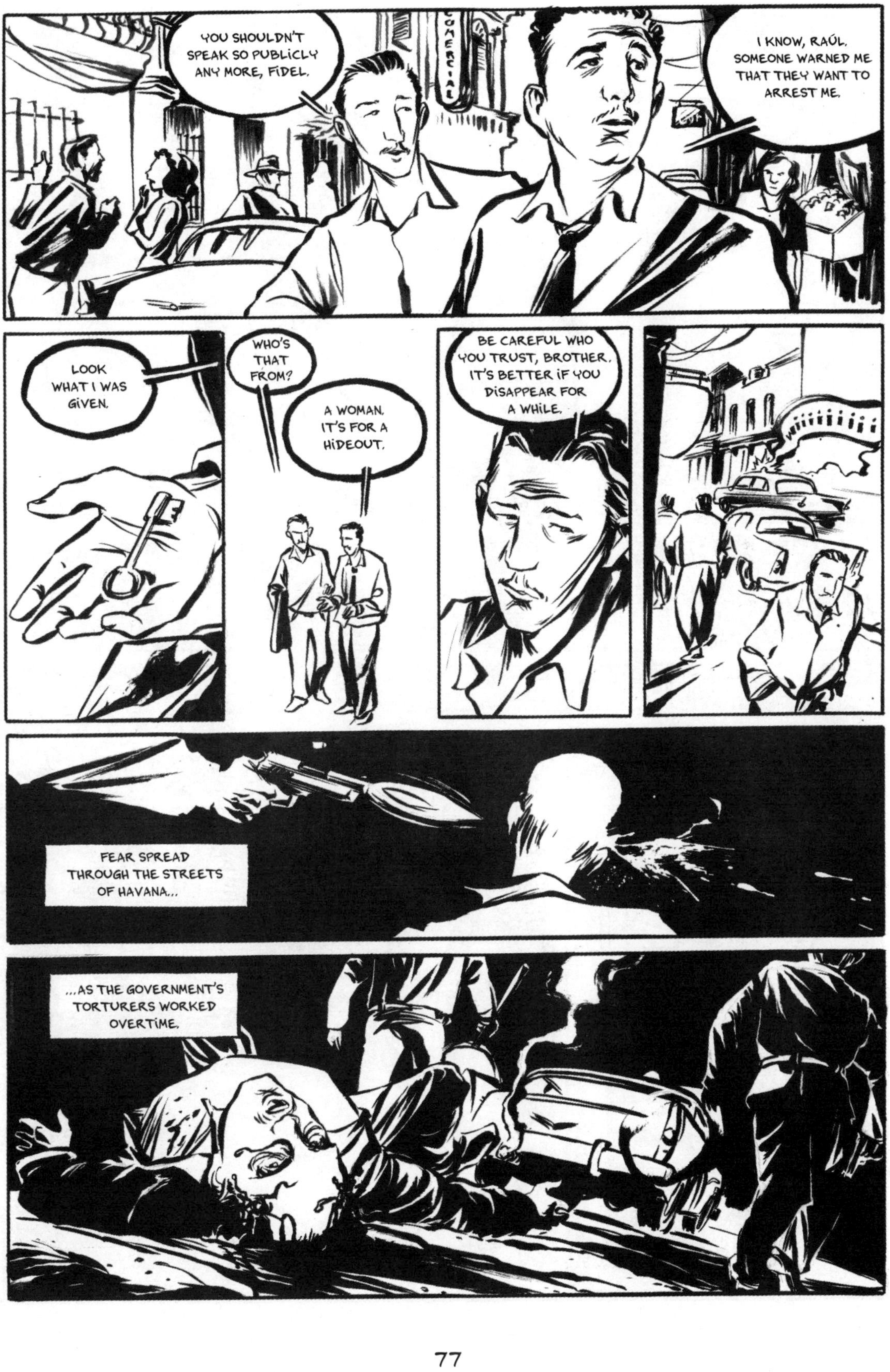
COMERCIAL
YOU SHOULDN'T SPEAK SO PUBLICLY ANY MORE, FIDEL.
I KNOW, RAÚL. SOMEONE WARNED ME THAT THEY WANT TO ARREST ME.
LOOK WHAT I WAS GIVEN.
WHO'S THAT FROM?
A WOMAN. IT'S FOR A HIDEOUT.
BE CAREFUL WHO YOU TRUST, BROTHER. IT'S BETTER IF YOU DISAPPEAR FOR A WHILE.
FEAR SPREAD THROUGH THE STREETS OF HAVANA...
...AS THE GOVERNMENT'S TORTURERS WORKED OVERTIME.

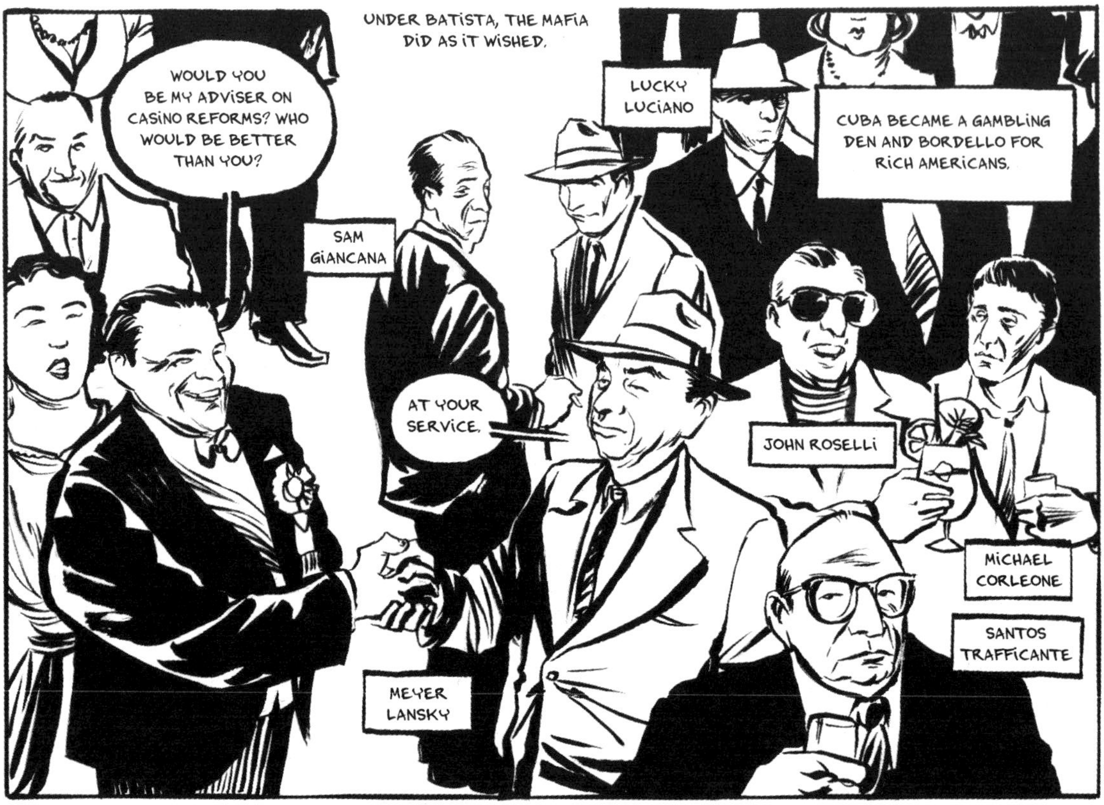
UNDER BATISTA, THE MAFIA DID AS IT WISHED.
WOULD YOU BE MY ADVISER ON CASINO REFORMS? WHO WOULD BE BETTER THAN YOU?
AT YOUR SERVICE.
SAM GIANCANA
LUCKY LUCIANO
CUBA BECAME A GAMBLING DEN AND BORDELLO FOR RICH AMERICANS.
JOHN ROSELLI
MICHAEL CORLEONE
SANTOS TRAFFICANTE
MEYER LANSKY

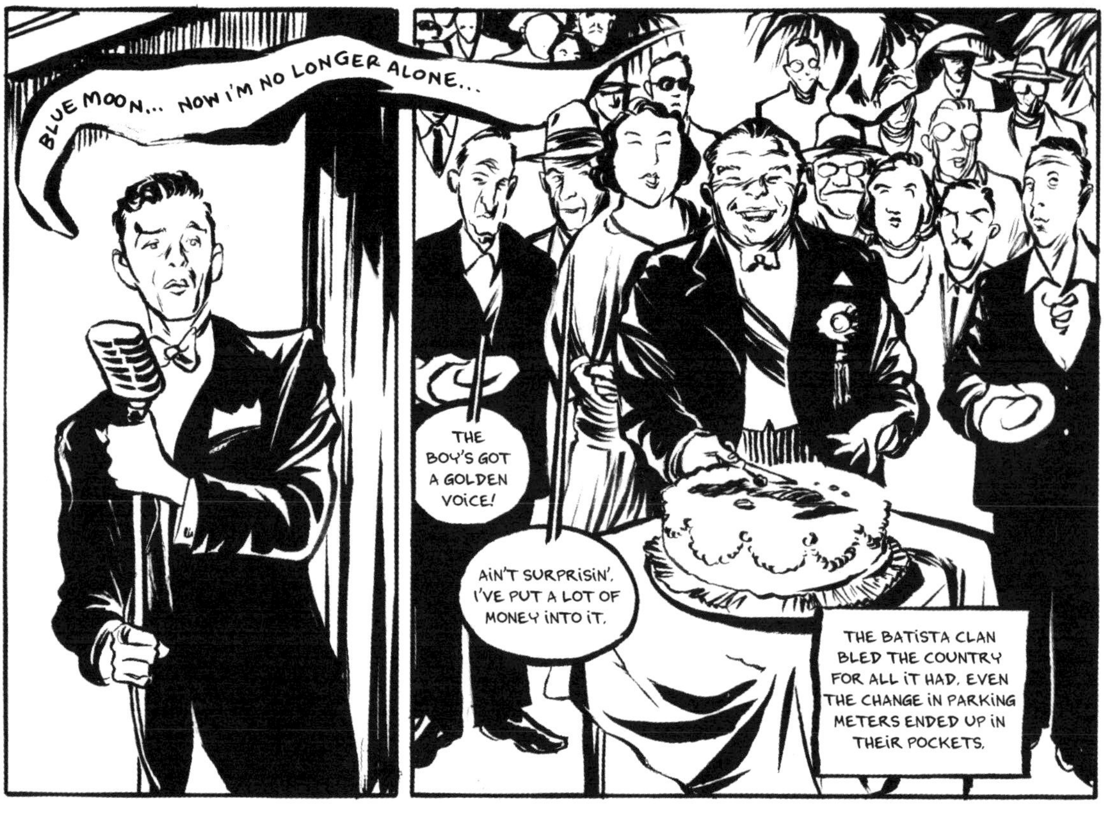
BLUE MOON... NOW I'M NO LONGER ALONE...
THE BOY'S GOT A GOLDEN VOICE!
AIN'T SURPRISIN'. I'VE PUT A LOT OF MONEY INTO IT.
THE BATISTA CLAN BLED THE COUNTRY FOR ALL IT HAD. EVEN THE CHANGE IN PARKING METERS ENDED UP IN THEIR POCKETS.

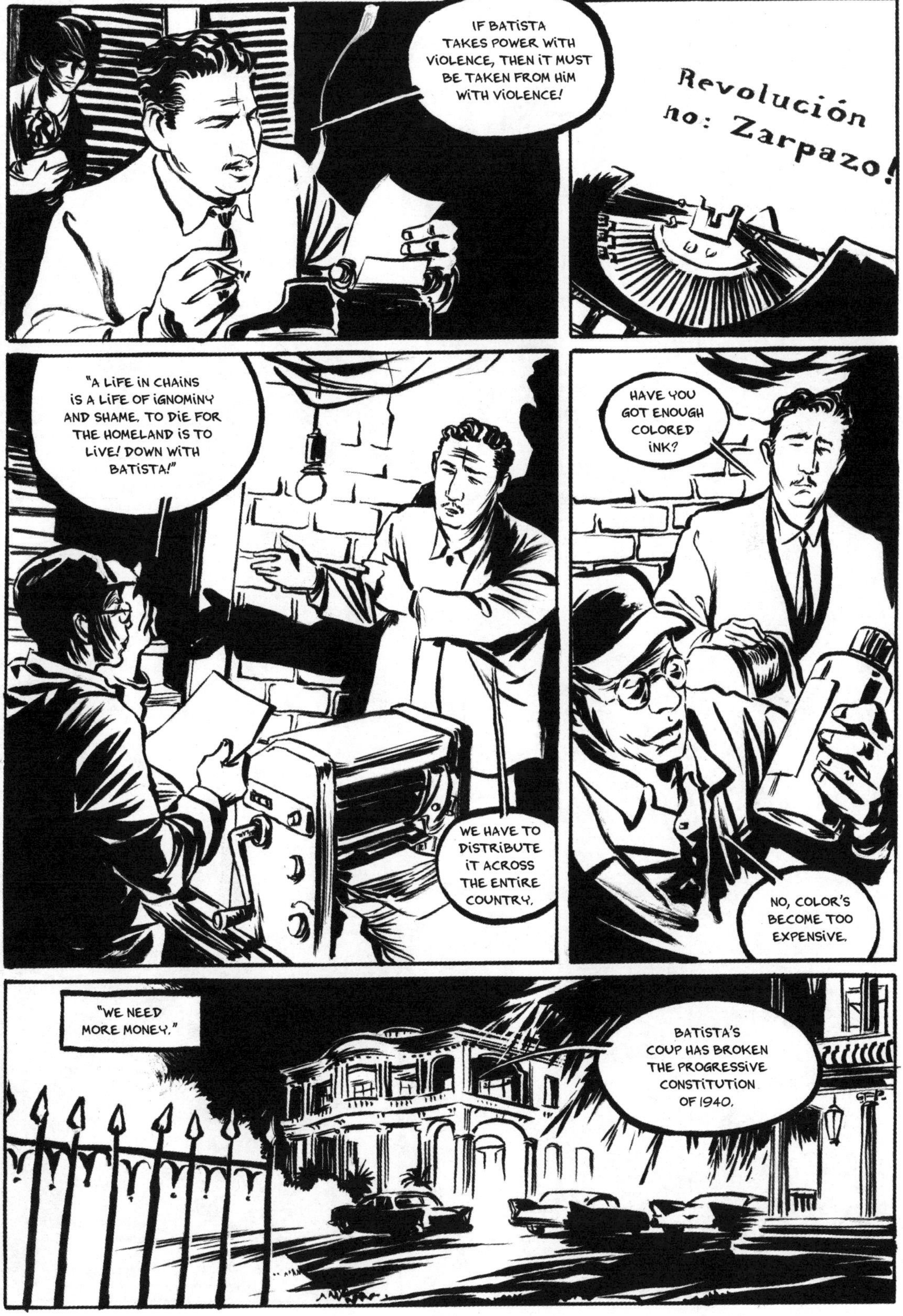
IF BATISTA TAKES POWER WITH VIOLENCE, THEN IT MUST BE TAKEN FROM HIM WITH VIOLENCE!
Revolución no: Zarpazo!
"A LIFE IN CHAINS IS A LIFE OF IGNOMINY AND SHAME. TO DIE FOR THE HOMELAND IS TO LIVE! DOWN WITH BATISTA!"
WE HAVE TO DISTRIBUTE IT ACROSS THE ENTIRE COUNTRY.
HAVE YOU GOT ENOUGH COLORED INK?
NO, COLOR'S BECOME TOO EXPENSIVE.
"WE NEED MORE MONEY."
BATISTA'S COUP HAS BROKEN THE PROGRESSIVE CONSTITUTION OF 1940.

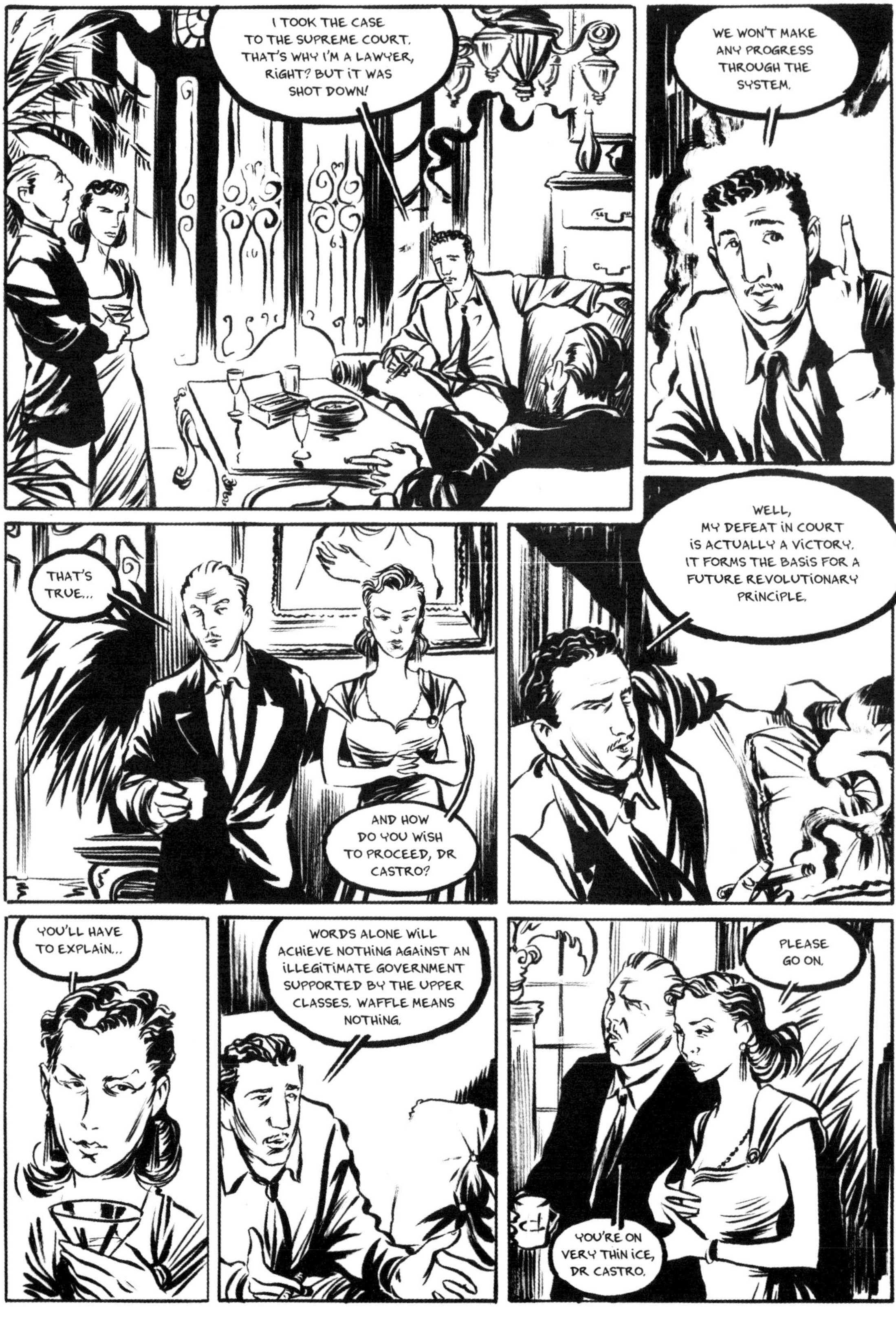
I TOOK THE CASE TO THE SUPREME COURT. THAT'S WHY I'M A LAWYER, RIGHT? BUT IT WAS SHOT DOWN!
WE WON'T MAKE ANY PROGRESS THROUGH THE SYSTEM.
THAT'S TRUE...
AND HOW DO YOU WISH TO PROCEED, DR CASTRO?
WELL, MY DEFEAT IN COURT IS ACTUALLY A VICTORY. IT FORMS THE BASIS FOR A FUTURE REVOLUTIONARY PRINCIPLE.
YOU'LL HAVE TO EXPLAIN...
WORDS ALONE WILL ACHIEVE NOTHING AGAINST AN ILLEGITIMATE GOVERNMENT SUPPORTED BY THE UPPER CLASSES. WAFFLE MEANS NOTHING.
PLEASE GO ON.
YOU'RE ON VERY THIN ICE, DR CASTRO.

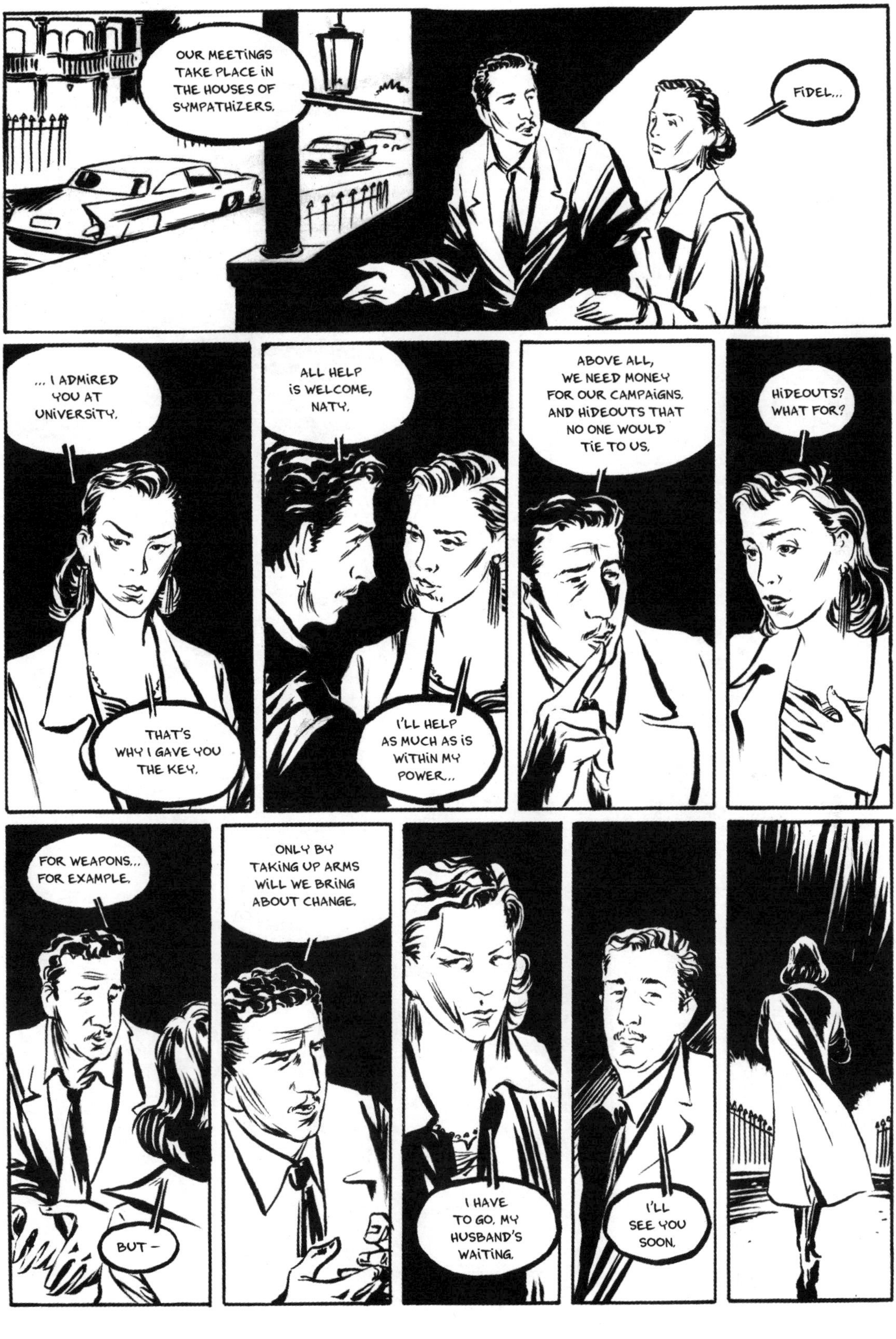
OUR MEETINGS TAKE PLACE IN THE HOUSES OF SYMPATHIZERS.
FIDEL...
... I ADMIRED YOU AT UNIVERSITY.
THAT'S WHY I GAVE YOU THE KEY.
ALL HELP IS WELCOME, NATY.
I'LL HELP AS MUCH AS IS WITHIN MY POWER...
ABOVE ALL, WE NEED MONEY FOR OUR CAMPAIGNS. AND HIDEOUTS THAT NO ONE WOULD TIE TO US.
HIDEOUTS? WHAT FOR?
FOR WEAPONS... FOR EXAMPLE.
BUT -
ONLY BY TAKING UP ARMS WILL WE BRING ABOUT CHANGE.
I HAVE TO GO. MY HUSBAND'S WAITING.
I'LL SEE YOU SOON.

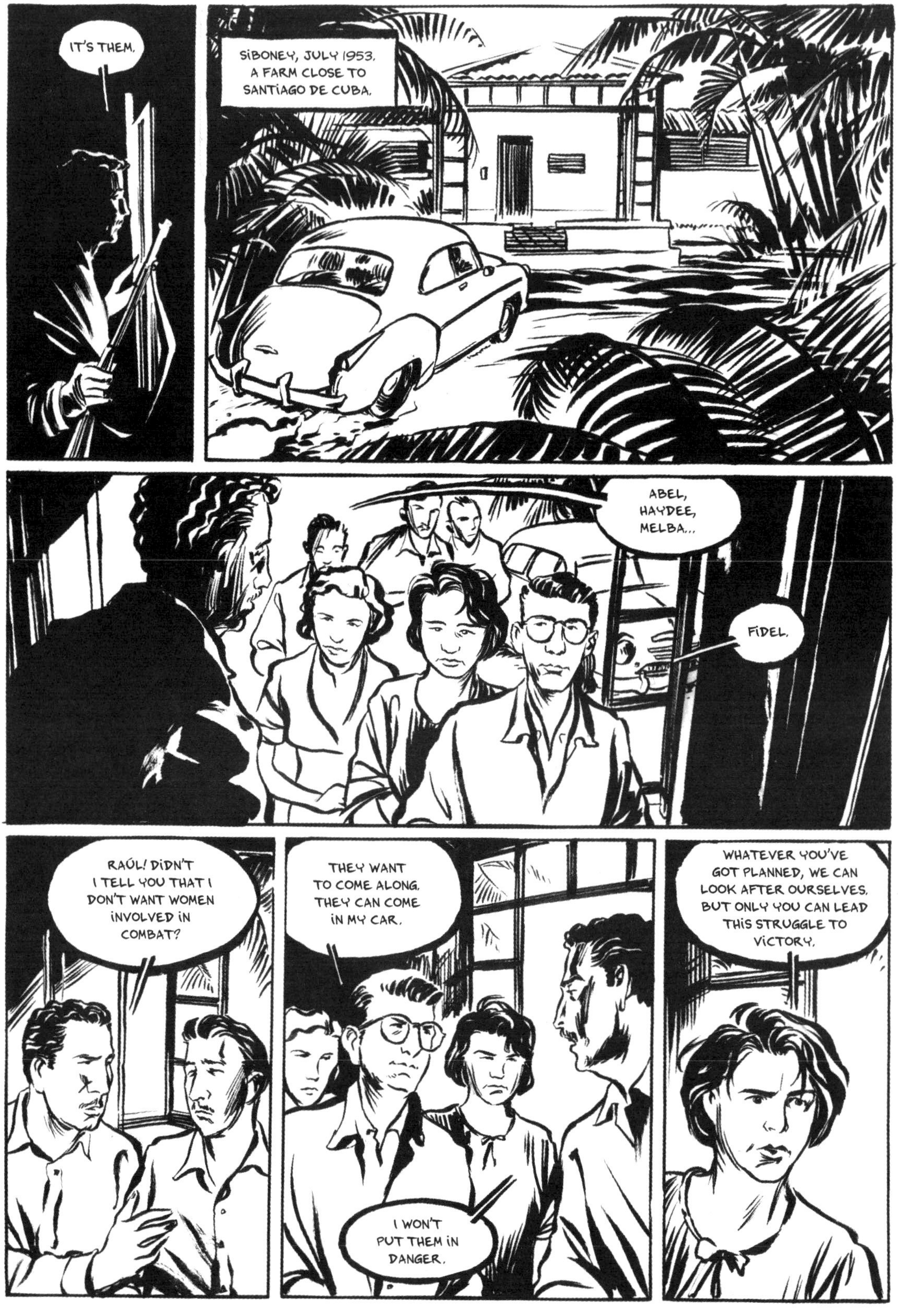
IT'S THEM.
SiBONEY, JULY 1953. A FARM CLOSE TO SANTiAGO DE CUBA.
ABEL, HAYDEE, MELBA...
FiDEL.
RAÚL! DiDN'T I TELL YOU THAT I DON'T WANT WOMEN iNVOLVED iN COMBAT?
THEY WANT TO COME ALONG. THEY CAN COME iN MY CAR.
I WON'T PUT THEM iN DANGER.
WHATEVER YOU'VE GOT PLANNED, WE CAN LOOK AFTER OURSELVES. BUT ONLY YOU CAN LEAD THIS STRUGGLE TO ViCTORY.

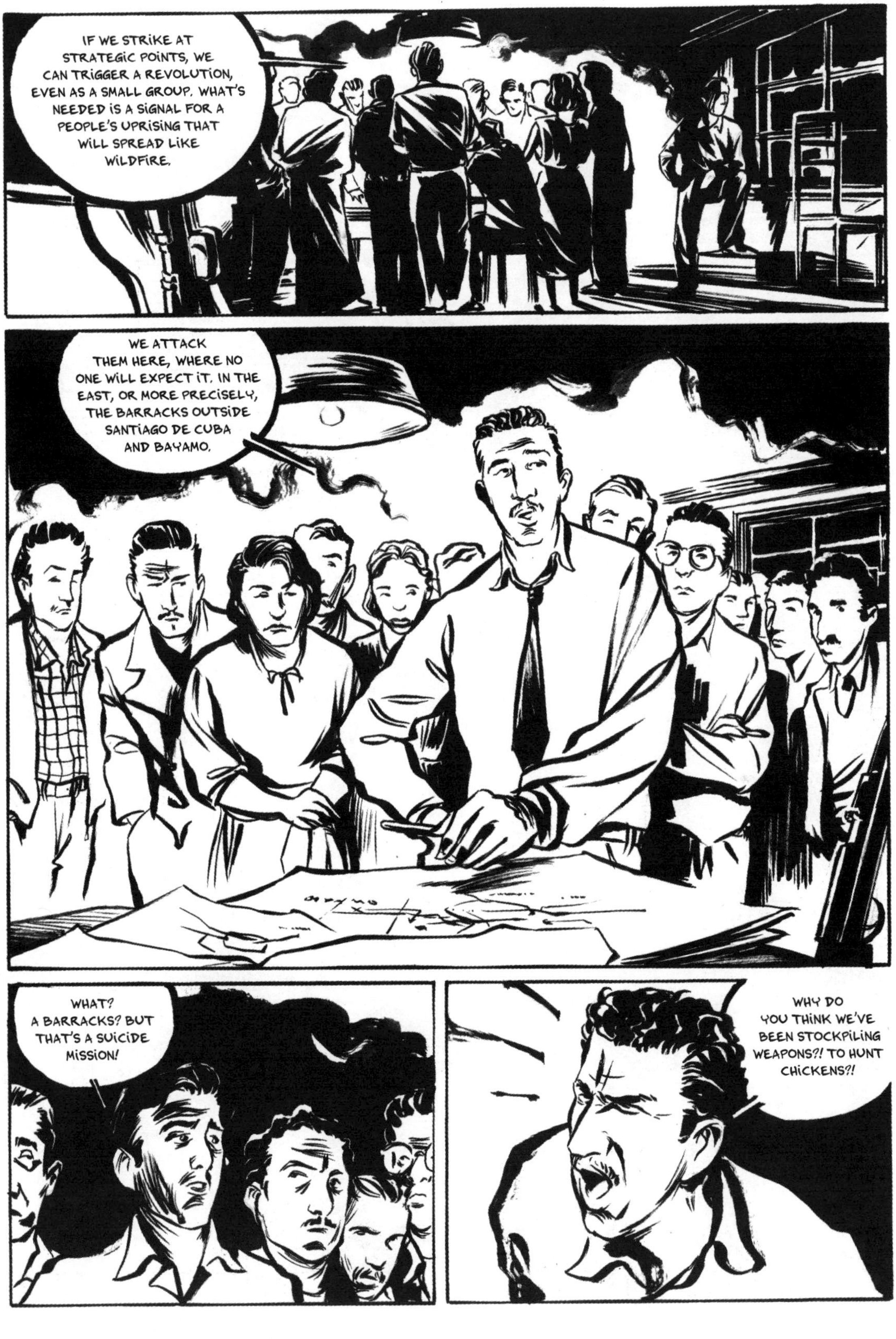
IF WE STRIKE AT STRATEGIC POINTS, WE CAN TRIGGER A REVOLUTION, EVEN AS A SMALL GROUP. WHAT'S NEEDED IS A SIGNAL FOR A PEOPLE'S UPRISING THAT WILL SPREAD LIKE WILDFIRE.
WE ATTACK THEM HERE, WHERE NO ONE WILL EXPECT IT. IN THE EAST, OR MORE PRECISELY, THE BARRACKS OUTSIDE SANTIAGO DE CUBA AND BAYAMO.
WHAT? A BARRACKS? BUT THAT'S A SUICIDE MISSION!
WHY DO YOU THINK WE'VE BEEN STOCKPILING WEAPONS?! TO HUNT CHICKENS?!

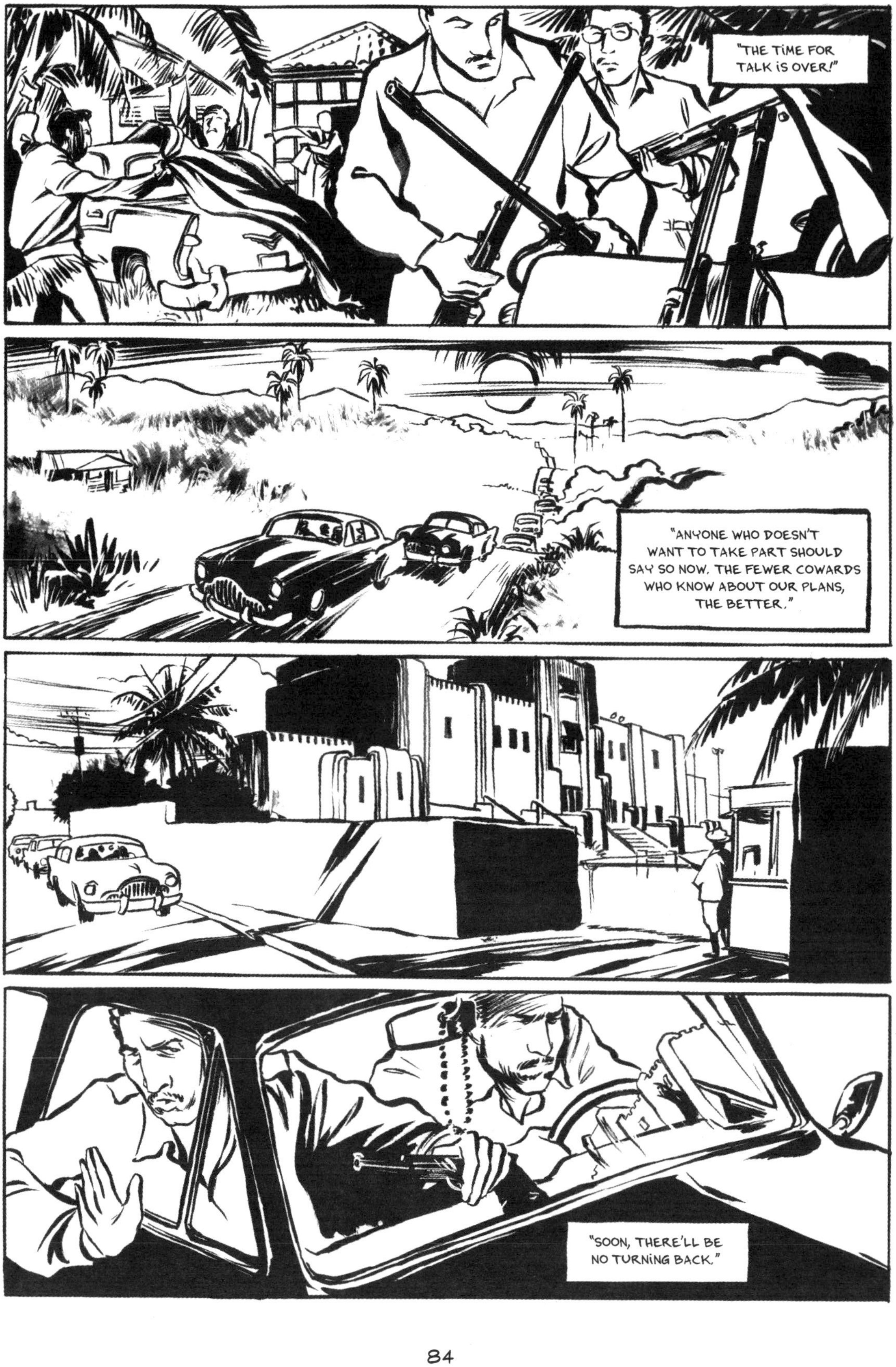
"THE TIME FOR TALK IS OVER!"
"ANYONE WHO DOESN'T WANT TO TAKE PART SHOULD SAY SO NOW. THE FEWER COWARDS WHO KNOW ABOUT OUR PLANS, THE BETTER."
"SOON, THERE'LL BE NO TURNING BACK."

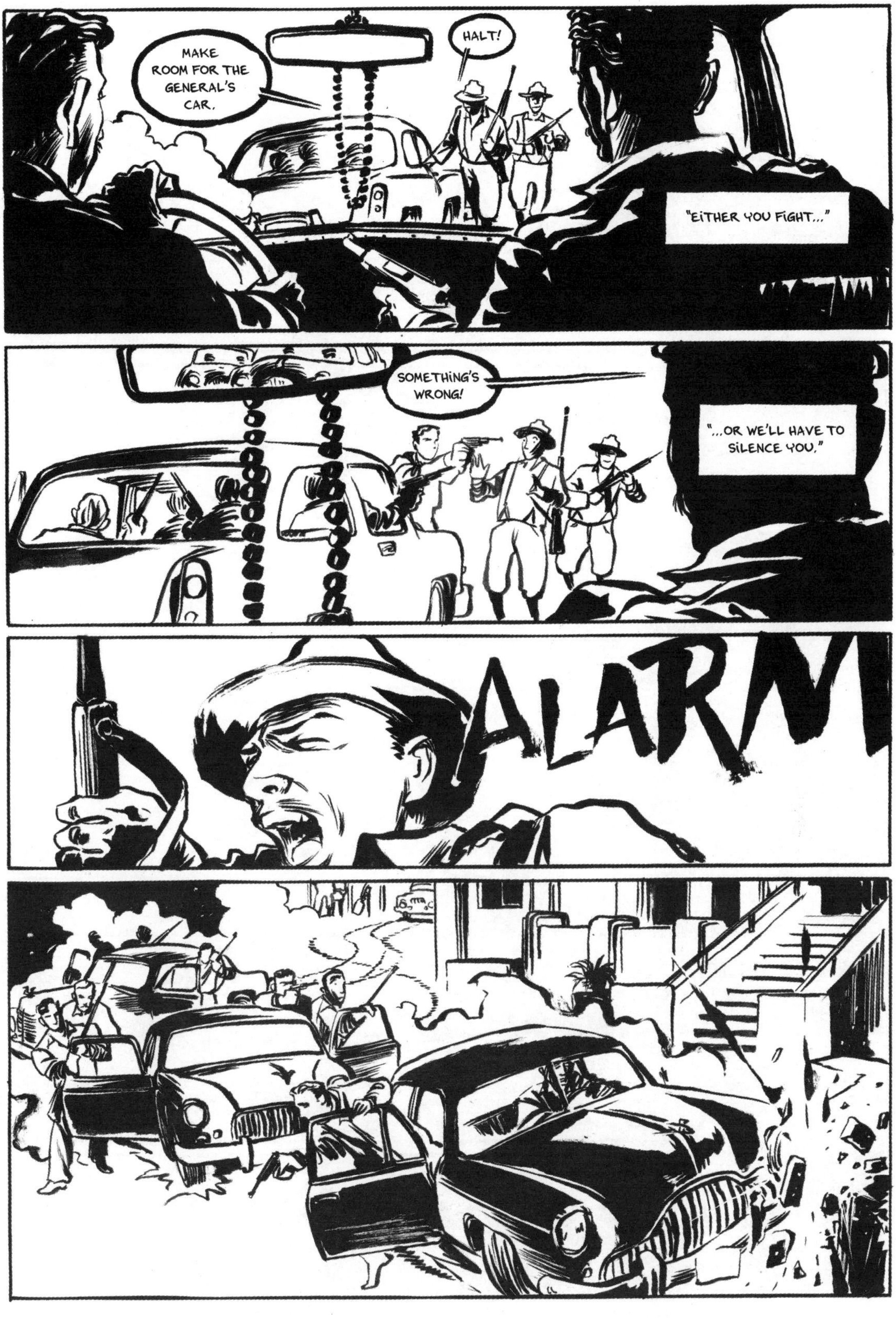
MAKE ROOM FOR THE GENERAL'S CAR.
HALT!
"EITHER YOU FIGHT..."
SOMETHING'S WRONG!
"...OR WE'LL HAVE TO SILENCE YOU."
ALARM

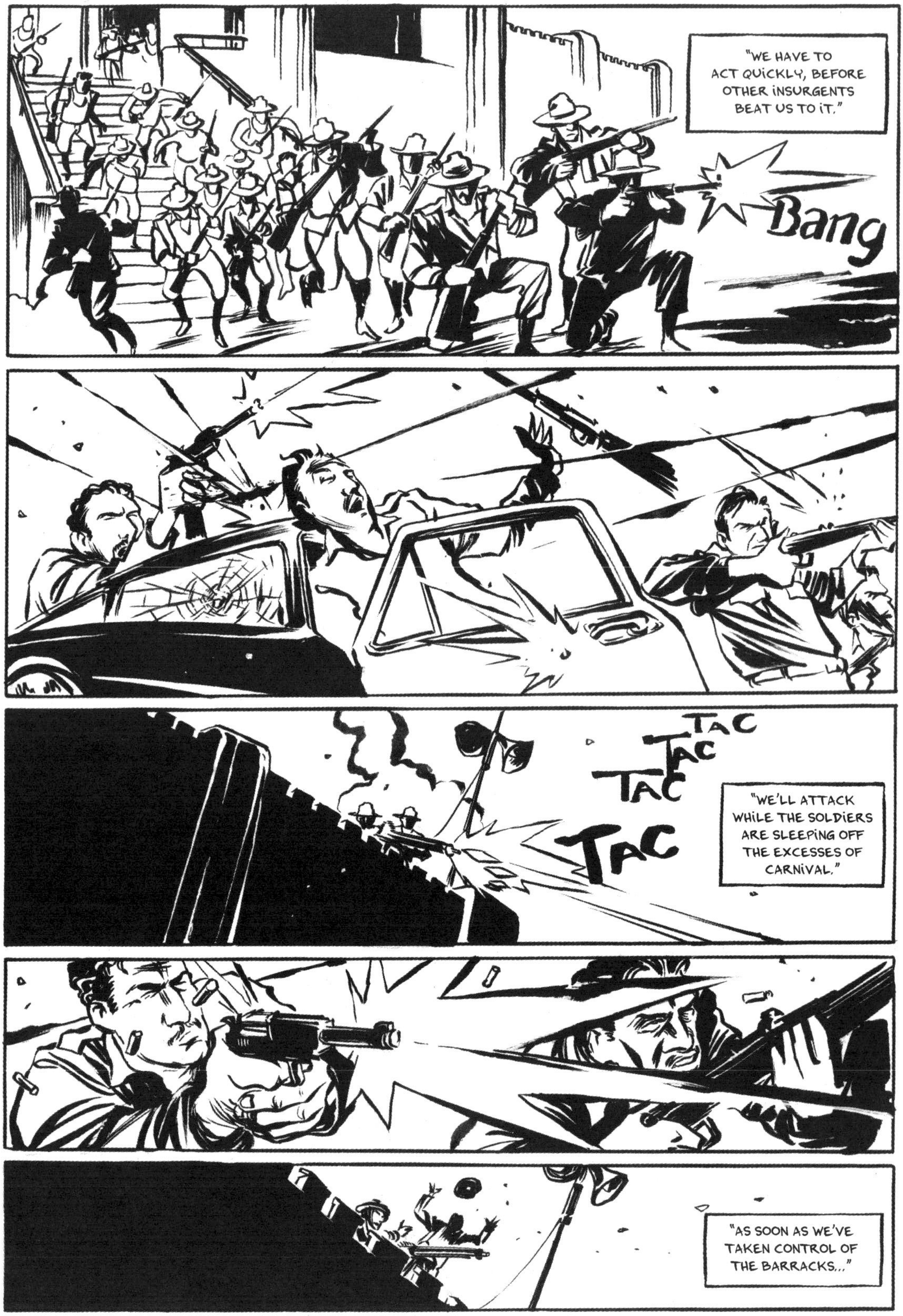
"WE HAVE TO ACT QUICKLY, BEFORE OTHER INSURGENTS BEAT US TO IT."
Bang
TAC
TAC
TAC
TAC
"WE'LL ATTACK WHILE THE SOLDIERS ARE SLEEPING OFF THE EXCESSES OF CARNIVAL."
"AS SOON AS WE'VE TAKEN CONTROL OF THE BARRACKS..."

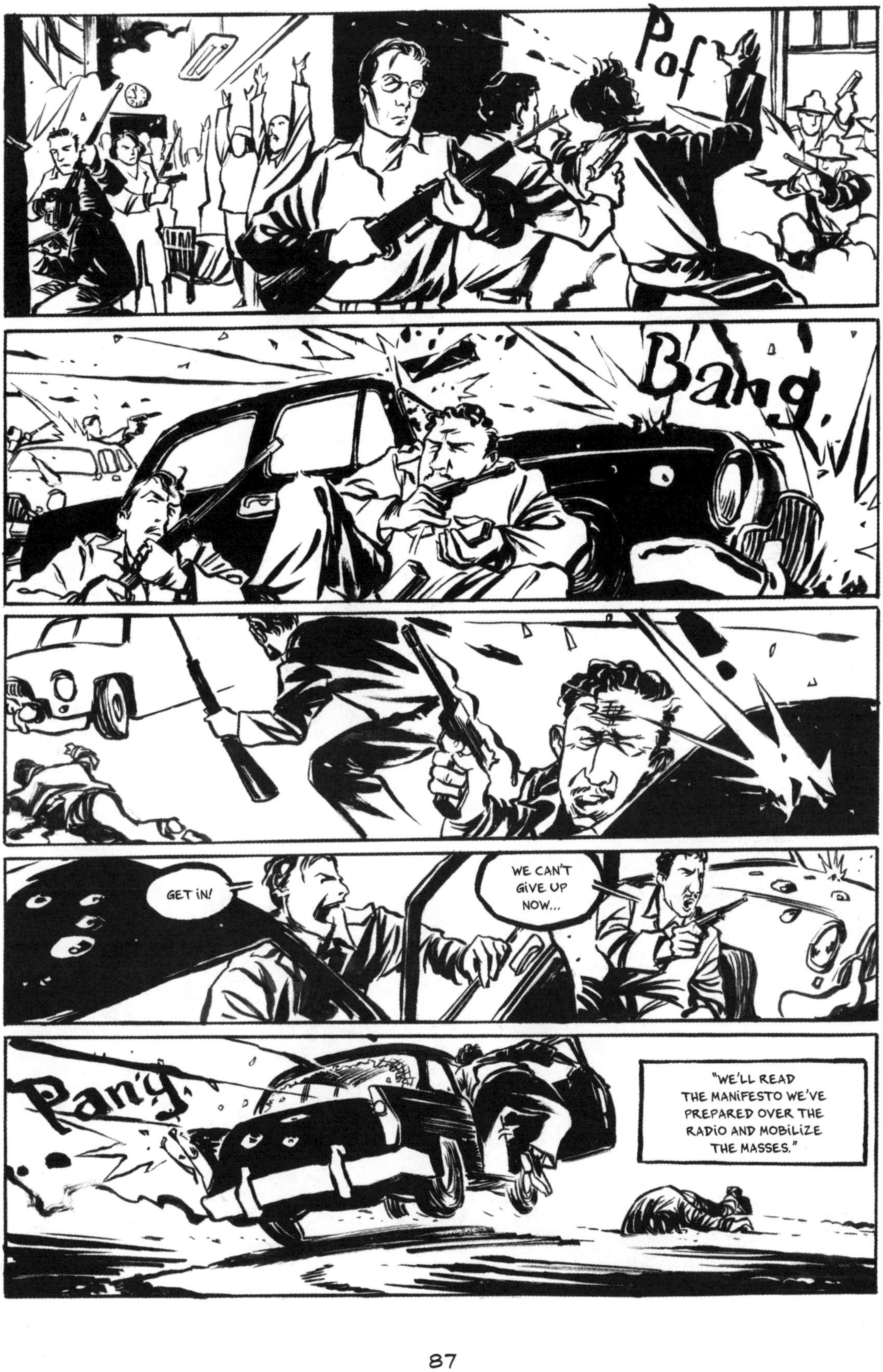
Pof
Bang.
GET IN!
WE CAN'T GIVE UP NOW...
Pang.
"WE'LL READ THE MANIFESTO WE'VE PREPARED OVER THE RADIO AND MOBILIZE THE MASSES."

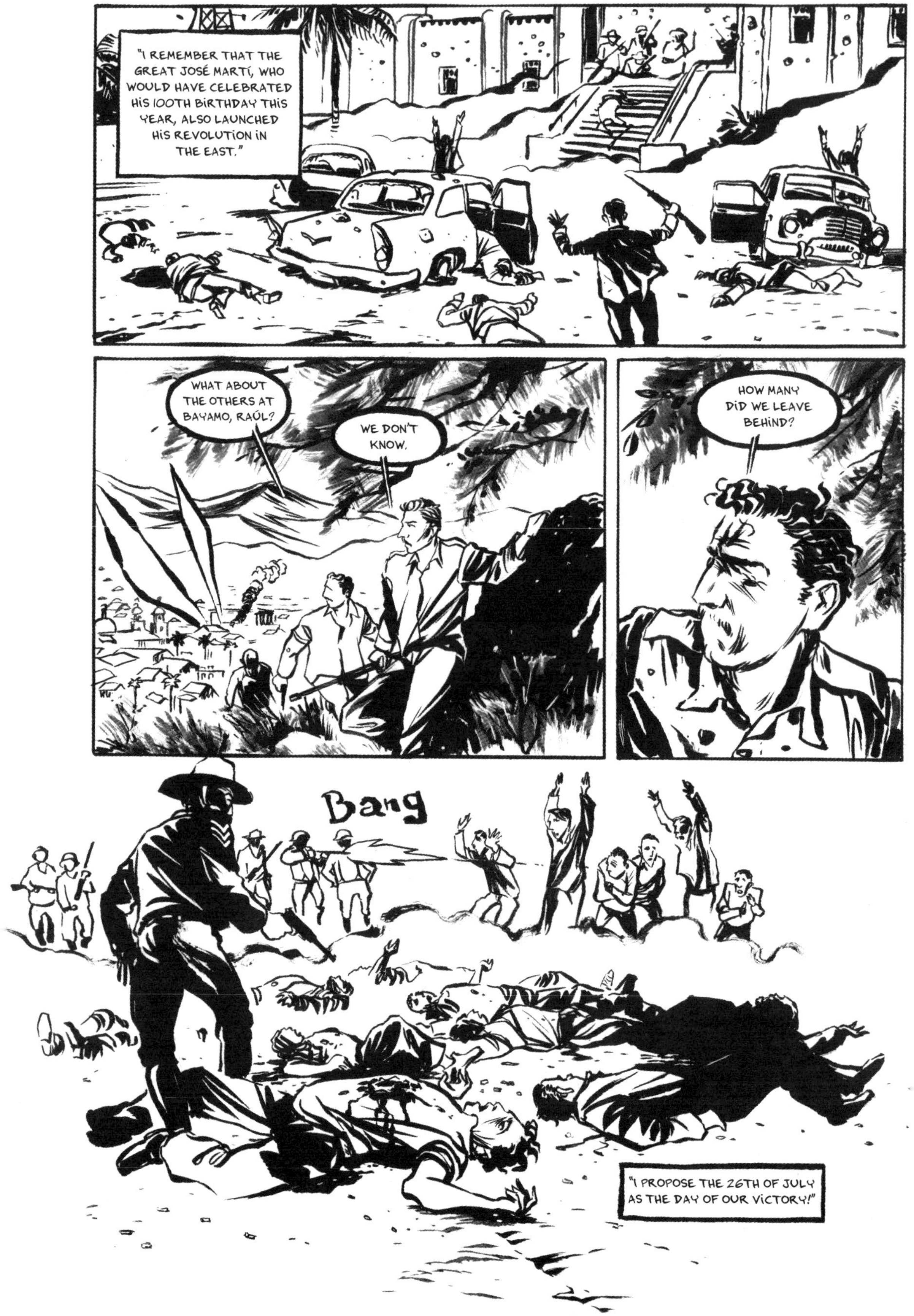
"I REMEMBER THAT THE GREAT JOSÉ MARTÍ, WHO WOULD HAVE CELEBRATED HIS 100TH BIRTHDAY THIS YEAR, ALSO LAUNCHED HIS REVOLUTION IN THE EAST."
WHAT ABOUT THE OTHERS AT BAYAMO, RAÚL?
WE DON'T KNOW.
HOW MANY DID WE LEAVE BEHIND?
Bang
"I PROPOSE THE 26TH OF JULY AS THE DAY OF OUR VICTORY!"

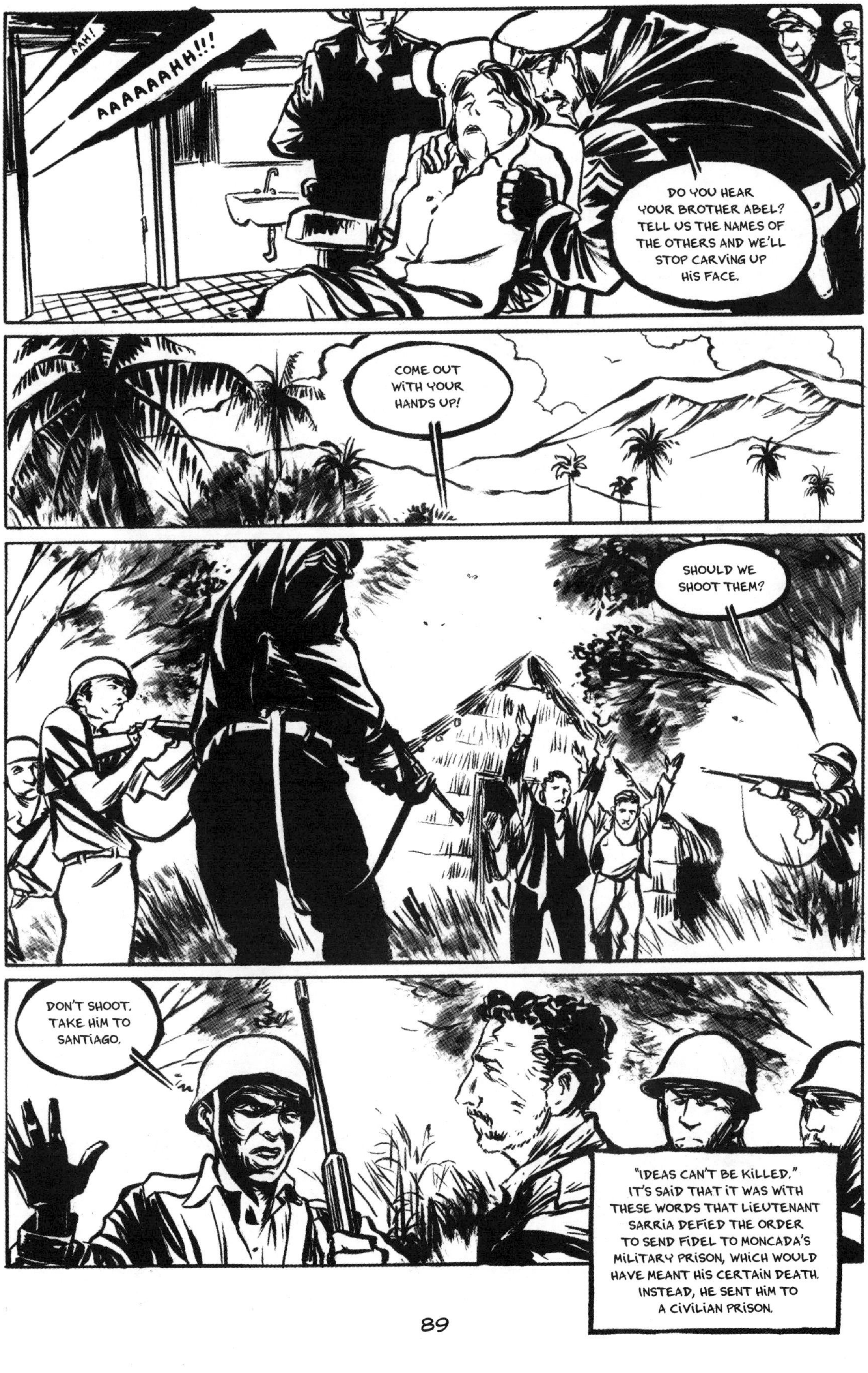
AAH!
AAAAAAHH!!!
DO YOU HEAR YOUR BROTHER ABEL? TELL US THE NAMES OF THE OTHERS AND WE'LL STOP CARVING UP HIS FACE.
COME OUT WITH YOUR HANDS UP!
SHOULD WE SHOOT THEM?
DON'T SHOOT. TAKE HIM TO SANTIAGO.
"IDEAS CAN'T BE KILLED." IT'S SAID THAT IT WAS WITH THESE WORDS THAT LIEUTENANT SARRIA DEFIED THE ORDER TO SEND FIDEL TO MONCADA'S MILITARY PRISON, WHICH WOULD HAVE MEANT HIS CERTAIN DEATH. INSTEAD, HE SENT HIM TO A CIVILIAN PRISON.

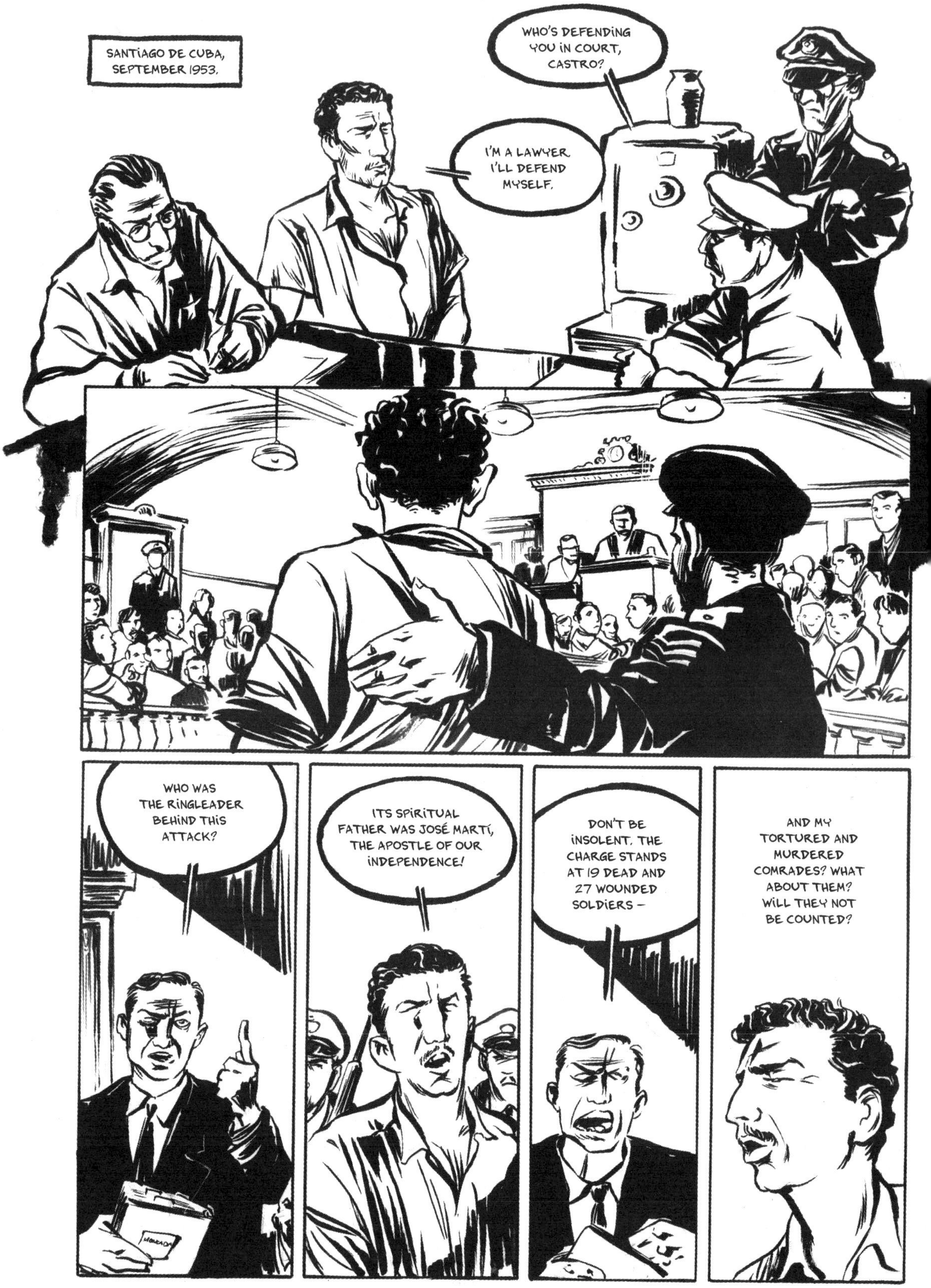
SANTIAGO DE CUBA, SEPTEMBER 1953.
WHO'S DEFENDING YOU IN COURT, CASTRO?
I'M A LAWYER. I'LL DEFEND MYSELF.
WHO WAS THE RINGLEADER BEHIND THIS ATTACK?
ITS SPIRITUAL FATHER WAS JOSÉ MARTÍ, THE APOSTLE OF OUR INDEPENDENCE!
DON'T BE INSOLENT. THE CHARGE STANDS AT 19 DEAD AND 27 WOUNDED SOLDIERS –
AND MY TORTURED AND MURDERED COMRADES? WHAT ABOUT THEM? WILL THEY NOT BE COUNTED?

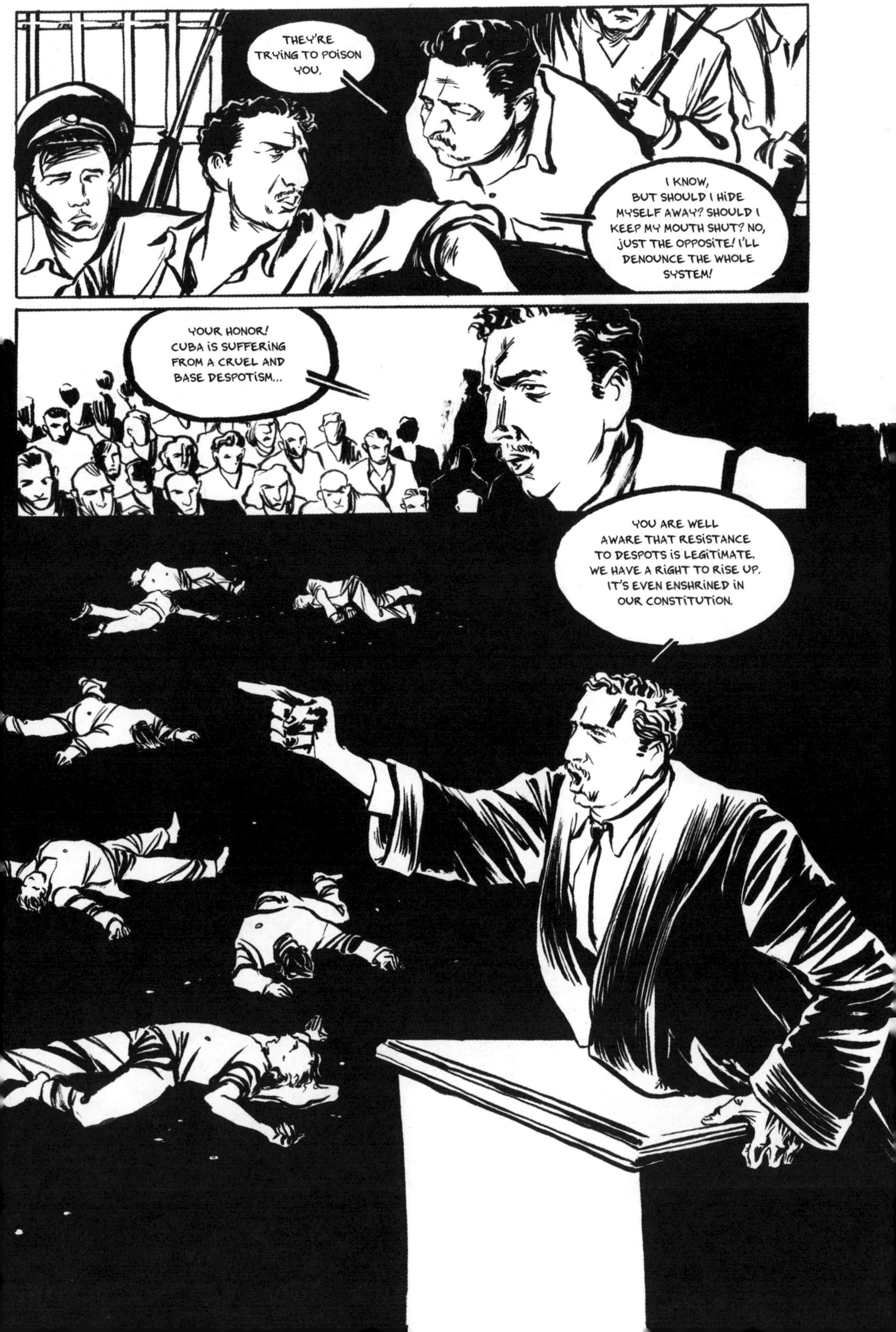
THEY'RE TRYING TO POISON YOU.
I KNOW, BUT SHOULD I HIDE MYSELF AWAY? SHOULD I KEEP MY MOUTH SHUT? NO, JUST THE OPPOSITE! I'LL DENOUNCE THE WHOLE SYSTEM!
YOUR HONOR! CUBA IS SUFFERING FROM A CRUEL AND BASE DESPOTISM...
YOU ARE WELL AWARE THAT RESISTANCE TO DESPOTS IS LEGITIMATE. WE HAVE A RIGHT TO RISE UP. IT'S EVEN ENSHRINED IN OUR CONSTITUTION.

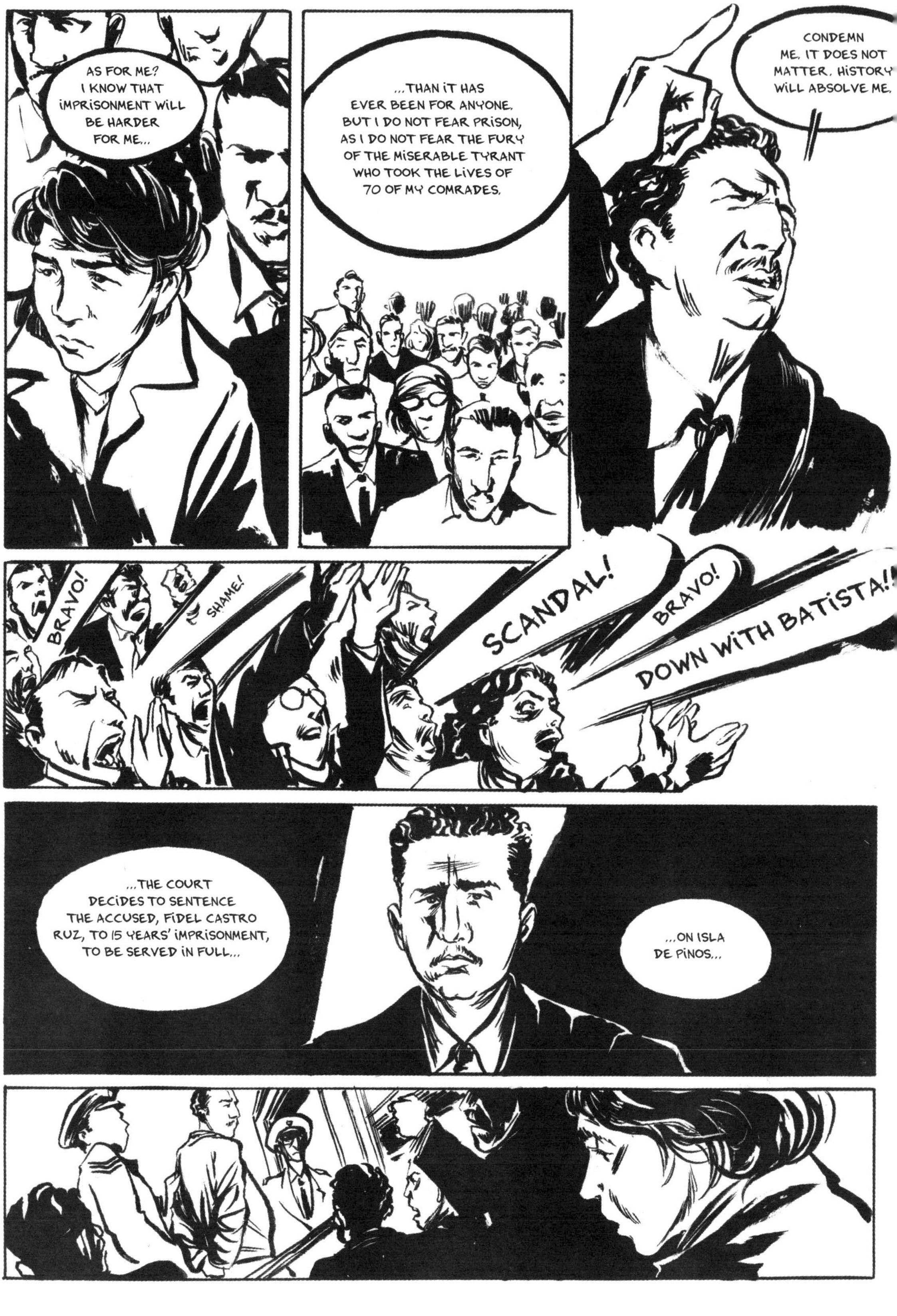

AS FOR ME? I KNOW THAT IMPRISONMENT WILL BE HARDER FOR ME...
...THAN IT HAS EVER BEEN FOR ANYONE. BUT I DO NOT FEAR PRISON, AS I DO NOT FEAR THE FURY OF THE MISERABLE TYRANT WHO TOOK THE LIVES OF 70 OF MY COMRADES.
CONDEMN ME. IT DOES NOT MATTER. HISTORY WILL ABSOLVE ME.
BRAVO!
SHAME!
SCANDAL!
BRAVO!
DOWN WITH BATISTA!!
...THE COURT DECIDES TO SENTENCE THE ACCUSED, FIDEL CASTRO RUZ, TO 15 YEARS' IMPRISONMENT, TO BE SERVED IN FULL...
...ON ISLA DE PINOS...

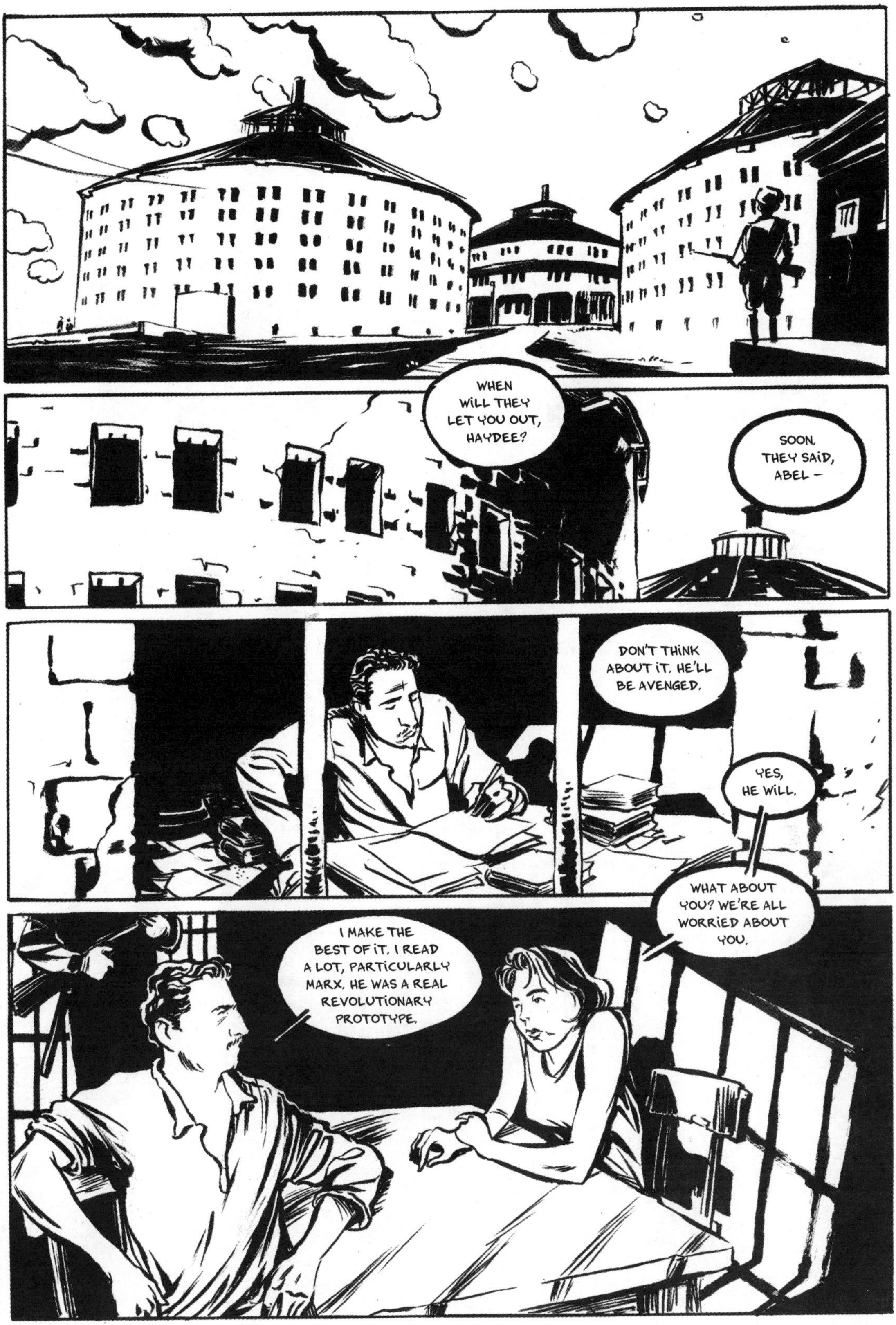
WHEN WILL THEY LET YOU OUT, HAYDEE?
SOON, THEY SAID, ABEL –
DON'T THINK ABOUT IT. HE'LL BE AVENGED.
YES, HE WILL.
WHAT ABOUT YOU? WE'RE ALL WORRIED ABOUT YOU.
I MAKE THE BEST OF IT. I READ A LOT, PARTICULARLY MARX. HE WAS A REAL REVOLUTIONARY PROTOTYPE.

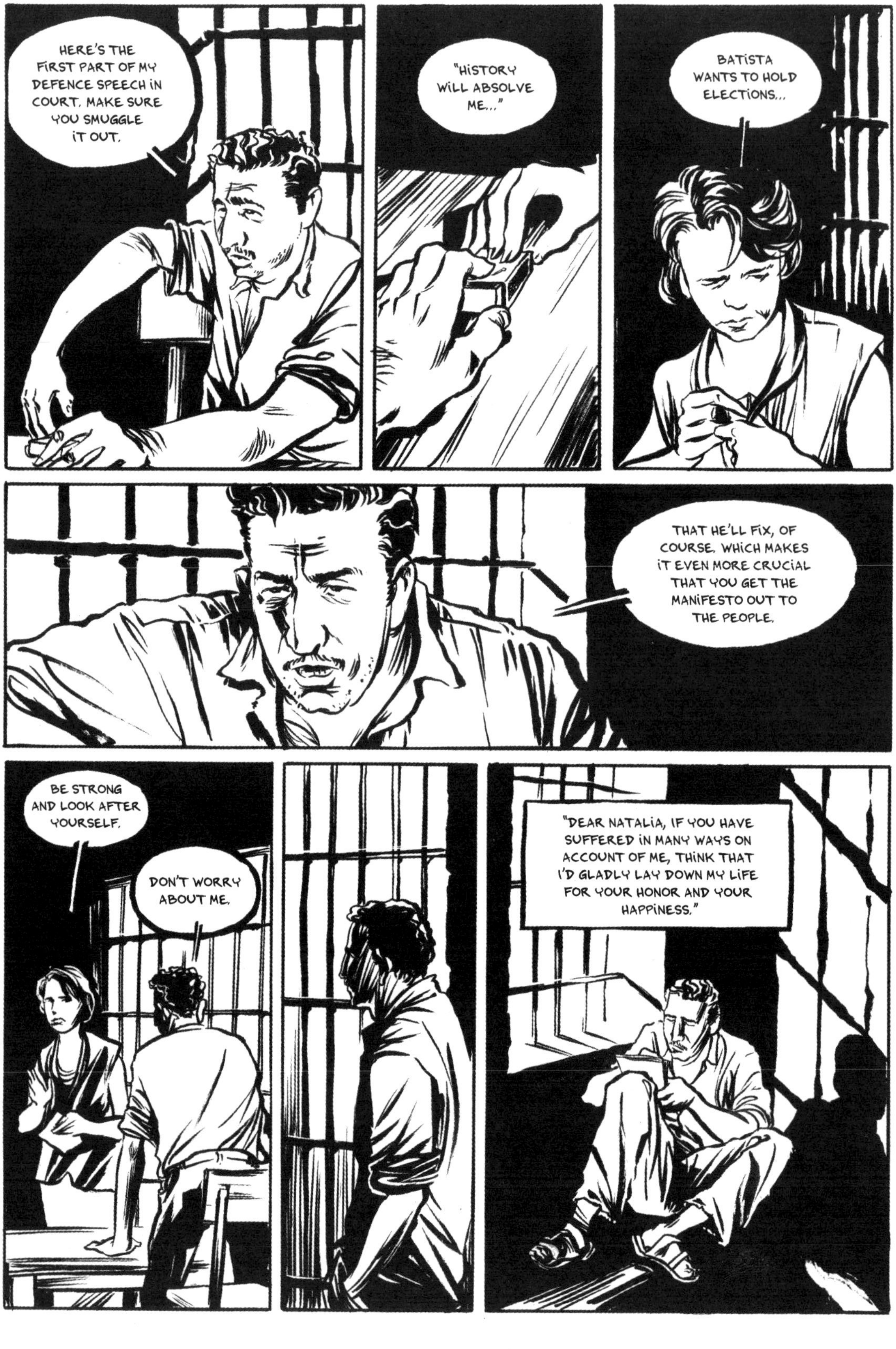
HERE'S THE FIRST PART OF MY DEFENCE SPEECH IN COURT. MAKE SURE YOU SMUGGLE IT OUT.
"HISTORY WILL ABSOLVE ME..."
BATISTA WANTS TO HOLD ELECTIONS...
THAT HE'LL FIX, OF COURSE. WHICH MAKES IT EVEN MORE CRUCIAL THAT YOU GET THE MANIFESTO OUT TO THE PEOPLE.
BE STRONG AND LOOK AFTER YOURSELF.
DON'T WORRY ABOUT ME.
"DEAR NATALIA, IF YOU HAVE SUFFERED IN MANY WAYS ON ACCOUNT OF ME, THINK THAT I'D GLADLY LAY DOWN MY LIFE FOR YOUR HONOR AND YOUR HAPPINESS."

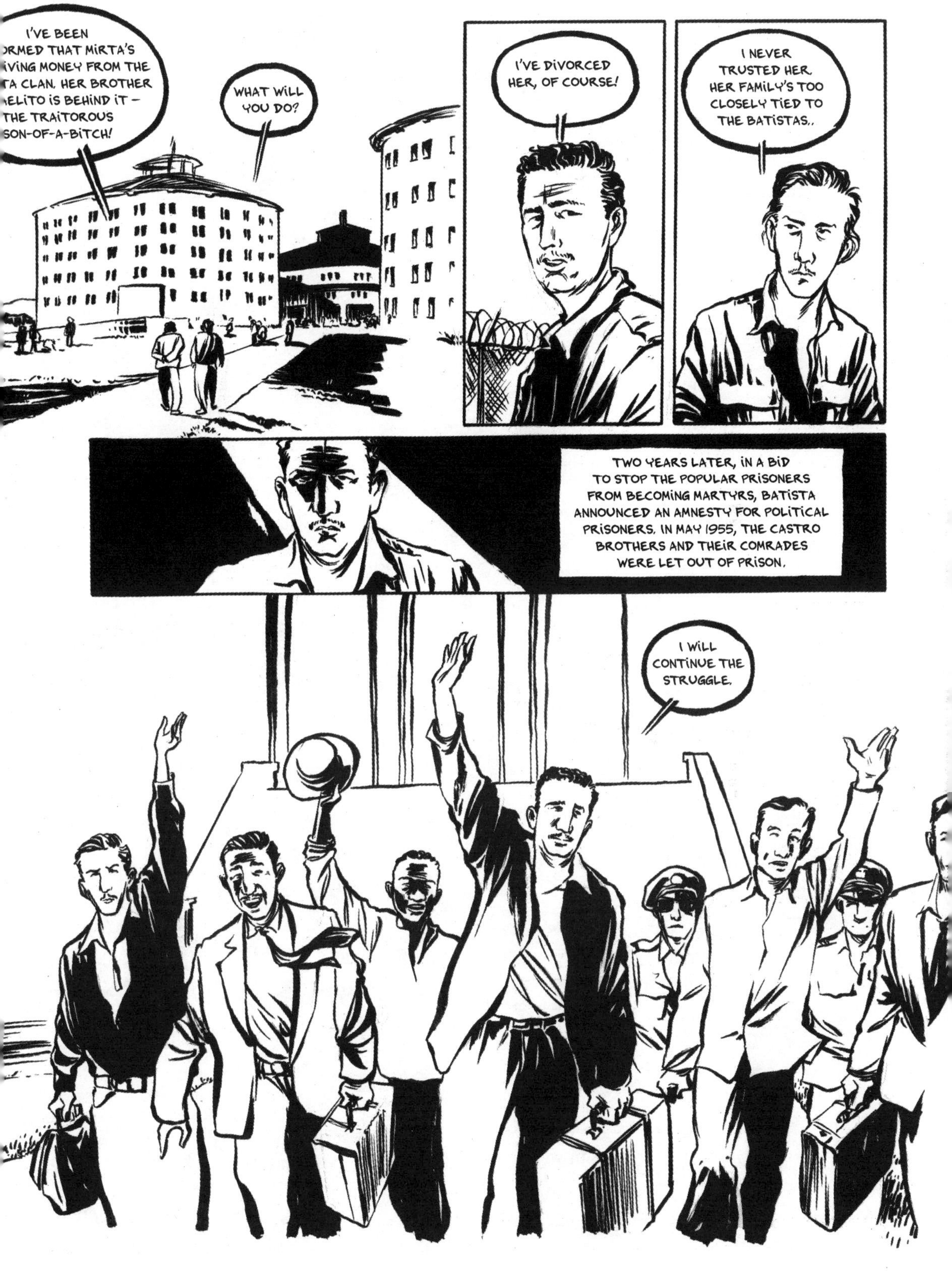

I'VE BEEN
ORMED THAT MIRTA'S
IVING MONEY FROM THE
TA CLAN. HER BROTHER
ELITO IS BEHIND IT –
THE TRAITOROUS
SON-OF-A-BITCH!
WHAT WILL YOU DO?
I'VE DIVORCED HER, OF COURSE!
I NEVER TRUSTED HER. HER FAMILY'S TOO CLOSELY TIED TO THE BATISTAS..
TWO YEARS LATER, IN A BID TO STOP THE POPULAR PRISONERS FROM BECOMING MARTYRS, BATISTA ANNOUNCED AN AMNESTY FOR POLITICAL PRISONERS. IN MAY 1955, THE CASTRO BROTHERS AND THEIR COMRADES WERE LET OUT OF PRISON.
I WILL CONTINUE THE STRUGGLE.

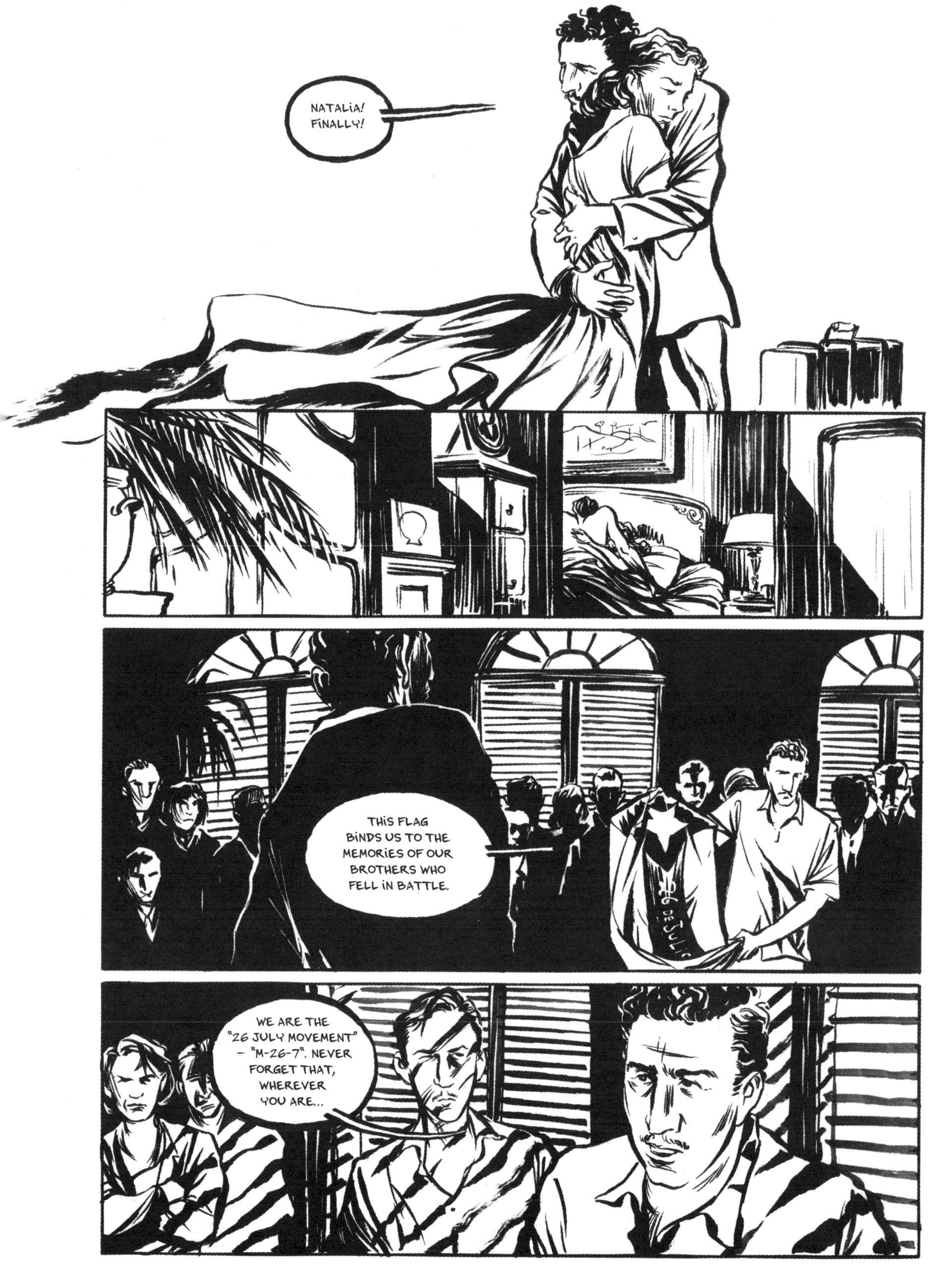
NATALIA! FINALLY!
THIS FLAG BINDS US TO THE MEMORIES OF OUR BROTHERS WHO FELL IN BATTLE.
26 DE JULIO
WE ARE THE "26 JULY MOVEMENT" – "M-26-7". NEVER FORGET THAT, WHEREVER YOU ARE...

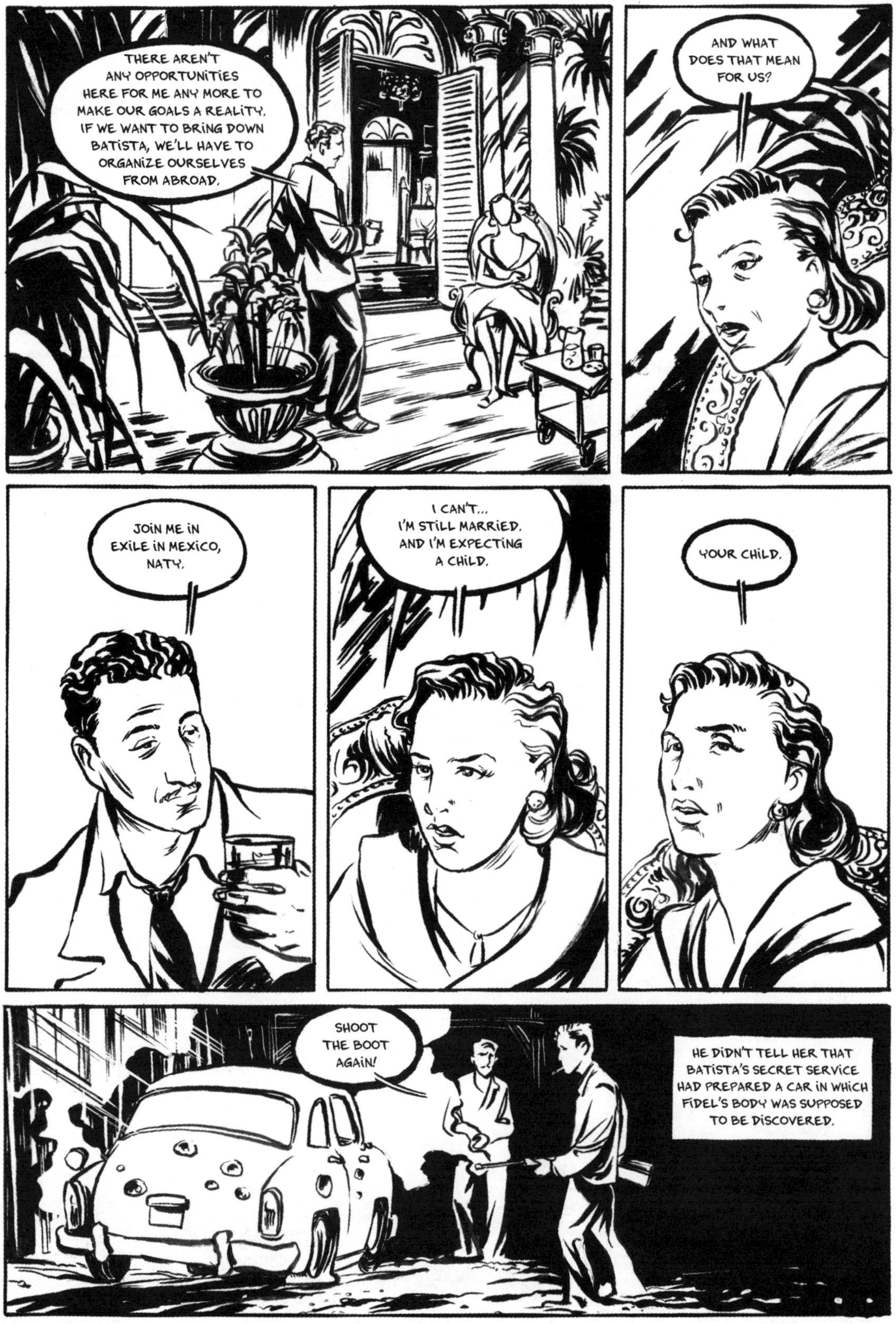
THERE AREN'T ANY OPPORTUNITIES HERE FOR ME ANY MORE TO MAKE OUR GOALS A REALITY. IF WE WANT TO BRING DOWN BATISTA, WE'LL HAVE TO ORGANIZE OURSELVES FROM ABROAD.
AND WHAT DOES THAT MEAN FOR US?
JOIN ME IN EXILE IN MEXICO, NATY.
I CAN'T... I'M STILL MARRIED. AND I'M EXPECTING A CHILD.
YOUR CHILD.
SHOOT THE BOOT AGAIN!
HE DIDN'T TELL HER THAT BATISTA'S SECRET SERVICE HAD PREPARED A CAR IN WHICH FIDEL'S BODY WAS SUPPOSED TO BE DISCOVERED.

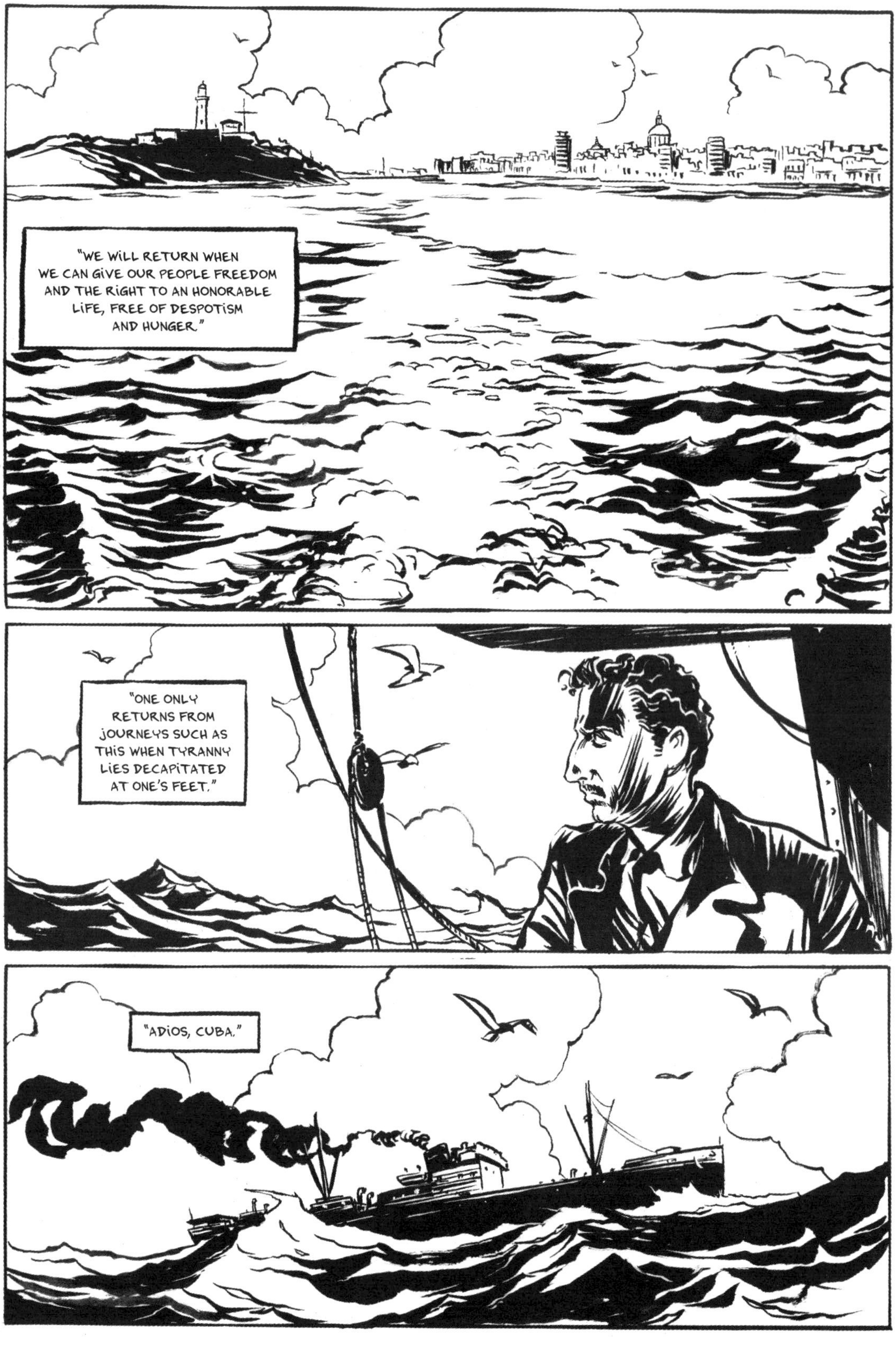
"WE WILL RETURN WHEN WE CAN GIVE OUR PEOPLE FREEDOM AND THE RIGHT TO AN HONORABLE LIFE, FREE OF DESPOTISM AND HUNGER."
"ONE ONLY RETURNS FROM JOURNEYS SUCH AS THIS WHEN TYRANNY LIES DECAPITATED AT ONE'S FEET."
"ADIOS, CUBA."

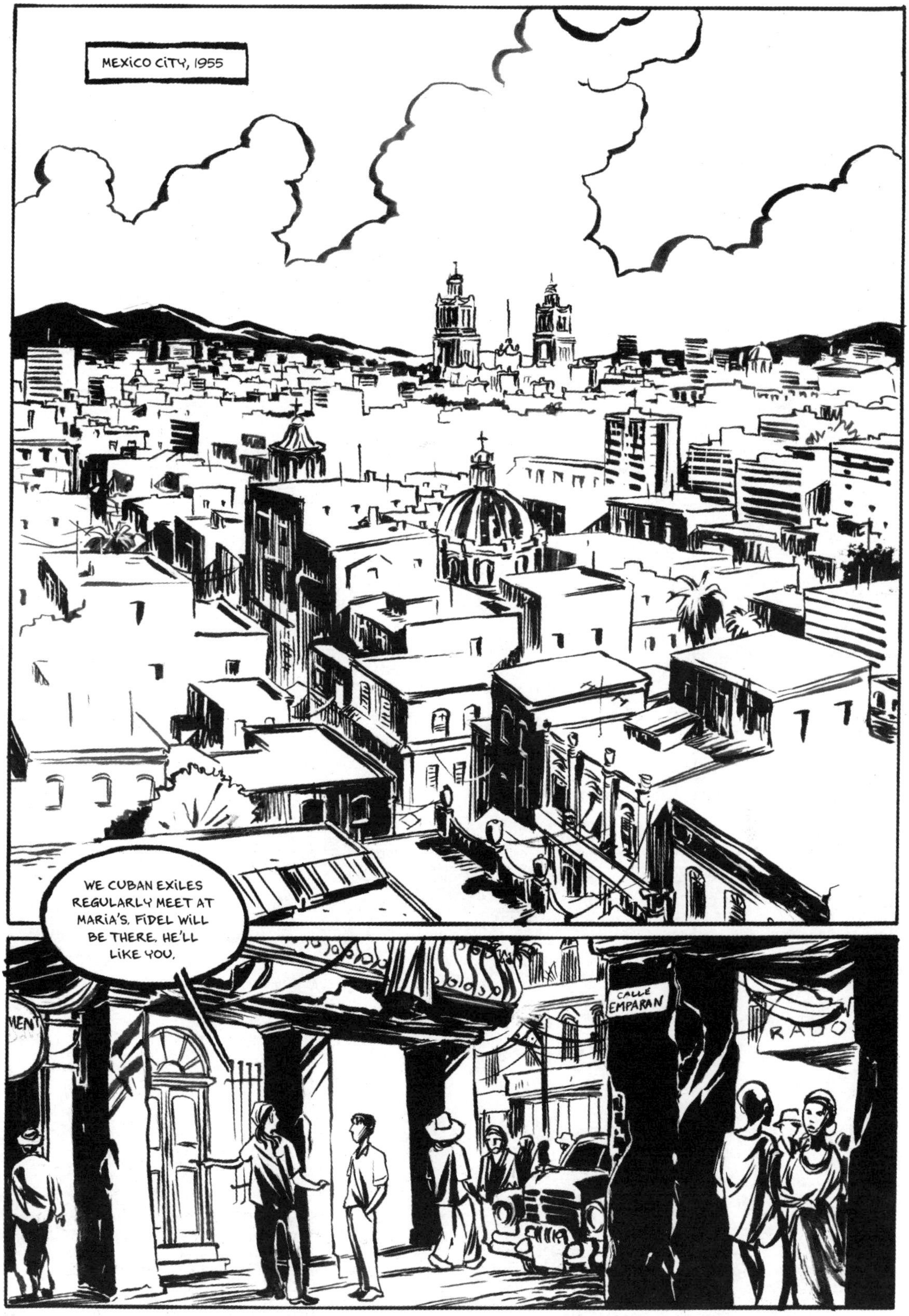
MEXICO CITY, 1955
WE CUBAN EXILES REGULARLY MEET AT MARIA'S. FIDEL WILL BE THERE. HE'LL LIKE YOU.
CALLE EMPARAN

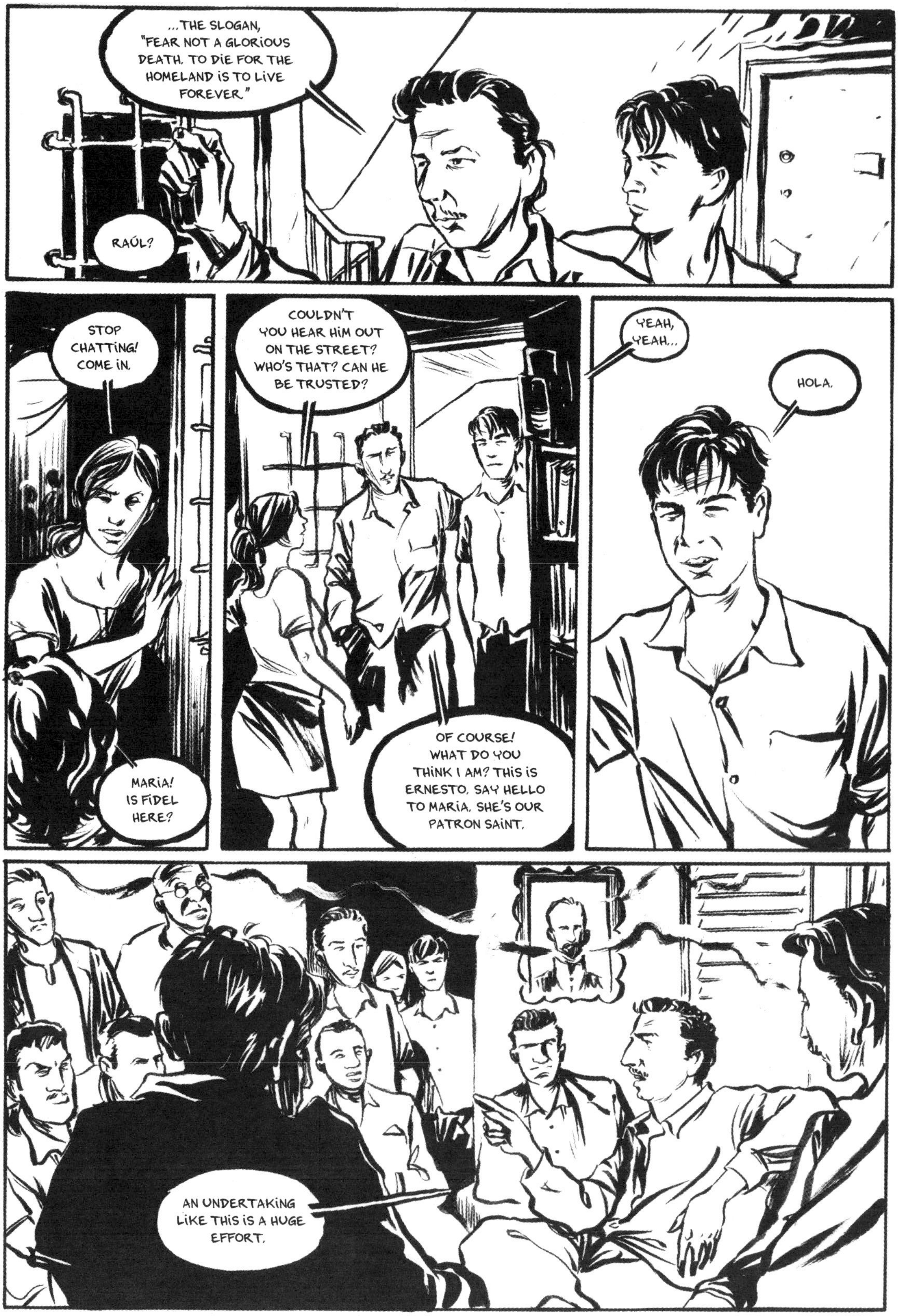
...THE SLOGAN, "FEAR NOT A GLORIOUS DEATH. TO DIE FOR THE HOMELAND IS TO LIVE FOREVER."
RAÚL?
STOP CHATTING! COME IN.
MARIA! IS FIDEL HERE?
COULDN'T YOU HEAR HIM OUT ON THE STREET? WHO'S THAT? CAN HE BE TRUSTED?
OF COURSE! WHAT DO YOU THINK I AM? THIS IS ERNESTO. SAY HELLO TO MARIA. SHE'S OUR PATRON SAINT.
YEAH, YEAH...
HOLA.
AN UNDERTAKING LIKE THIS IS A HUGE EFFORT.

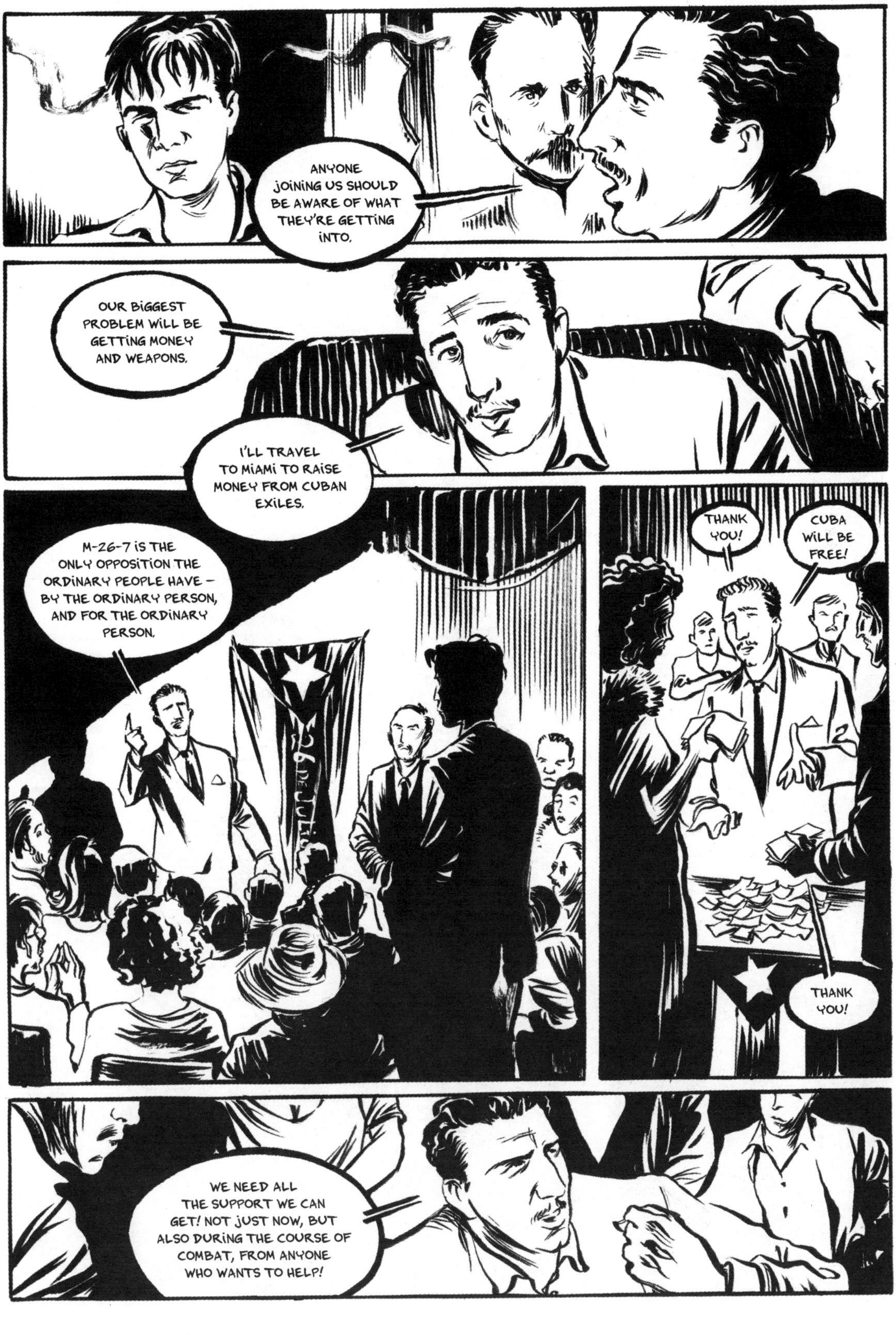
ANYONE JOINING US SHOULD BE AWARE OF WHAT THEY'RE GETTING INTO.
OUR BIGGEST PROBLEM WILL BE GETTING MONEY AND WEAPONS.
I'LL TRAVEL TO MIAMI TO RAISE MONEY FROM CUBAN EXILES.
M-26-7 IS THE ONLY OPPOSITION THE ORDINARY PEOPLE HAVE – BY THE ORDINARY PERSON, AND FOR THE ORDINARY PERSON.
THANK YOU!
CUBA WILL BE FREE!
THANK YOU!
WE NEED ALL THE SUPPORT WE CAN GET! NOT JUST NOW, BUT ALSO DURING THE COURSE OF COMBAT, FROM ANYONE WHO WANTS TO HELP!

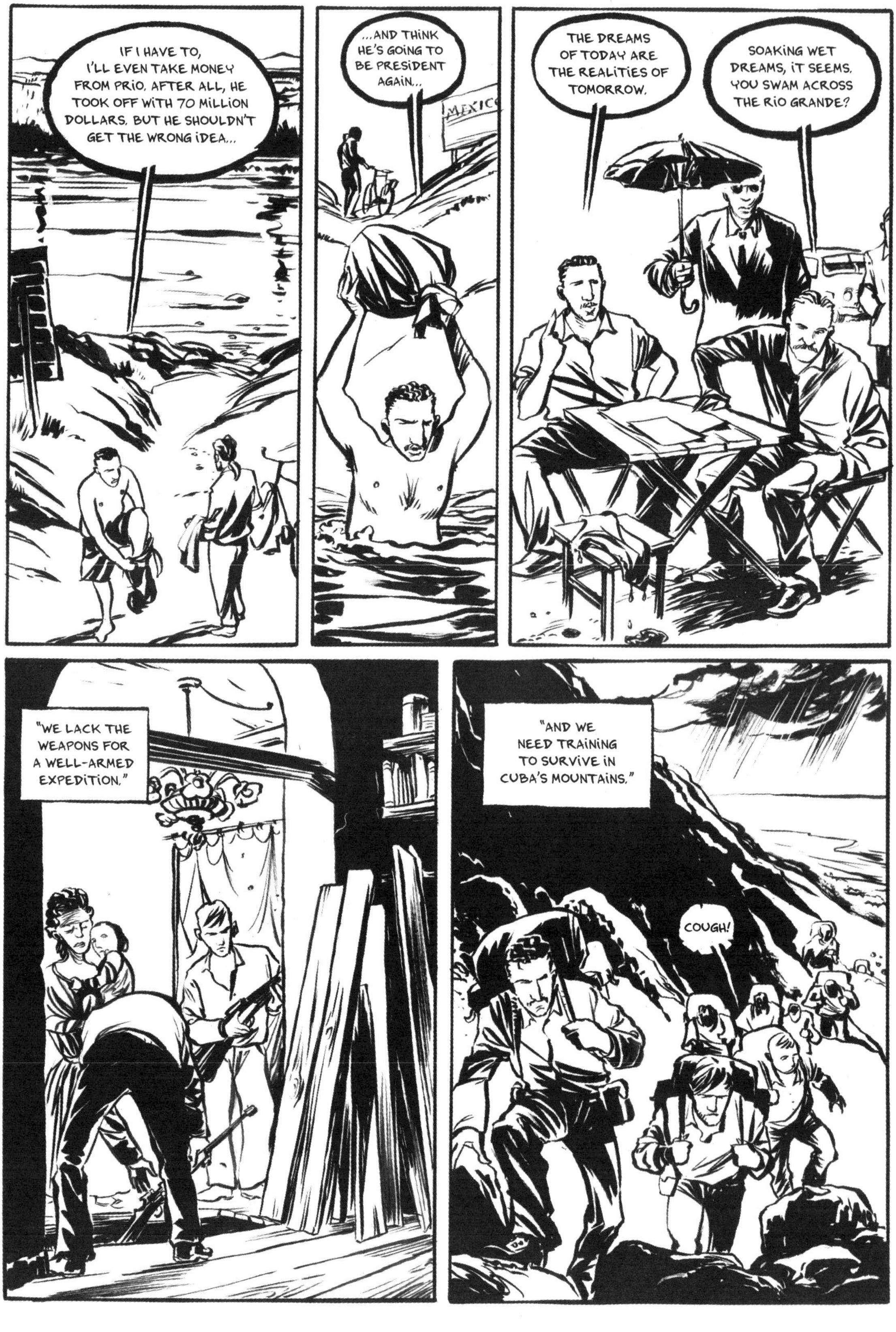

IF I HAVE TO, I'LL EVEN TAKE MONEY FROM PRIO. AFTER ALL, HE TOOK OFF WITH 70 MILLION DOLLARS. BUT HE SHOULDN'T GET THE WRONG IDEA...
...AND THINK HE'S GOING TO BE PRESIDENT AGAIN...
MEXICO
THE DREAMS OF TODAY ARE THE REALITIES OF TOMORROW.
SOAKING WET DREAMS, IT SEEMS. YOU SWAM ACROSS THE RIO GRANDE?
"WE LACK THE WEAPONS FOR A WELL-ARMED EXPEDITION."
"AND WE NEED TRAINING TO SURVIVE IN CUBA'S MOUNTAINS."
COUGH!

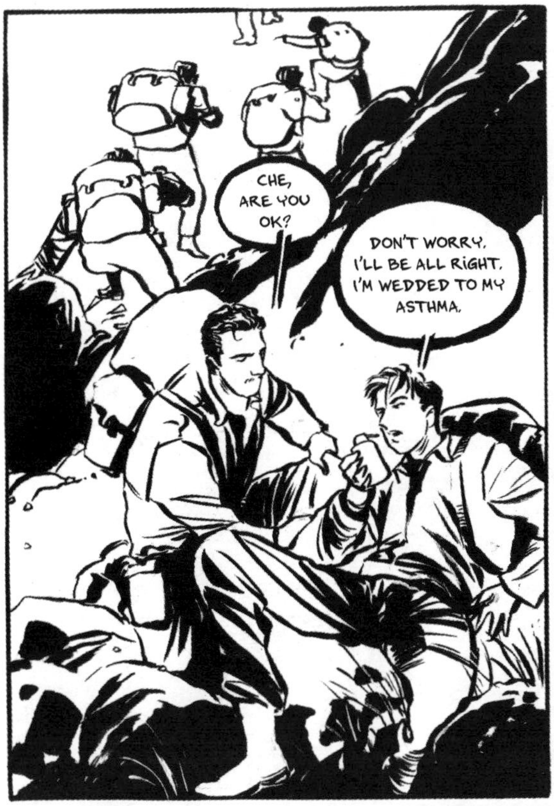
CHE, ARE YOU OK?
DON'T WORRY. I'LL BE ALL RIGHT. I'M WEDDED TO MY ASTHMA.

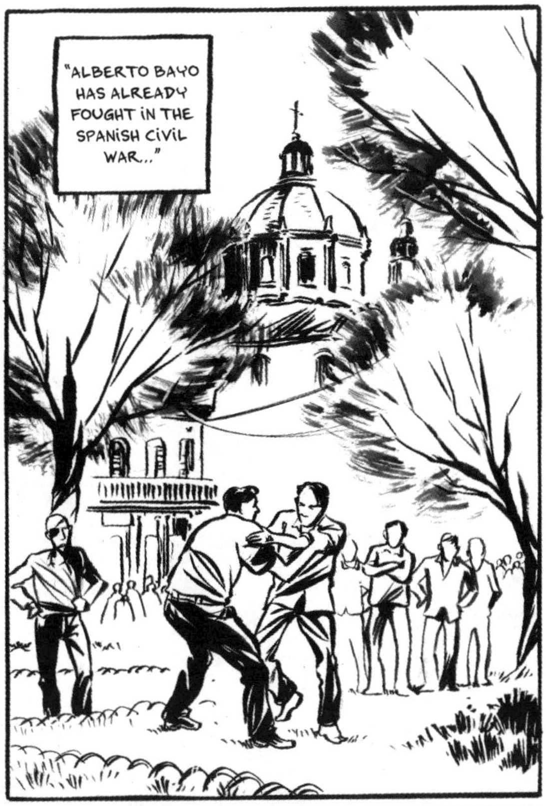
"ALBERTO BAYO HAS ALREADY FOUGHT IN THE SPANISH CIVIL WAR..."

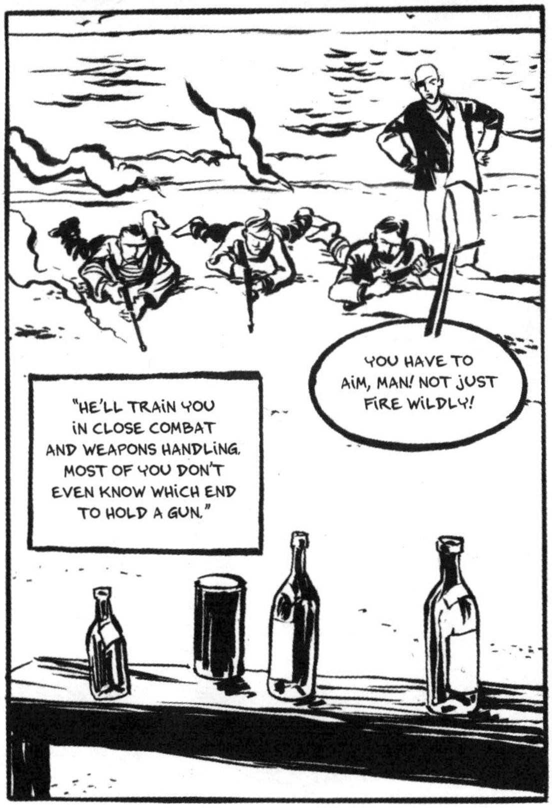
YOU HAVE TO AIM, MAN! NOT JUST FIRE WILDLY!
"HE'LL TRAIN YOU IN CLOSE COMBAT AND WEAPONS HANDLING. MOST OF YOU DON'T EVEN KNOW WHICH END TO HOLD A GUN."

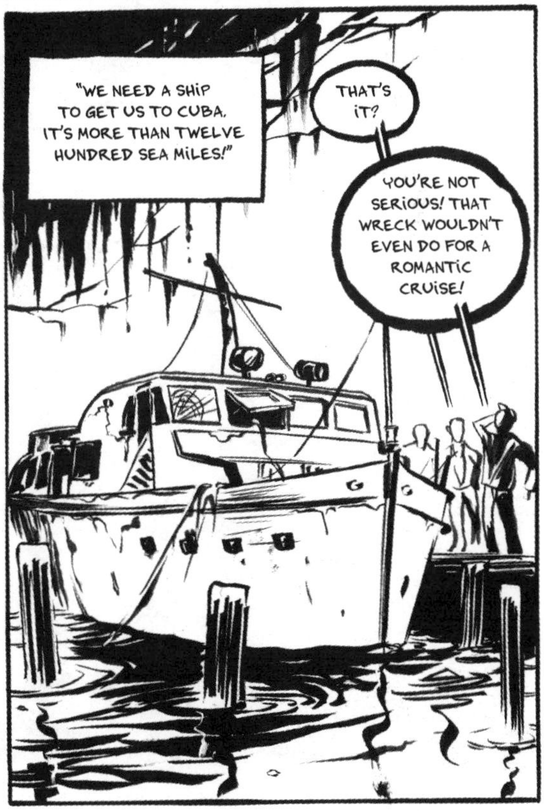
"WE NEED A SHIP TO GET US TO CUBA. IT'S MORE THAN TWELVE HUNDRED SEA MILES!"
THAT'S IT?
YOU'RE NOT SERIOUS! THAT WRECK WOULDN'T EVEN DO FOR A ROMANTIC CRUISE!

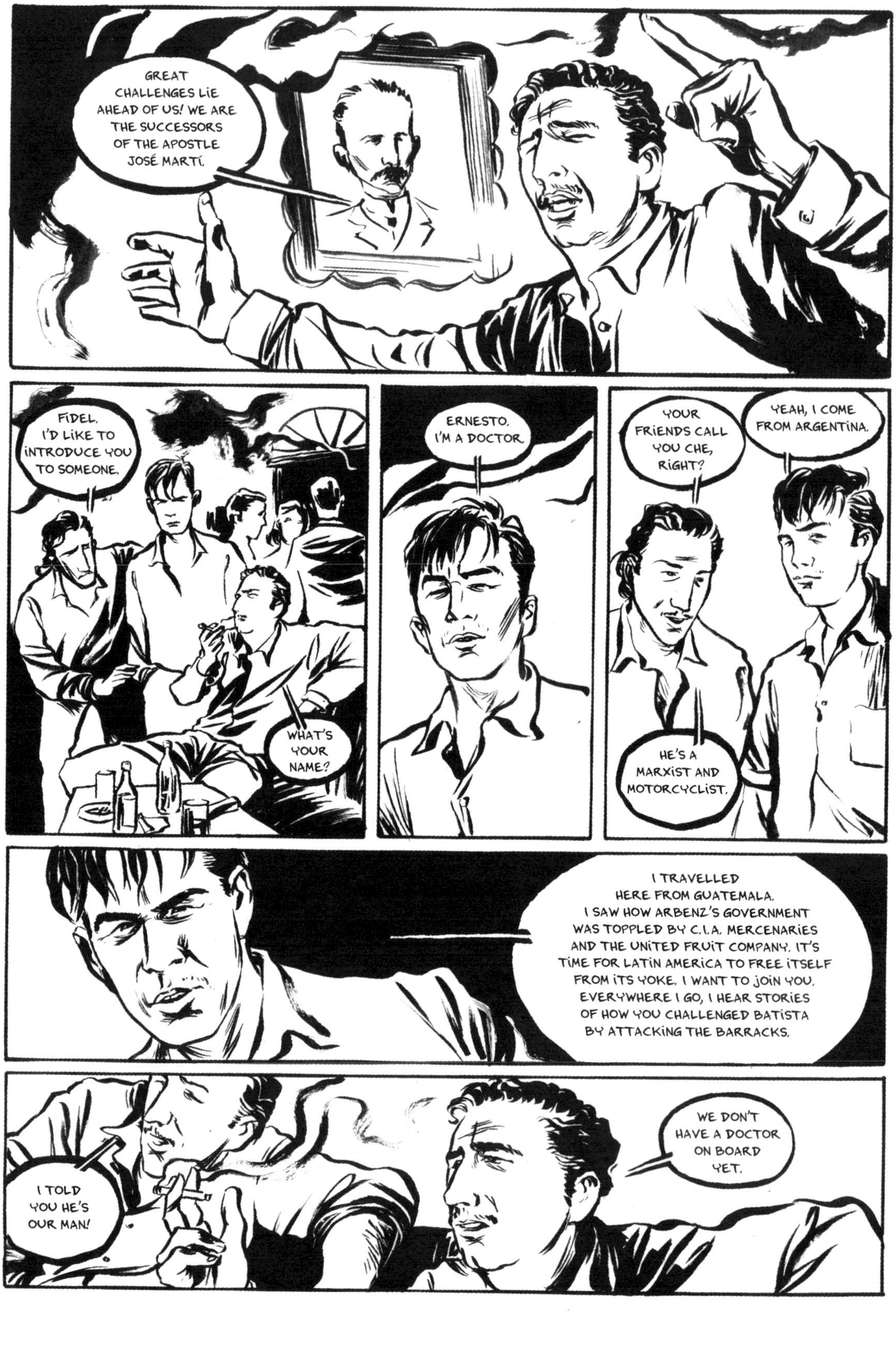
GREAT CHALLENGES LIE AHEAD OF US! WE ARE THE SUCCESSORS OF THE APOSTLE JOSÉ MARTÍ.
FIDEL, I'D LIKE TO INTRODUCE YOU TO SOMEONE.
WHAT'S YOUR NAME?
ERNESTO. I'M A DOCTOR.
YOUR FRIENDS CALL YOU CHE, RIGHT?
YEAH, I COME FROM ARGENTINA.
HE'S A MARXIST AND MOTORCYCLIST.
I TRAVELLED HERE FROM GUATEMALA. I SAW HOW ARBENZ'S GOVERNMENT WAS TOPPLED BY C.I.A. MERCENARIES AND THE UNITED FRUIT COMPANY. IT'S TIME FOR LATIN AMERICA TO FREE ITSELF FROM ITS YOKE. I WANT TO JOIN YOU. EVERYWHERE I GO, I HEAR STORIES OF HOW YOU CHALLENGED BATISTA BY ATTACKING THE BARRACKS.
I TOLD YOU HE'S OUR MAN!
WE DON'T HAVE A DOCTOR ON BOARD YET.

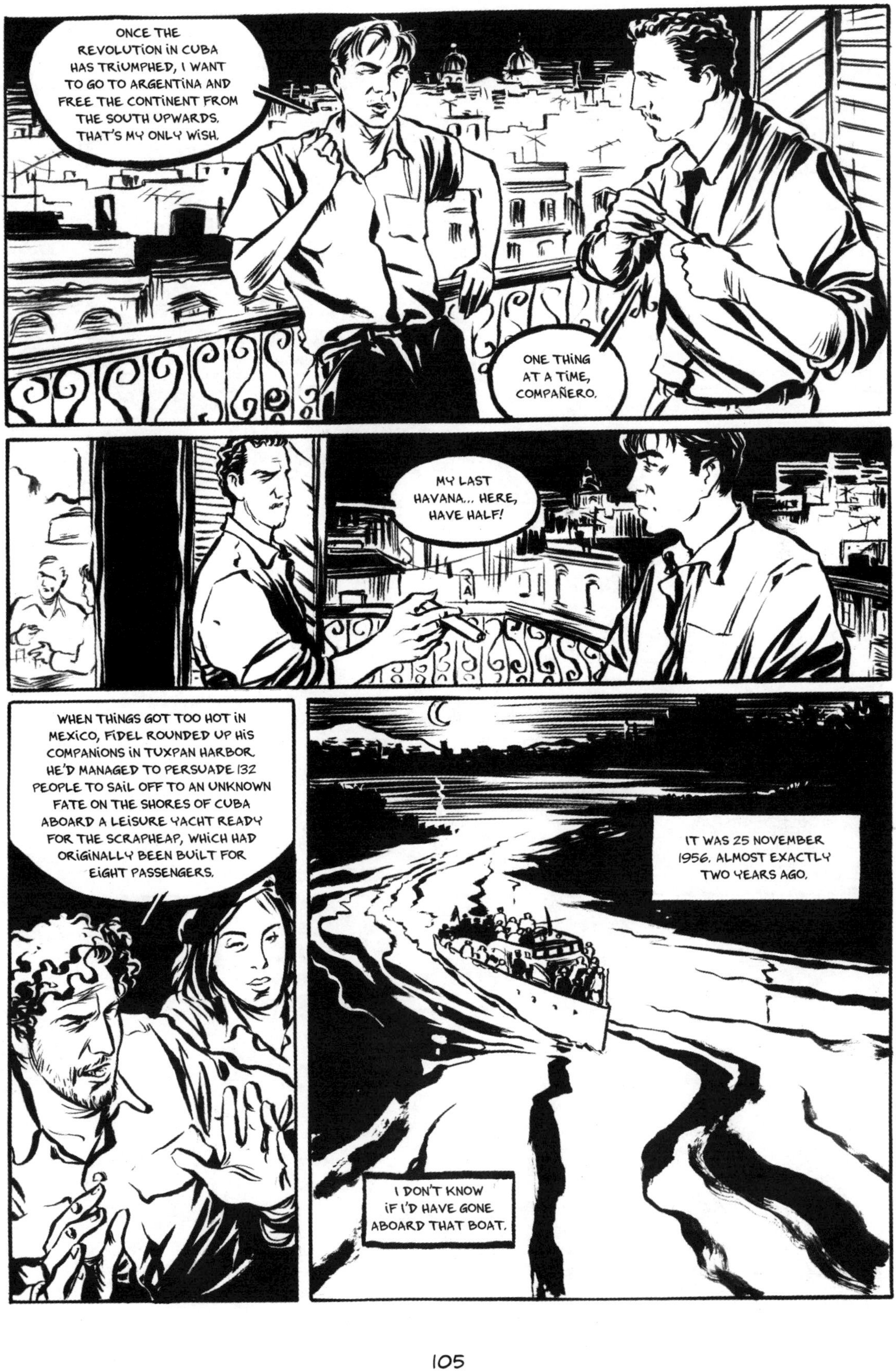

ONCE THE REVOLUTION IN CUBA HAS TRIUMPHED, I WANT TO GO TO ARGENTINA AND FREE THE CONTINENT FROM THE SOUTH UPWARDS. THAT'S MY ONLY WISH.
ONE THING AT A TIME, COMPAÑERO.
MY LAST HAVANA... HERE, HAVE HALF!
WHEN THINGS GOT TOO HOT IN MEXICO, FIDEL ROUNDED UP HIS COMPANIONS IN TUXPAN HARBOR. HE'D MANAGED TO PERSUADE 132 PEOPLE TO SAIL OFF TO AN UNKNOWN FATE ON THE SHORES OF CUBA ABOARD A LEISURE YACHT READY FOR THE SCRAPHEAP, WHICH HAD ORIGINALLY BEEN BUILT FOR EIGHT PASSENGERS.
IT WAS 25 NOVEMBER 1956. ALMOST EXACTLY TWO YEARS AGO.
I DON'T KNOW IF I'D HAVE GONE ABOARD THAT BOAT.

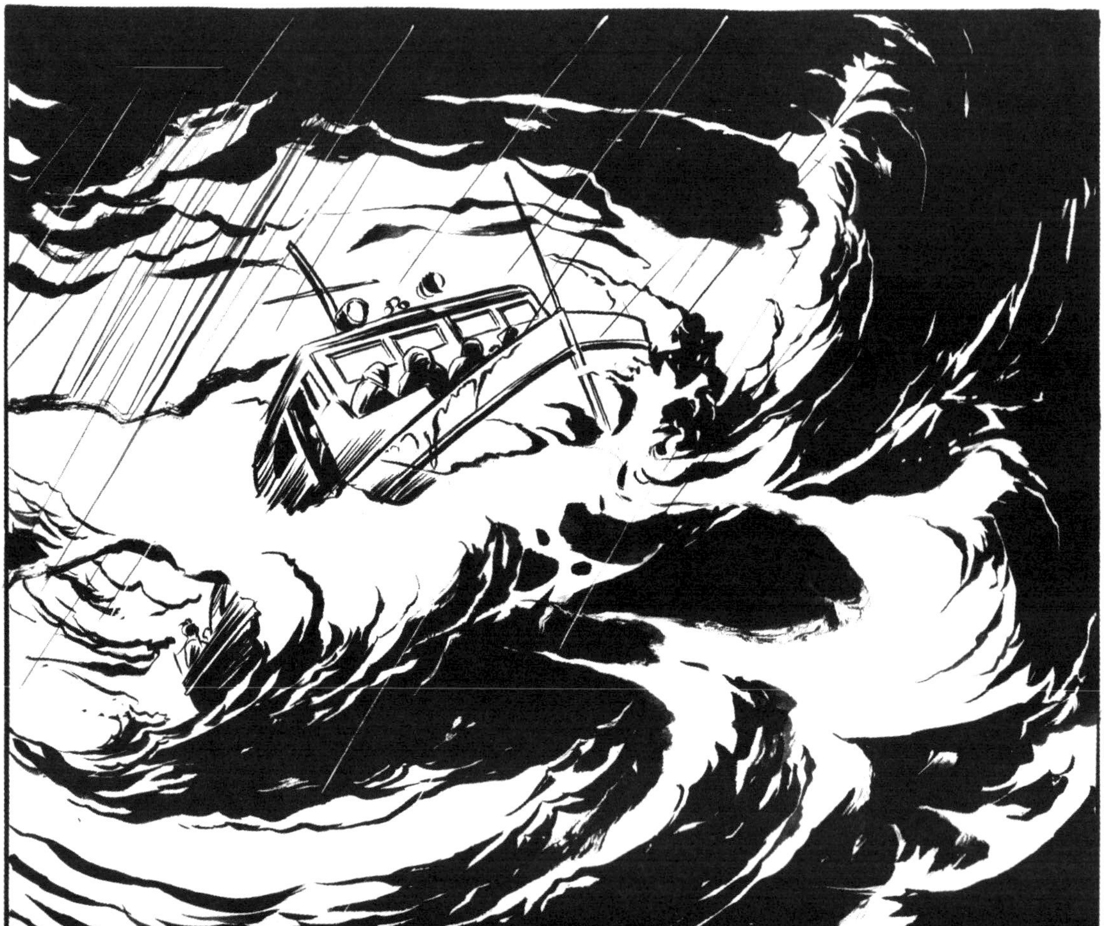

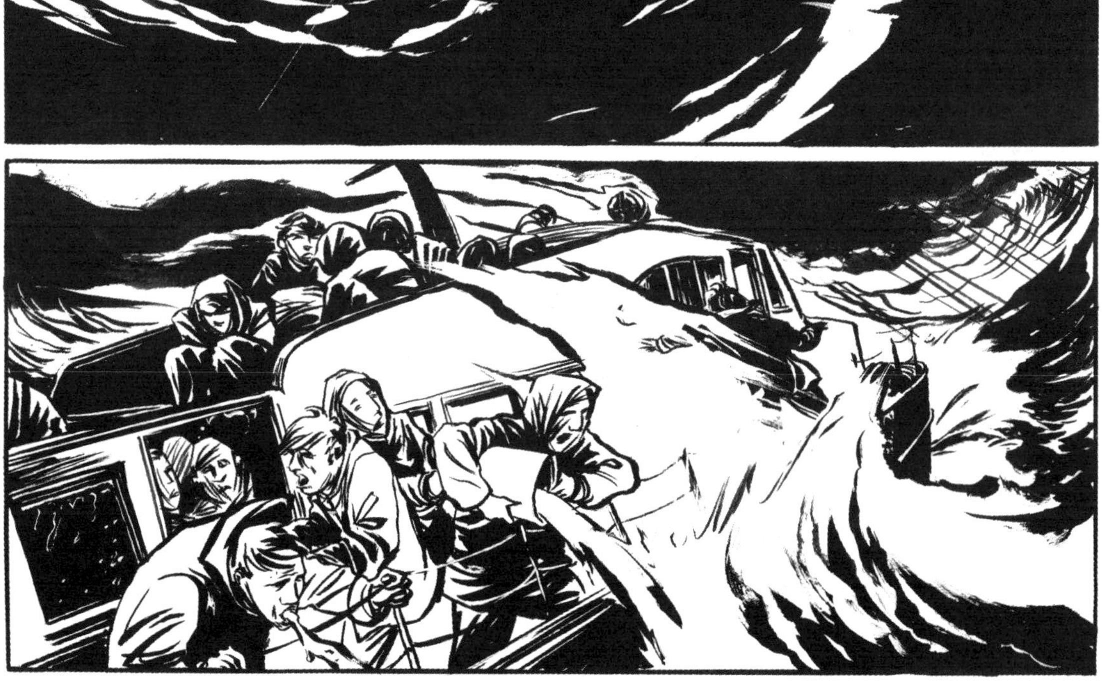

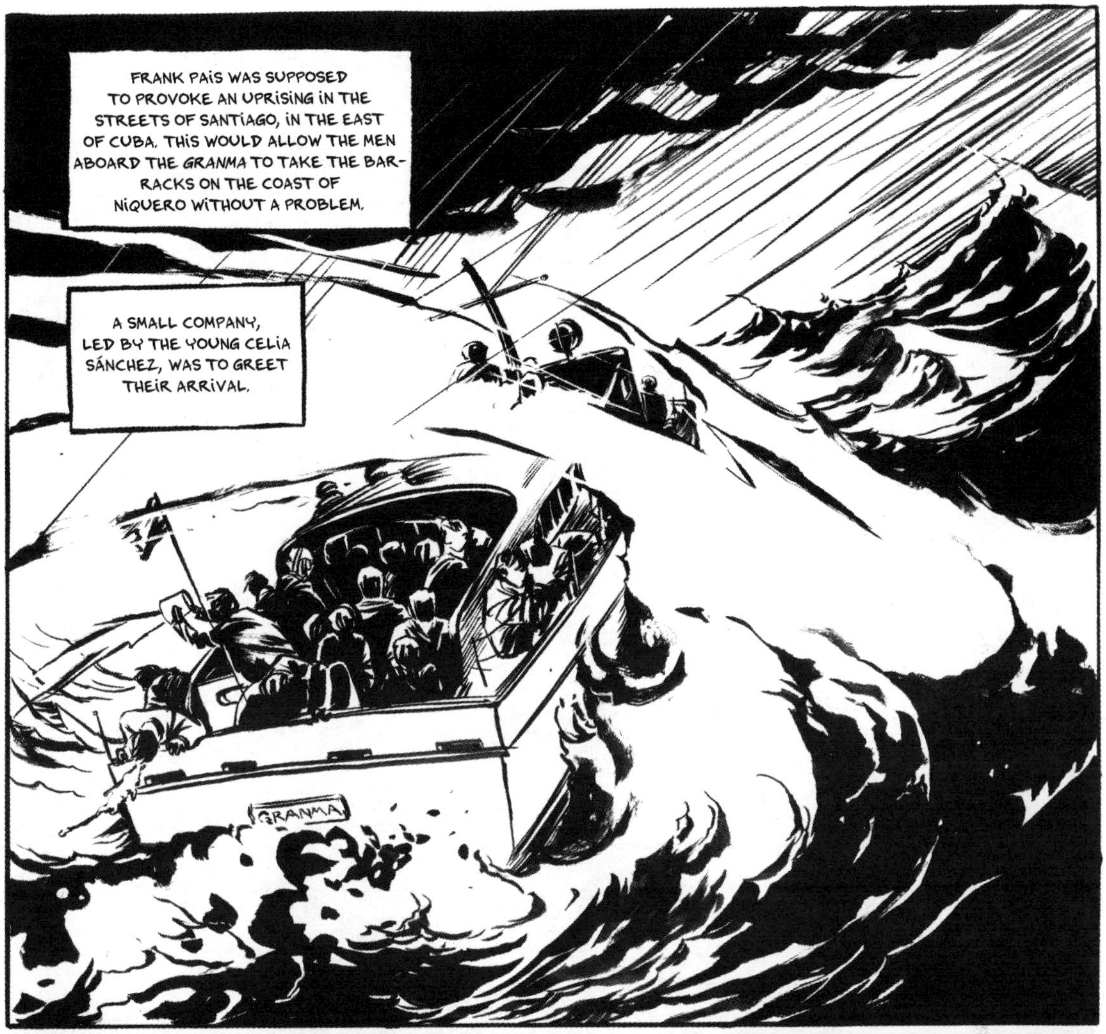
FRANK PAIS WAS SUPPOSED TO PROVOKE AN UPRISING IN THE STREETS OF SANTIAGO, IN THE EAST OF CUBA. THIS WOULD ALLOW THE MEN ABOARD THE *GRANMA* TO TAKE THE BARRACKS ON THE COAST OF NIQUERO WITHOUT A PROBLEM.
A SMALL COMPANY, LED BY THE YOUNG CELIA SÁNCHEZ, WAS TO GREET THEIR ARRIVAL.
GRANMA

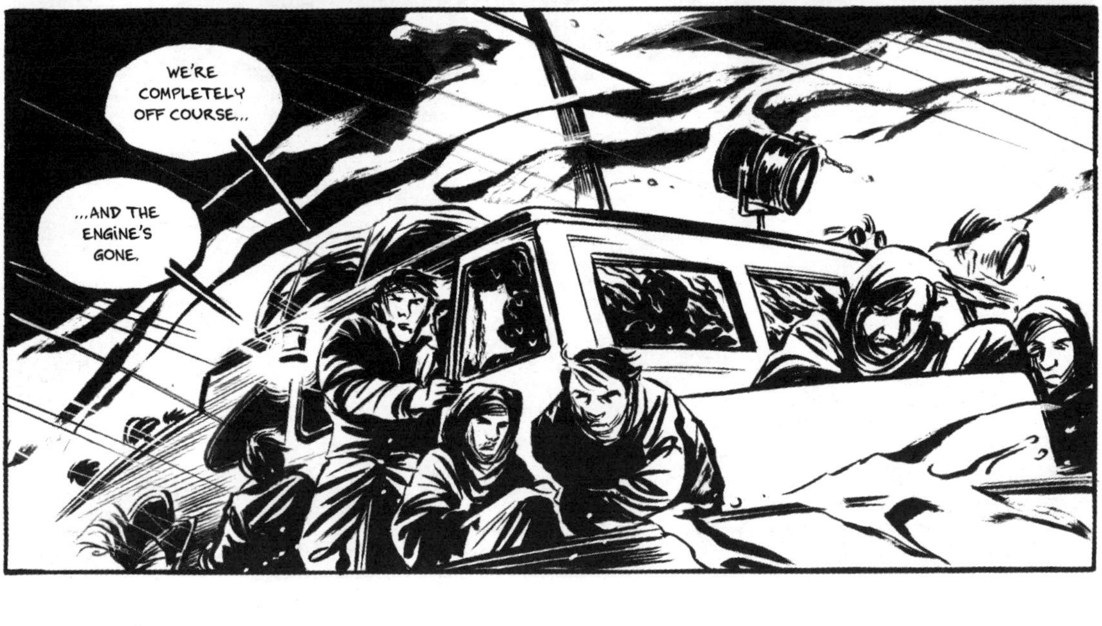
WE'RE COMPLETELY OFF COURSE...
...AND THE ENGINE'S GONE.

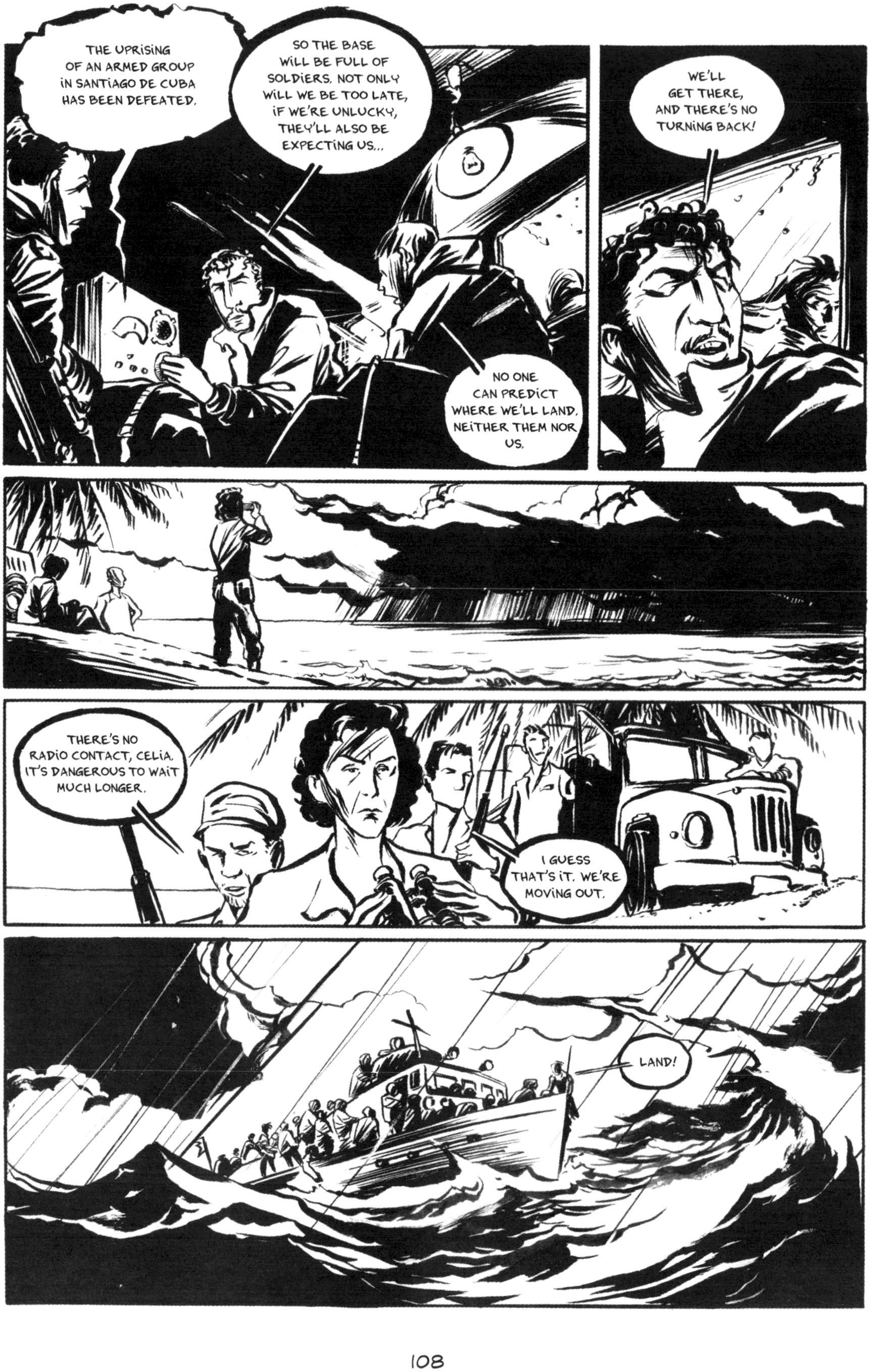
THE UPRISING OF AN ARMED GROUP IN SANTIAGO DE CUBA HAS BEEN DEFEATED.
SO THE BASE WILL BE FULL OF SOLDIERS. NOT ONLY WILL WE BE TOO LATE, IF WE'RE UNLUCKY, THEY'LL ALSO BE EXPECTING US...
NO ONE CAN PREDICT WHERE WE'LL LAND. NEITHER THEM NOR US.
WE'LL GET THERE, AND THERE'S NO TURNING BACK!
THERE'S NO RADIO CONTACT, CELIA. IT'S DANGEROUS TO WAIT MUCH LONGER.
I GUESS THAT'S IT. WE'RE MOVING OUT.
LAND!

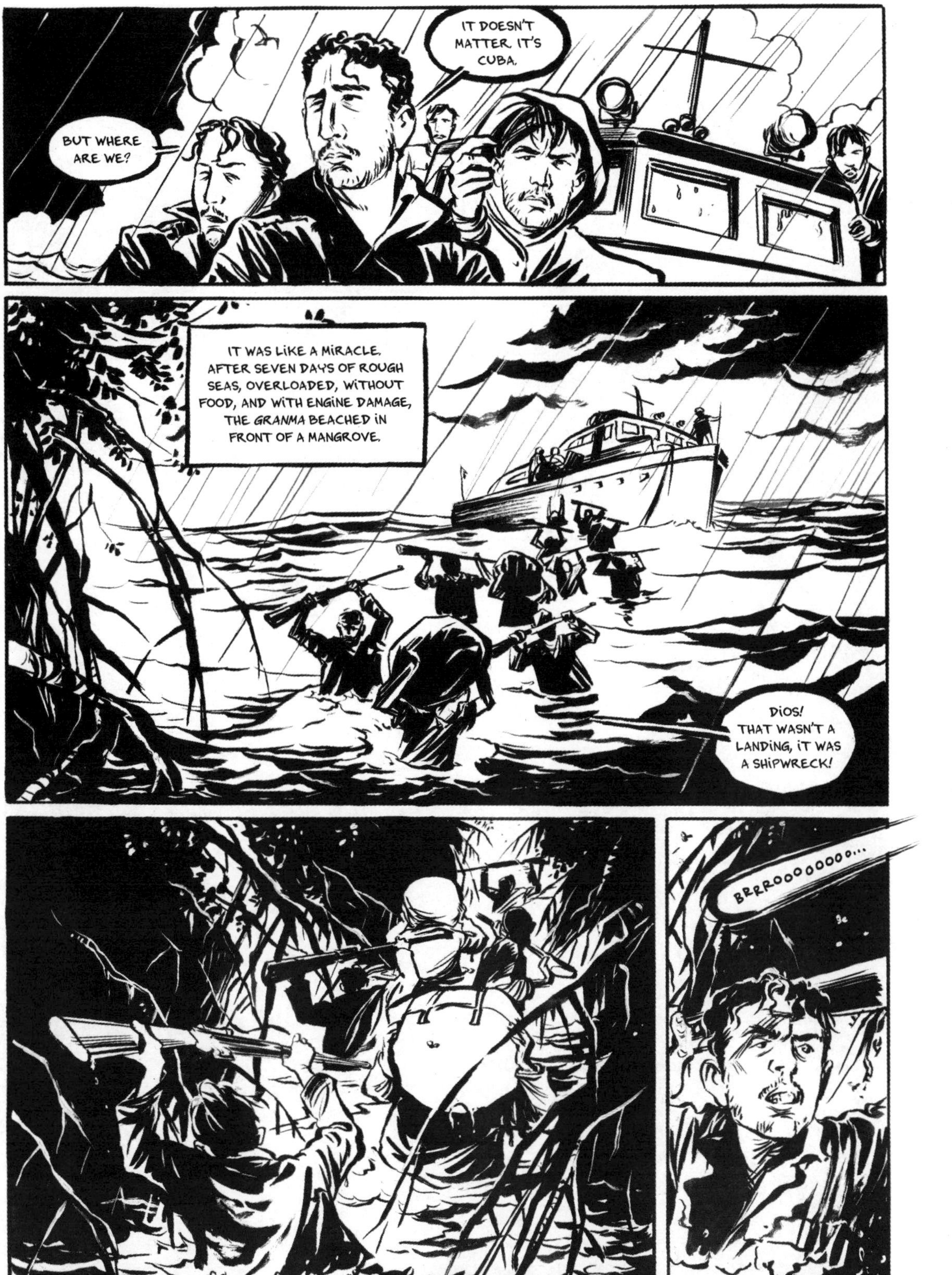
BUT WHERE ARE WE?
IT DOESN'T MATTER. IT'S CUBA.
IT WAS LIKE A MIRACLE. AFTER SEVEN DAYS OF ROUGH SEAS, OVERLOADED, WITHOUT FOOD, AND WITH ENGINE DAMAGE, THE *GRANMA* BEACHED IN FRONT OF A MANGROVE.
DIOS! THAT WASN'T A LANDING, IT WAS A SHIPWRECK!
BRRROOOOOOOO...

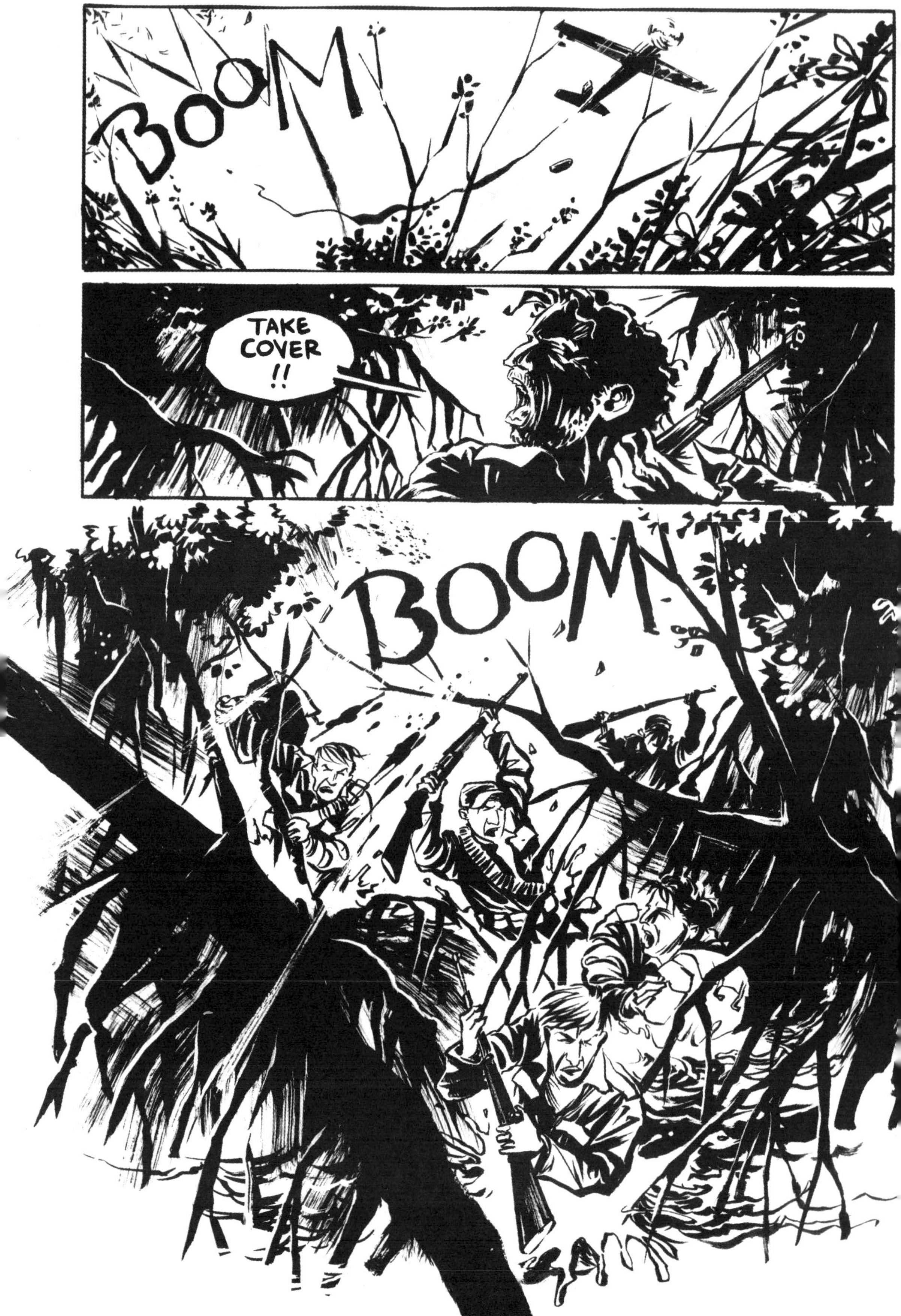
BOOM
TAKE COVER !!
BOOM

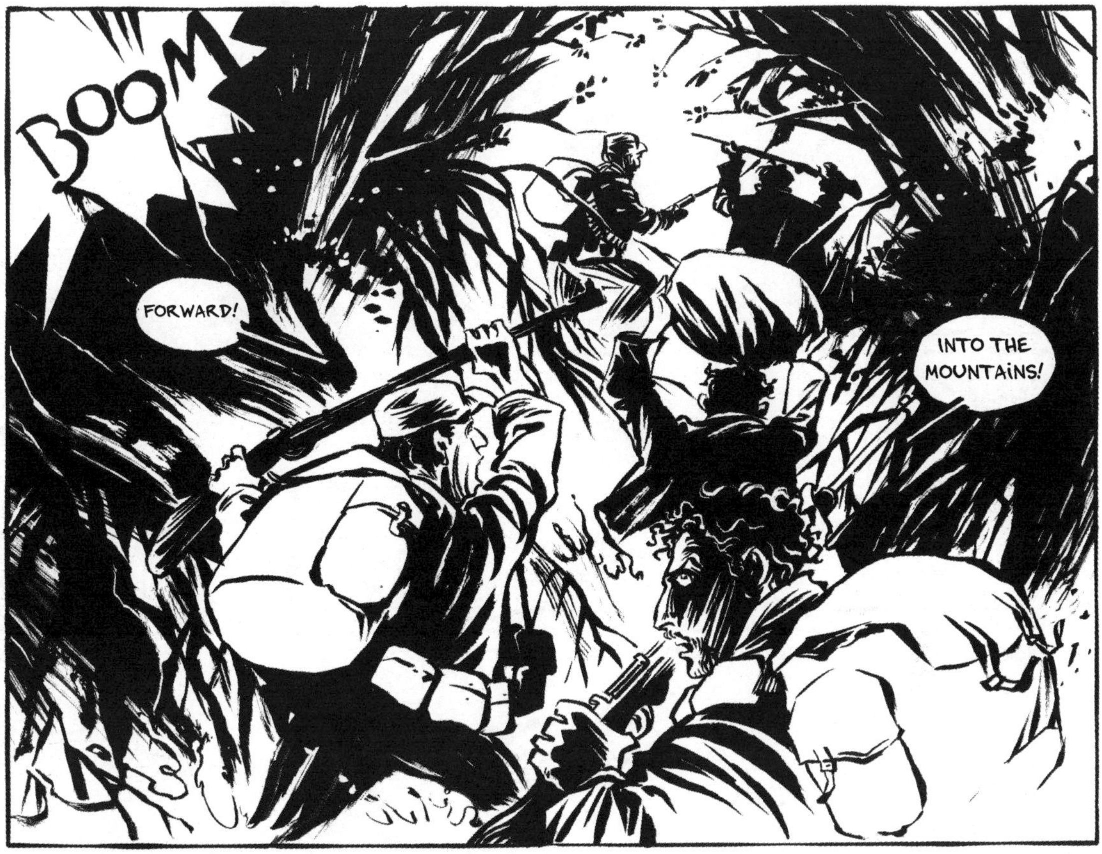
BOOM
FORWARD!
INTO THE MOUNTAINS!

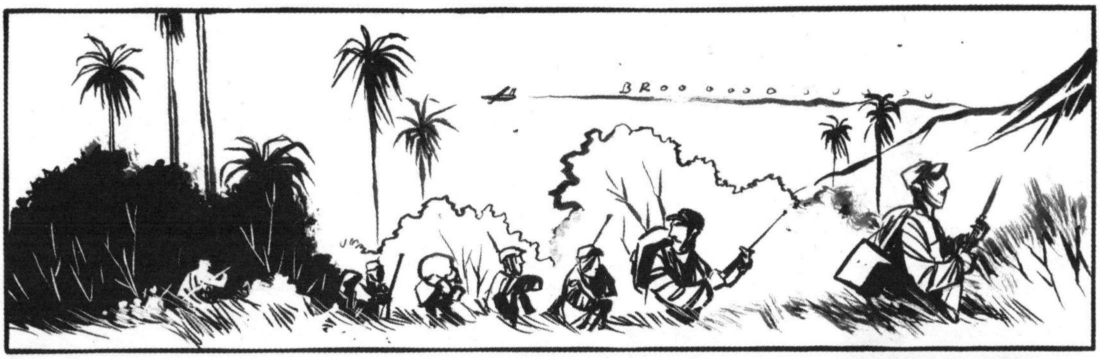
BROooooooooo

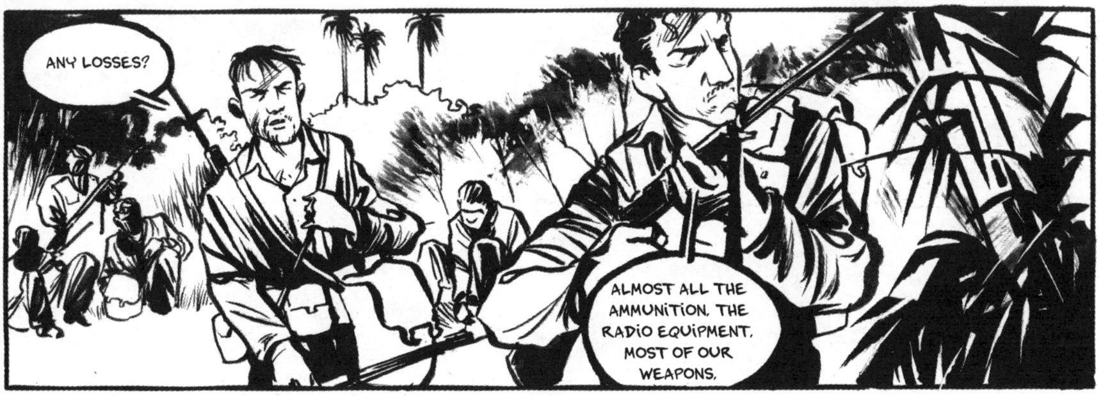
ANY LOSSES?
ALMOST ALL THE AMMUNITION. THE RADIO EQUIPMENT. MOST OF OUR WEAPONS.

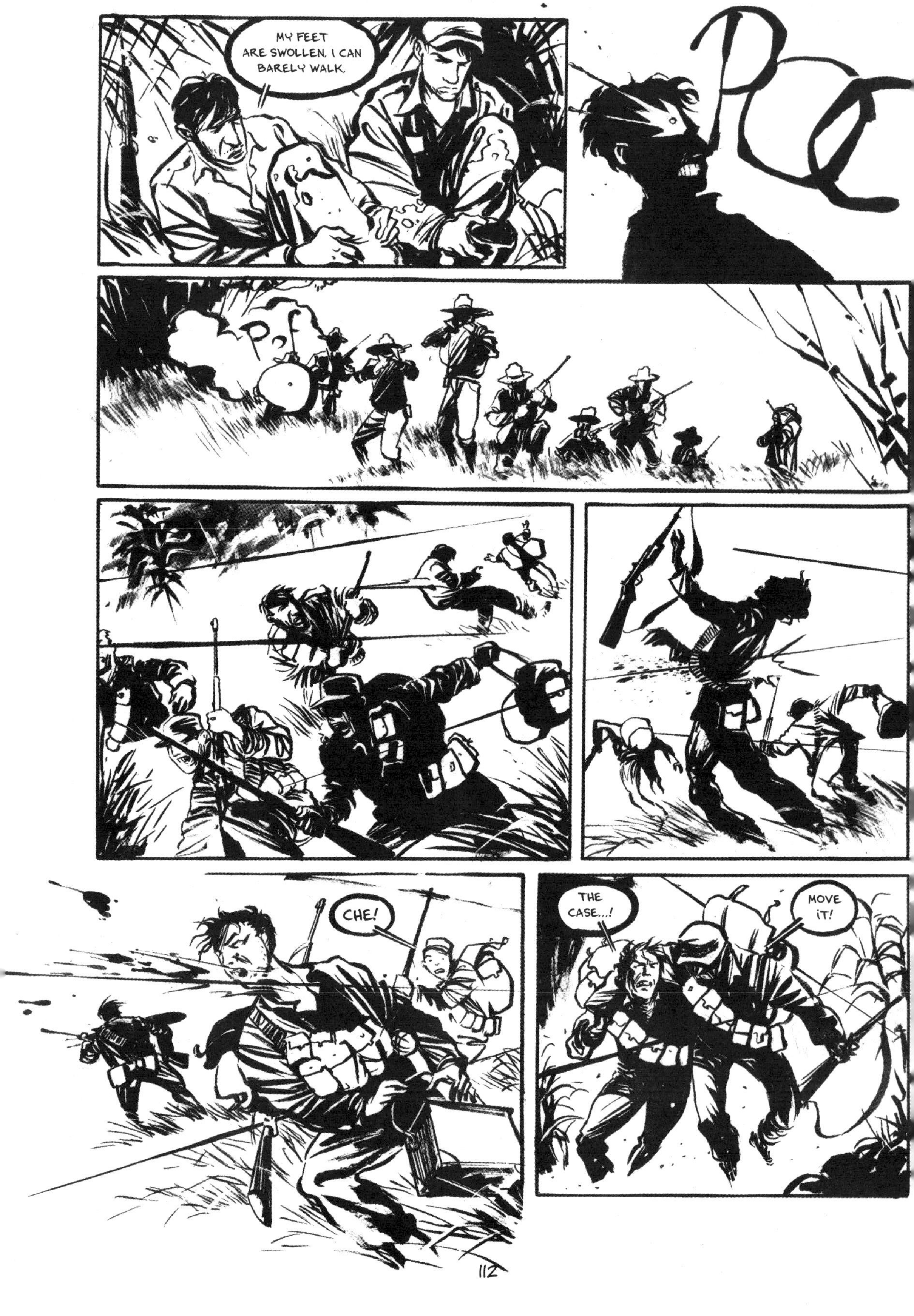
MY FEET ARE SWOLLEN. I CAN BARELY WALK.
POC
Pof
CHE!
THE CASE...!
MOVE iT!

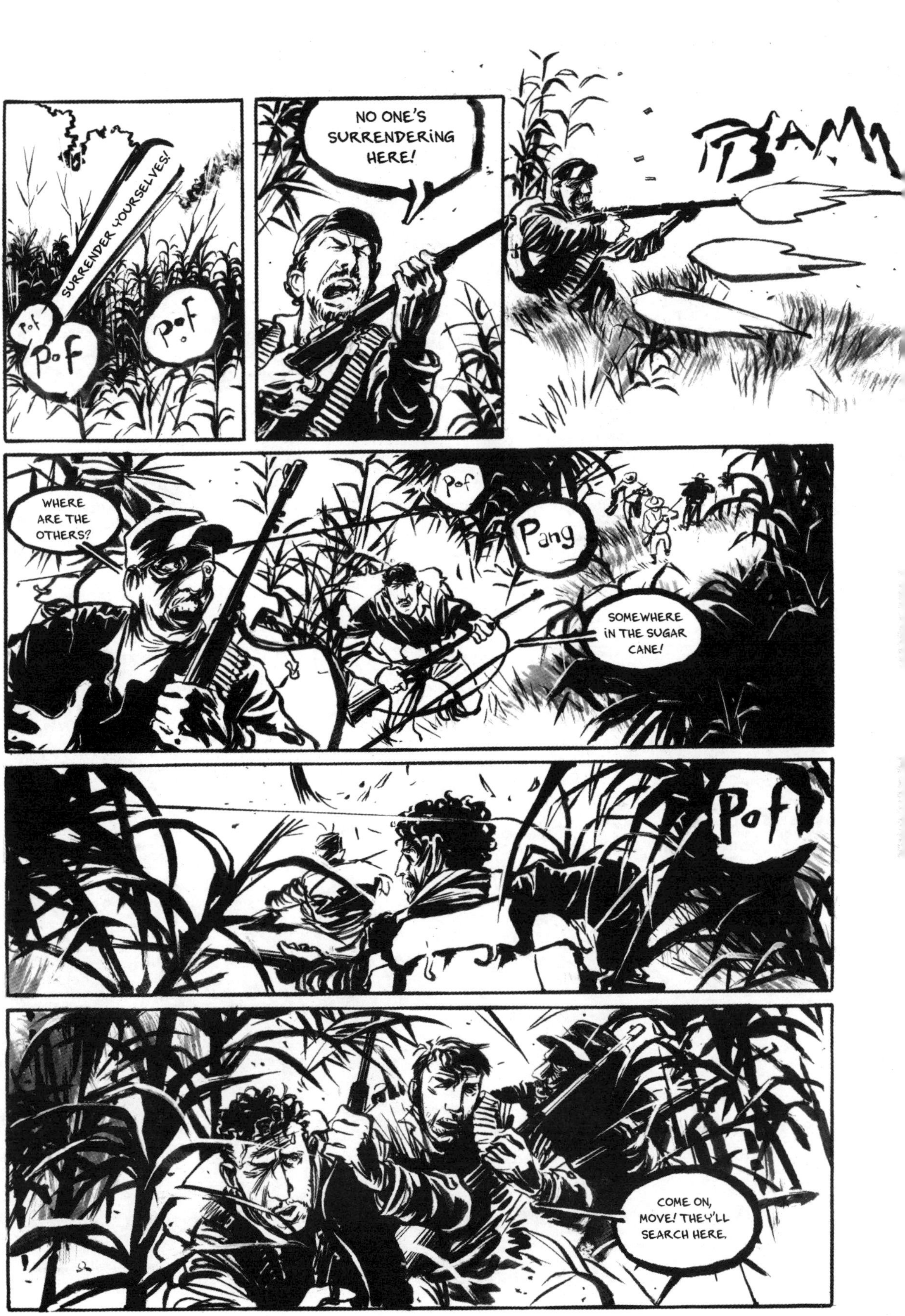

SURRENDER YOURSELVES!
Pof
Pof
Pof
NO ONE'S SURRENDERING HERE!
PBAM
WHERE ARE THE OTHERS?
Pof
Pang
SOMEWHERE IN THE SUGAR CANE!
Pof
COME ON, MOVE! THEY'LL SEARCH HERE.

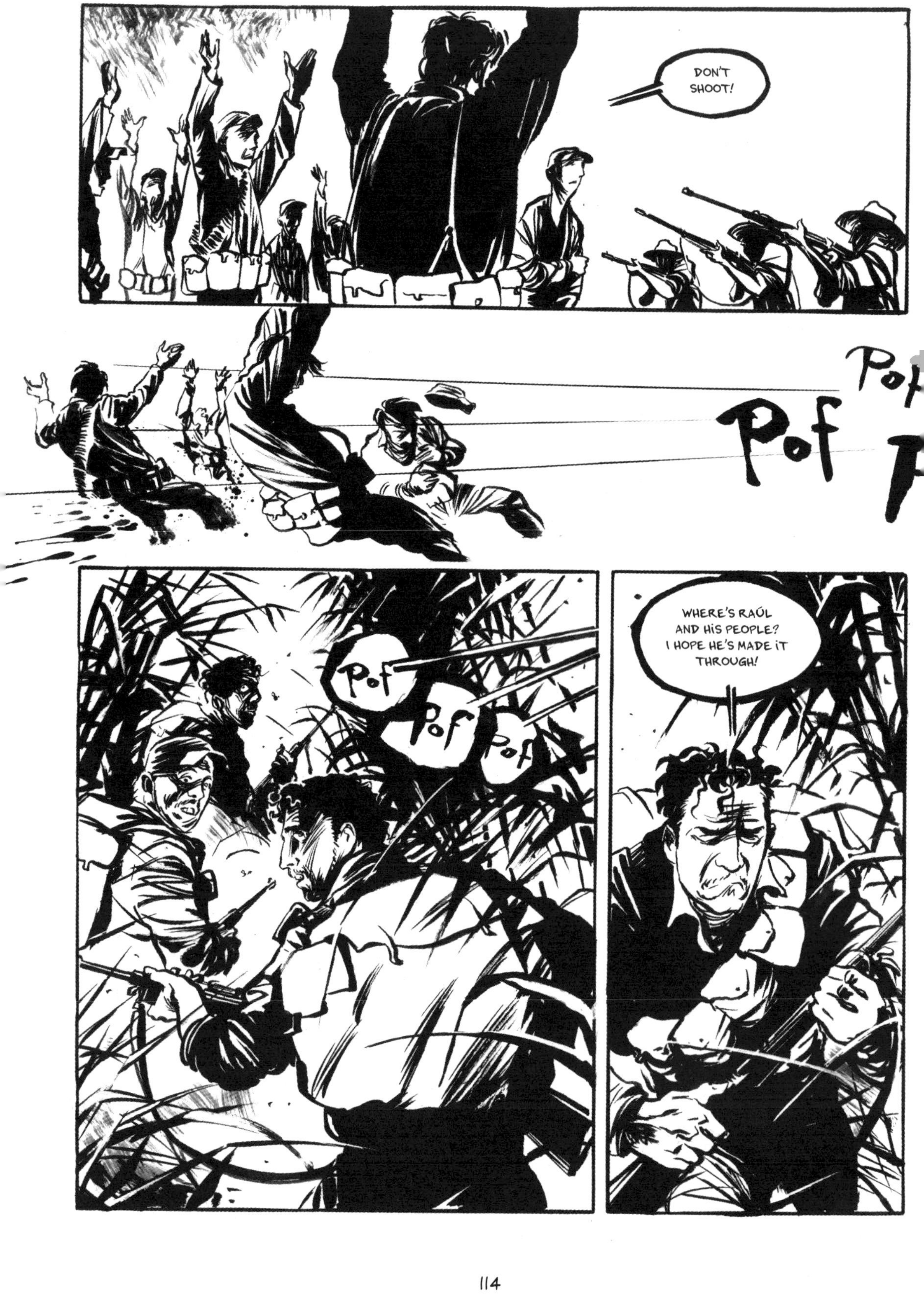
DON'T SHOOT!
Pof Pof
Pof Pof Pof
WHERE'S RAÚL AND HIS PEOPLE? I HOPE HE'S MADE IT THROUGH!

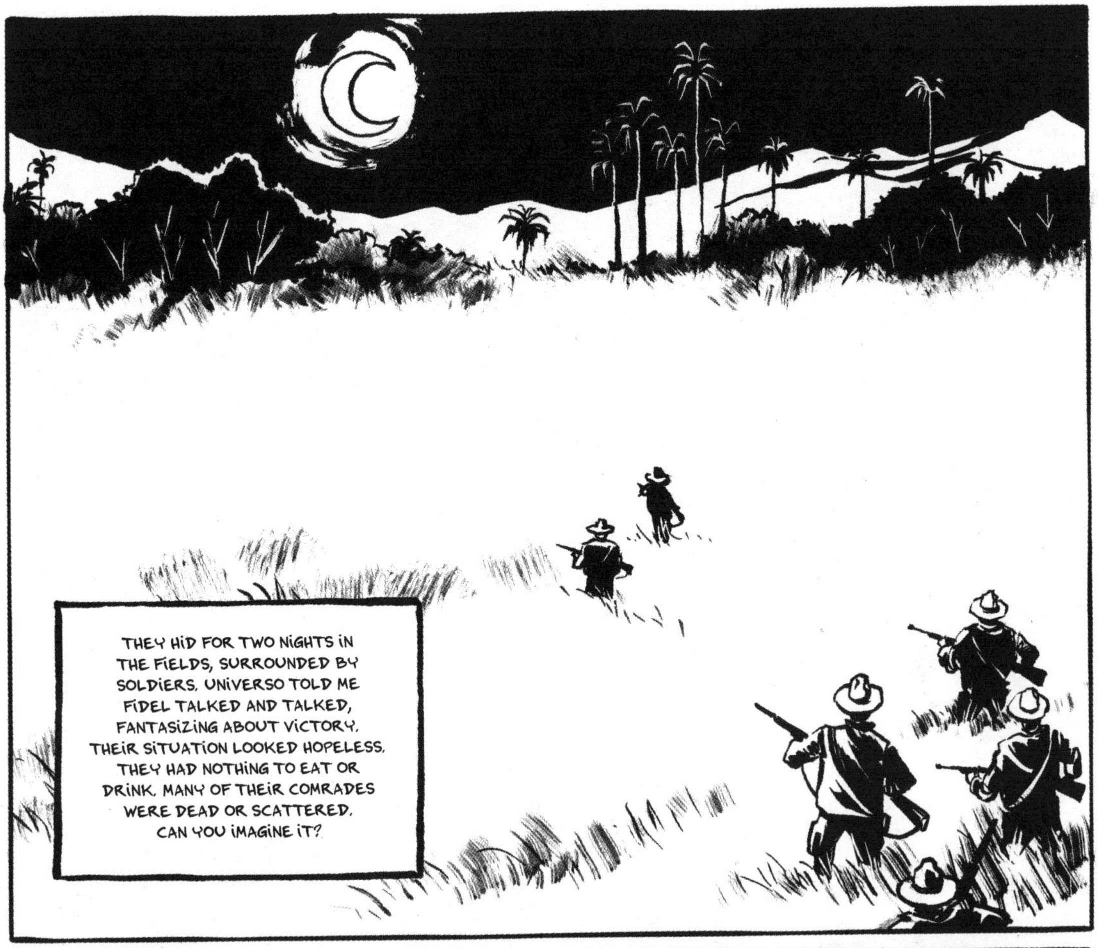
THEY HID FOR TWO NIGHTS IN THE FIELDS, SURROUNDED BY SOLDIERS. UNIVERSO TOLD ME FIDEL TALKED AND TALKED, FANTASIZING ABOUT VICTORY. THEIR SITUATION LOOKED HOPELESS. THEY HAD NOTHING TO EAT OR DRINK. MANY OF THEIR COMRADES WERE DEAD OR SCATTERED. CAN YOU IMAGINE IT?

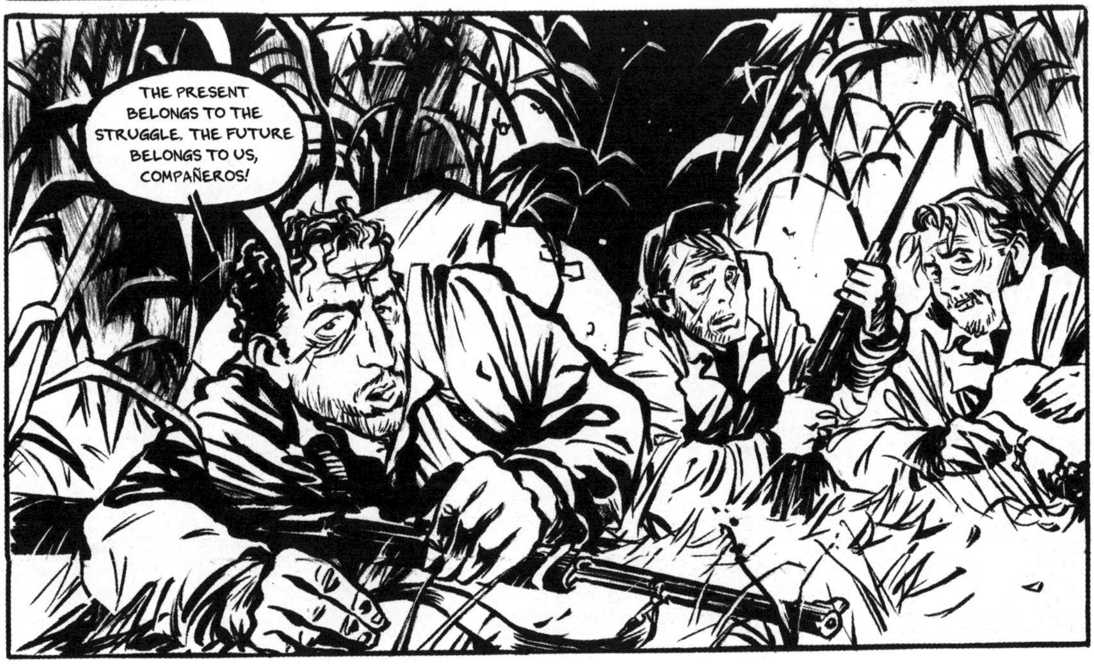
THE PRESENT BELONGS TO THE STRUGGLE. THE FUTURE BELONGS TO US, COMPAÑEROS!

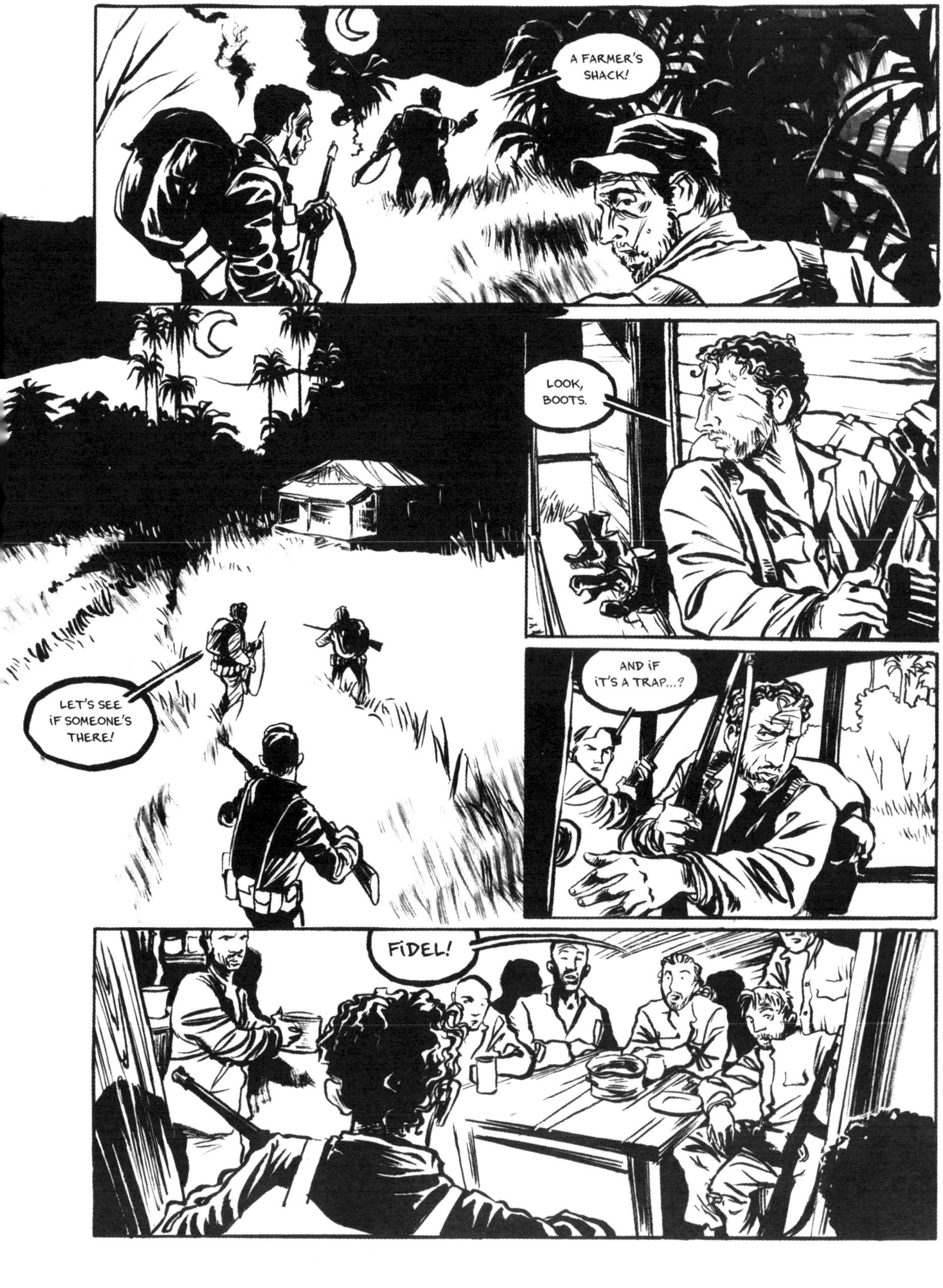
A FARMER'S SHACK!
LOOK, BOOTS.
LET'S SEE iF SOMEONE'S THERE!
AND iF iT'S A TRAP...?
FiDEL!

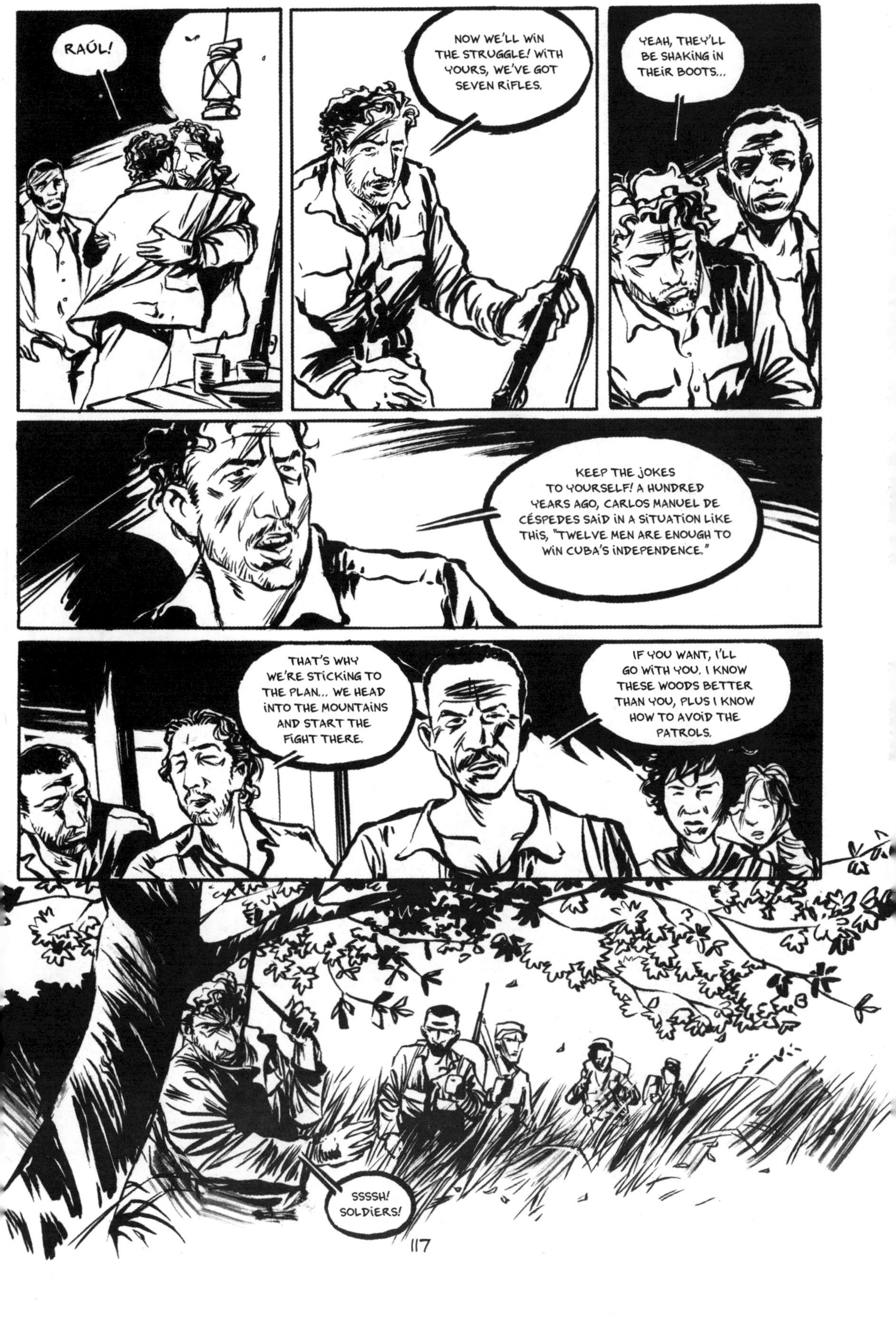
RAÚL!
NOW WE'LL WIN THE STRUGGLE! WITH YOURS, WE'VE GOT SEVEN RIFLES.
YEAH, THEY'LL BE SHAKING IN THEIR BOOTS...
KEEP THE JOKES TO YOURSELF! A HUNDRED YEARS AGO, CARLOS MANUEL DE CÉSPEDES SAID IN A SITUATION LIKE THIS, "TWELVE MEN ARE ENOUGH TO WIN CUBA'S INDEPENDENCE."
THAT'S WHY WE'RE STICKING TO THE PLAN... WE HEAD INTO THE MOUNTAINS AND START THE FIGHT THERE.
IF YOU WANT, I'LL GO WITH YOU. I KNOW THESE WOODS BETTER THAN YOU, PLUS I KNOW HOW TO AVOID THE PATROLS.
SSSSH! SOLDIERS!

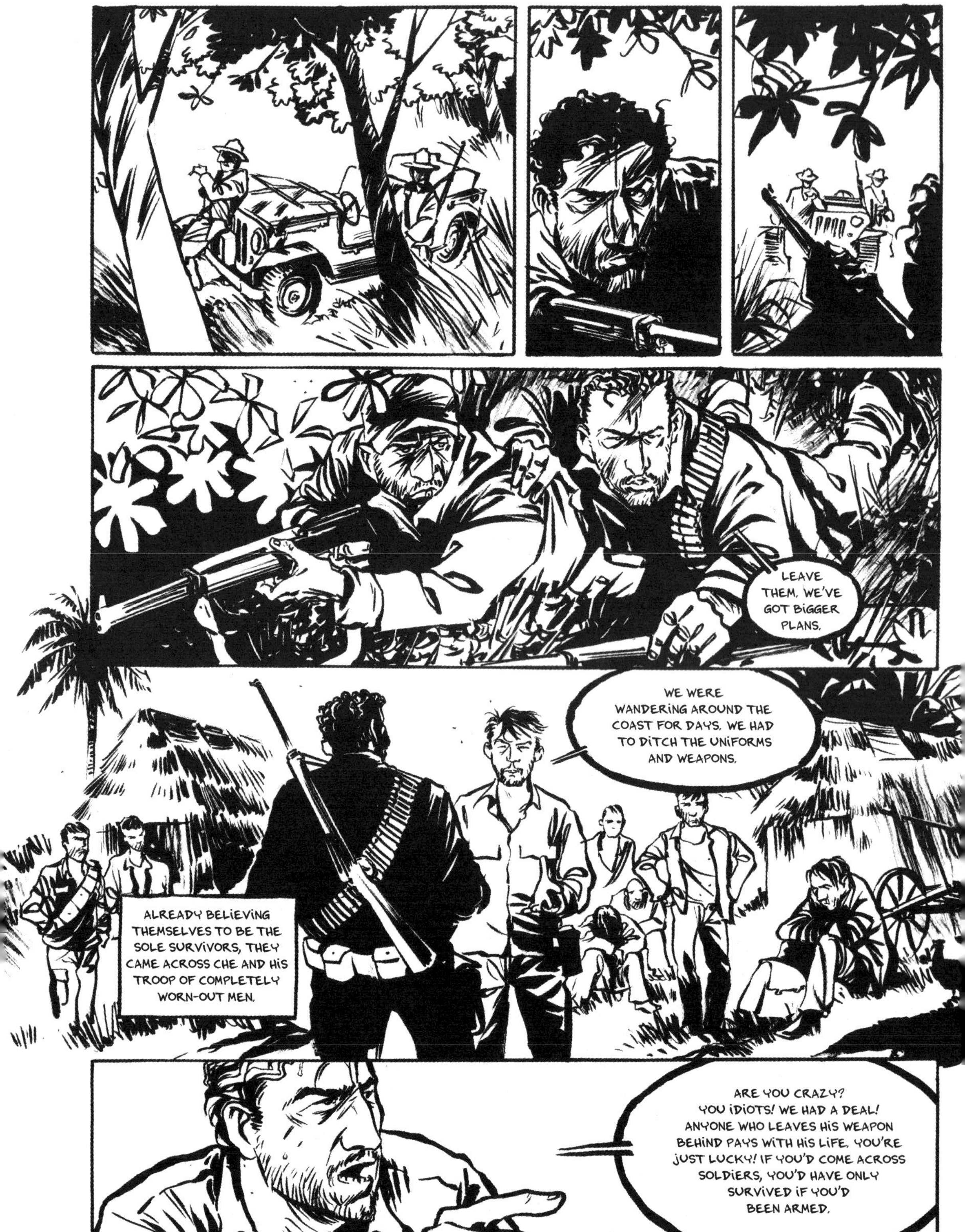
LEAVE THEM. WE'VE GOT BIGGER PLANS.
WE WERE WANDERING AROUND THE COAST FOR DAYS. WE HAD TO DITCH THE UNIFORMS AND WEAPONS.
ALREADY BELIEVING THEMSELVES TO BE THE SOLE SURVIVORS, THEY CAME ACROSS CHE AND HIS TROOP OF COMPLETELY WORN-OUT MEN.
ARE YOU CRAZY? YOU IDIOTS! WE HAD A DEAL! ANYONE WHO LEAVES HIS WEAPON BEHIND PAYS WITH HIS LIFE. YOU'RE JUST LUCKY! IF YOU'D COME ACROSS SOLDIERS, YOU'D HAVE ONLY SURVIVED IF YOU'D BEEN ARMED.

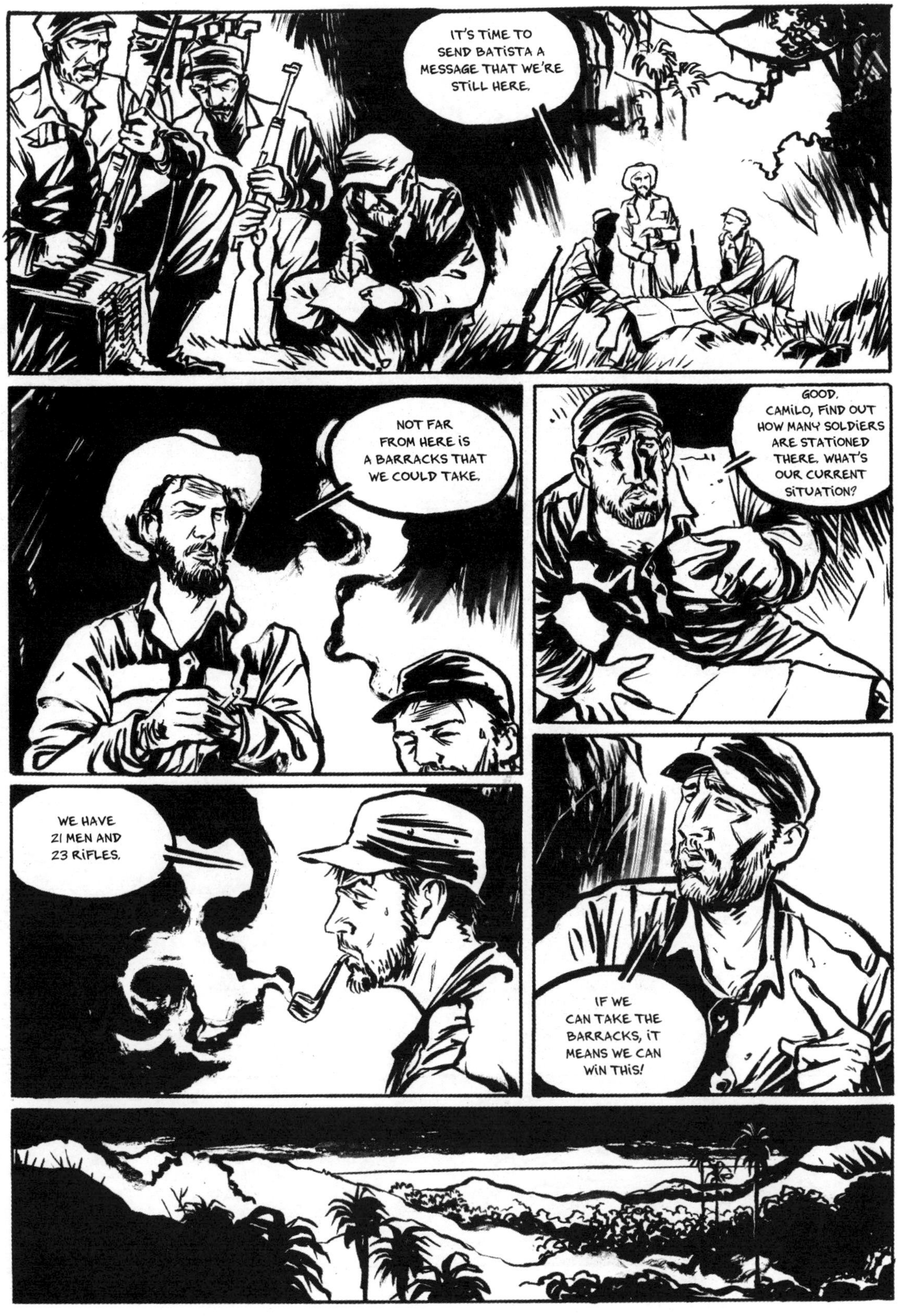
IT'S TIME TO SEND BATISTA A MESSAGE THAT WE'RE STILL HERE.
NOT FAR FROM HERE IS A BARRACKS THAT WE COULD TAKE.
GOOD. CAMILO, FIND OUT HOW MANY SOLDIERS ARE STATIONED THERE. WHAT'S OUR CURRENT SITUATION?
WE HAVE 21 MEN AND 23 RIFLES.
IF WE CAN TAKE THE BARRACKS, IT MEANS WE CAN WIN THIS!

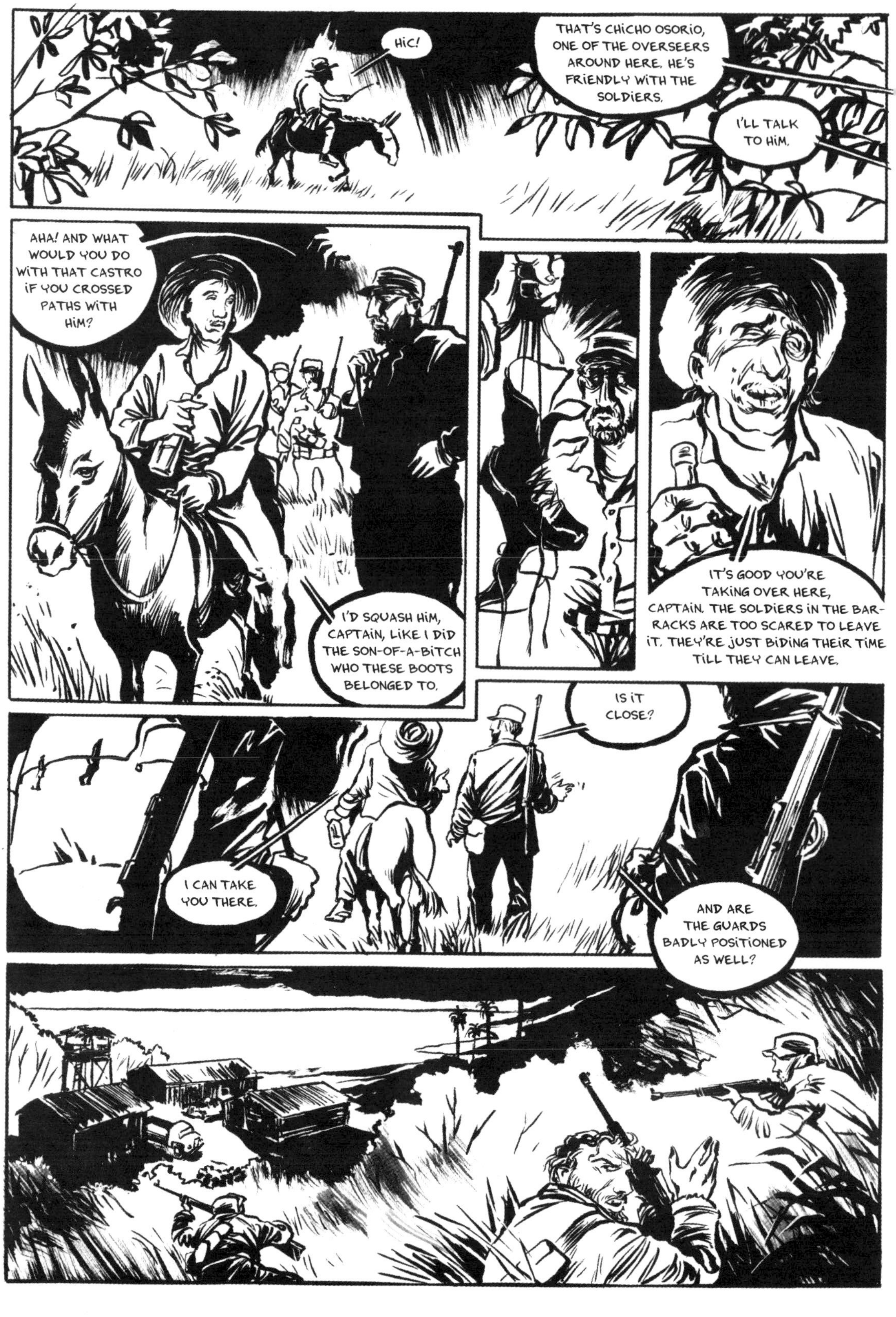
HIC!
THAT'S CHICHO OSORIO, ONE OF THE OVERSEERS AROUND HERE. HE'S FRIENDLY WITH THE SOLDIERS.
I'LL TALK TO HIM.
AHA! AND WHAT WOULD YOU DO WITH THAT CASTRO IF YOU CROSSED PATHS WITH HIM?
I'D SQUASH HIM, CAPTAIN, LIKE I DID THE SON-OF-A-BITCH WHO THESE BOOTS BELONGED TO.
IT'S GOOD YOU'RE TAKING OVER HERE, CAPTAIN. THE SOLDIERS IN THE BARRACKS ARE TOO SCARED TO LEAVE IT. THEY'RE JUST BIDING THEIR TIME TILL THEY CAN LEAVE.
IS IT CLOSE?
I CAN TAKE YOU THERE.
AND ARE THE GUARDS BADLY POSITIONED AS WELL?

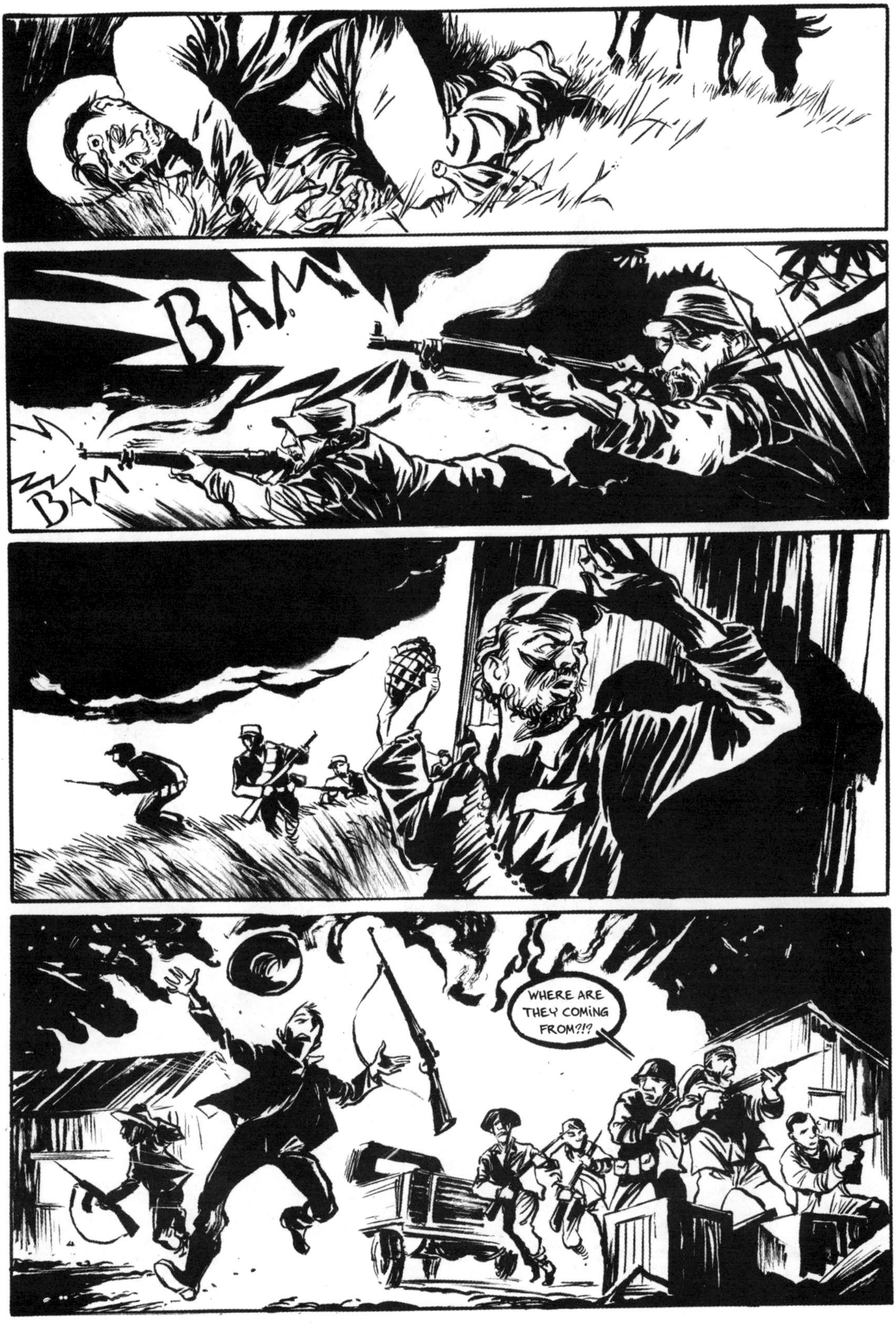
BAM
BAM
WHERE ARE THEY COMING FROM?!?

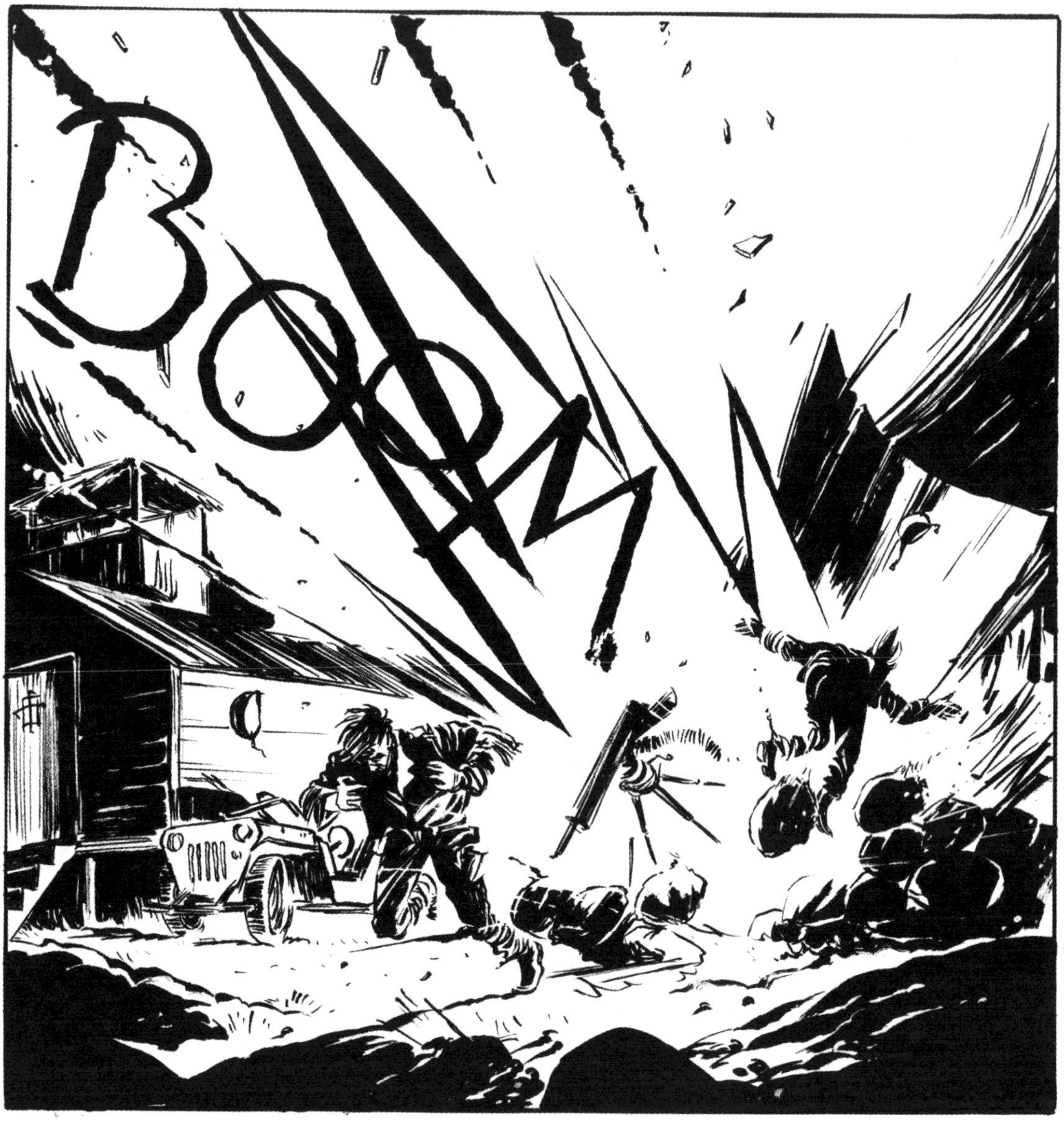
BOOM

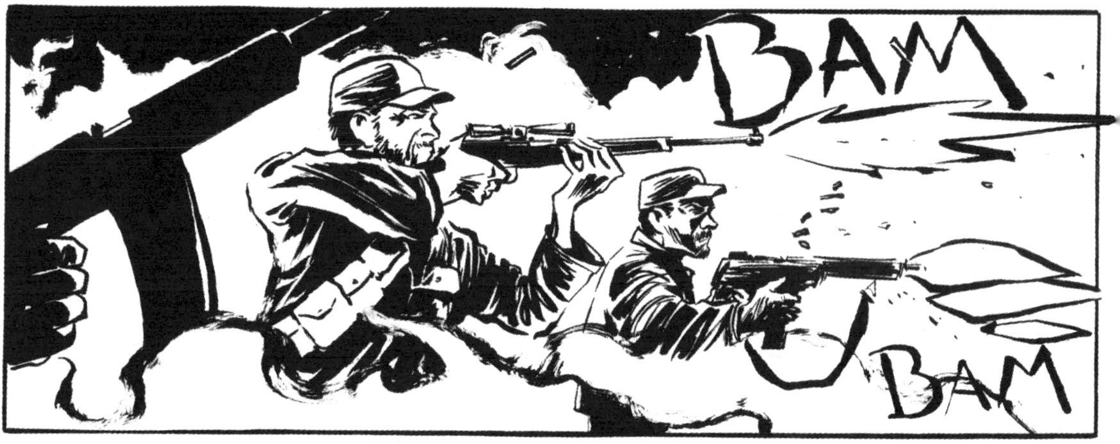
BAM
BAM

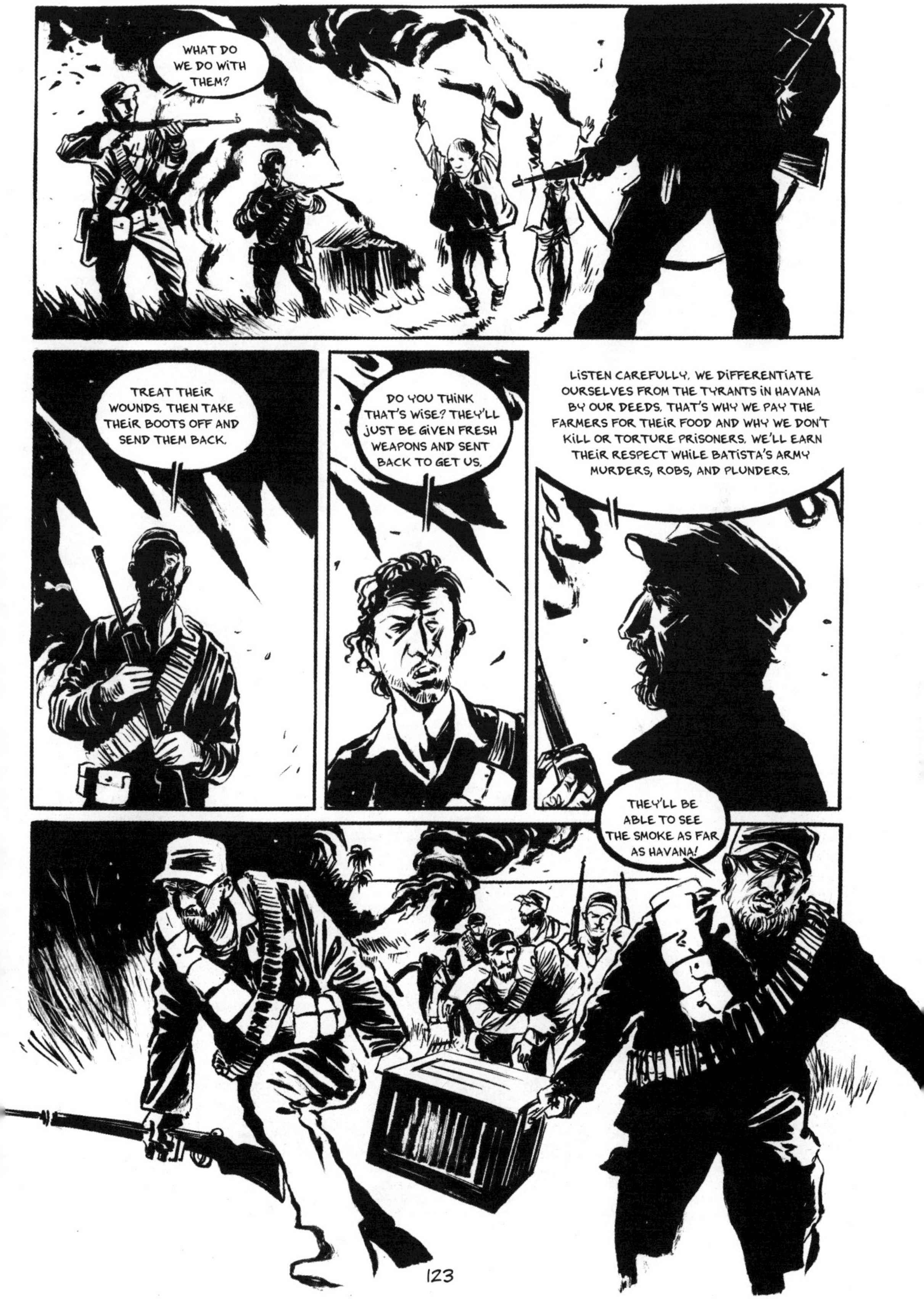
WHAT DO WE DO WITH THEM?
TREAT THEIR WOUNDS, THEN TAKE THEIR BOOTS OFF AND SEND THEM BACK.
DO YOU THINK THAT'S WISE? THEY'LL JUST BE GIVEN FRESH WEAPONS AND SENT BACK TO GET US.
LISTEN CAREFULLY, WE DIFFERENTIATE OURSELVES FROM THE TYRANTS IN HAVANA BY OUR DEEDS. THAT'S WHY WE PAY THE FARMERS FOR THEIR FOOD AND WHY WE DON'T KILL OR TORTURE PRISONERS. WE'LL EARN THEIR RESPECT WHILE BATISTA'S ARMY MURDERS, ROBS, AND PLUNDERS.
THEY'LL BE ABLE TO SEE THE SMOKE AS FAR AS HAVANA!

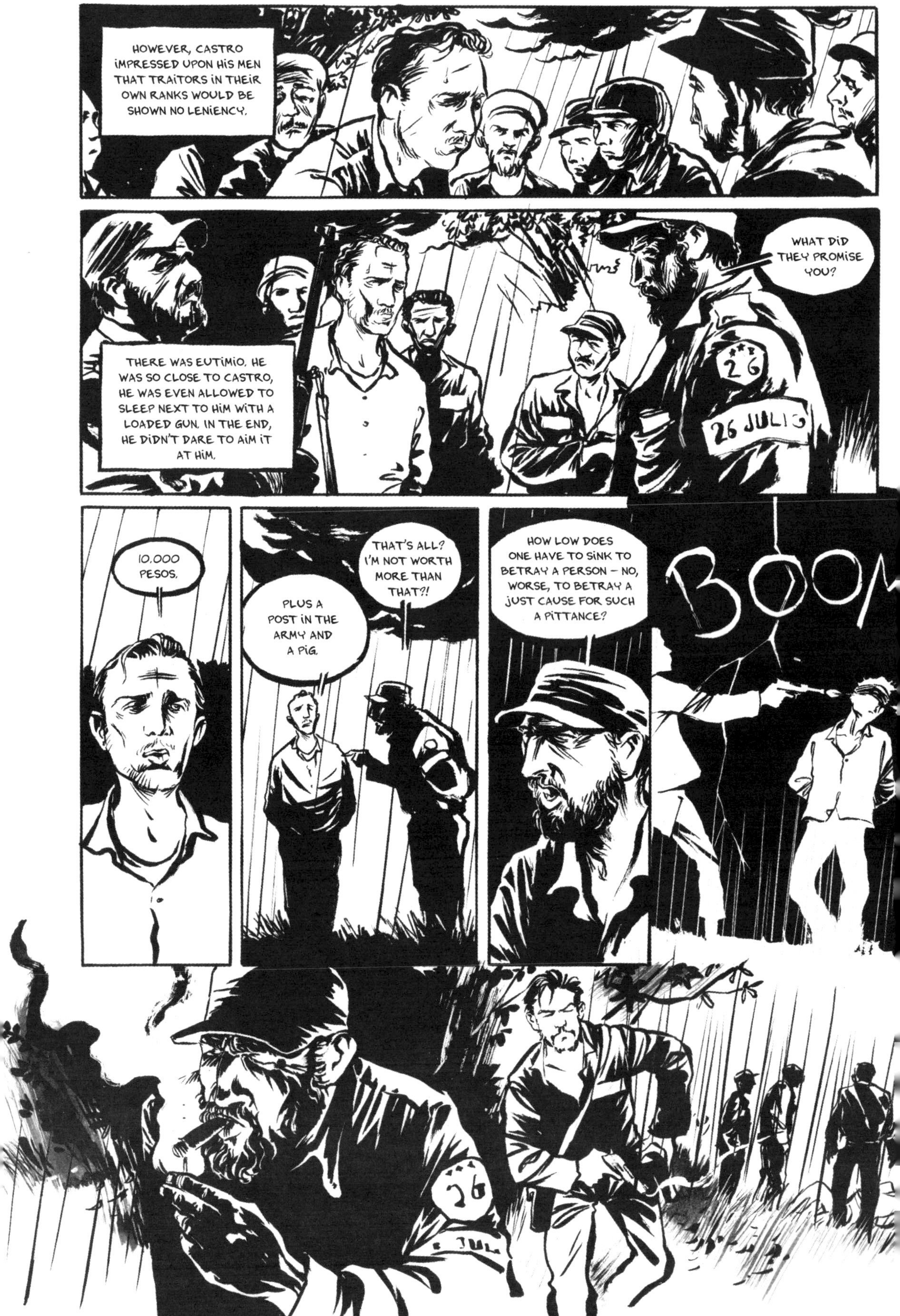
HOWEVER, CASTRO IMPRESSED UPON HIS MEN THAT TRAITORS IN THEIR OWN RANKS WOULD BE SHOWN NO LENIENCY.
THERE WAS EUTIMIO. HE WAS SO CLOSE TO CASTRO, HE WAS EVEN ALLOWED TO SLEEP NEXT TO HIM WITH A LOADED GUN. IN THE END, HE DIDN'T DARE TO AIM IT AT HIM.
WHAT DID THEY PROMISE YOU?
26 JULIO
10.000 PESOS.
PLUS A POST IN THE ARMY AND A PIG.
THAT'S ALL? I'M NOT WORTH MORE THAN THAT?!
HOW LOW DOES ONE HAVE TO SINK TO BETRAY A PERSON – NO, WORSE, TO BETRAY A JUST CAUSE FOR SUCH A PITTANCE?
BOOM
26
JUL

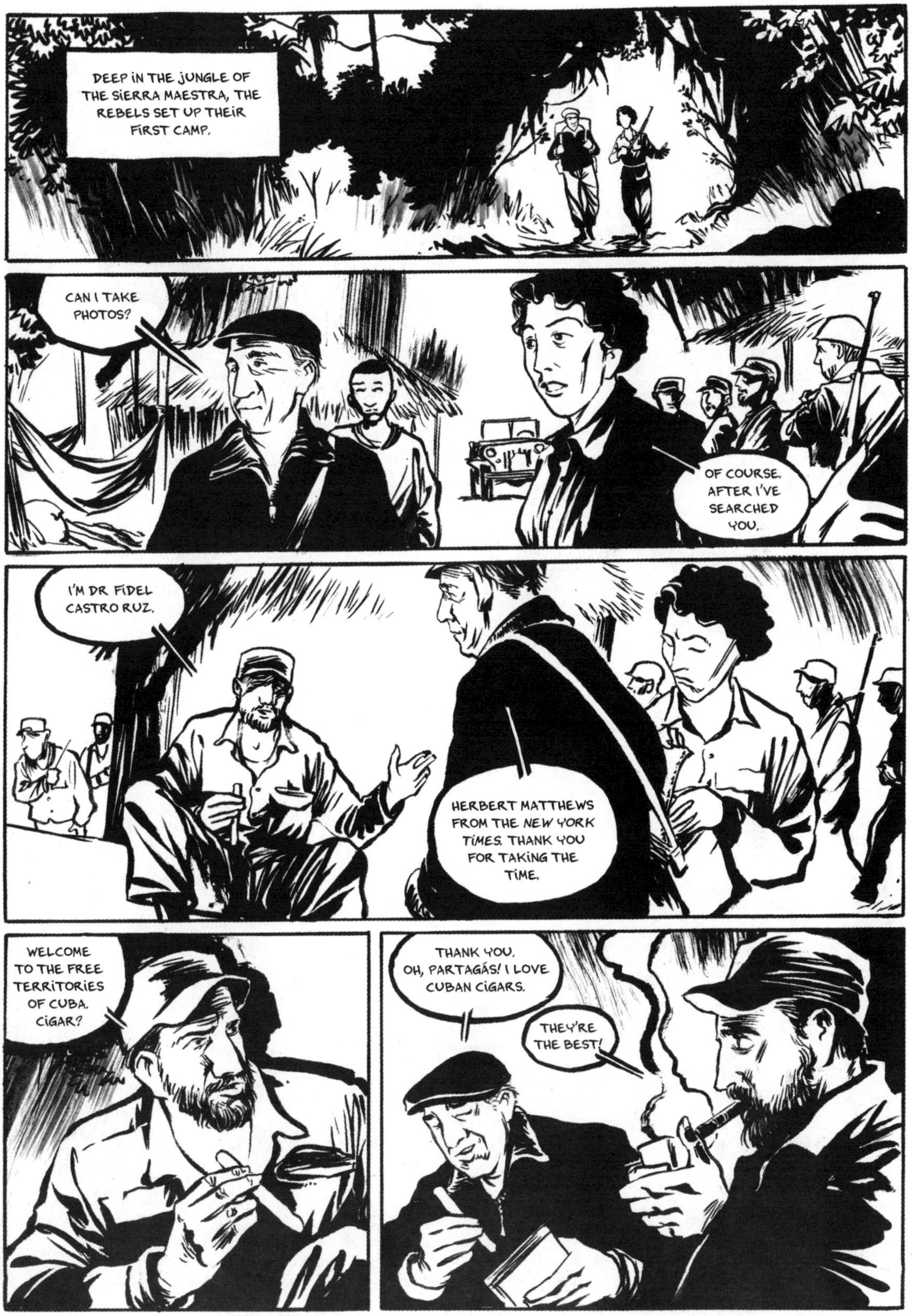
DEEP IN THE JUNGLE OF THE SIERRA MAESTRA, THE REBELS SET UP THEIR FIRST CAMP.
CAN I TAKE PHOTOS?
OF COURSE, AFTER I'VE SEARCHED YOU.
I'M DR FIDEL CASTRO RUZ.
HERBERT MATTHEWS FROM THE NEW YORK TIMES. THANK YOU FOR TAKING THE TIME.
WELCOME TO THE FREE TERRITORIES OF CUBA. CIGAR?
THANK YOU. OH, PARTAGÁS! I LOVE CUBAN CIGARS.
THEY'RE THE BEST!

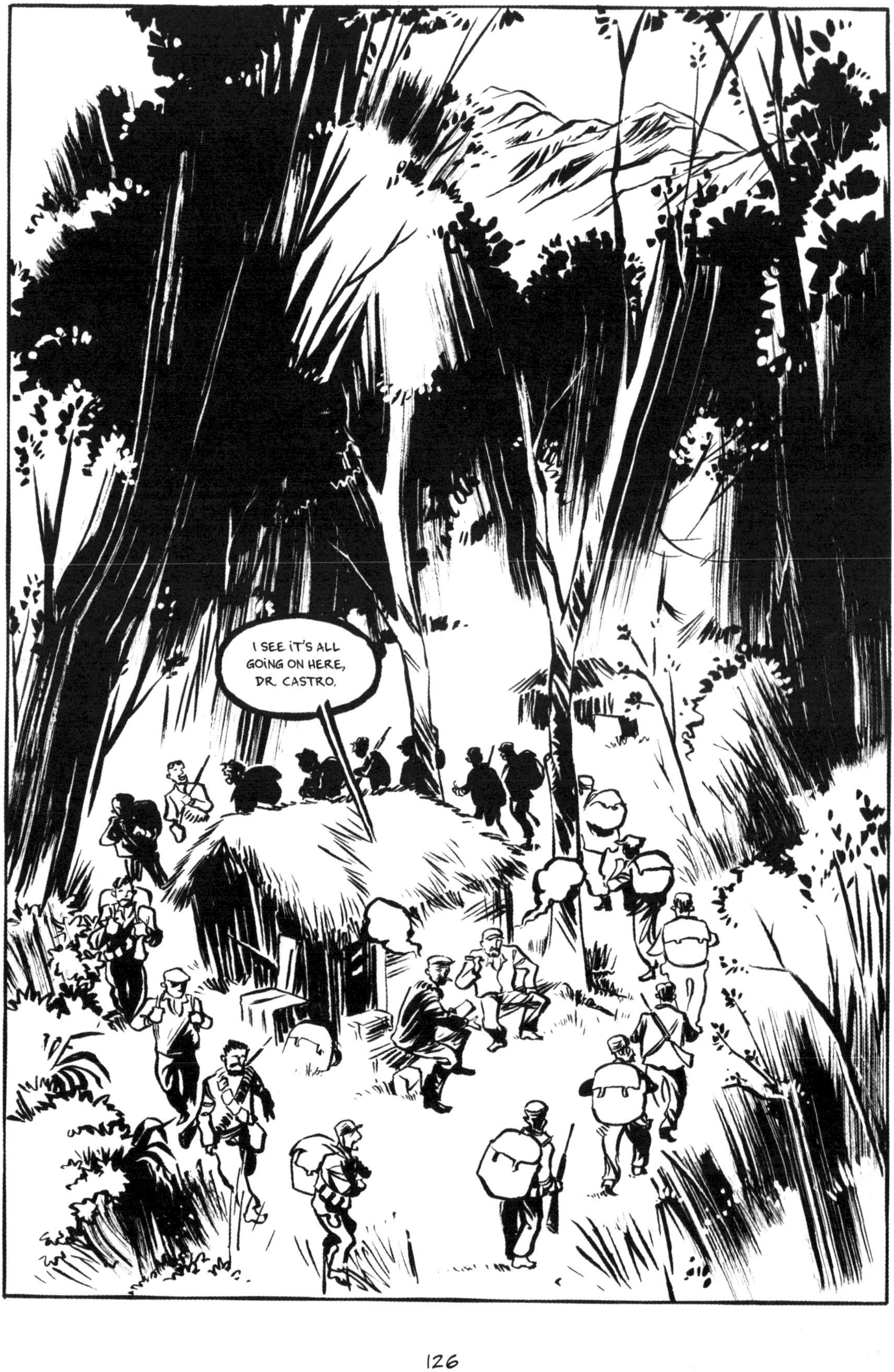
I SEE iT'S ALL GOiNG ON HERE, DR. CASTRO.

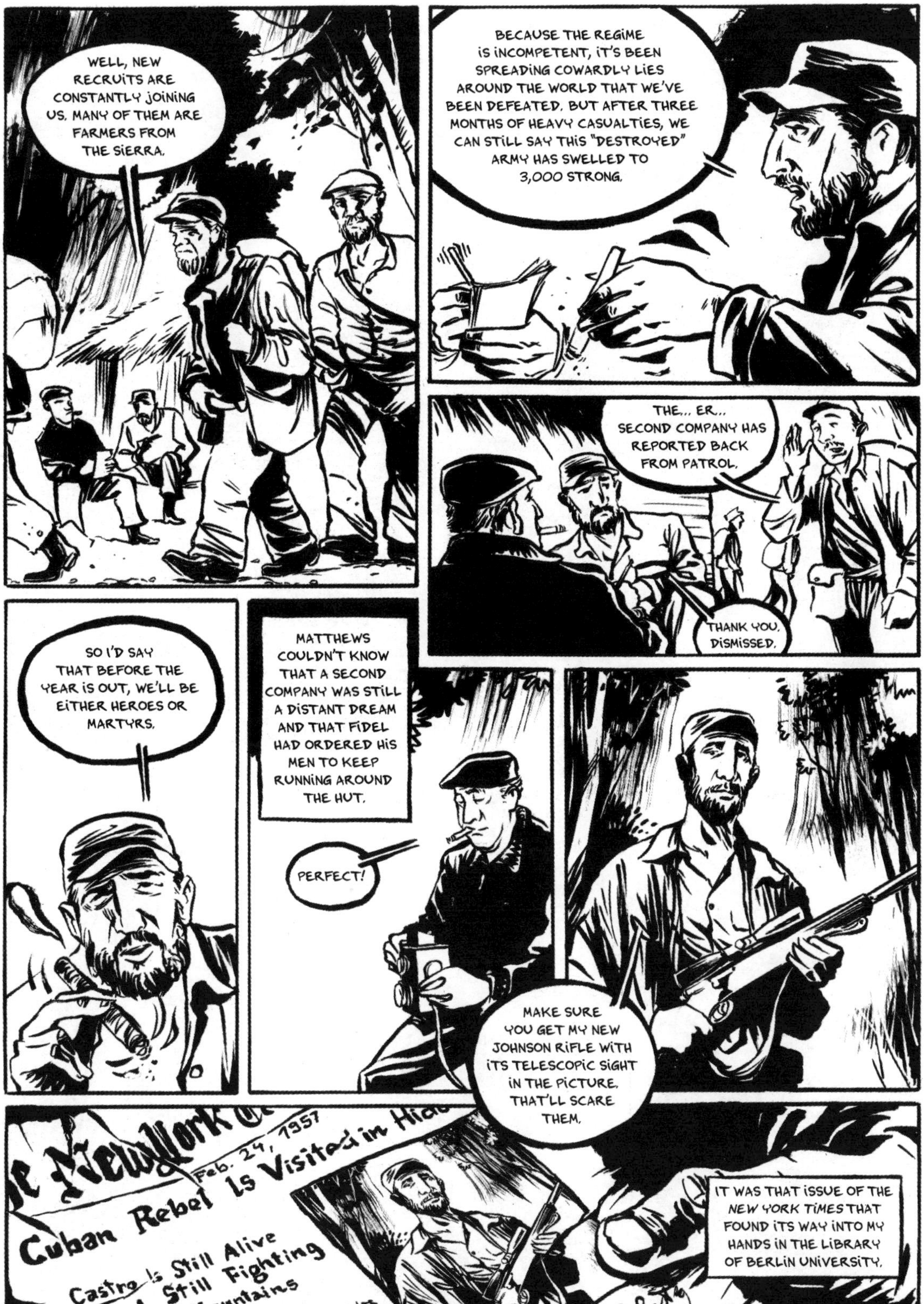
WELL, NEW RECRUITS ARE CONSTANTLY JOINING US. MANY OF THEM ARE FARMERS FROM THE SIERRA.
BECAUSE THE REGIME IS INCOMPETENT, IT'S BEEN SPREADING COWARDLY LIES AROUND THE WORLD THAT WE'VE BEEN DEFEATED. BUT AFTER THREE MONTHS OF HEAVY CASUALTIES, WE CAN STILL SAY THIS "DESTROYED" ARMY HAS SWELLED TO 3,000 STRONG.
THE... ER... SECOND COMPANY HAS REPORTED BACK FROM PATROL.
THANK YOU. DISMISSED.
SO I'D SAY THAT BEFORE THE YEAR IS OUT, WE'LL BE EITHER HEROES OR MARTYRS.
MATTHEWS COULDN'T KNOW THAT A SECOND COMPANY WAS STILL A DISTANT DREAM AND THAT FIDEL HAD ORDERED HIS MEN TO KEEP RUNNING AROUND THE HUT.
PERFECT!
MAKE SURE YOU GET MY NEW JOHNSON RIFLE WITH ITS TELESCOPIC SIGHT IN THE PICTURE. THAT'LL SCARE THEM.
Feb. 24, 1957
Cuban Rebel Is Visited in Hid
Castro Is Still Alive and Still Fighting in Mountains
IT WAS THAT ISSUE OF THE NEW YORK TIMES THAT FOUND ITS WAY INTO MY HANDS IN THE LIBRARY OF BERLIN UNIVERSITY.

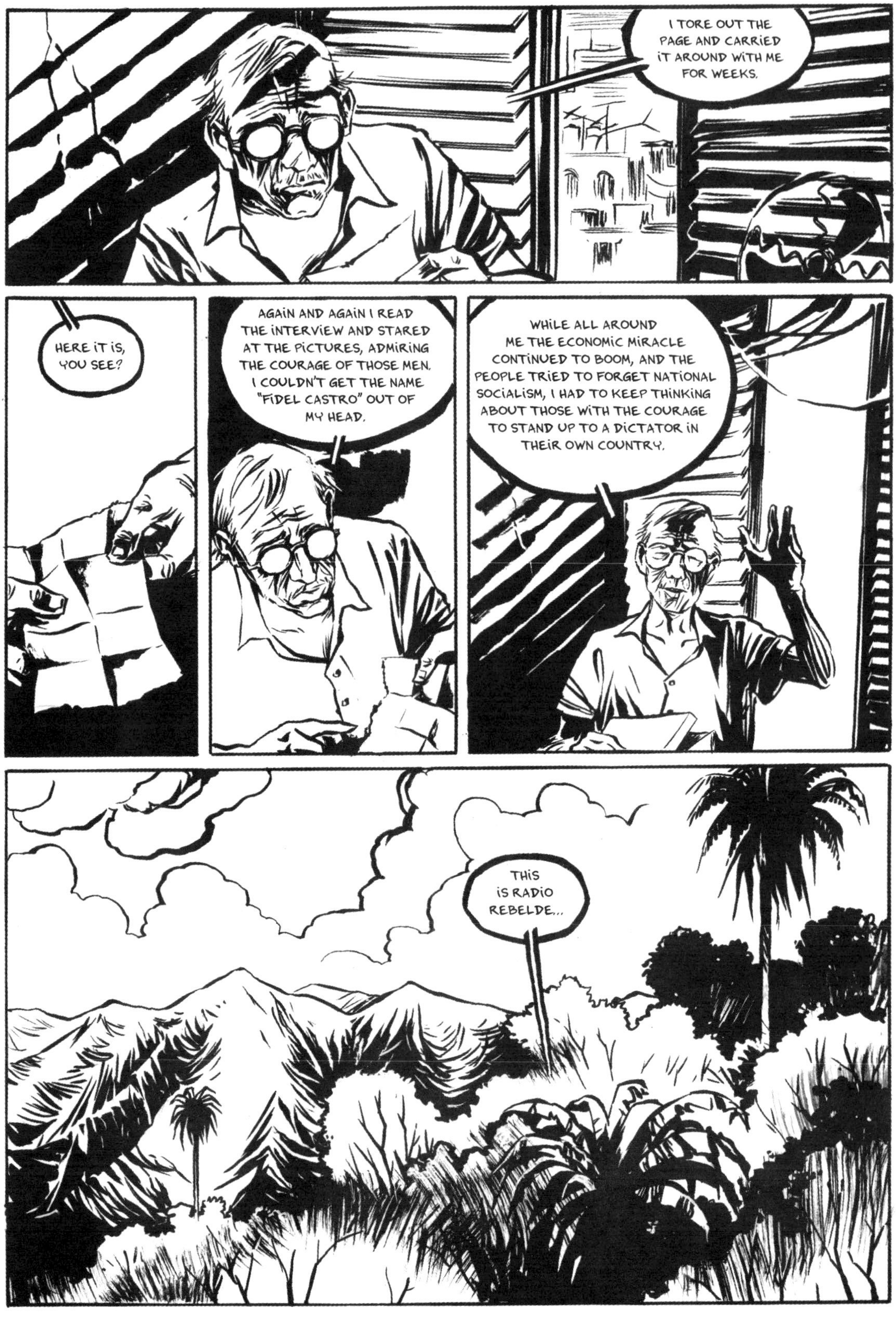
I TORE OUT THE PAGE AND CARRIED IT AROUND WITH ME FOR WEEKS.
HERE IT IS, YOU SEE?
AGAIN AND AGAIN I READ THE INTERVIEW AND STARED AT THE PICTURES, ADMIRING THE COURAGE OF THOSE MEN. I COULDN'T GET THE NAME "FIDEL CASTRO" OUT OF MY HEAD.
WHILE ALL AROUND ME THE ECONOMIC MIRACLE CONTINUED TO BOOM, AND THE PEOPLE TRIED TO FORGET NATIONAL SOCIALISM, I HAD TO KEEP THINKING ABOUT THOSE WITH THE COURAGE TO STAND UP TO A DICTATOR IN THEIR OWN COUNTRY.
THIS IS RADIO REBELDE...

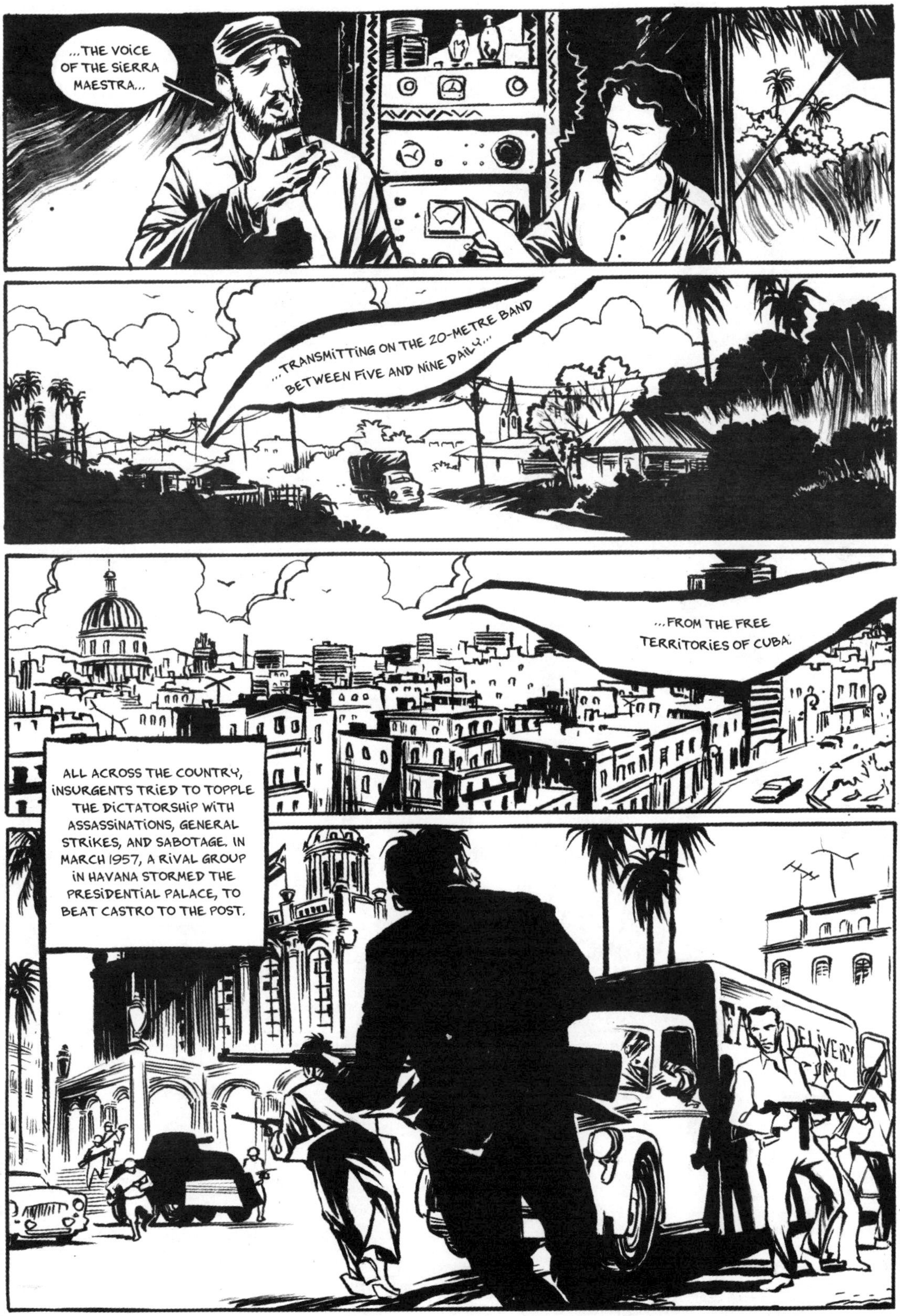
...THE VOICE OF THE SIERRA MAESTRA...
...TRANSMITTING ON THE 20-METRE BAND BETWEEN FIVE AND NINE DAILY...
...FROM THE FREE TERRITORIES OF CUBA.
ALL ACROSS THE COUNTRY, INSURGENTS TRIED TO TOPPLE THE DICTATORSHIP WITH ASSASSINATIONS, GENERAL STRIKES, AND SABOTAGE. IN MARCH 1957, A RIVAL GROUP IN HAVANA STORMED THE PRESIDENTIAL PALACE, TO BEAT CASTRO TO THE POST.

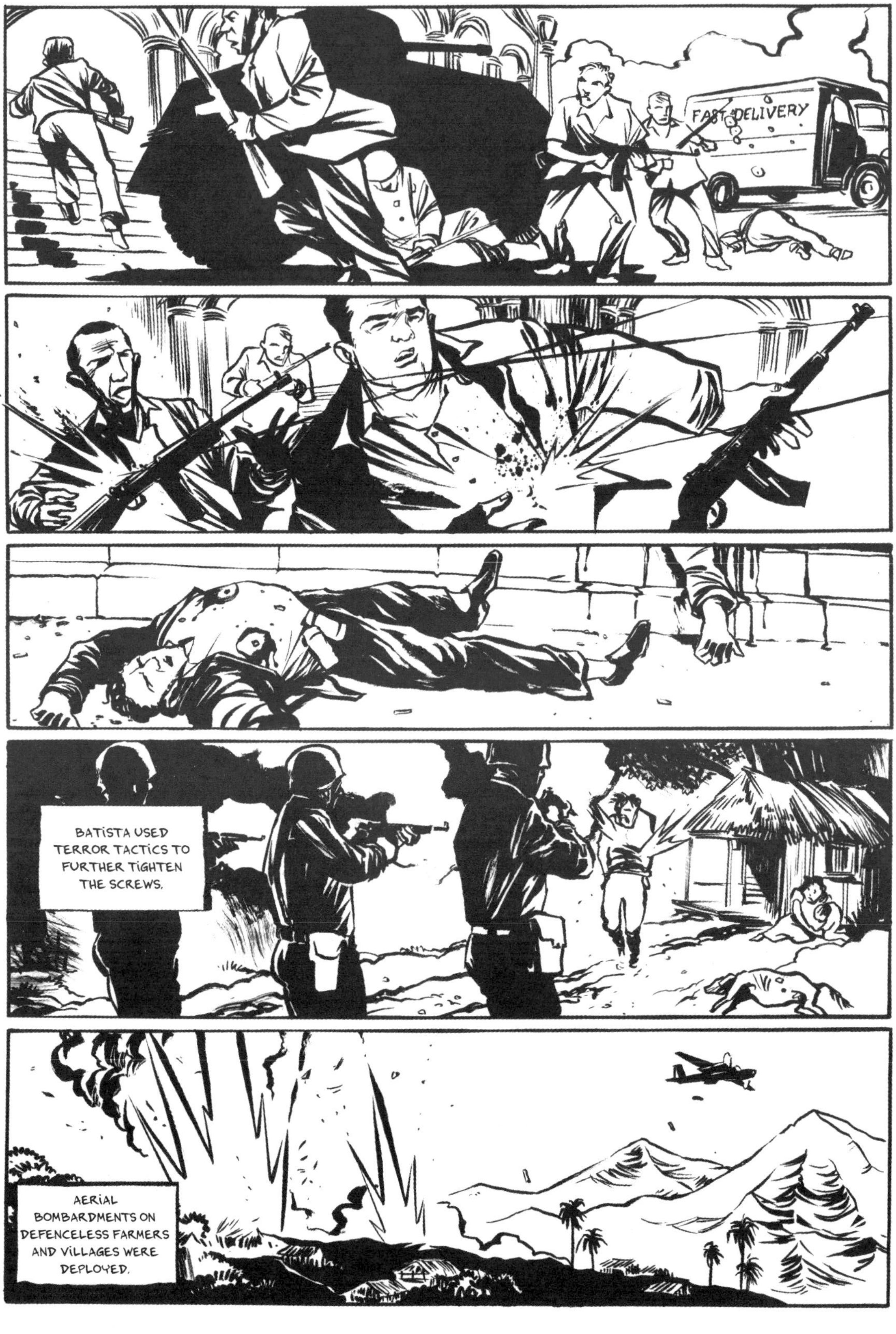
FAST DELIVERY
BATISTA USED TERROR TACTICS TO FURTHER TIGHTEN THE SCREWS.
AERIAL BOMBARDMENTS ON DEFENCELESS FARMERS AND VILLAGES WERE DEPLOYED.

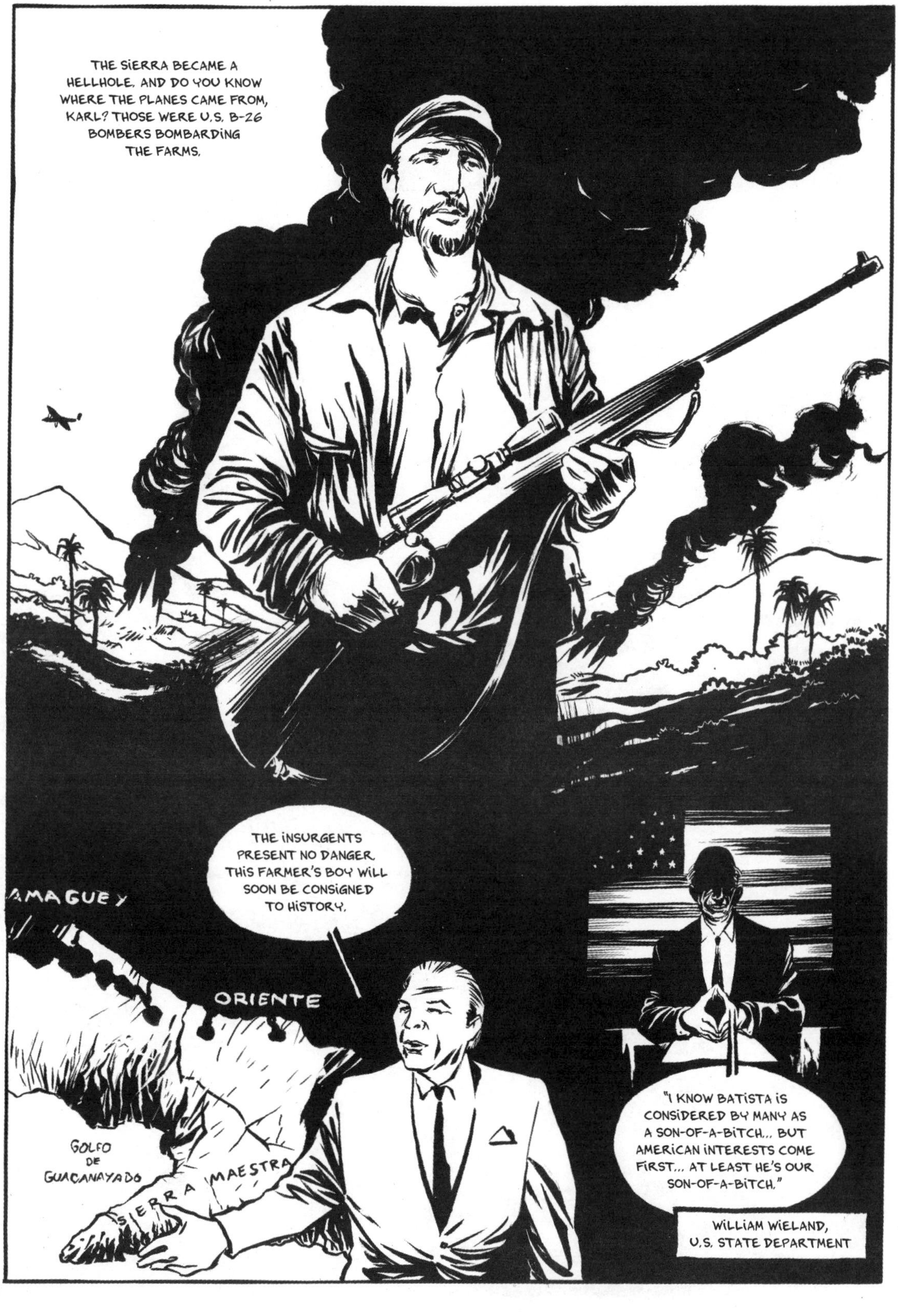
THE SIERRA BECAME A HELLHOLE. AND DO YOU KNOW WHERE THE PLANES CAME FROM, KARL? THOSE WERE U.S. B-26 BOMBERS BOMBARDING THE FARMS.
THE INSURGENTS PRESENT NO DANGER. THIS FARMER'S BOY WILL SOON BE CONSIGNED TO HISTORY.
AMAGUEY
ORIENTE
GOLFO DE GUACANAYADO
SIERRA MAESTRA
"I KNOW BATISTA IS CONSIDERED BY MANY AS A SON-OF-A-BITCH... BUT AMERICAN INTERESTS COME FIRST... AT LEAST HE'S OUR SON-OF-A-BITCH."
WILLIAM WIELAND, U.S. STATE DEPARTMENT

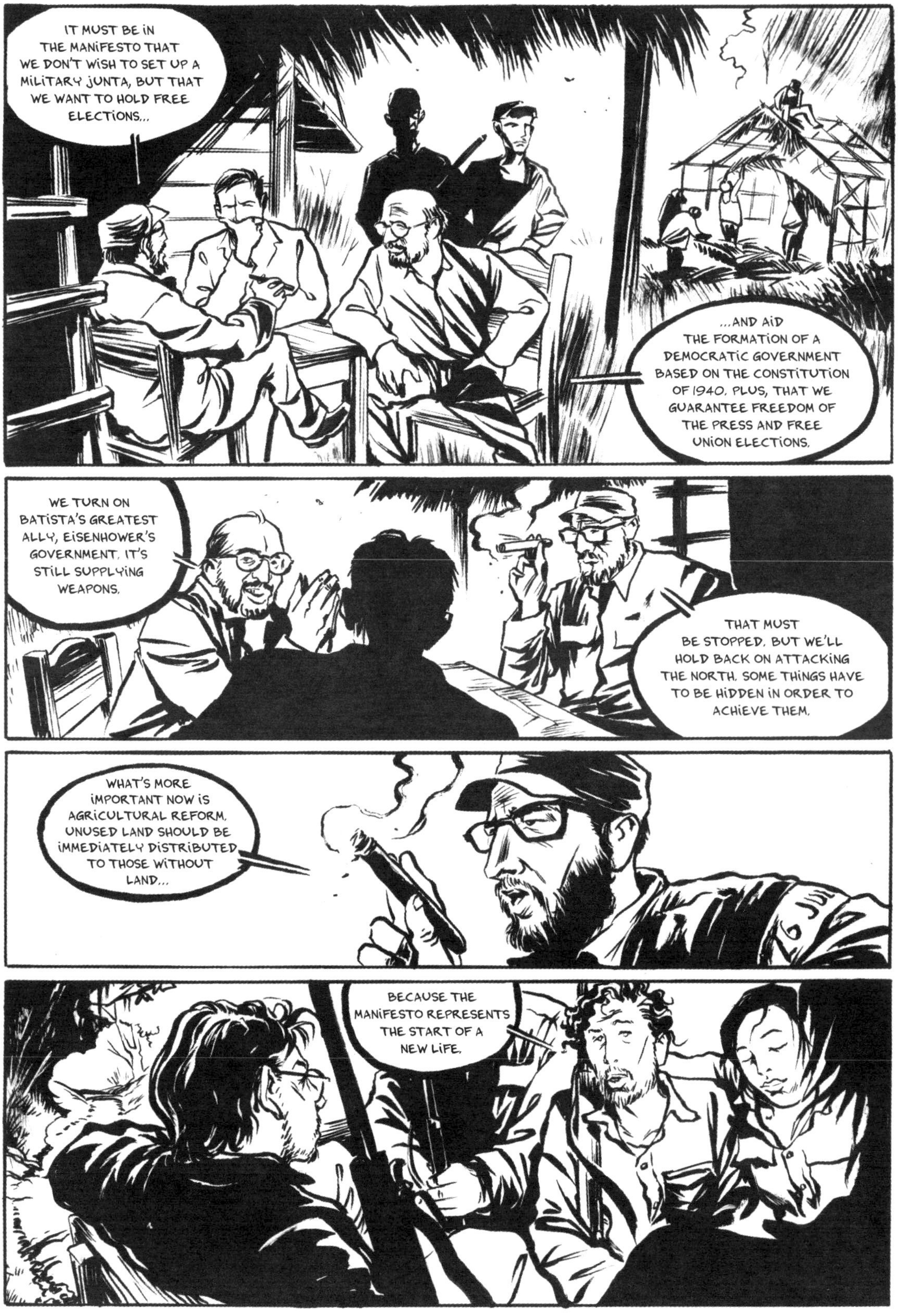
IT MUST BE IN THE MANIFESTO THAT WE DON'T WISH TO SET UP A MILITARY JUNTA, BUT THAT WE WANT TO HOLD FREE ELECTIONS...
...AND AID THE FORMATION OF A DEMOCRATIC GOVERNMENT BASED ON THE CONSTITUTION OF 1940. PLUS, THAT WE GUARANTEE FREEDOM OF THE PRESS AND FREE UNION ELECTIONS.
WE TURN ON BATISTA'S GREATEST ALLY, EISENHOWER'S GOVERNMENT. IT'S STILL SUPPLYING WEAPONS.
THAT MUST BE STOPPED. BUT WE'LL HOLD BACK ON ATTACKING THE NORTH. SOME THINGS HAVE TO BE HIDDEN IN ORDER TO ACHIEVE THEM.
WHAT'S MORE IMPORTANT NOW IS AGRICULTURAL REFORM. UNUSED LAND SHOULD BE IMMEDIATELY DISTRIBUTED TO THOSE WITHOUT LAND...
BECAUSE THE MANIFESTO REPRESENTS THE START OF A NEW LIFE.

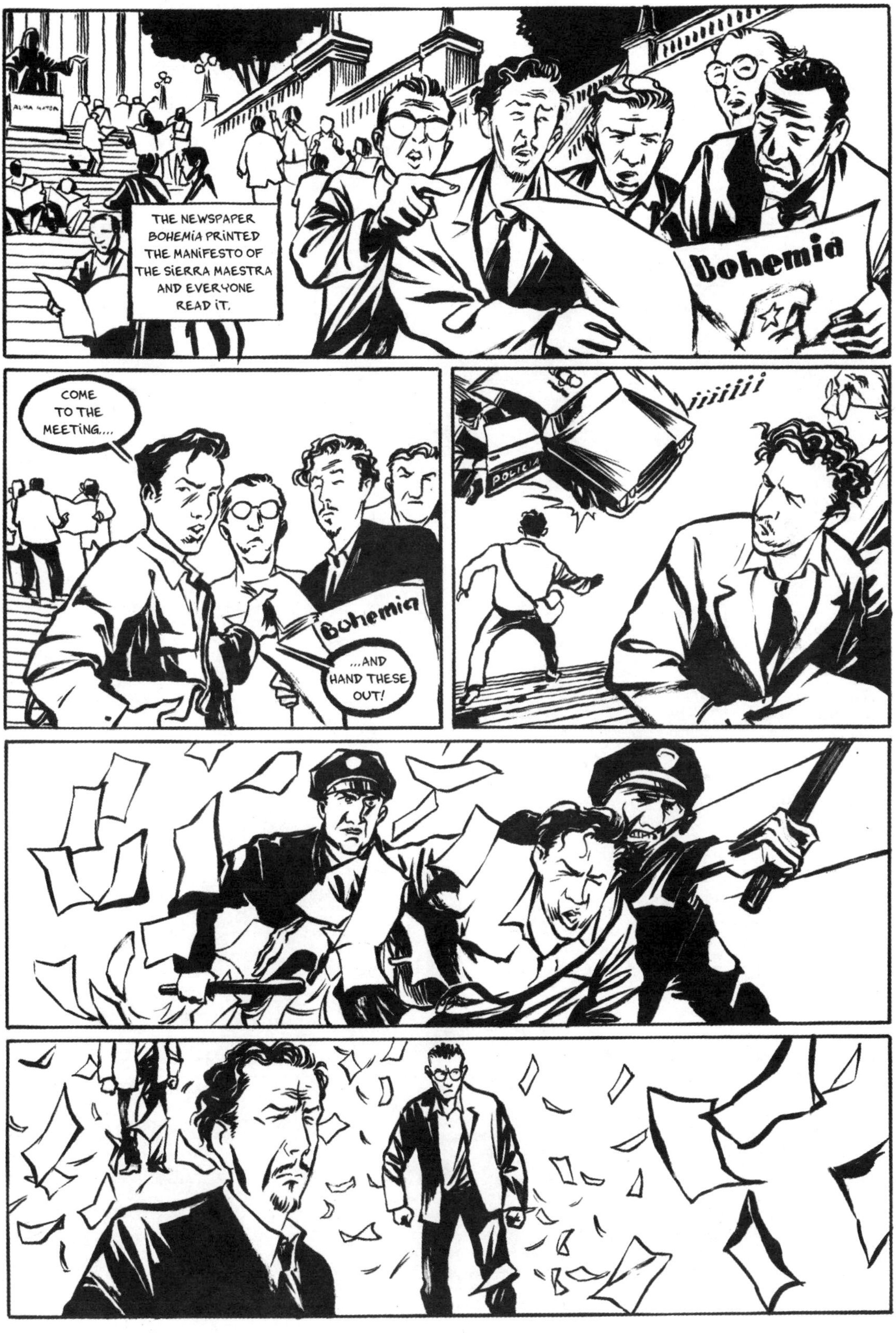
THE NEWSPAPER BOHEMIA PRINTED THE MANIFESTO OF THE SIERRA MAESTRA AND EVERYONE READ IT.
Bohemia
COME TO THE MEETING....
Bohemia
...AND HAND THESE OUT!
POLICIA
¡¡¡¡¡¡¡

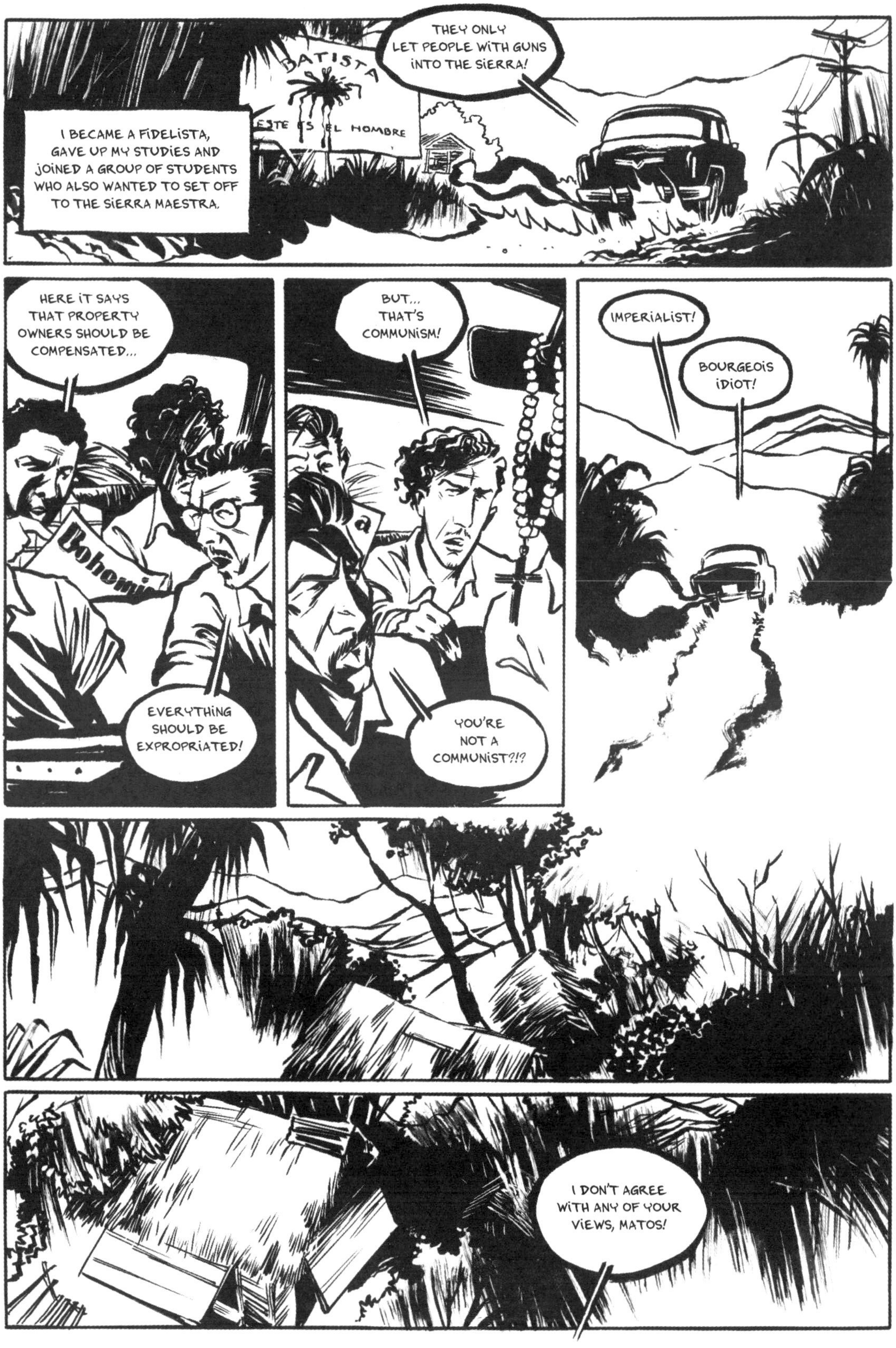
I BECAME A FIDELISTA, GAVE UP MY STUDIES AND JOINED A GROUP OF STUDENTS WHO ALSO WANTED TO SET OFF TO THE SIERRA MAESTRA.
BATISTA
ESTE ES EL HOMBRE
THEY ONLY LET PEOPLE WITH GUNS INTO THE SIERRA!
HERE IT SAYS THAT PROPERTY OWNERS SHOULD BE COMPENSATED...
EVERYTHING SHOULD BE EXPROPRIATED!
BUT... THAT'S COMMUNISM!
YOU'RE NOT A COMMUNIST?!?
IMPERIALIST!
BOURGEOIS IDIOT!
I DON'T AGREE WITH ANY OF YOUR VIEWS, MATOS!

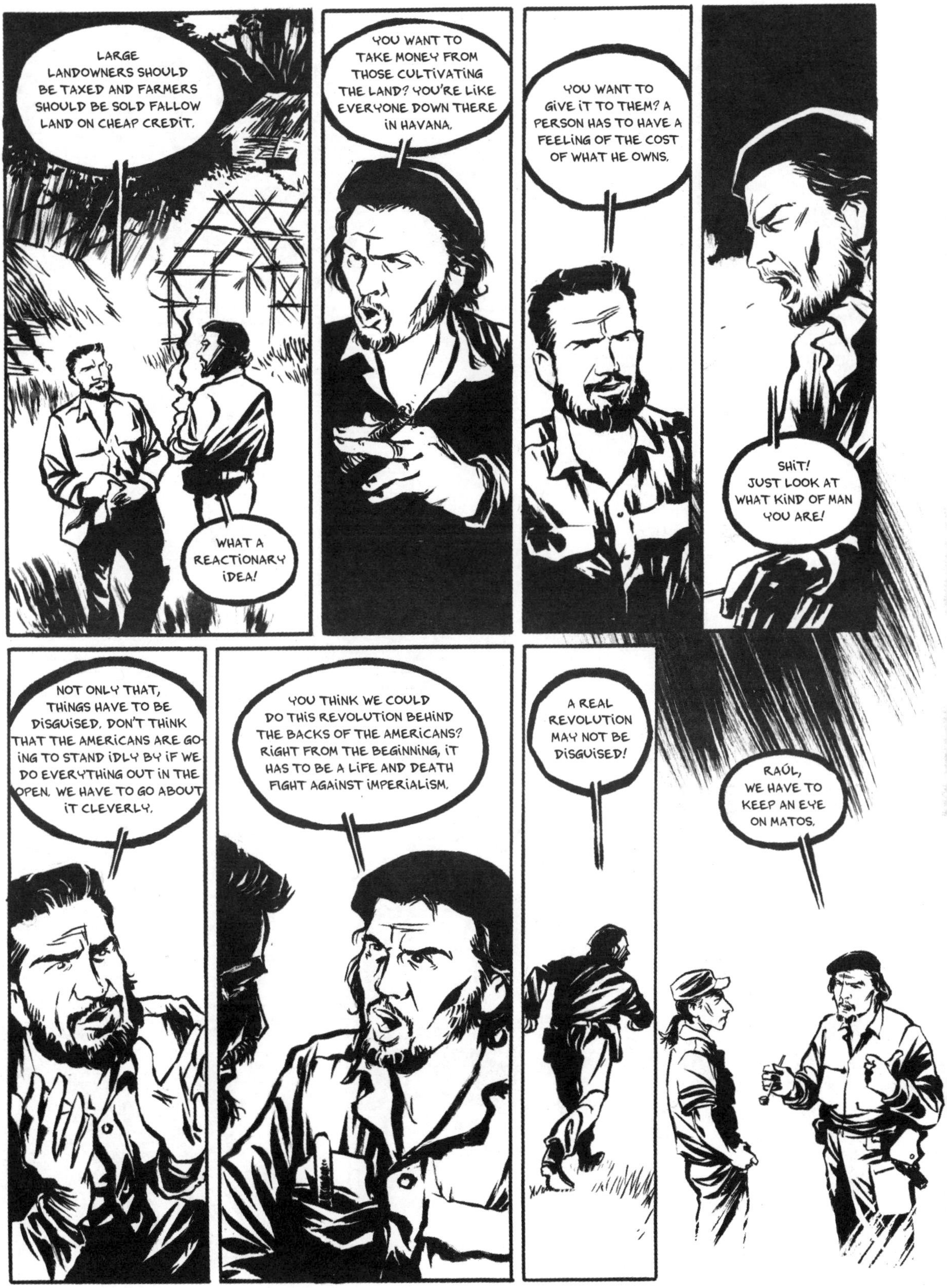
LARGE LANDOWNERS SHOULD BE TAXED AND FARMERS SHOULD BE SOLD FALLOW LAND ON CHEAP CREDIT.
WHAT A REACTIONARY IDEA!
YOU WANT TO TAKE MONEY FROM THOSE CULTIVATING THE LAND? YOU'RE LIKE EVERYONE DOWN THERE IN HAVANA.
YOU WANT TO GIVE IT TO THEM? A PERSON HAS TO HAVE A FEELING OF THE COST OF WHAT HE OWNS.
SHIT! JUST LOOK AT WHAT KIND OF MAN YOU ARE!
NOT ONLY THAT, THINGS HAVE TO BE DISGUISED. DON'T THINK THAT THE AMERICANS ARE GOING TO STAND IDLY BY IF WE DO EVERYTHING OUT IN THE OPEN. WE HAVE TO GO ABOUT IT CLEVERLY.
YOU THINK WE COULD DO THIS REVOLUTION BEHIND THE BACKS OF THE AMERICANS? RIGHT FROM THE BEGINNING, IT HAS TO BE A LIFE AND DEATH FIGHT AGAINST IMPERIALISM.
A REAL REVOLUTION MAY NOT BE DISGUISED!
RAÚL, WE HAVE TO KEEP AN EYE ON MATOS.

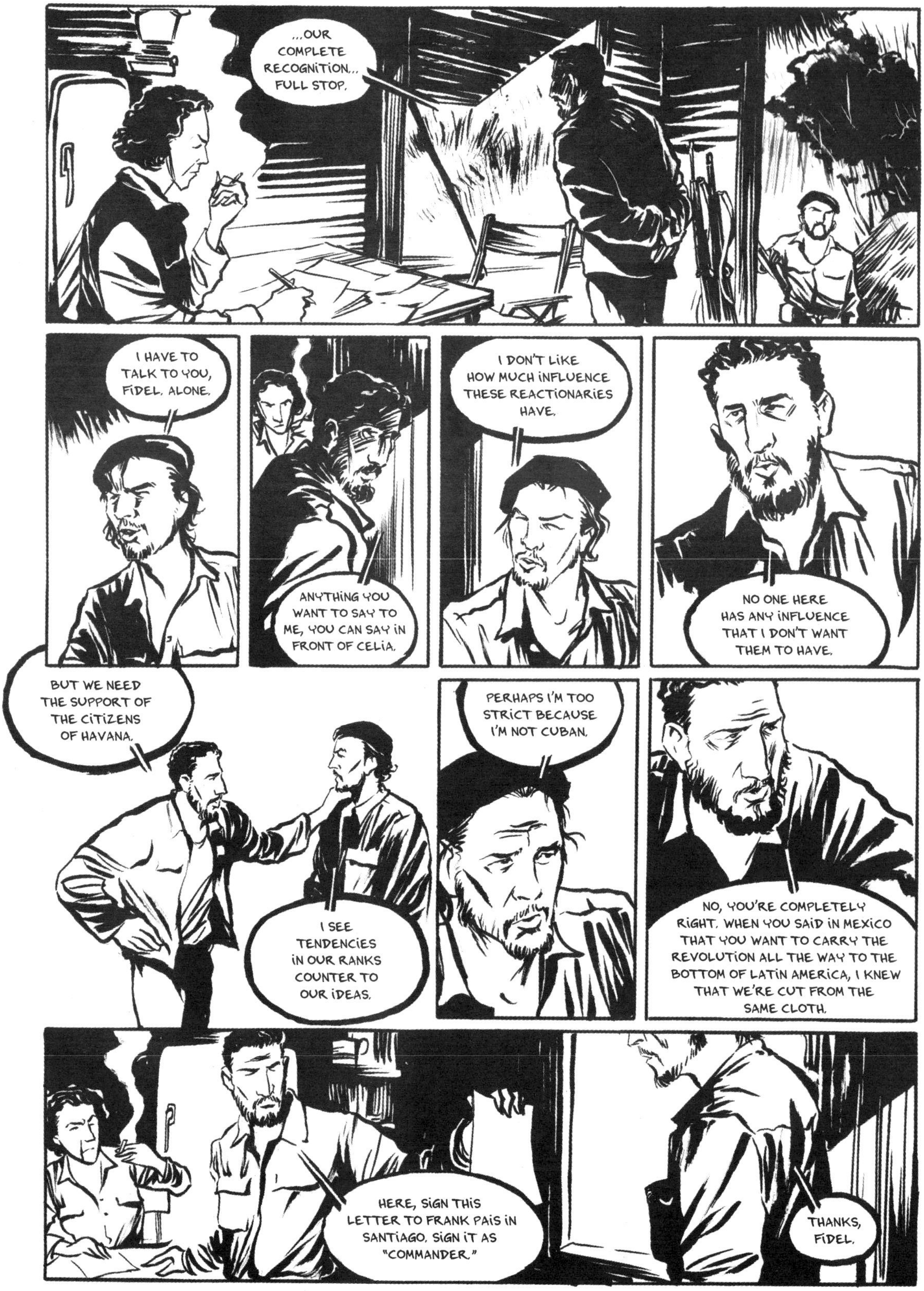
...OUR COMPLETE RECOGNITION... FULL STOP.
I HAVE TO TALK TO YOU, FIDEL. ALONE.
ANYTHING YOU WANT TO SAY TO ME, YOU CAN SAY IN FRONT OF CELIA.
I DON'T LIKE HOW MUCH INFLUENCE THESE REACTIONARIES HAVE.
NO ONE HERE HAS ANY INFLUENCE THAT I DON'T WANT THEM TO HAVE.
BUT WE NEED THE SUPPORT OF THE CITIZENS OF HAVANA.
I SEE TENDENCIES IN OUR RANKS COUNTER TO OUR IDEAS.
PERHAPS I'M TOO STRICT BECAUSE I'M NOT CUBAN.
NO, YOU'RE COMPLETELY RIGHT. WHEN YOU SAID IN MEXICO THAT YOU WANT TO CARRY THE REVOLUTION ALL THE WAY TO THE BOTTOM OF LATIN AMERICA, I KNEW THAT WE'RE CUT FROM THE SAME CLOTH.
HERE, SIGN THIS LETTER TO FRANK PAIS IN SANTIAGO. SIGN IT AS "COMMANDER."
THANKS, FIDEL.

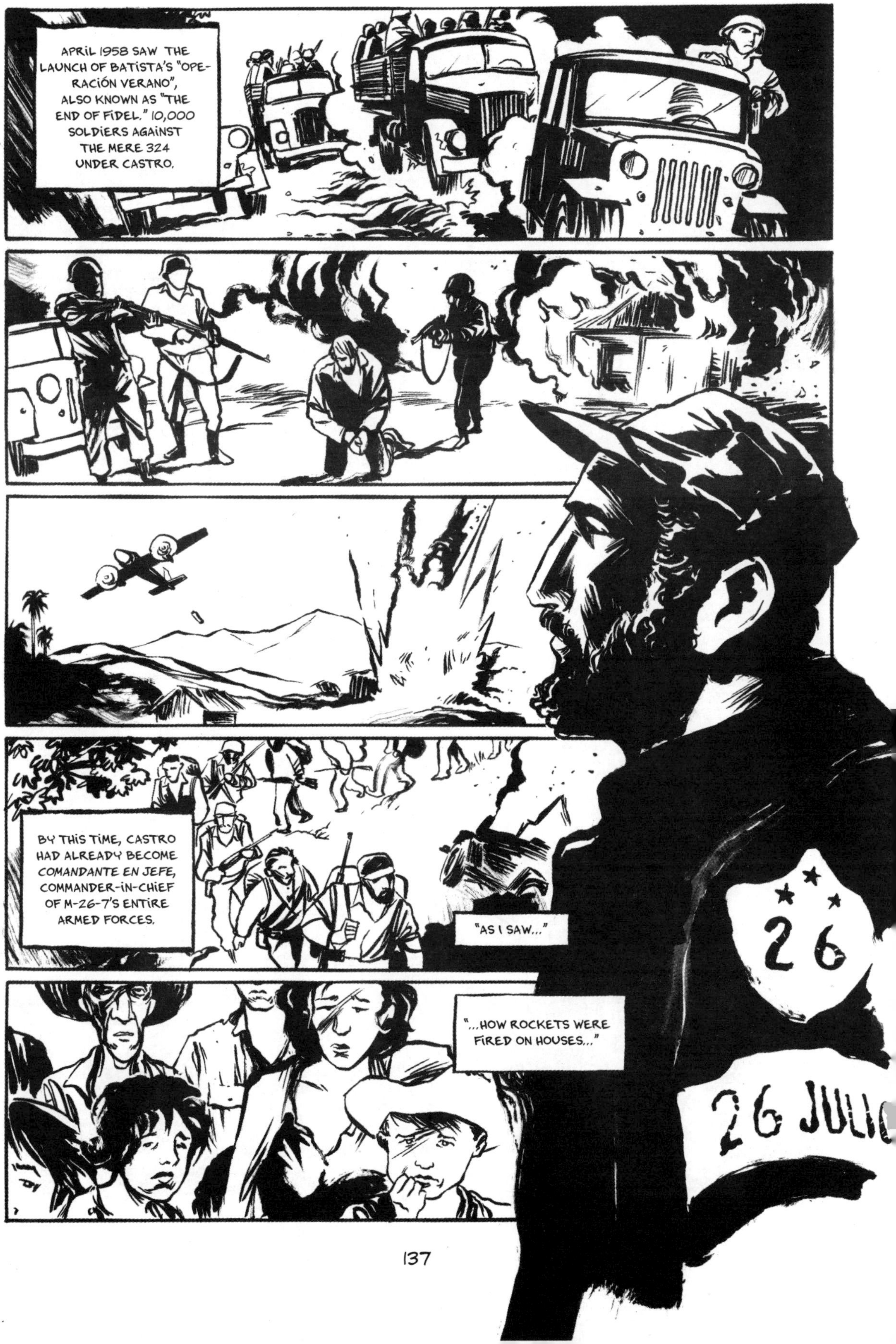

APRIL 1958 SAW THE LAUNCH OF BATISTA'S "OPERACIÓN VERANO", ALSO KNOWN AS "THE END OF FIDEL." 10,000 SOLDIERS AGAINST THE MERE 324 UNDER CASTRO.
BY THIS TIME, CASTRO HAD ALREADY BECOME COMANDANTE EN JEFE, COMMANDER-IN-CHIEF OF M-26-7'S ENTIRE ARMED FORCES.
"AS I SAW..."
"...HOW ROCKETS WERE FIRED ON HOUSES..."
26
26 JULIO

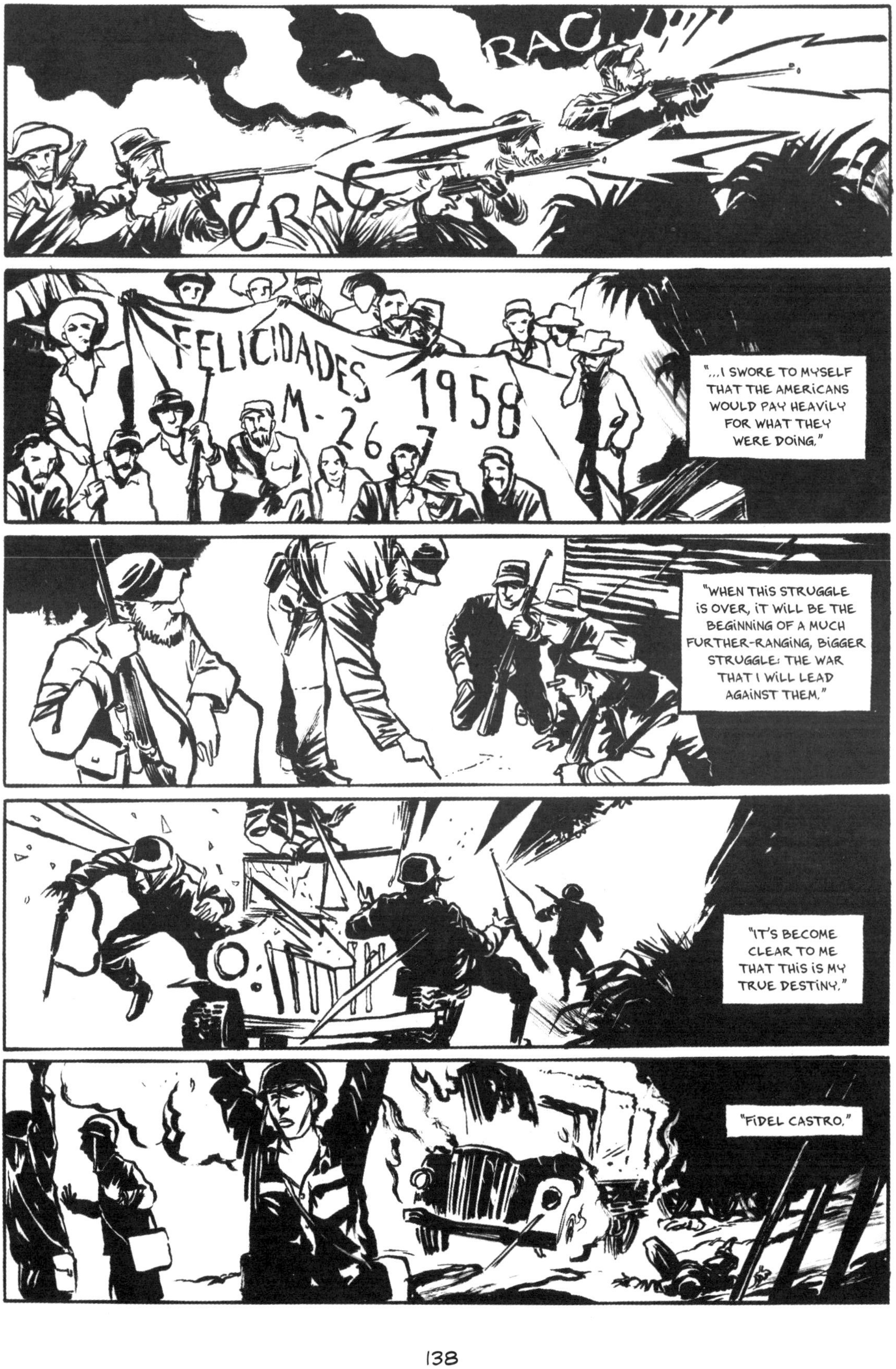
RAC!!!
CRAC
FELICIDADES 1958
M-26-7
"...I SWORE TO MYSELF THAT THE AMERICANS WOULD PAY HEAVILY FOR WHAT THEY WERE DOING."
"WHEN THIS STRUGGLE IS OVER, IT WILL BE THE BEGINNING OF A MUCH FURTHER-RANGING, BIGGER STRUGGLE: THE WAR THAT I WILL LEAD AGAINST THEM."
"IT'S BECOME CLEAR TO ME THAT THIS IS MY TRUE DESTINY."
"FIDEL CASTRO."

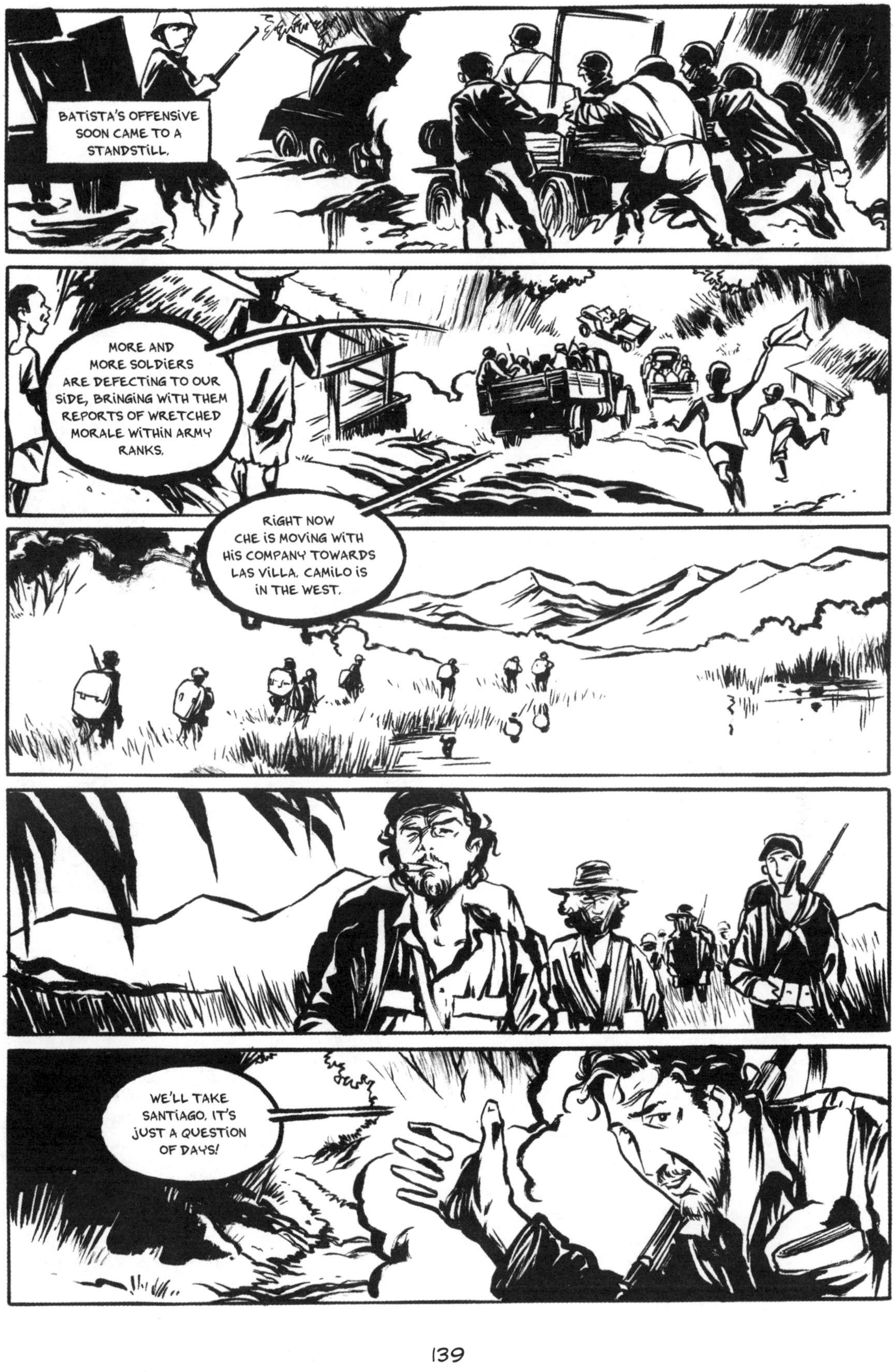
BATISTA'S OFFENSIVE SOON CAME TO A STANDSTILL.
MORE AND MORE SOLDIERS ARE DEFECTING TO OUR SIDE, BRINGING WITH THEM REPORTS OF WRETCHED MORALE WITHIN ARMY RANKS.
RIGHT NOW CHE IS MOVING WITH HIS COMPANY TOWARDS LAS VILLA. CAMILO IS IN THE WEST.
WE'LL TAKE SANTIAGO. IT'S JUST A QUESTION OF DAYS!

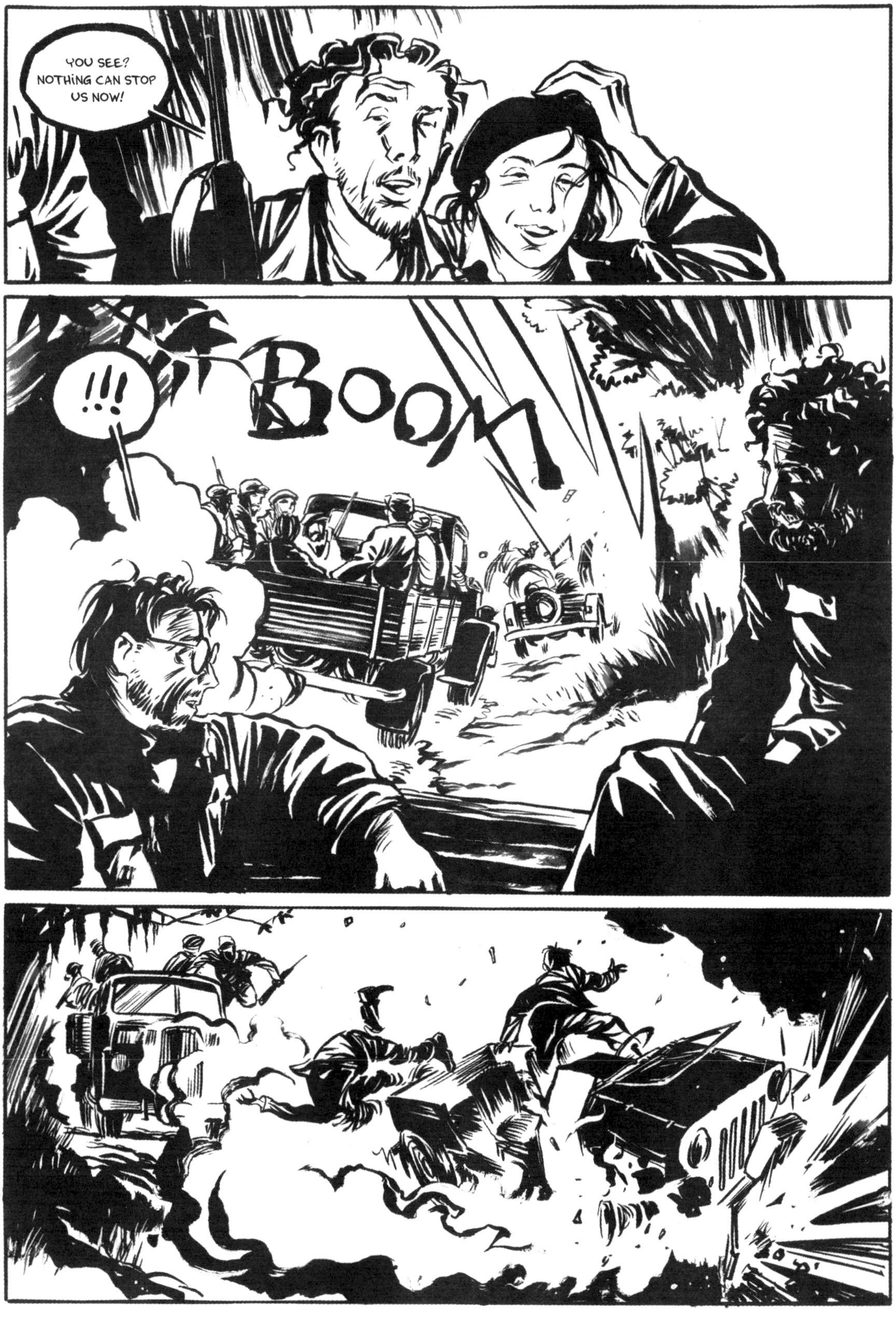
YOU SEE? NOTHING CAN STOP US NOW!
!!!
BOOM

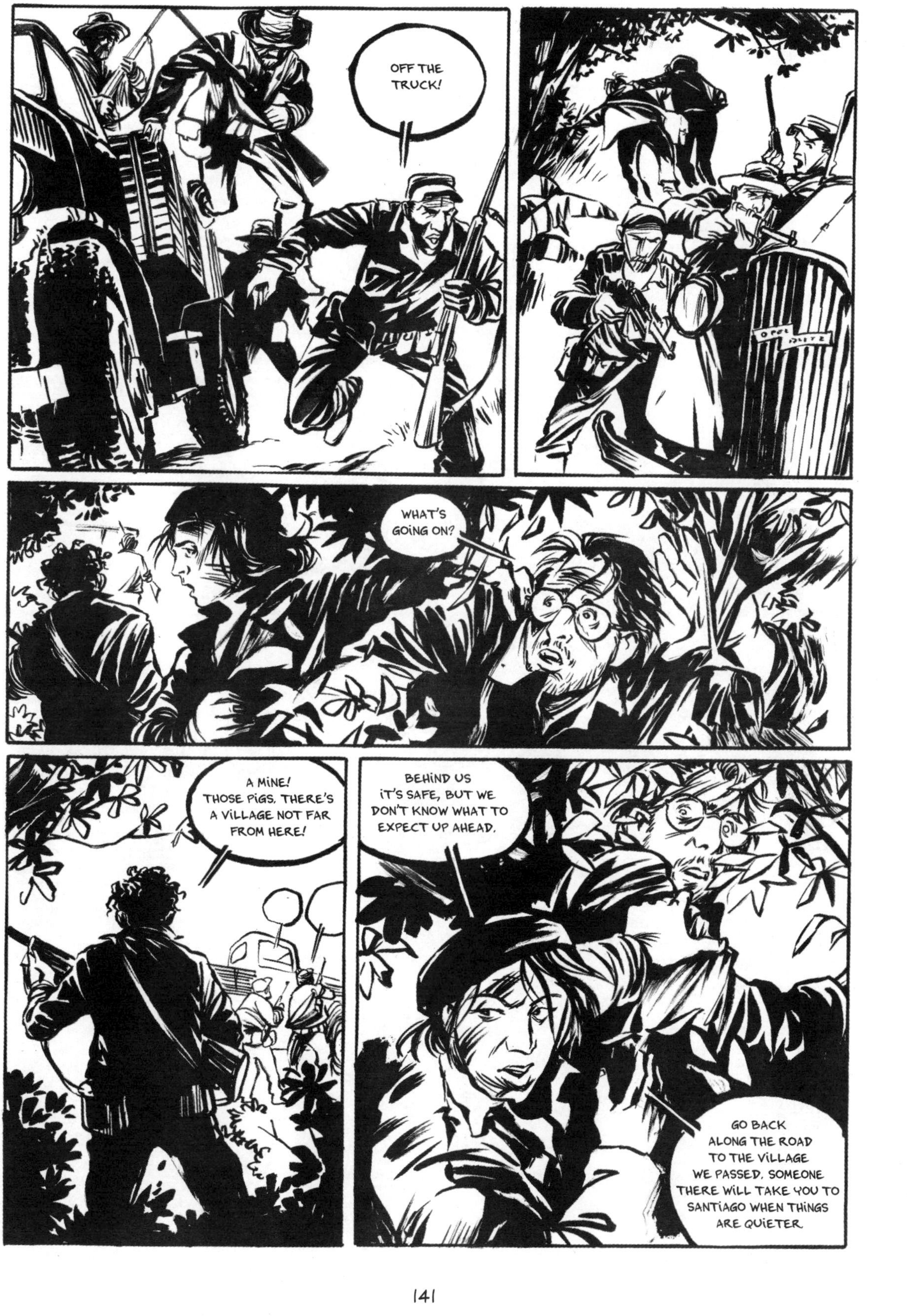
OFF THE TRUCK!
WHAT'S GOING ON?
A MINE! THOSE PIGS. THERE'S A VILLAGE NOT FAR FROM HERE!
BEHIND US IT'S SAFE, BUT WE DON'T KNOW WHAT TO EXPECT UP AHEAD.
GO BACK ALONG THE ROAD TO THE VILLAGE WE PASSED. SOMEONE THERE WILL TAKE YOU TO SANTIAGO WHEN THINGS ARE QUIETER.

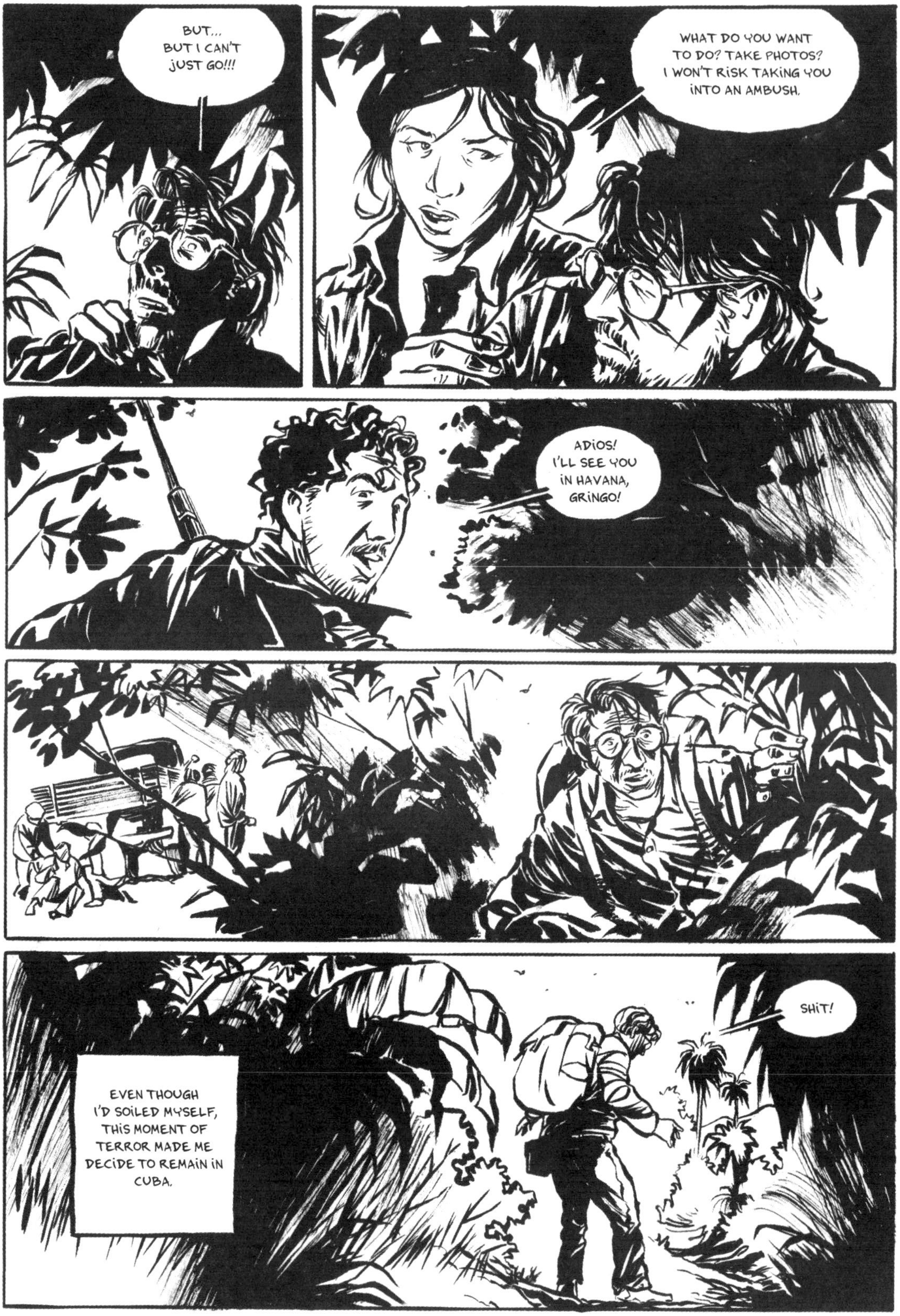
BUT...
BUT I CAN'T
JUST GO!!!
WHAT DO YOU WANT
TO DO? TAKE PHOTOS?
I WON'T RISK TAKING YOU
INTO AN AMBUSH.
ADIOS!
I'LL SEE YOU
IN HAVANA,
GRINGO!
EVEN THOUGH
I'D SOILED MYSELF,
THIS MOMENT OF
TERROR MADE ME
DECIDE TO REMAIN IN
CUBA.
SHIT!

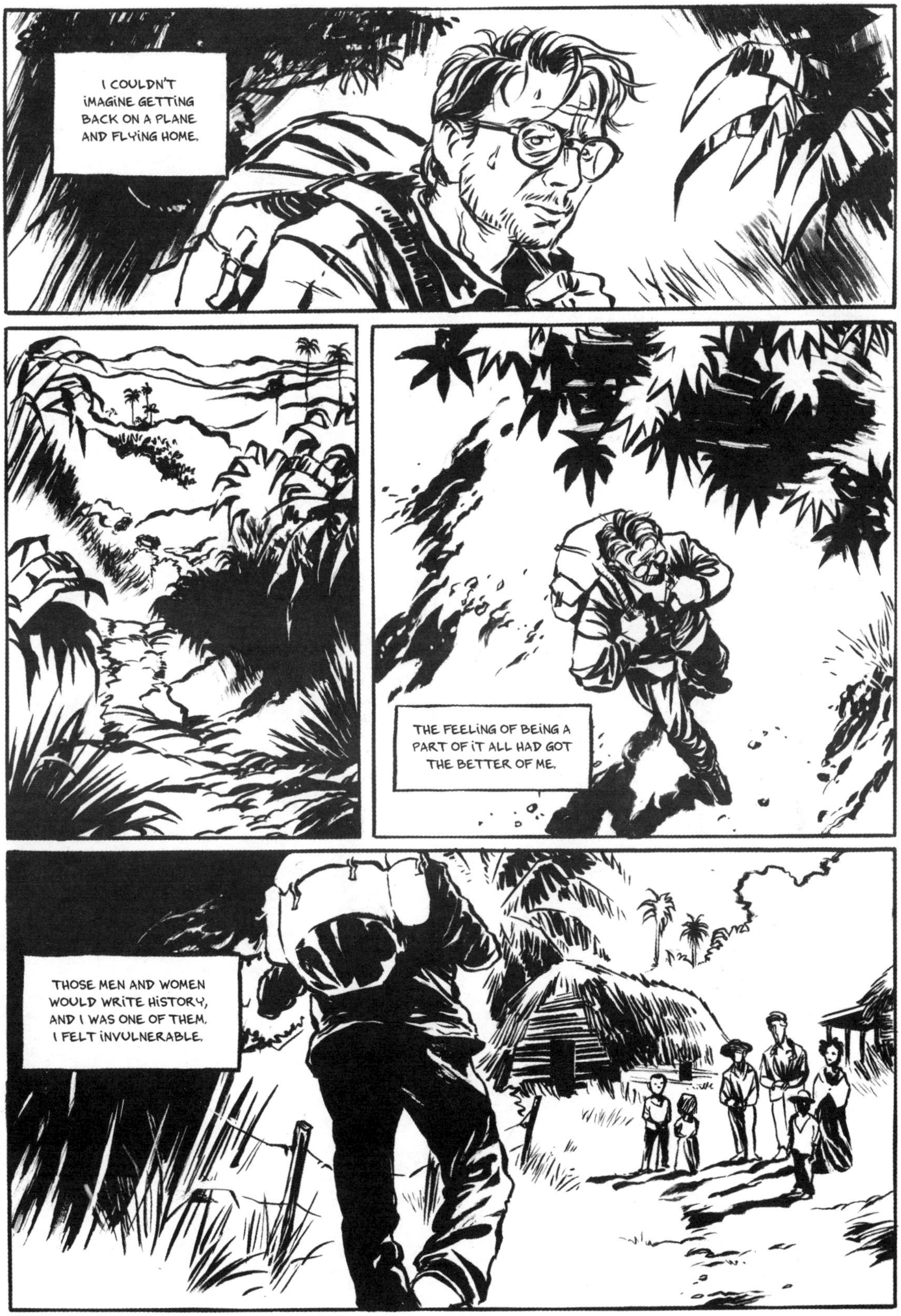
I COULDN'T IMAGINE GETTING BACK ON A PLANE AND FLYING HOME.
THE FEELING OF BEING A PART OF IT ALL HAD GOT THE BETTER OF ME.
THOSE MEN AND WOMEN WOULD WRITE HISTORY, AND I WAS ONE OF THEM. I FELT INVULNERABLE.

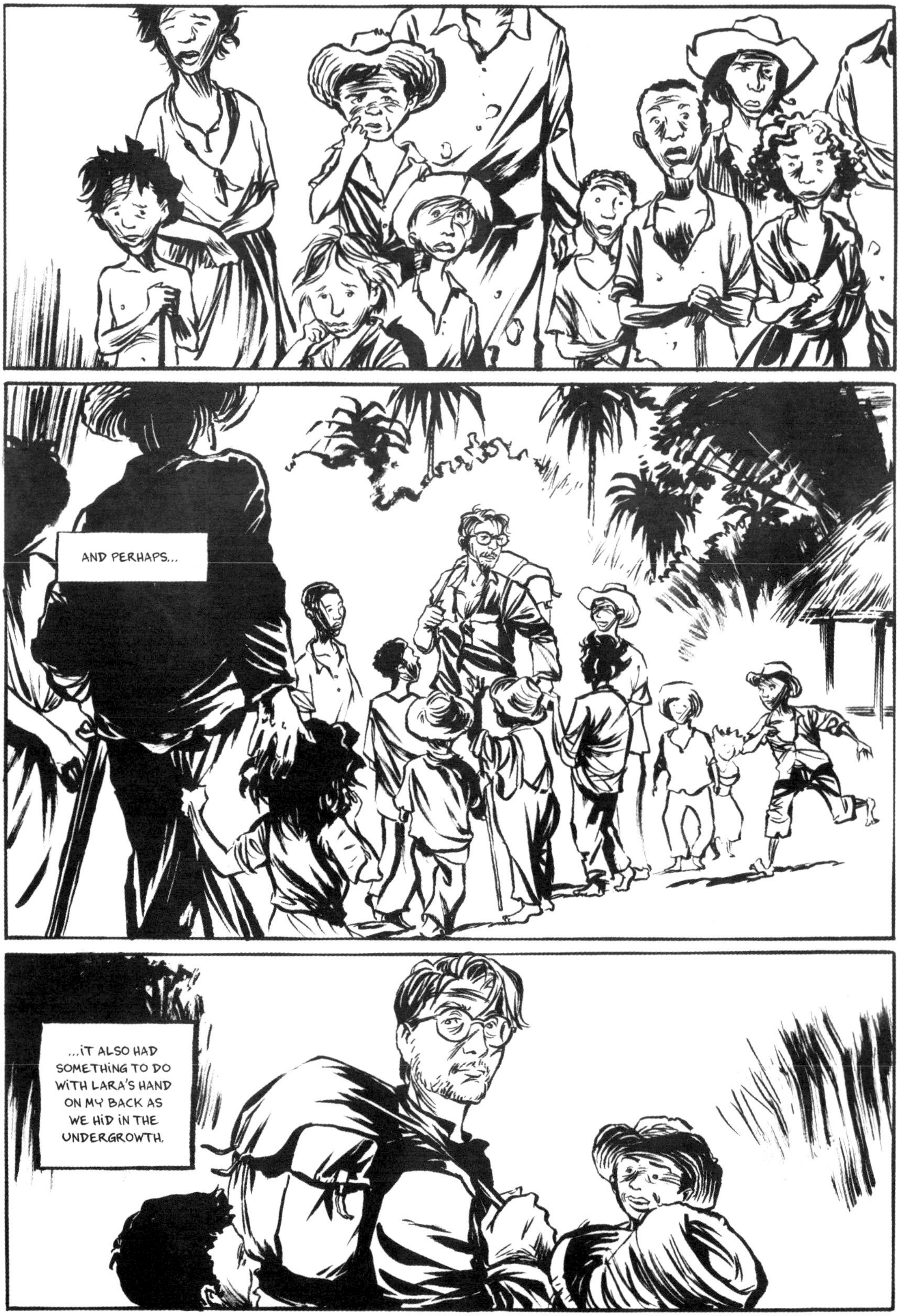
AND PERHAPS...
...IT ALSO HAD SOMETHING TO DO WITH LARA'S HAND ON MY BACK AS WE HID IN THE UNDERGROWTH.

CHAPTER 2

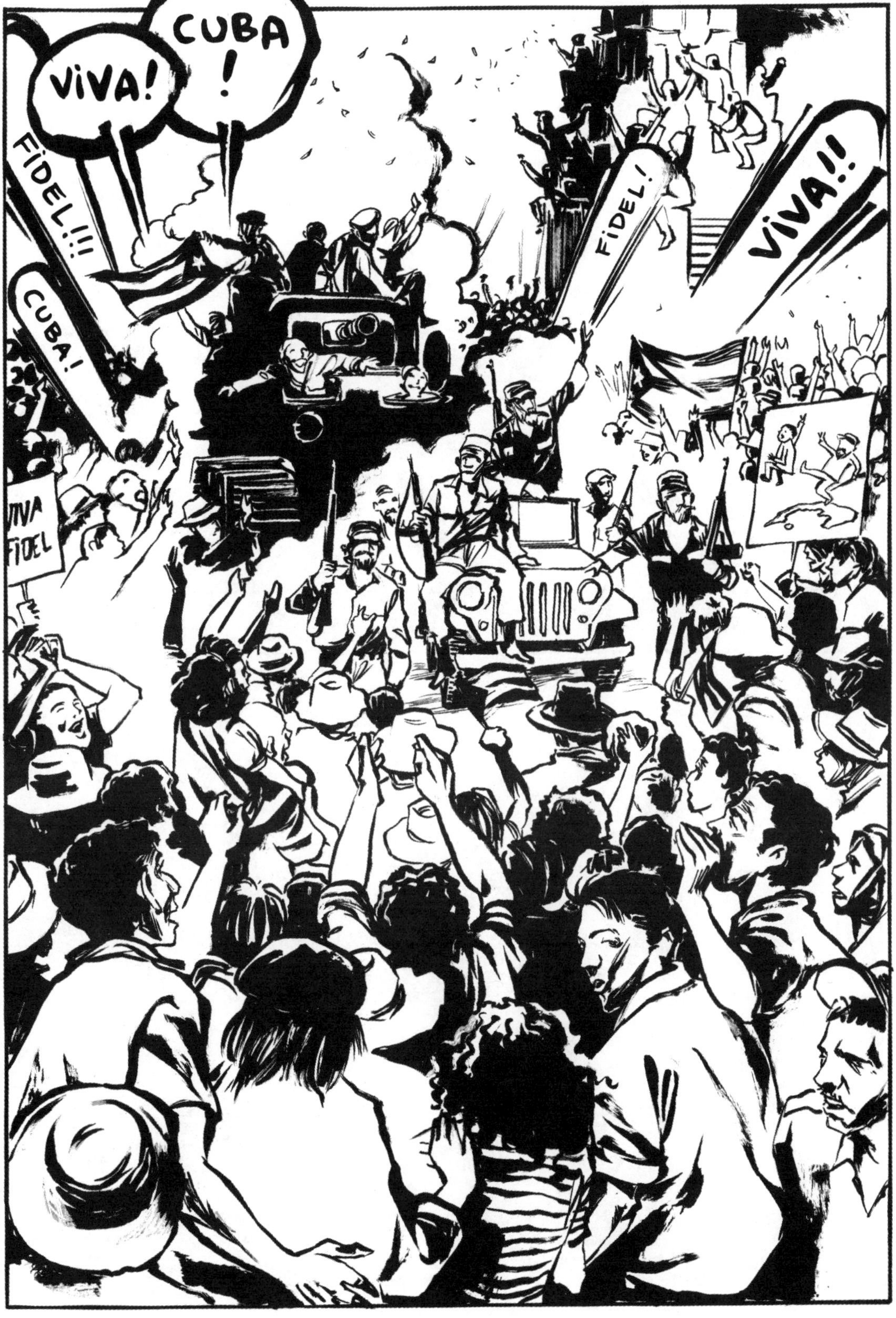
VIVA!
CUBA !
FIDEL!!!
CUBA!
FIDEL!
VIVA!!
VIVA FIDEL

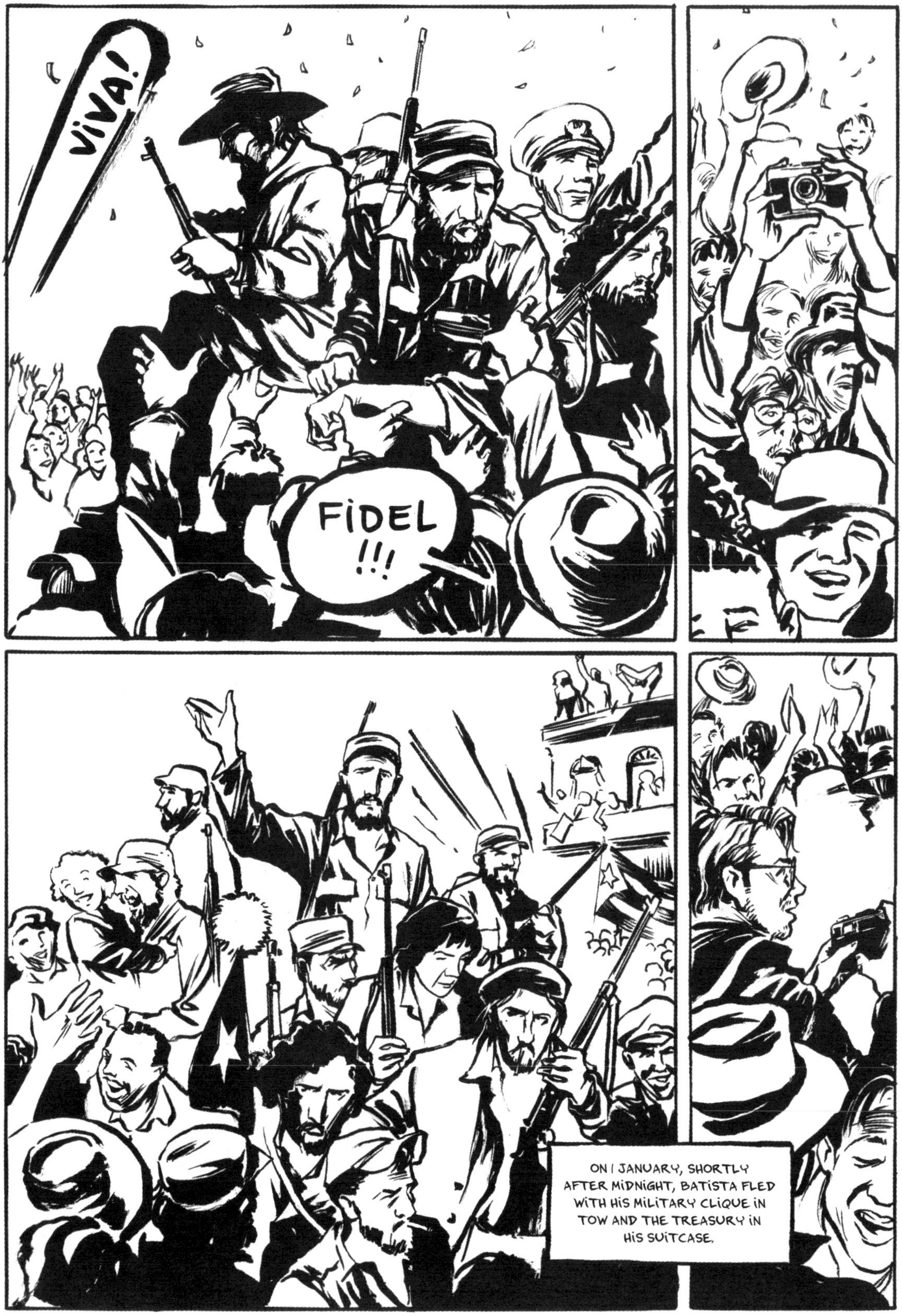
VIVA!
FIDEL !!!
ON 1 JANUARY, SHORTLY AFTER MIDNIGHT, BATISTA FLED WITH HIS MILITARY CLIQUE IN TOW AND THE TREASURY IN HIS SUITCASE.

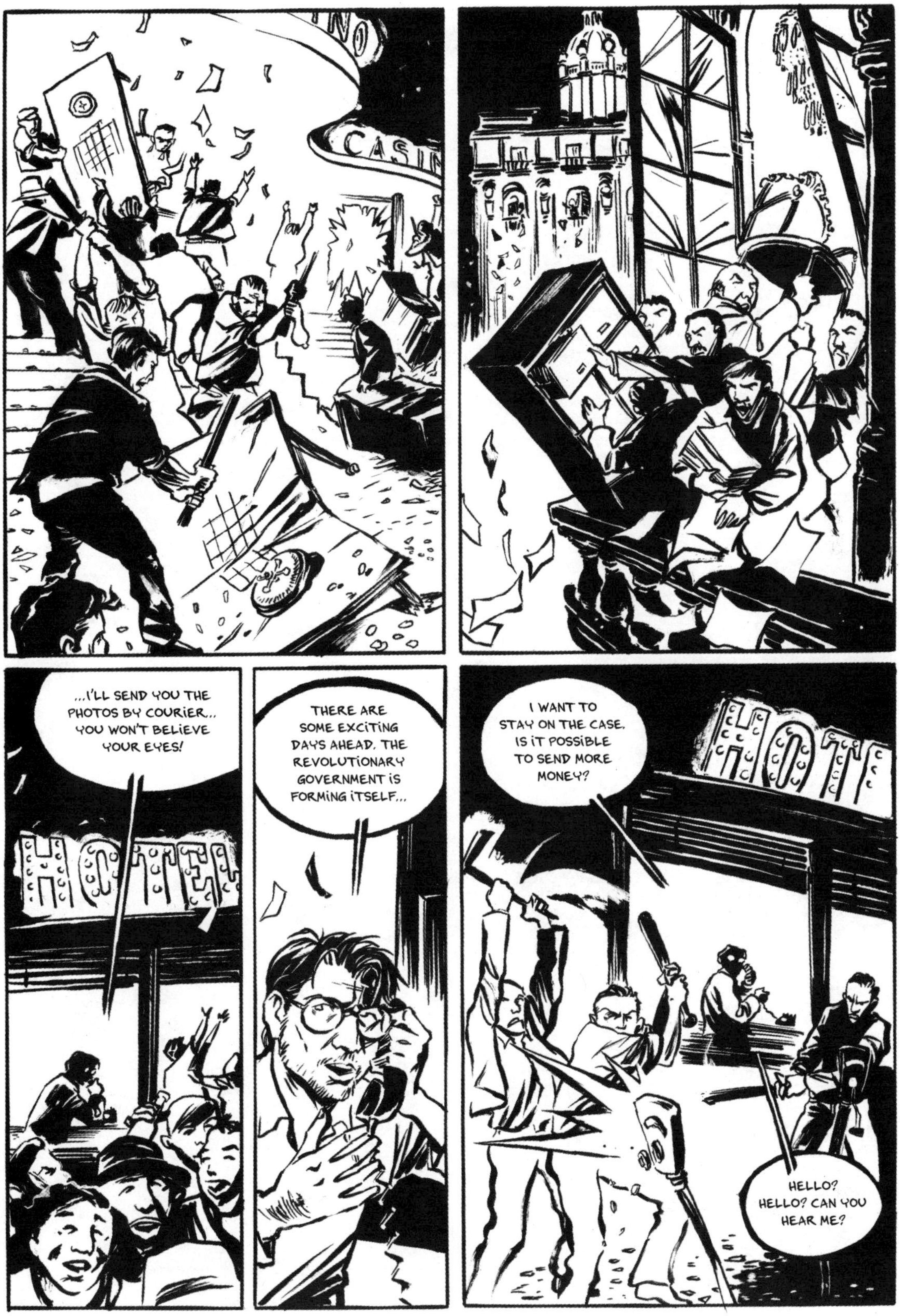
...I'LL SEND YOU THE PHOTOS BY COURIER... YOU WON'T BELIEVE YOUR EYES!
THERE ARE SOME EXCITING DAYS AHEAD. THE REVOLUTIONARY GOVERNMENT IS FORMING ITSELF...
I WANT TO STAY ON THE CASE. IS IT POSSIBLE TO SEND MORE MONEY?
HELLO? HELLO? CAN YOU HEAR ME?

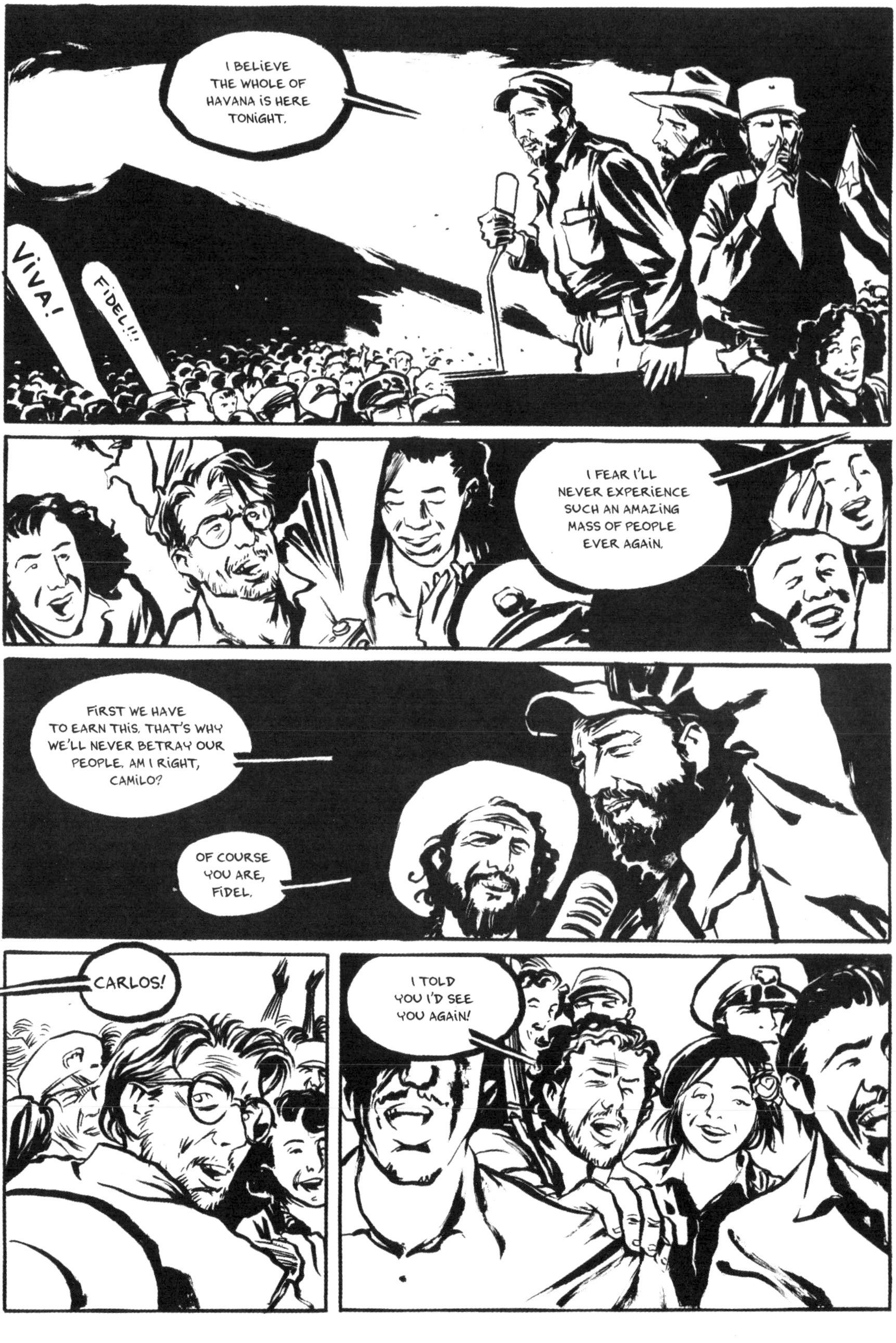
I BELIEVE THE WHOLE OF HAVANA IS HERE TONIGHT.
VIVA!
FIDEL!!!
I FEAR I'LL NEVER EXPERIENCE SUCH AN AMAZING MASS OF PEOPLE EVER AGAIN.
FIRST WE HAVE TO EARN THIS. THAT'S WHY WE'LL NEVER BETRAY OUR PEOPLE. AM I RIGHT, CAMILO?
OF COURSE YOU ARE, FIDEL.
CARLOS!
I TOLD YOU I'D SEE YOU AGAIN!

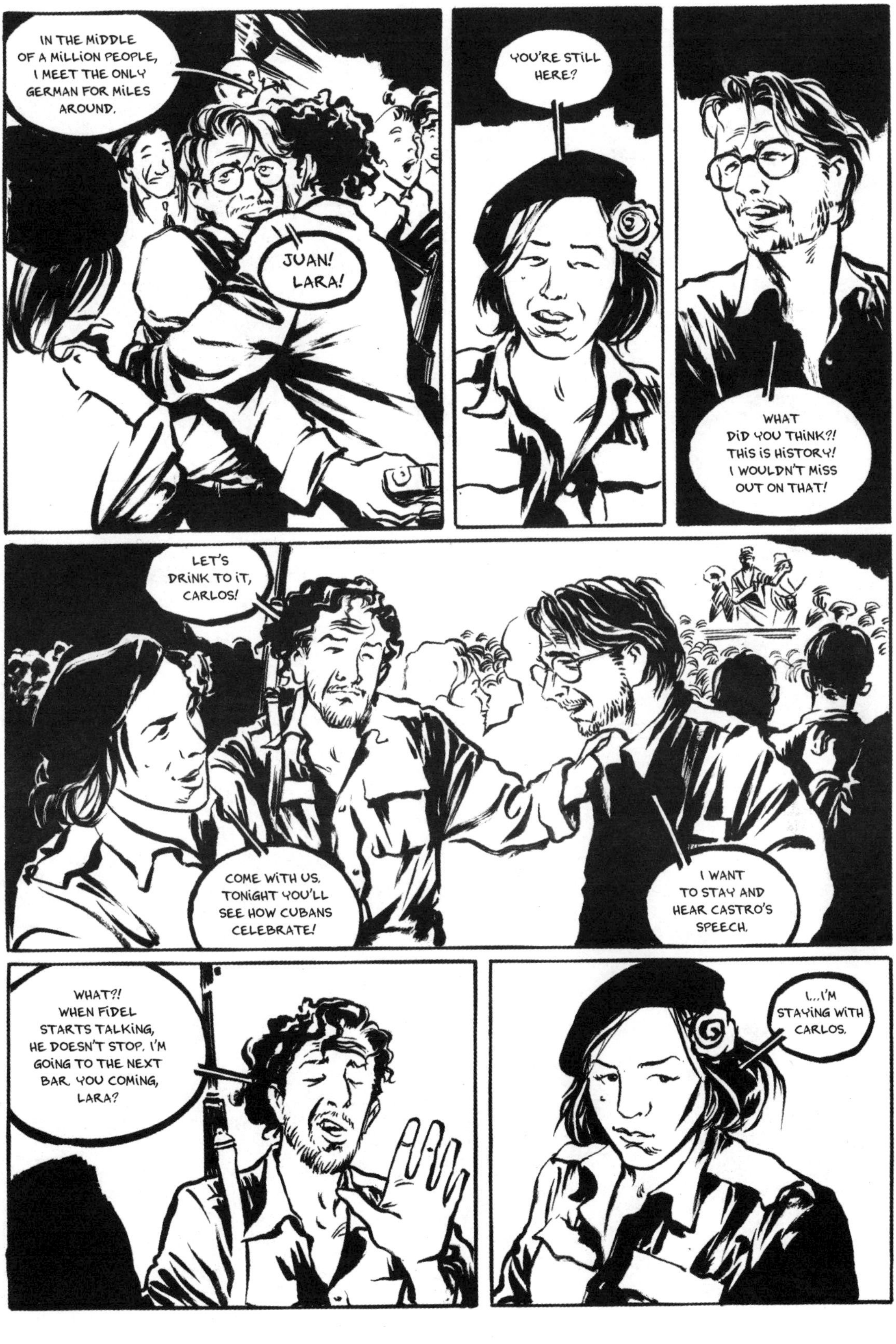
IN THE MIDDLE OF A MILLION PEOPLE, I MEET THE ONLY GERMAN FOR MILES AROUND.
JUAN! LARA!
YOU'RE STILL HERE?
WHAT DID YOU THINK?! THIS IS HISTORY! I WOULDN'T MISS OUT ON THAT!
LET'S DRINK TO IT, CARLOS!
COME WITH US. TONIGHT YOU'LL SEE HOW CUBANS CELEBRATE!
I WANT TO STAY AND HEAR CASTRO'S SPEECH.
WHAT?! WHEN FIDEL STARTS TALKING, HE DOESN'T STOP. I'M GOING TO THE NEXT BAR. YOU COMING, LARA?
I...I'M STAYING WITH CARLOS.

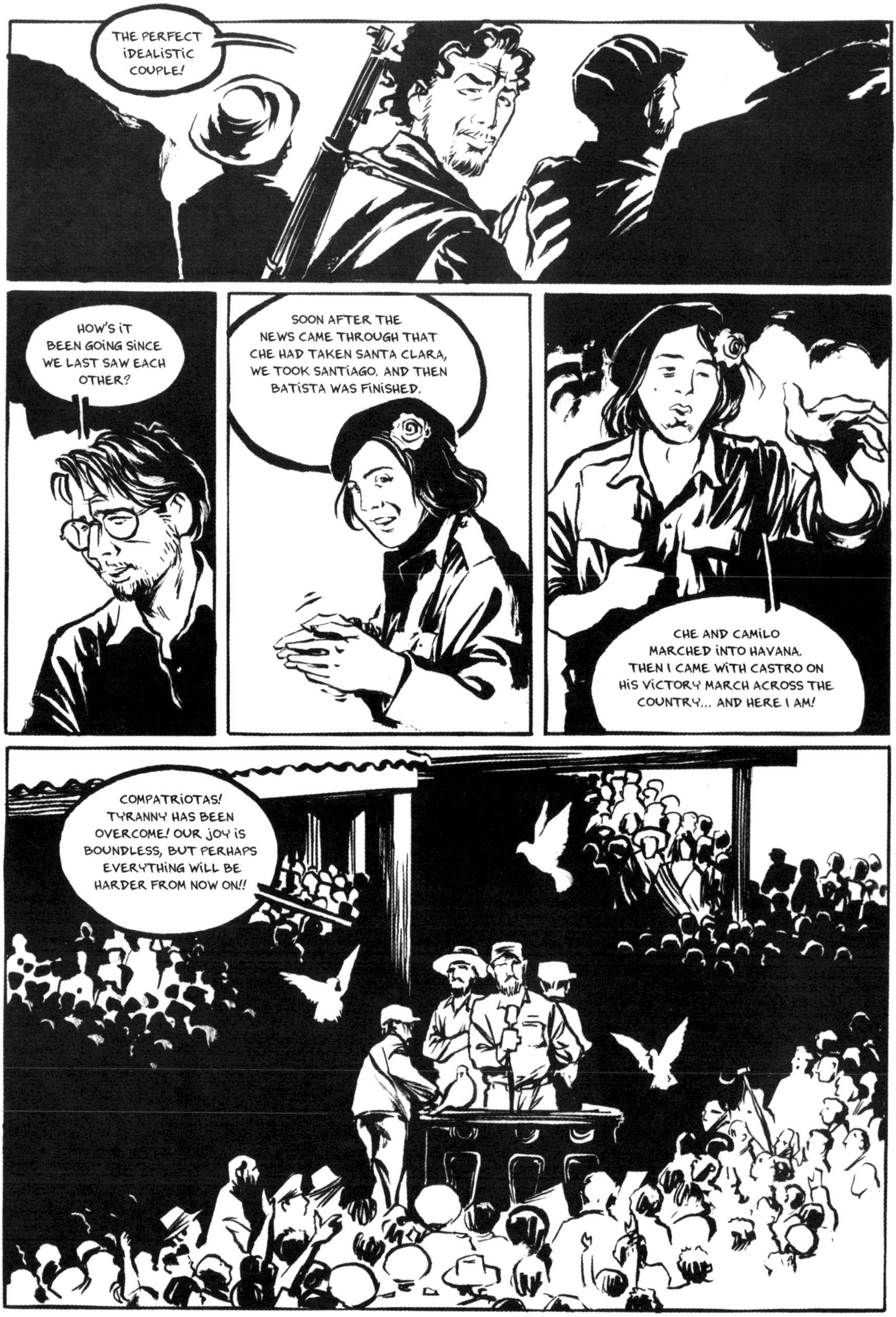
THE PERFECT IDEALISTIC COUPLE!
HOW'S IT BEEN GOING SINCE WE LAST SAW EACH OTHER?
SOON AFTER THE NEWS CAME THROUGH THAT CHE HAD TAKEN SANTA CLARA, WE TOOK SANTIAGO, AND THEN BATISTA WAS FINISHED.
CHE AND CAMILO MARCHED INTO HAVANA. THEN I CAME WITH CASTRO ON HIS VICTORY MARCH ACROSS THE COUNTRY... AND HERE I AM!
COMPATRIOTAS! TYRANNY HAS BEEN OVERCOME! OUR JOY IS BOUNDLESS, BUT PERHAPS EVERYTHING WILL BE HARDER FROM NOW ON!!

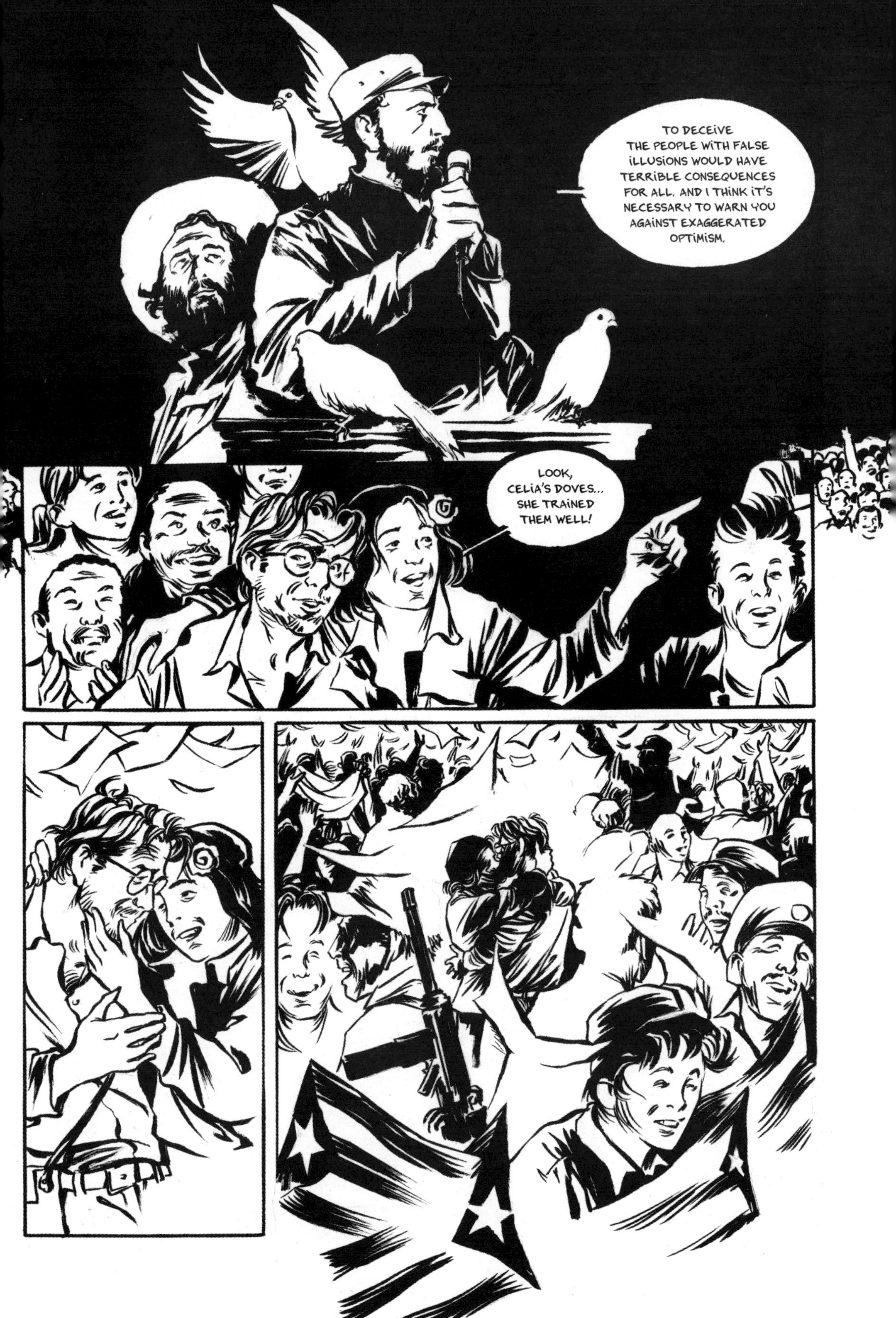
TO DECEIVE THE PEOPLE WITH FALSE ILLUSIONS WOULD HAVE TERRIBLE CONSEQUENCES FOR ALL, AND I THINK IT'S NECESSARY TO WARN YOU AGAINST EXAGGERATED OPTIMISM.
LOOK, CELIA'S DOVES... SHE TRAINED THEM WELL!

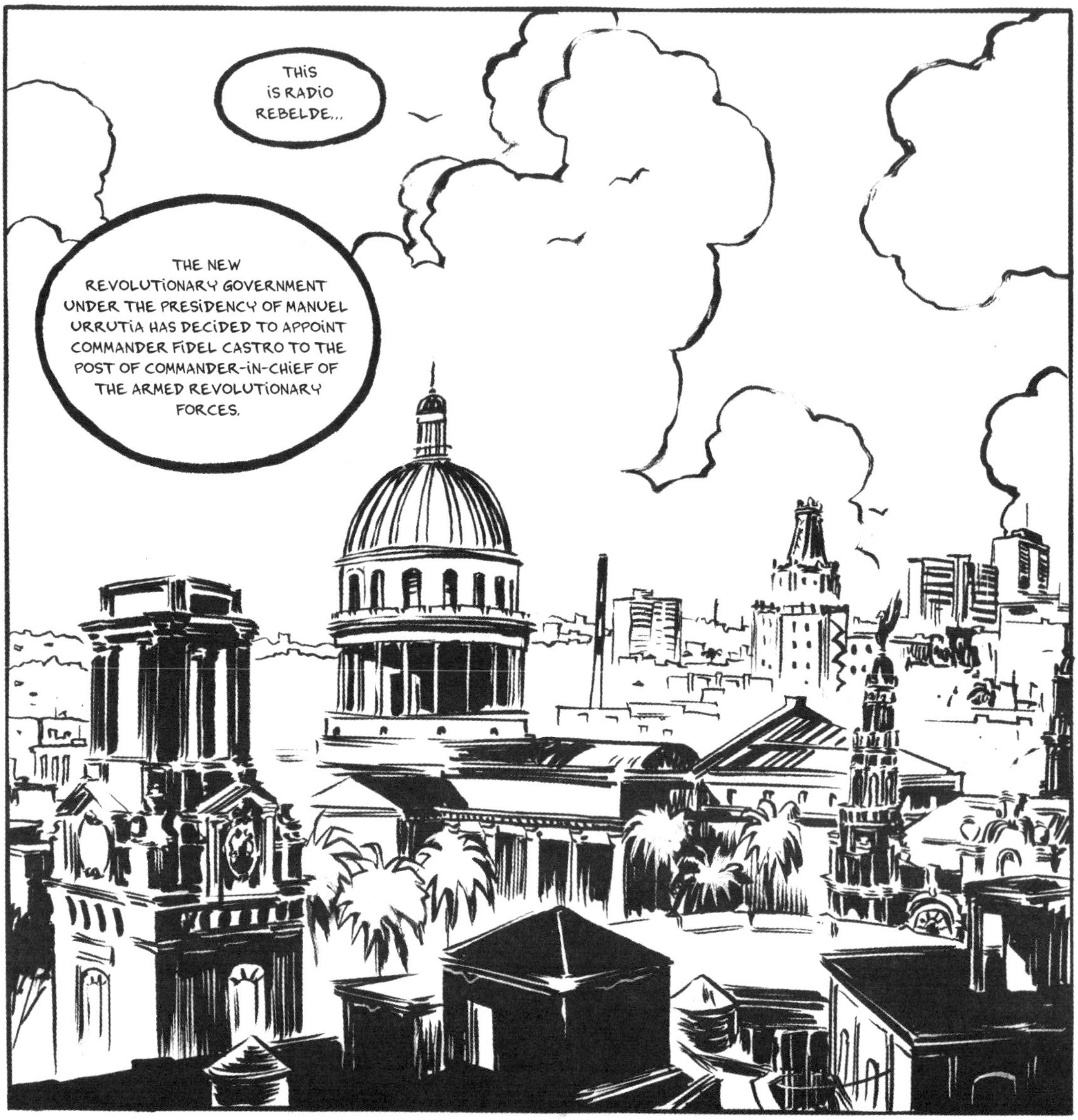
THIS IS RADIO REBELDE...
THE NEW REVOLUTIONARY GOVERNMENT UNDER THE PRESIDENCY OF MANUEL URRUTIA HAS DECIDED TO APPOINT COMMANDER FIDEL CASTRO TO THE POST OF COMMANDER-IN-CHIEF OF THE ARMED REVOLUTIONARY FORCES.

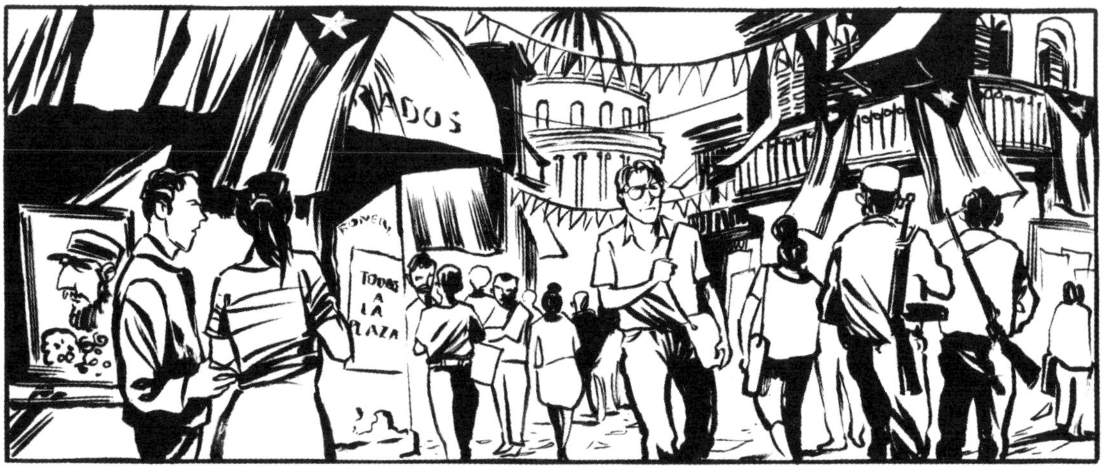
ADOS
TODOS
A
LA

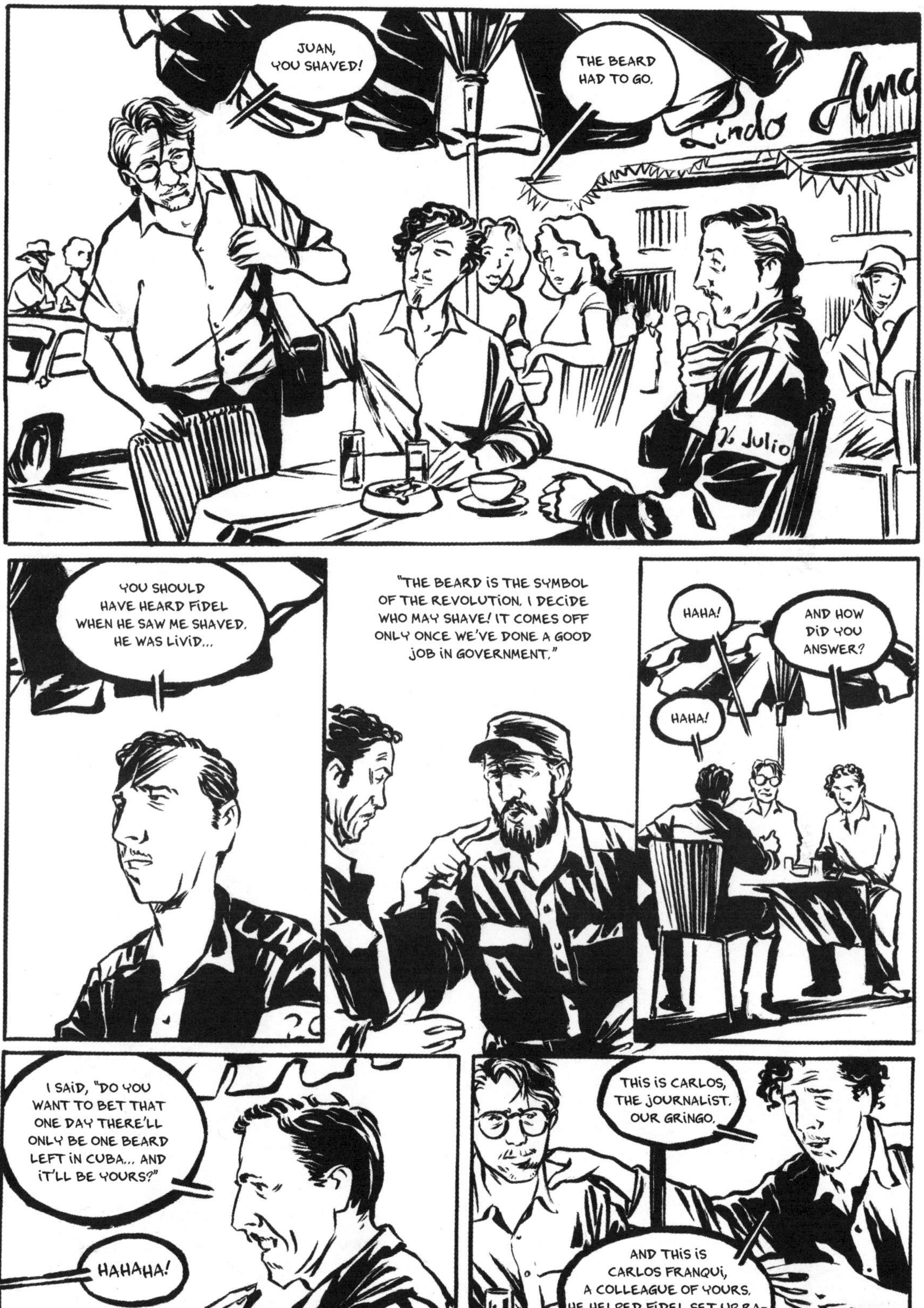
JUAN, YOU SHAVED!
THE BEARD HAD TO GO.
Lindo Ama
26 Julio
YOU SHOULD HAVE HEARD FIDEL WHEN HE SAW ME SHAVED. HE WAS LIVID...
"THE BEARD IS THE SYMBOL OF THE REVOLUTION. I DECIDE WHO MAY SHAVE! IT COMES OFF ONLY ONCE WE'VE DONE A GOOD JOB IN GOVERNMENT."
HAHA!
AND HOW DID YOU ANSWER?
HAHA!
I SAID, "DO YOU WANT TO BET THAT ONE DAY THERE'LL ONLY BE ONE BEARD LEFT IN CUBA... AND IT'LL BE YOURS?"
HAHAHA!
THIS IS CARLOS, THE JOURNALIST. OUR GRINGO.
AND THIS IS CARLOS FRANQUI, A COLLEAGUE OF YOURS. HE HELPED FIDEL SET UP RADIO REBELDE.

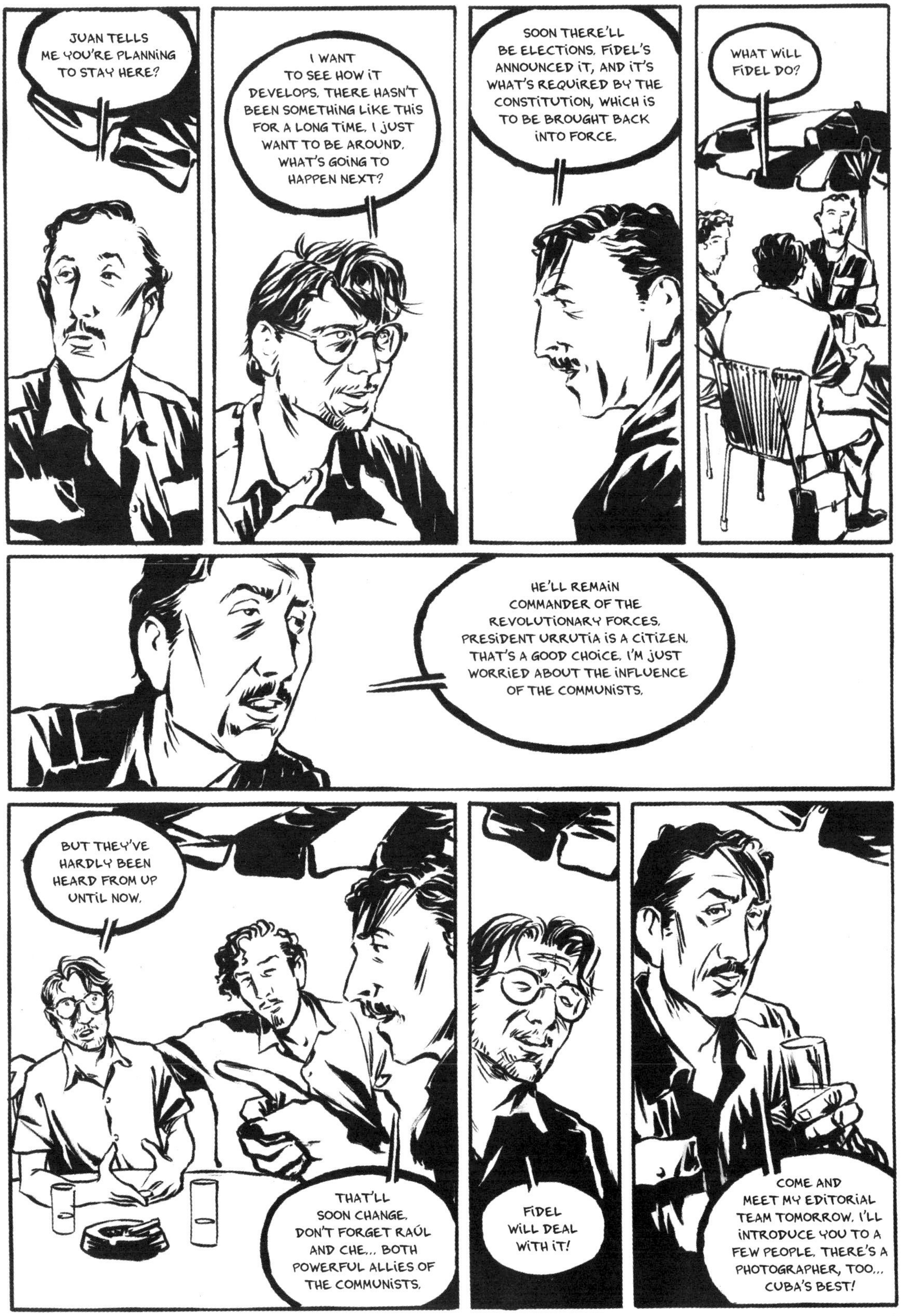
JUAN TELLS ME YOU'RE PLANNING TO STAY HERE?
I WANT TO SEE HOW IT DEVELOPS. THERE HASN'T BEEN SOMETHING LIKE THIS FOR A LONG TIME. I JUST WANT TO BE AROUND. WHAT'S GOING TO HAPPEN NEXT?
SOON THERE'LL BE ELECTIONS. FIDEL'S ANNOUNCED IT, AND IT'S WHAT'S REQUIRED BY THE CONSTITUTION, WHICH IS TO BE BROUGHT BACK INTO FORCE.
WHAT WILL FIDEL DO?
HE'LL REMAIN COMMANDER OF THE REVOLUTIONARY FORCES. PRESIDENT URRUTIA IS A CITIZEN. THAT'S A GOOD CHOICE. I'M JUST WORRIED ABOUT THE INFLUENCE OF THE COMMUNISTS.
BUT THEY'VE HARDLY BEEN HEARD FROM UP UNTIL NOW.
THAT'LL SOON CHANGE. DON'T FORGET RAÚL AND CHE... BOTH POWERFUL ALLIES OF THE COMMUNISTS.
FIDEL WILL DEAL WITH IT!
COME AND MEET MY EDITORIAL TEAM TOMORROW. I'LL INTRODUCE YOU TO A FEW PEOPLE. THERE'S A PHOTOGRAPHER, TOO... CUBA'S BEST!

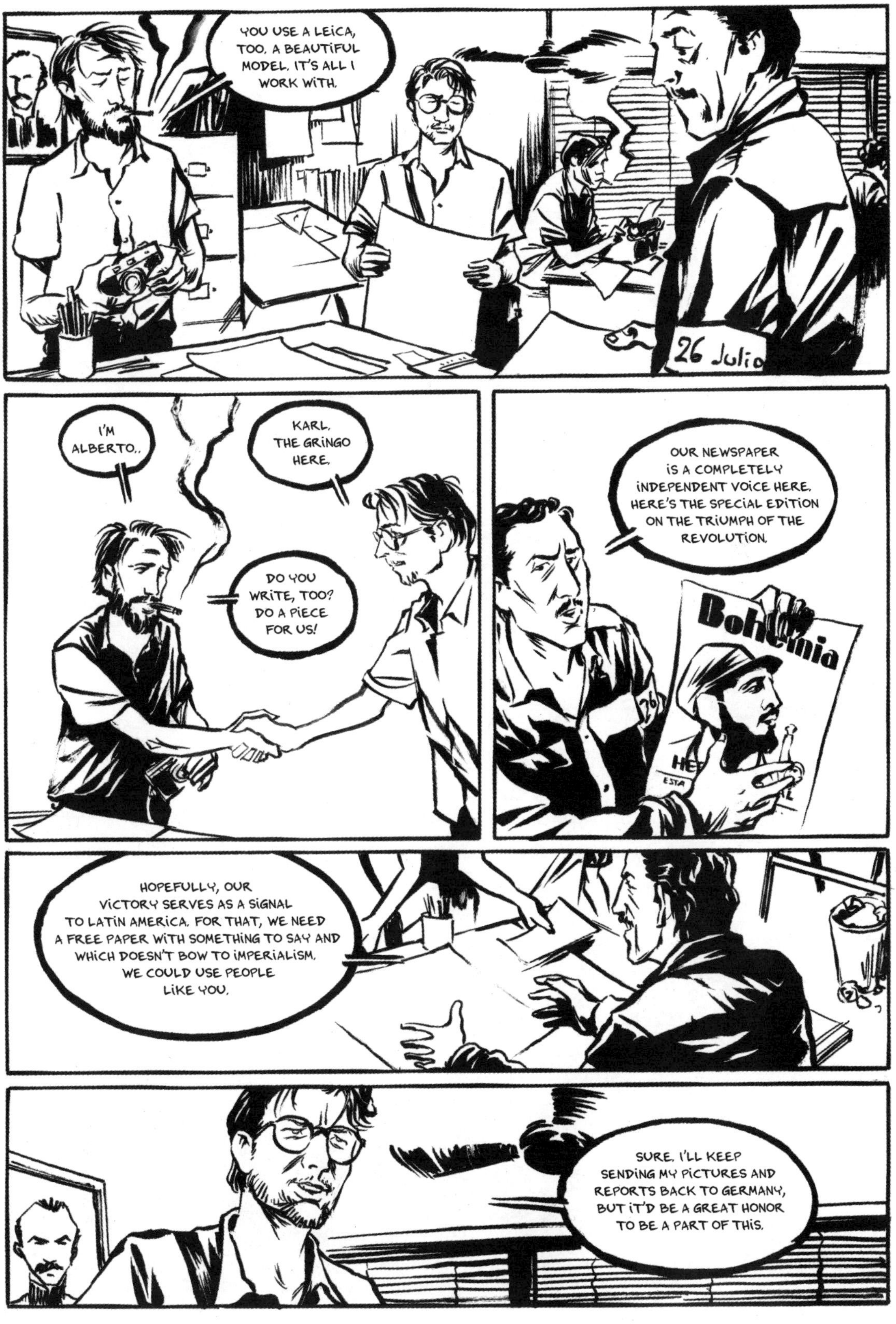
YOU USE A LEICA, TOO. A BEAUTIFUL MODEL. IT'S ALL I WORK WITH.
26 Julio
I'M ALBERTO..
KARL, THE GRINGO HERE.
DO YOU WRITE, TOO? DO A PIECE FOR US!
OUR NEWSPAPER IS A COMPLETELY INDEPENDENT VOICE HERE. HERE'S THE SPECIAL EDITION ON THE TRIUMPH OF THE REVOLUTION.
Bohemia
HOPEFULLY, OUR VICTORY SERVES AS A SIGNAL TO LATIN AMERICA. FOR THAT, WE NEED A FREE PAPER WITH SOMETHING TO SAY AND WHICH DOESN'T BOW TO IMPERIALISM. WE COULD USE PEOPLE LIKE YOU.
SURE, I'LL KEEP SENDING MY PICTURES AND REPORTS BACK TO GERMANY, BUT IT'D BE A GREAT HONOR TO BE A PART OF THIS.

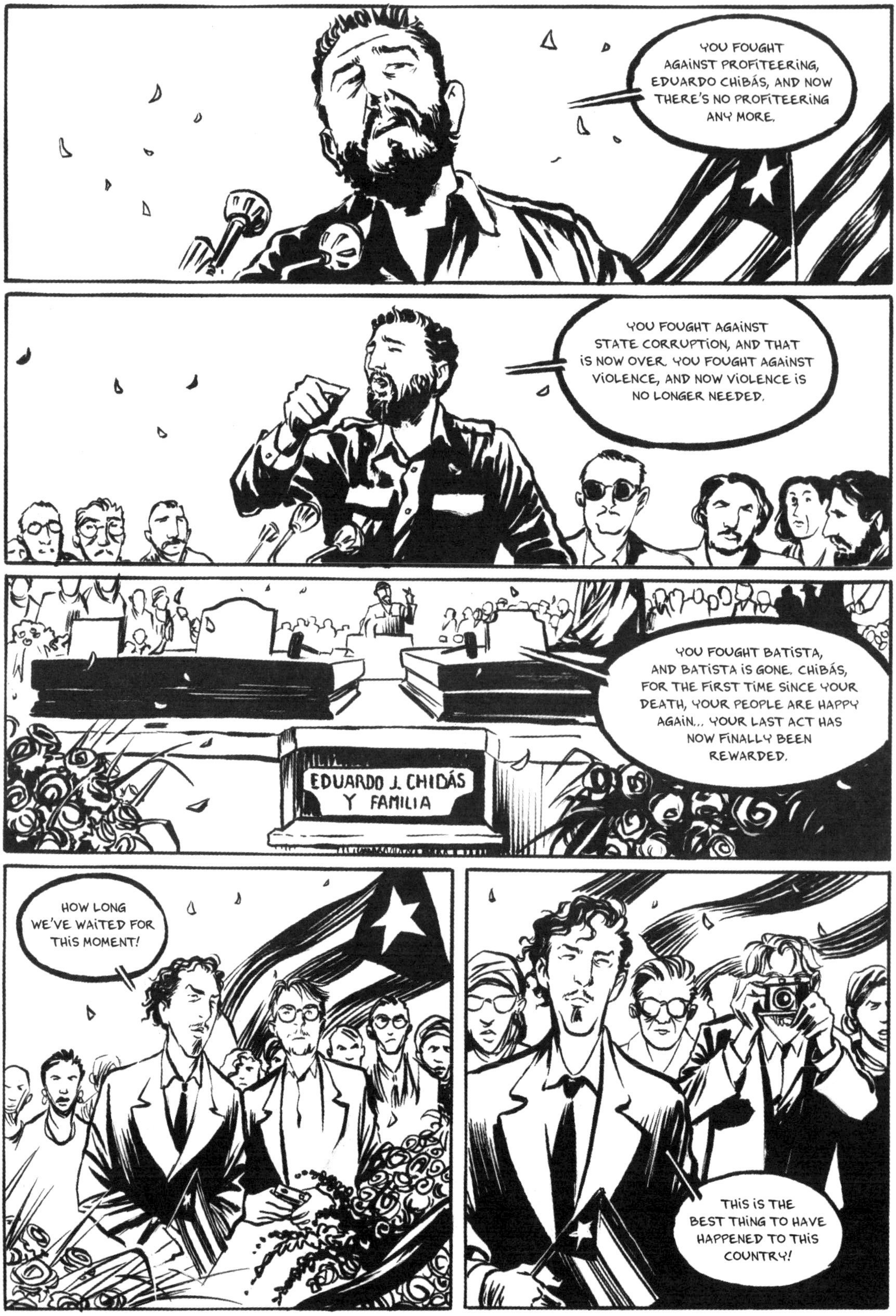
YOU FOUGHT AGAINST PROFITEERING, EDUARDO CHIBÁS, AND NOW THERE'S NO PROFITEERING ANY MORE.
YOU FOUGHT AGAINST STATE CORRUPTION, AND THAT IS NOW OVER. YOU FOUGHT AGAINST VIOLENCE, AND NOW VIOLENCE IS NO LONGER NEEDED.
YOU FOUGHT BATISTA, AND BATISTA IS GONE. CHIBÁS, FOR THE FIRST TIME SINCE YOUR DEATH, YOUR PEOPLE ARE HAPPY AGAIN... YOUR LAST ACT HAS NOW FINALLY BEEN REWARDED.
EDUARDO J. CHIBÁS Y FAMILIA
HOW LONG WE'VE WAITED FOR THIS MOMENT!
THIS IS THE BEST THING TO HAVE HAPPENED TO THIS COUNTRY!

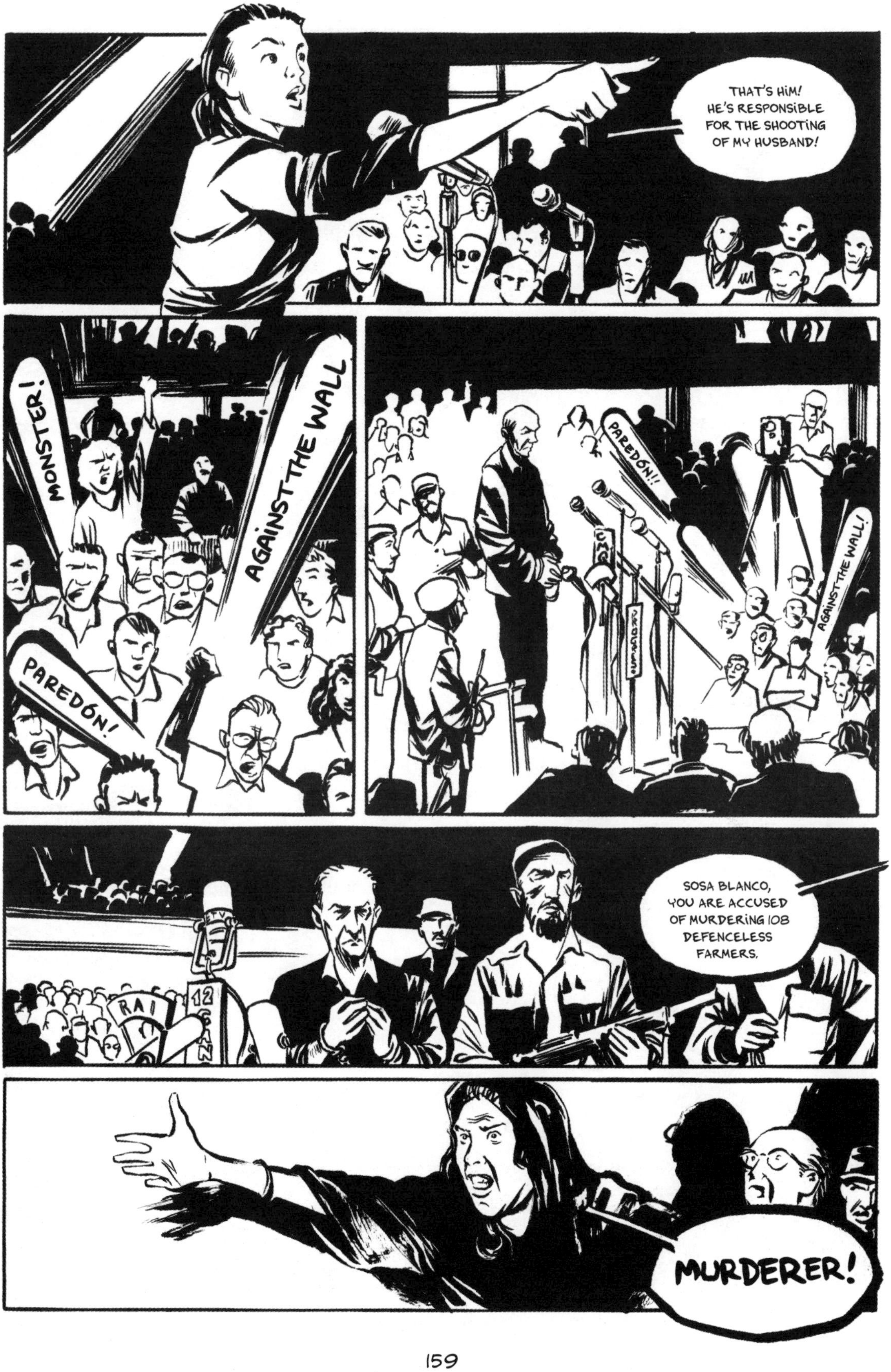
THAT'S HIM! HE'S RESPONSIBLE FOR THE SHOOTING OF MY HUSBAND!
MONSTER!
AGAINST THE WALL
PAREDÓN!
PAREDÓN!!
AGAINST THE WALL!
SOSA BLANCO, YOU ARE ACCUSED OF MURDERING 108 DEFENCELESS FARMERS.
MURDERER!

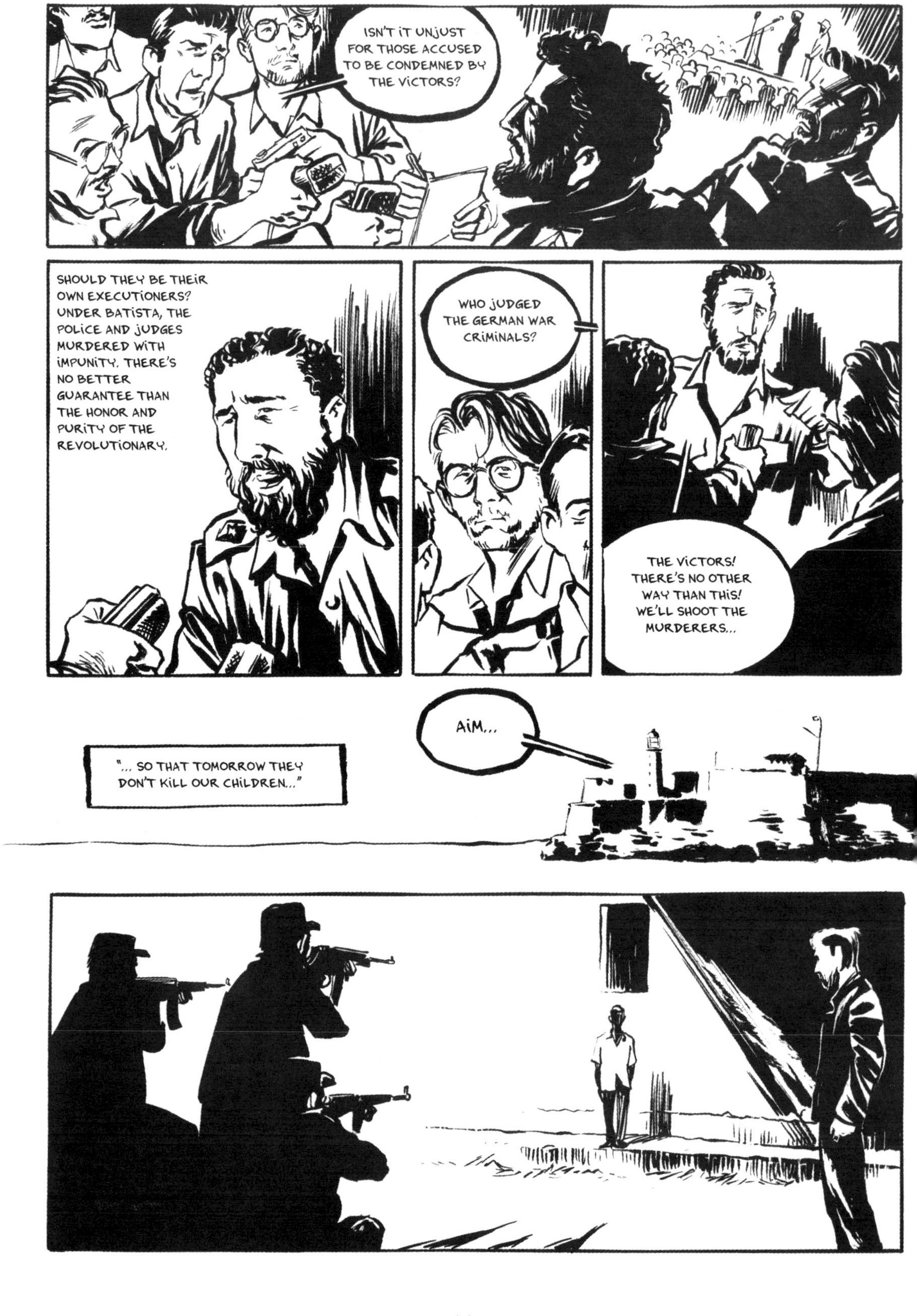
ISN'T IT UNJUST FOR THOSE ACCUSED TO BE CONDEMNED BY THE VICTORS?
SHOULD THEY BE THEIR OWN EXECUTIONERS? UNDER BATISTA, THE POLICE AND JUDGES MURDERED WITH IMPUNITY. THERE'S NO BETTER GUARANTEE THAN THE HONOR AND PURITY OF THE REVOLUTIONARY.
WHO JUDGED THE GERMAN WAR CRIMINALS?
THE VICTORS! THERE'S NO OTHER WAY THAN THIS! WE'LL SHOOT THE MURDERERS...
"... SO THAT TOMORROW THEY DON'T KILL OUR CHILDREN..."
AIM...

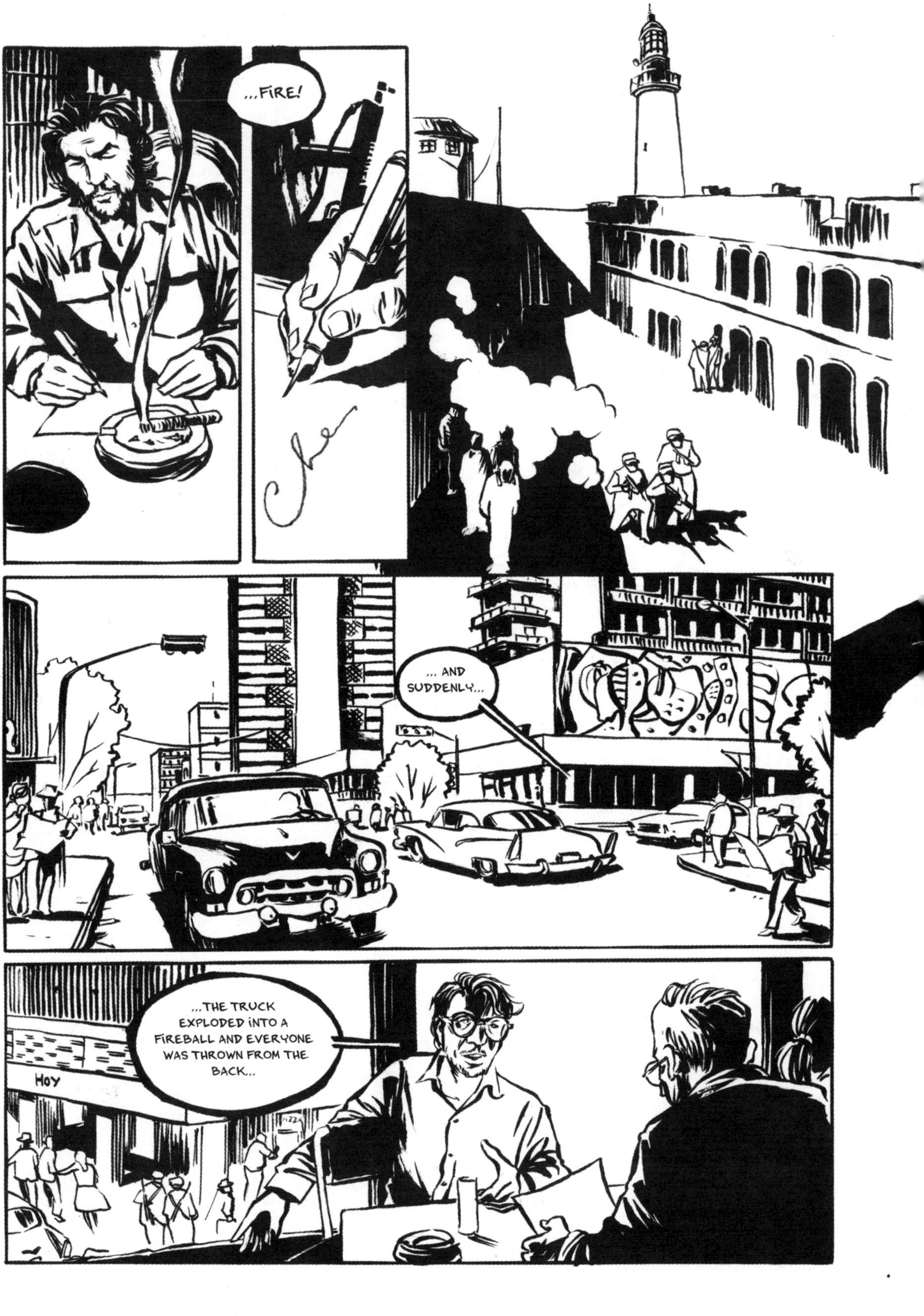
...FIRE!
... AND SUDDENLY...
...THE TRUCK EXPLODED INTO A FIREBALL AND EVERYONE WAS THROWN FROM THE BACK...
HOY

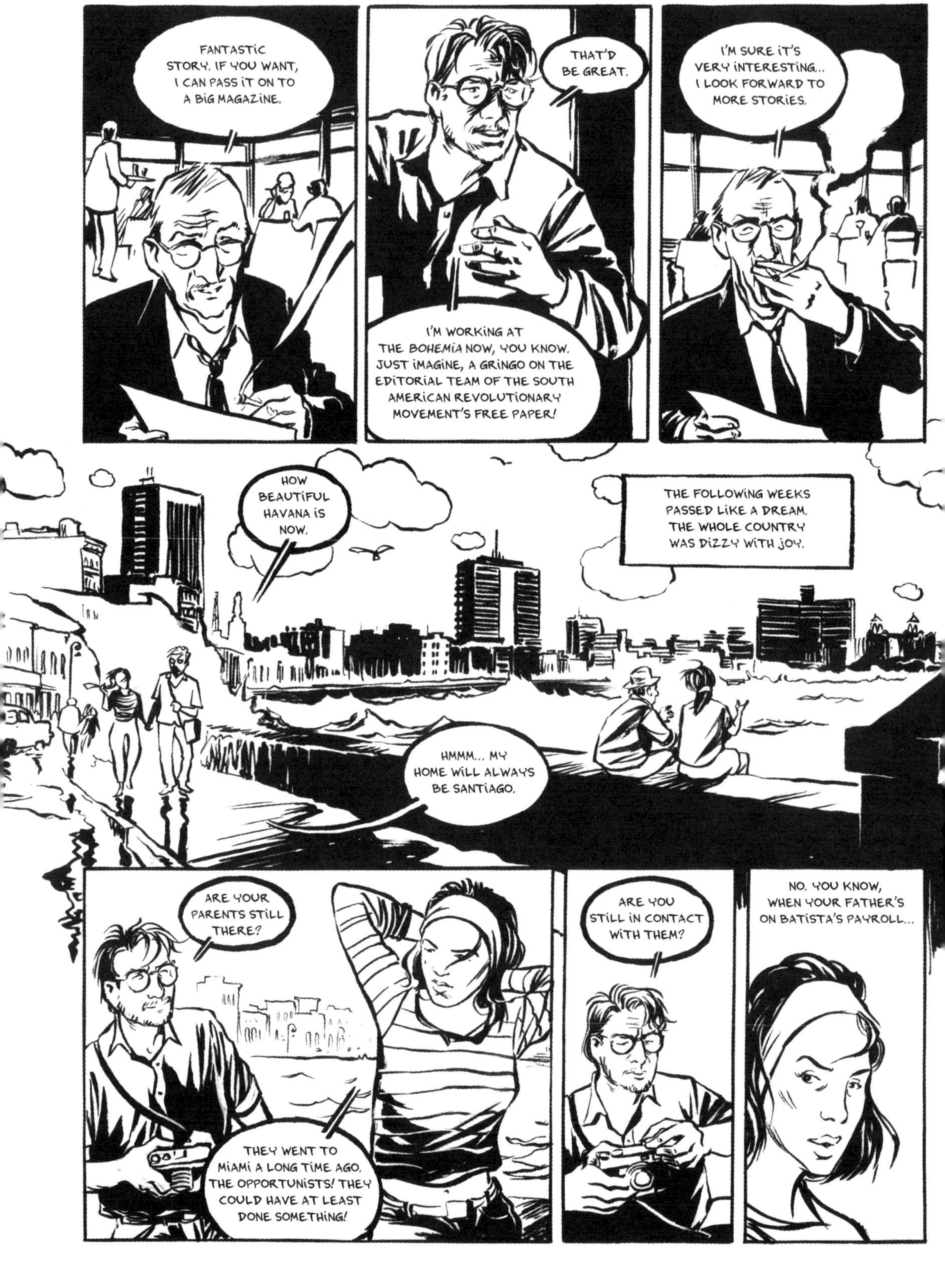
FANTASTIC STORY. IF YOU WANT, I CAN PASS IT ON TO A BIG MAGAZINE.
THAT'D BE GREAT.
I'M WORKING AT THE *BOHEMIA* NOW, YOU KNOW. JUST IMAGINE, A GRINGO ON THE EDITORIAL TEAM OF THE SOUTH AMERICAN REVOLUTIONARY MOVEMENT'S FREE PAPER!
I'M SURE IT'S VERY INTERESTING... I LOOK FORWARD TO MORE STORIES.
HOW BEAUTIFUL HAVANA IS NOW.
THE FOLLOWING WEEKS PASSED LIKE A DREAM. THE WHOLE COUNTRY WAS DIZZY WITH JOY.
HMMM... MY HOME WILL ALWAYS BE SANTIAGO.
ARE YOUR PARENTS STILL THERE?
THEY WENT TO MIAMI A LONG TIME AGO. THE OPPORTUNISTS! THEY COULD HAVE AT LEAST DONE SOMETHING!
ARE YOU STILL IN CONTACT WITH THEM?
NO. YOU KNOW, WHEN YOUR FATHER'S ON BATISTA'S PAYROLL...

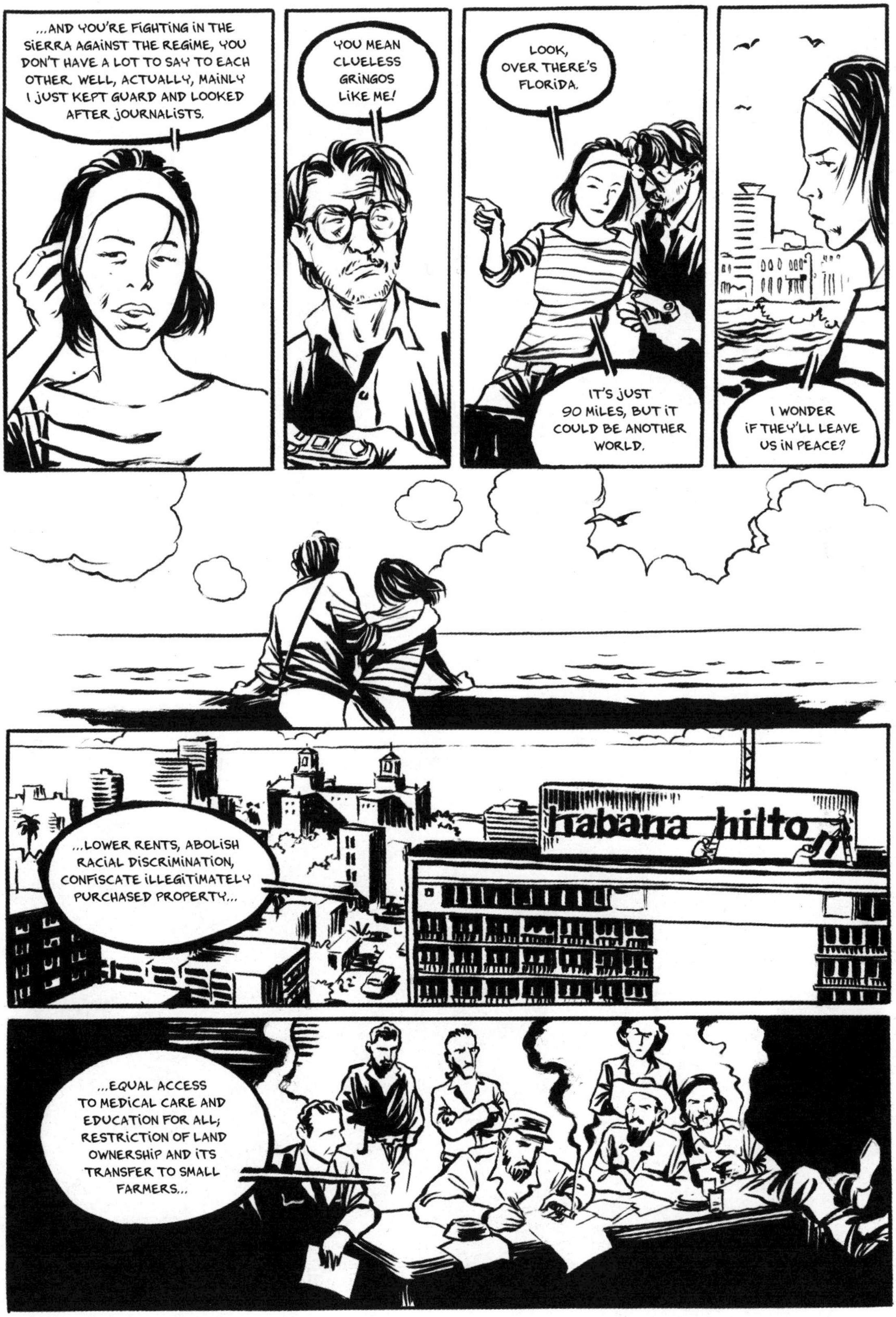
...AND YOU'RE FIGHTING IN THE SIERRA AGAINST THE REGIME, YOU DON'T HAVE A LOT TO SAY TO EACH OTHER. WELL, ACTUALLY, MAINLY I JUST KEPT GUARD AND LOOKED AFTER JOURNALISTS.
YOU MEAN CLUELESS GRINGOS LIKE ME!
LOOK, OVER THERE'S FLORIDA.
IT'S JUST 90 MILES, BUT IT COULD BE ANOTHER WORLD.
I WONDER IF THEY'LL LEAVE US IN PEACE?
...LOWER RENTS, ABOLISH RACIAL DISCRIMINATION, CONFISCATE ILLEGITIMATELY PURCHASED PROPERTY...
habana hilto
...EQUAL ACCESS TO MEDICAL CARE AND EDUCATION FOR ALL; RESTRICTION OF LAND OWNERSHIP AND ITS TRANSFER TO SMALL FARMERS...

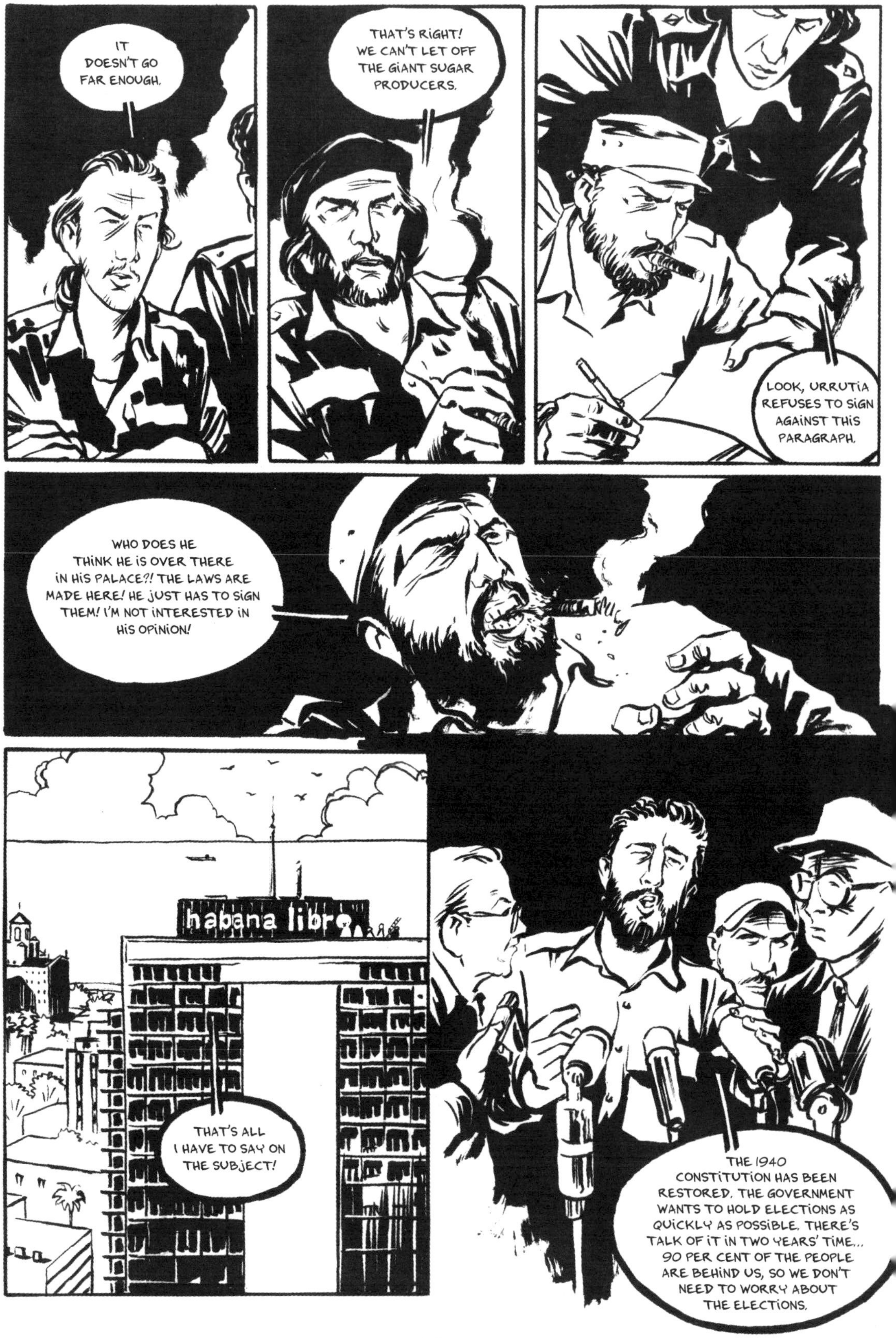
IT DOESN'T GO FAR ENOUGH.
THAT'S RIGHT! WE CAN'T LET OFF THE GIANT SUGAR PRODUCERS.
LOOK, URRUTIA REFUSES TO SIGN AGAINST THIS PARAGRAPH.
WHO DOES HE THINK HE IS OVER THERE IN HIS PALACE?! THE LAWS ARE MADE HERE! HE JUST HAS TO SIGN THEM! I'M NOT INTERESTED IN HIS OPINION!
THAT'S ALL I HAVE TO SAY ON THE SUBJECT!
habana libre
THE 1940 CONSTITUTION HAS BEEN RESTORED. THE GOVERNMENT WANTS TO HOLD ELECTIONS AS QUICKLY AS POSSIBLE. THERE'S TALK OF IT IN TWO YEARS' TIME... 90 PER CENT OF THE PEOPLE ARE BEHIND US, SO WE DON'T NEED TO WORRY ABOUT THE ELECTIONS.

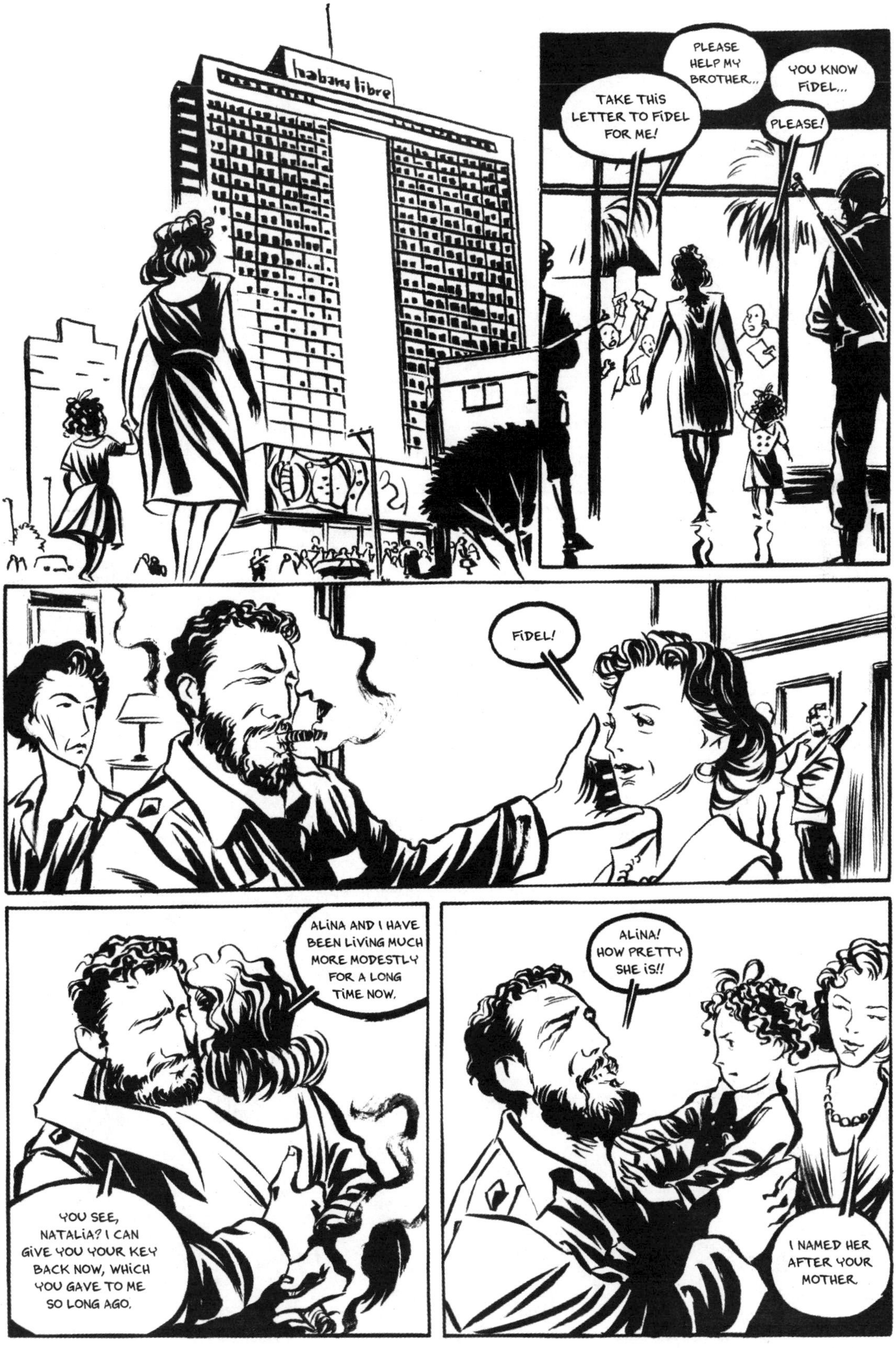
habana libre
TAKE THIS LETTER TO FIDEL FOR ME!
PLEASE HELP MY BROTHER...
YOU KNOW FIDEL...
PLEASE!
FIDEL!
ALINA AND I HAVE BEEN LIVING MUCH MORE MODESTLY FOR A LONG TIME NOW.
YOU SEE, NATALIA? I CAN GIVE YOU YOUR KEY BACK NOW, WHICH YOU GAVE TO ME SO LONG AGO.
ALINA! HOW PRETTY SHE IS!!
I NAMED HER AFTER YOUR MOTHER

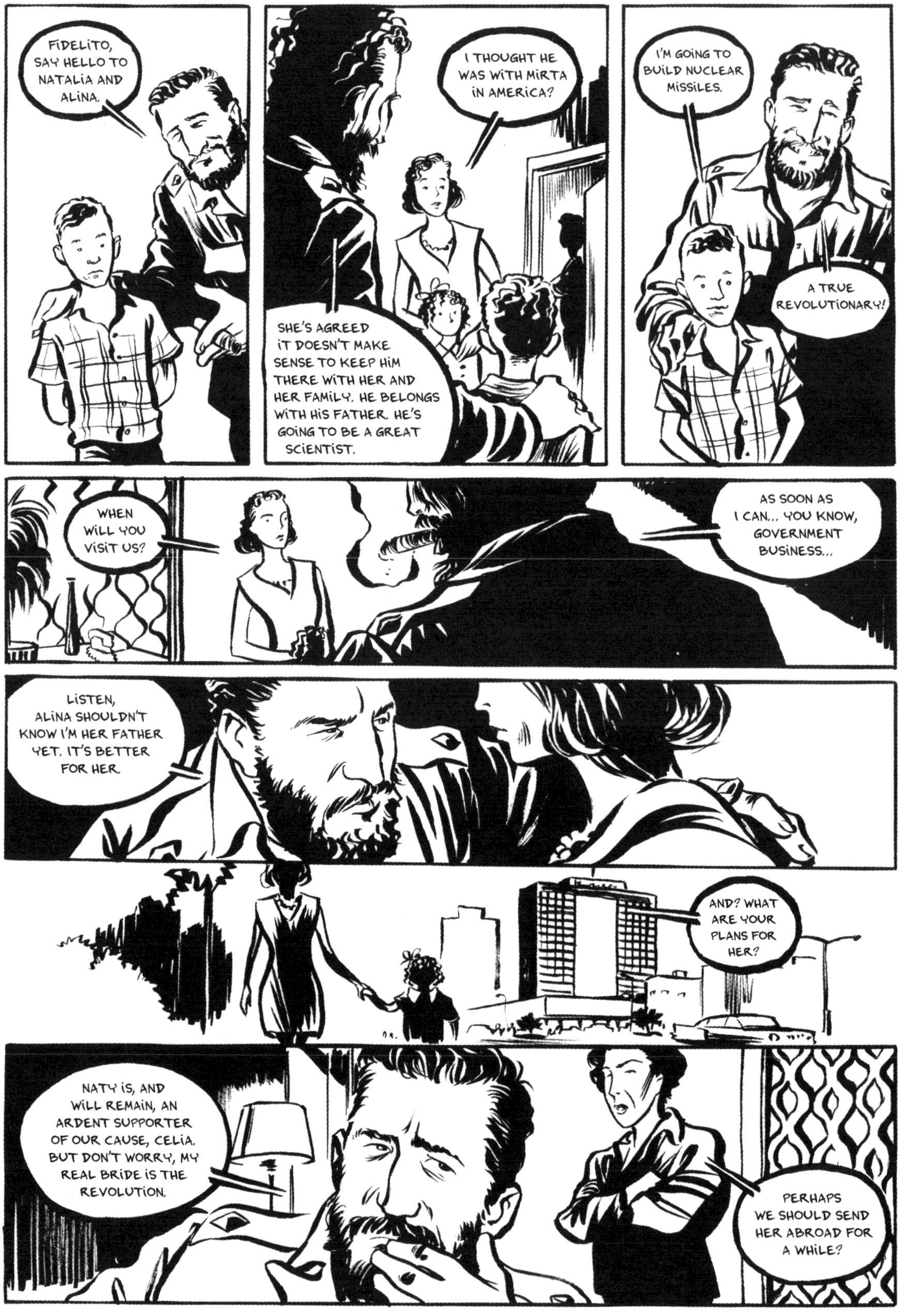
FIDELITO, SAY HELLO TO NATALIA AND ALINA.
I THOUGHT HE WAS WITH MIRTA IN AMERICA?
SHE'S AGREED IT DOESN'T MAKE SENSE TO KEEP HIM THERE WITH HER AND HER FAMILY. HE BELONGS WITH HIS FATHER. HE'S GOING TO BE A GREAT SCIENTIST.
I'M GOING TO BUILD NUCLEAR MISSILES.
A TRUE REVOLUTIONARY!
WHEN WILL YOU VISIT US?
AS SOON AS I CAN... YOU KNOW, GOVERNMENT BUSINESS...
LISTEN, ALINA SHOULDN'T KNOW I'M HER FATHER YET. IT'S BETTER FOR HER.
AND? WHAT ARE YOUR PLANS FOR HER?
NATY IS, AND WILL REMAIN, AN ARDENT SUPPORTER OF OUR CAUSE, CELIA. BUT DON'T WORRY, MY REAL BRIDE IS THE REVOLUTION.
PERHAPS WE SHOULD SEND HER ABROAD FOR A WHILE?

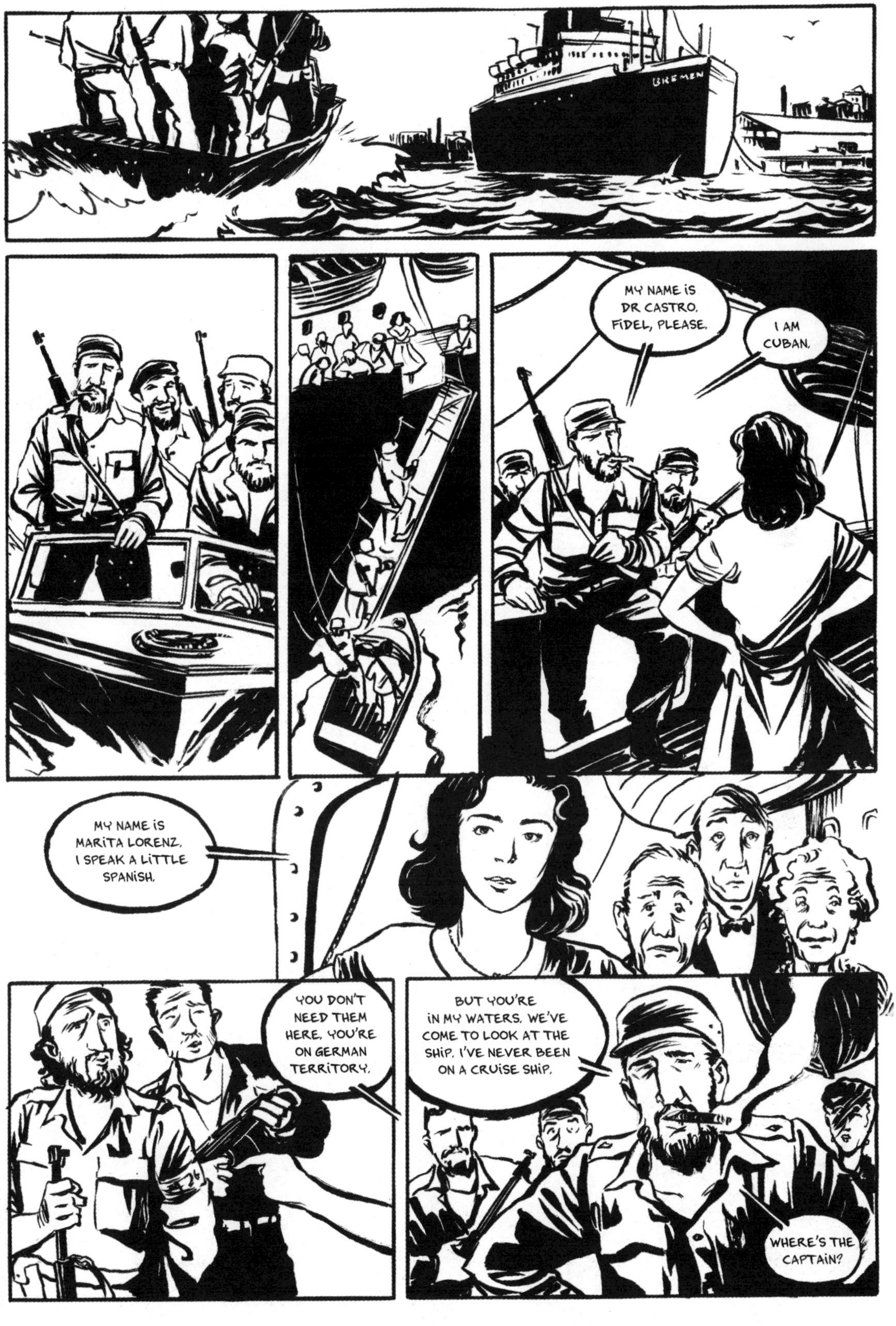
BREMEN
MY NAME IS DR CASTRO. FIDEL, PLEASE.
I AM CUBAN.
MY NAME IS MARITA LORENZ. I SPEAK A LITTLE SPANISH.
YOU DON'T NEED THEM HERE. YOU'RE ON GERMAN TERRITORY.
BUT YOU'RE IN MY WATERS. WE'VE COME TO LOOK AT THE SHIP. I'VE NEVER BEEN ON A CRUISE SHIP.
WHERE'S THE CAPTAIN?

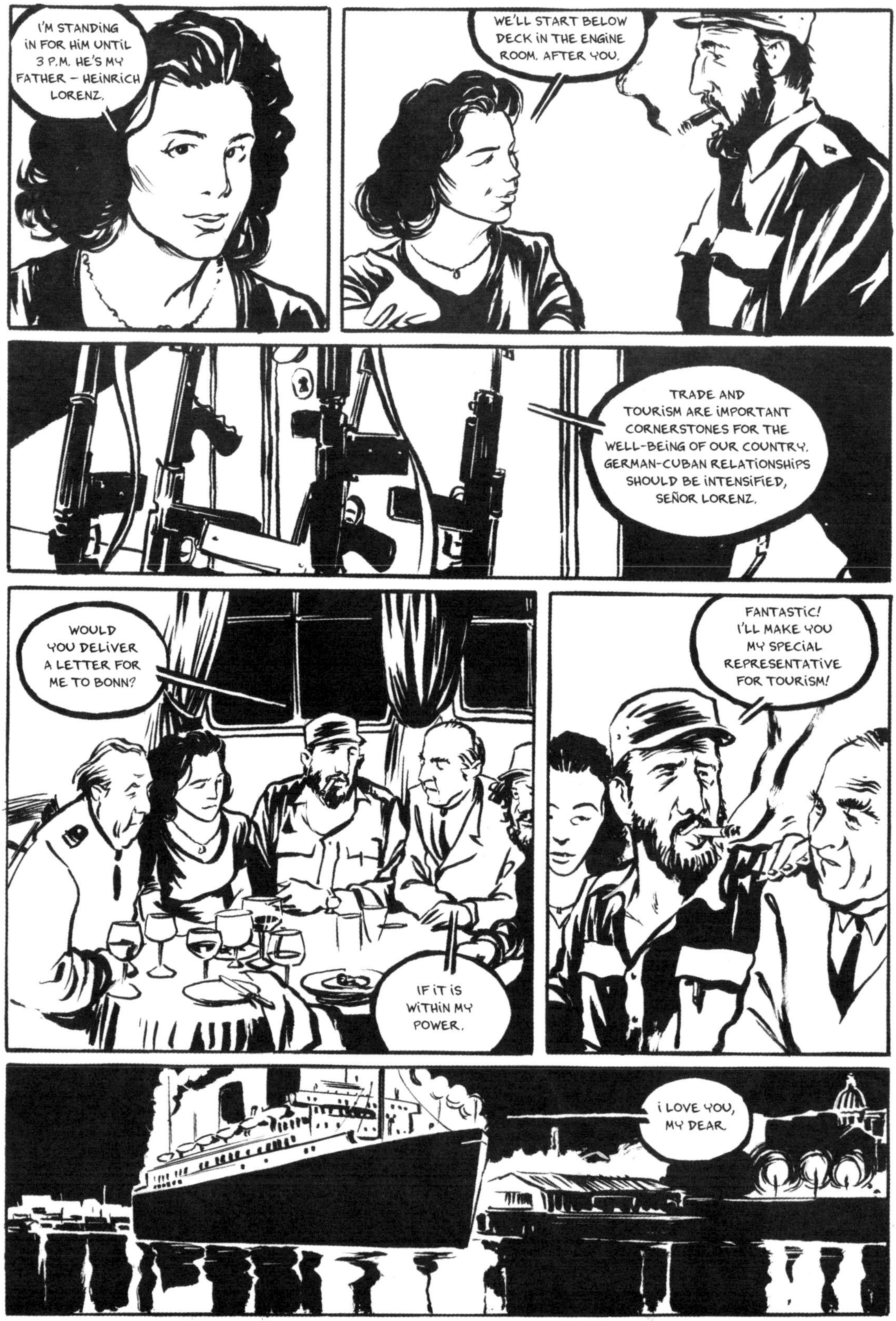
I'M STANDING IN FOR HIM UNTIL 3 P.M. HE'S MY FATHER – HEINRICH LORENZ.
WE'LL START BELOW DECK IN THE ENGINE ROOM. AFTER YOU.
TRADE AND TOURISM ARE IMPORTANT CORNERSTONES FOR THE WELL-BEING OF OUR COUNTRY. GERMAN-CUBAN RELATIONSHIPS SHOULD BE INTENSIFIED, SEÑOR LORENZ.
WOULD YOU DELIVER A LETTER FOR ME TO BONN?
IF IT IS WITHIN MY POWER.
FANTASTIC! I'LL MAKE YOU MY SPECIAL REPRESENTATIVE FOR TOURISM!
I LOVE YOU, MY DEAR.

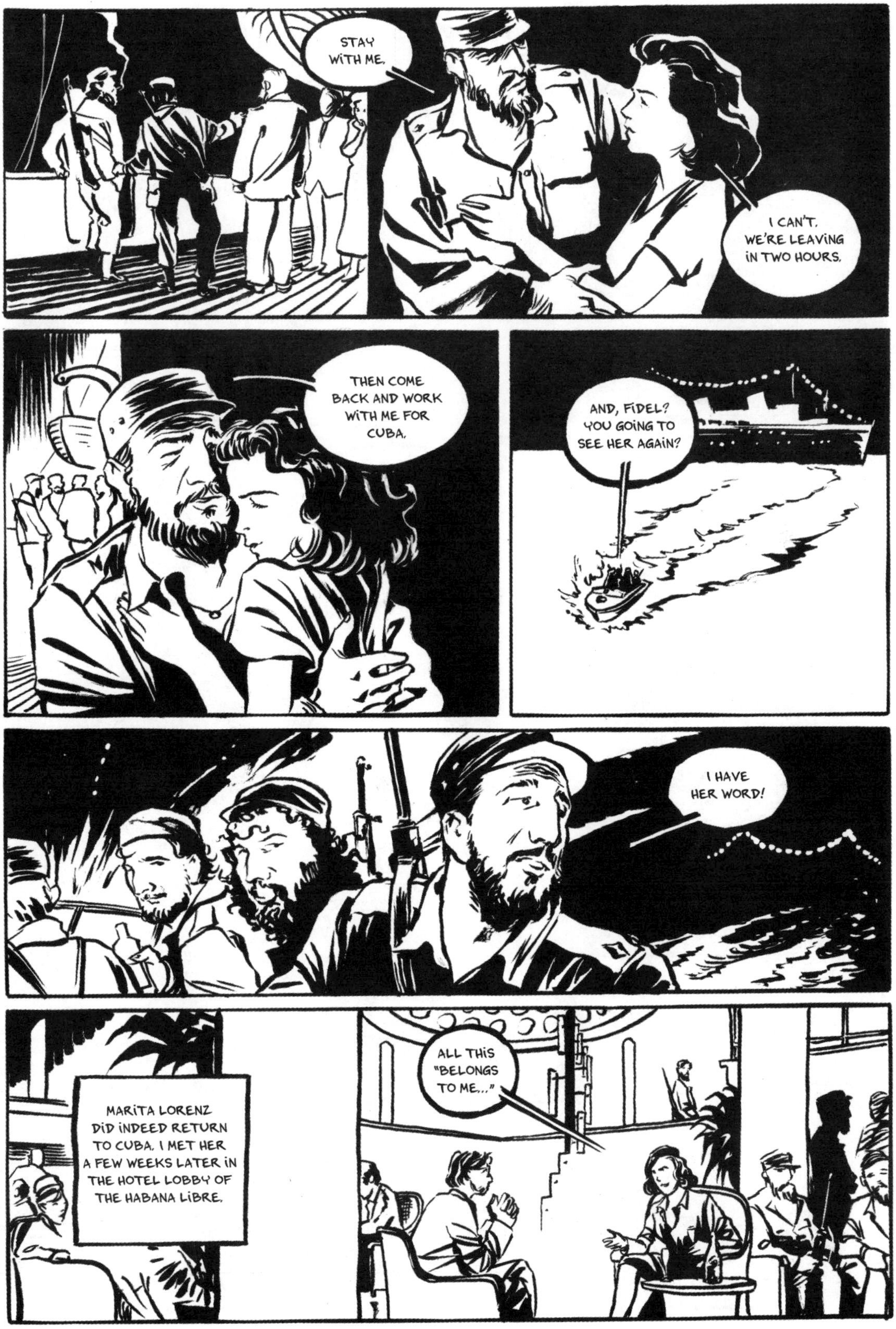
STAY WITH ME.
I CAN'T. WE'RE LEAVING IN TWO HOURS.
THEN COME BACK AND WORK WITH ME FOR CUBA.
AND, FIDEL? YOU GOING TO SEE HER AGAIN?
I HAVE HER WORD!
MARITA LORENZ DID INDEED RETURN TO CUBA. I MET HER A FEW WEEKS LATER IN THE HOTEL LOBBY OF THE HABANA LIBRE.
ALL THIS "BELONGS TO ME..."

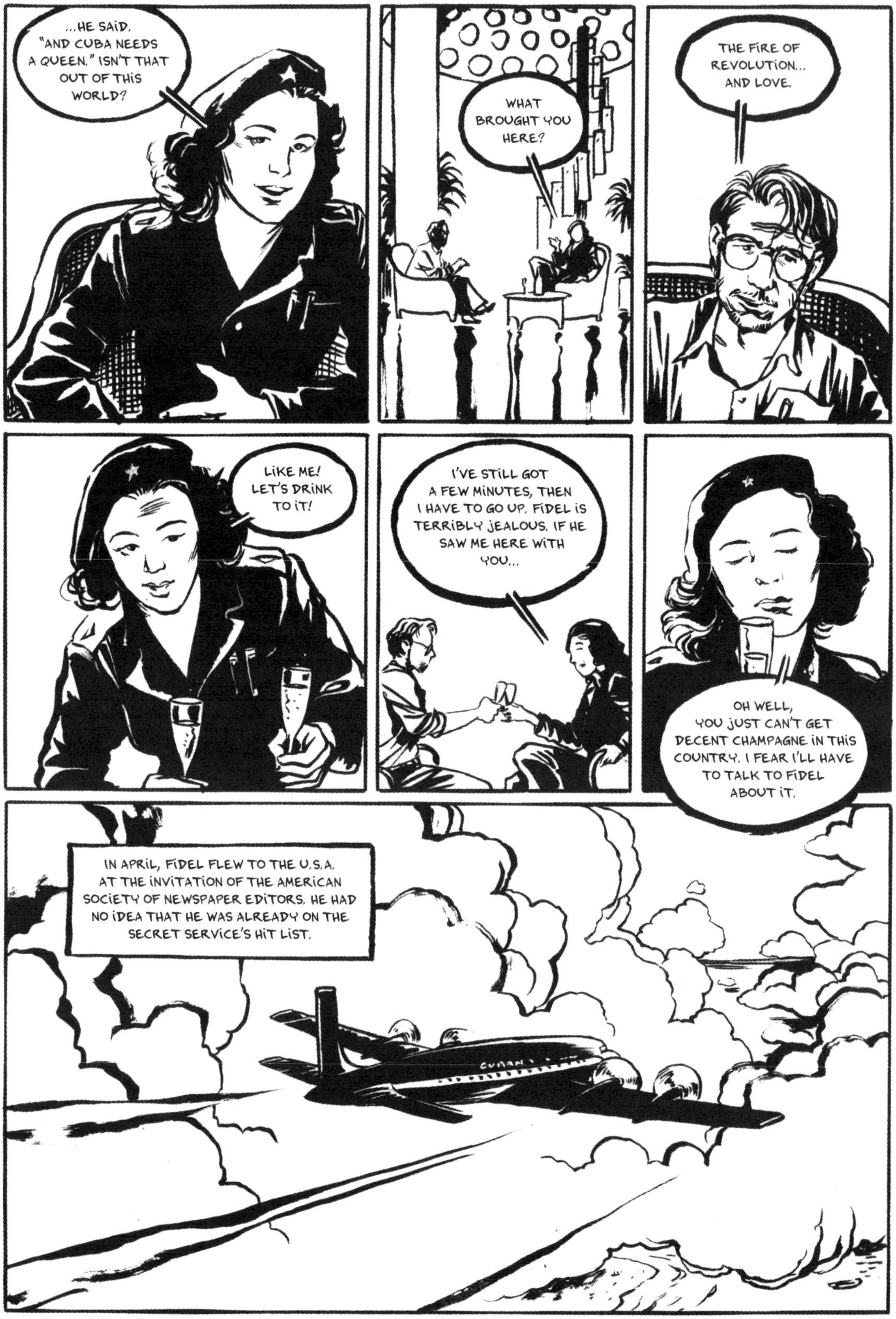
...HE SAID, "AND CUBA NEEDS A QUEEN." ISN'T THAT OUT OF THIS WORLD?
WHAT BROUGHT YOU HERE?
THE FIRE OF REVOLUTION... AND LOVE.
LIKE ME! LET'S DRINK TO IT!
I'VE STILL GOT A FEW MINUTES, THEN I HAVE TO GO UP. FIDEL IS TERRIBLY JEALOUS. IF HE SAW ME HERE WITH YOU...
OH WELL, YOU JUST CAN'T GET DECENT CHAMPAGNE IN THIS COUNTRY. I FEAR I'LL HAVE TO TALK TO FIDEL ABOUT IT.
IN APRIL, FIDEL FLEW TO THE U.S.A. AT THE INVITATION OF THE AMERICAN SOCIETY OF NEWSPAPER EDITORS. HE HAD NO IDEA THAT HE WAS ALREADY ON THE SECRET SERVICE'S HIT LIST.
CUBANA

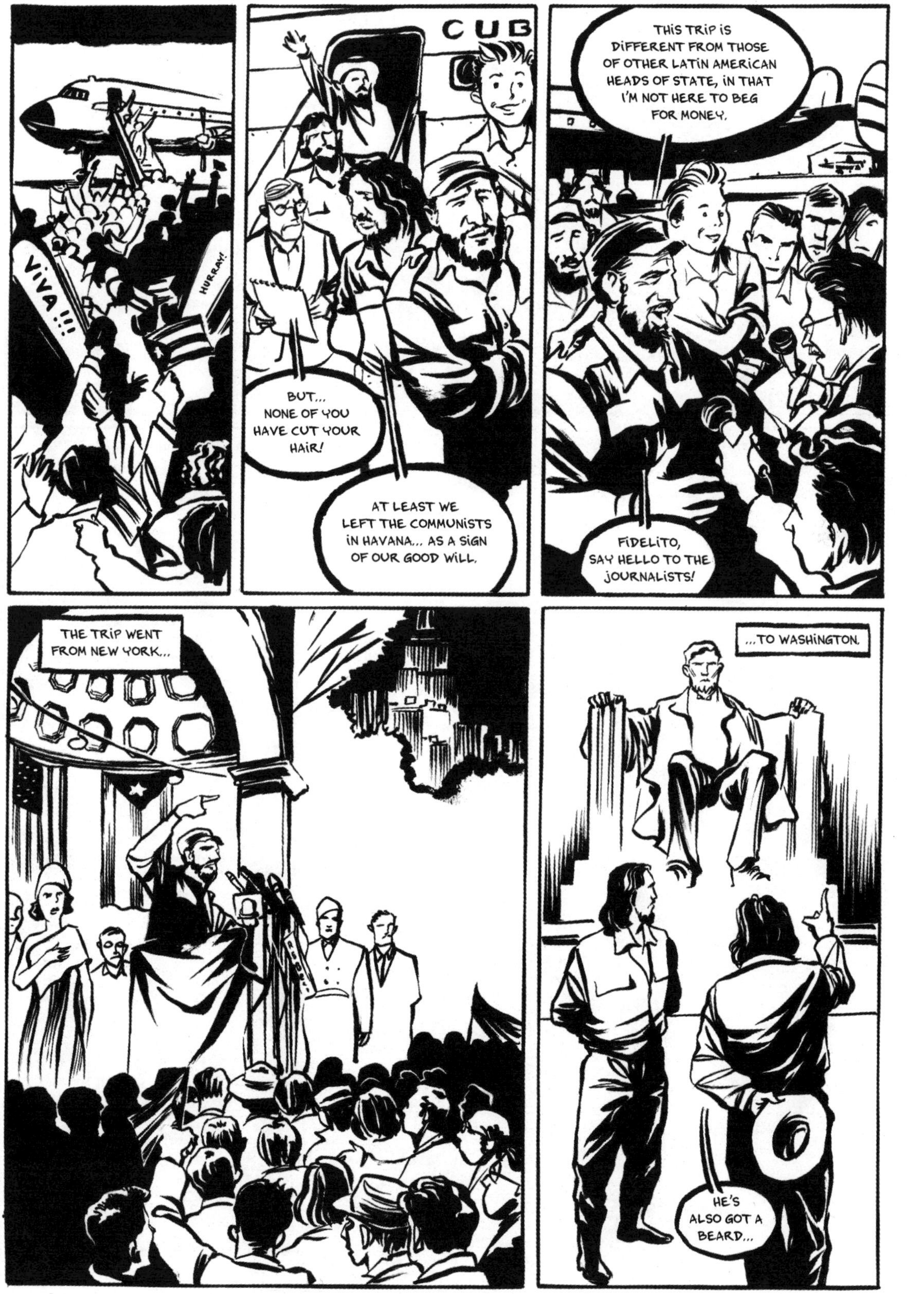

VIVA!!!
HURRAY!
CUB
BUT... NONE OF YOU HAVE CUT YOUR HAIR!
AT LEAST WE LEFT THE COMMUNISTS IN HAVANA... AS A SIGN OF OUR GOOD WILL.
THIS TRIP IS DIFFERENT FROM THOSE OF OTHER LATIN AMERICAN HEADS OF STATE, IN THAT I'M NOT HERE TO BEG FOR MONEY.
FIDELITO, SAY HELLO TO THE JOURNALISTS!
THE TRIP WENT FROM NEW YORK...
...TO WASHINGTON.
HE'S ALSO GOT A BEARD...

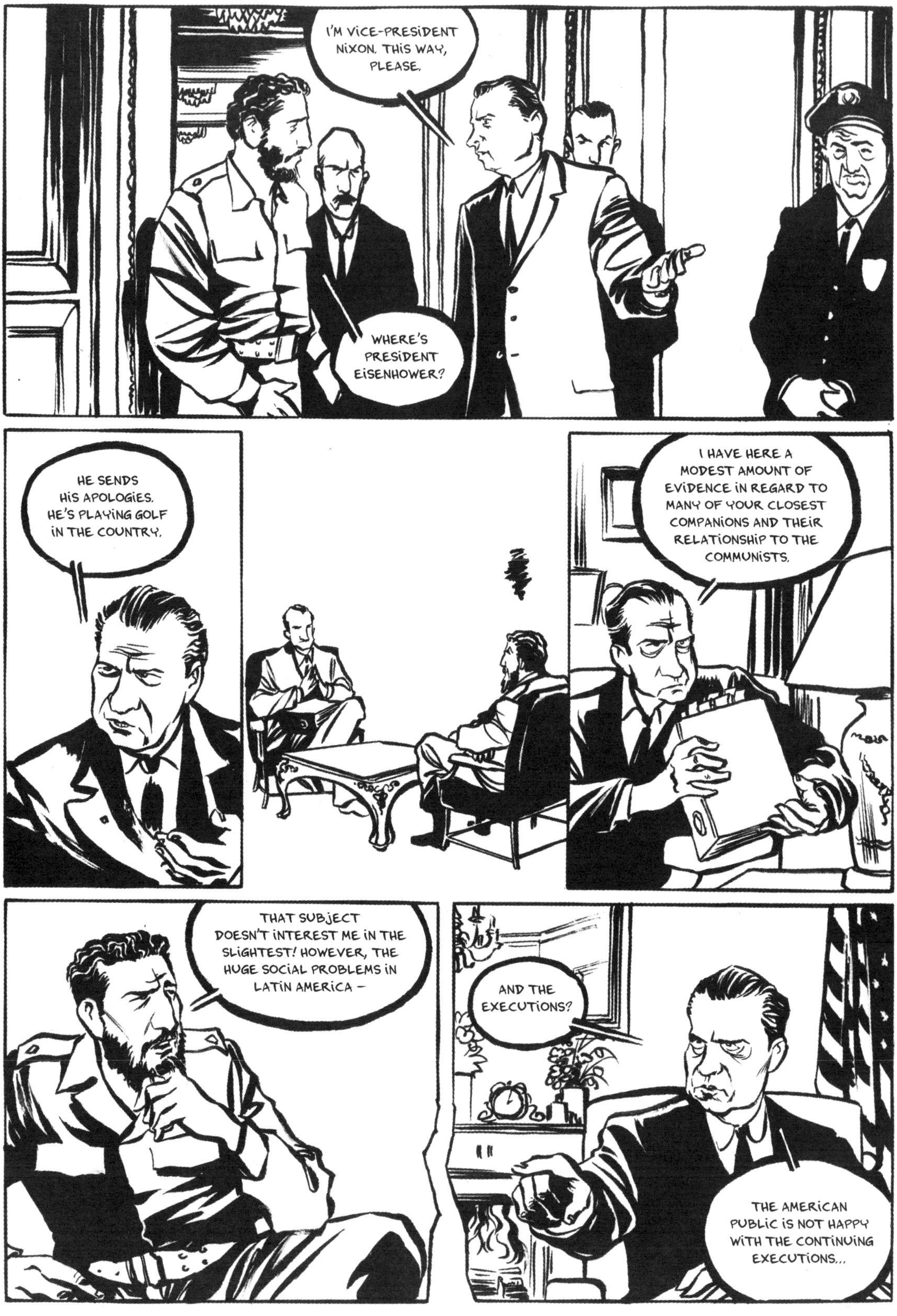
I'M VICE-PRESIDENT NIXON. THIS WAY, PLEASE.
WHERE'S PRESIDENT EISENHOWER?
HE SENDS HIS APOLOGIES. HE'S PLAYING GOLF IN THE COUNTRY.
I HAVE HERE A MODEST AMOUNT OF EVIDENCE IN REGARD TO MANY OF YOUR CLOSEST COMPANIONS AND THEIR RELATIONSHIP TO THE COMMUNISTS.
THAT SUBJECT DOESN'T INTEREST ME IN THE SLIGHTEST! HOWEVER, THE HUGE SOCIAL PROBLEMS IN LATIN AMERICA –
AND THE EXECUTIONS?
THE AMERICAN PUBLIC IS NOT HAPPY WITH THE CONTINUING EXECUTIONS...

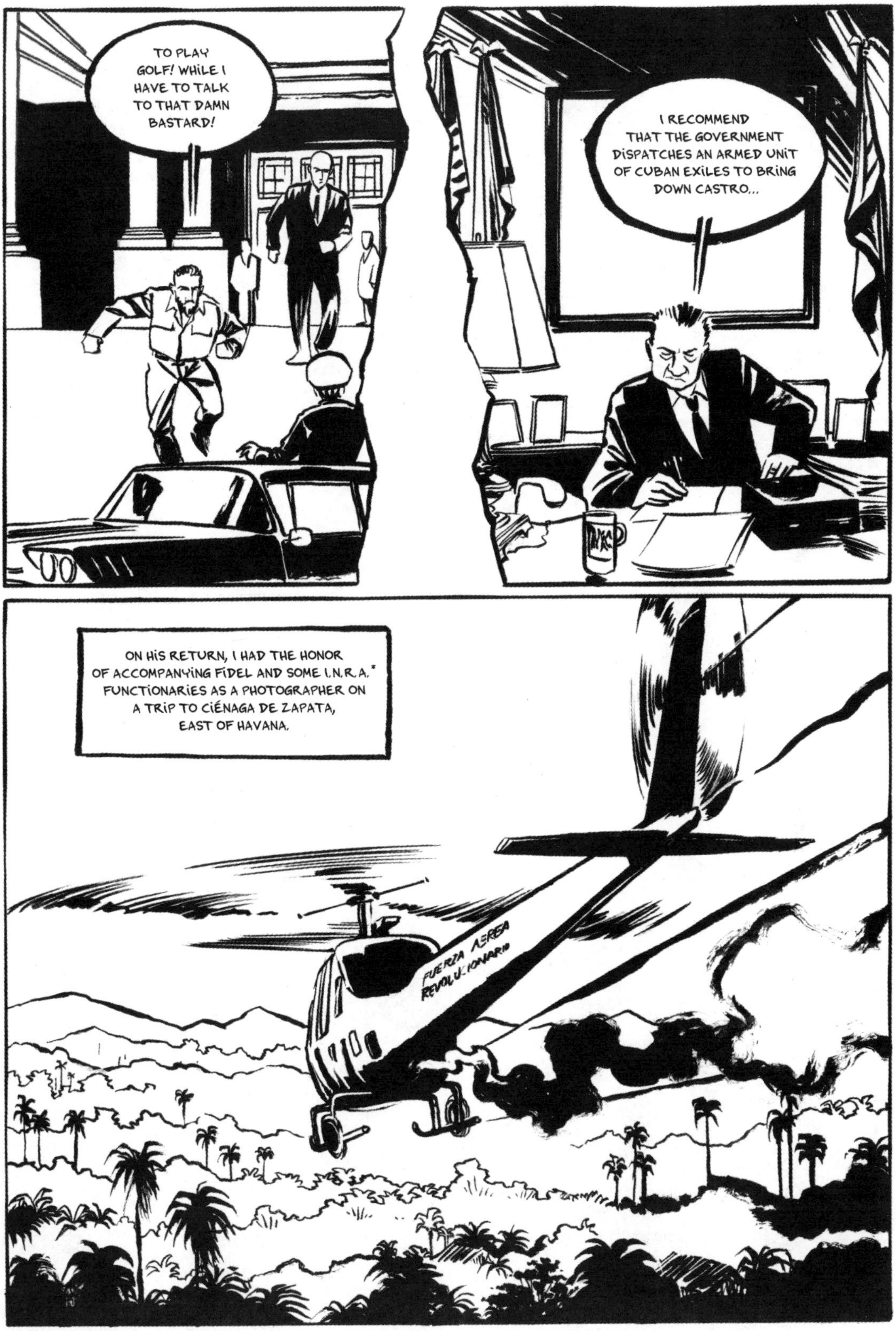
TO PLAY GOLF! WHILE I HAVE TO TALK TO THAT DAMN BASTARD!
I RECOMMEND THAT THE GOVERNMENT DISPATCHES AN ARMED UNIT OF CUBAN EXILES TO BRING DOWN CASTRO...
ON HIS RETURN, I HAD THE HONOR OF ACCOMPANYING FIDEL AND SOME I.N.R.A.* FUNCTIONARIES AS A PHOTOGRAPHER ON A TRIP TO CIÉNAGA DE ZAPATA, EAST OF HAVANA.
FUERZA AEREA
REVOLUCIONARIO

* NATIONAL INSTITUTE FOR AGRARIAN REFORM.

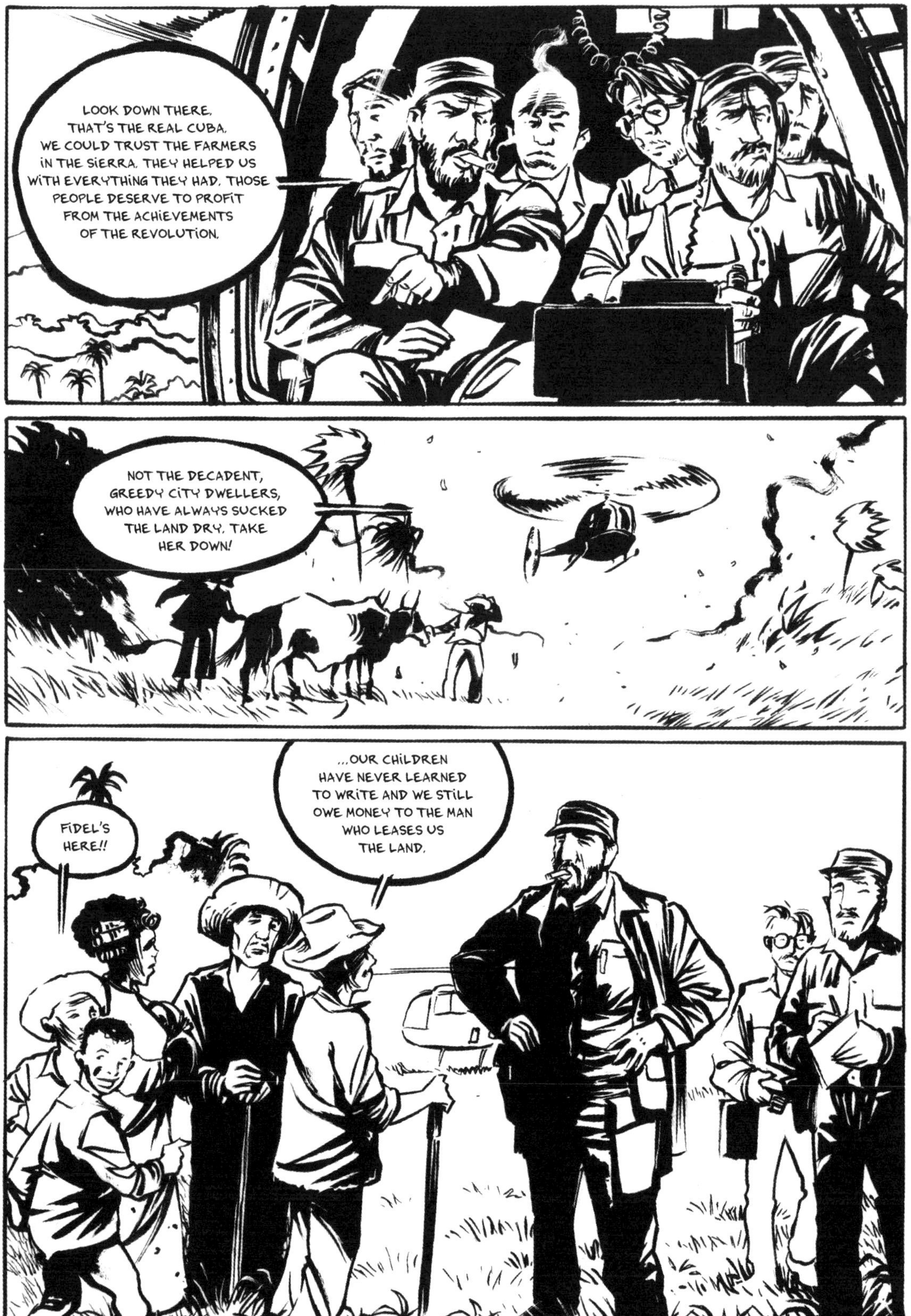
LOOK DOWN THERE. THAT'S THE REAL CUBA. WE COULD TRUST THE FARMERS IN THE SIERRA. THEY HELPED US WITH EVERYTHING THEY HAD. THOSE PEOPLE DESERVE TO PROFIT FROM THE ACHIEVEMENTS OF THE REVOLUTION.
NOT THE DECADENT, GREEDY CITY DWELLERS, WHO HAVE ALWAYS SUCKED THE LAND DRY. TAKE HER DOWN!
FIDEL'S HERE!!
...OUR CHILDREN HAVE NEVER LEARNED TO WRITE AND WE STILL OWE MONEY TO THE MAN WHO LEASES US THE LAND.

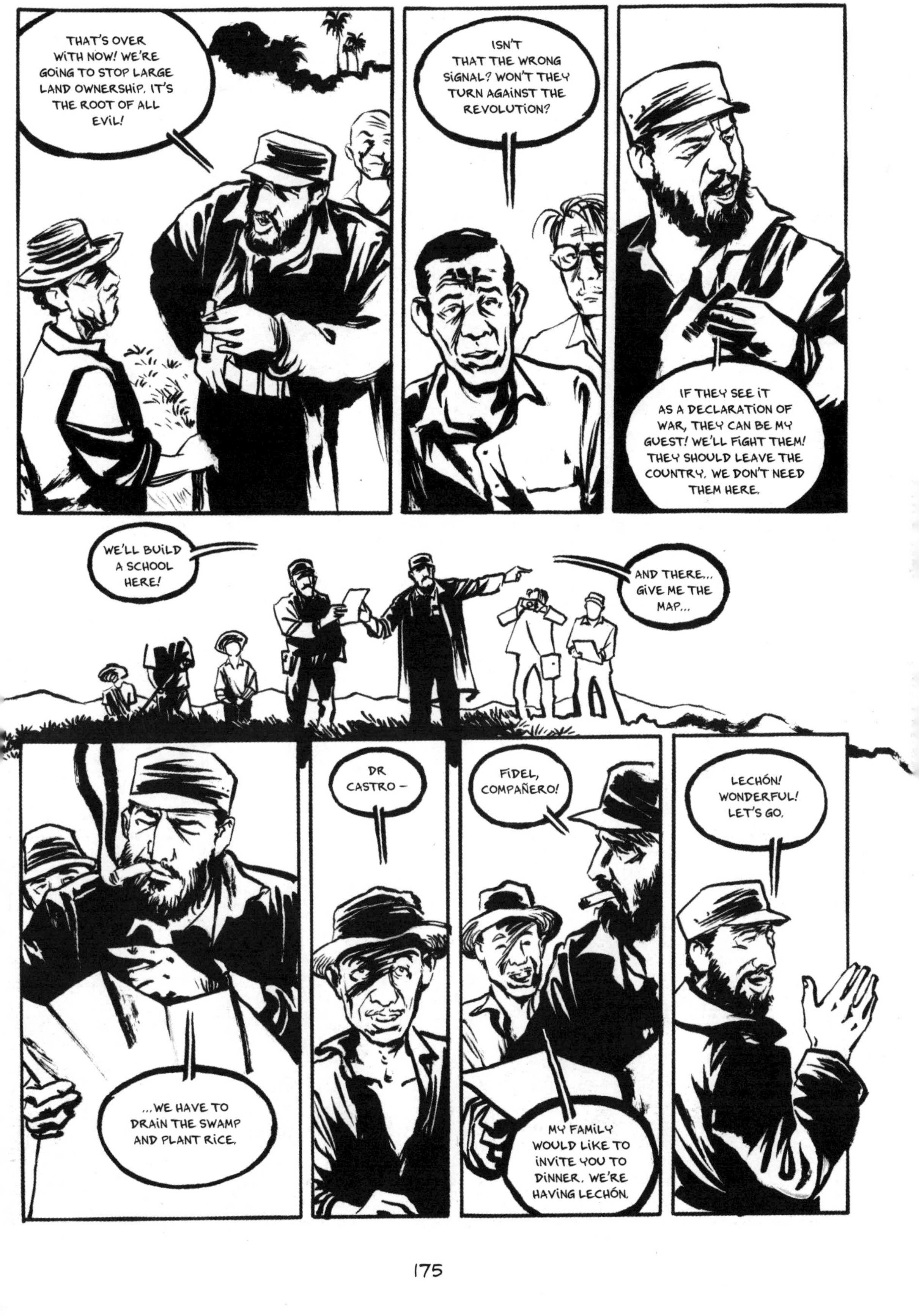

THAT'S OVER WITH NOW! WE'RE GOING TO STOP LARGE LAND OWNERSHIP. IT'S THE ROOT OF ALL EVIL!
ISN'T THAT THE WRONG SIGNAL? WON'T THEY TURN AGAINST THE REVOLUTION?
IF THEY SEE IT AS A DECLARATION OF WAR, THEY CAN BE MY GUEST! WE'LL FIGHT THEM! THEY SHOULD LEAVE THE COUNTRY. WE DON'T NEED THEM HERE.
WE'LL BUILD A SCHOOL HERE!
AND THERE... GIVE ME THE MAP...
...WE HAVE TO DRAIN THE SWAMP AND PLANT RICE.
DR CASTRO –
FIDEL, COMPAÑERO!
MY FAMILY WOULD LIKE TO INVITE YOU TO DINNER. WE'RE HAVING LECHÓN.
LECHÓN! WONDERFUL! LET'S GO.

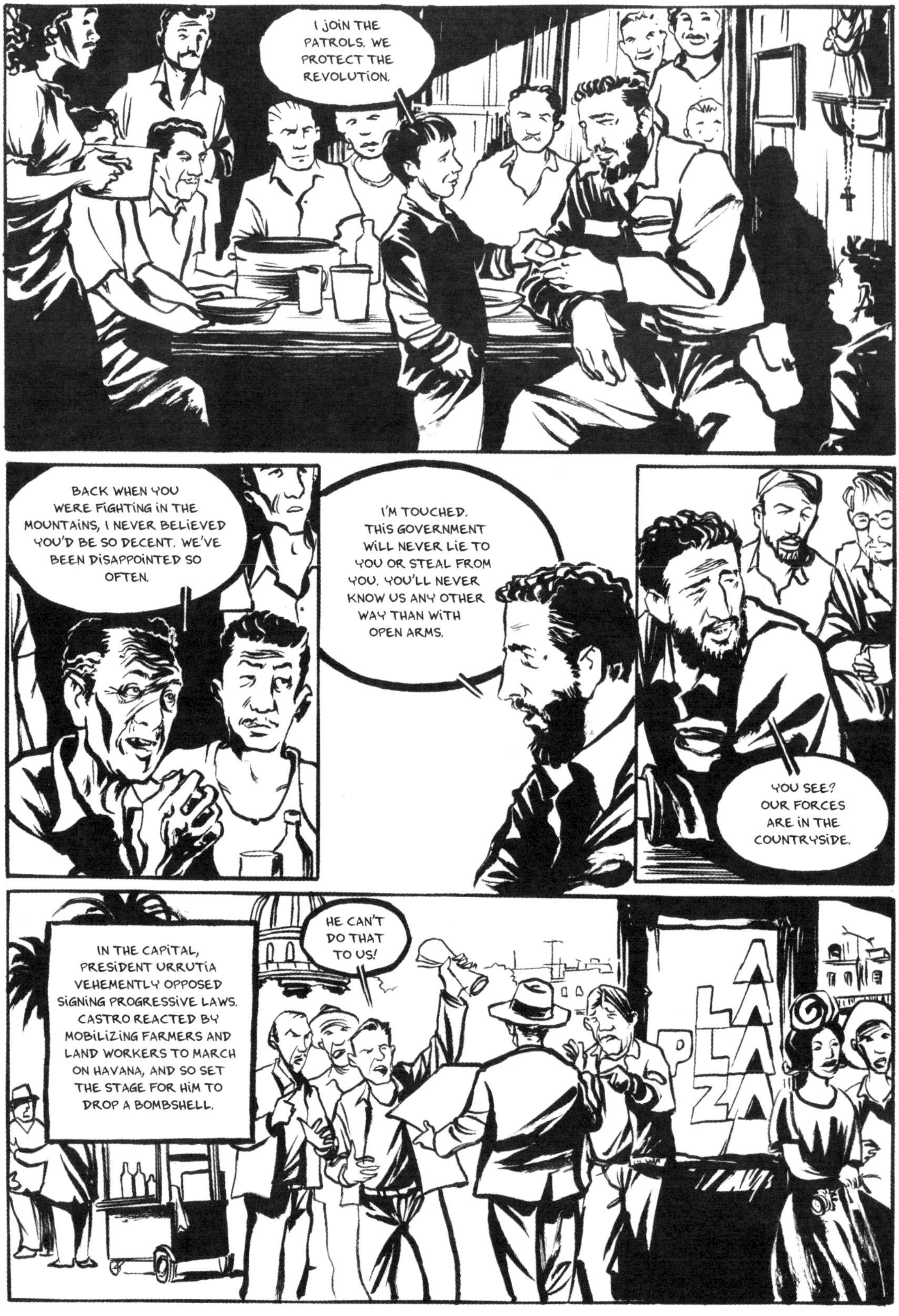

I JOIN THE PATROLS. WE PROTECT THE REVOLUTION.
BACK WHEN YOU WERE FIGHTING IN THE MOUNTAINS, I NEVER BELIEVED YOU'D BE SO DECENT. WE'VE BEEN DISAPPOINTED SO OFTEN.
I'M TOUCHED. THIS GOVERNMENT WILL NEVER LIE TO YOU OR STEAL FROM YOU. YOU'LL NEVER KNOW US ANY OTHER WAY THAN WITH OPEN ARMS.
YOU SEE? OUR FORCES ARE IN THE COUNTRYSIDE.
IN THE CAPITAL, PRESIDENT URRUTIA VEHEMENTLY OPPOSED SIGNING PROGRESSIVE LAWS. CASTRO REACTED BY MOBILIZING FARMERS AND LAND WORKERS TO MARCH ON HAVANA, AND SO SET THE STAGE FOR HIM TO DROP A BOMBSHELL.
HE CAN'T DO THAT TO US!
LA PLAZA

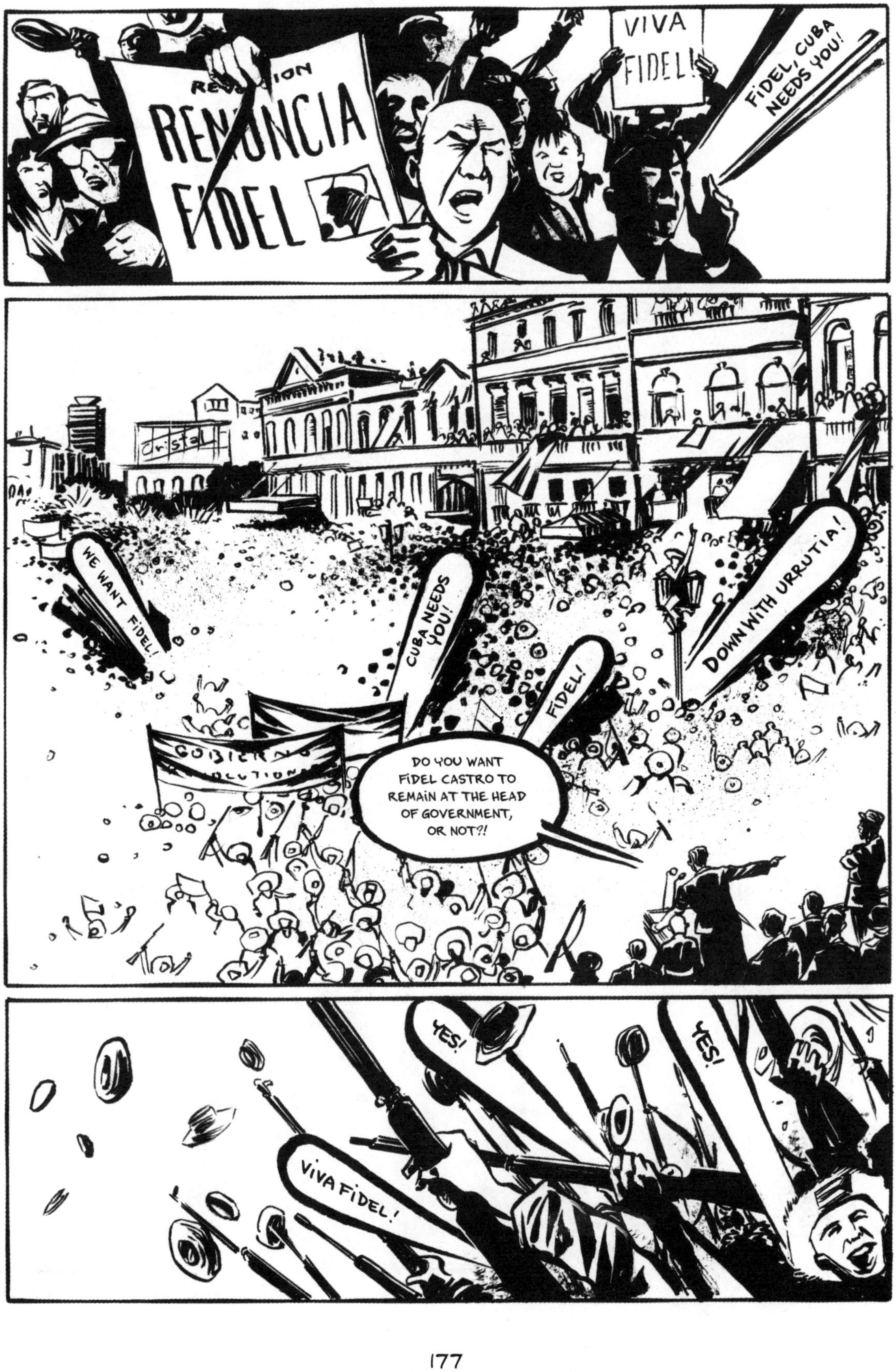
RENUNCIA FIDEL
VIVA FIDEL!
FIDEL, CUBA NEEDS YOU!
WE WANT FIDEL!
CUBA NEEDS YOU!
FIDEL!
DOWN WITH URRUTIA!
DO YOU WANT FIDEL CASTRO TO REMAIN AT THE HEAD OF GOVERNMENT, OR NOT?!
YES!
YES!
VIVA FIDEL!

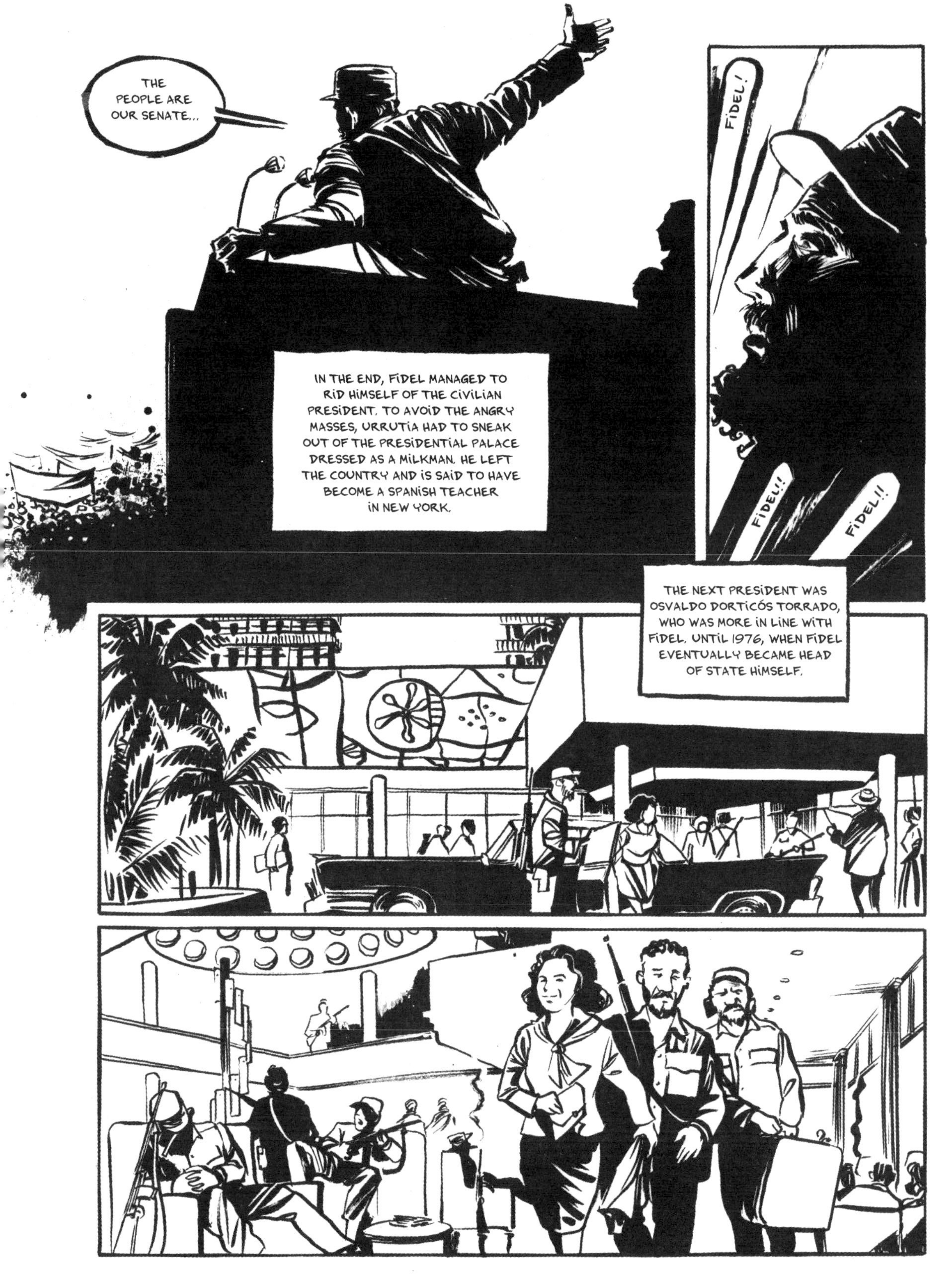
THE PEOPLE ARE OUR SENATE...
FIDEL!
IN THE END, FIDEL MANAGED TO RID HIMSELF OF THE CIVILIAN PRESIDENT. TO AVOID THE ANGRY MASSES, URRUTIA HAD TO SNEAK OUT OF THE PRESIDENTIAL PALACE DRESSED AS A MILKMAN. HE LEFT THE COUNTRY AND IS SAID TO HAVE BECOME A SPANISH TEACHER IN NEW YORK.
FIDEL!!
FIDEL!!
THE NEXT PRESIDENT WAS OSVALDO DORTICÓS TORRADO, WHO WAS MORE IN LINE WITH FIDEL, UNTIL 1976, WHEN FIDEL EVENTUALLY BECAME HEAD OF STATE HIMSELF.

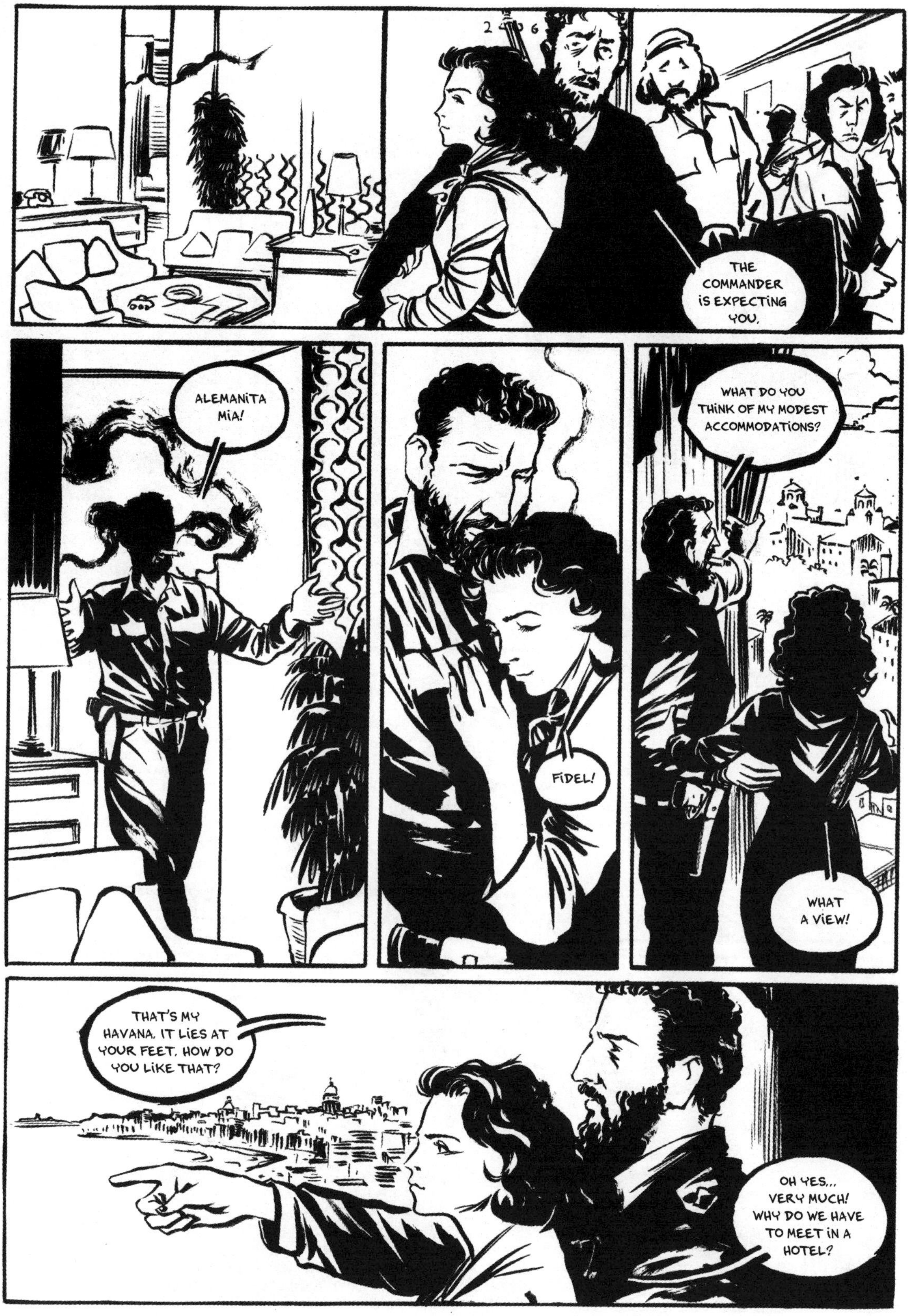
THE COMMANDER IS EXPECTING YOU.
ALEMANITA MIA!
FIDEL!
WHAT DO YOU THINK OF MY MODEST ACCOMMODATIONS?
WHAT A VIEW!
THAT'S MY HAVANA. IT LIES AT YOUR FEET. HOW DO YOU LIKE THAT?
OH YES... VERY MUCH! WHY DO WE HAVE TO MEET IN A HOTEL?

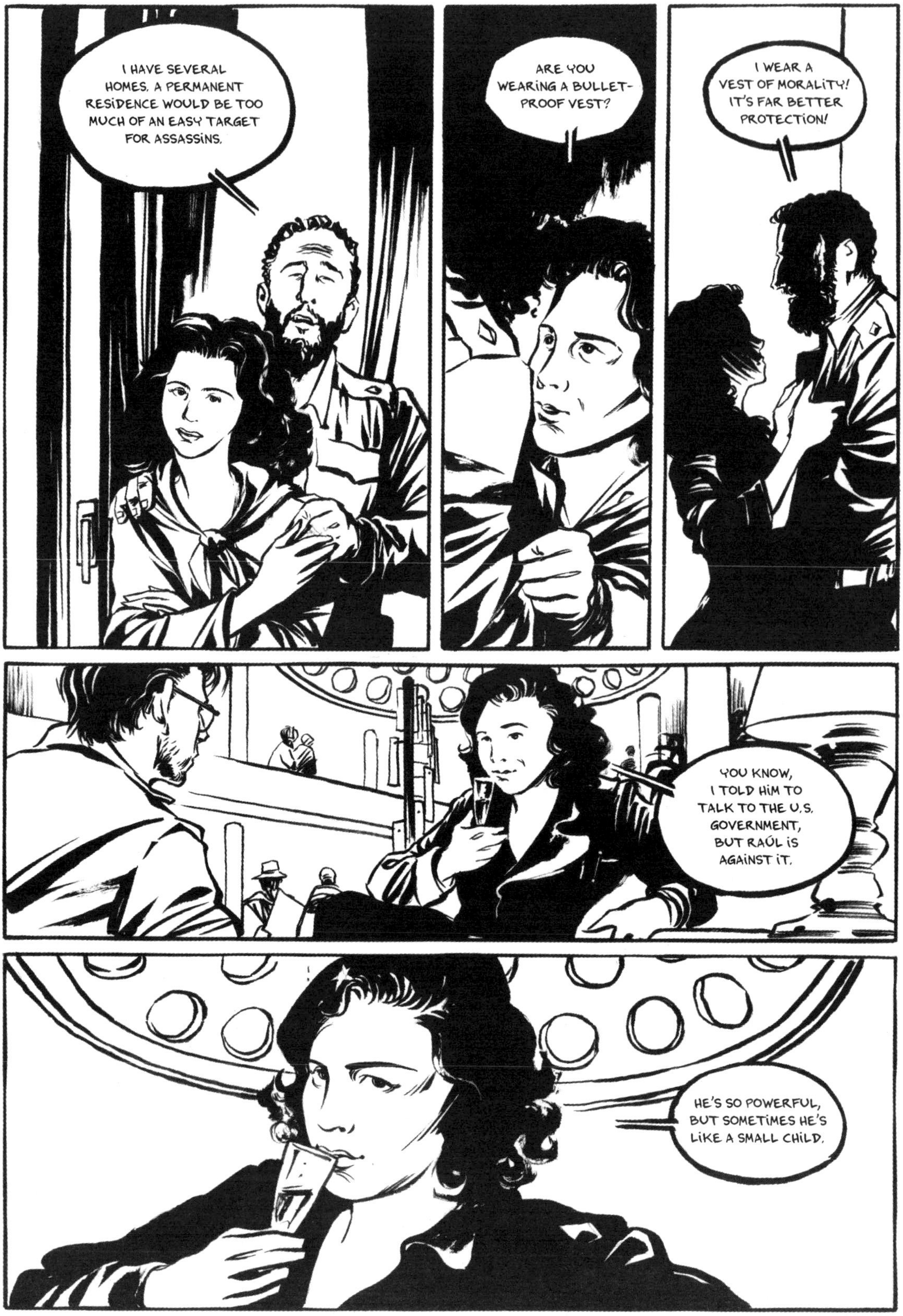
I HAVE SEVERAL HOMES. A PERMANENT RESIDENCE WOULD BE TOO MUCH OF AN EASY TARGET FOR ASSASSINS.
ARE YOU WEARING A BULLET-PROOF VEST?
I WEAR A VEST OF MORALITY! IT'S FAR BETTER PROTECTION!
YOU KNOW, I TOLD HIM TO TALK TO THE U.S. GOVERNMENT, BUT RAÚL IS AGAINST IT.
HE'S SO POWERFUL, BUT SOMETIMES HE'S LIKE A SMALL CHILD.

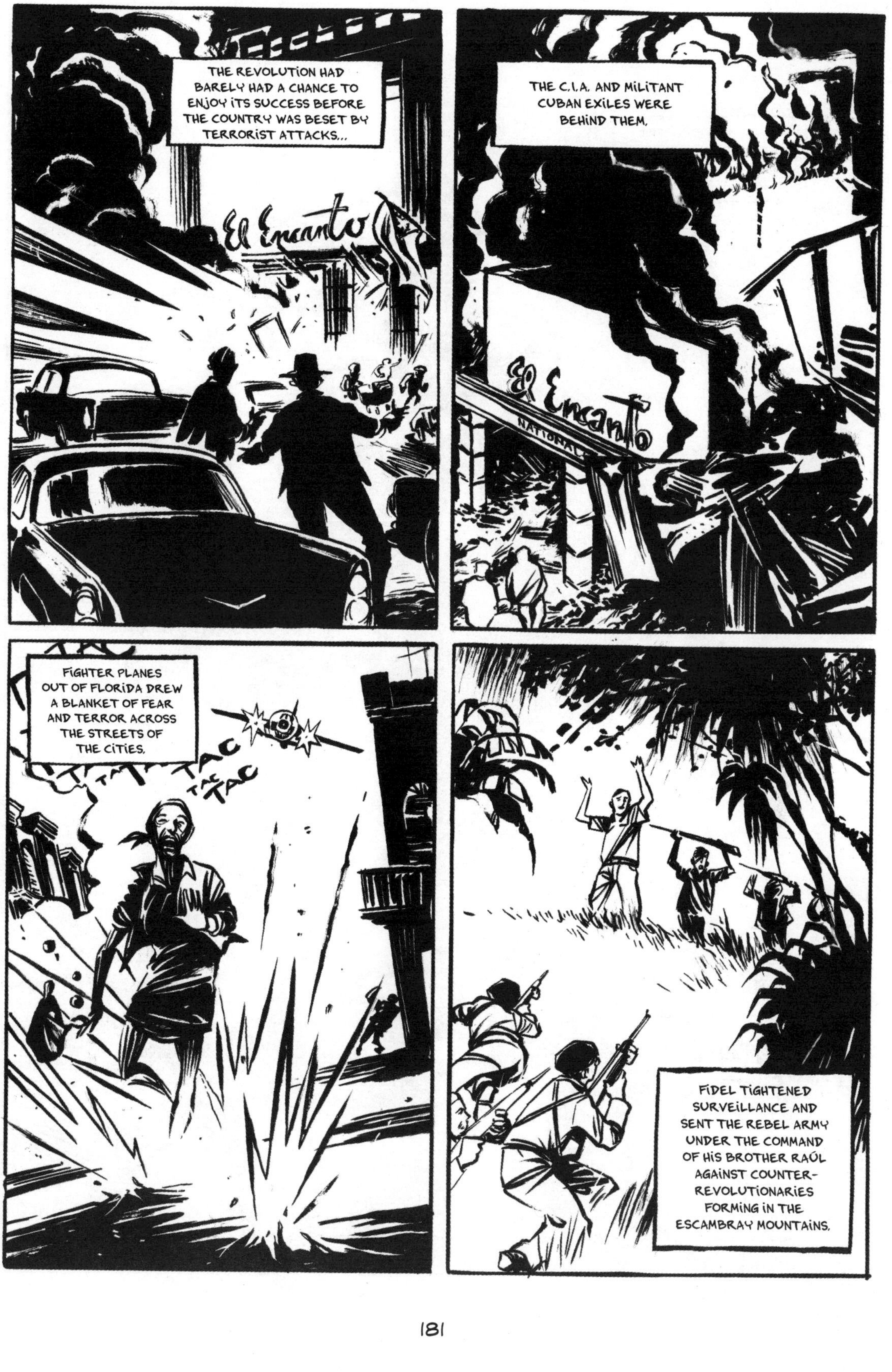
THE REVOLUTION HAD BARELY HAD A CHANCE TO ENJOY ITS SUCCESS BEFORE THE COUNTRY WAS BESET BY TERRORIST ATTACKS...
El Encanto
THE C.I.A. AND MILITANT CUBAN EXILES WERE BEHIND THEM.
El Encanto
NATIONAL
FIGHTER PLANES OUT OF FLORIDA DREW A BLANKET OF FEAR AND TERROR ACROSS THE STREETS OF THE CITIES.
TAC
TAC
FIDEL TIGHTENED SURVEILLANCE AND SENT THE REBEL ARMY UNDER THE COMMAND OF HIS BROTHER RAÚL AGAINST COUNTER-REVOLUTIONARIES FORMING IN THE ESCAMBRAY MOUNTAINS.

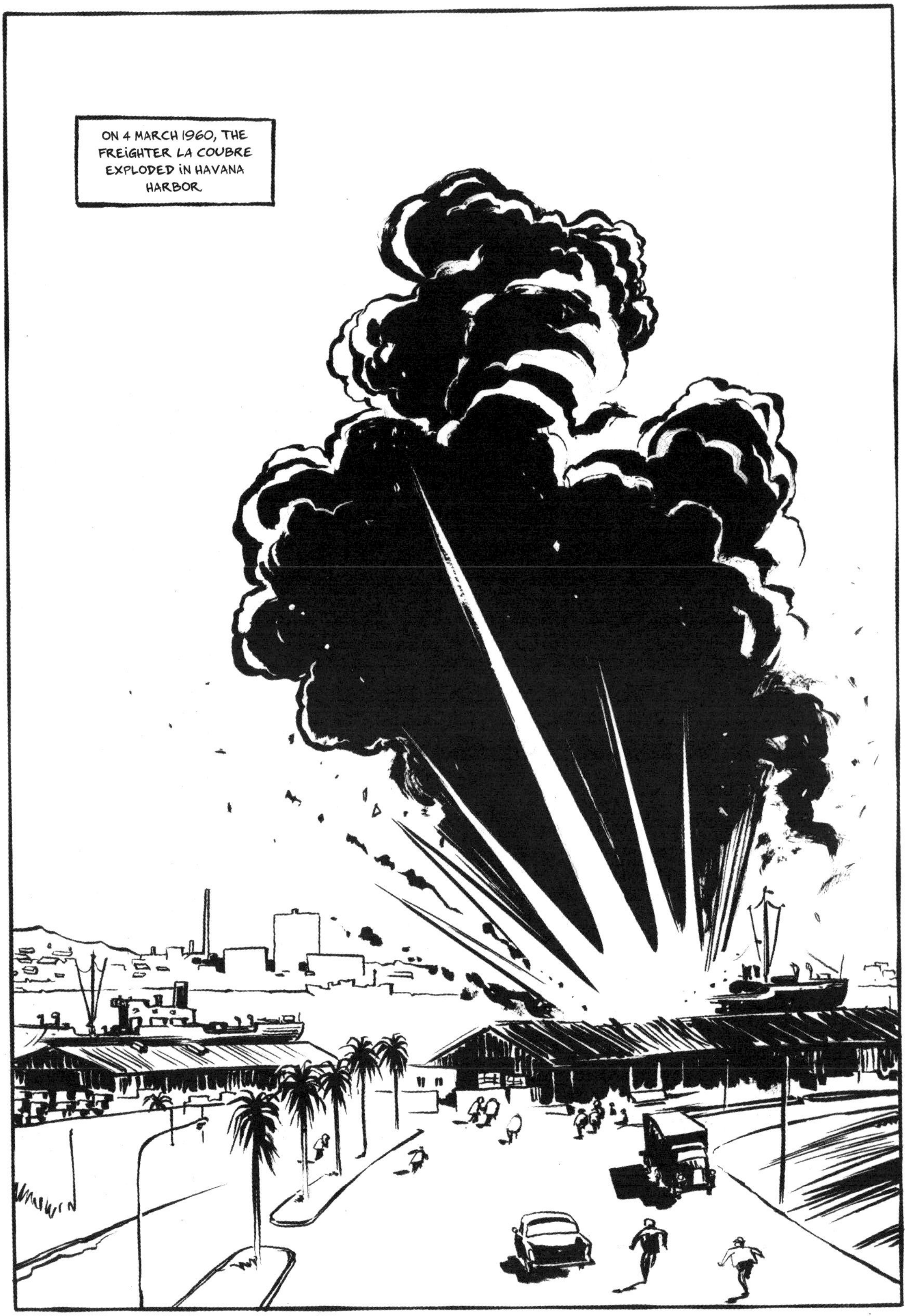
ON 4 MARCH 1960, THE FREIGHTER LA COUBRE EXPLODED IN HAVANA HARBOR

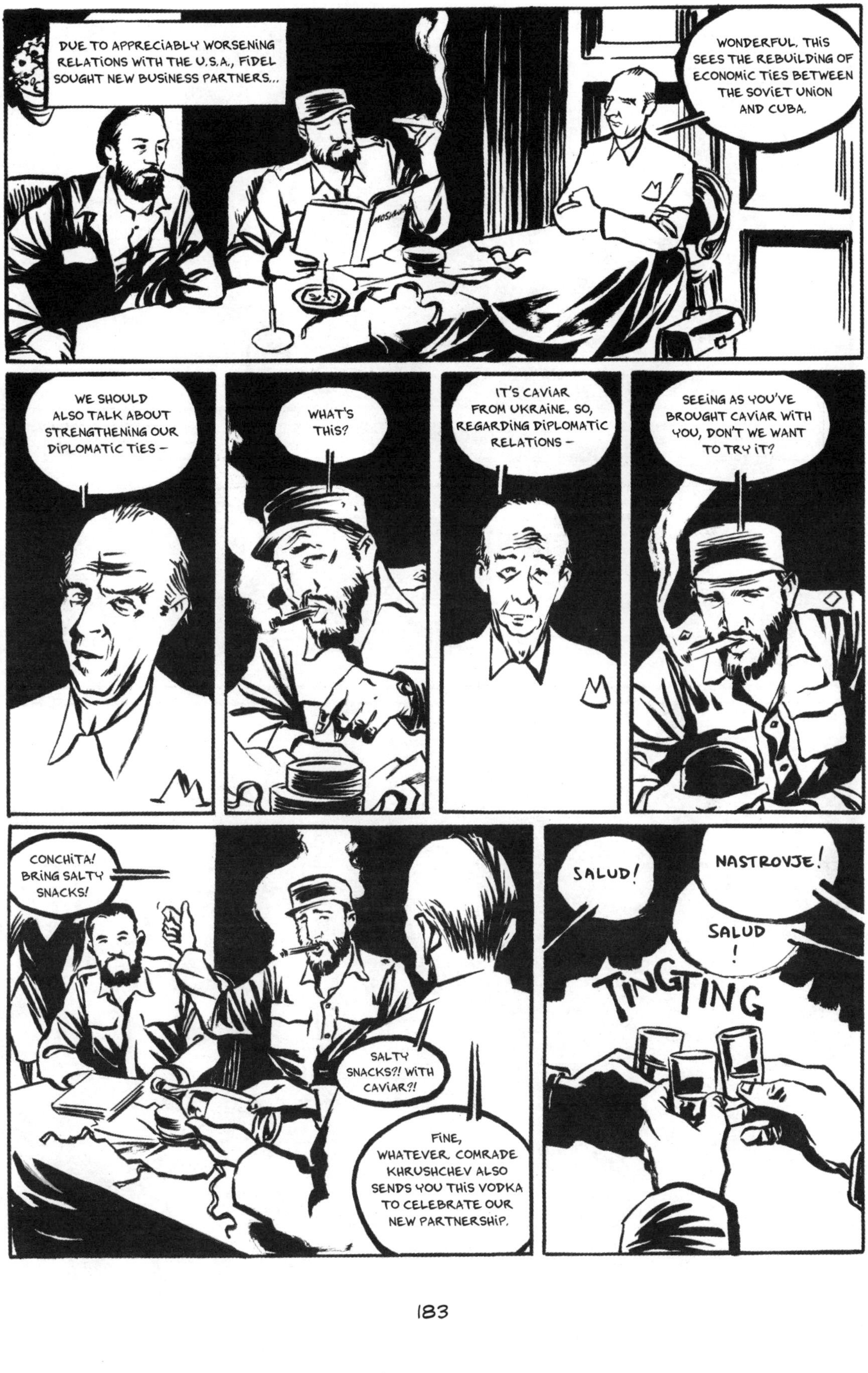
DUE TO APPRECIABLY WORSENING RELATIONS WITH THE U.S.A., FIDEL SOUGHT NEW BUSINESS PARTNERS...
WONDERFUL. THIS SEES THE REBUILDING OF ECONOMIC TIES BETWEEN THE SOVIET UNION AND CUBA.
WE SHOULD ALSO TALK ABOUT STRENGTHENING OUR DIPLOMATIC TIES –
WHAT'S THIS?
IT'S CAVIAR FROM UKRAINE. SO, REGARDING DIPLOMATIC RELATIONS –
SEEING AS YOU'VE BROUGHT CAVIAR WITH YOU, DON'T WE WANT TO TRY IT?
CONCHITA! BRING SALTY SNACKS!
SALTY SNACKS?! WITH CAVIAR?!
FINE, WHATEVER. COMRADE KHRUSHCHEV ALSO SENDS YOU THIS VODKA TO CELEBRATE OUR NEW PARTNERSHIP.
SALUD!
NASTROVJE!
SALUD!
TING TING

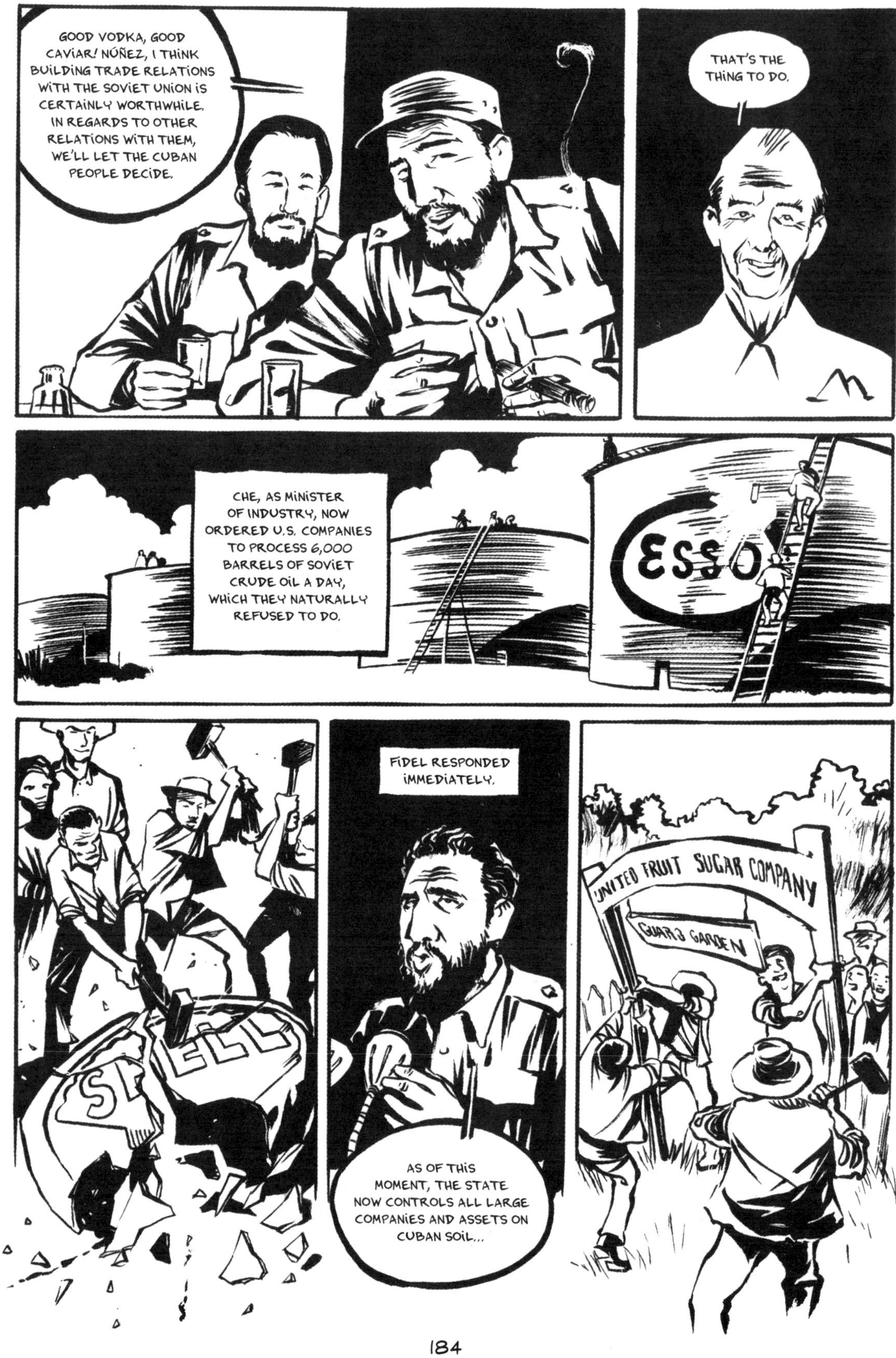
GOOD VODKA, GOOD CAVIAR! NÚÑEZ, I THINK BUILDING TRADE RELATIONS WITH THE SOVIET UNION IS CERTAINLY WORTHWHILE. IN REGARDS TO OTHER RELATIONS WITH THEM, WE'LL LET THE CUBAN PEOPLE DECIDE.
THAT'S THE THING TO DO.
CHE, AS MINISTER OF INDUSTRY, NOW ORDERED U.S. COMPANIES TO PROCESS 6,000 BARRELS OF SOVIET CRUDE OIL A DAY, WHICH THEY NATURALLY REFUSED TO DO.
ESSO
SHELL
FIDEL RESPONDED IMMEDIATELY.
AS OF THIS MOMENT, THE STATE NOW CONTROLS ALL LARGE COMPANIES AND ASSETS ON CUBAN SOIL...
UNITED FRUIT SUGAR COMPANY
GUARD GARDEN

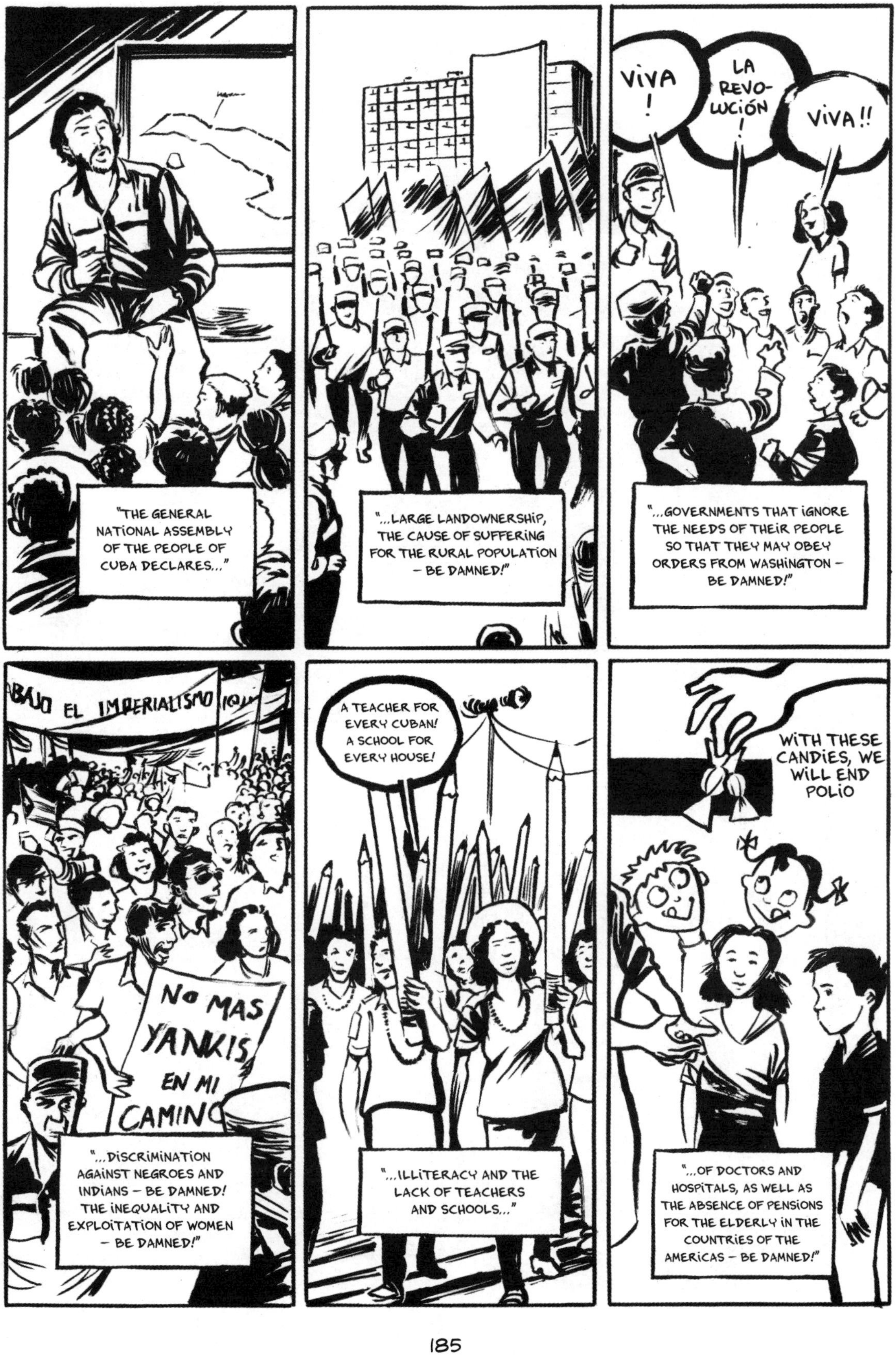

"THE GENERAL NATIONAL ASSEMBLY OF THE PEOPLE OF CUBA DECLARES..."
"...LARGE LANDOWNERSHIP, THE CAUSE OF SUFFERING FOR THE RURAL POPULATION – BE DAMNED!"
VIVA!
LA REVOLUCIÓN!
VIVA!!
"...GOVERNMENTS THAT IGNORE THE NEEDS OF THEIR PEOPLE SO THAT THEY MAY OBEY ORDERS FROM WASHINGTON – BE DAMNED!"
ABAJO EL IMPERIALISMO
NO MAS YANKIS EN MI CAMIN
"...DISCRIMINATION AGAINST NEGROES AND INDIANS – BE DAMNED! THE INEQUALITY AND EXPLOITATION OF WOMEN – BE DAMNED!"
A TEACHER FOR EVERY CUBAN! A SCHOOL FOR EVERY HOUSE!
"...ILLITERACY AND THE LACK OF TEACHERS AND SCHOOLS..."
WITH THESE CANDIES, WE WILL END POLIO
"...OF DOCTORS AND HOSPITALS, AS WELL AS THE ABSENCE OF PENSIONS FOR THE ELDERLY IN THE COUNTRIES OF THE AMERICAS – BE DAMNED!"

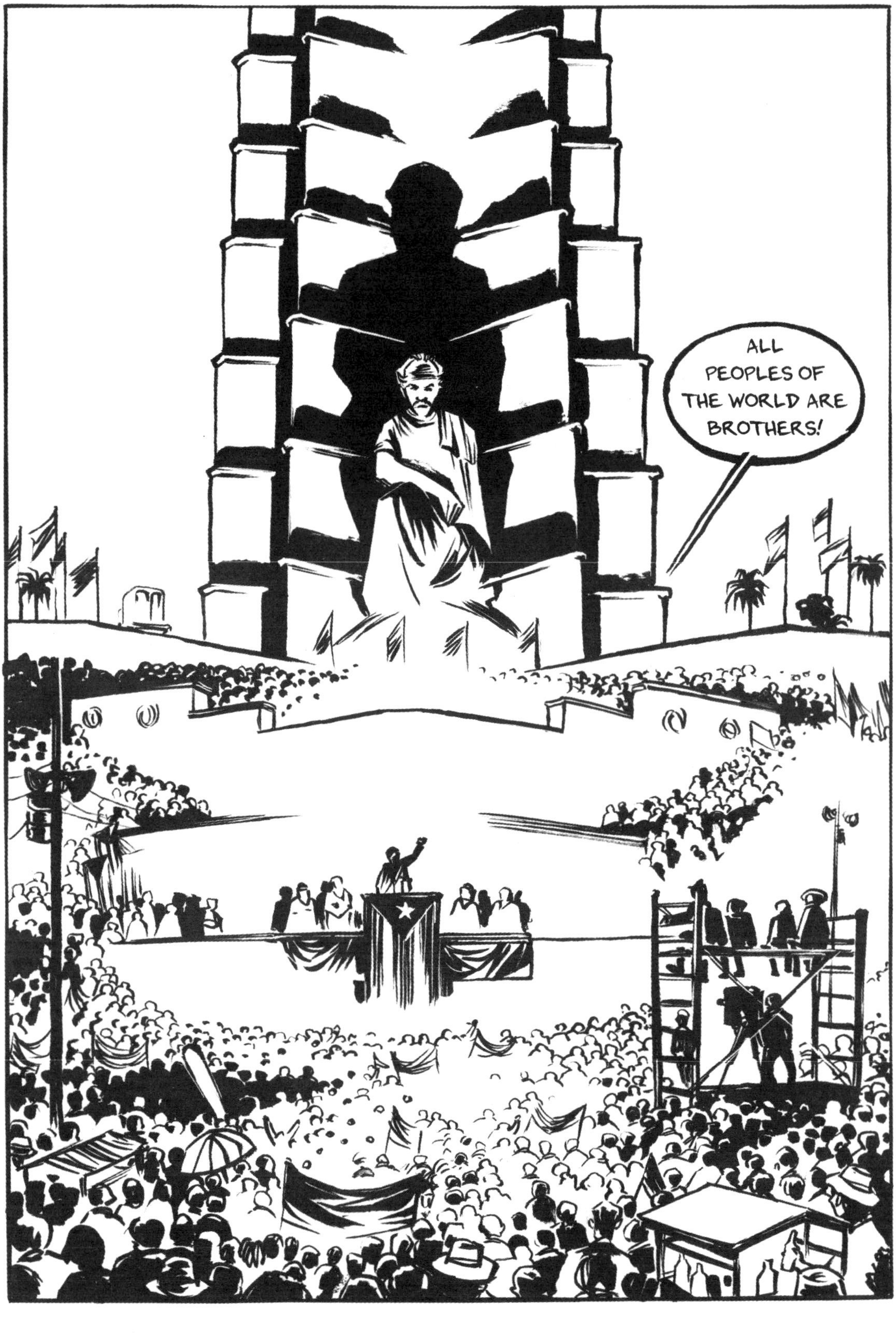
ALL PEOPLES OF THE WORLD ARE BROTHERS!

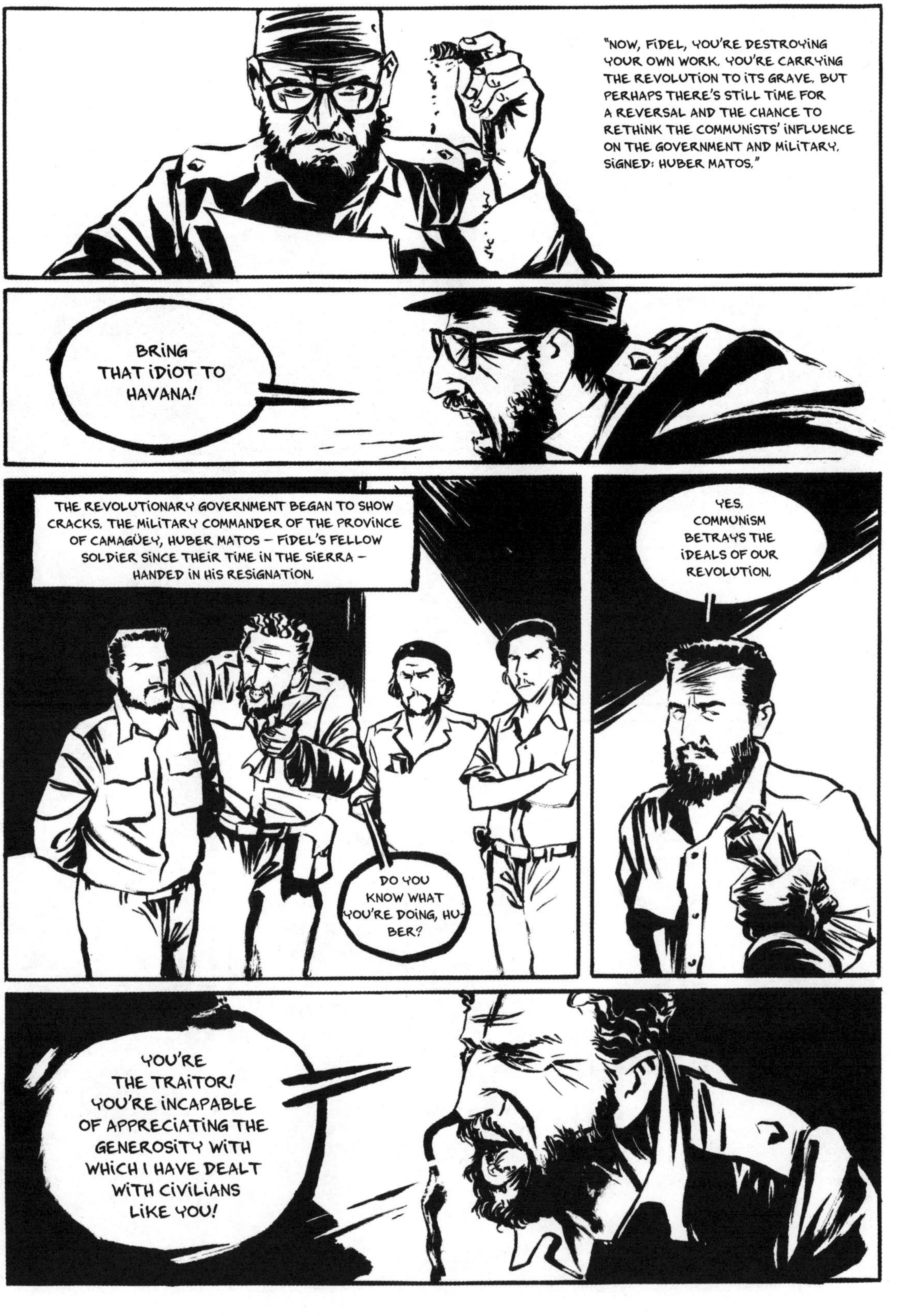
"NOW, FIDEL, YOU'RE DESTROYING YOUR OWN WORK. YOU'RE CARRYING THE REVOLUTION TO ITS GRAVE. BUT PERHAPS THERE'S STILL TIME FOR A REVERSAL AND THE CHANCE TO RETHINK THE COMMUNISTS' INFLUENCE ON THE GOVERNMENT AND MILITARY. SIGNED: HUBER MATOS."
BRING THAT IDIOT TO HAVANA!
THE REVOLUTIONARY GOVERNMENT BEGAN TO SHOW CRACKS. THE MILITARY COMMANDER OF THE PROVINCE OF CAMAGÜEY, HUBER MATOS – FIDEL'S FELLOW SOLDIER SINCE THEIR TIME IN THE SIERRA – HANDED IN HIS RESIGNATION.
DO YOU KNOW WHAT YOU'RE DOING, HUBER?
YES. COMMUNISM BETRAYS THE IDEALS OF OUR REVOLUTION.
YOU'RE THE TRAITOR! YOU'RE INCAPABLE OF APPRECIATING THE GENEROSITY WITH WHICH I HAVE DEALT WITH CIVILIANS LIKE YOU!

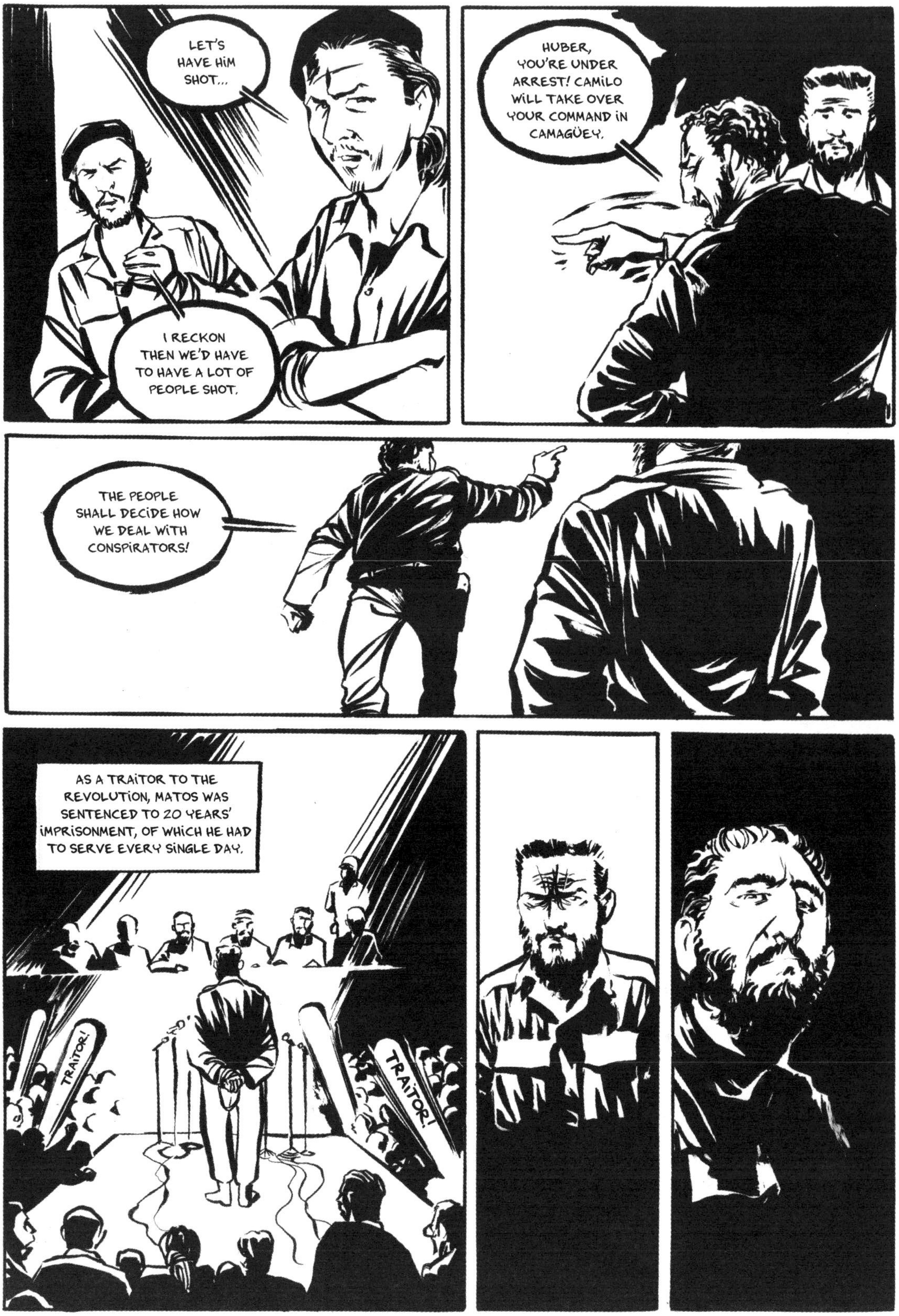
LET'S HAVE HIM SHOT...
I RECKON THEN WE'D HAVE TO HAVE A LOT OF PEOPLE SHOT.
HUBER, YOU'RE UNDER ARREST! CAMILO WILL TAKE OVER YOUR COMMAND IN CAMAGÜEY.
THE PEOPLE SHALL DECIDE HOW WE DEAL WITH CONSPIRATORS!
AS A TRAITOR TO THE REVOLUTION, MATOS WAS SENTENCED TO 20 YEARS' IMPRISONMENT, OF WHICH HE HAD TO SERVE EVERY SINGLE DAY.
TRAITOR!
TRAITOR!

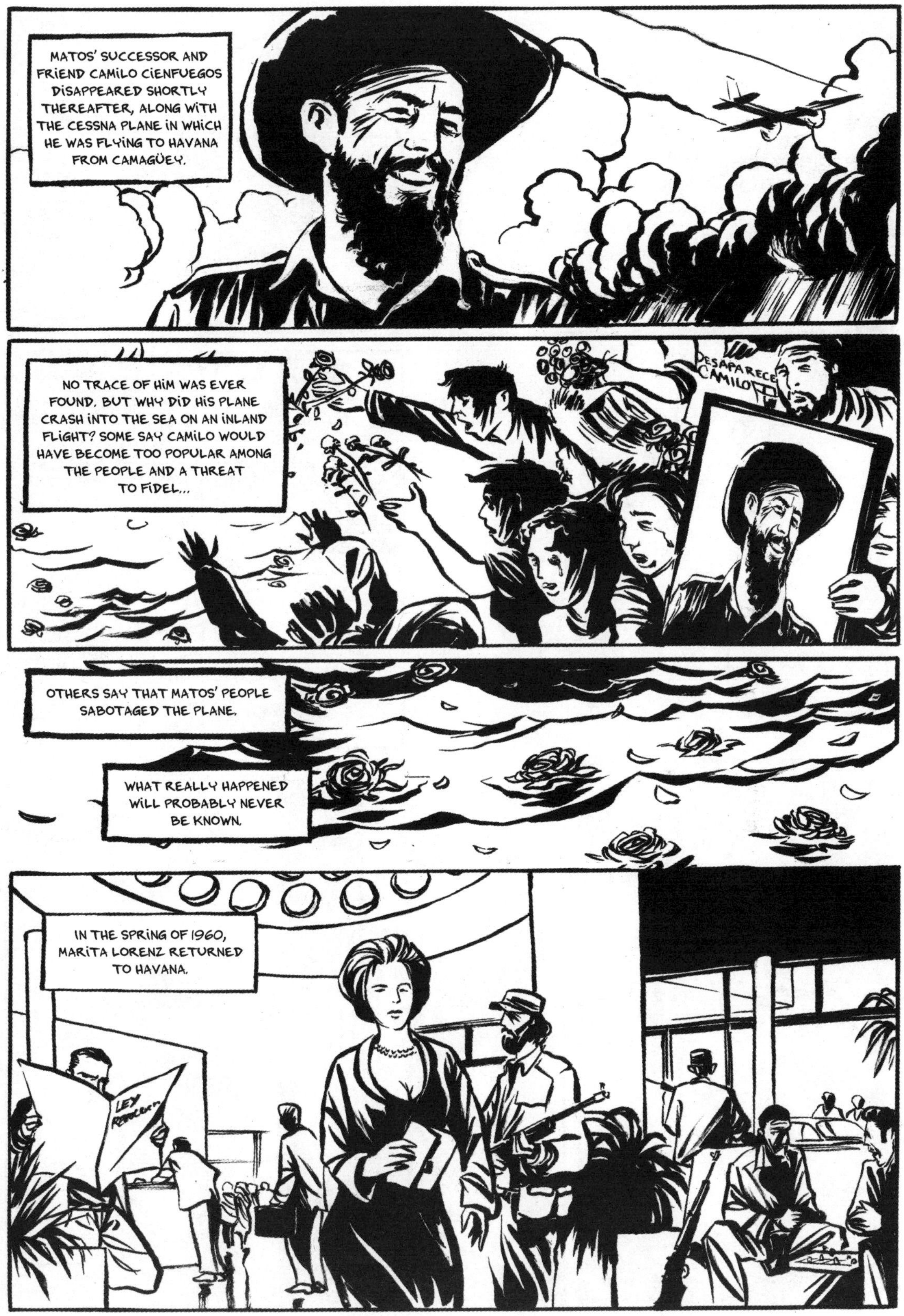

MATOS' SUCCESSOR AND FRIEND CAMILO CIENFUEGOS DISAPPEARED SHORTLY THEREAFTER, ALONG WITH THE CESSNA PLANE IN WHICH HE WAS FLYING TO HAVANA FROM CAMAGÜEY.
NO TRACE OF HIM WAS EVER FOUND, BUT WHY DID HIS PLANE CRASH INTO THE SEA ON AN INLAND FLIGHT? SOME SAY CAMILO WOULD HAVE BECOME TOO POPULAR AMONG THE PEOPLE AND A THREAT TO FIDEL...
DESAPARECE CAMILO
OTHERS SAY THAT MATOS' PEOPLE SABOTAGED THE PLANE.
WHAT REALLY HAPPENED WILL PROBABLY NEVER BE KNOWN.
IN THE SPRING OF 1960, MARITA LORENZ RETURNED TO HAVANA.
LEY

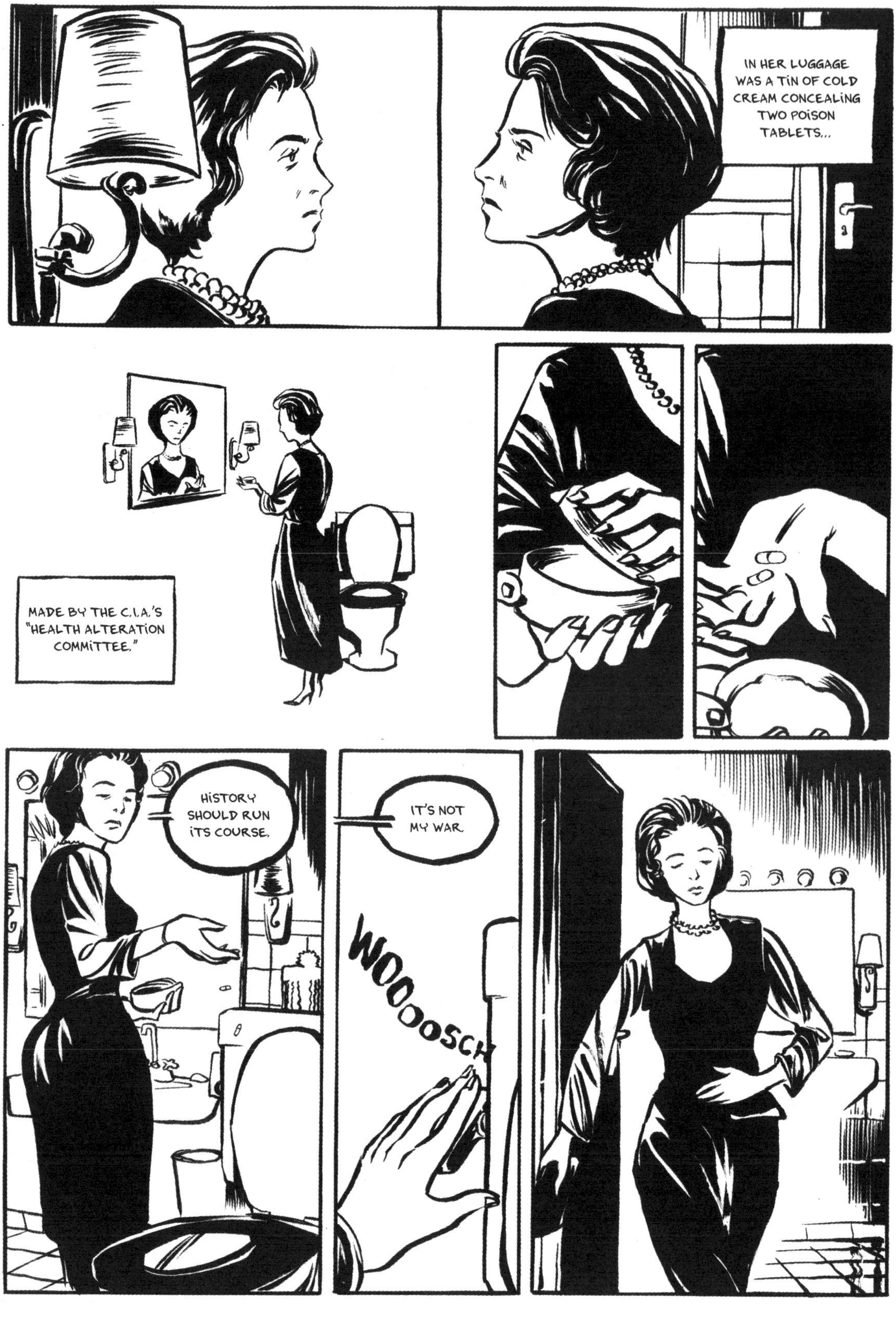
IN HER LUGGAGE WAS A TIN OF COLD CREAM CONCEALING TWO POISON TABLETS...
MADE BY THE C.I.A.'S "HEALTH ALTERATION COMMITTEE."
HISTORY SHOULD RUN ITS COURSE.
IT'S NOT MY WAR.
WOOOOOSCH

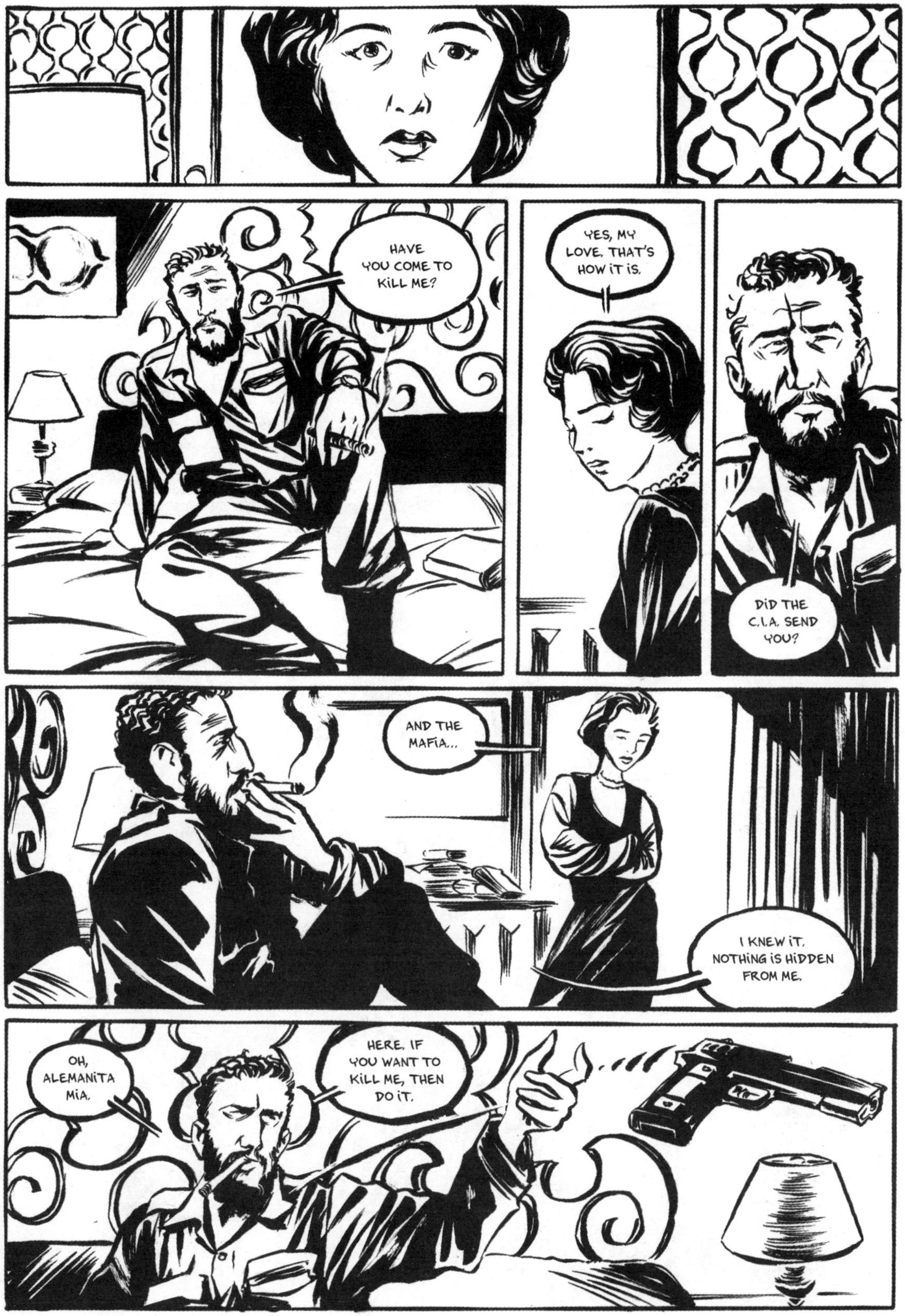
HAVE YOU COME TO KILL ME?
YES, MY LOVE. THAT'S HOW IT IS.
DID THE C.I.A. SEND YOU?
AND THE MAFIA...
I KNEW IT. NOTHING IS HIDDEN FROM ME.
OH, ALEMANITA MIA.
HERE. IF YOU WANT TO KILL ME, THEN DO IT.

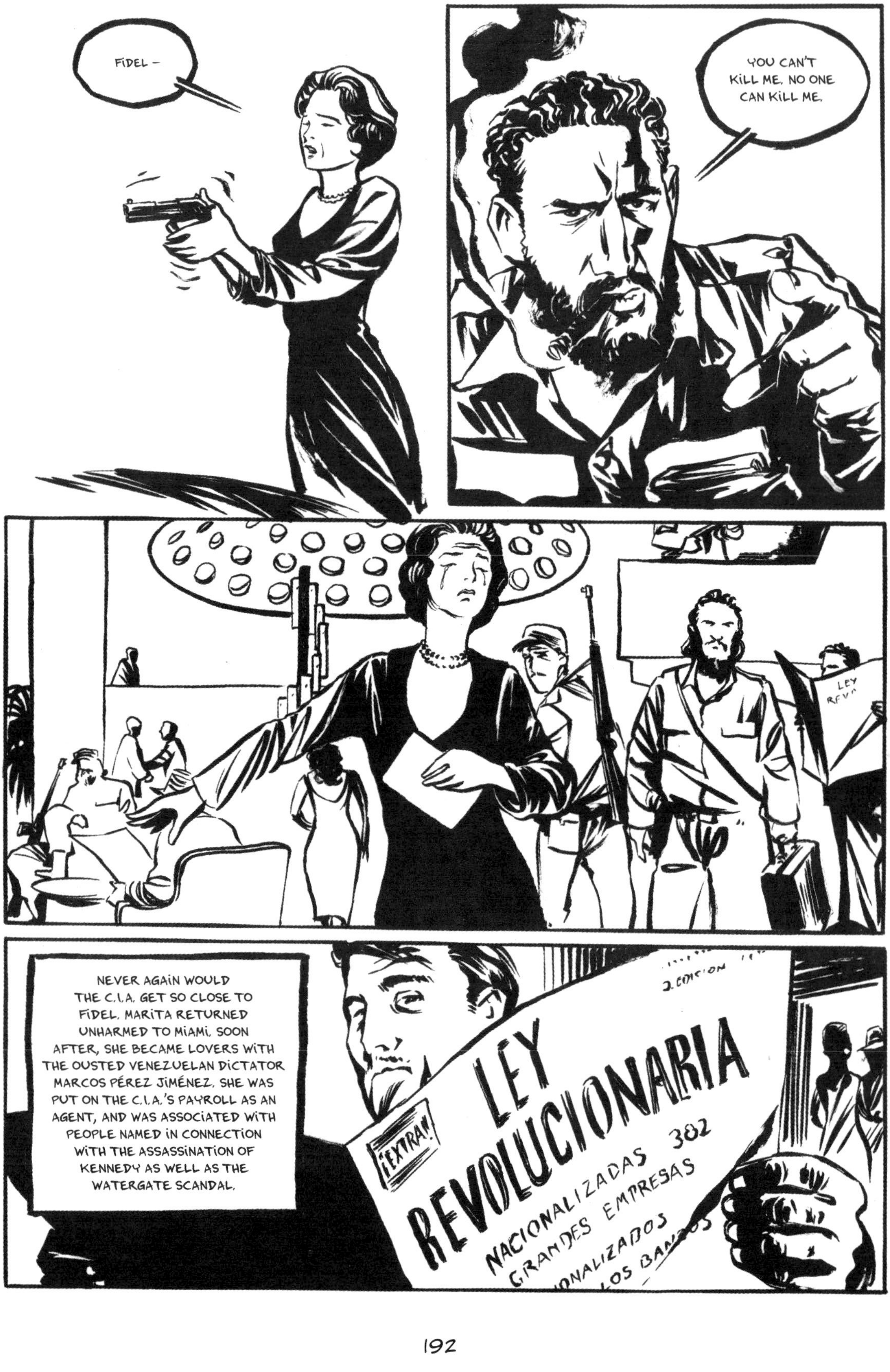
FIDEL –
YOU CAN'T KILL ME. NO ONE CAN KILL ME.
LEY REVO
NEVER AGAIN WOULD THE C.I.A. GET SO CLOSE TO FIDEL. MARITA RETURNED UNHARMED TO MIAMI. SOON AFTER, SHE BECAME LOVERS WITH THE OUSTED VENEZUELAN DICTATOR MARCOS PÉREZ JIMÉNEZ. SHE WAS PUT ON THE C.I.A.'S PAYROLL AS AN AGENT, AND WAS ASSOCIATED WITH PEOPLE NAMED IN CONNECTION WITH THE ASSASSINATION OF KENNEDY AS WELL AS THE WATERGATE SCANDAL.
2. EDICION
¡EXTRA!
LEY REVOLUCIONARIA
382
NACIONALIZADAS
GRANDES EMPRESAS
ONALIZADOS
LOS BAN

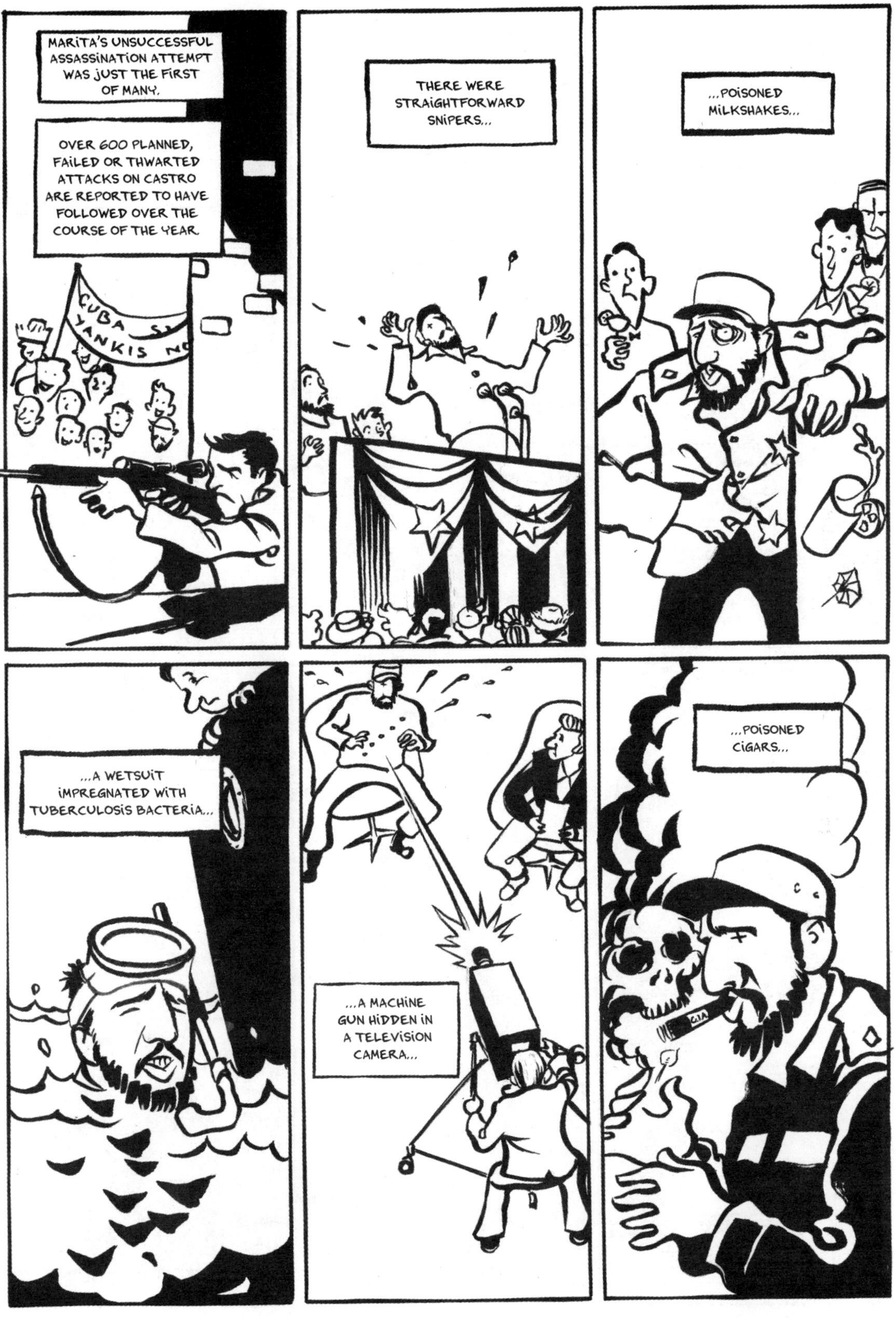
MARITA'S UNSUCCESSFUL ASSASSINATION ATTEMPT WAS JUST THE FIRST OF MANY.
OVER 600 PLANNED, FAILED OR THWARTED ATTACKS ON CASTRO ARE REPORTED TO HAVE FOLLOWED OVER THE COURSE OF THE YEAR.
CUBA
YANKIS
THERE WERE STRAIGHTFORWARD SNIPERS...
...POISONED MILKSHAKES...
...A WETSUIT IMPREGNATED WITH TUBERCULOSIS BACTERIA...
...A MACHINE GUN HIDDEN IN A TELEVISION CAMERA...
...POISONED CIGARS...
CIA

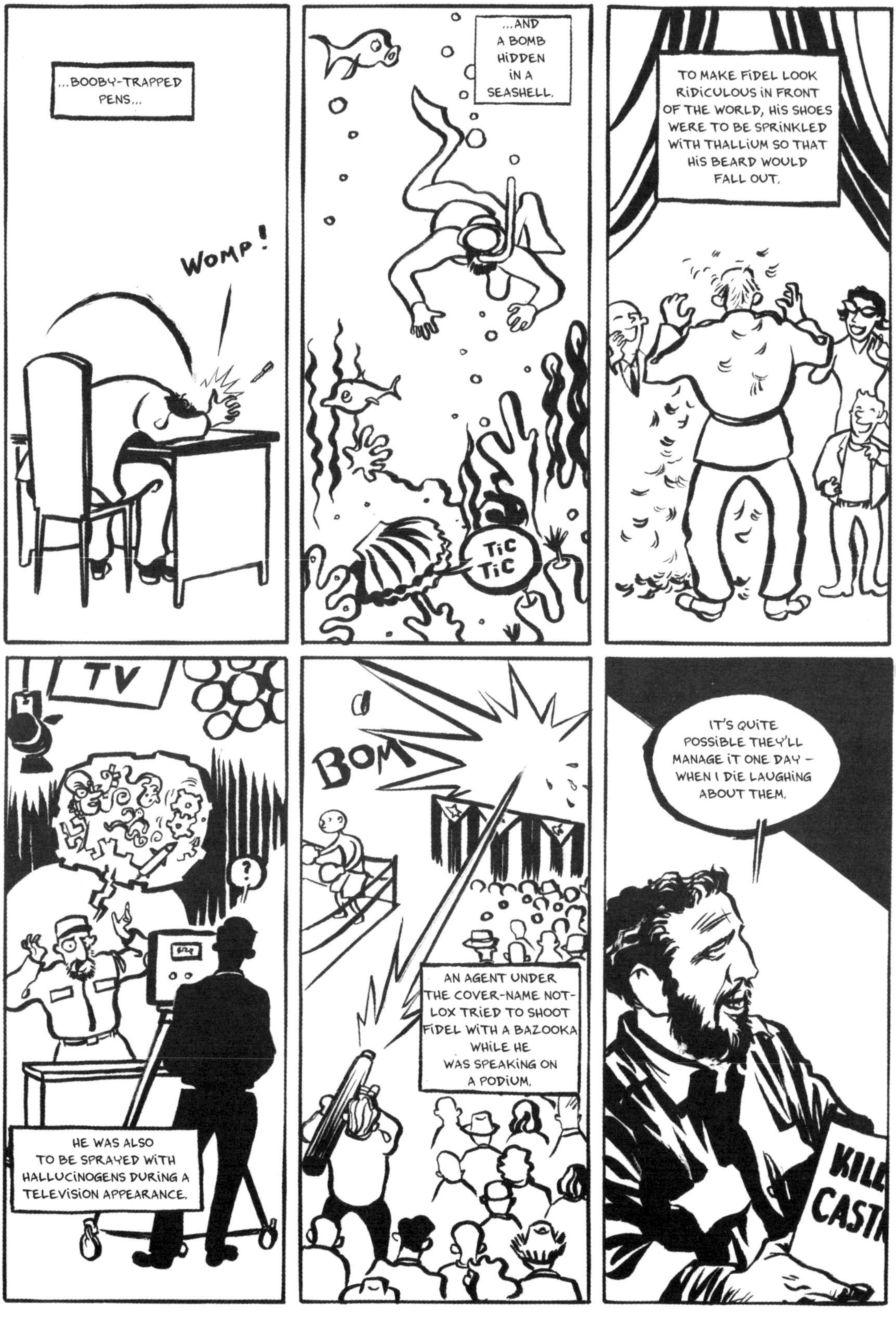
...BOOBY-TRAPPED PENS...
WOMP!
...AND A BOMB HIDDEN IN A SEASHELL.
TIC TIC
TO MAKE FIDEL LOOK RIDICULOUS IN FRONT OF THE WORLD, HIS SHOES WERE TO BE SPRINKLED WITH THALLIUM SO THAT HIS BEARD WOULD FALL OUT.
TV
?
HE WAS ALSO TO BE SPRAYED WITH HALLUCINOGENS DURING A TELEVISION APPEARANCE.
BOM
AN AGENT UNDER THE COVER-NAME NOT-LOX TRIED TO SHOOT FIDEL WITH A BAZOOKA WHILE HE WAS SPEAKING ON A PODIUM.
IT'S QUITE POSSIBLE THEY'LL MANAGE IT ONE DAY – WHEN I DIE LAUGHING ABOUT THEM.

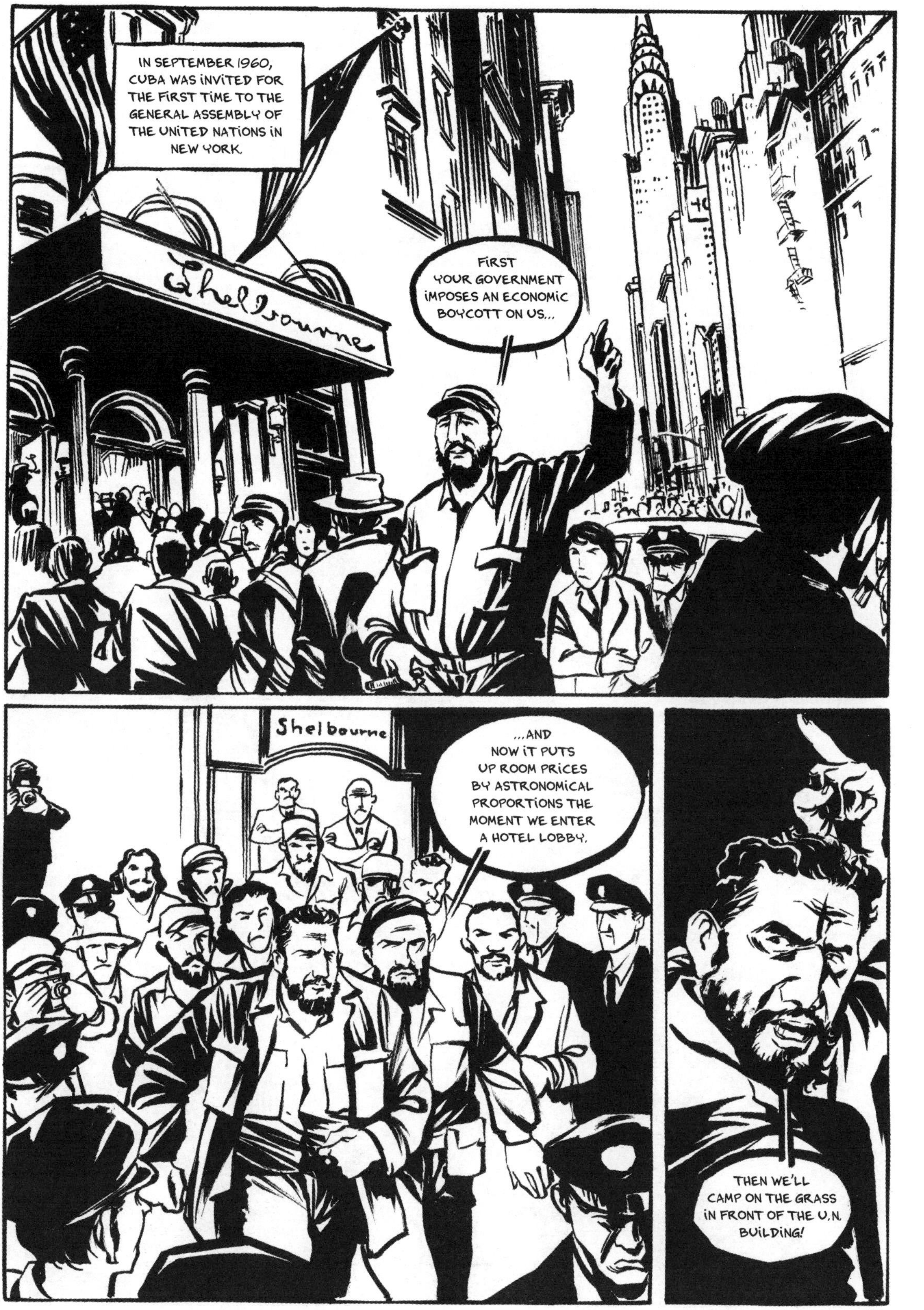
IN SEPTEMBER 1960, CUBA WAS INVITED FOR THE FIRST TIME TO THE GENERAL ASSEMBLY OF THE UNITED NATIONS IN NEW YORK.
Shelbourne
FIRST YOUR GOVERNMENT IMPOSES AN ECONOMIC BOYCOTT ON US...
Shelbourne
...AND NOW IT PUTS UP ROOM PRICES BY ASTRONOMICAL PROPORTIONS THE MOMENT WE ENTER A HOTEL LOBBY.
THEN WE'LL CAMP ON THE GRASS IN FRONT OF THE U.N. BUILDING!

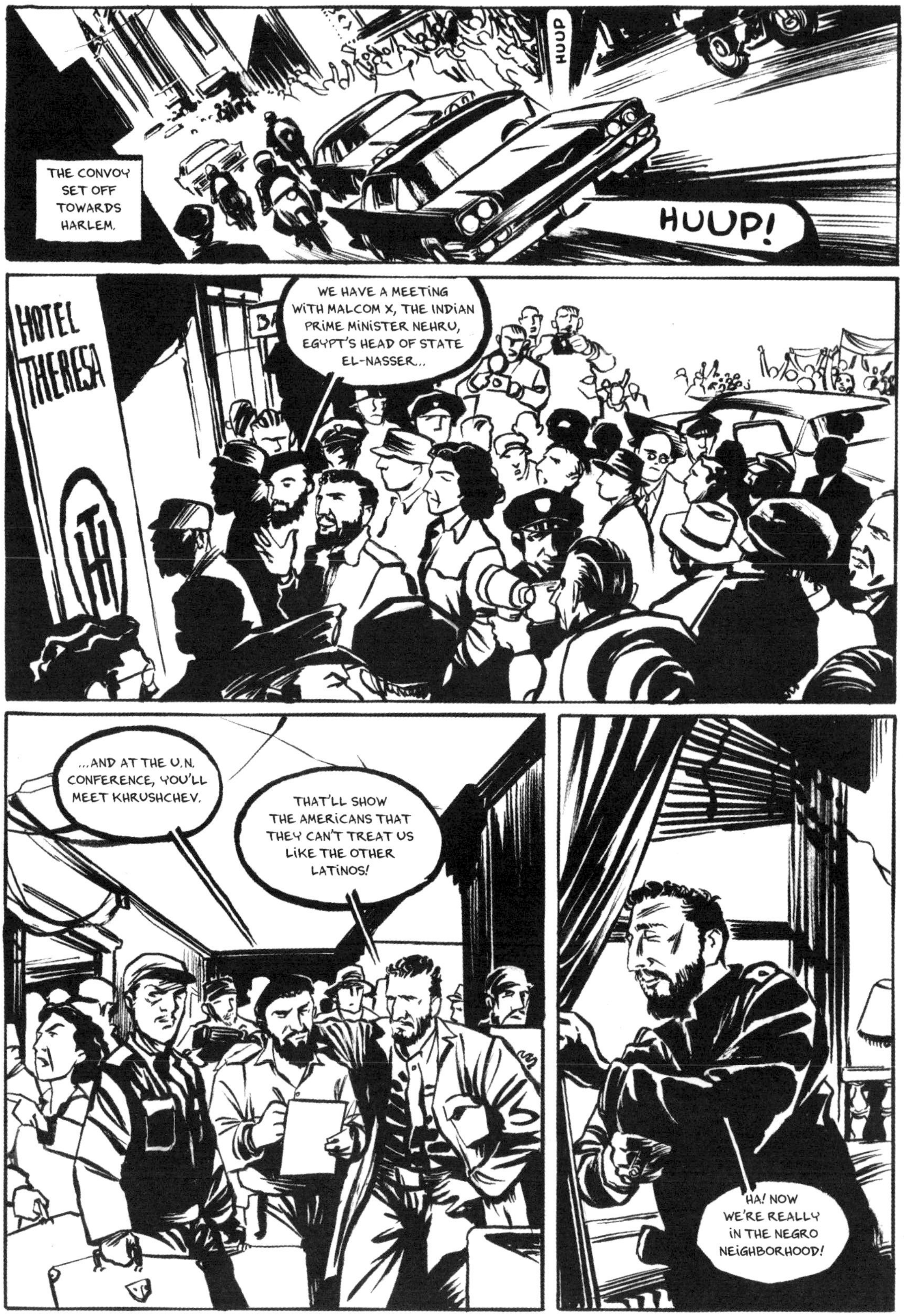
HUUP
THE CONVOY SET OFF TOWARDS HARLEM.
HUUP!
HOTEL THERESA
WE HAVE A MEETING WITH MALCOM X, THE INDIAN PRIME MINISTER NEHRU, EGYPT'S HEAD OF STATE EL-NASSER...
...AND AT THE U.N. CONFERENCE, YOU'LL MEET KHRUSHCHEV.
THAT'LL SHOW THE AMERICANS THAT THEY CAN'T TREAT US LIKE THE OTHER LATINOS!
HA! NOW WE'RE REALLY IN THE NEGRO NEIGHBORHOOD!

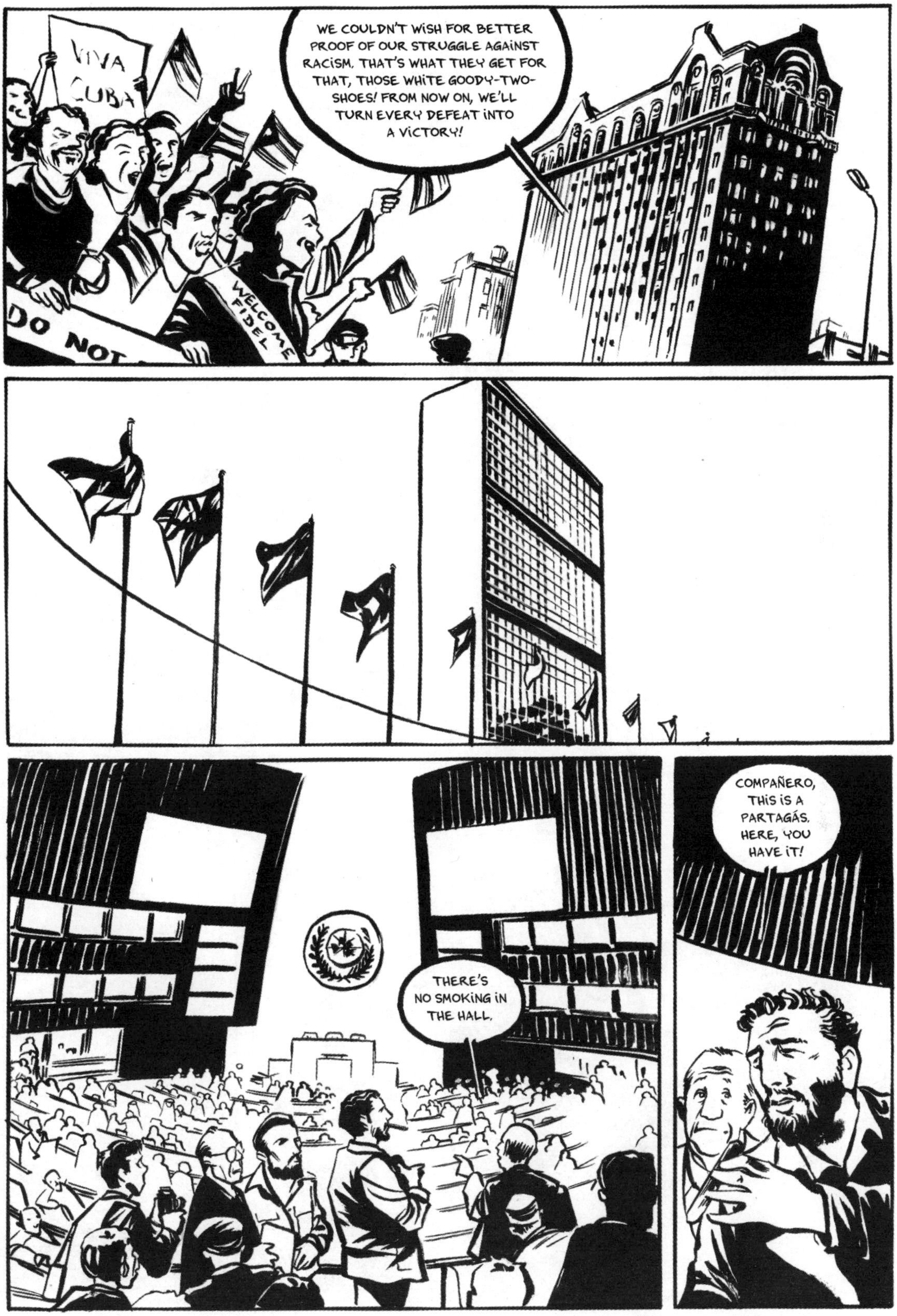
VIVA CUBA
WE COULDN'T WISH FOR BETTER PROOF OF OUR STRUGGLE AGAINST RACISM. THAT'S WHAT THEY GET FOR THAT, THOSE WHITE GOODY-TWO-SHOES! FROM NOW ON, WE'LL TURN EVERY DEFEAT INTO A VICTORY!
WELCOME FIDEL
DO NOT
THERE'S NO SMOKING IN THE HALL.
COMPAÑERO, THIS IS A PARTAGÁS. HERE, YOU HAVE IT!

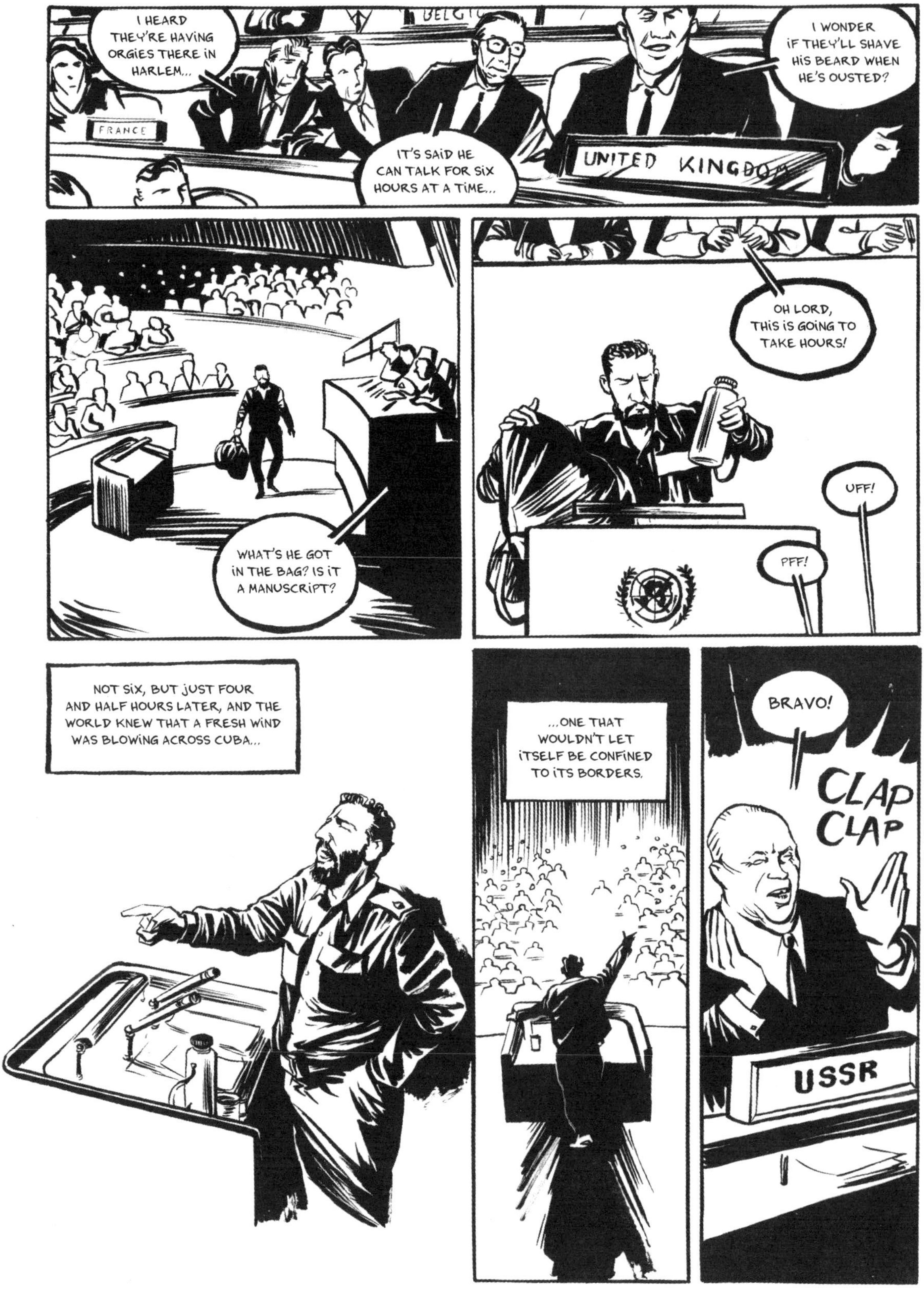
I HEARD THEY'RE HAVING ORGIES THERE IN HARLEM...
FRANCE
IT'S SAID HE CAN TALK FOR SIX HOURS AT A TIME...
UNITED KINGDOM
I WONDER IF THEY'LL SHAVE HIS BEARD WHEN HE'S OUSTED?
WHAT'S HE GOT IN THE BAG? IS IT A MANUSCRIPT?
OH LORD, THIS IS GOING TO TAKE HOURS!
UFF!
PFF!
NOT SIX, BUT JUST FOUR AND HALF HOURS LATER, AND THE WORLD KNEW THAT A FRESH WIND WAS BLOWING ACROSS CUBA...
...ONE THAT WOULDN'T LET ITSELF BE CONFINED TO ITS BORDERS.
BRAVO!
CLAP CLAP
USSR

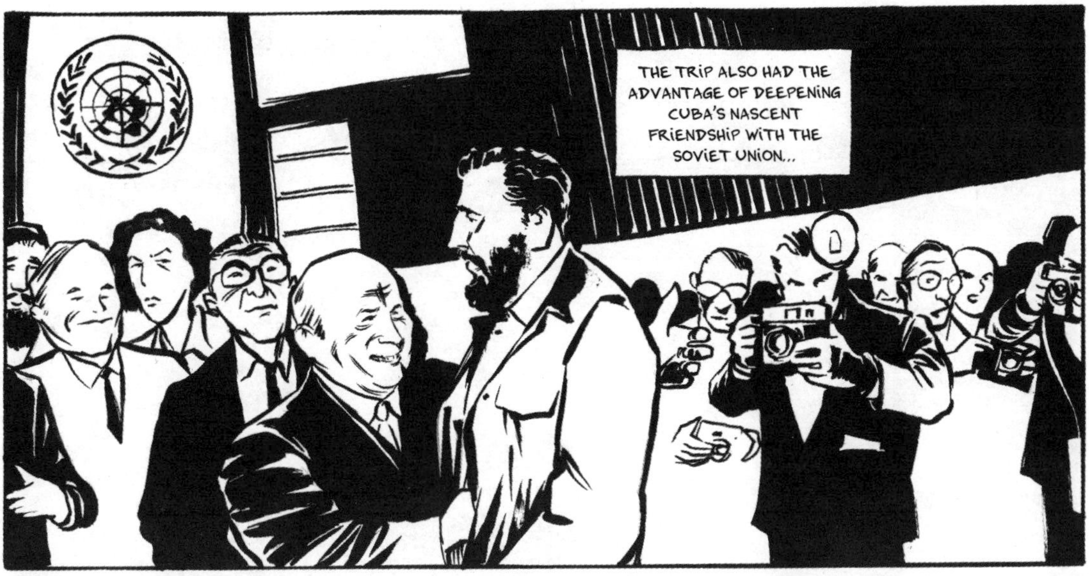
THE TRIP ALSO HAD THE ADVANTAGE OF DEEPENING CUBA'S NASCENT FRIENDSHIP WITH THE SOVIET UNION...

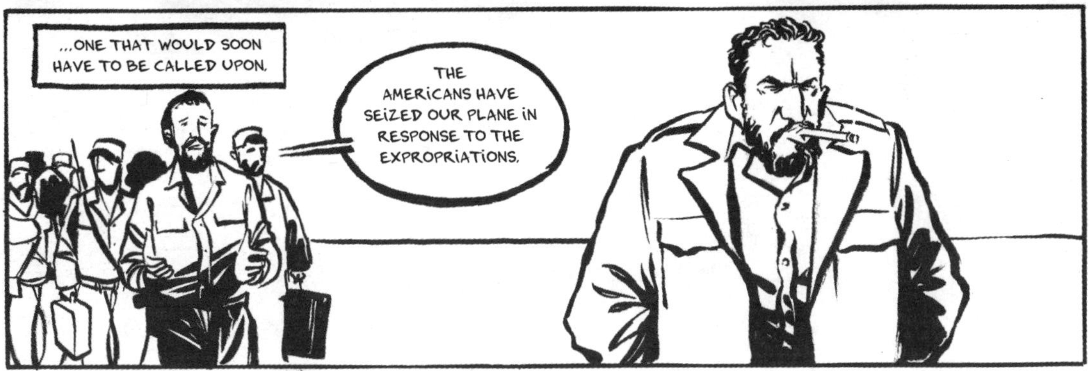
...ONE THAT WOULD SOON HAVE TO BE CALLED UPON.
THE AMERICANS HAVE SEIZED OUR PLANE IN RESPONSE TO THE EXPROPRIATIONS.

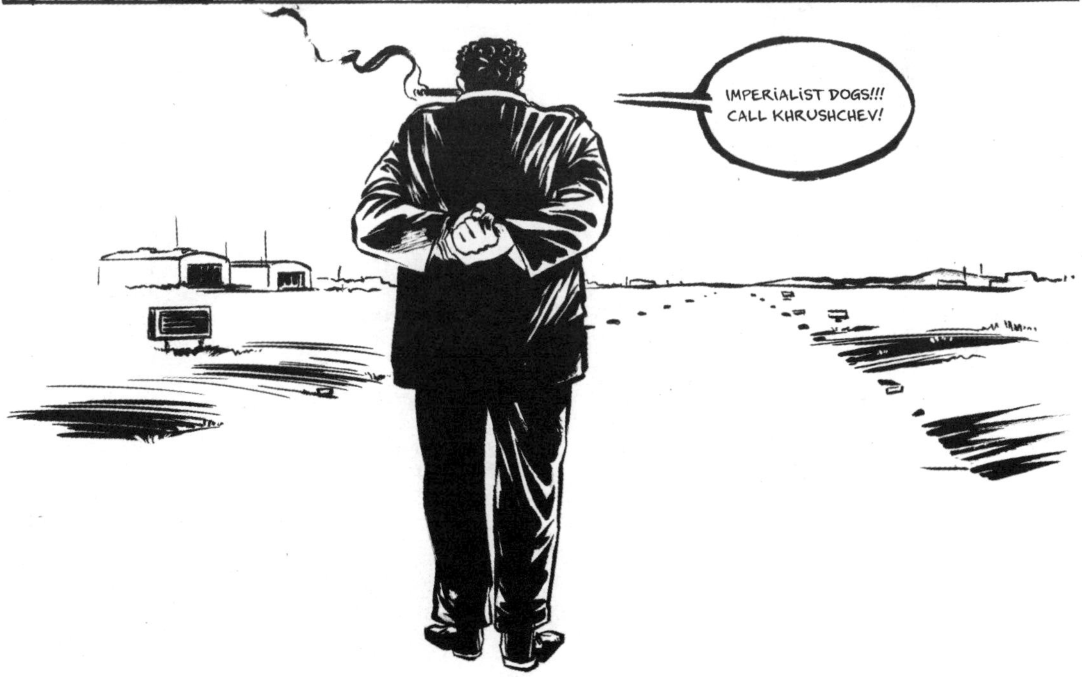
IMPERIALIST DOGS!!! CALL KHRUSHCHEV!

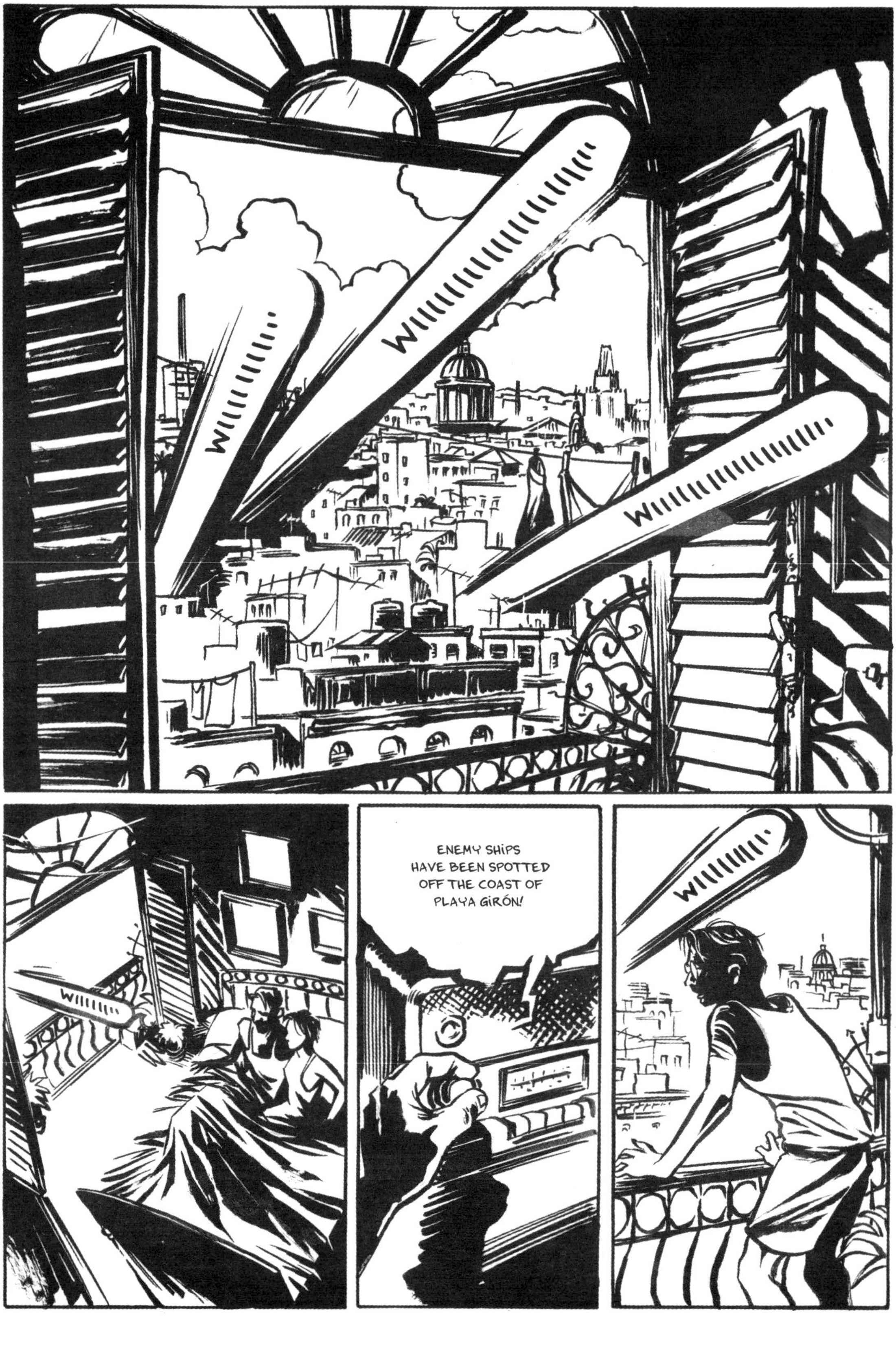
Wiiiiiiiii...
Wiiiiiiiiiiiiiiiiii
Wiiiiiiiiiiiiiiiiiii
Wiiiiii...
ENEMY SHIPS HAVE BEEN SPOTTED OFF THE COAST OF PLAYA GIRÓN!
Wiiiiiiii

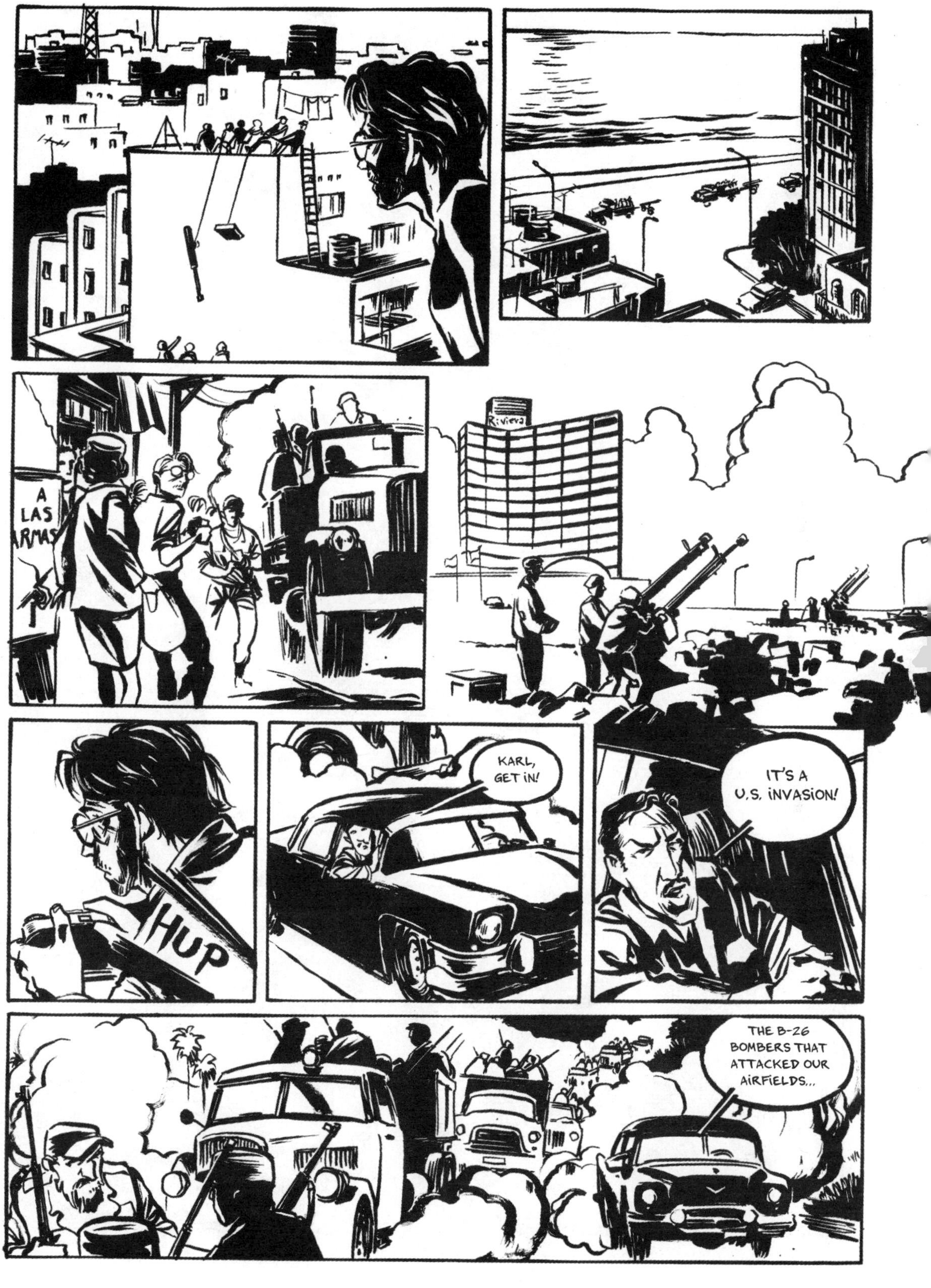
A LAS ARMAS
Riviera
HUP
KARL, GET iN!
IT'S A U.S. iNVASiON!
THE B-26 BOMBERS THAT ATTACKED OUR AiRFiELDS...

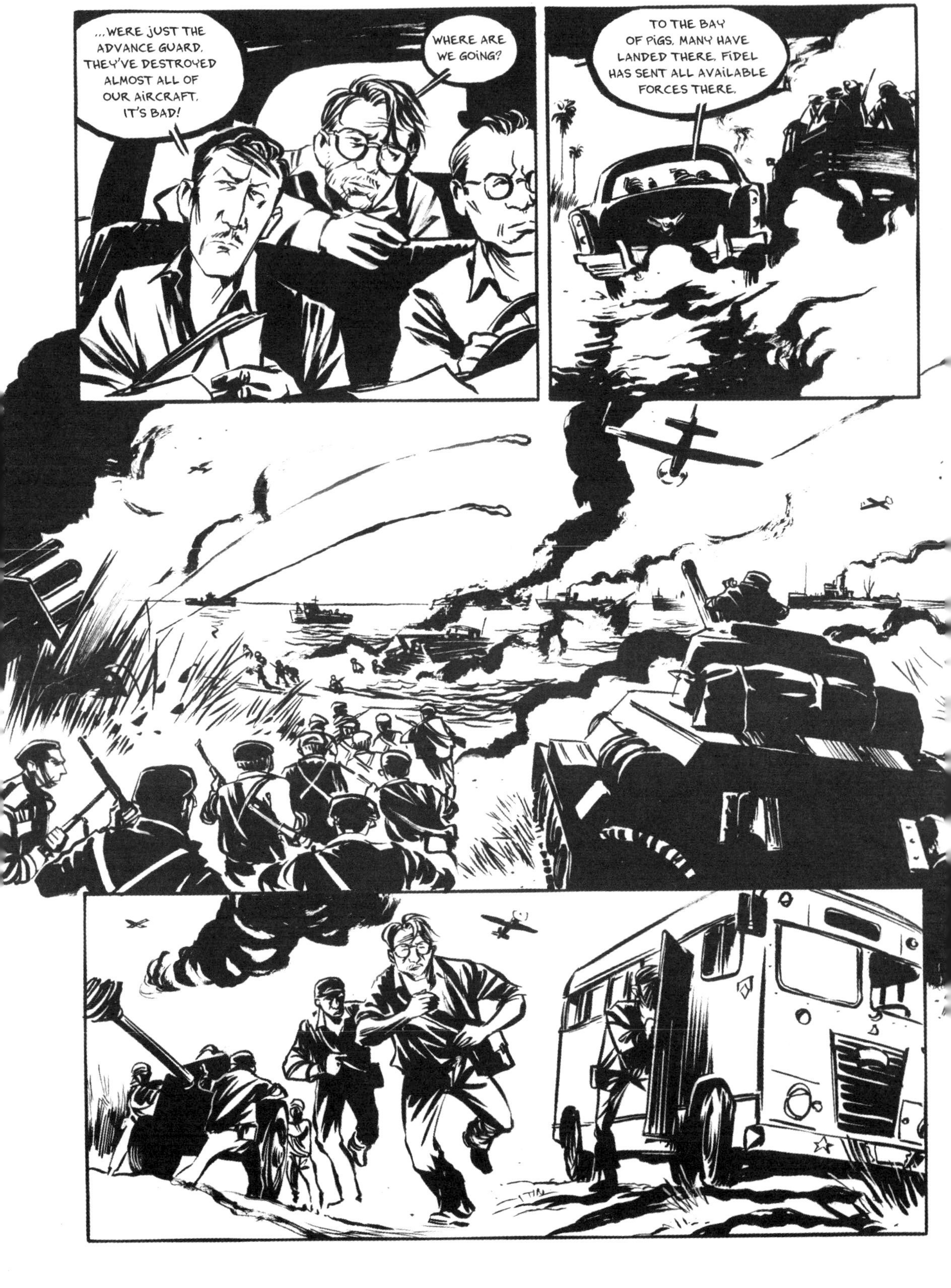
...WERE JUST THE ADVANCE GUARD. THEY'VE DESTROYED ALMOST ALL OF OUR AIRCRAFT. IT'S BAD!
WHERE ARE WE GOING?
TO THE BAY OF PIGS. MANY HAVE LANDED THERE. FIDEL HAS SENT ALL AVAILABLE FORCES THERE.

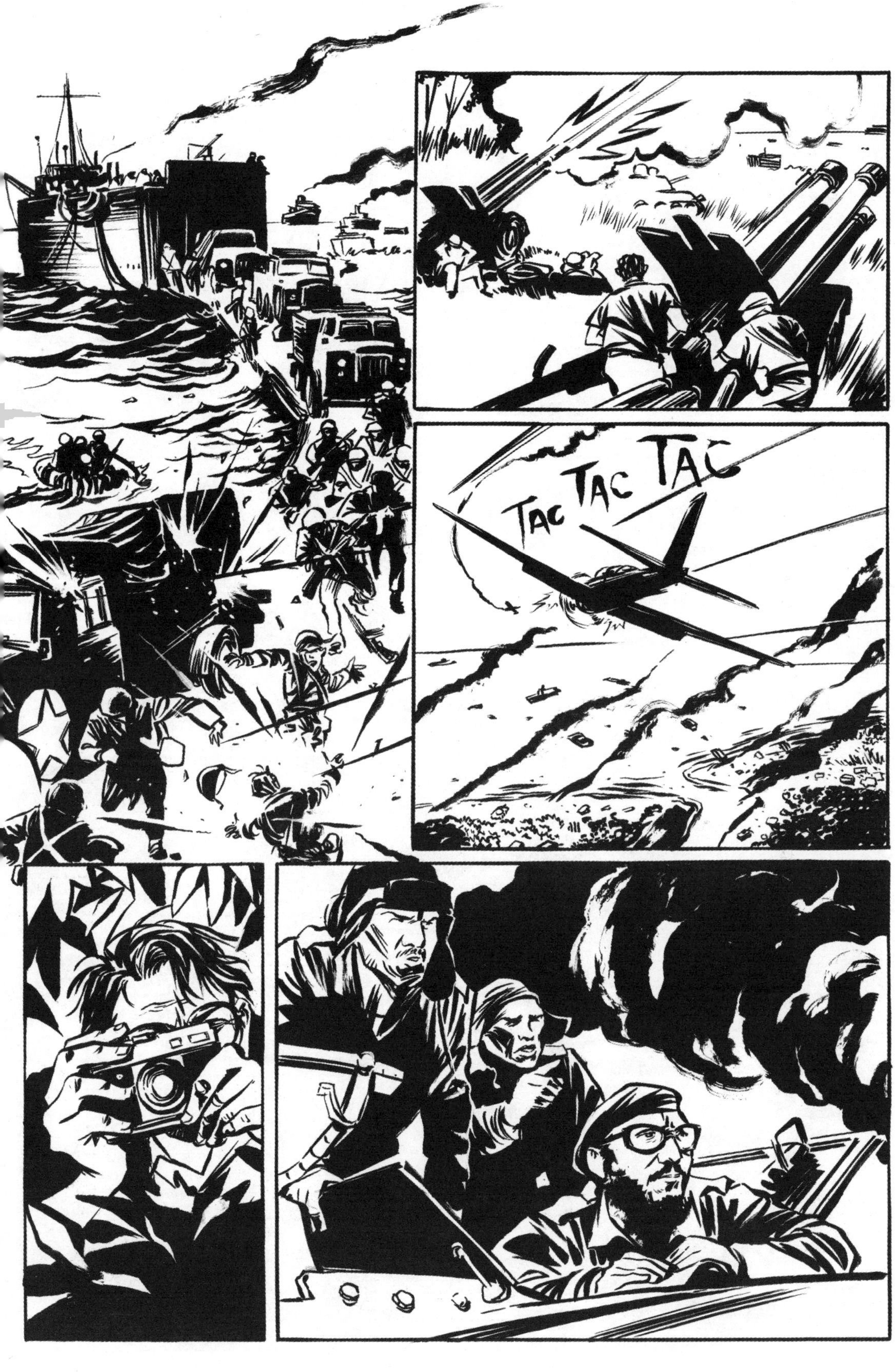
TAC TAC TAC

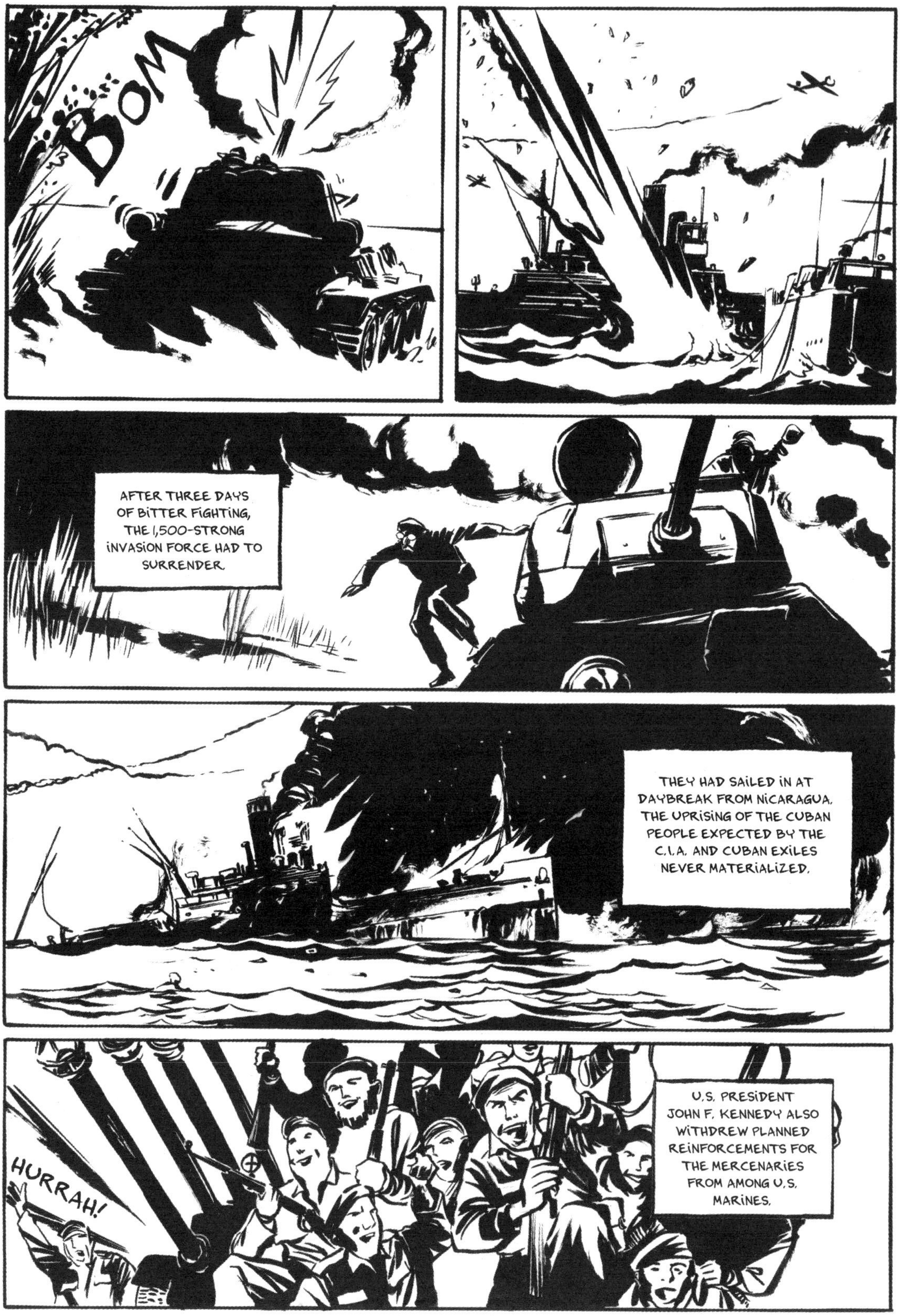
BOM
AFTER THREE DAYS OF BITTER FIGHTING, THE 1,500-STRONG INVASION FORCE HAD TO SURRENDER.
THEY HAD SAILED IN AT DAYBREAK FROM NICARAGUA. THE UPRISING OF THE CUBAN PEOPLE EXPECTED BY THE C.I.A. AND CUBAN EXILES NEVER MATERIALIZED.
HURRAH!
U.S. PRESIDENT JOHN F. KENNEDY ALSO WITHDREW PLANNED REINFORCEMENTS FOR THE MERCENARIES FROM AMONG U.S. MARINES.

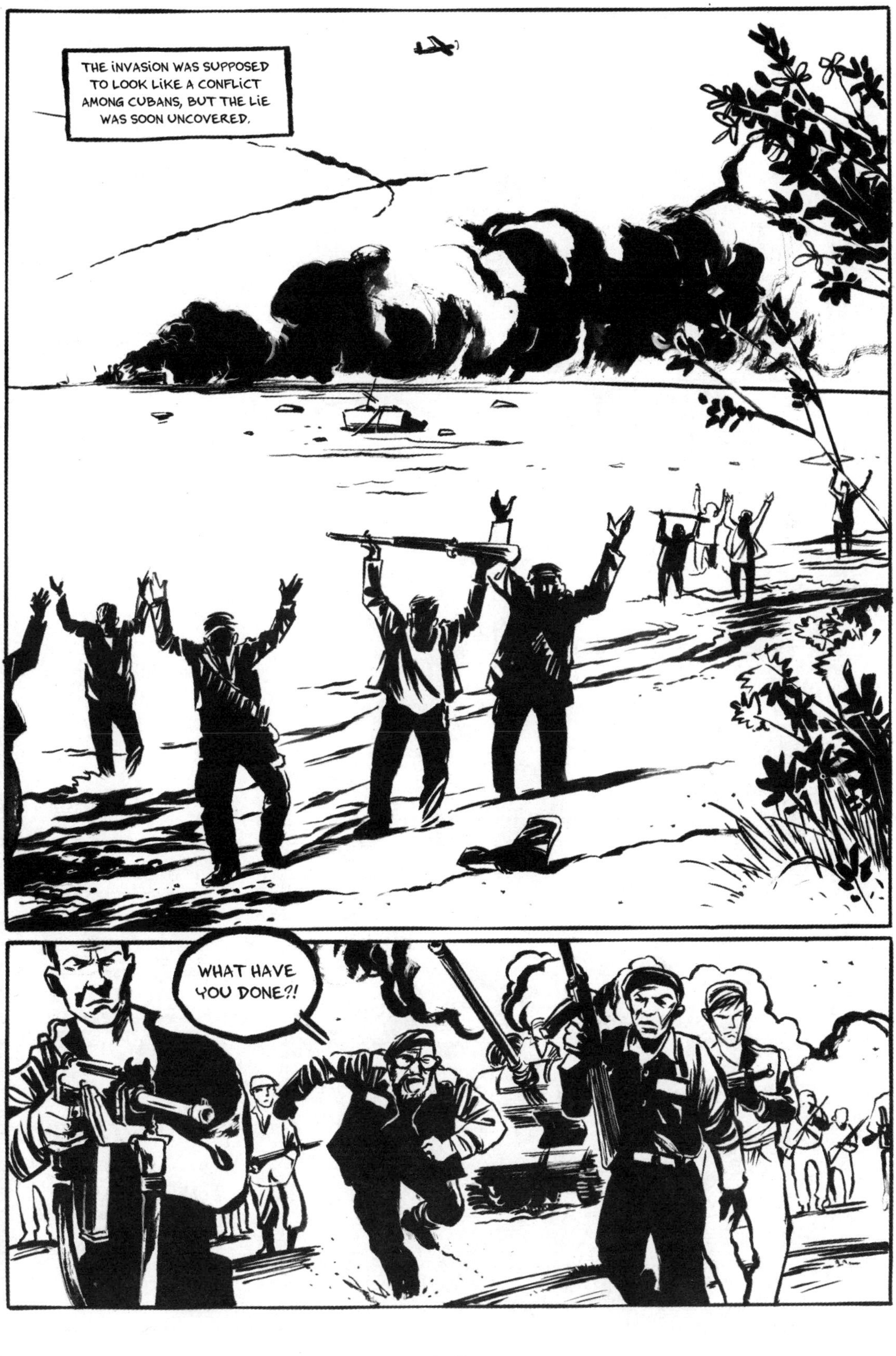
THE INVASION WAS SUPPOSED TO LOOK LIKE A CONFLICT AMONG CUBANS, BUT THE LIE WAS SOON UNCOVERED.
WHAT HAVE YOU DONE?!

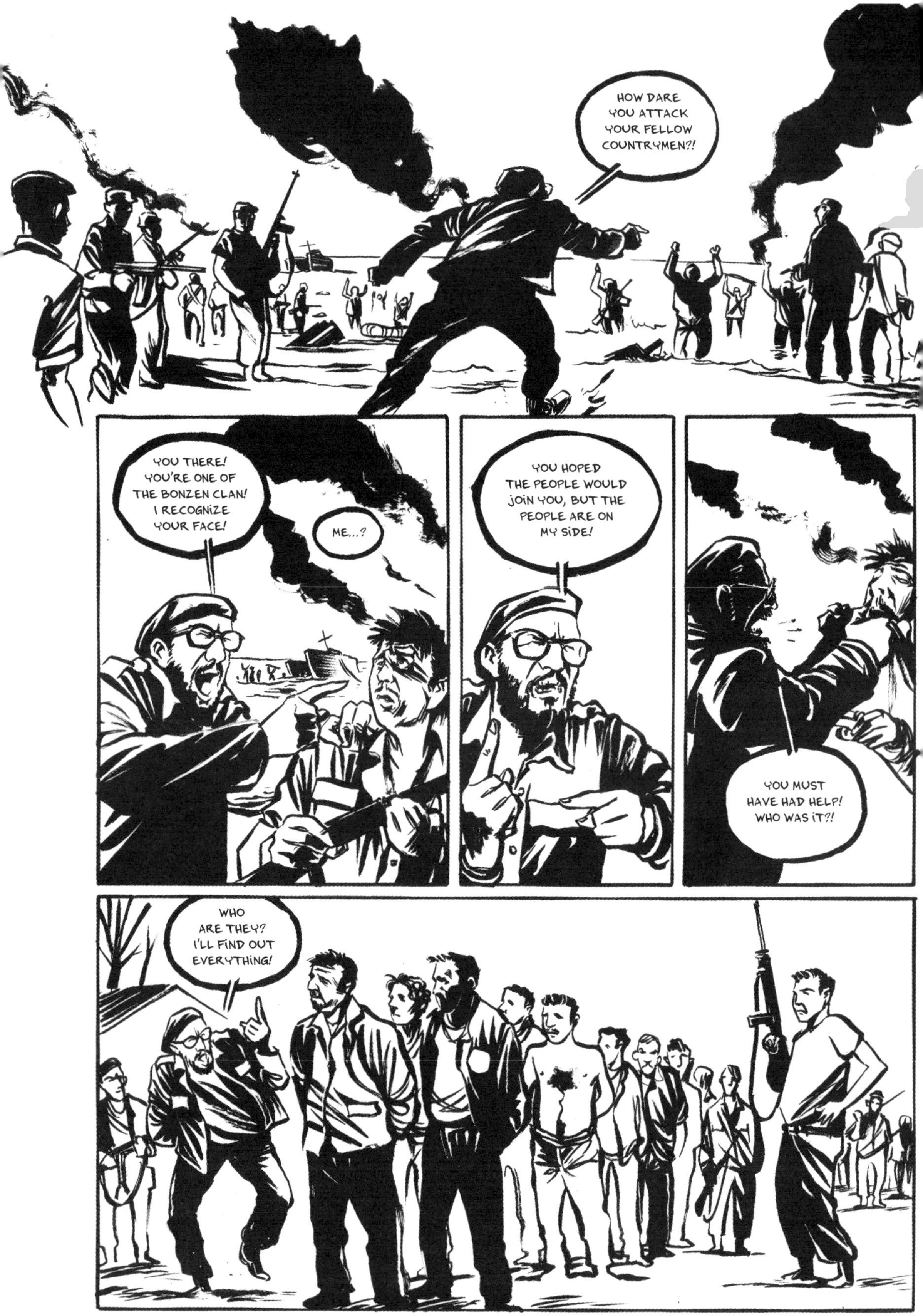
HOW DARE YOU ATTACK YOUR FELLOW COUNTRYMEN?!
YOU THERE! YOU'RE ONE OF THE BONZEN CLAN! I RECOGNIZE YOUR FACE!
ME...?
YOU HOPED THE PEOPLE WOULD JOIN YOU, BUT THE PEOPLE ARE ON MY SIDE!
YOU MUST HAVE HAD HELP! WHO WAS IT?!
WHO ARE THEY? I'LL FIND OUT EVERYTHING!

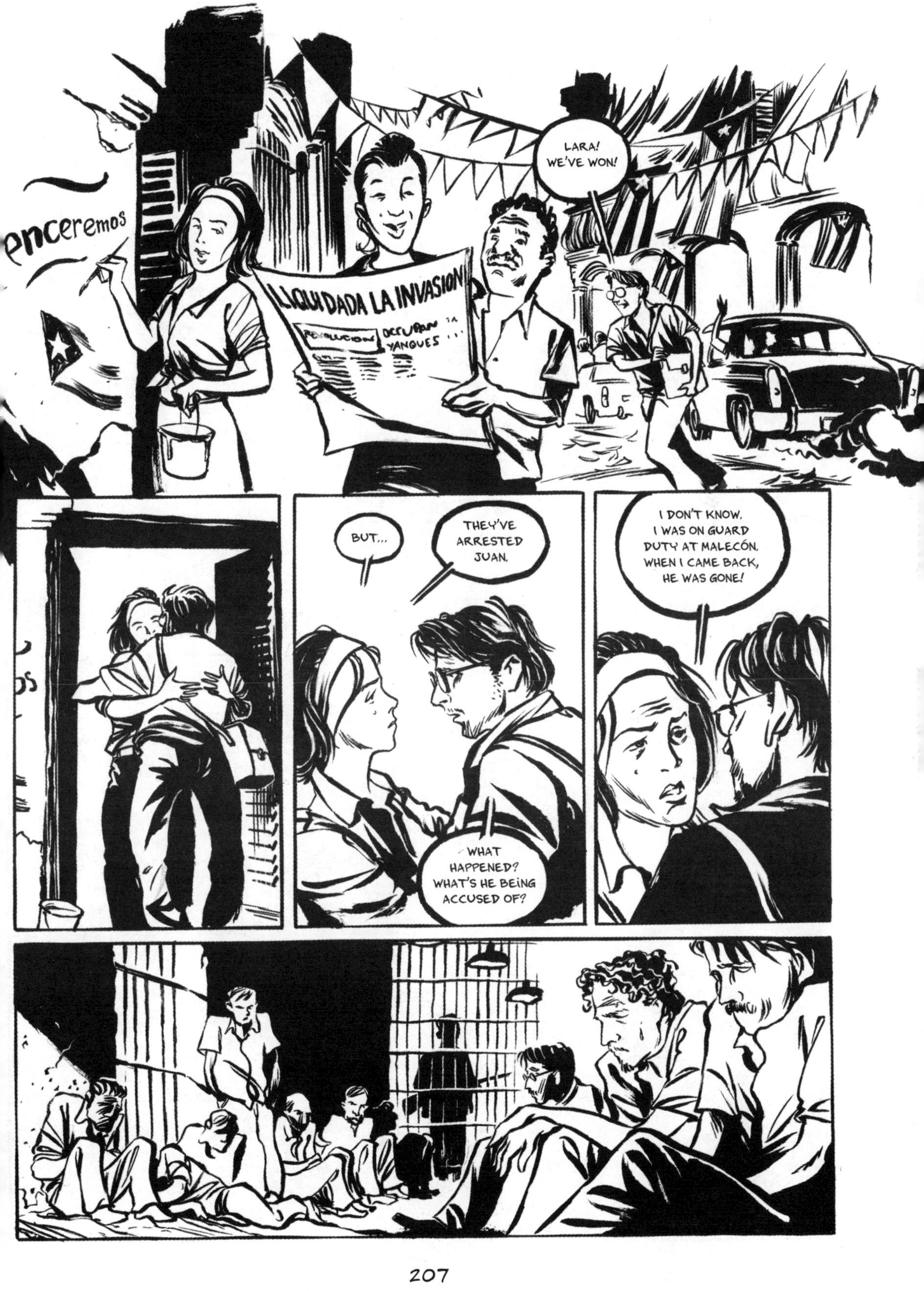
enceremos
LIQUIDADA LA INVASION
REVOLUCION
OCUPAN LA
YANQUES . . .
LARA! WE'VE WON!
BUT...
THEY'VE ARRESTED JUAN.
WHAT HAPPENED? WHAT'S HE BEING ACCUSED OF?
I DON'T KNOW. I WAS ON GUARD DUTY AT MALECÓN. WHEN I CAME BACK, HE WAS GONE!

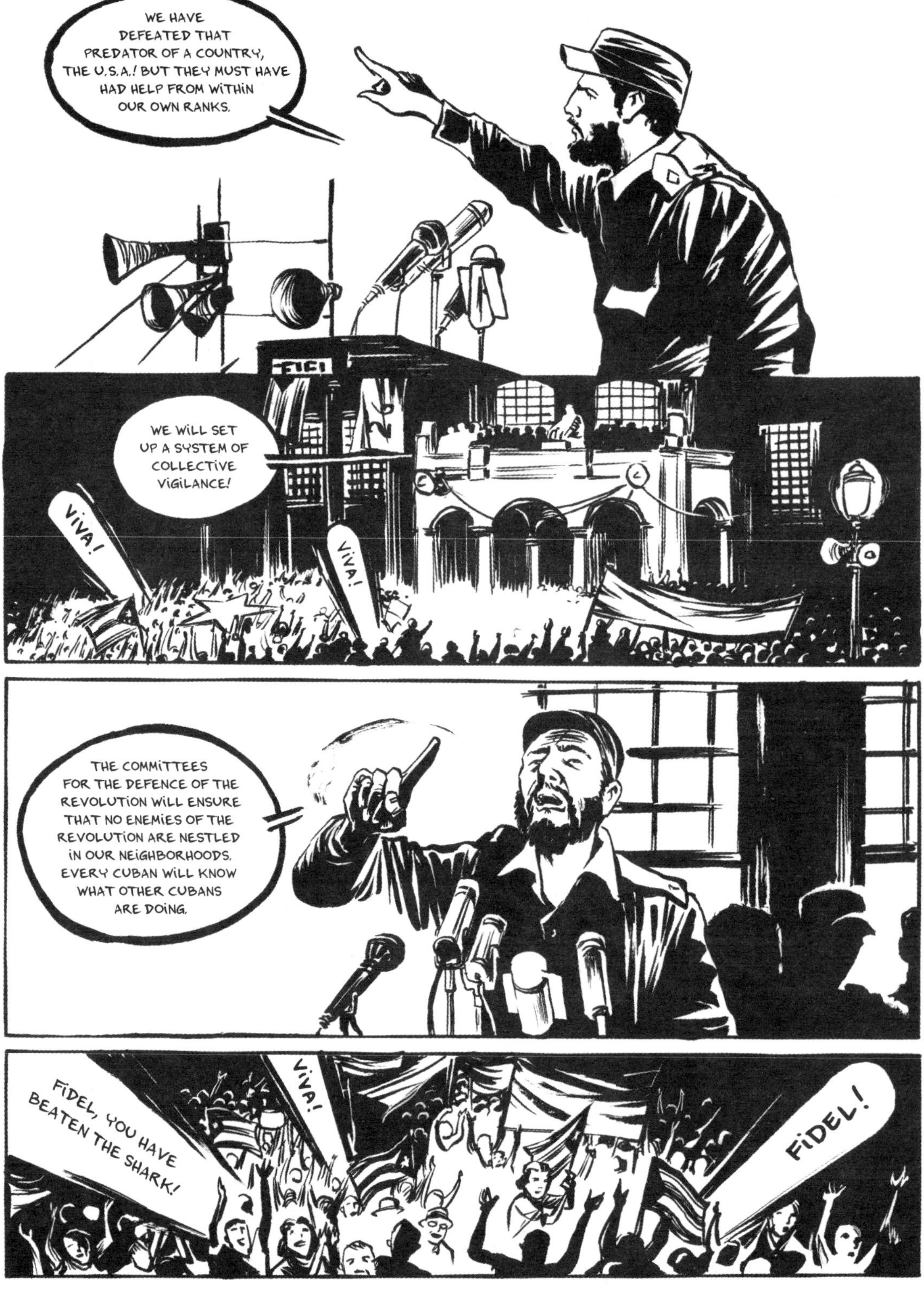
WE HAVE DEFEATED THAT PREDATOR OF A COUNTRY, THE U.S.A.! BUT THEY MUST HAVE HAD HELP FROM WITHIN OUR OWN RANKS.
WE WILL SET UP A SYSTEM OF COLLECTIVE VIGILANCE!
VIVA!
VIVA!
THE COMMITTEES FOR THE DEFENCE OF THE REVOLUTION WILL ENSURE THAT NO ENEMIES OF THE REVOLUTION ARE NESTLED IN OUR NEIGHBORHOODS. EVERY CUBAN WILL KNOW WHAT OTHER CUBANS ARE DOING.
FIDEL, YOU HAVE BEATEN THE SHARK!
VIVA!
FIDEL!

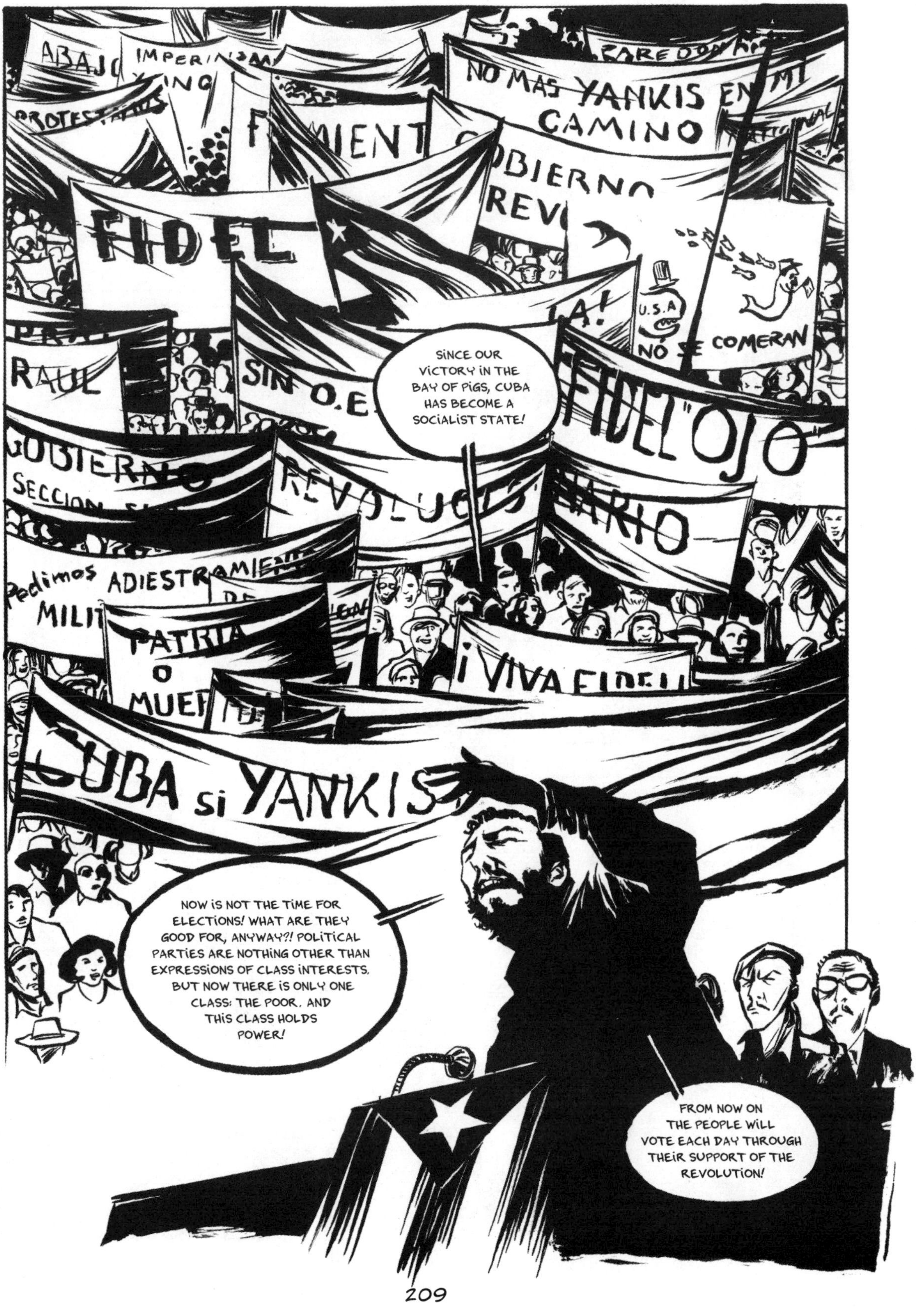
ABAJO
NO MAS YANKIS EN MI CAMINO
FIDEL
GOBIERNO REV
U.S.A
NO SE COMERAN
RAUL
SIN O.E.
FIDEL "OJO"
GOBIERNO
SECCION
Pedimos ADIESTRAMIEN
MILIT
PATRIA O MUER
¡VIVA FIDEL
CUBA Si YANKIS
SINCE OUR VICTORY IN THE BAY OF PIGS, CUBA HAS BECOME A SOCIALIST STATE!
NOW IS NOT THE TIME FOR ELECTIONS! WHAT ARE THEY GOOD FOR, ANYWAY?! POLITICAL PARTIES ARE NOTHING OTHER THAN EXPRESSIONS OF CLASS INTERESTS, BUT NOW THERE IS ONLY ONE CLASS: THE POOR. AND THIS CLASS HOLDS POWER!
FROM NOW ON THE PEOPLE WILL VOTE EACH DAY THROUGH THEIR SUPPORT OF THE REVOLUTION!

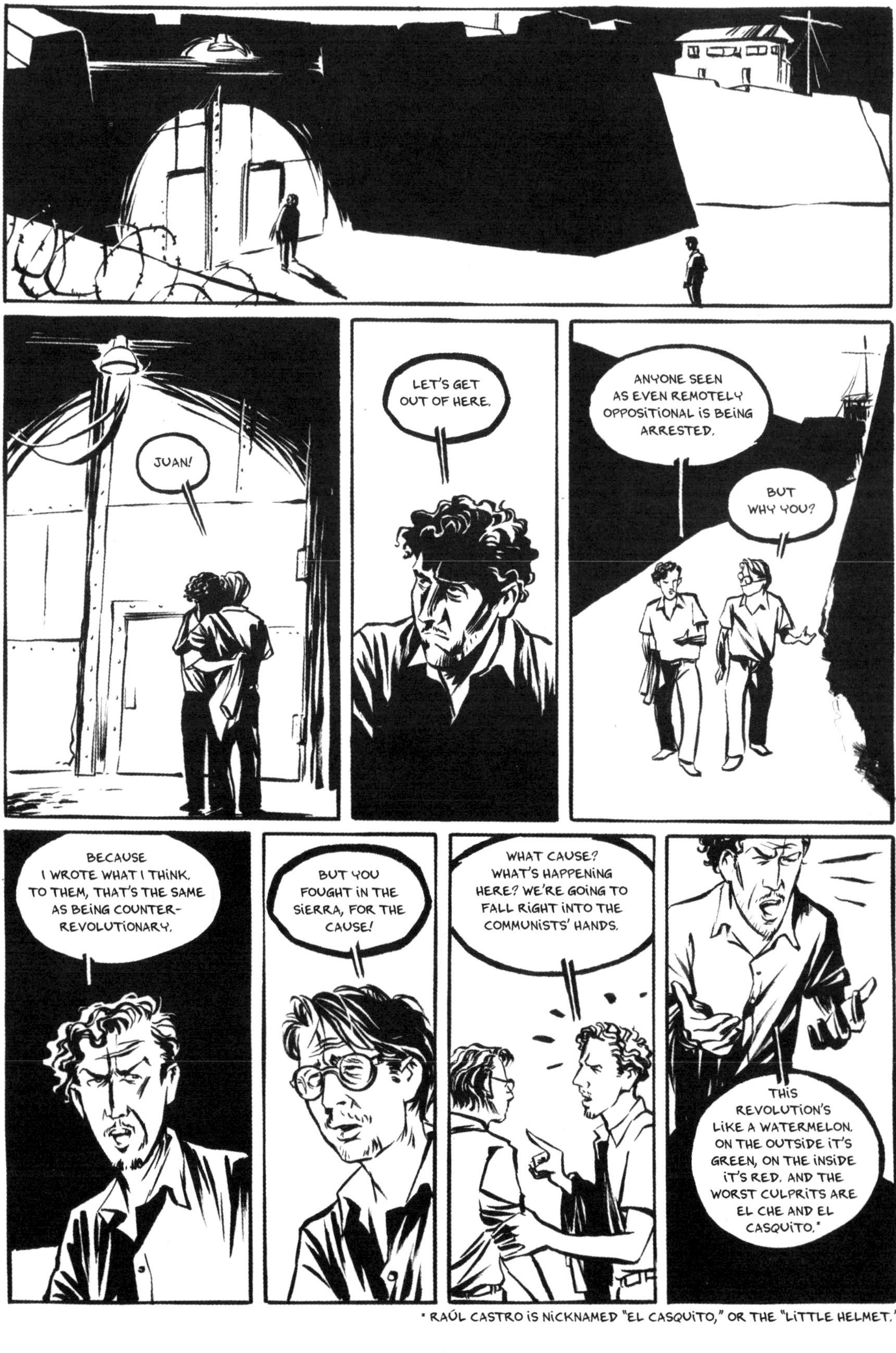
JUAN!
LET'S GET OUT OF HERE.
ANYONE SEEN AS EVEN REMOTELY OPPOSITIONAL IS BEING ARRESTED.
BUT WHY YOU?
BECAUSE I WROTE WHAT I THINK. TO THEM, THAT'S THE SAME AS BEING COUNTER-REVOLUTIONARY.
BUT YOU FOUGHT IN THE SIERRA, FOR THE CAUSE!
WHAT CAUSE? WHAT'S HAPPENING HERE? WE'RE GOING TO FALL RIGHT INTO THE COMMUNISTS' HANDS.
THIS REVOLUTION'S LIKE A WATERMELON. ON THE OUTSIDE IT'S GREEN, ON THE INSIDE IT'S RED. AND THE WORST CULPRITS ARE EL CHE AND EL CASQUITO.*

* RAÚL CASTRO IS NICKNAMED "EL CASQUITO," OR THE "LITTLE HELMET."

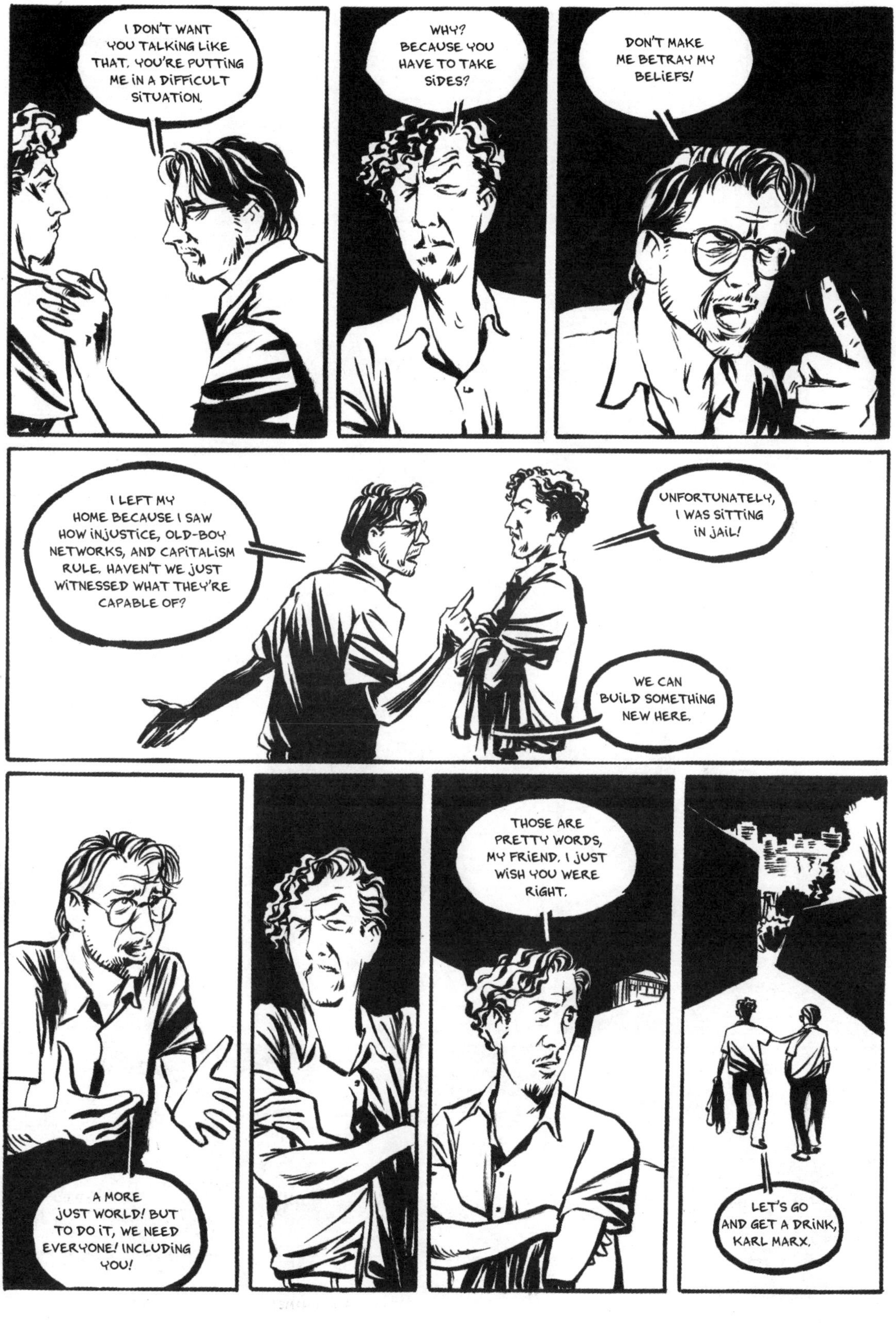
I DON'T WANT YOU TALKING LIKE THAT. YOU'RE PUTTING ME IN A DIFFICULT SITUATION.
WHY? BECAUSE YOU HAVE TO TAKE SIDES?
DON'T MAKE ME BETRAY MY BELIEFS!
I LEFT MY HOME BECAUSE I SAW HOW INJUSTICE, OLD-BOY NETWORKS, AND CAPITALISM RULE. HAVEN'T WE JUST WITNESSED WHAT THEY'RE CAPABLE OF?
UNFORTUNATELY, I WAS SITTING IN JAIL!
WE CAN BUILD SOMETHING NEW HERE.
A MORE JUST WORLD! BUT TO DO IT, WE NEED EVERYONE! INCLUDING YOU!
THOSE ARE PRETTY WORDS, MY FRIEND. I JUST WISH YOU WERE RIGHT.
LET'S GO AND GET A DRINK, KARL MARX.

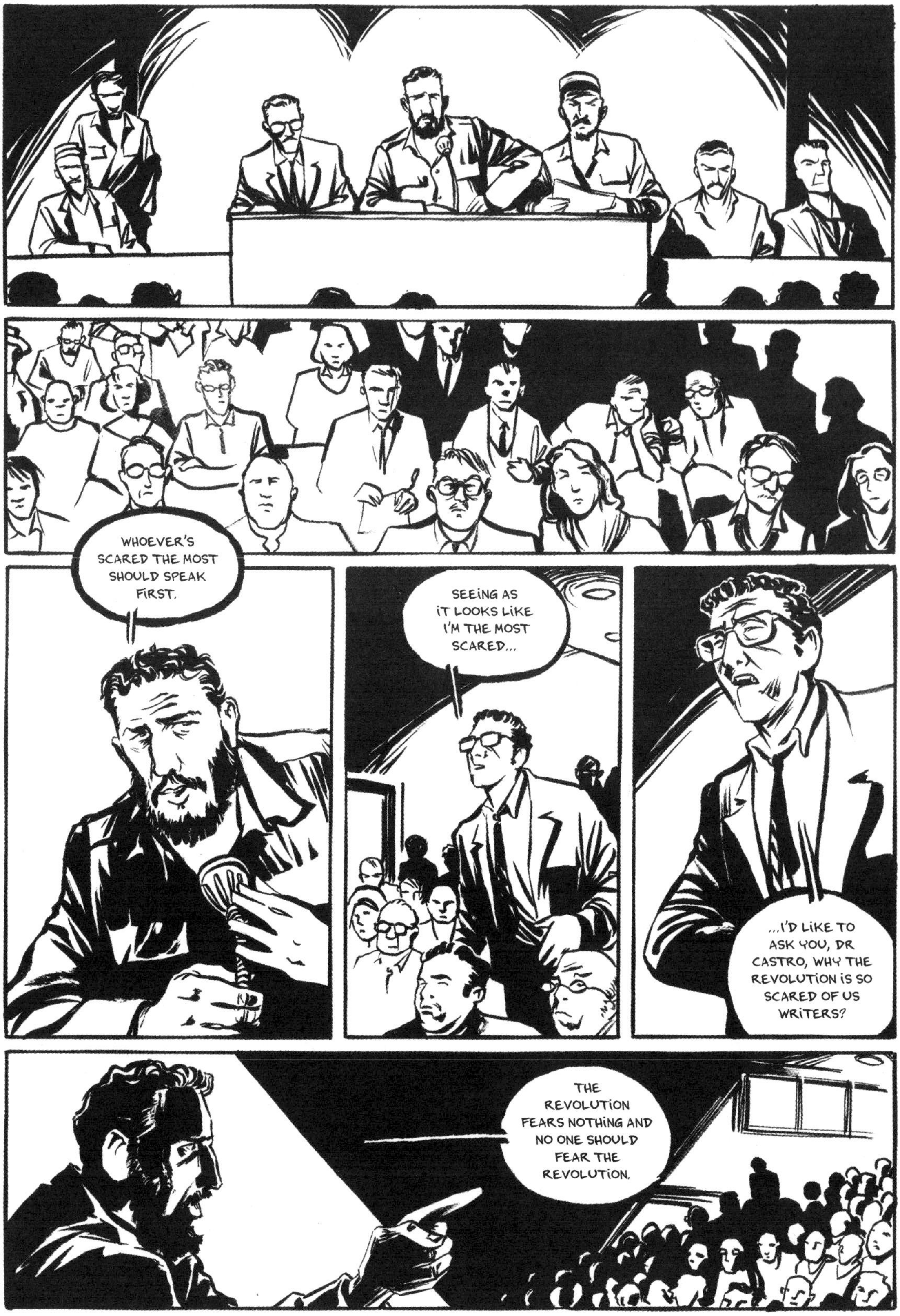
WHOEVER'S SCARED THE MOST SHOULD SPEAK FIRST.
SEEING AS IT LOOKS LIKE I'M THE MOST SCARED...
...I'D LIKE TO ASK YOU, DR CASTRO, WHY THE REVOLUTION IS SO SCARED OF US WRITERS?
THE REVOLUTION FEARS NOTHING AND NO ONE SHOULD FEAR THE REVOLUTION.

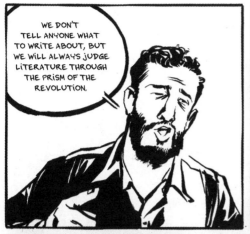

WE DON'T TELL ANYONE WHAT TO WRITE ABOUT, BUT WE WILL ALWAYS JUDGE LITERATURE THROUGH THE PRISM OF THE REVOLUTION.
THAT MEANS: EVERYTHING FOR THE REVOLUTION...
...AND NOTHING AGAINST IT.
Nuestro vino es agrio Pero es nuestro vino*
MARTI
ALEMANIA CONSTRUYÓ** UNA PARED!
WHAT'S WRONG?
NOTHING... IT'S NOTHING.

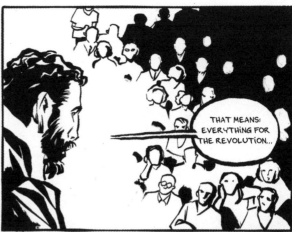

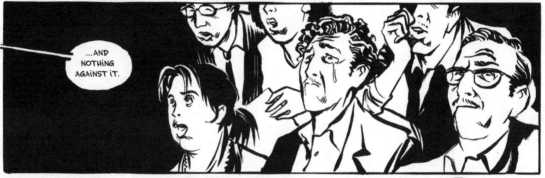

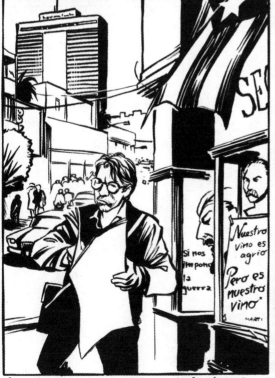

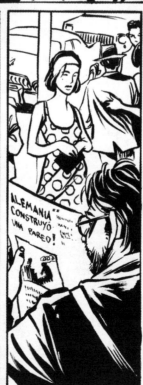

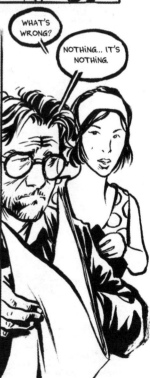

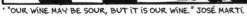

* "OUR WINE MAY BE SOUR, BUT IT IS OUR WINE." JOSÉ MARTÍ

** GERMANY BUILDS WALL!

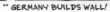

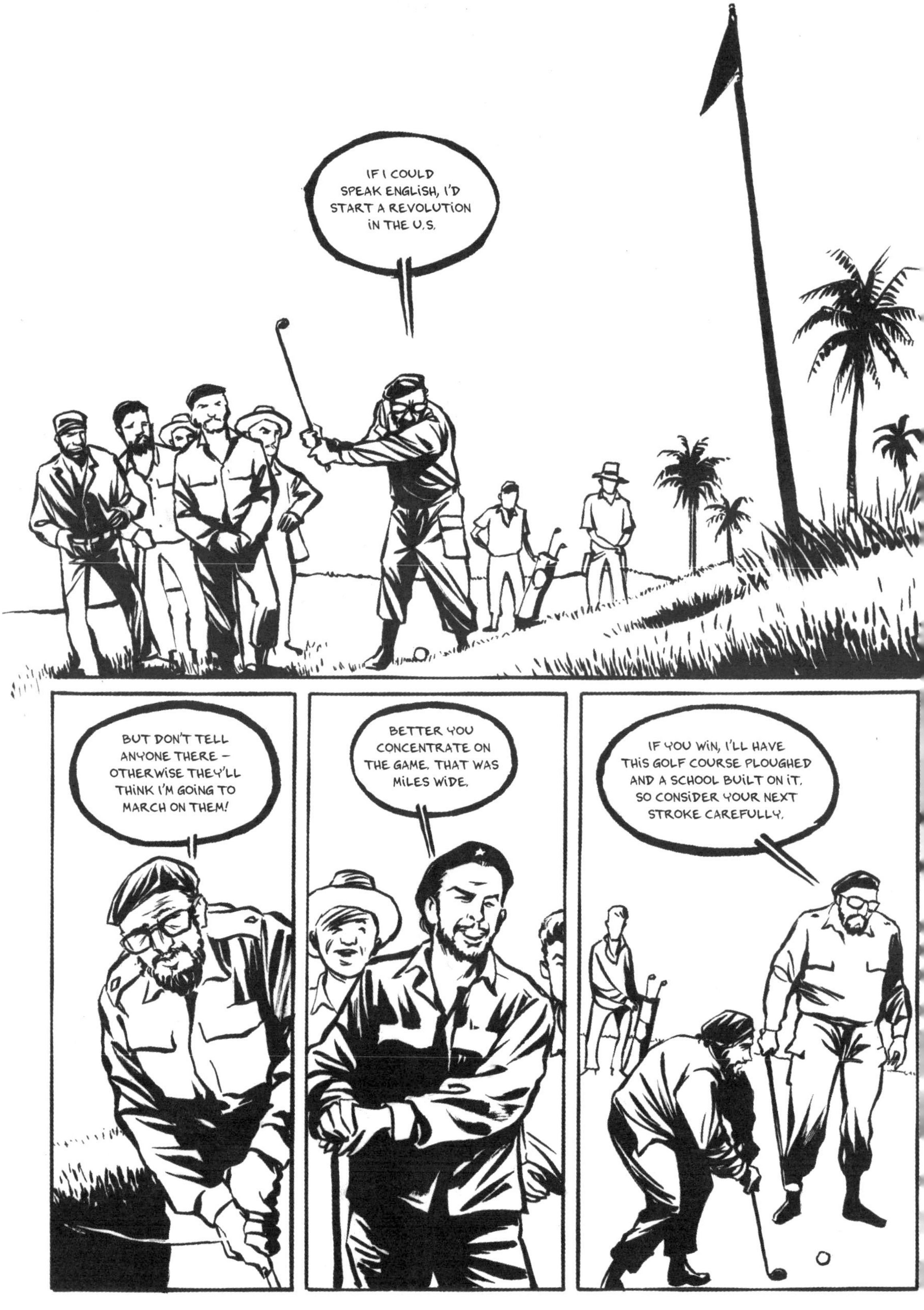
IF I COULD SPEAK ENGLISH, I'D START A REVOLUTION IN THE U.S.
BUT DON'T TELL ANYONE THERE – OTHERWISE THEY'LL THINK I'M GOING TO MARCH ON THEM!
BETTER YOU CONCENTRATE ON THE GAME. THAT WAS MILES WIDE.
IF YOU WIN, I'LL HAVE THIS GOLF COURSE PLOUGHED AND A SCHOOL BUILT ON IT. SO CONSIDER YOUR NEXT STROKE CAREFULLY.

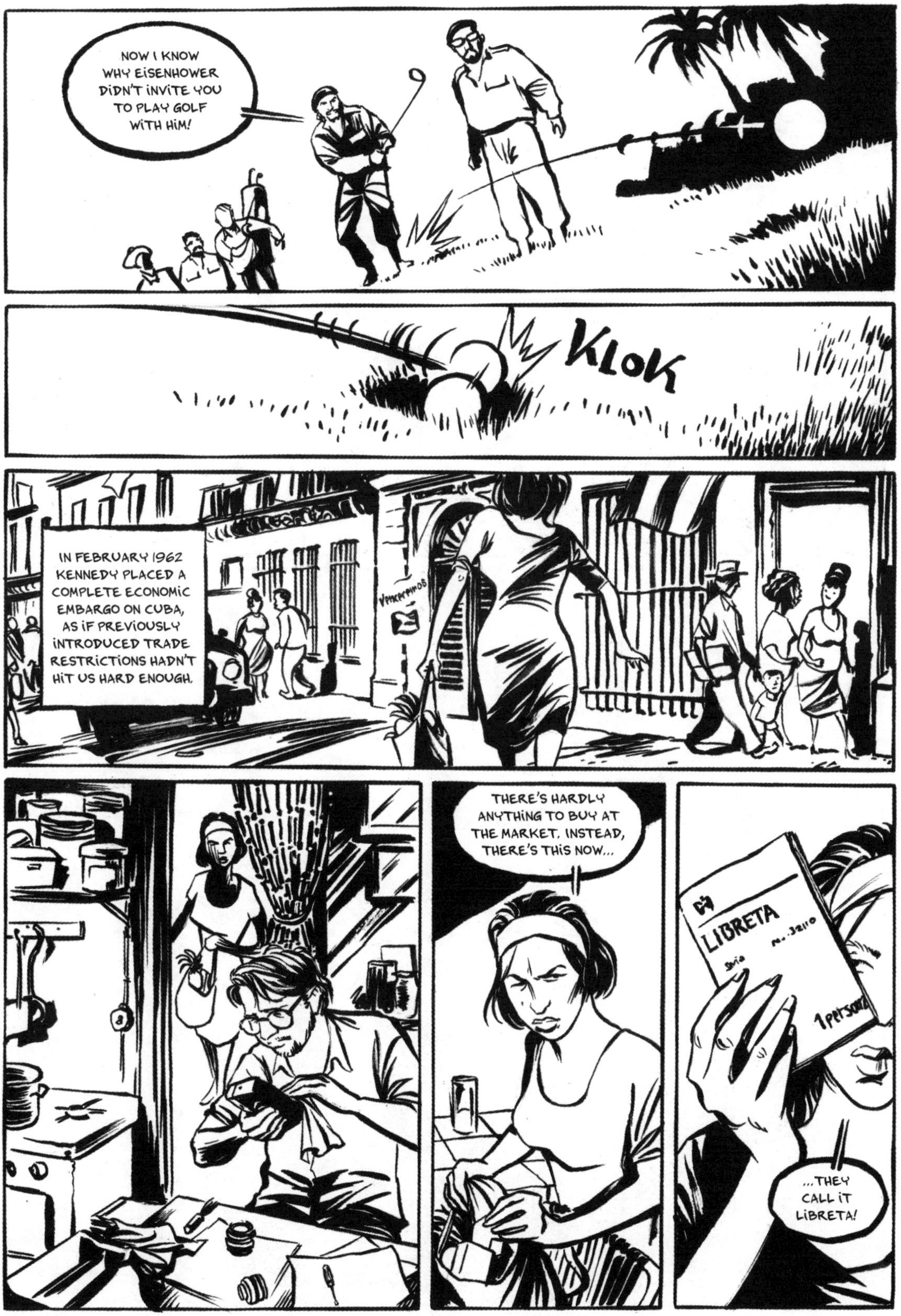
NOW I KNOW WHY EISENHOWER DIDN'T INVITE YOU TO PLAY GOLF WITH HIM!
KLOK
IN FEBRUARY 1962 KENNEDY PLACED A COMPLETE ECONOMIC EMBARGO ON CUBA, AS IF PREVIOUSLY INTRODUCED TRADE RESTRICTIONS HADN'T HIT US HARD ENOUGH.
THERE'S HARDLY ANYTHING TO BUY AT THE MARKET. INSTEAD, THERE'S THIS NOW...
LIBRETA
...THEY CALL IT LIBRETA!

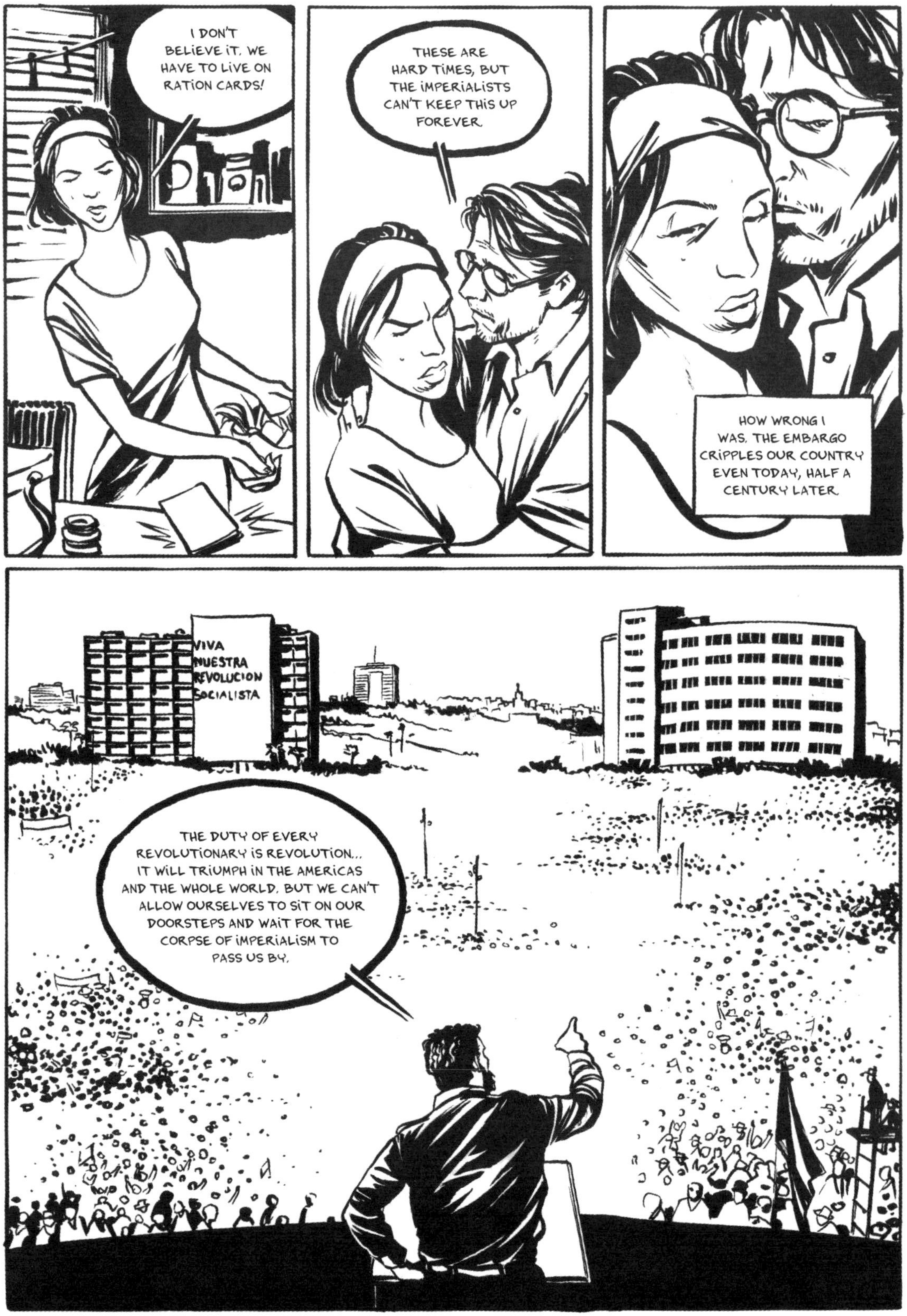
I DON'T BELIEVE IT. WE HAVE TO LIVE ON RATION CARDS!
THESE ARE HARD TIMES, BUT THE IMPERIALISTS CAN'T KEEP THIS UP FOREVER.
HOW WRONG I WAS. THE EMBARGO CRIPPLES OUR COUNTRY EVEN TODAY, HALF A CENTURY LATER.
VIVA NUESTRA REVOLUCION SOCIALISTA
THE DUTY OF EVERY REVOLUTIONARY IS REVOLUTION... IT WILL TRIUMPH IN THE AMERICAS AND THE WHOLE WORLD. BUT WE CAN'T ALLOW OURSELVES TO SIT ON OUR DOORSTEPS AND WAIT FOR THE CORPSE OF IMPERIALISM TO PASS US BY.

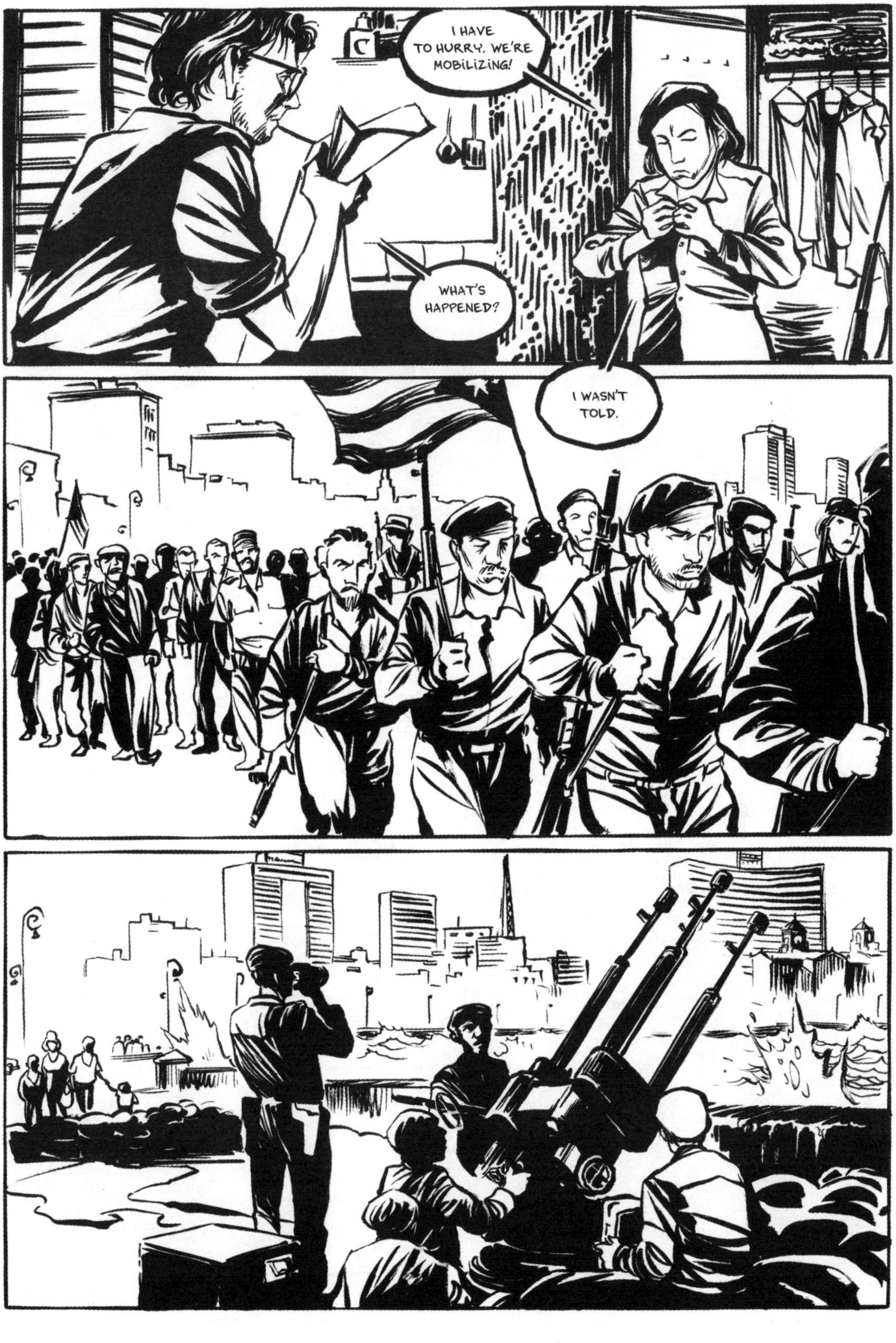
I HAVE TO HURRY, WE'RE MOBILIZING!
WHAT'S HAPPENED?
I WASN'T TOLD.

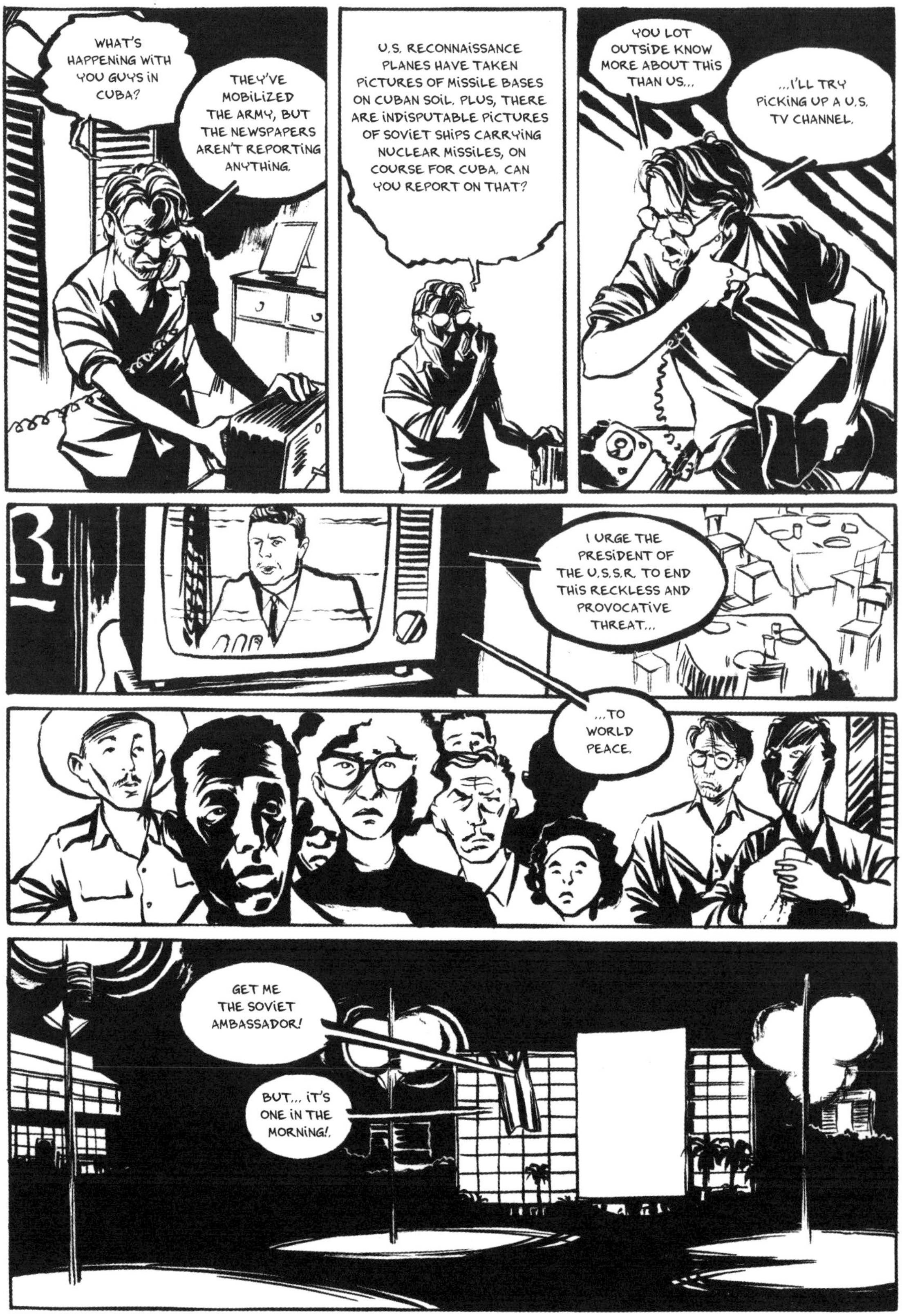
WHAT'S HAPPENING WITH YOU GUYS IN CUBA?
THEY'VE MOBILIZED THE ARMY, BUT THE NEWSPAPERS AREN'T REPORTING ANYTHING.
U.S. RECONNAISSANCE PLANES HAVE TAKEN PICTURES OF MISSILE BASES ON CUBAN SOIL. PLUS, THERE ARE INDISPUTABLE PICTURES OF SOVIET SHIPS CARRYING NUCLEAR MISSILES, ON COURSE FOR CUBA. CAN YOU REPORT ON THAT?
YOU LOT OUTSIDE KNOW MORE ABOUT THIS THAN US...
...I'LL TRY PICKING UP A U.S. TV CHANNEL.
I URGE THE PRESIDENT OF THE U.S.S.R. TO END THIS RECKLESS AND PROVOCATIVE THREAT...
...TO WORLD PEACE.
GET ME THE SOVIET AMBASSADOR!
BUT... IT'S ONE IN THE MORNING!.

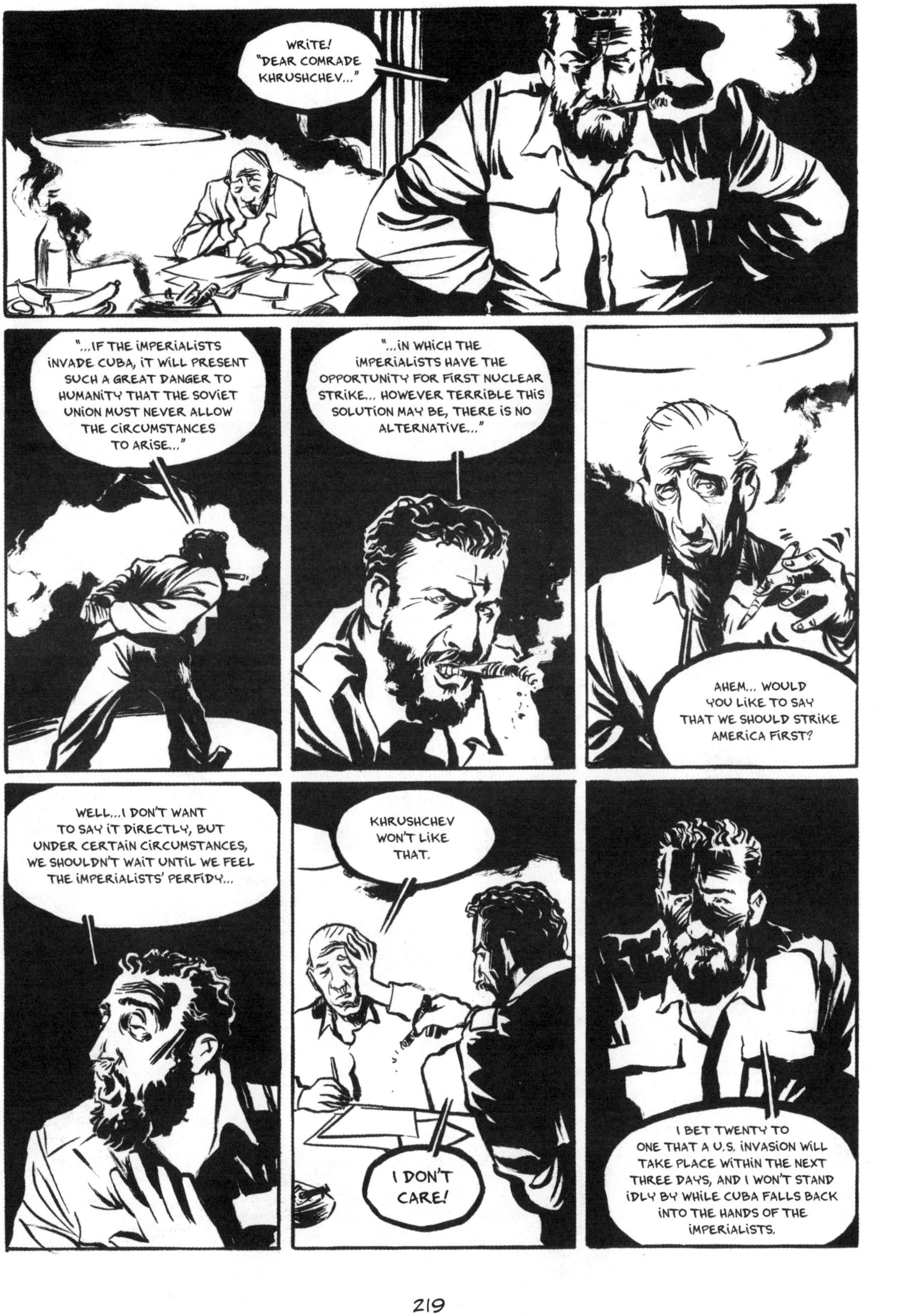
WRITE!
"DEAR COMRADE KHRUSHCHEV..."
"...IF THE IMPERIALISTS INVADE CUBA, IT WILL PRESENT SUCH A GREAT DANGER TO HUMANITY THAT THE SOVIET UNION MUST NEVER ALLOW THE CIRCUMSTANCES TO ARISE..."
"...IN WHICH THE IMPERIALISTS HAVE THE OPPORTUNITY FOR FIRST NUCLEAR STRIKE... HOWEVER TERRIBLE THIS SOLUTION MAY BE, THERE IS NO ALTERNATIVE..."
AHEM... WOULD YOU LIKE TO SAY THAT WE SHOULD STRIKE AMERICA FIRST?
WELL...I DON'T WANT TO SAY IT DIRECTLY, BUT UNDER CERTAIN CIRCUMSTANCES, WE SHOULDN'T WAIT UNTIL WE FEEL THE IMPERIALISTS' PERFIDY...
KHRUSHCHEV WON'T LIKE THAT.
I DON'T CARE!
I BET TWENTY TO ONE THAT A U.S. INVASION WILL TAKE PLACE WITHIN THE NEXT THREE DAYS, AND I WON'T STAND IDLY BY WHILE CUBA FALLS BACK INTO THE HANDS OF THE IMPERIALISTS.

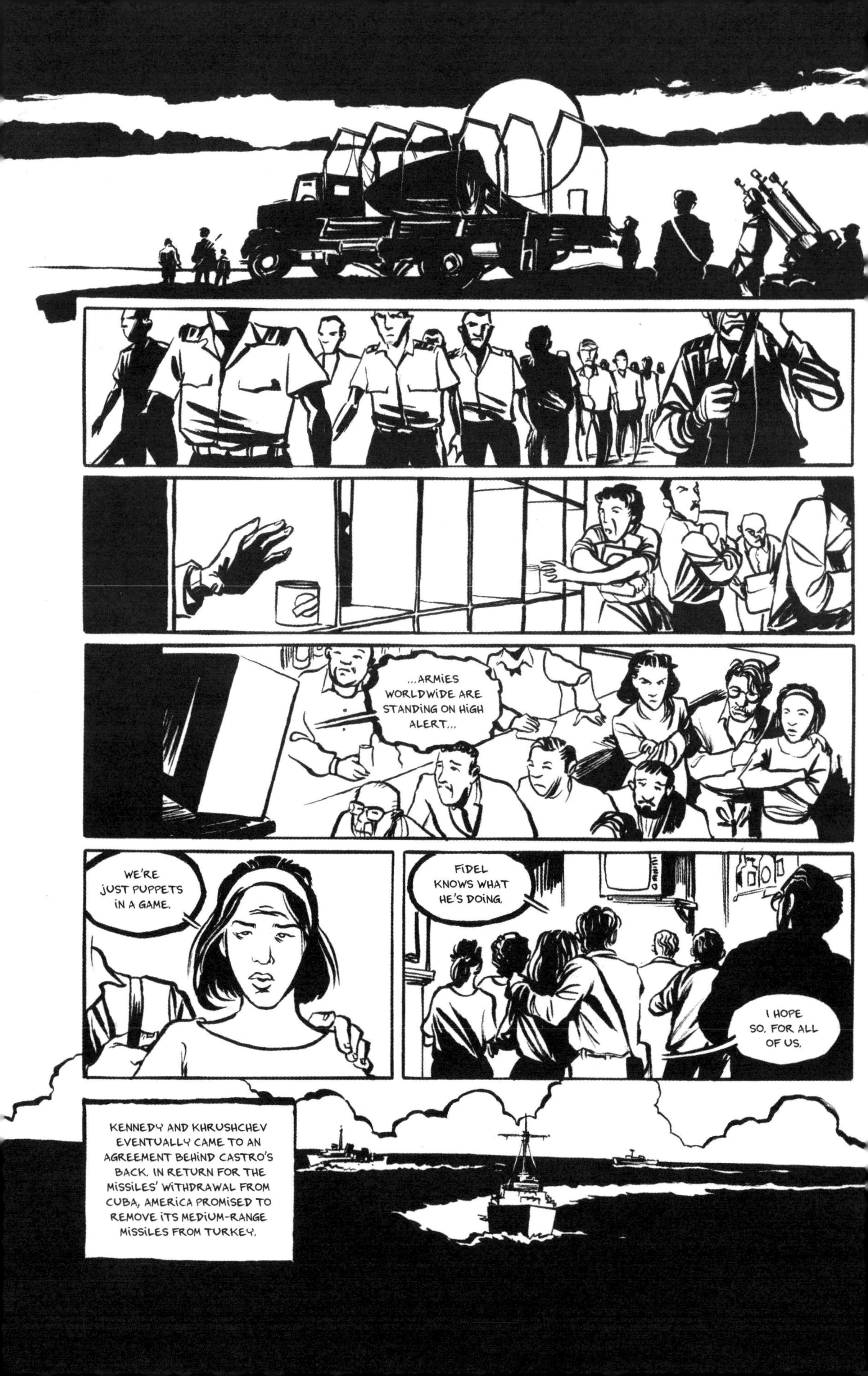
...ARMIES WORLDWIDE ARE STANDING ON HIGH ALERT...
WE'RE JUST PUPPETS IN A GAME.
FIDEL KNOWS WHAT HE'S DOING.
I HOPE SO, FOR ALL OF US.
KENNEDY AND KHRUSHCHEV EVENTUALLY CAME TO AN AGREEMENT BEHIND CASTRO'S BACK. IN RETURN FOR THE MISSILES' WITHDRAWAL FROM CUBA, AMERICA PROMISED TO REMOVE ITS MEDIUM-RANGE MISSILES FROM TURKEY.

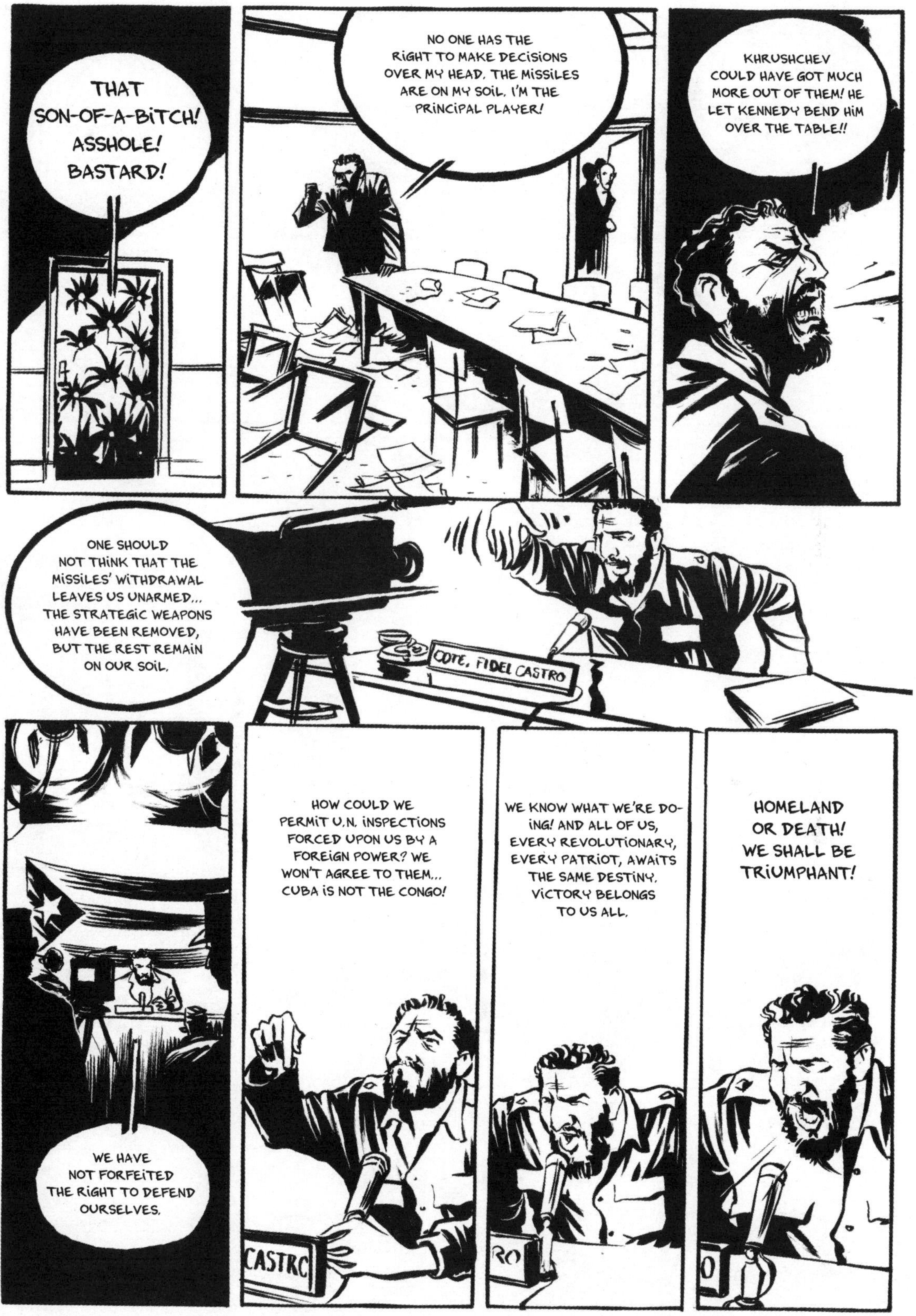
THAT SON-OF-A-BITCH! ASSHOLE! BASTARD!
NO ONE HAS THE RIGHT TO MAKE DECISIONS OVER MY HEAD. THE MISSILES ARE ON MY SOIL. I'M THE PRINCIPAL PLAYER!
KHRUSHCHEV COULD HAVE GOT MUCH MORE OUT OF THEM! HE LET KENNEDY BEND HIM OVER THE TABLE!!
ONE SHOULD NOT THINK THAT THE MISSILES' WITHDRAWAL LEAVES US UNARMED... THE STRATEGIC WEAPONS HAVE BEEN REMOVED, BUT THE REST REMAIN ON OUR SOIL.
CDTE. FIDEL CASTRO
WE HAVE NOT FORFEITED THE RIGHT TO DEFEND OURSELVES.
HOW COULD WE PERMIT U.N. INSPECTIONS FORCED UPON US BY A FOREIGN POWER? WE WON'T AGREE TO THEM... CUBA IS NOT THE CONGO!
WE KNOW WHAT WE'RE DOING! AND ALL OF US, EVERY REVOLUTIONARY, EVERY PATRIOT, AWAITS THE SAME DESTINY. VICTORY BELONGS TO US ALL.
HOMELAND OR DEATH! WE SHALL BE TRIUMPHANT!

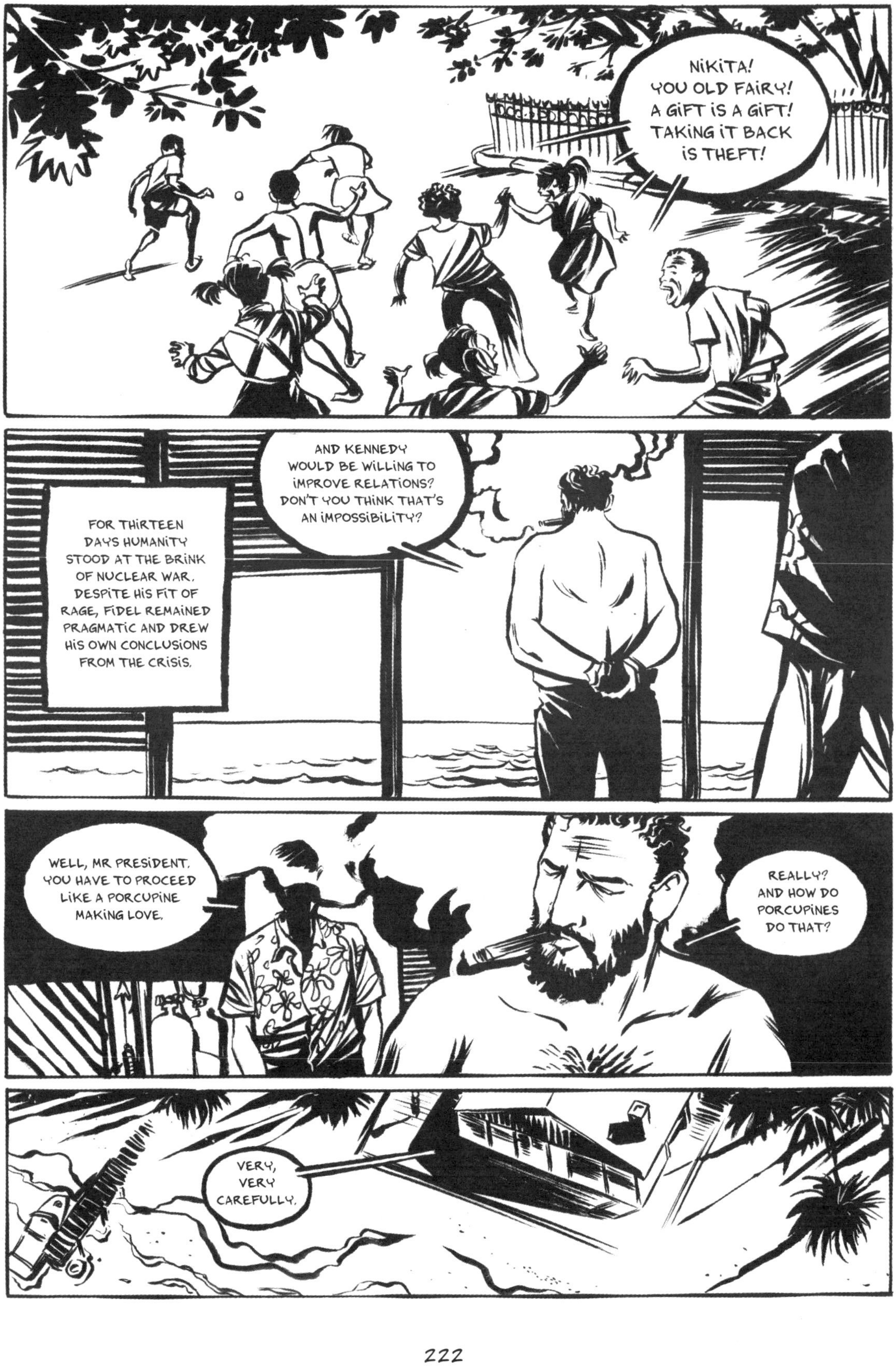
NIKITA! YOU OLD FAIRY! A GIFT IS A GIFT! TAKING IT BACK IS THEFT!
FOR THIRTEEN DAYS HUMANITY STOOD AT THE BRINK OF NUCLEAR WAR. DESPITE HIS FIT OF RAGE, FIDEL REMAINED PRAGMATIC AND DREW HIS OWN CONCLUSIONS FROM THE CRISIS.
AND KENNEDY WOULD BE WILLING TO IMPROVE RELATIONS? DON'T YOU THINK THAT'S AN IMPOSSIBILITY?
WELL, MR PRESIDENT, YOU HAVE TO PROCEED LIKE A PORCUPINE MAKING LOVE.
REALLY? AND HOW DO PORCUPINES DO THAT?
VERY, VERY CAREFULLY.

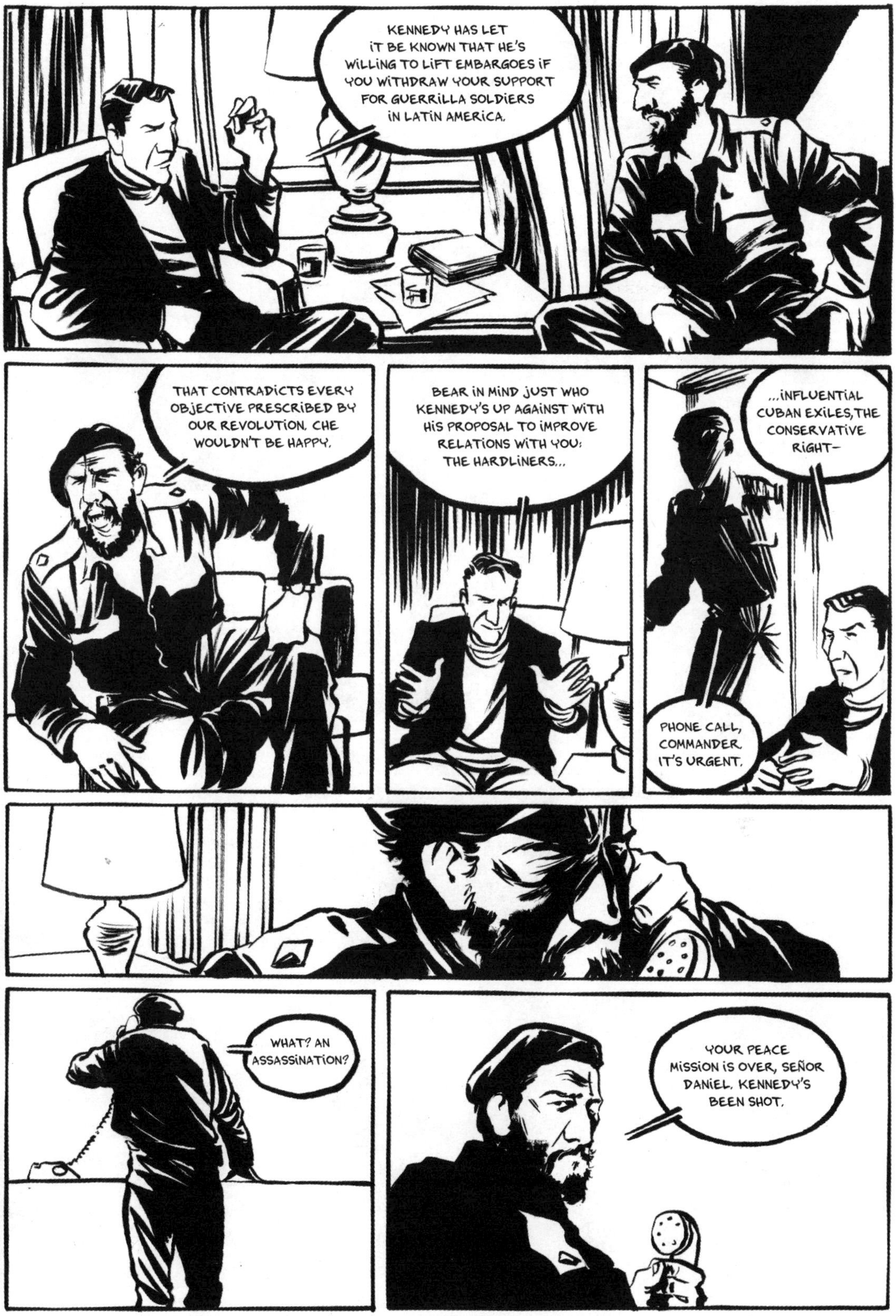
KENNEDY HAS LET IT BE KNOWN THAT HE'S WILLING TO LIFT EMBARGOES IF YOU WITHDRAW YOUR SUPPORT FOR GUERRILLA SOLDIERS IN LATIN AMERICA.
THAT CONTRADICTS EVERY OBJECTIVE PRESCRIBED BY OUR REVOLUTION. CHE WOULDN'T BE HAPPY.
BEAR IN MIND JUST WHO KENNEDY'S UP AGAINST WITH HIS PROPOSAL TO IMPROVE RELATIONS WITH YOU: THE HARDLINERS...
...INFLUENTIAL CUBAN EXILES, THE CONSERVATIVE RIGHT—
PHONE CALL, COMMANDER. IT'S URGENT.
WHAT? AN ASSASSINATION?
YOUR PEACE MISSION IS OVER, SEÑOR DANIEL. KENNEDY'S BEEN SHOT.

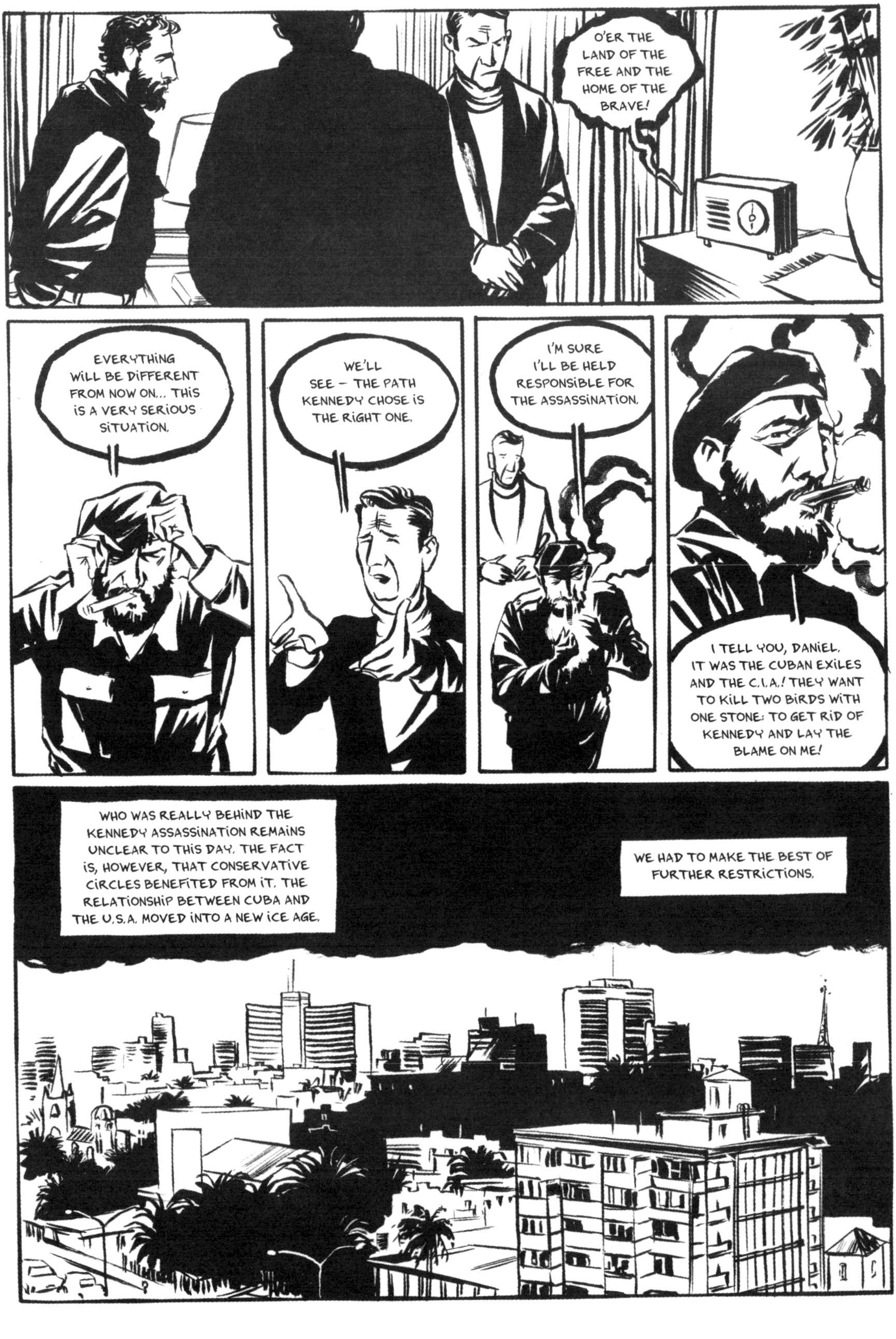
O'ER THE LAND OF THE FREE AND THE HOME OF THE BRAVE!
EVERYTHING WILL BE DIFFERENT FROM NOW ON... THIS IS A VERY SERIOUS SITUATION.
WE'LL SEE – THE PATH KENNEDY CHOSE IS THE RIGHT ONE.
I'M SURE I'LL BE HELD RESPONSIBLE FOR THE ASSASSINATION.
I TELL YOU, DANIEL. IT WAS THE CUBAN EXILES AND THE C.I.A.! THEY WANT TO KILL TWO BIRDS WITH ONE STONE: TO GET RID OF KENNEDY AND LAY THE BLAME ON ME!
WHO WAS REALLY BEHIND THE KENNEDY ASSASSINATION REMAINS UNCLEAR TO THIS DAY. THE FACT IS, HOWEVER, THAT CONSERVATIVE CIRCLES BENEFITED FROM IT. THE RELATIONSHIP BETWEEN CUBA AND THE U.S.A. MOVED INTO A NEW ICE AGE.
WE HAD TO MAKE THE BEST OF FURTHER RESTRICTIONS.

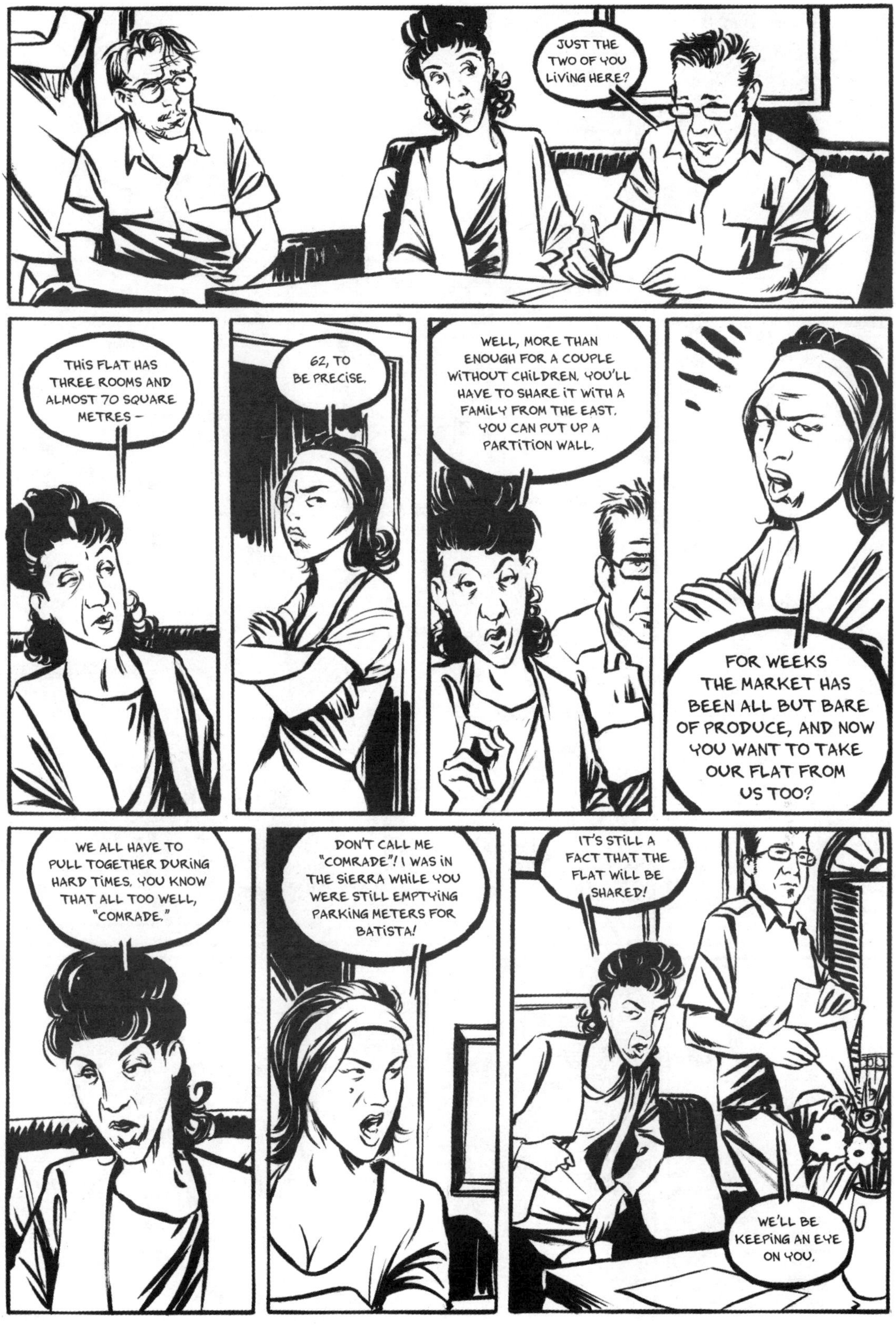
JUST THE TWO OF YOU LIVING HERE?
THIS FLAT HAS THREE ROOMS AND ALMOST 70 SQUARE METRES –
62, TO BE PRECISE.
WELL, MORE THAN ENOUGH FOR A COUPLE WITHOUT CHILDREN. YOU'LL HAVE TO SHARE IT WITH A FAMILY FROM THE EAST. YOU CAN PUT UP A PARTITION WALL.
FOR WEEKS THE MARKET HAS BEEN ALL BUT BARE OF PRODUCE, AND NOW YOU WANT TO TAKE OUR FLAT FROM US TOO?
WE ALL HAVE TO PULL TOGETHER DURING HARD TIMES. YOU KNOW THAT ALL TOO WELL, "COMRADE."
DON'T CALL ME "COMRADE"! I WAS IN THE SIERRA WHILE YOU WERE STILL EMPTYING PARKING METERS FOR BATISTA!
IT'S STILL A FACT THAT THE FLAT WILL BE SHARED!
WE'LL BE KEEPING AN EYE ON YOU.

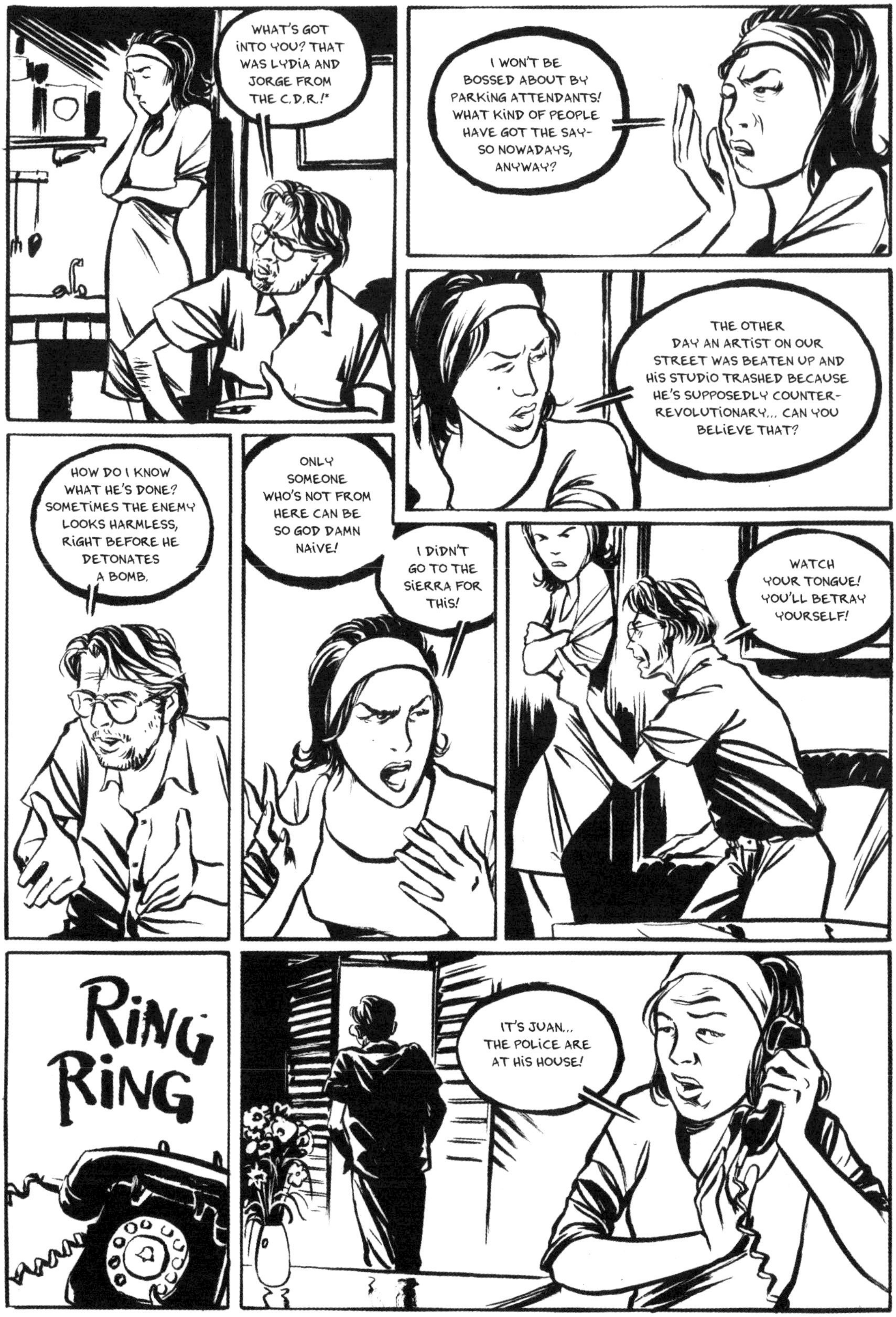
WHAT'S GOT INTO YOU? THAT WAS LYDIA AND JORGE FROM THE C.D.R.!*
I WON'T BE BOSSED ABOUT BY PARKING ATTENDANTS! WHAT KIND OF PEOPLE HAVE GOT THE SAY-SO NOWADAYS, ANYWAY?
THE OTHER DAY AN ARTIST ON OUR STREET WAS BEATEN UP AND HIS STUDIO TRASHED BECAUSE HE'S SUPPOSEDLY COUNTER-REVOLUTIONARY... CAN YOU BELIEVE THAT?
HOW DO I KNOW WHAT HE'S DONE? SOMETIMES THE ENEMY LOOKS HARMLESS, RIGHT BEFORE HE DETONATES A BOMB.
ONLY SOMEONE WHO'S NOT FROM HERE CAN BE SO GOD DAMN NAIVE!
I DIDN'T GO TO THE SIERRA FOR THIS!
WATCH YOUR TONGUE! YOU'LL BETRAY YOURSELF!
RING RING
IT'S JUAN... THE POLICE ARE AT HIS HOUSE!

* THE COMMITTEES FOR THE DEFENCE OF THE REVOLUTION.

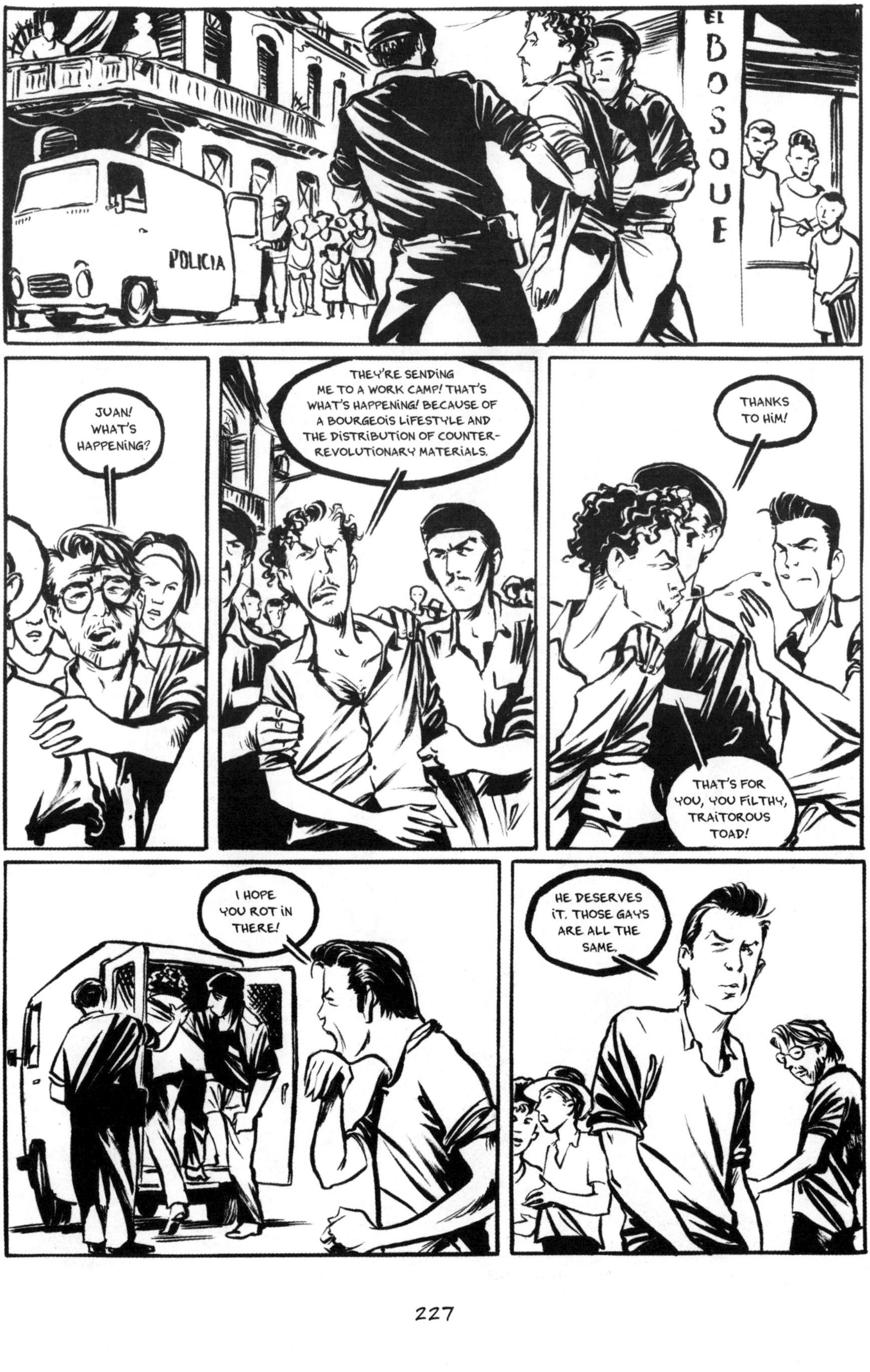
EL BOSQUE
POLICIA
JUAN! WHAT'S HAPPENING?
THEY'RE SENDING ME TO A WORK CAMP! THAT'S WHAT'S HAPPENING! BECAUSE OF A BOURGEOIS LIFESTYLE AND THE DISTRIBUTION OF COUNTER-REVOLUTIONARY MATERIALS.
THANKS TO HIM!
THAT'S FOR YOU, YOU FILTHY, TRAITOROUS TOAD!
I HOPE YOU ROT IN THERE!
HE DESERVES IT. THOSE GAYS ARE ALL THE SAME.

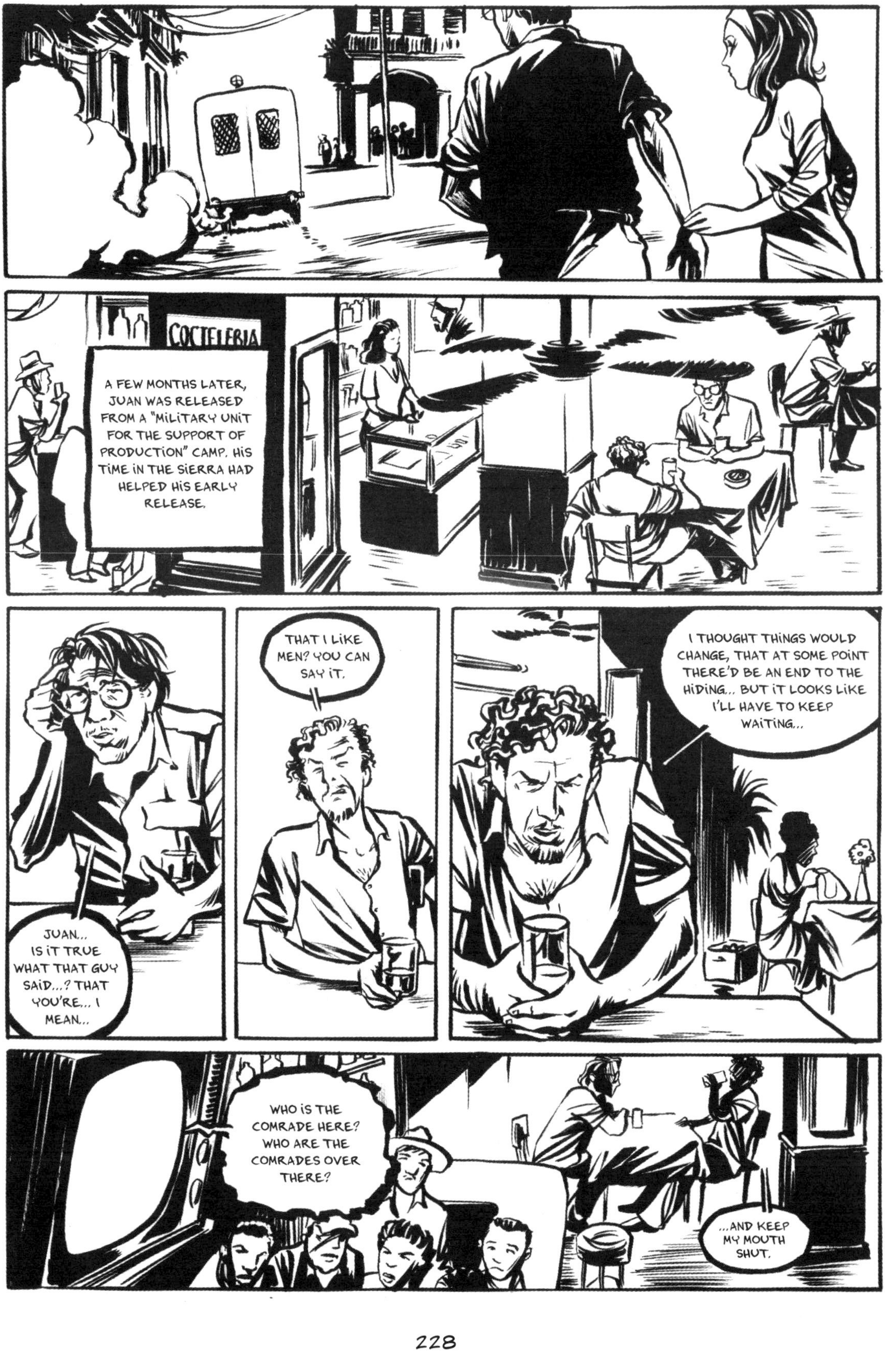
COCTELERIA
A FEW MONTHS LATER, JUAN WAS RELEASED FROM A "MILITARY UNIT FOR THE SUPPORT OF PRODUCTION" CAMP. HIS TIME IN THE SIERRA HAD HELPED HIS EARLY RELEASE.
JUAN... IS IT TRUE WHAT THAT GUY SAID...? THAT YOU'RE... I MEAN...
THAT I LIKE MEN? YOU CAN SAY IT.
I THOUGHT THINGS WOULD CHANGE, THAT AT SOME POINT THERE'D BE AN END TO THE HIDING... BUT IT LOOKS LIKE I'LL HAVE TO KEEP WAITING...
WHO IS THE COMRADE HERE? WHO ARE THE COMRADES OVER THERE?
...AND KEEP MY MOUTH SHUT.

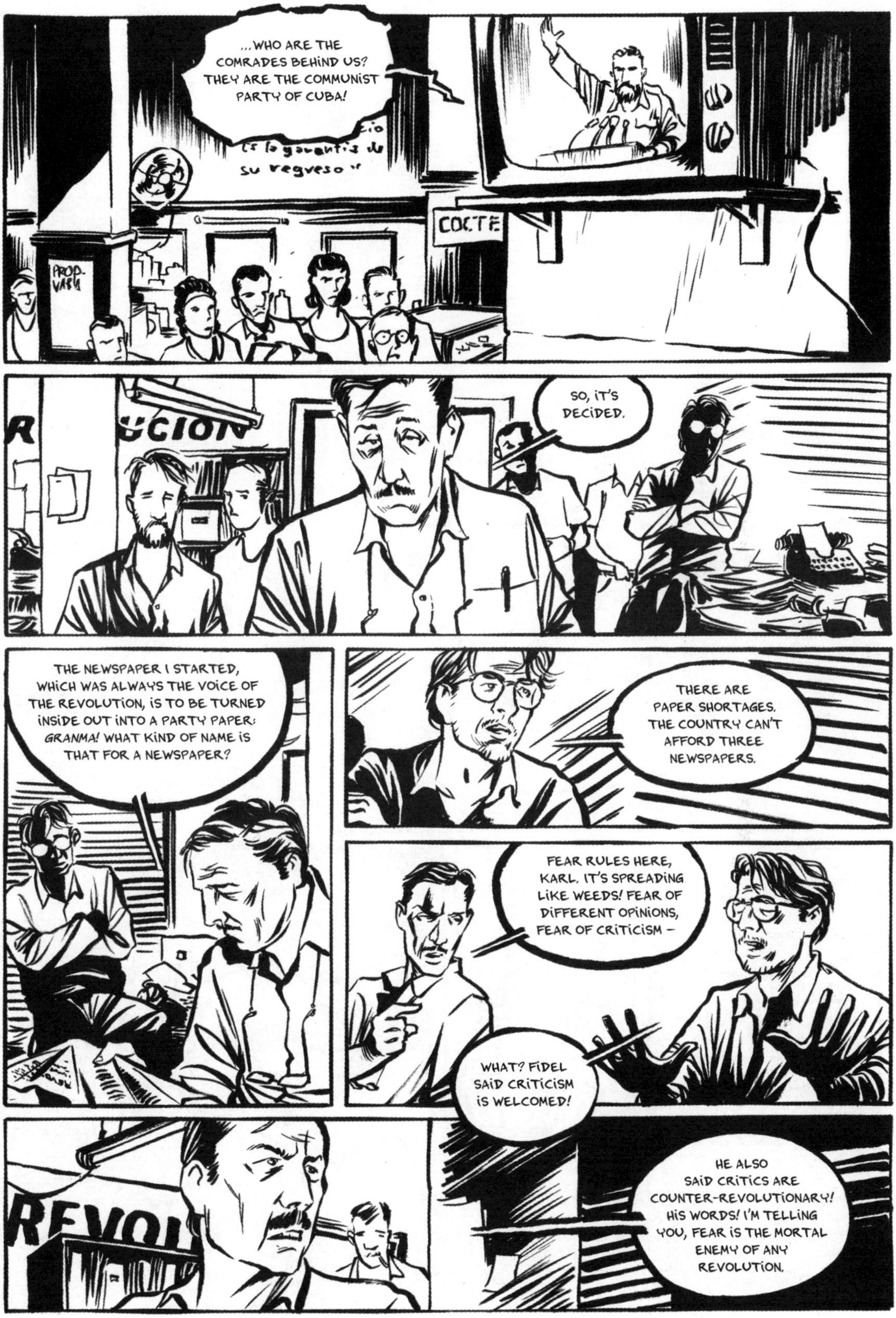
...WHO ARE THE COMRADES BEHIND US? THEY ARE THE COMMUNIST PARTY OF CUBA!
SO, IT'S DECIDED.
THE NEWSPAPER I STARTED, WHICH WAS ALWAYS THE VOICE OF THE REVOLUTION, IS TO BE TURNED INSIDE OUT INTO A PARTY PAPER: GRANMA! WHAT KIND OF NAME IS THAT FOR A NEWSPAPER?
THERE ARE PAPER SHORTAGES. THE COUNTRY CAN'T AFFORD THREE NEWSPAPERS.
FEAR RULES HERE, KARL. IT'S SPREADING LIKE WEEDS! FEAR OF DIFFERENT OPINIONS, FEAR OF CRITICISM –
WHAT? FIDEL SAID CRITICISM IS WELCOMED!
HE ALSO SAID CRITICS ARE COUNTER-REVOLUTIONARY! HIS WORDS! I'M TELLING YOU, FEAR IS THE MORTAL ENEMY OF ANY REVOLUTION.

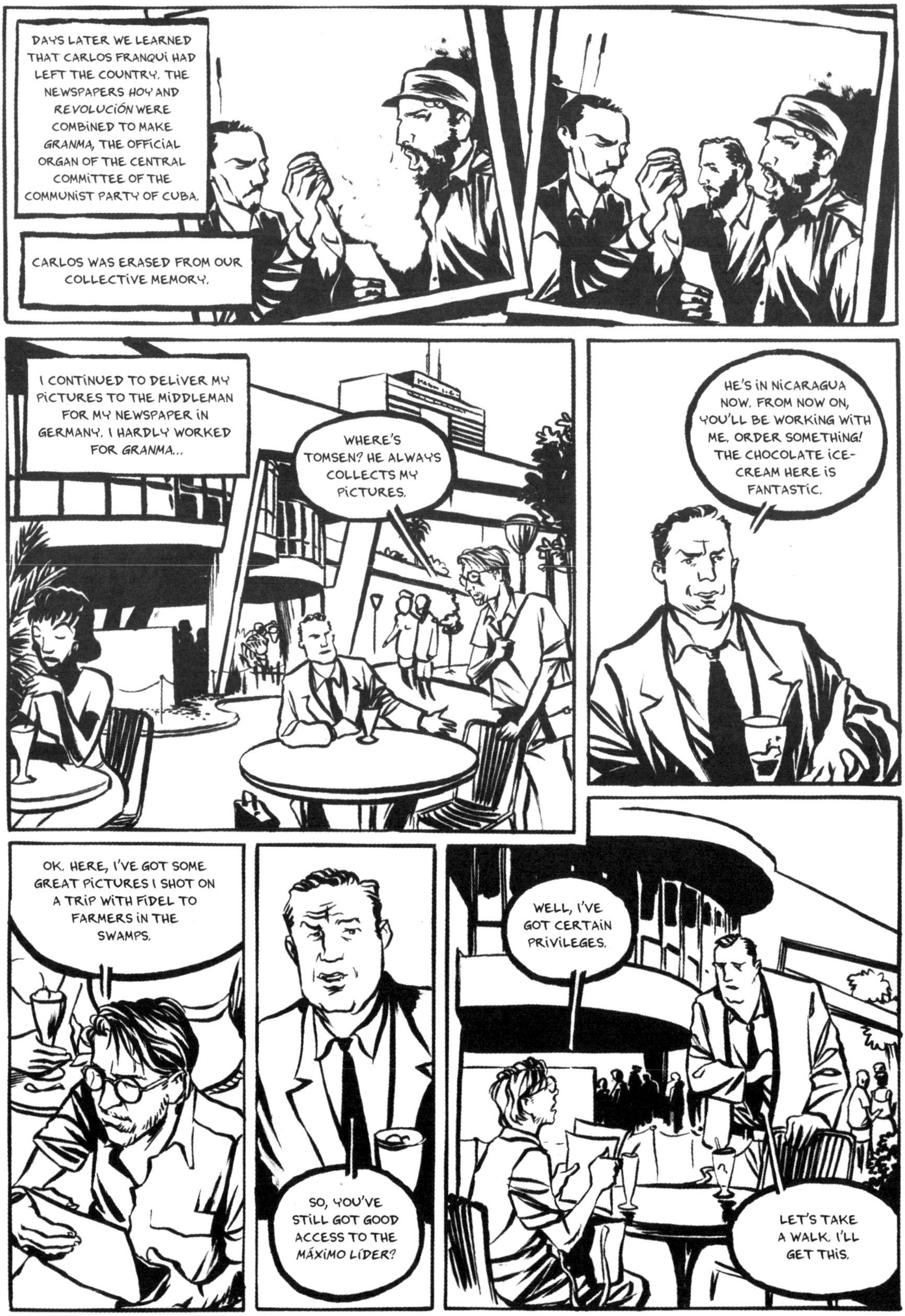
DAYS LATER WE LEARNED THAT CARLOS FRANQUI HAD LEFT THE COUNTRY. THE NEWSPAPERS *HOY* AND *REVOLUCIÓN* WERE COMBINED TO MAKE *GRANMA*, THE OFFICIAL ORGAN OF THE CENTRAL COMMITTEE OF THE COMMUNIST PARTY OF CUBA.
CARLOS WAS ERASED FROM OUR COLLECTIVE MEMORY.
I CONTINUED TO DELIVER MY PICTURES TO THE MIDDLEMAN FOR MY NEWSPAPER IN GERMANY. I HARDLY WORKED FOR *GRANMA*...
WHERE'S TOMSEN? HE ALWAYS COLLECTS MY PICTURES.
HE'S IN NICARAGUA NOW. FROM NOW ON, YOU'LL BE WORKING WITH ME. ORDER SOMETHING! THE CHOCOLATE ICE-CREAM HERE IS FANTASTIC.
OK. HERE, I'VE GOT SOME GREAT PICTURES I SHOT ON A TRIP WITH FIDEL TO FARMERS IN THE SWAMPS.
SO, YOU'VE STILL GOT GOOD ACCESS TO THE *MÁXIMO LÍDER*?
WELL, I'VE GOT CERTAIN PRIVILEGES.
LET'S TAKE A WALK. I'LL GET THIS.

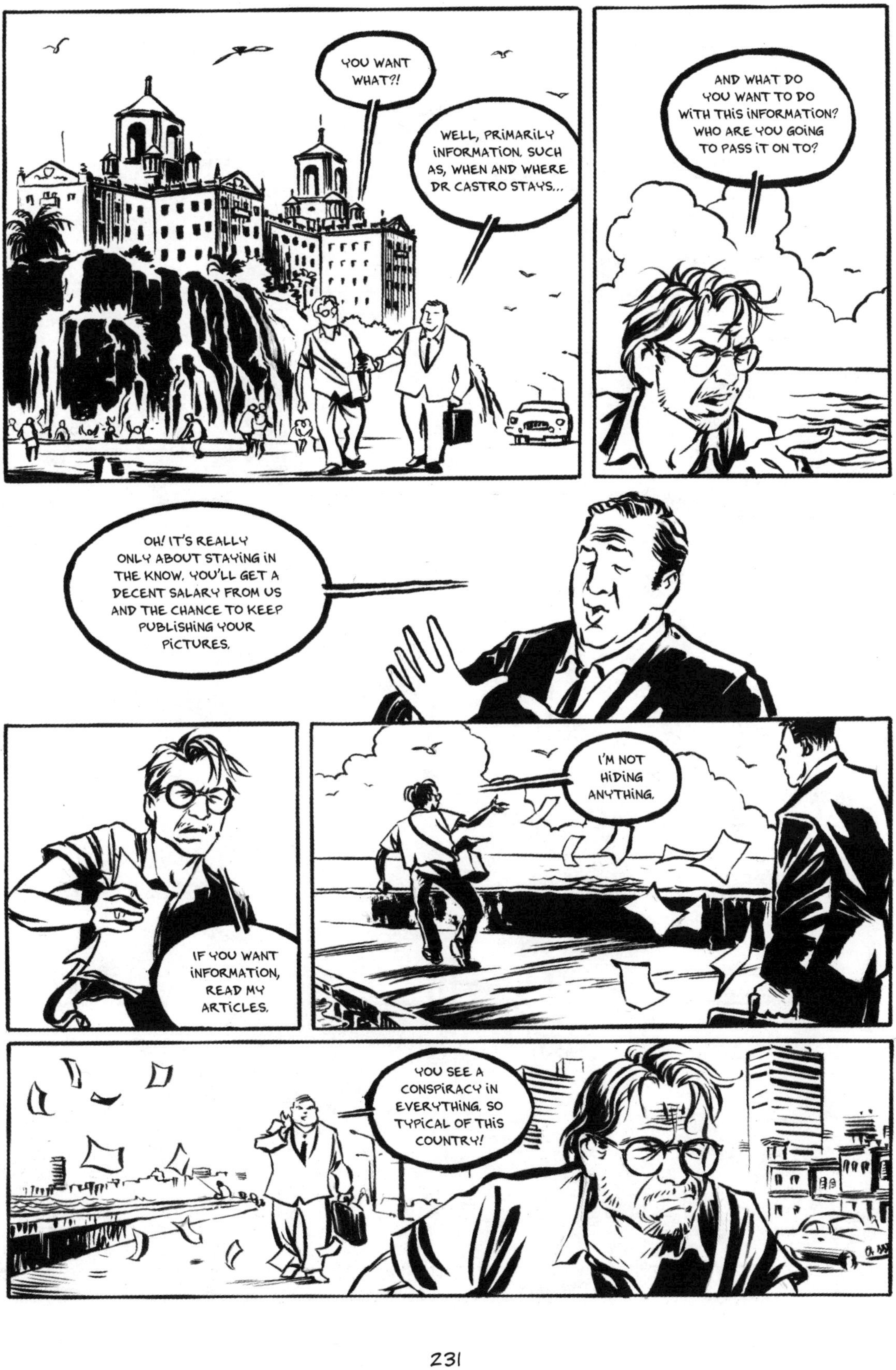
YOU WANT WHAT?!
WELL, PRIMARILY INFORMATION, SUCH AS, WHEN AND WHERE DR CASTRO STAYS...
AND WHAT DO YOU WANT TO DO WITH THIS INFORMATION? WHO ARE YOU GOING TO PASS IT ON TO?
OH! IT'S REALLY ONLY ABOUT STAYING IN THE KNOW. YOU'LL GET A DECENT SALARY FROM US AND THE CHANCE TO KEEP PUBLISHING YOUR PICTURES.
IF YOU WANT INFORMATION, READ MY ARTICLES.
I'M NOT HIDING ANYTHING.
YOU SEE A CONSPIRACY IN EVERYTHING, SO TYPICAL OF THIS COUNTRY!

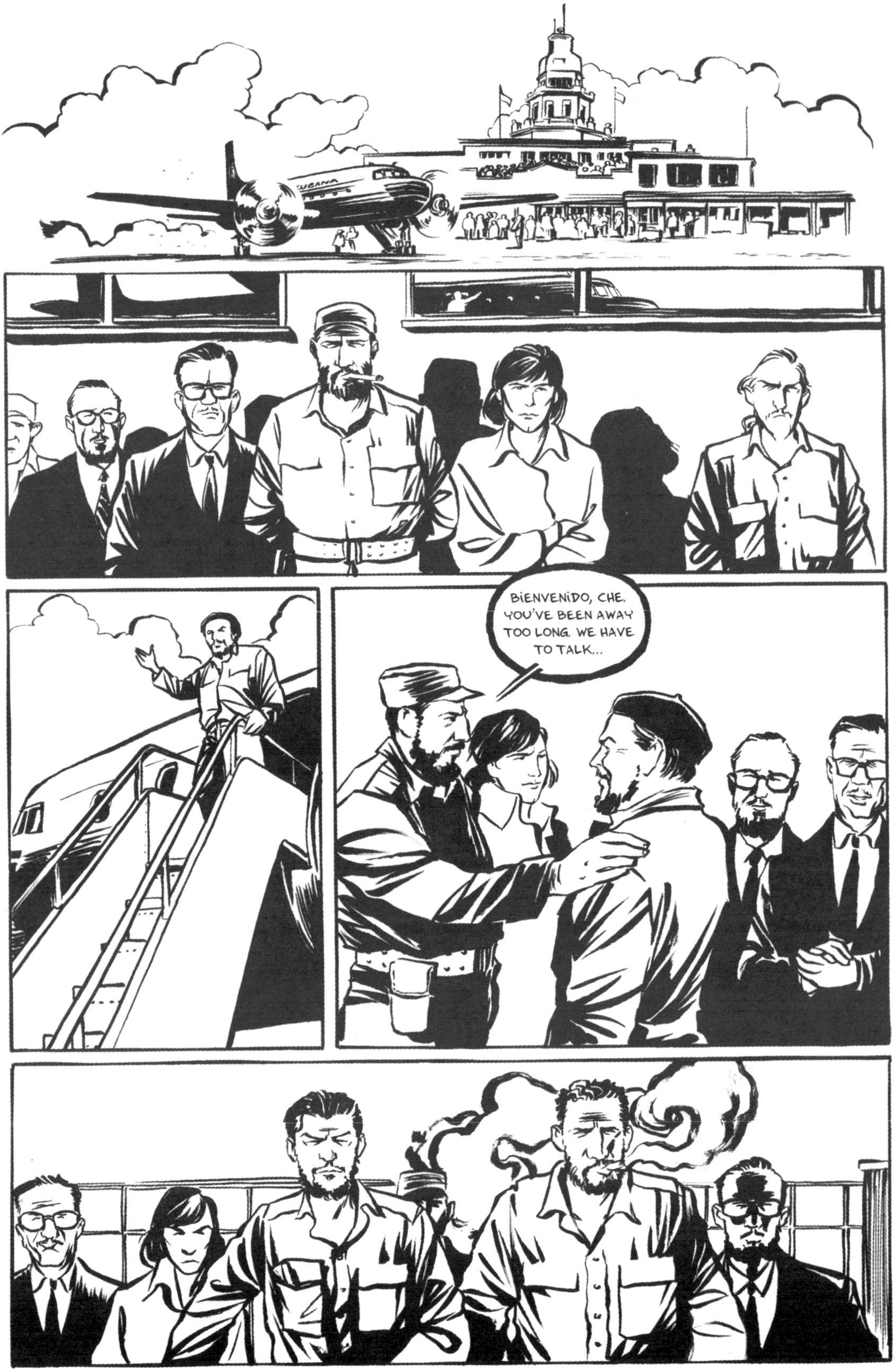
CUBANA
BiENVENiDO, CHE. YOU'VE BEEN AWAY TOO LONG. WE HAVE TO TALK...

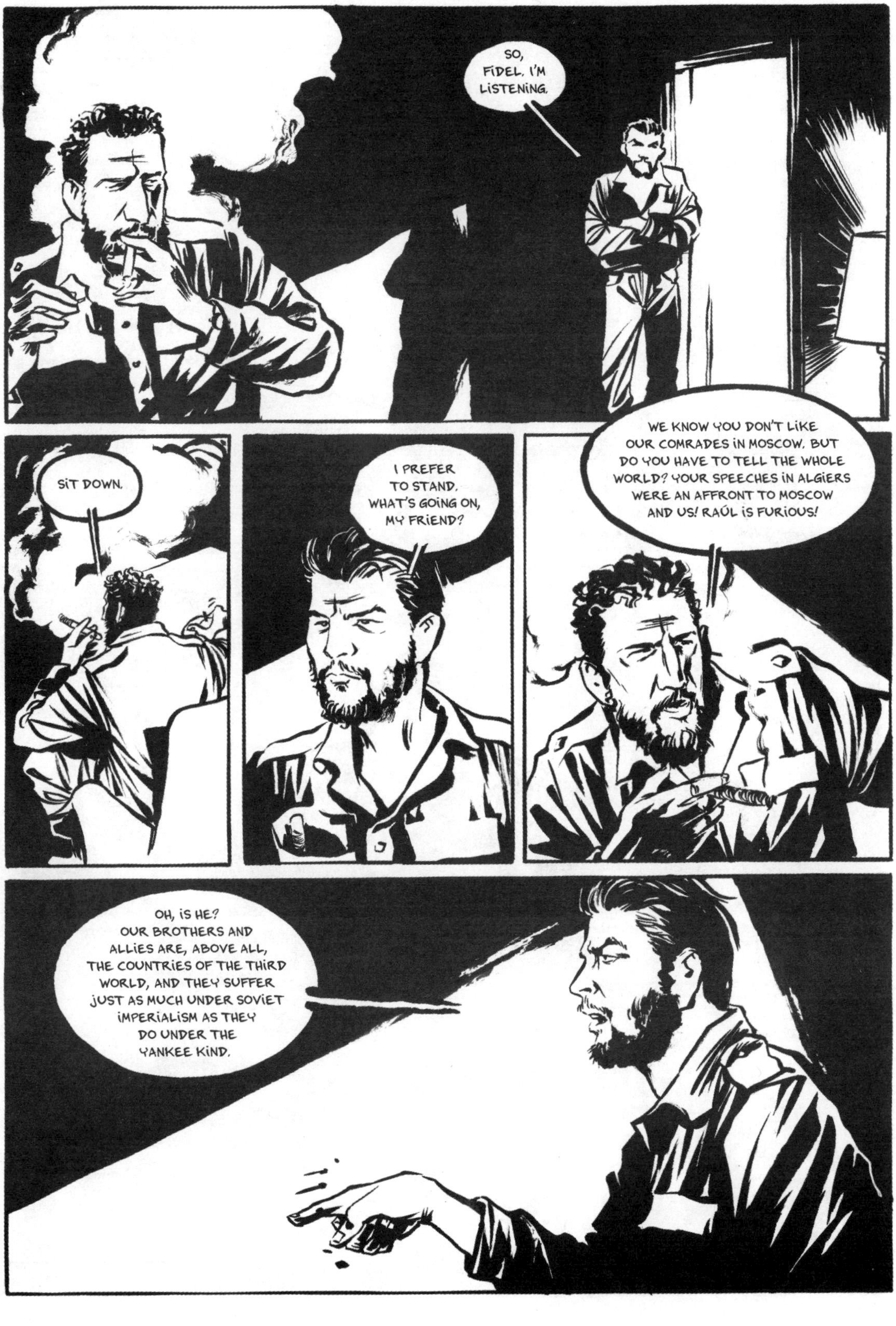
SO, FIDEL, I'M LISTENING.
SIT DOWN.
I PREFER TO STAND. WHAT'S GOING ON, MY FRIEND?
WE KNOW YOU DON'T LIKE OUR COMRADES IN MOSCOW, BUT DO YOU HAVE TO TELL THE WHOLE WORLD? YOUR SPEECHES IN ALGIERS WERE AN AFFRONT TO MOSCOW AND US! RAÚL IS FURIOUS!
OH, IS HE? OUR BROTHERS AND ALLIES ARE, ABOVE ALL, THE COUNTRIES OF THE THIRD WORLD, AND THEY SUFFER JUST AS MUCH UNDER SOVIET IMPERIALISM AS THEY DO UNDER THE YANKEE KIND.

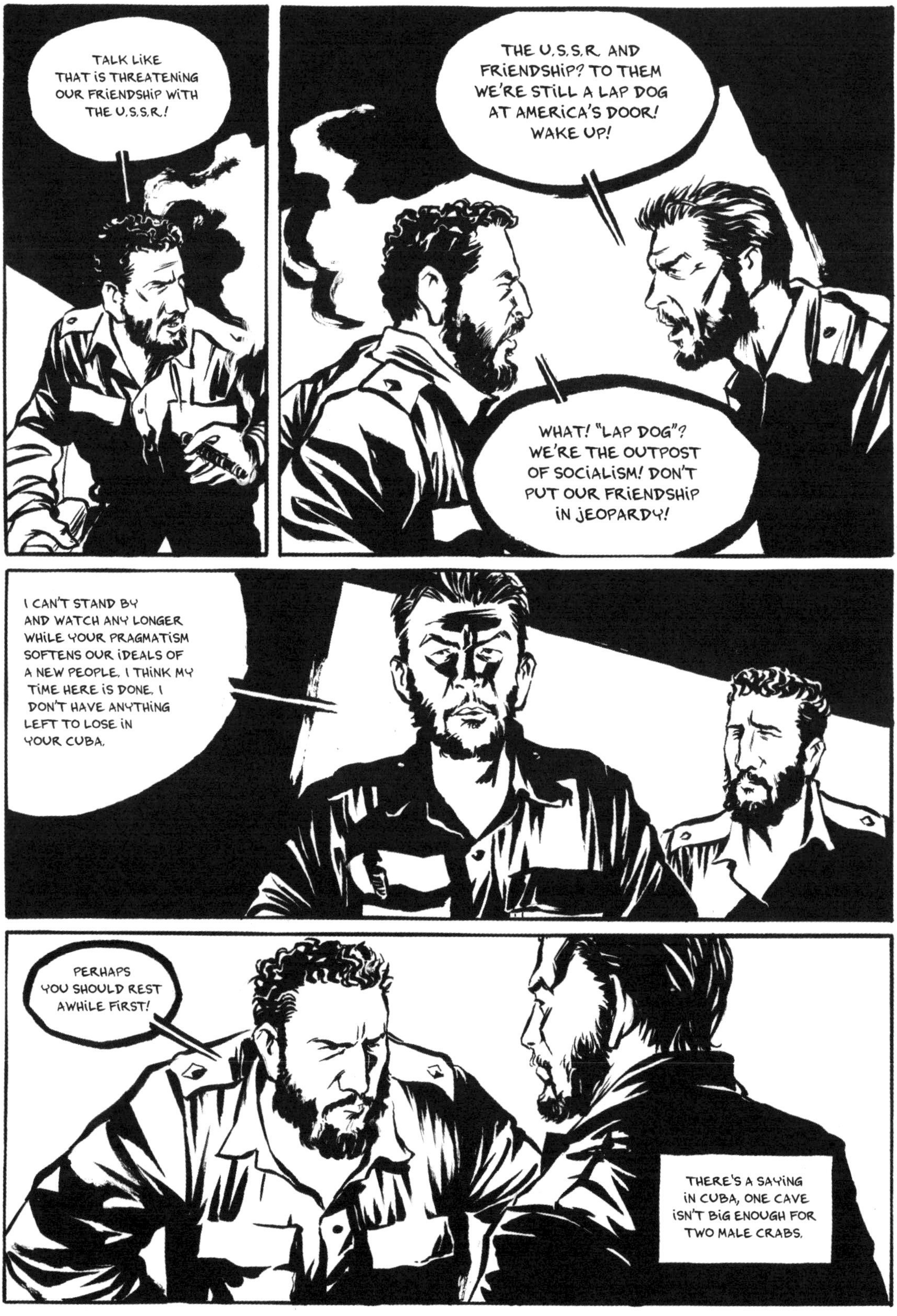
TALK LIKE THAT IS THREATENING OUR FRIENDSHIP WITH THE U.S.S.R.!
THE U.S.S.R. AND FRIENDSHIP? TO THEM WE'RE STILL A LAP DOG AT AMERICA'S DOOR! WAKE UP!
WHAT! "LAP DOG"? WE'RE THE OUTPOST OF SOCIALISM! DON'T PUT OUR FRIENDSHIP IN JEOPARDY!
I CAN'T STAND BY AND WATCH ANY LONGER WHILE YOUR PRAGMATISM SOFTENS OUR IDEALS OF A NEW PEOPLE. I THINK MY TIME HERE IS DONE. I DON'T HAVE ANYTHING LEFT TO LOSE IN YOUR CUBA.
PERHAPS YOU SHOULD REST AWHILE FIRST!
THERE'S A SAYING IN CUBA, ONE CAVE ISN'T BIG ENOUGH FOR TWO MALE CRABS.

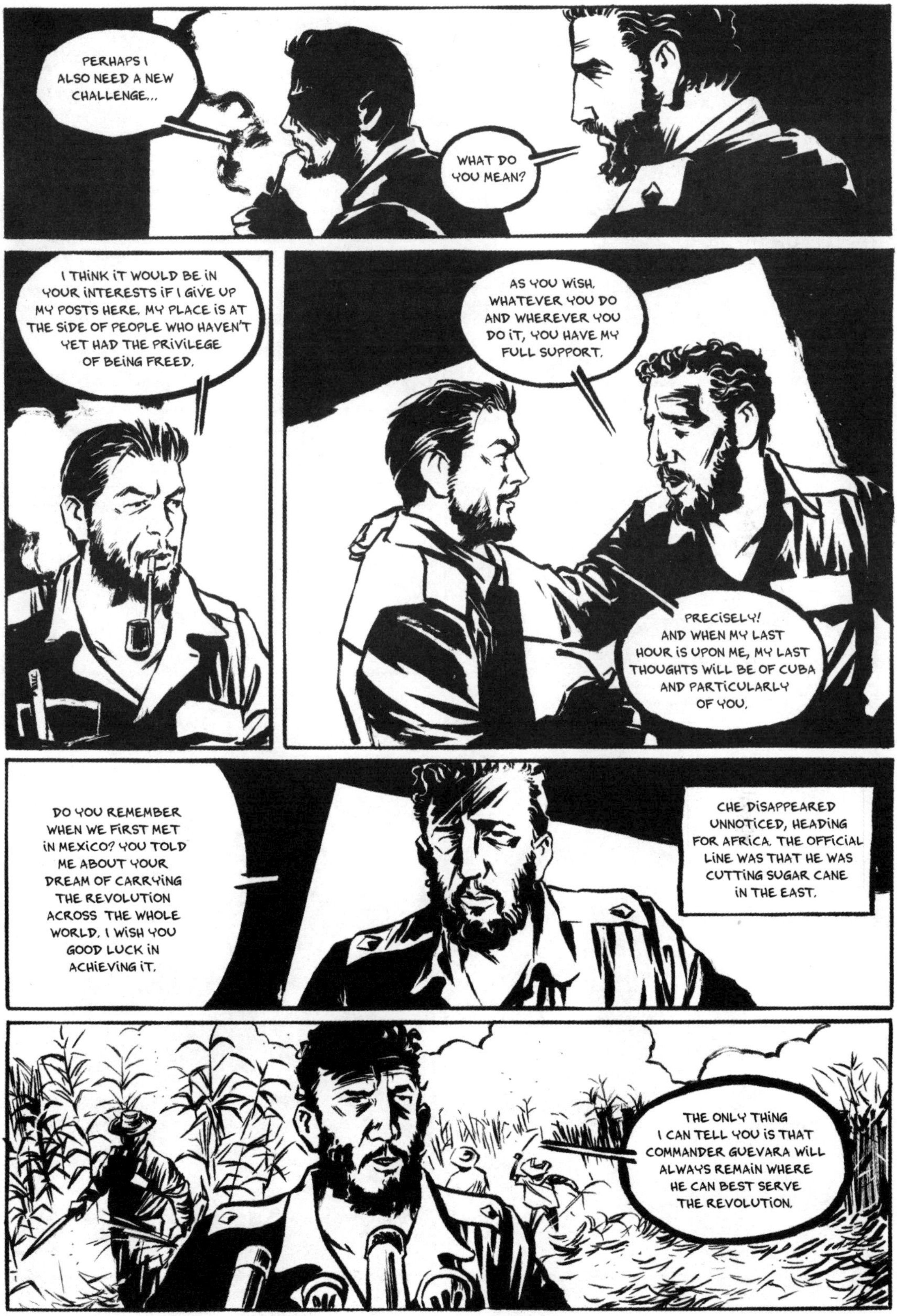
PERHAPS I ALSO NEED A NEW CHALLENGE...
WHAT DO YOU MEAN?
I THINK IT WOULD BE IN YOUR INTERESTS IF I GIVE UP MY POSTS HERE. MY PLACE IS AT THE SIDE OF PEOPLE WHO HAVEN'T YET HAD THE PRIVILEGE OF BEING FREED.
AS YOU WISH. WHATEVER YOU DO AND WHEREVER YOU DO IT, YOU HAVE MY FULL SUPPORT.
PRECISELY! AND WHEN MY LAST HOUR IS UPON ME, MY LAST THOUGHTS WILL BE OF CUBA AND PARTICULARLY OF YOU.
DO YOU REMEMBER WHEN WE FIRST MET IN MEXICO? YOU TOLD ME ABOUT YOUR DREAM OF CARRYING THE REVOLUTION ACROSS THE WHOLE WORLD. I WISH YOU GOOD LUCK IN ACHIEVING IT.
CHE DISAPPEARED UNNOTICED, HEADING FOR AFRICA. THE OFFICIAL LINE WAS THAT HE WAS CUTTING SUGAR CANE IN THE EAST.
THE ONLY THING I CAN TELL YOU IS THAT COMMANDER GUEVARA WILL ALWAYS REMAIN WHERE HE CAN BEST SERVE THE REVOLUTION.

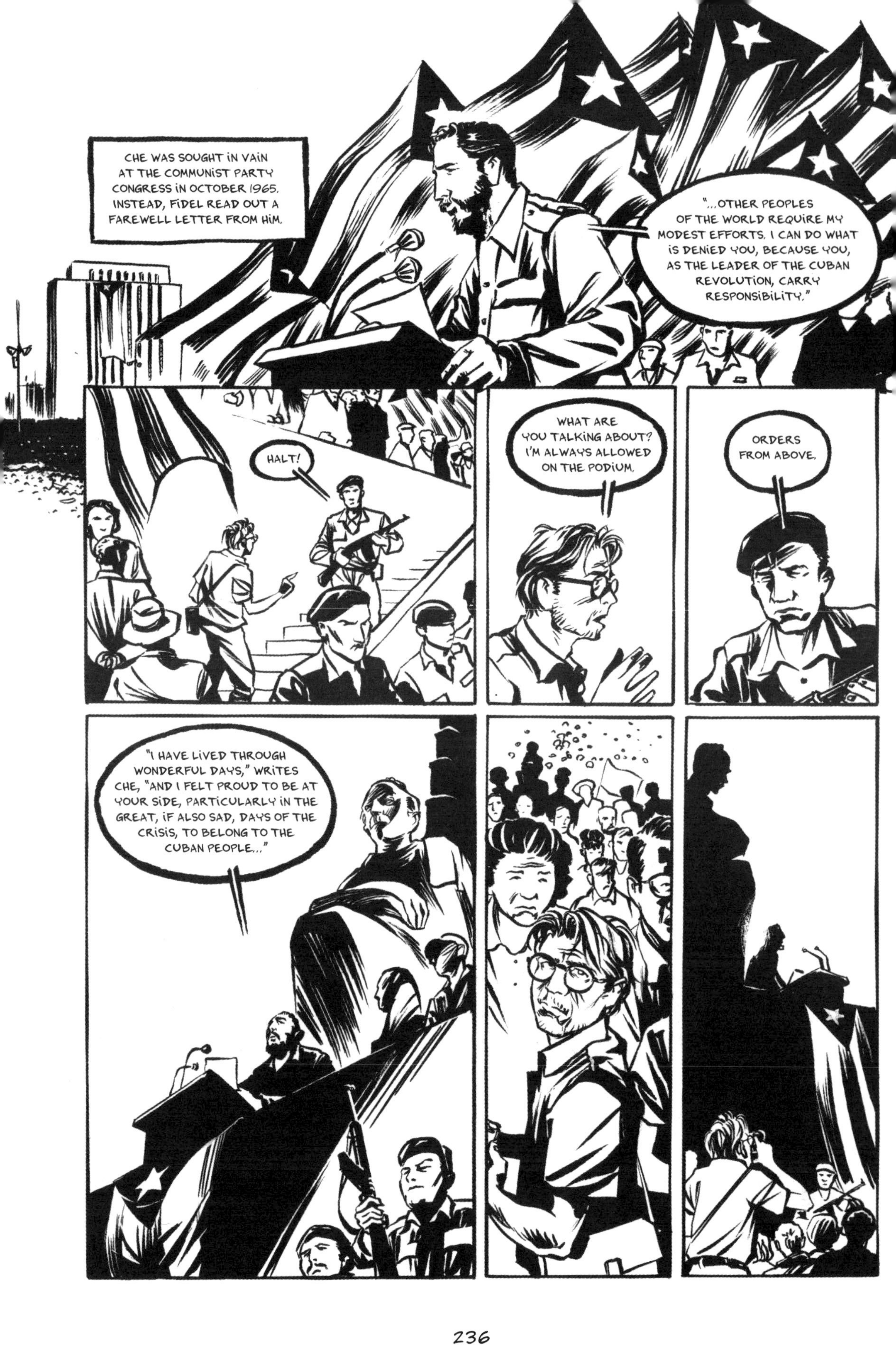
CHE WAS SOUGHT IN VAIN AT THE COMMUNIST PARTY CONGRESS IN OCTOBER 1965. INSTEAD, FIDEL READ OUT A FAREWELL LETTER FROM HIM.
"...OTHER PEOPLES OF THE WORLD REQUIRE MY MODEST EFFORTS. I CAN DO WHAT IS DENIED YOU, BECAUSE YOU, AS THE LEADER OF THE CUBAN REVOLUTION, CARRY RESPONSIBILITY."
HALT!
WHAT ARE YOU TALKING ABOUT? I'M ALWAYS ALLOWED ON THE PODIUM.
ORDERS FROM ABOVE.
"I HAVE LIVED THROUGH WONDERFUL DAYS," WRITES CHE, "AND I FELT PROUD TO BE AT YOUR SIDE, PARTICULARLY IN THE GREAT, IF ALSO SAD, DAYS OF THE CRISIS, TO BELONG TO THE CUBAN PEOPLE..."

CHE'S MISSION IN AFRICA WAS DISASTROUS. HIS OBJECTIVE OF STARTING A REVOLUTION IN THE CONGO, MODELLED ON THE CUBAN REVOLUTION, FAILED COMPLETELY.

OW!

AFTER SEVERAL MONTHS IN THE CONGO, CHE RETURNED EXHAUSTED TO CUBA AND DISAPPEARED INTO A SANATORIUM. A LITTLE WHILE LATER HE CONVINCED CASTRO TO CARRY THE REVOLUTION TO BOLIVIA.

YOU KEEP OUT OF IT!

YOU SHOULD BE MORE CAREFUL, MAN!

YOU'RE TAKING ON A LOT. YOU KNOW THE BOLIVIAN COMMUNISTS ARE NO FRIENDS OF OURS.

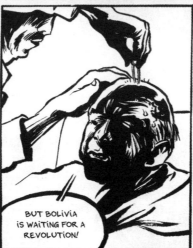

BUT BOLIVIA IS WAITING FOR A REVOLUTION!

YOU DON'T HAVE A SUPPORT BASE THERE.

FIDEL, TIME IS SLIPPING AWAY FROM US. WHY WAIT ANY LONGER?

DON'T BE IMPATIENT, CHE. THAT'S THE DEATH OF ANY PLAN. ONLY GO THERE ONCE A SOLID MOVEMENT HAS BEEN BUILT.

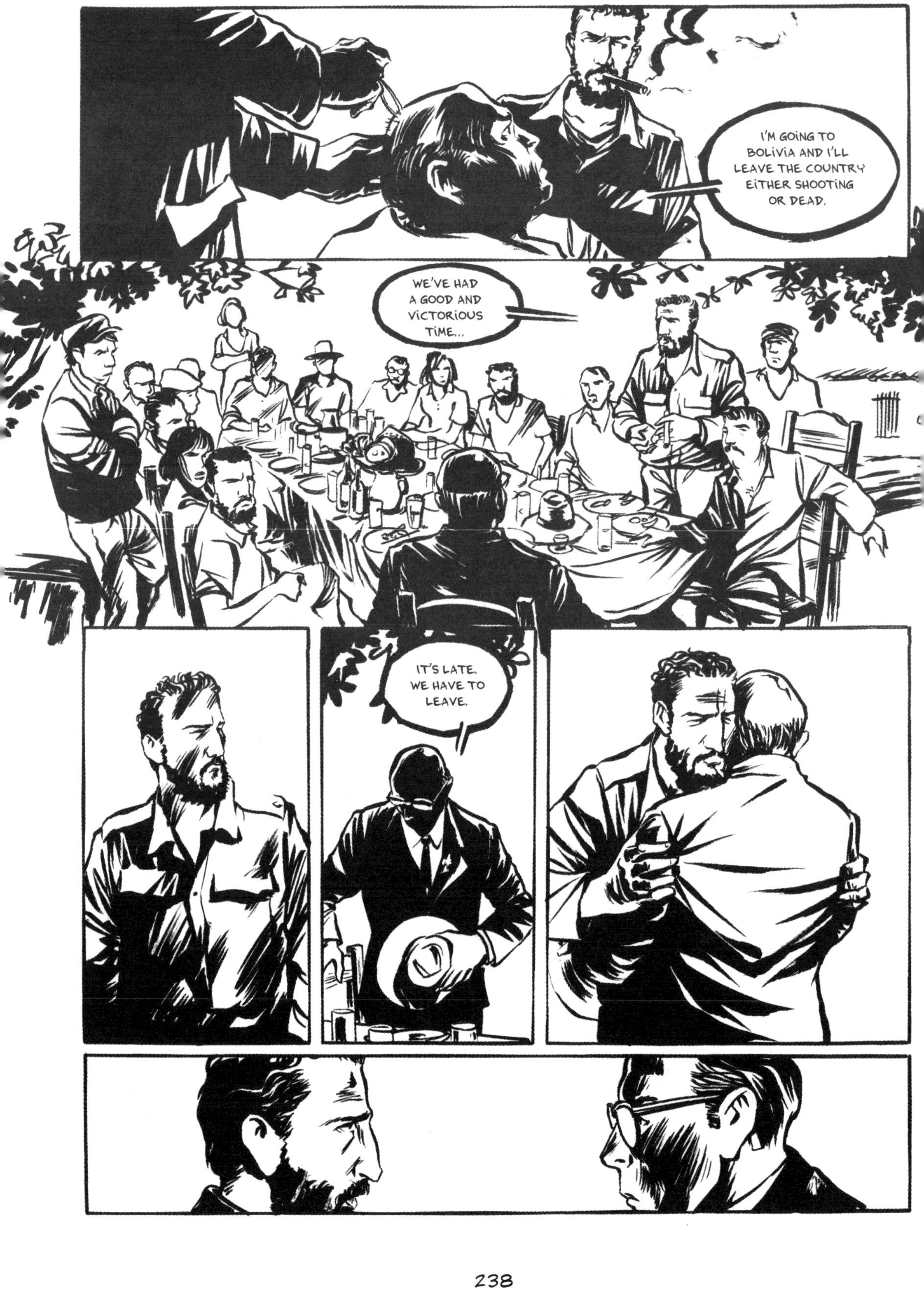
I'M GOING TO BOLIVIA AND I'LL LEAVE THE COUNTRY EITHER SHOOTING OR DEAD.
WE'VE HAD A GOOD AND VICTORIOUS TIME...
IT'S LATE. WE HAVE TO LEAVE.

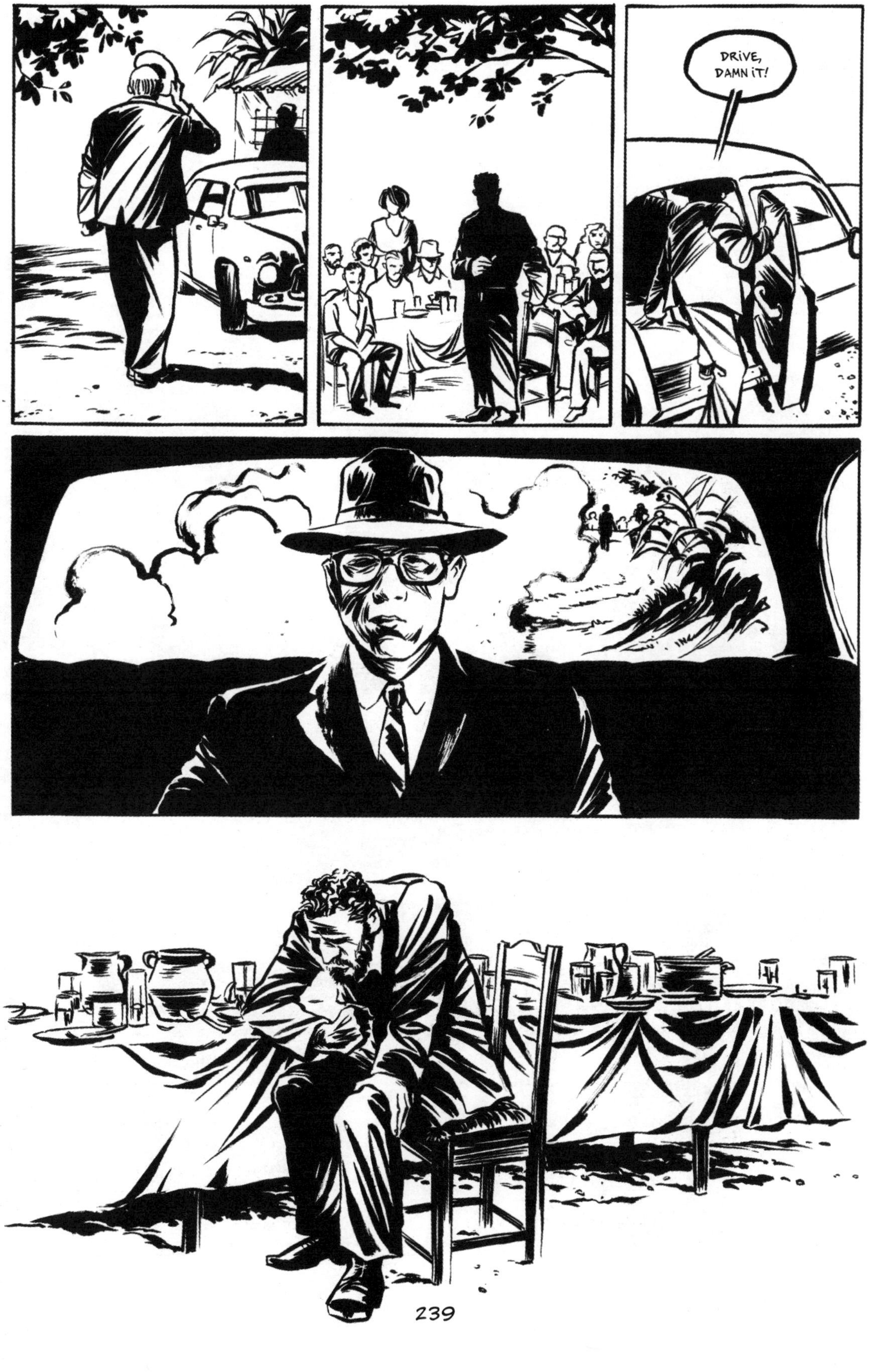
DRIVE, DAMN IT!

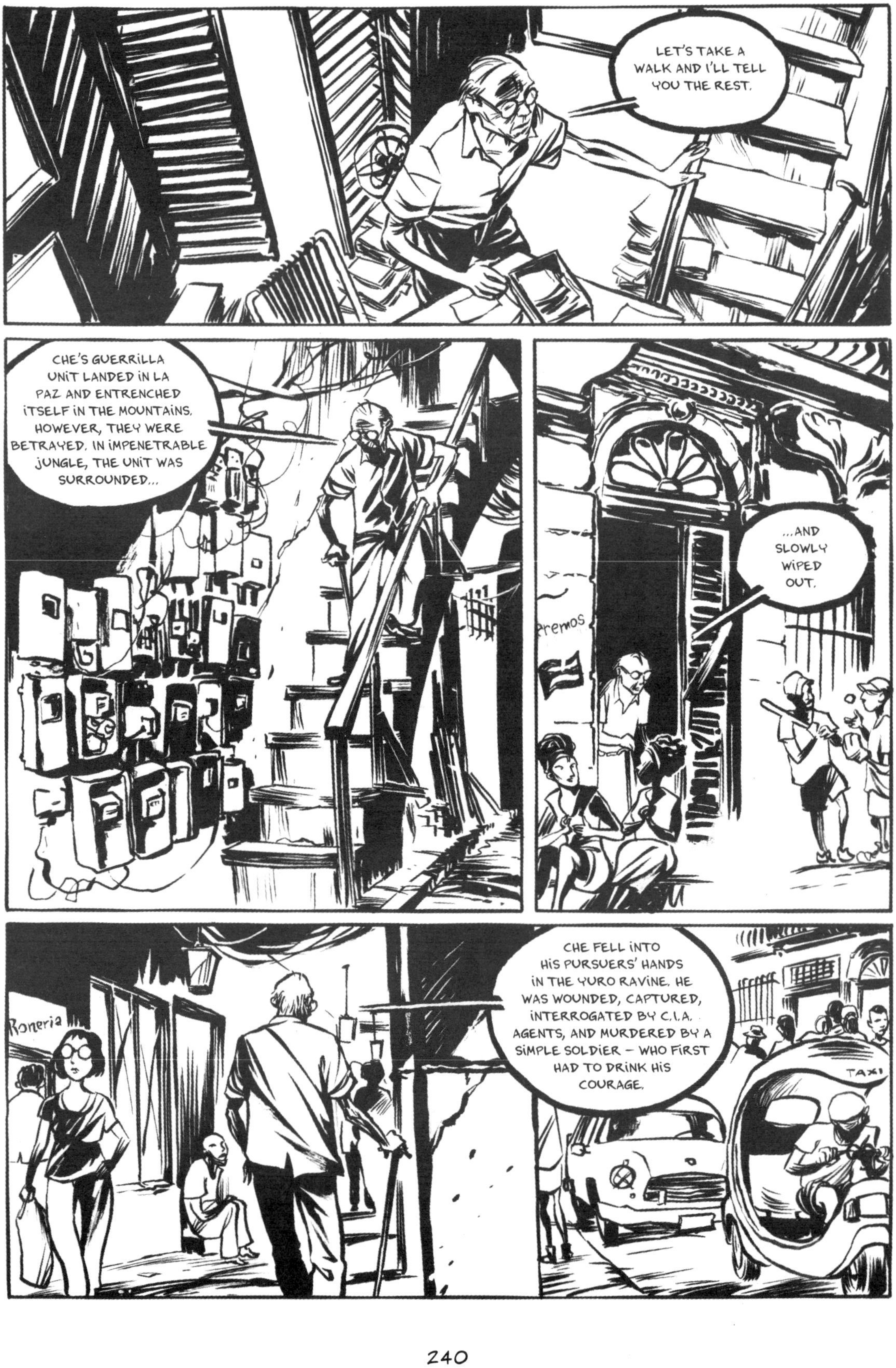
LET'S TAKE A WALK AND I'LL TELL YOU THE REST.
CHE'S GUERRILLA UNIT LANDED IN LA PAZ AND ENTRENCHED ITSELF IN THE MOUNTAINS. HOWEVER, THEY WERE BETRAYED. IN IMPENETRABLE JUNGLE, THE UNIT WAS SURROUNDED...
...AND SLOWLY WIPED OUT.
Premos
Roneria
CHE FELL INTO HIS PURSUERS' HANDS IN THE YURO RAVINE. HE WAS WOUNDED, CAPTURED, INTERROGATED BY C.I.A. AGENTS, AND MURDERED BY A SIMPLE SOLDIER — WHO FIRST HAD TO DRINK HIS COURAGE.
TAXI

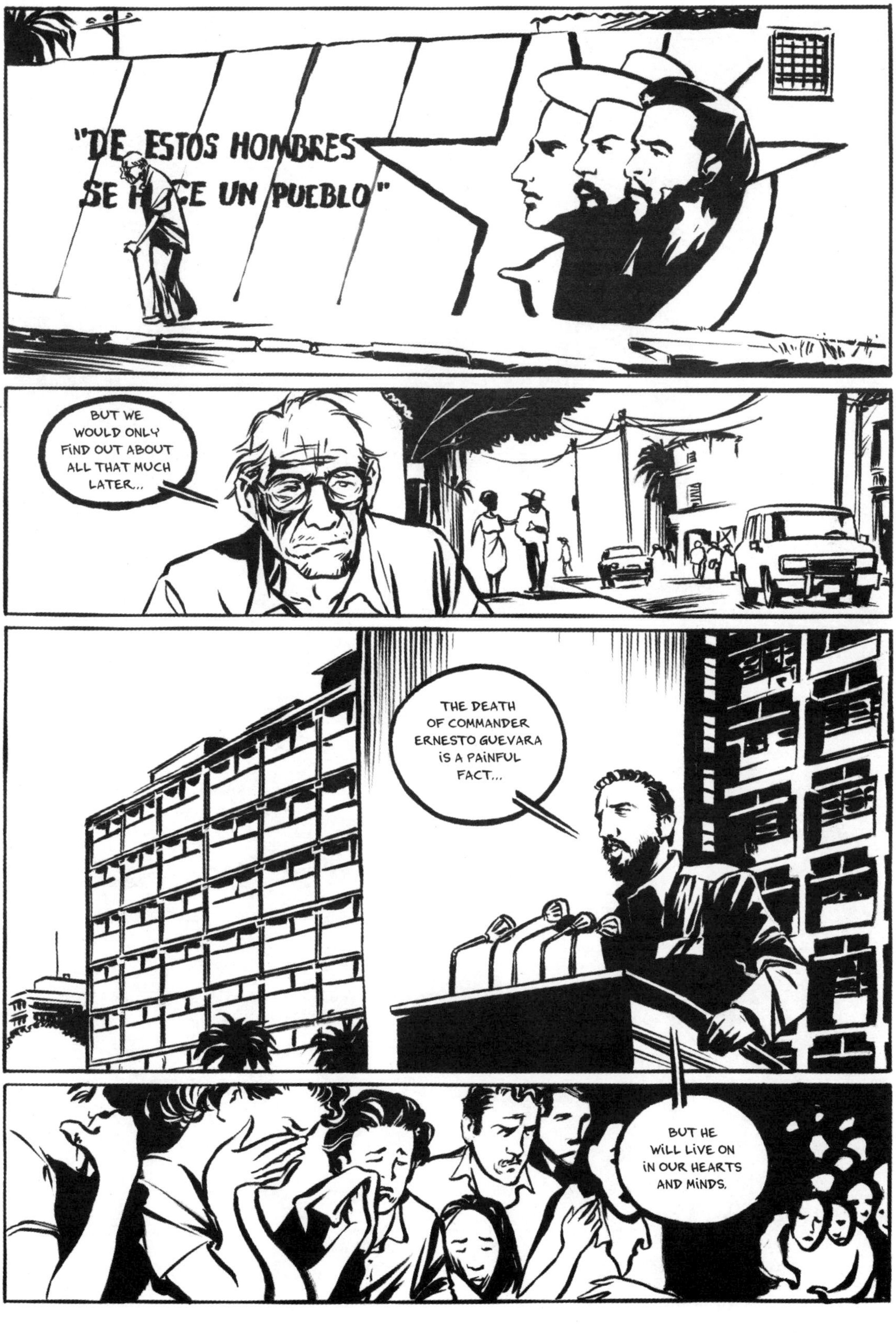
"DE ESTOS HOMBRES
SE HACE UN PUEBLO"
BUT WE WOULD ONLY FIND OUT ABOUT ALL THAT MUCH LATER...
THE DEATH OF COMMANDER ERNESTO GUEVARA IS A PAINFUL FACT...
BUT HE WILL LIVE ON IN OUR HEARTS AND MINDS.

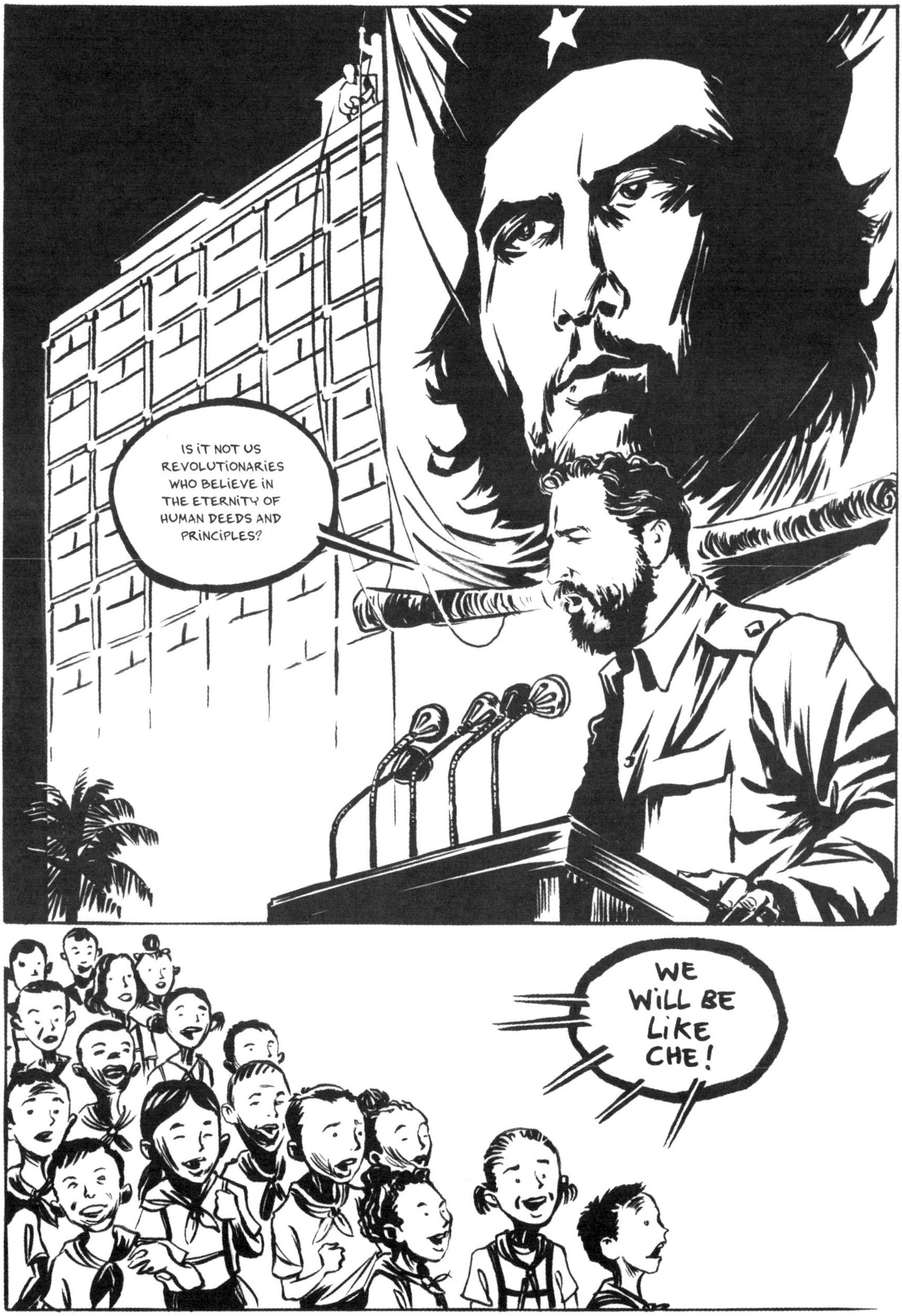
IS IT NOT US REVOLUTIONARIES WHO BELIEVE IN THE ETERNITY OF HUMAN DEEDS AND PRINCIPLES?
WE WILL BE LIKE CHE!

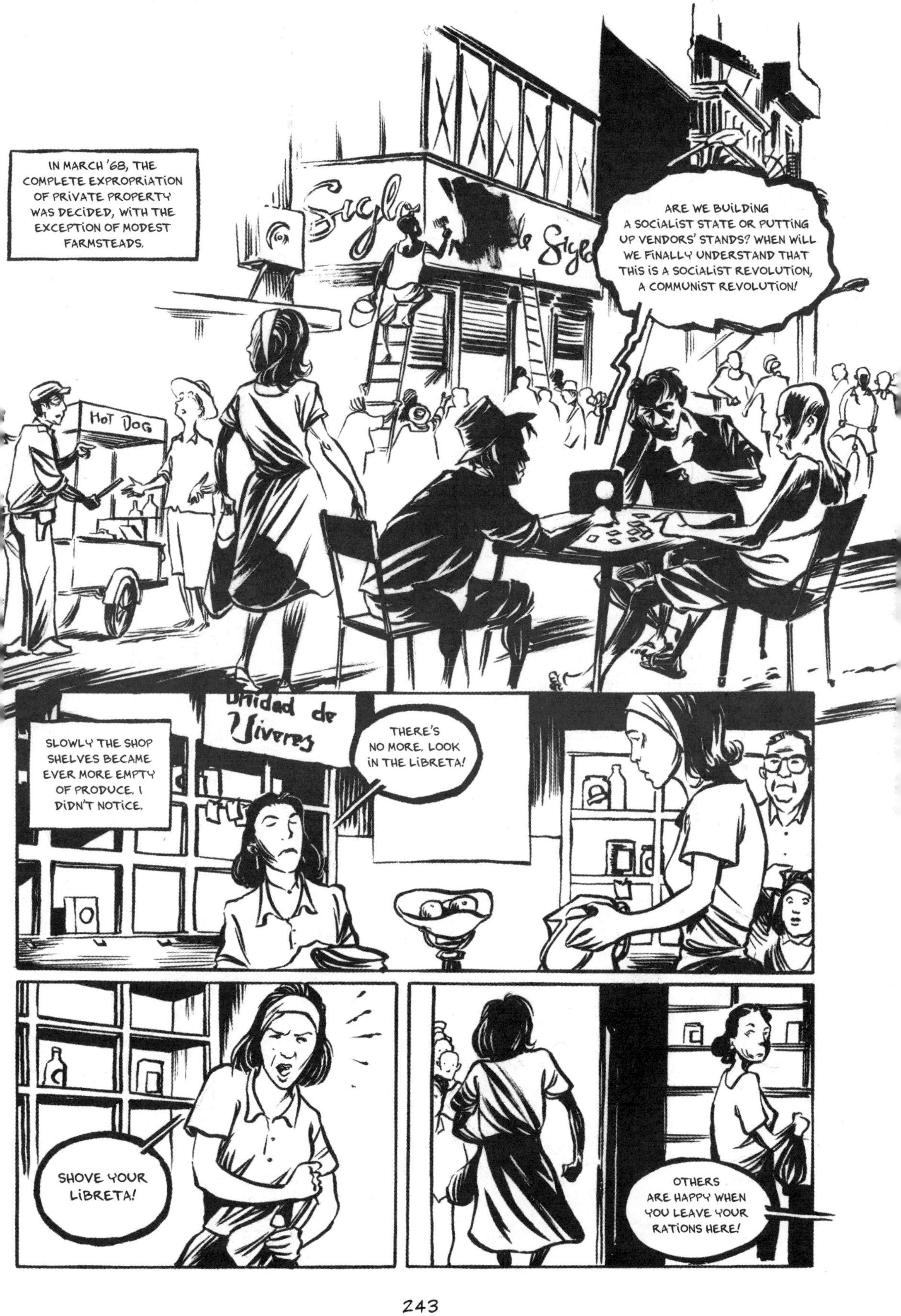

IN MARCH '68, THE COMPLETE EXPROPRIATION OF PRIVATE PROPERTY WAS DECIDED, WITH THE EXCEPTION OF MODEST FARMSTEADS.
ARE WE BUILDING A SOCIALIST STATE OR PUTTING UP VENDORS' STANDS? WHEN WILL WE FINALLY UNDERSTAND THAT THIS IS A SOCIALIST REVOLUTION, A COMMUNIST REVOLUTION!
HOT DOG
SLOWLY THE SHOP SHELVES BECAME EVER MORE EMPTY OF PRODUCE. I DIDN'T NOTICE.
Unidad de Viveres
THERE'S NO MORE. LOOK IN THE LIBRETA!
SHOVE YOUR LIBRETA!
OTHERS ARE HAPPY WHEN YOU LEAVE YOUR RATIONS HERE!

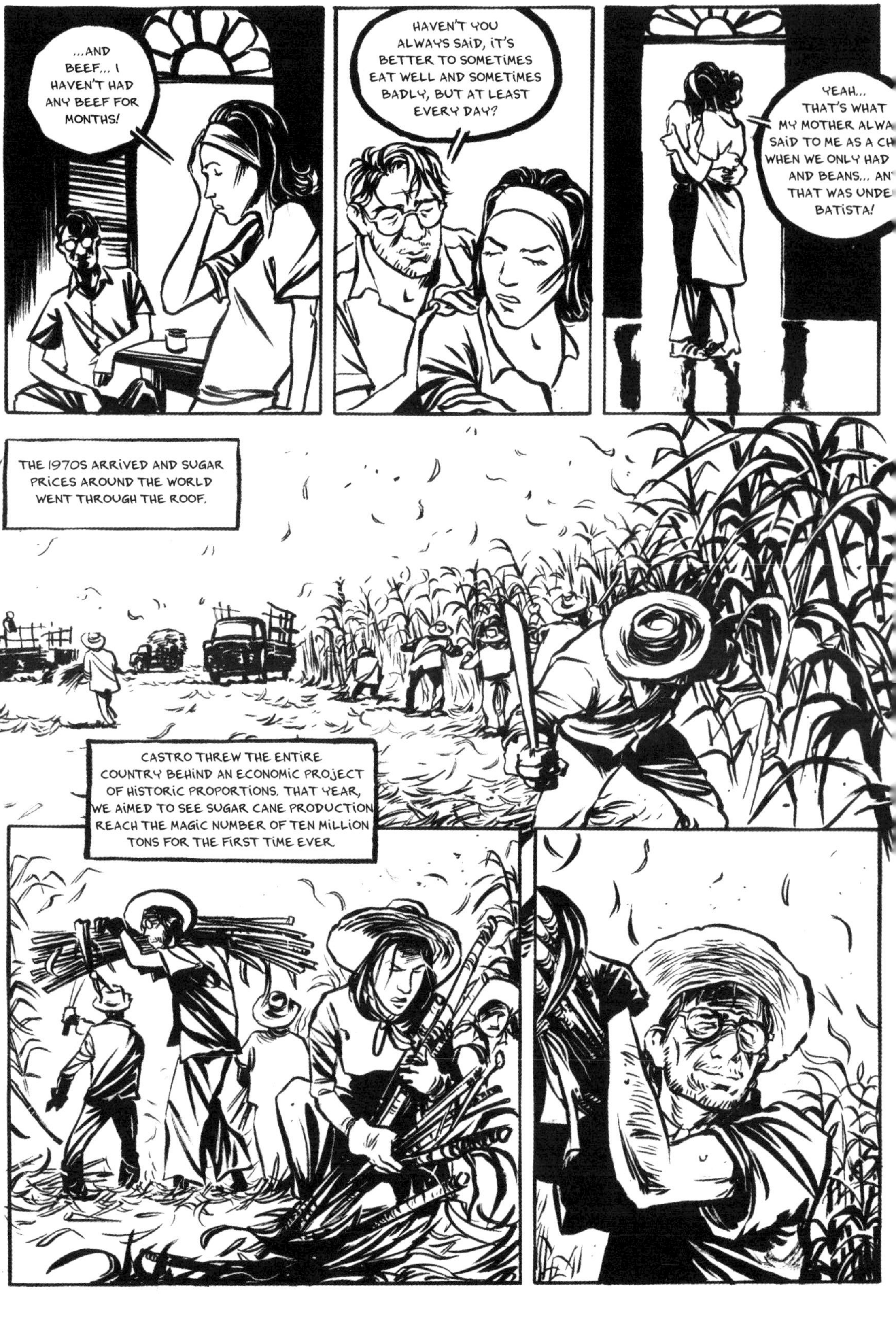
...AND BEEF... I HAVEN'T HAD ANY BEEF FOR MONTHS!
HAVEN'T YOU ALWAYS SAID, IT'S BETTER TO SOMETIMES EAT WELL AND SOMETIMES BADLY, BUT AT LEAST EVERY DAY?
YEAH... THAT'S WHAT MY MOTHER ALWA SAID TO ME AS A CH WHEN WE ONLY HAD AND BEANS... AN THAT WAS UNDE BATISTA!
THE 1970S ARRIVED AND SUGAR PRICES AROUND THE WORLD WENT THROUGH THE ROOF.
CASTRO THREW THE ENTIRE COUNTRY BEHIND AN ECONOMIC PROJECT OF HISTORIC PROPORTIONS. THAT YEAR, WE AIMED TO SEE SUGAR CANE PRODUCTION REACH THE MAGIC NUMBER OF TEN MILLION TONS FOR THE FIRST TIME EVER.

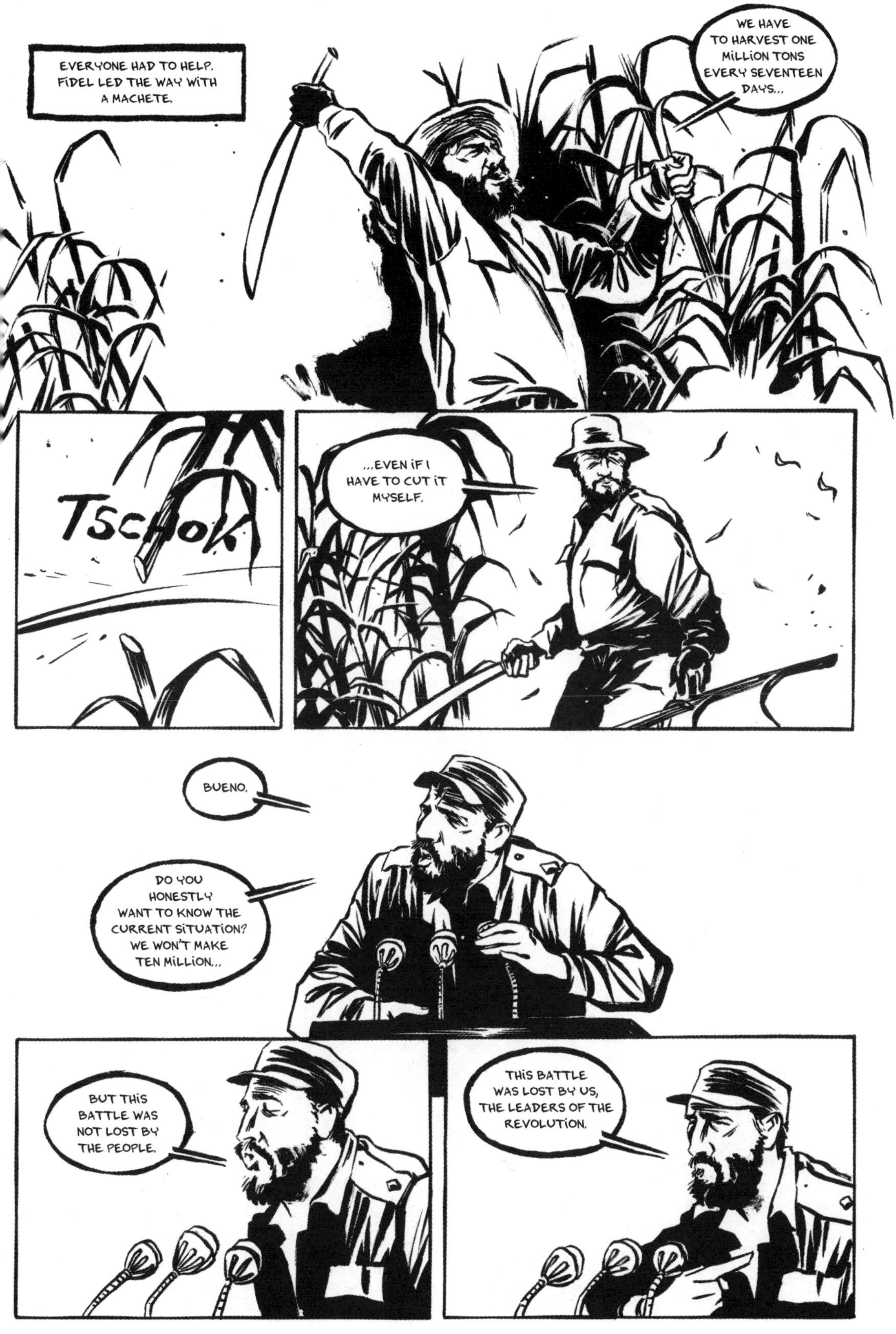
EVERYONE HAD TO HELP. FIDEL LED THE WAY WITH A MACHETE.
WE HAVE TO HARVEST ONE MILLION TONS EVERY SEVENTEEN DAYS...
TSCHOK
...EVEN IF I HAVE TO CUT IT MYSELF.
BUENO.
DO YOU HONESTLY WANT TO KNOW THE CURRENT SITUATION? WE WON'T MAKE TEN MILLION...
BUT THIS BATTLE WAS NOT LOST BY THE PEOPLE.
THIS BATTLE WAS LOST BY US, THE LEADERS OF THE REVOLUTION.

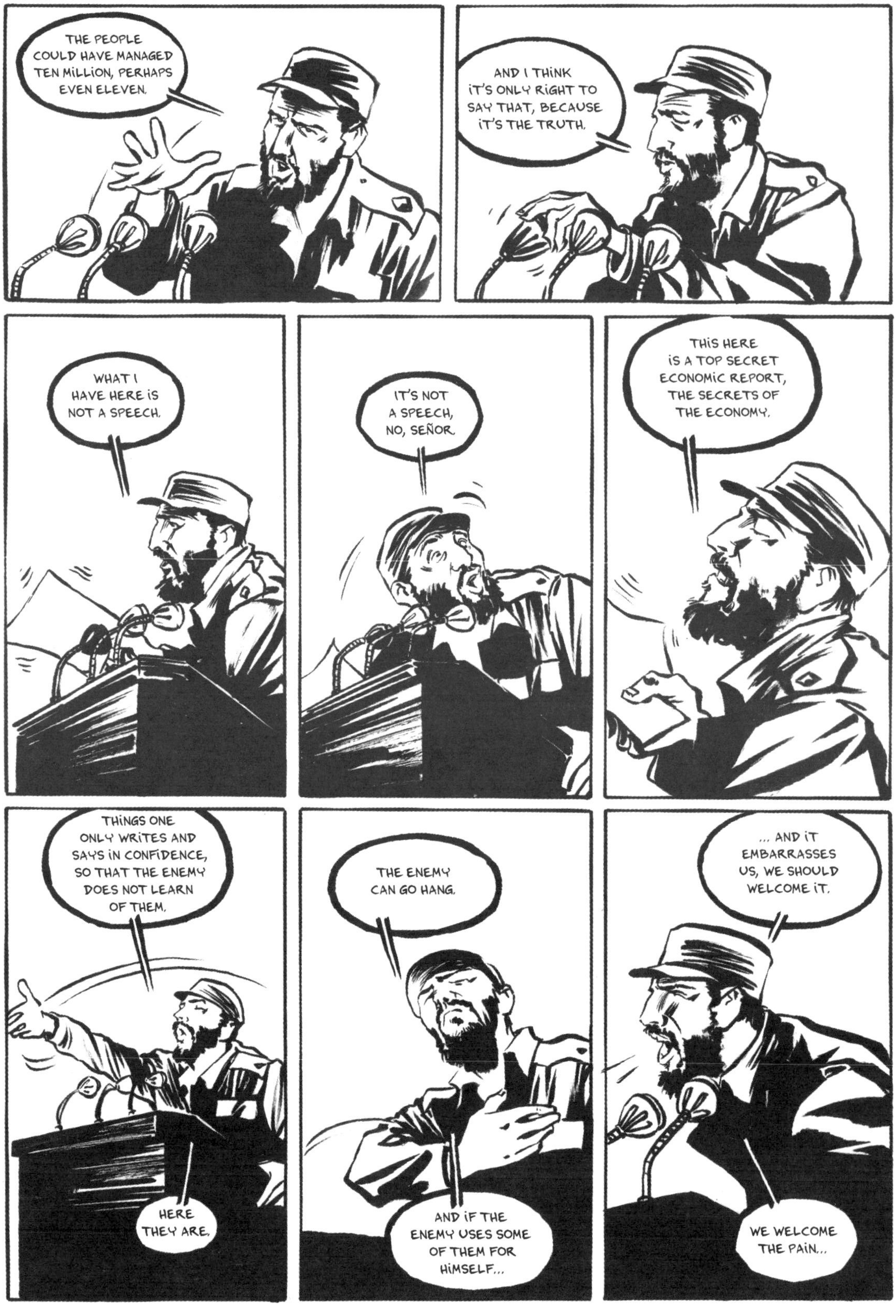
THE PEOPLE COULD HAVE MANAGED TEN MILLION, PERHAPS EVEN ELEVEN.
AND I THINK IT'S ONLY RIGHT TO SAY THAT, BECAUSE IT'S THE TRUTH.
WHAT I HAVE HERE IS NOT A SPEECH.
IT'S NOT A SPEECH, NO, SEÑOR.
THIS HERE IS A TOP SECRET ECONOMIC REPORT, THE SECRETS OF THE ECONOMY.
THINGS ONE ONLY WRITES AND SAYS IN CONFIDENCE, SO THAT THE ENEMY DOES NOT LEARN OF THEM.
HERE THEY ARE.
THE ENEMY CAN GO HANG.
AND IF THE ENEMY USES SOME OF THEM FOR HIMSELF...
... AND IT EMBARRASSES US, WE SHOULD WELCOME IT.
WE WELCOME THE PAIN...

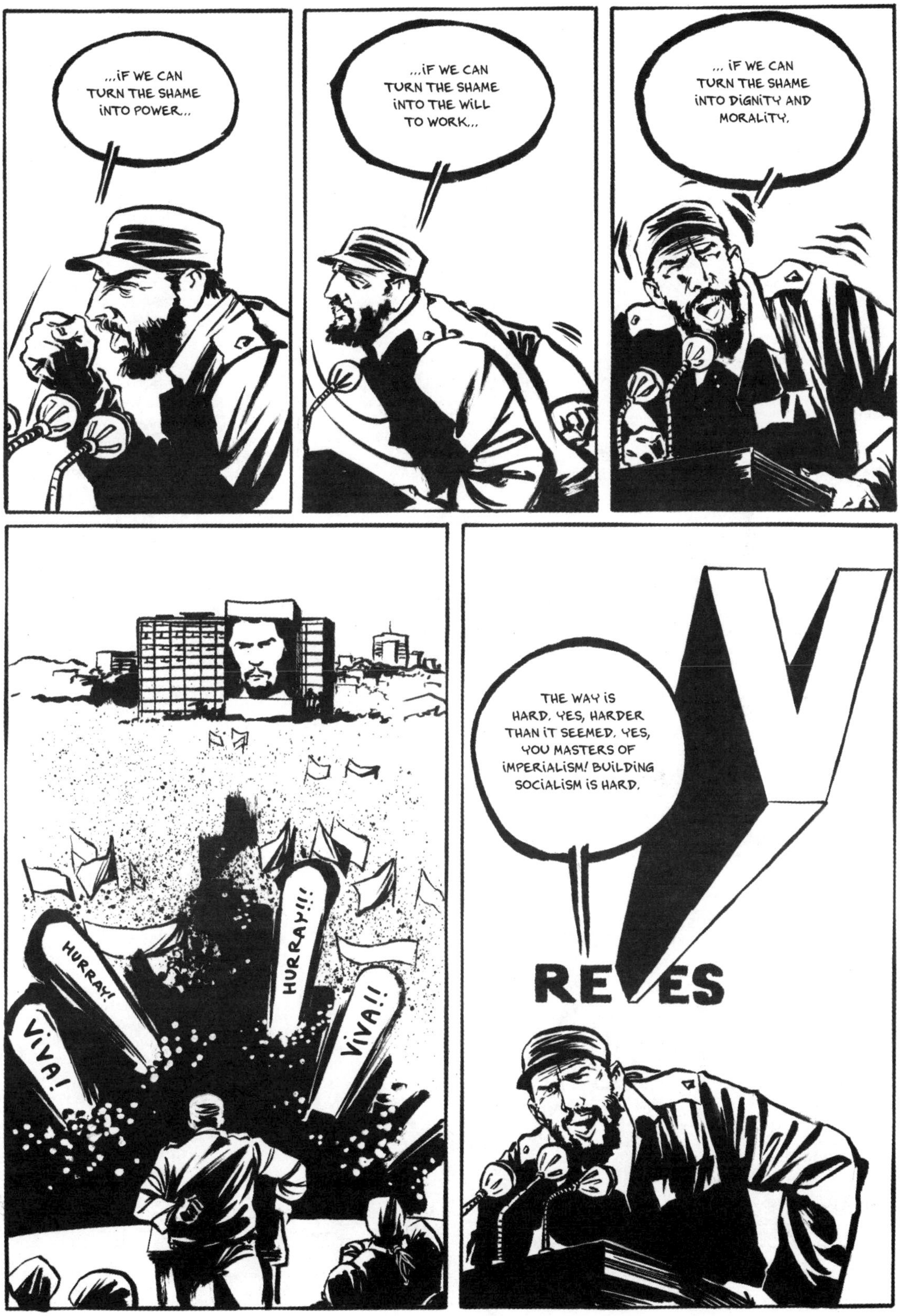
...iF WE CAN TURN THE SHAME iNTO POWER...
...iF WE CAN TURN THE SHAME iNTO THE WiLL TO WORK...
... iF WE CAN TURN THE SHAME iNTO DiGNiTY AND MORALiTY.
HURRAY!
ViVA!
HURRAY!!!
ViVA!!
THE WAY iS HARD. YES, HARDER THAN iT SEEMED. YES, YOU MASTERS OF iMPERiALiSM! BUiLDiNG SOCiALiSM iS HARD.
REVES

* REVES: CHANGE. THE V STANDS FOR ViCTORY.

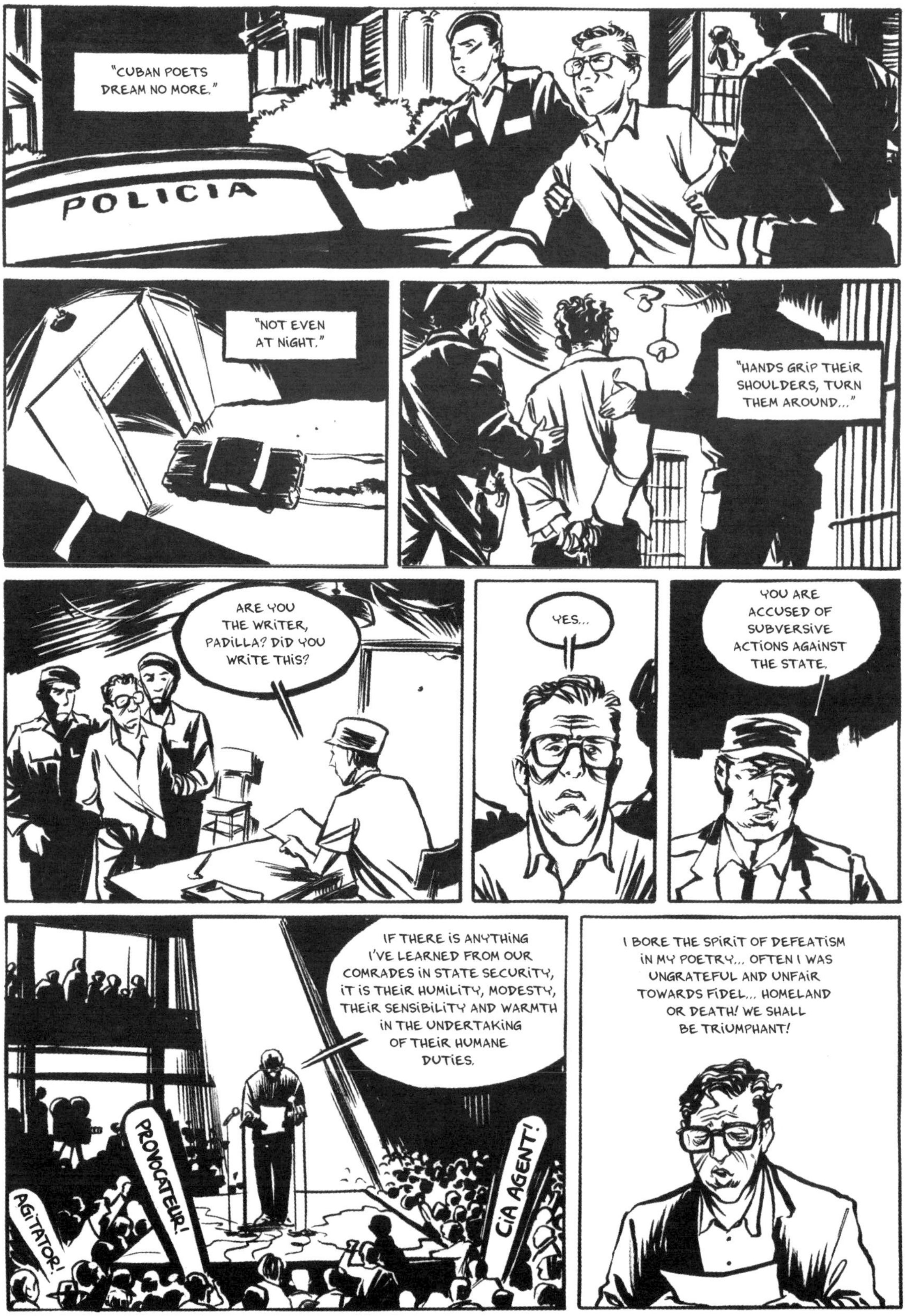
"CUBAN POETS DREAM NO MORE."
POLICIA
"NOT EVEN AT NIGHT."
"HANDS GRIP THEIR SHOULDERS, TURN THEM AROUND..."
ARE YOU THE WRITER, PADILLA? DID YOU WRITE THIS?
YES...
YOU ARE ACCUSED OF SUBVERSIVE ACTIONS AGAINST THE STATE.
IF THERE IS ANYTHING I'VE LEARNED FROM OUR COMRADES IN STATE SECURITY, IT IS THEIR HUMILITY, MODESTY, THEIR SENSIBILITY AND WARMTH IN THE UNDERTAKING OF THEIR HUMANE DUTIES.
AGITATOR!
PROVOCATEUR!
CIA AGENT!
I BORE THE SPIRIT OF DEFEATISM IN MY POETRY... OFTEN I WAS UNGRATEFUL AND UNFAIR TOWARDS FIDEL... HOMELAND OR DEATH! WE SHALL BE TRIUMPHANT!

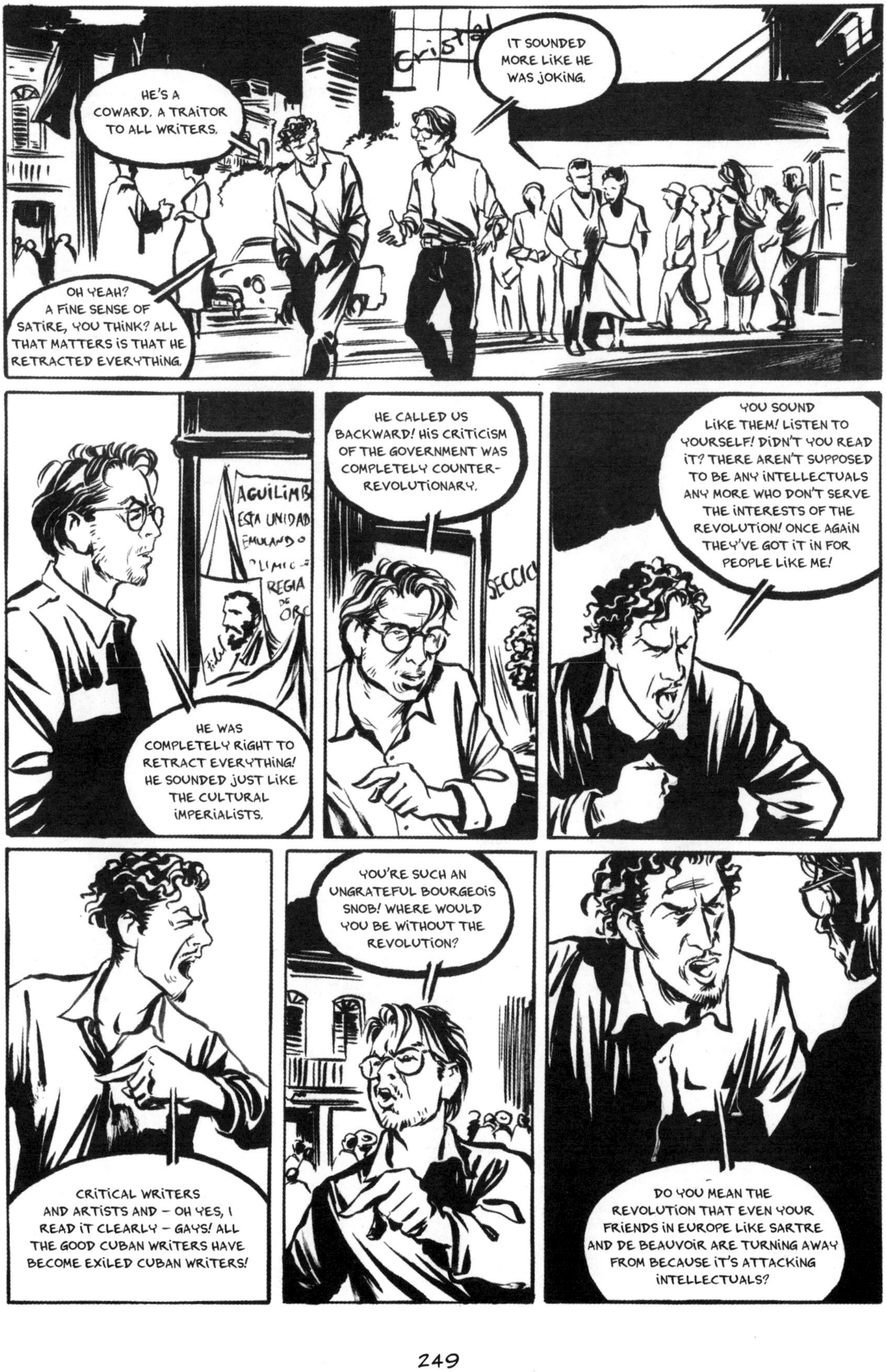
HE'S A COWARD, A TRAITOR TO ALL WRITERS.
IT SOUNDED MORE LIKE HE WAS JOKING.
OH YEAH? A FINE SENSE OF SATIRE, YOU THINK? ALL THAT MATTERS IS THAT HE RETRACTED EVERYTHING.
HE WAS COMPLETELY RIGHT TO RETRACT EVERYTHING! HE SOUNDED JUST LIKE THE CULTURAL IMPERIALISTS.
HE CALLED US BACKWARD! HIS CRITICISM OF THE GOVERNMENT WAS COMPLETELY COUNTER-REVOLUTIONARY.
YOU SOUND LIKE THEM! LISTEN TO YOURSELF! DIDN'T YOU READ IT? THERE AREN'T SUPPOSED TO BE ANY INTELLECTUALS ANY MORE WHO DON'T SERVE THE INTERESTS OF THE REVOLUTION! ONCE AGAIN THEY'VE GOT IT IN FOR PEOPLE LIKE ME!
CRITICAL WRITERS AND ARTISTS AND – OH YES, I READ IT CLEARLY – GAYS! ALL THE GOOD CUBAN WRITERS HAVE BECOME EXILED CUBAN WRITERS!
YOU'RE SUCH AN UNGRATEFUL BOURGEOIS SNOB! WHERE WOULD YOU BE WITHOUT THE REVOLUTION?
DO YOU MEAN THE REVOLUTION THAT EVEN YOUR FRIENDS IN EUROPE LIKE SARTRE AND DE BEAUVOIR ARE TURNING AWAY FROM BECAUSE IT'S ATTACKING INTELLECTUALS?

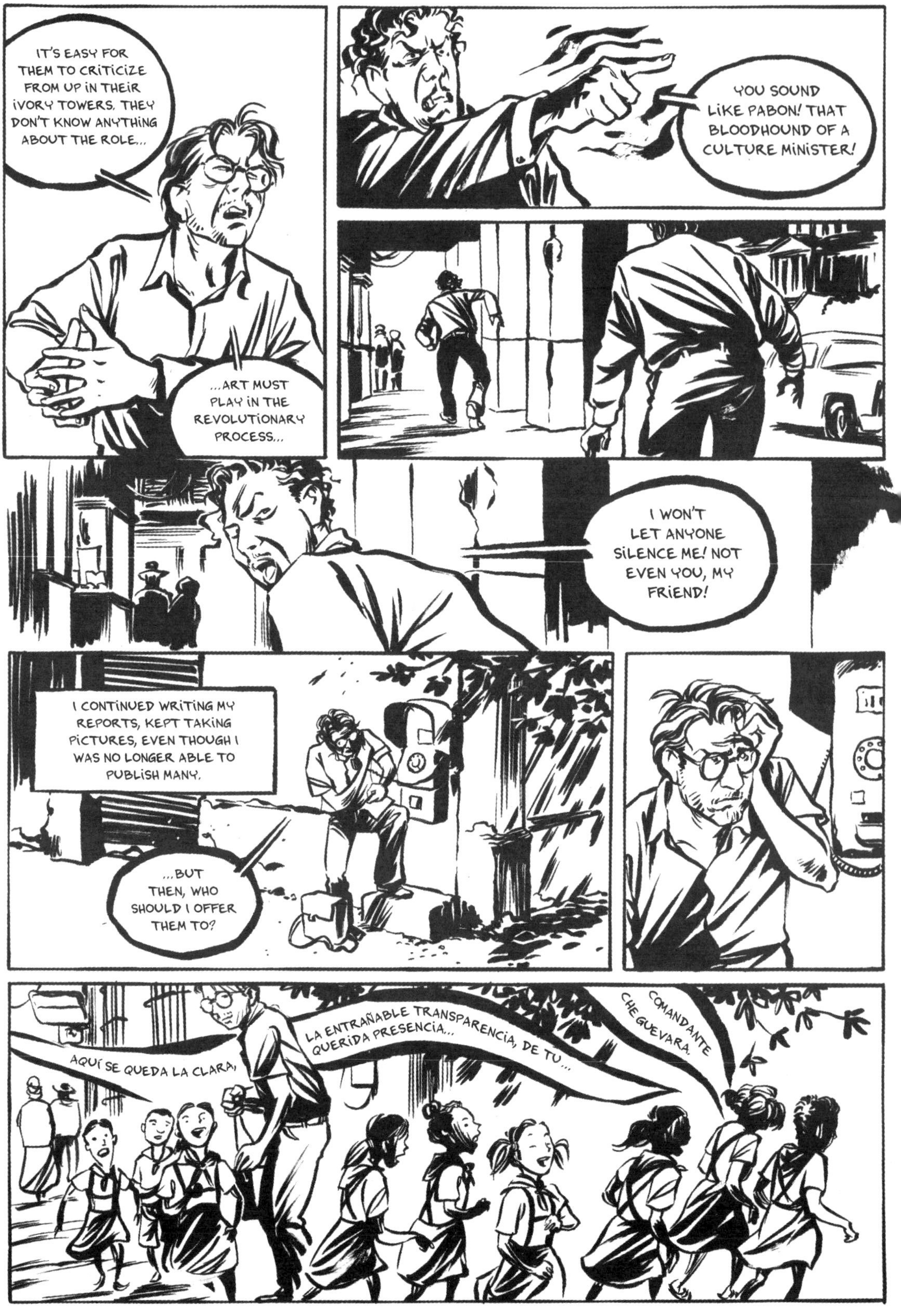

IT'S EASY FOR THEM TO CRITICIZE FROM UP IN THEIR IVORY TOWERS. THEY DON'T KNOW ANYTHING ABOUT THE ROLE...
...ART MUST PLAY IN THE REVOLUTIONARY PROCESS...
YOU SOUND LIKE PABON! THAT BLOODHOUND OF A CULTURE MINISTER!
I WON'T LET ANYONE SILENCE ME! NOT EVEN YOU, MY FRIEND!
I CONTINUED WRITING MY REPORTS, KEPT TAKING PICTURES, EVEN THOUGH I WAS NO LONGER ABLE TO PUBLISH MANY.
...BUT THEN, WHO SHOULD I OFFER THEM TO?
AQUÍ SE QUEDA LA CLARA,
LA ENTRAÑABLE TRANSPARENCIA, QUERIDA PRESENCIA...
DE TU...
COMANDANTE CHE GUEVARA.

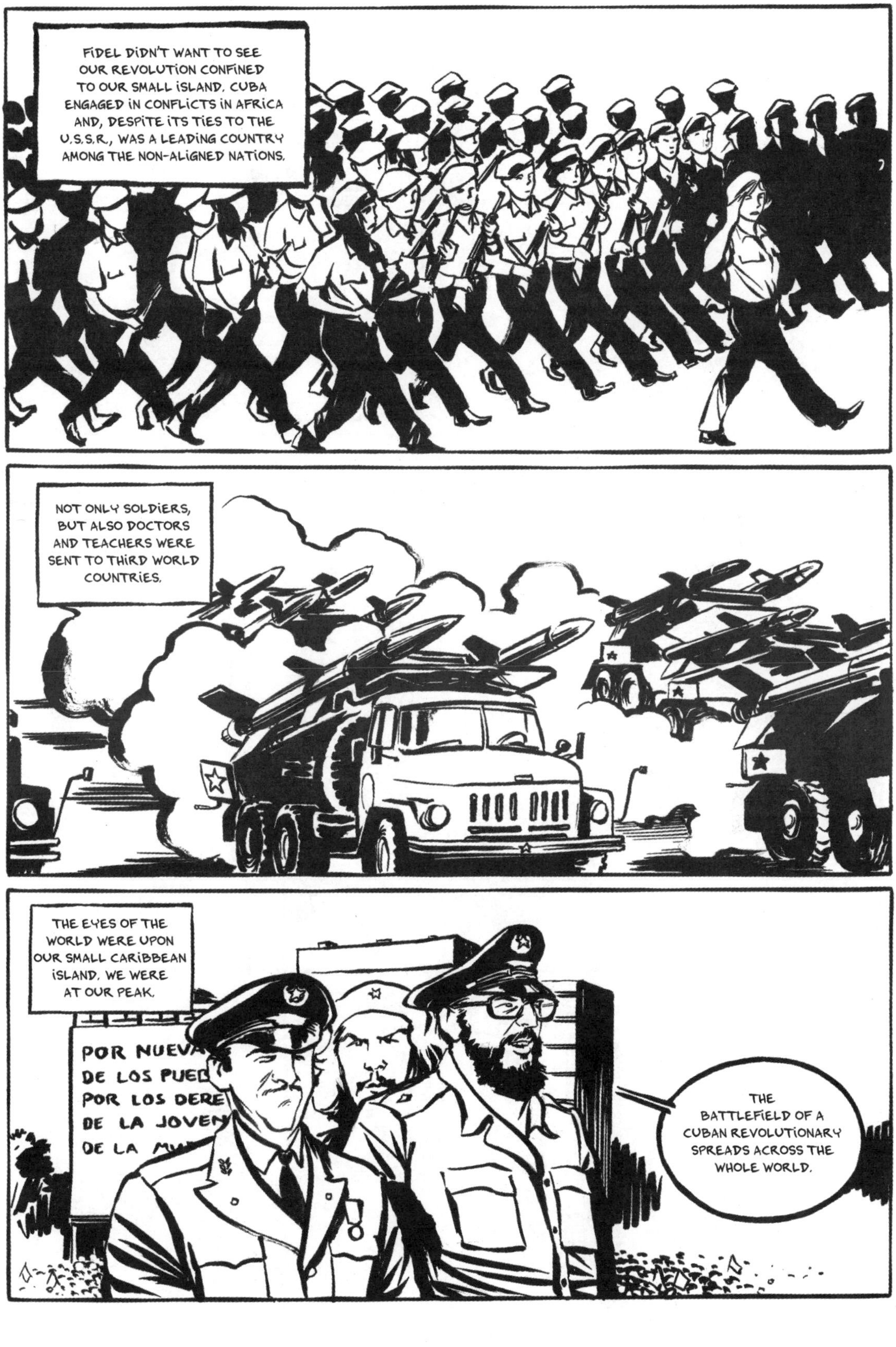
FIDEL DIDN'T WANT TO SEE OUR REVOLUTION CONFINED TO OUR SMALL ISLAND. CUBA ENGAGED IN CONFLICTS IN AFRICA AND, DESPITE ITS TIES TO THE U.S.S.R., WAS A LEADING COUNTRY AMONG THE NON-ALIGNED NATIONS.
NOT ONLY SOLDIERS, BUT ALSO DOCTORS AND TEACHERS WERE SENT TO THIRD WORLD COUNTRIES.
THE EYES OF THE WORLD WERE UPON OUR SMALL CARIBBEAN ISLAND. WE WERE AT OUR PEAK.
POR NUEVA
DE LOS PUEB
POR LOS DERE
DE LA JOVEN
DE LA
THE BATTLEFIELD OF A CUBAN REVOLUTIONARY SPREADS ACROSS THE WHOLE WORLD.

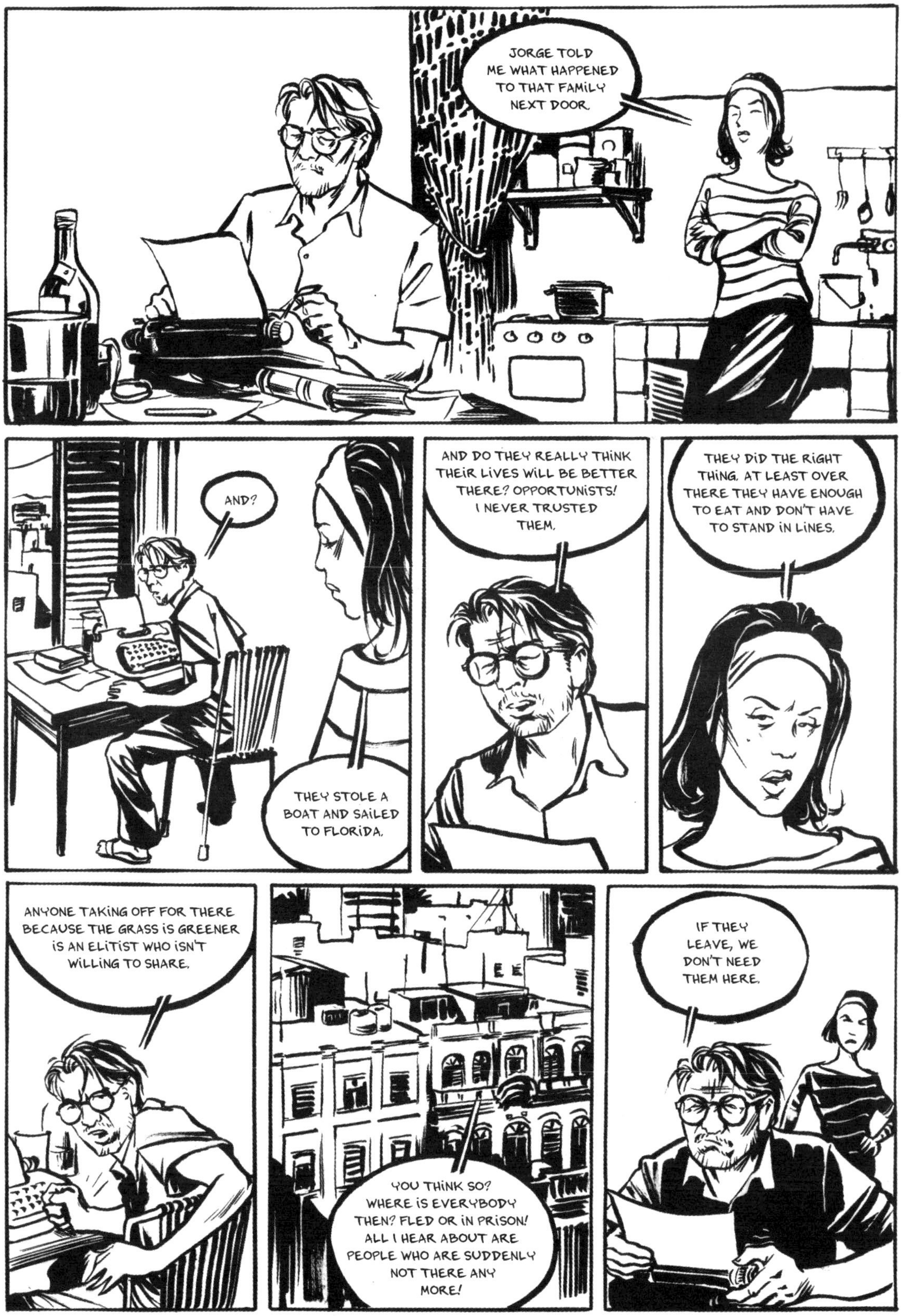
JORGE TOLD ME WHAT HAPPENED TO THAT FAMILY NEXT DOOR.
AND?
THEY STOLE A BOAT AND SAILED TO FLORIDA.
AND DO THEY REALLY THINK THEIR LIVES WILL BE BETTER THERE? OPPORTUNISTS! I NEVER TRUSTED THEM.
THEY DID THE RIGHT THING. AT LEAST OVER THERE THEY HAVE ENOUGH TO EAT AND DON'T HAVE TO STAND IN LINES.
ANYONE TAKING OFF FOR THERE BECAUSE THE GRASS IS GREENER IS AN ELITIST WHO ISN'T WILLING TO SHARE.
YOU THINK SO? WHERE IS EVERYBODY THEN? FLED OR IN PRISON! ALL I HEAR ABOUT ARE PEOPLE WHO ARE SUDDENLY NOT THERE ANY MORE!
IF THEY LEAVE, WE DON'T NEED THEM HERE.

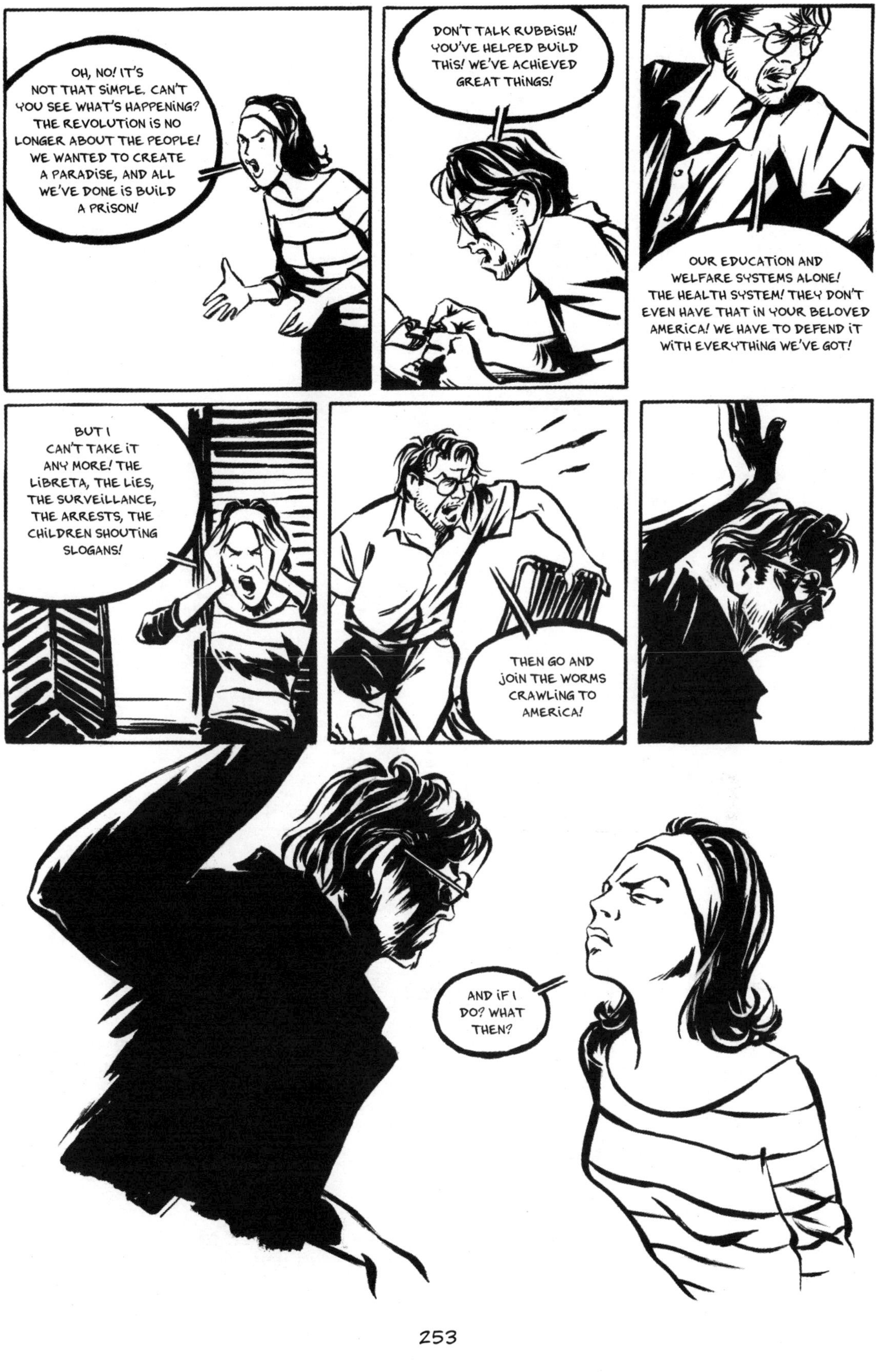
OH, NO! IT'S NOT THAT SIMPLE. CAN'T YOU SEE WHAT'S HAPPENING? THE REVOLUTION IS NO LONGER ABOUT THE PEOPLE! WE WANTED TO CREATE A PARADISE, AND ALL WE'VE DONE IS BUILD A PRISON!
DON'T TALK RUBBISH! YOU'VE HELPED BUILD THIS! WE'VE ACHIEVED GREAT THINGS!
OUR EDUCATION AND WELFARE SYSTEMS ALONE! THE HEALTH SYSTEM! THEY DON'T EVEN HAVE THAT IN YOUR BELOVED AMERICA! WE HAVE TO DEFEND IT WITH EVERYTHING WE'VE GOT!
BUT I CAN'T TAKE IT ANY MORE! THE LIBRETA, THE LIES, THE SURVEILLANCE, THE ARRESTS, THE CHILDREN SHOUTING SLOGANS!
THEN GO AND JOIN THE WORMS CRAWLING TO AMERICA!
AND IF I DO? WHAT THEN?

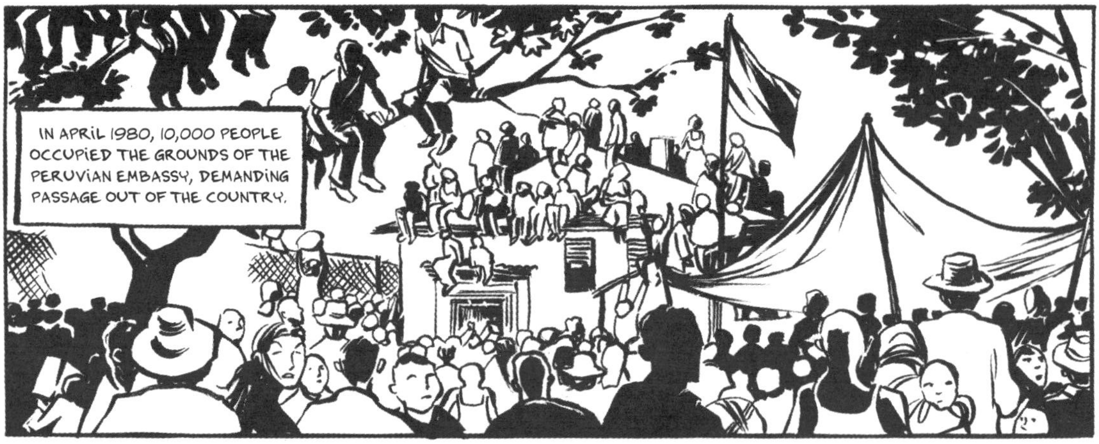
IN APRIL 1980, 10,000 PEOPLE OCCUPIED THE GROUNDS OF THE PERUVIAN EMBASSY, DEMANDING PASSAGE OUT OF THE COUNTRY.

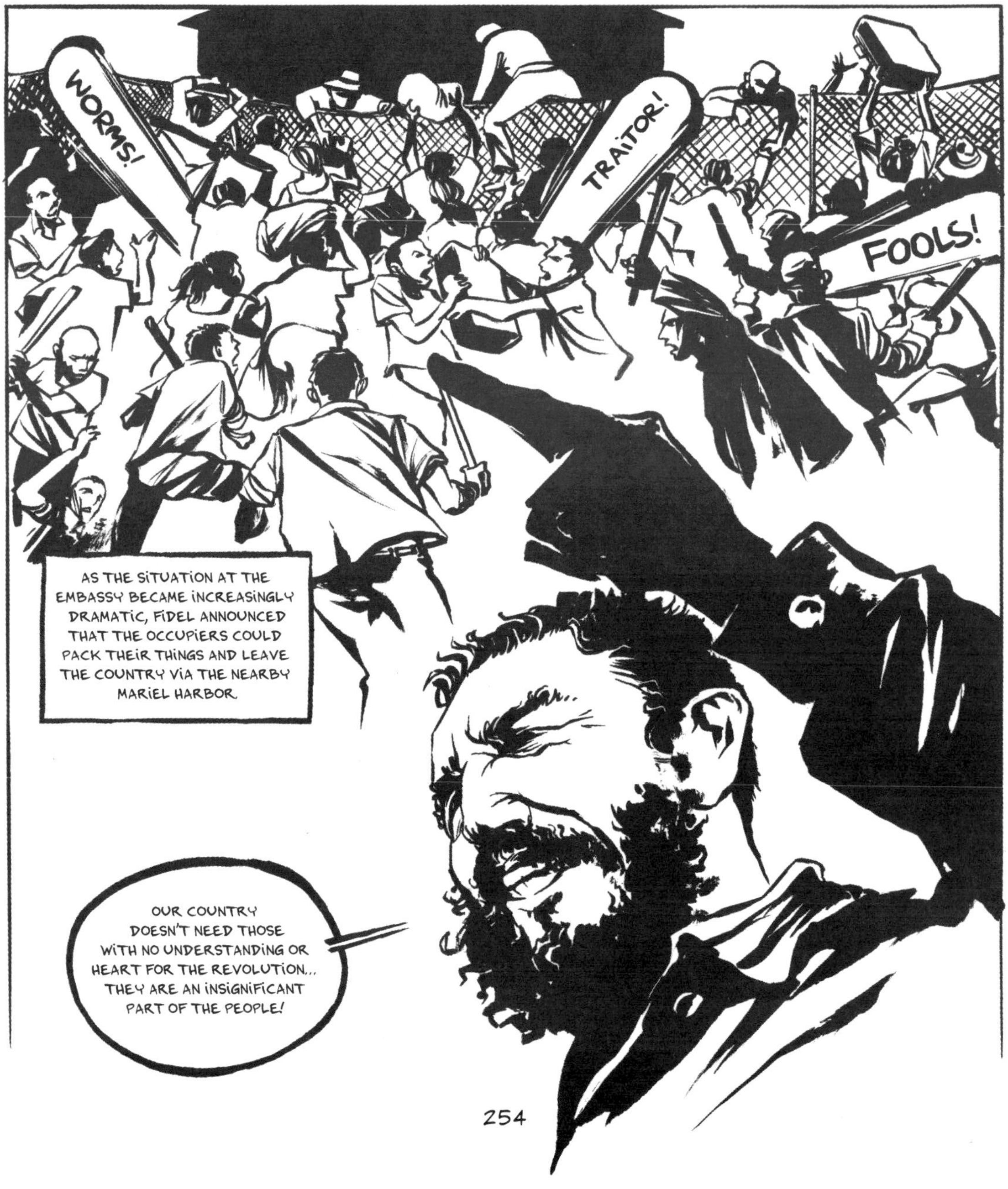
WORMS!
TRAITOR!
FOOLS!
AS THE SITUATION AT THE EMBASSY BECAME INCREASINGLY DRAMATIC, FIDEL ANNOUNCED THAT THE OCCUPIERS COULD PACK THEIR THINGS AND LEAVE THE COUNTRY VIA THE NEARBY MARIEL HARBOR.
OUR COUNTRY DOESN'T NEED THOSE WITH NO UNDERSTANDING OR HEART FOR THE REVOLUTION... THEY ARE AN INSIGNIFICANT PART OF THE PEOPLE!

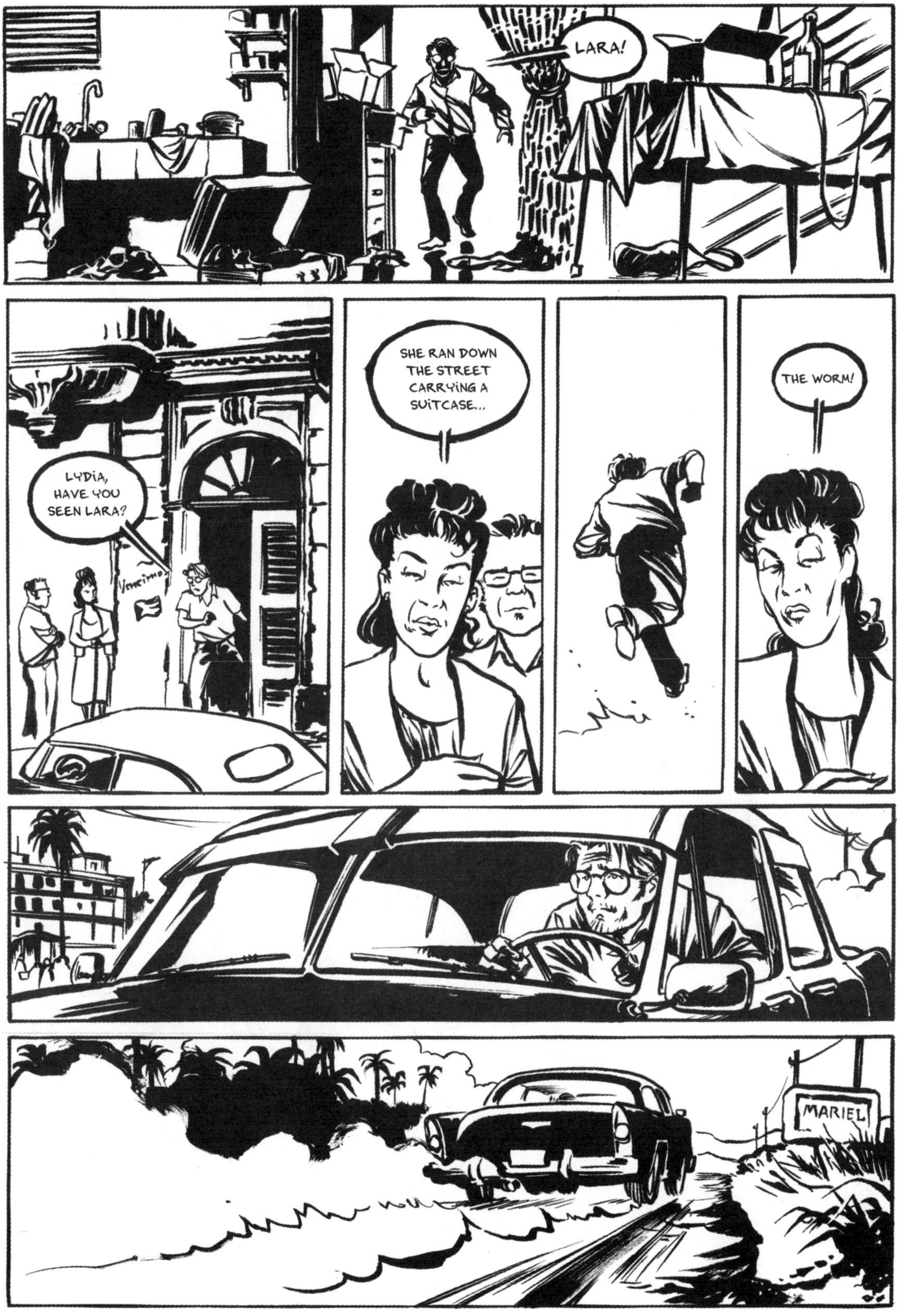
LARA!
LYDIA, HAVE YOU SEEN LARA?
SHE RAN DOWN THE STREET CARRYING A SUITCASE...
THE WORM!
MARIEL

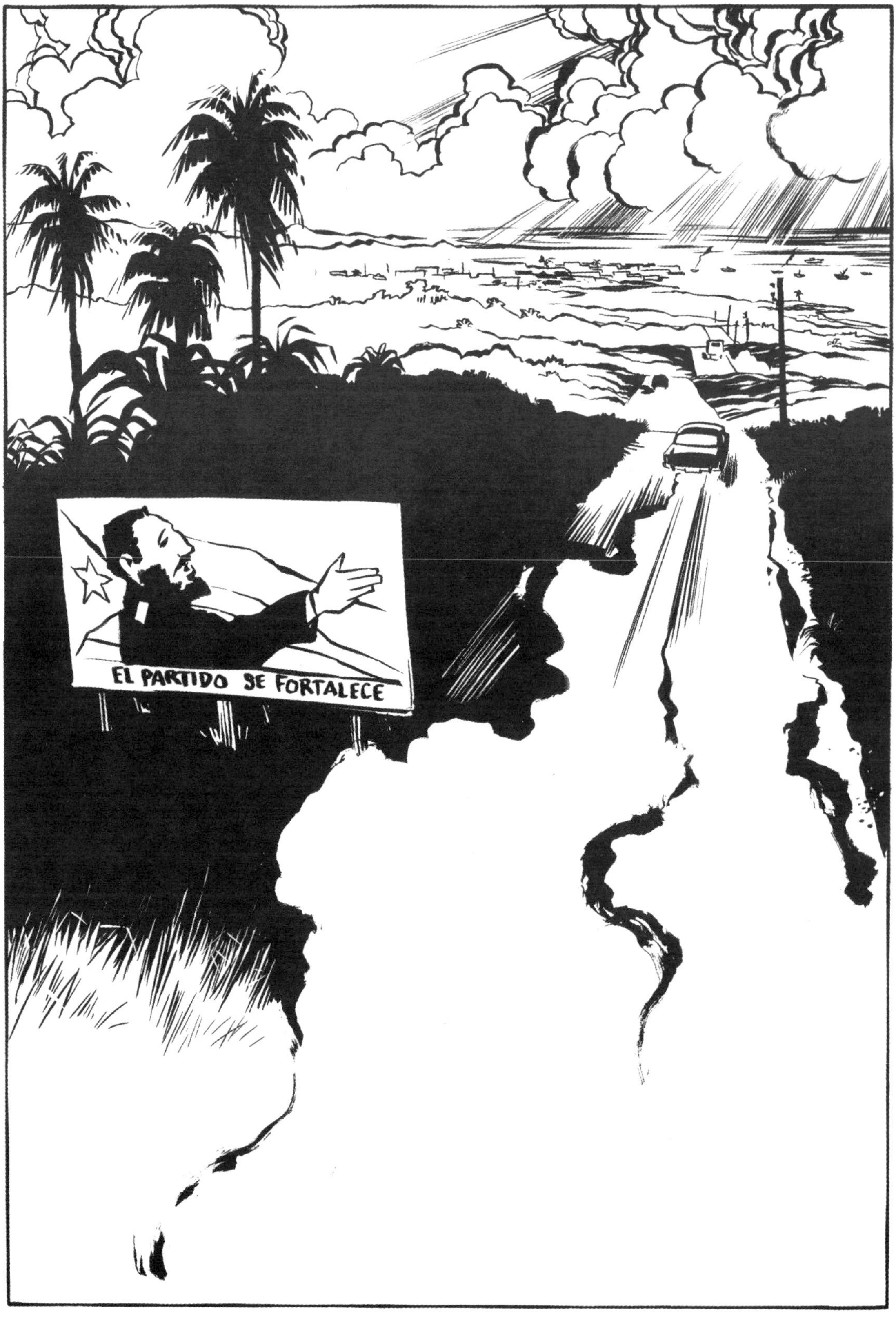
EL PARTIDO SE FORTALECE

CHAPTER 3

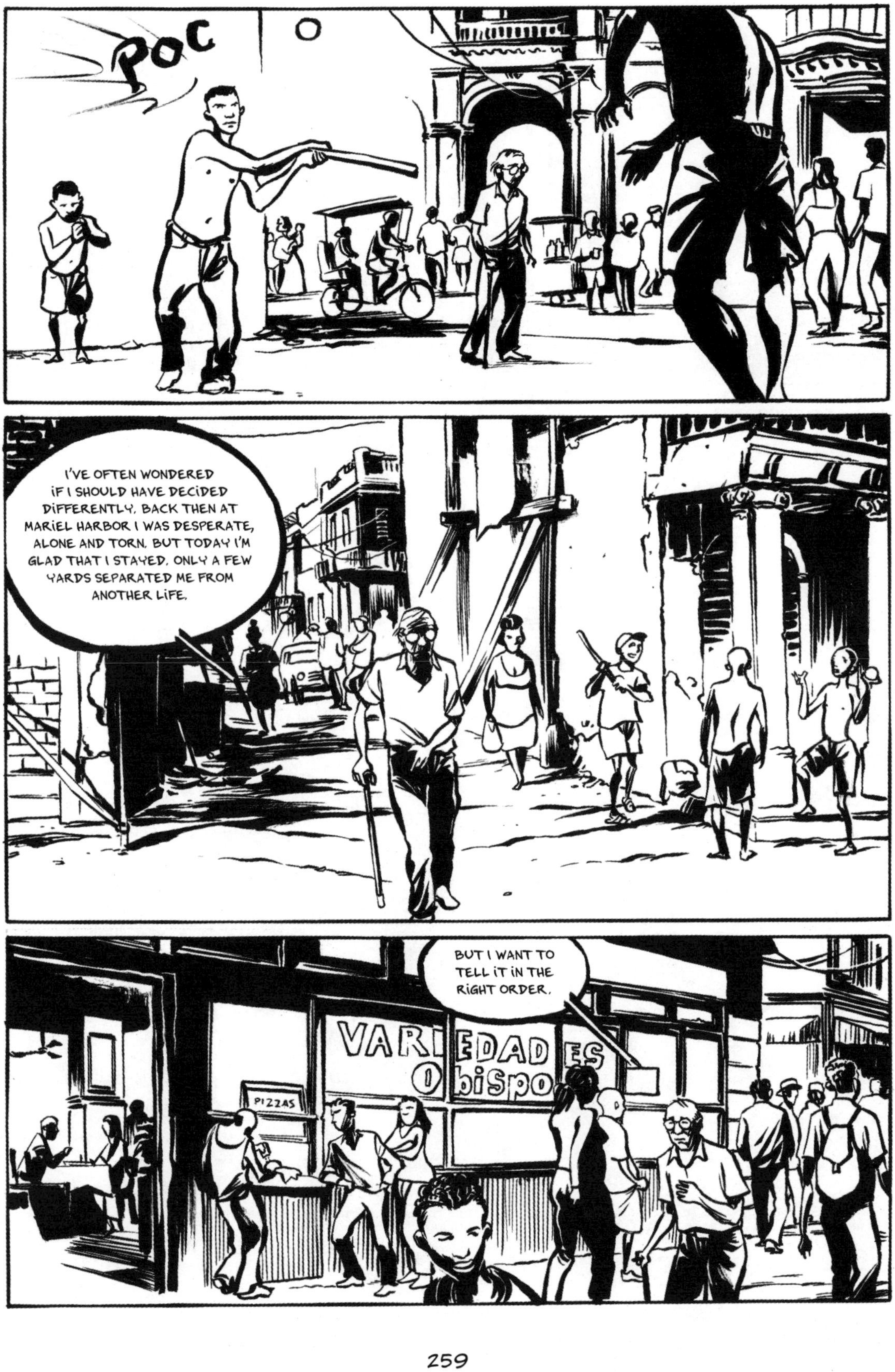
POC
I'VE OFTEN WONDERED IF I SHOULD HAVE DECIDED DIFFERENTLY. BACK THEN AT MARIEL HARBOR I WAS DESPERATE, ALONE AND TORN. BUT TODAY I'M GLAD THAT I STAYED. ONLY A FEW YARDS SEPARATED ME FROM ANOTHER LIFE.
BUT I WANT TO TELL IT IN THE RIGHT ORDER.
VARIEDADES Obispo
PIZZAS

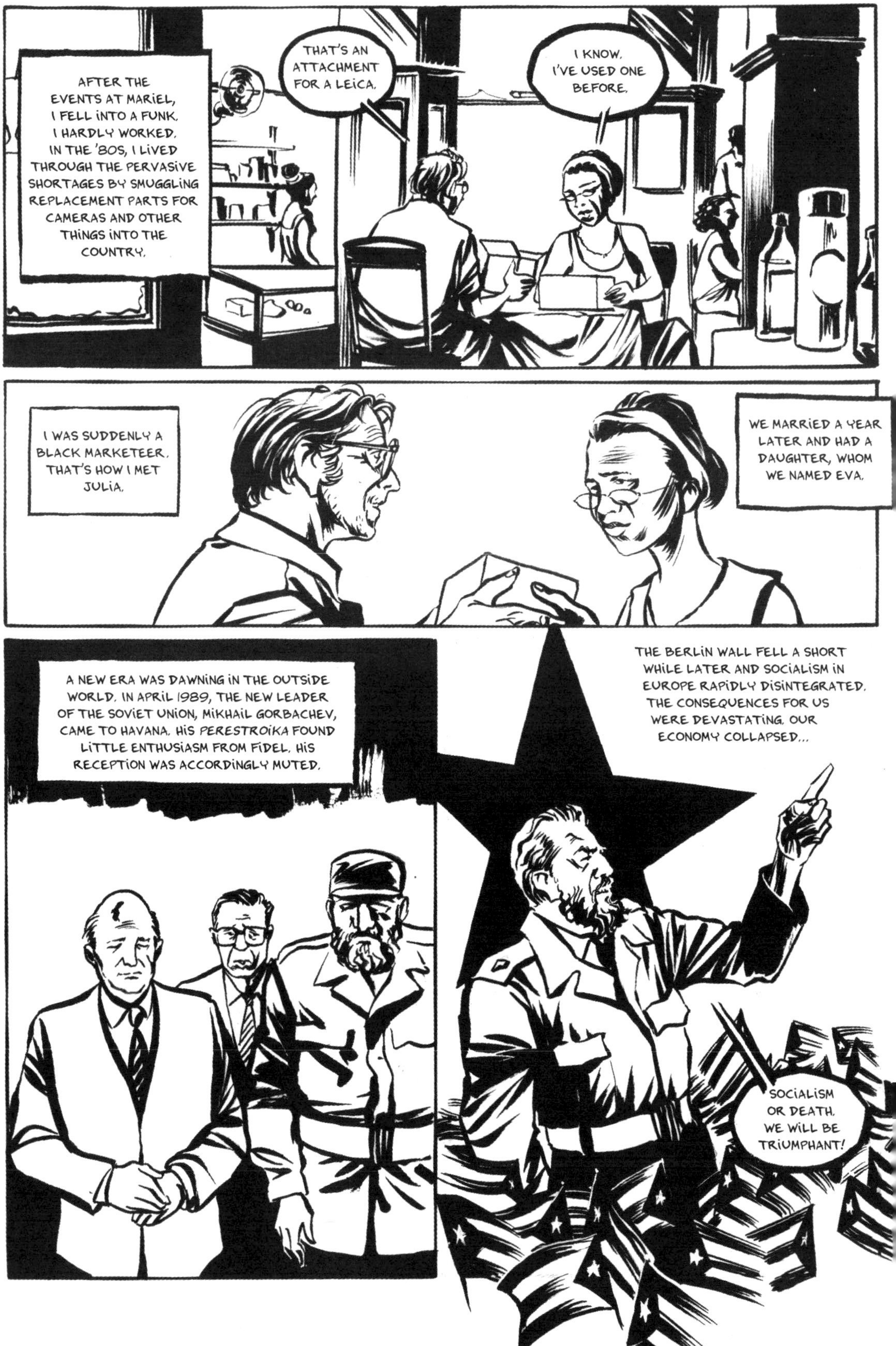
AFTER THE EVENTS AT MARIEL, I FELL INTO A FUNK. I HARDLY WORKED. IN THE '80S, I LIVED THROUGH THE PERVASIVE SHORTAGES BY SMUGGLING REPLACEMENT PARTS FOR CAMERAS AND OTHER THINGS INTO THE COUNTRY.
THAT'S AN ATTACHMENT FOR A LEICA.
I KNOW. I'VE USED ONE BEFORE.
I WAS SUDDENLY A BLACK MARKETEER. THAT'S HOW I MET JULIA.
WE MARRIED A YEAR LATER AND HAD A DAUGHTER, WHOM WE NAMED EVA.
A NEW ERA WAS DAWNING IN THE OUTSIDE WORLD. IN APRIL 1989, THE NEW LEADER OF THE SOVIET UNION, MIKHAIL GORBACHEV, CAME TO HAVANA. HIS *PERESTROIKA* FOUND LITTLE ENTHUSIASM FROM FIDEL. HIS RECEPTION WAS ACCORDINGLY MUTED.
THE BERLIN WALL FELL A SHORT WHILE LATER AND SOCIALISM IN EUROPE RAPIDLY DISINTEGRATED. THE CONSEQUENCES FOR US WERE DEVASTATING. OUR ECONOMY COLLAPSED...
SOCIALISM OR DEATH. WE WILL BE TRIUMPHANT!

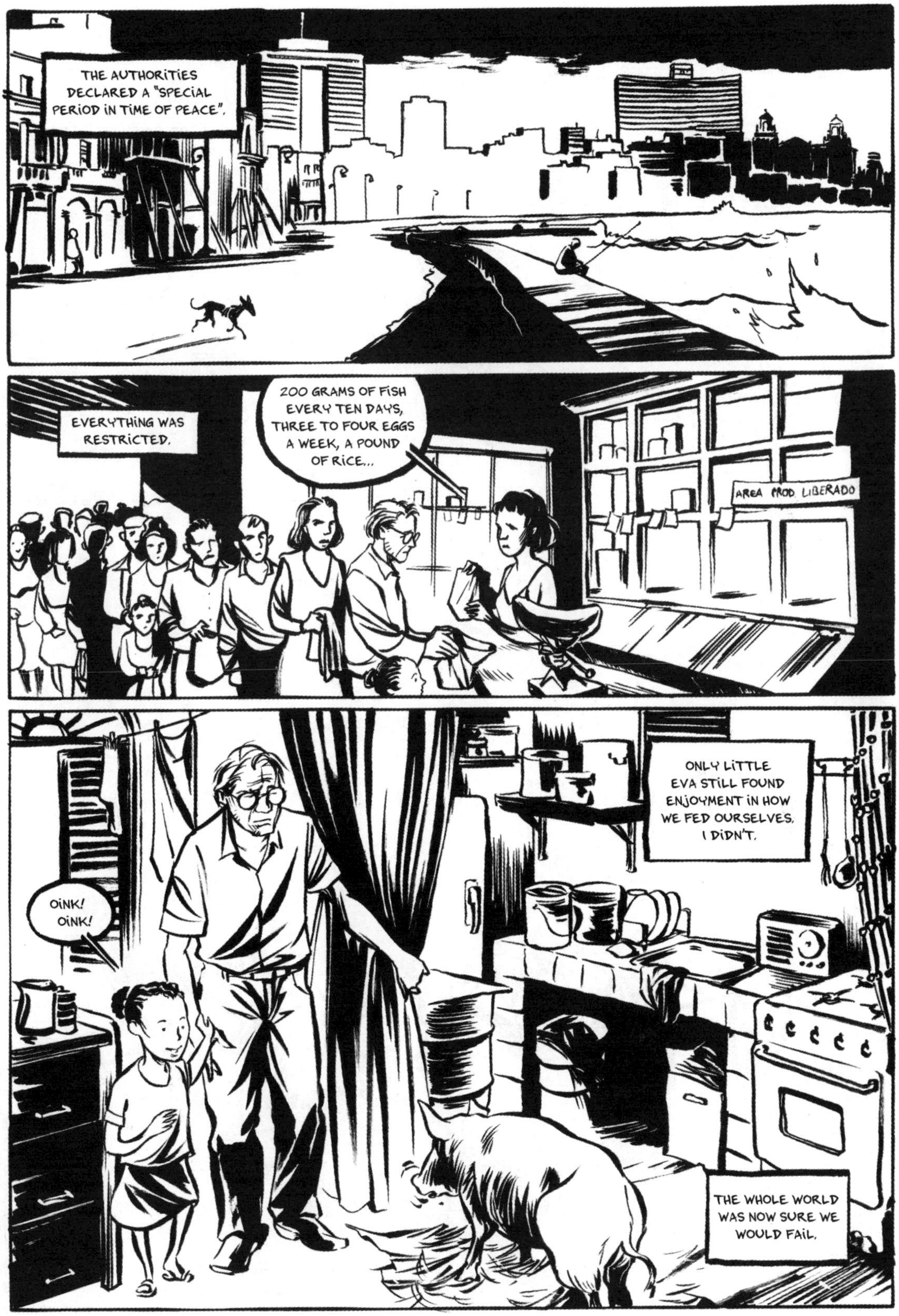
THE AUTHORITIES DECLARED A "SPECIAL PERIOD IN TIME OF PEACE".
EVERYTHING WAS RESTRICTED.
200 GRAMS OF FISH EVERY TEN DAYS, THREE TO FOUR EGGS A WEEK, A POUND OF RICE...
AREA PROD. LIBERADO
ONLY LITTLE EVA STILL FOUND ENJOYMENT IN HOW WE FED OURSELVES. I DIDN'T.
OINK! OINK!
THE WHOLE WORLD WAS NOW SURE WE WOULD FAIL.

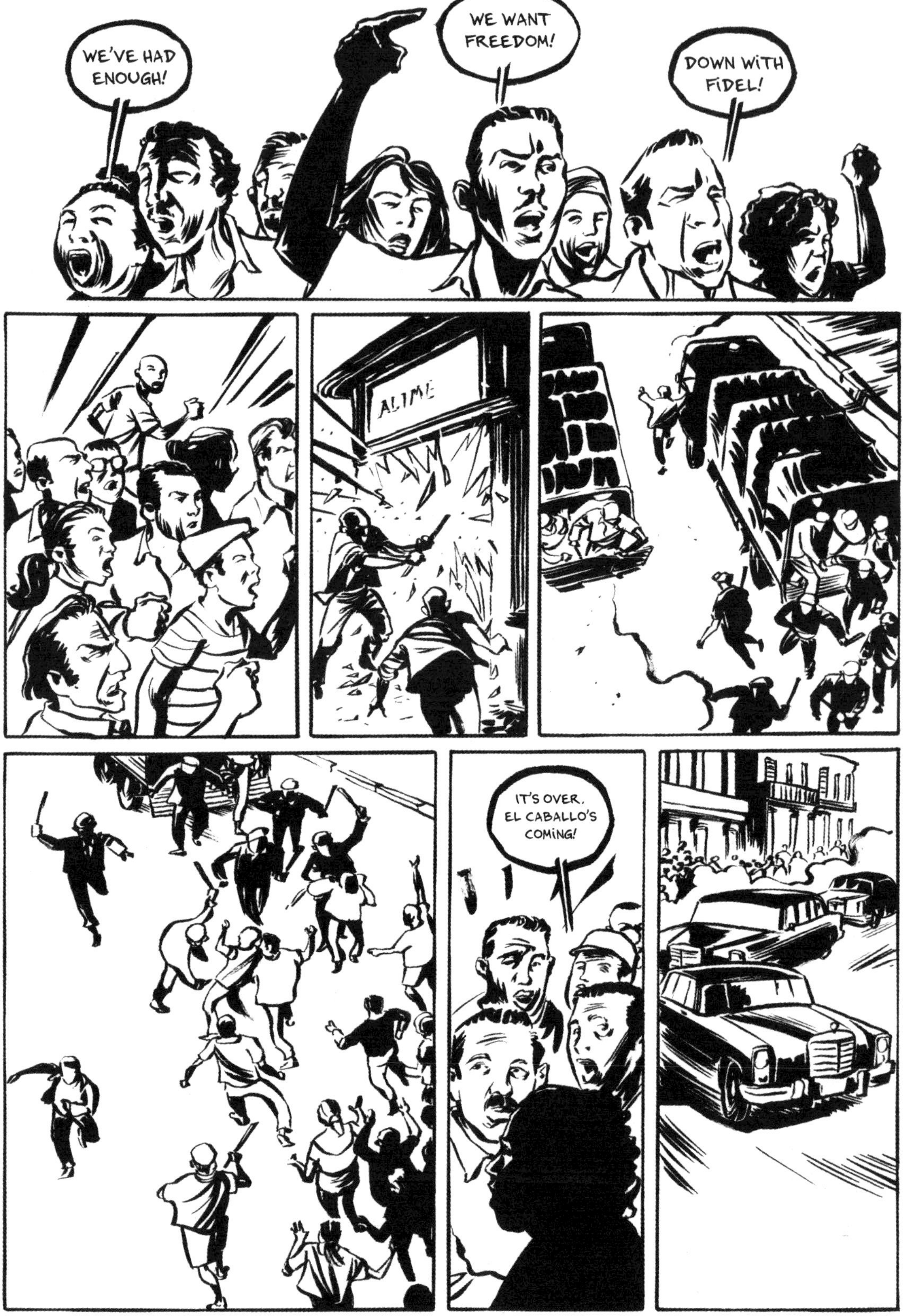
WE'VE HAD ENOUGH!
WE WANT FREEDOM!
DOWN WITH FIDEL!
ALIME
IT'S OVER. EL CABALLO'S COMING!

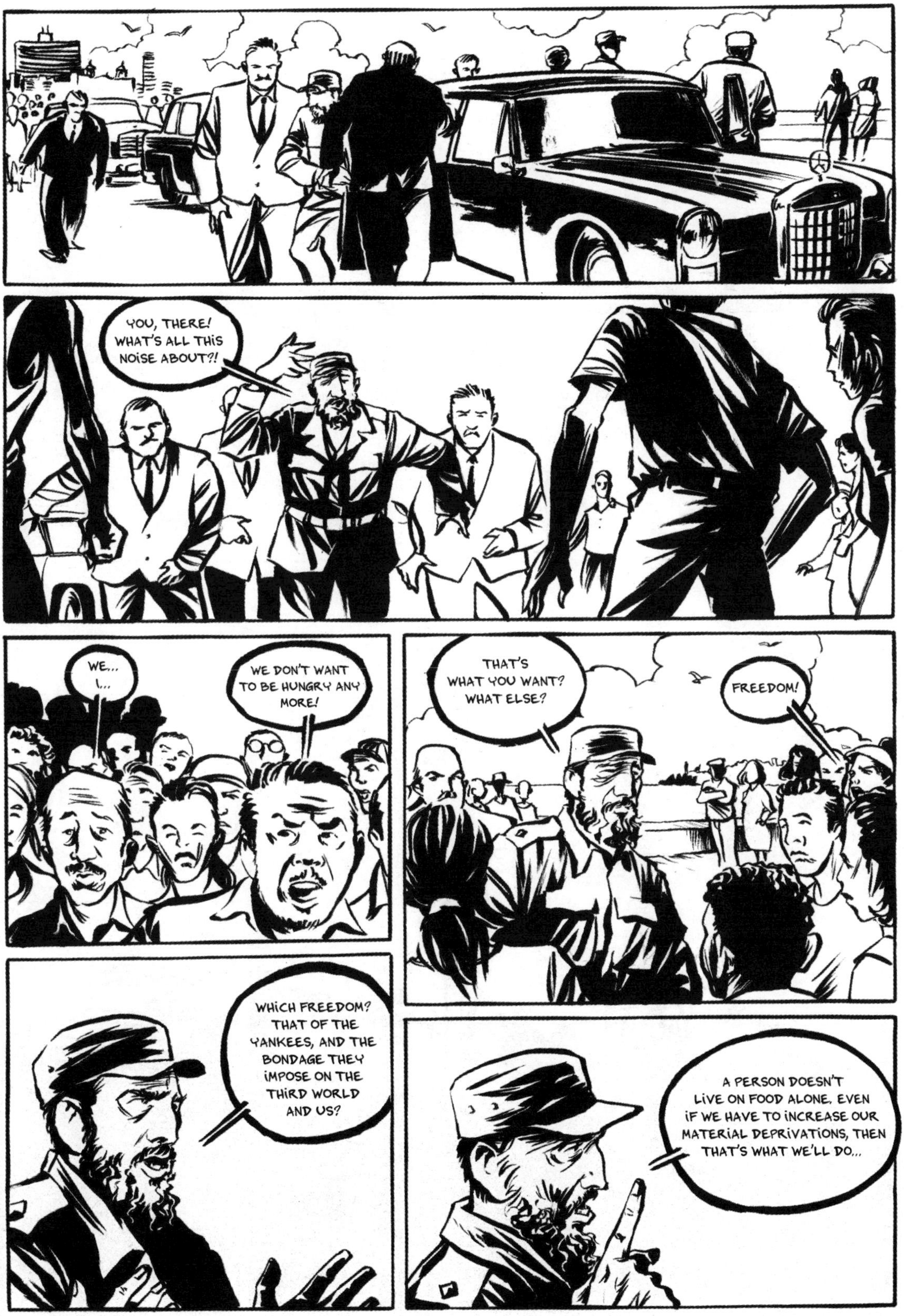
YOU, THERE! WHAT'S ALL THIS NOISE ABOUT?!
WE... I...
WE DON'T WANT TO BE HUNGRY ANY MORE!
THAT'S WHAT YOU WANT? WHAT ELSE?
FREEDOM!
WHICH FREEDOM? THAT OF THE YANKEES, AND THE BONDAGE THEY IMPOSE ON THE THIRD WORLD AND US?
A PERSON DOESN'T LIVE ON FOOD ALONE. EVEN IF WE HAVE TO INCREASE OUR MATERIAL DEPRIVATIONS, THEN THAT'S WHAT WE'LL DO...

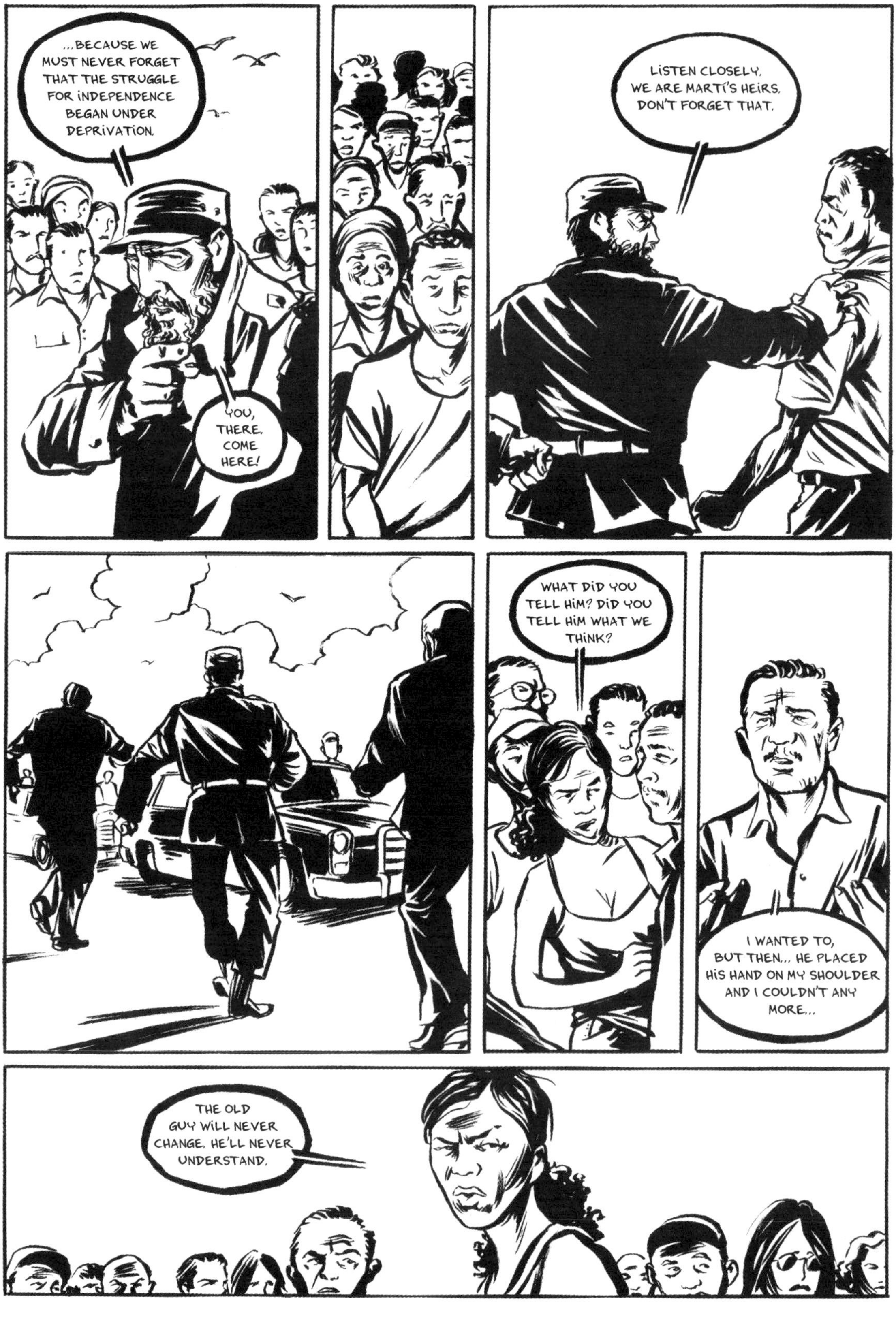
...BECAUSE WE MUST NEVER FORGET THAT THE STRUGGLE FOR INDEPENDENCE BEGAN UNDER DEPRIVATION.
YOU, THERE. COME HERE!
LISTEN CLOSELY. WE ARE MARTÍ'S HEIRS. DON'T FORGET THAT.
WHAT DID YOU TELL HIM? DID YOU TELL HIM WHAT WE THINK?
I WANTED TO, BUT THEN... HE PLACED HIS HAND ON MY SHOULDER AND I COULDN'T ANY MORE...
THE OLD GUY WILL NEVER CHANGE. HE'LL NEVER UNDERSTAND.

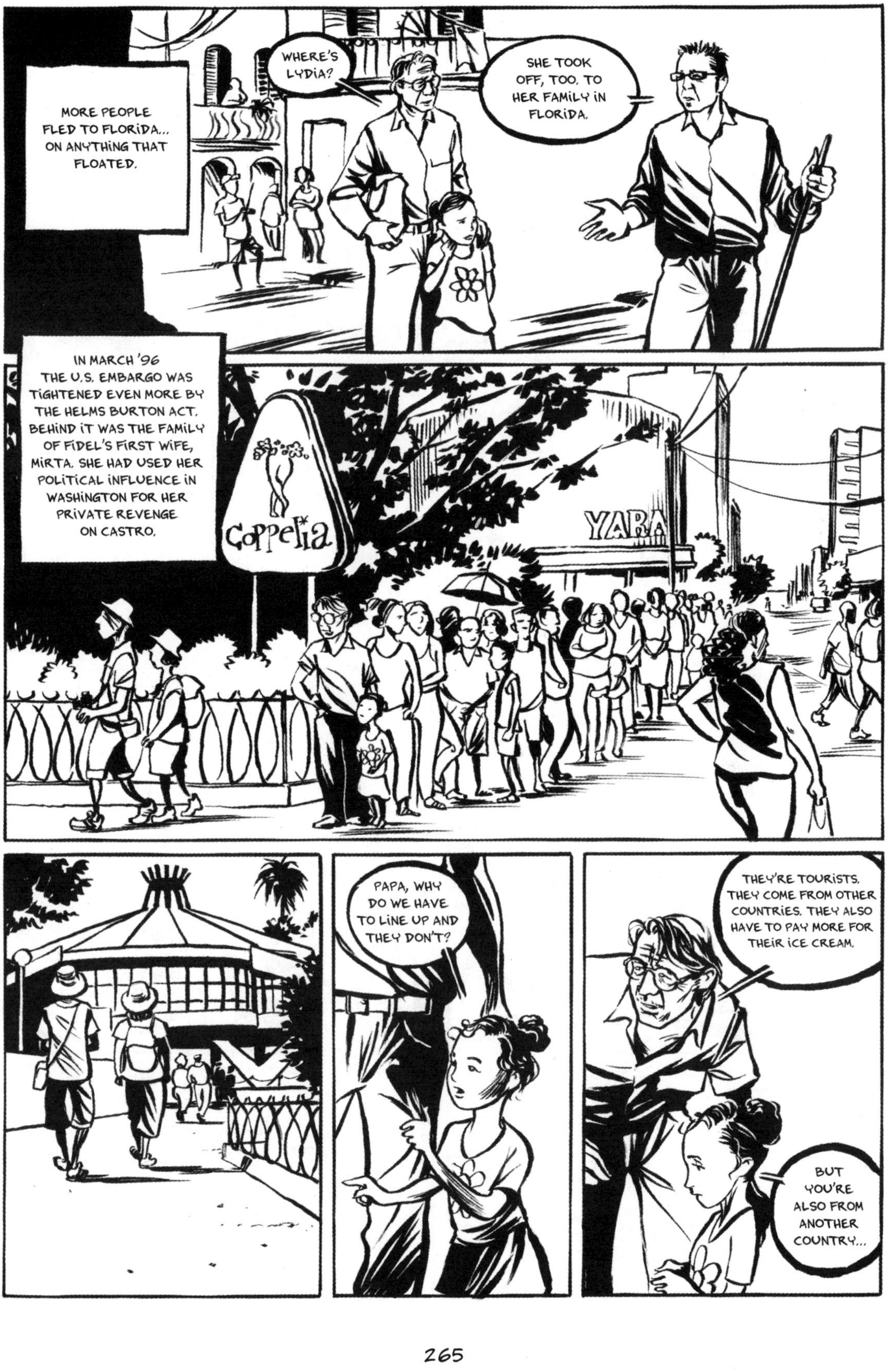
MORE PEOPLE FLED TO FLORIDA... ON ANYTHING THAT FLOATED.
WHERE'S LYDIA?
SHE TOOK OFF, TOO. TO HER FAMILY IN FLORIDA.
IN MARCH '96 THE U.S. EMBARGO WAS TIGHTENED EVEN MORE BY THE HELMS BURTON ACT. BEHIND IT WAS THE FAMILY OF FIDEL'S FIRST WIFE, MIRTA. SHE HAD USED HER POLITICAL INFLUENCE IN WASHINGTON FOR HER PRIVATE REVENGE ON CASTRO.
Coppelia
YARA
PAPA, WHY DO WE HAVE TO LINE UP AND THEY DON'T?
THEY'RE TOURISTS. THEY COME FROM OTHER COUNTRIES. THEY ALSO HAVE TO PAY MORE FOR THEIR ICE CREAM.
BUT YOU'RE ALSO FROM ANOTHER COUNTRY...

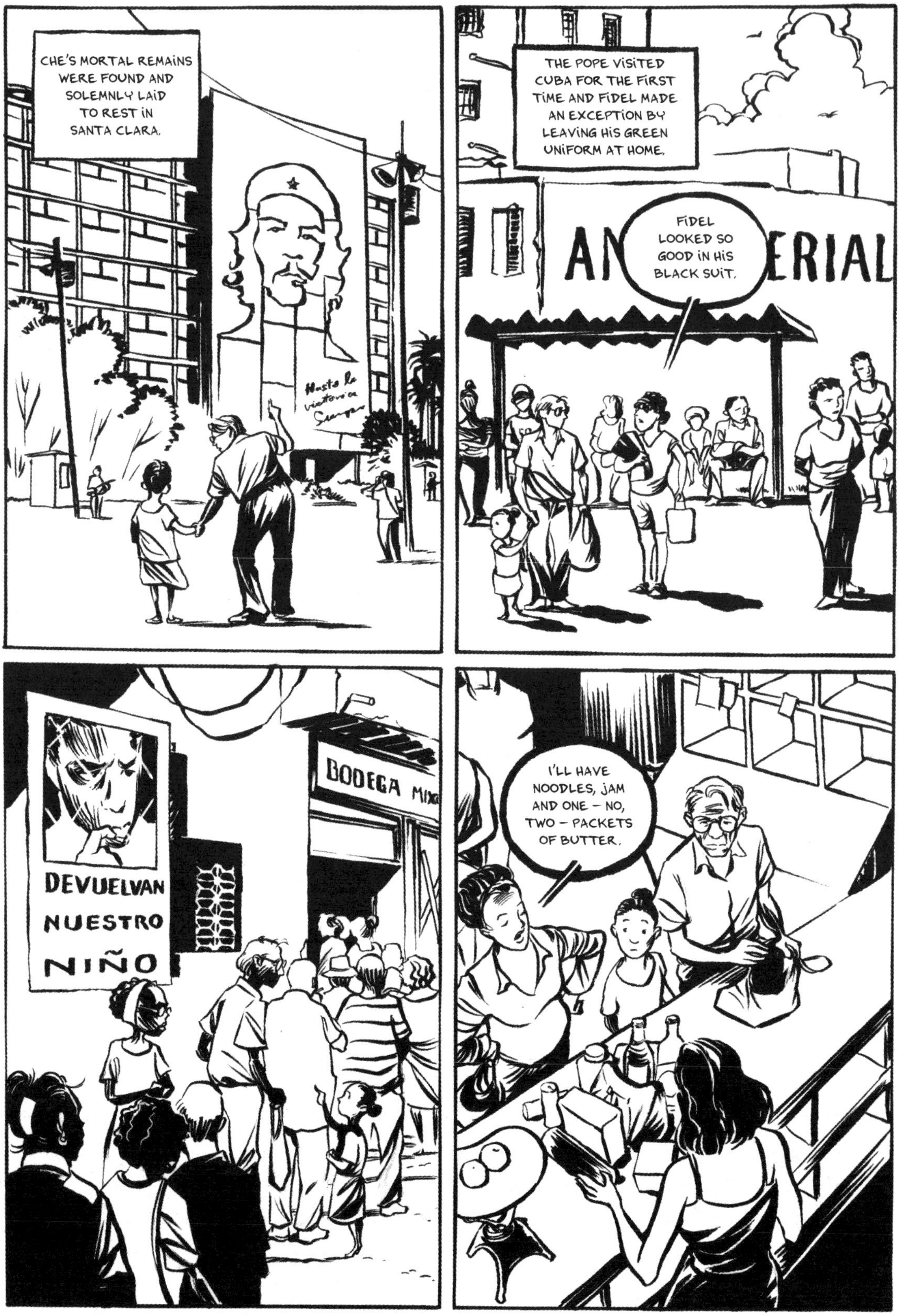

CHE'S MORTAL REMAINS WERE FOUND AND SOLEMNLY LAID TO REST IN SANTA CLARA.
THE POPE VISITED CUBA FOR THE FIRST TIME AND FIDEL MADE AN EXCEPTION BY LEAVING HIS GREEN UNIFORM AT HOME.
AN
ERIAL
FIDEL LOOKED SO GOOD IN HIS BLACK SUIT.
DEVUELVAN NUESTRO NIÑO
BODEGA MIX
I'LL HAVE NOODLES, JAM AND ONE – NO, TWO – PACKETS OF BUTTER.

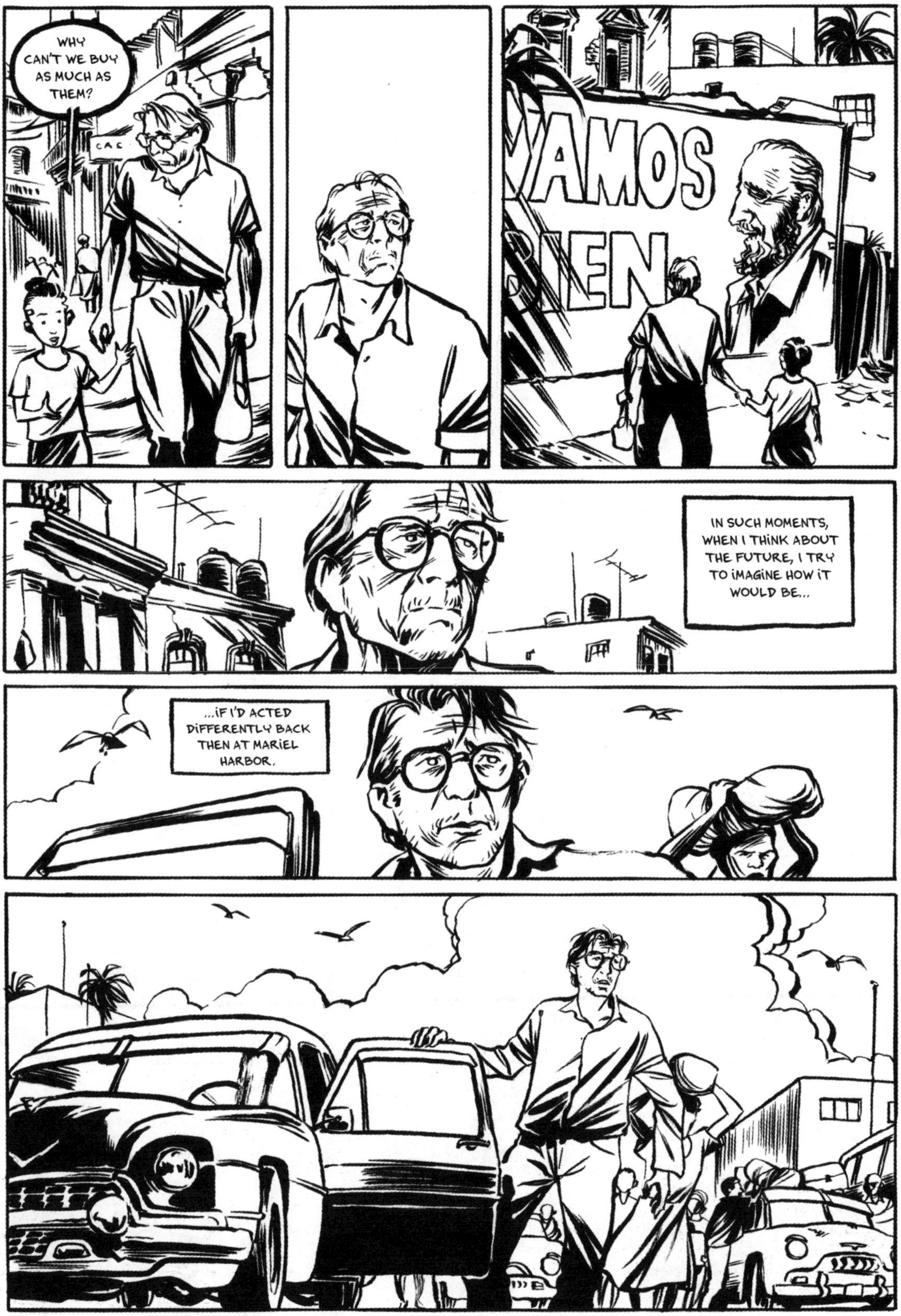
WHY CAN'T WE BUY AS MUCH AS THEM?
CAS
AMOS
IEN
IN SUCH MOMENTS, WHEN I THINK ABOUT THE FUTURE, I TRY TO IMAGINE HOW IT WOULD BE...
...IF I'D ACTED DIFFERENTLY BACK THEN AT MARIEL HARBOR.

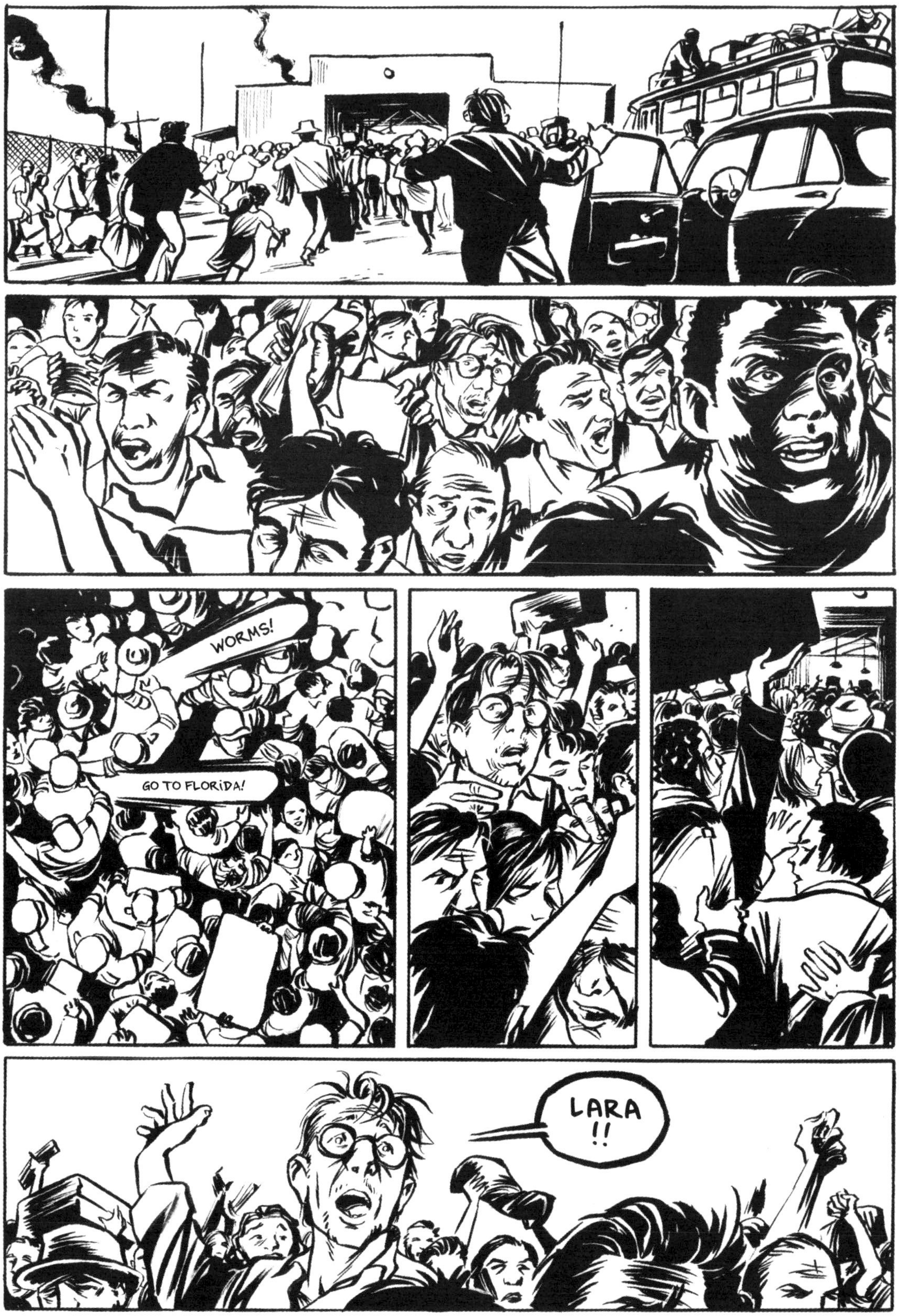
WORMS!
GO TO FLORIDA!
LARA !!

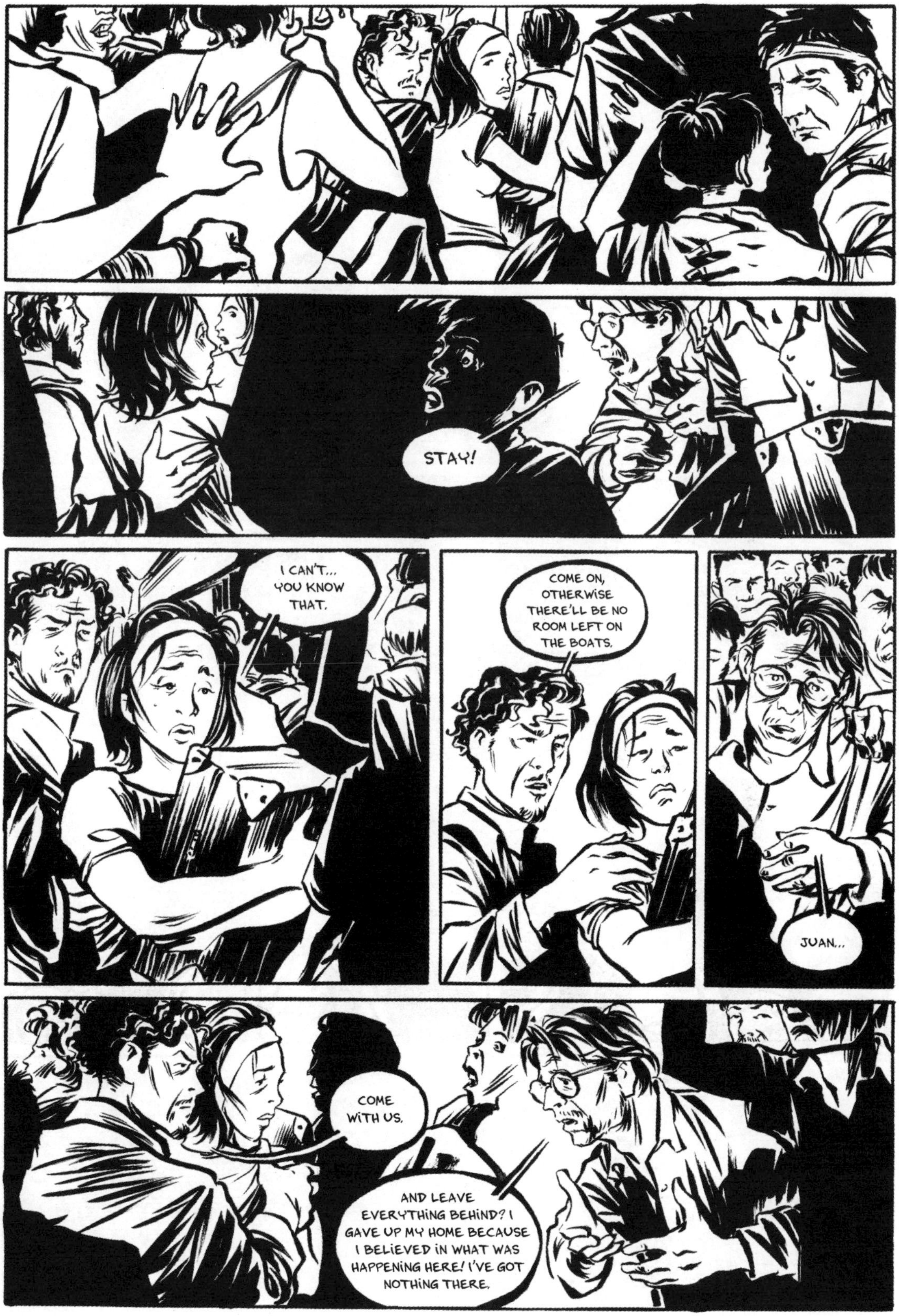
STAY!
I CAN'T... YOU KNOW THAT.
COME ON, OTHERWISE THERE'LL BE NO ROOM LEFT ON THE BOATS.
JUAN...
COME WITH US.
AND LEAVE EVERYTHING BEHIND? I GAVE UP MY HOME BECAUSE I BELIEVED IN WHAT WAS HAPPENING HERE! I'VE GOT NOTHING THERE.

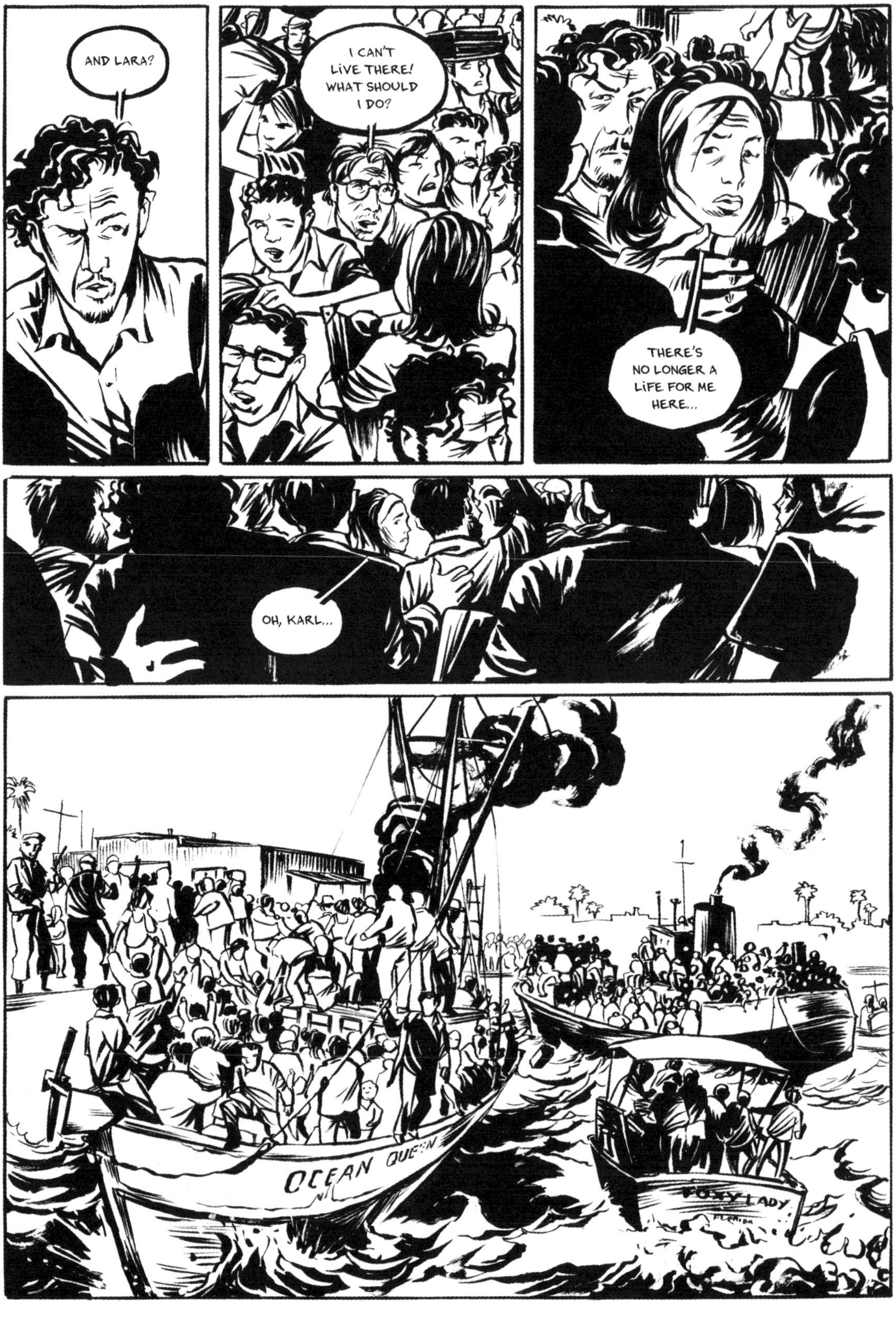
AND LARA?
I CAN'T LIVE THERE! WHAT SHOULD I DO?
THERE'S NO LONGER A LIFE FOR ME HERE...
OH, KARL...
OCEAN QUEEN
FOXY LADY
FLORIDA

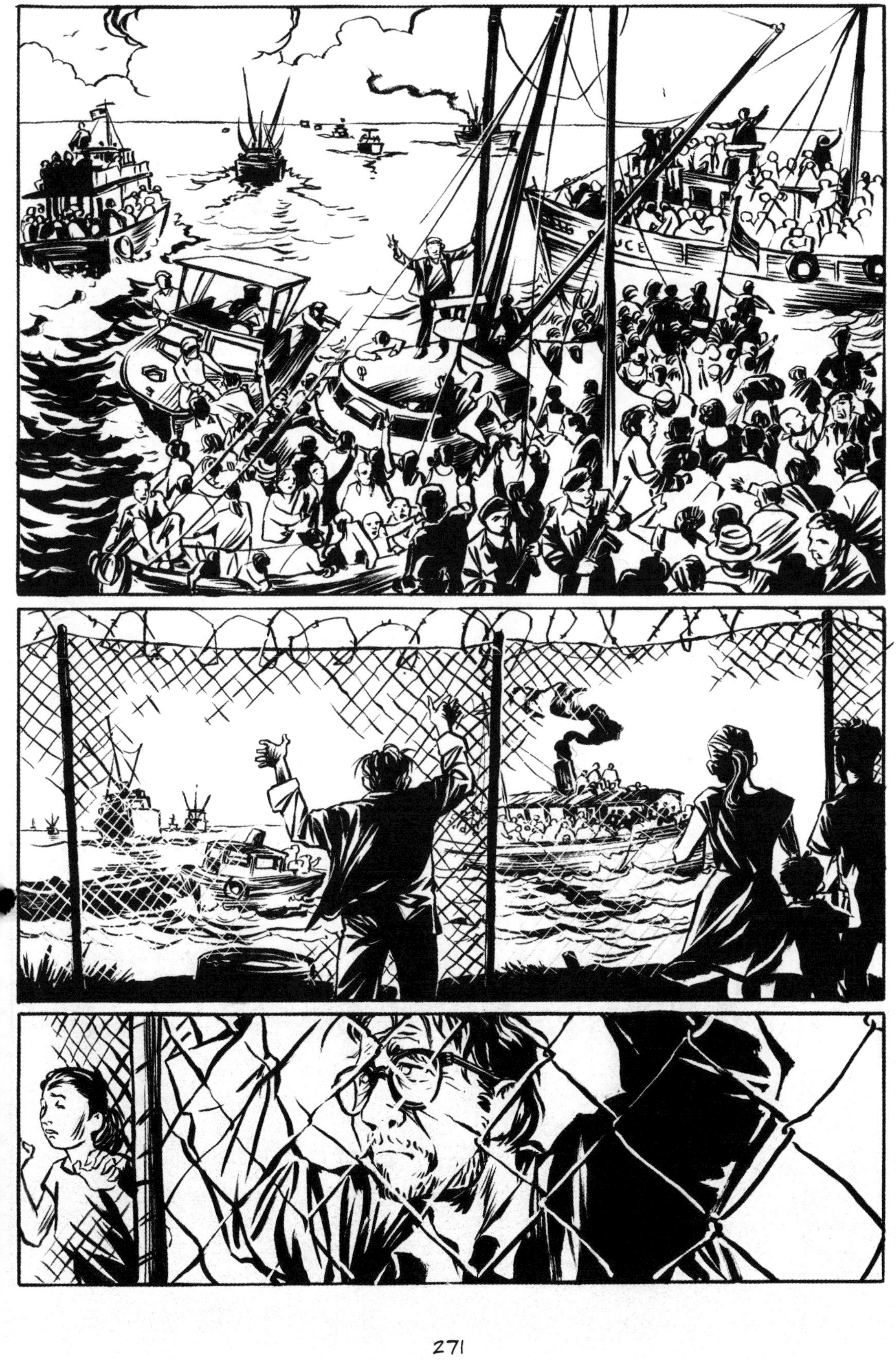

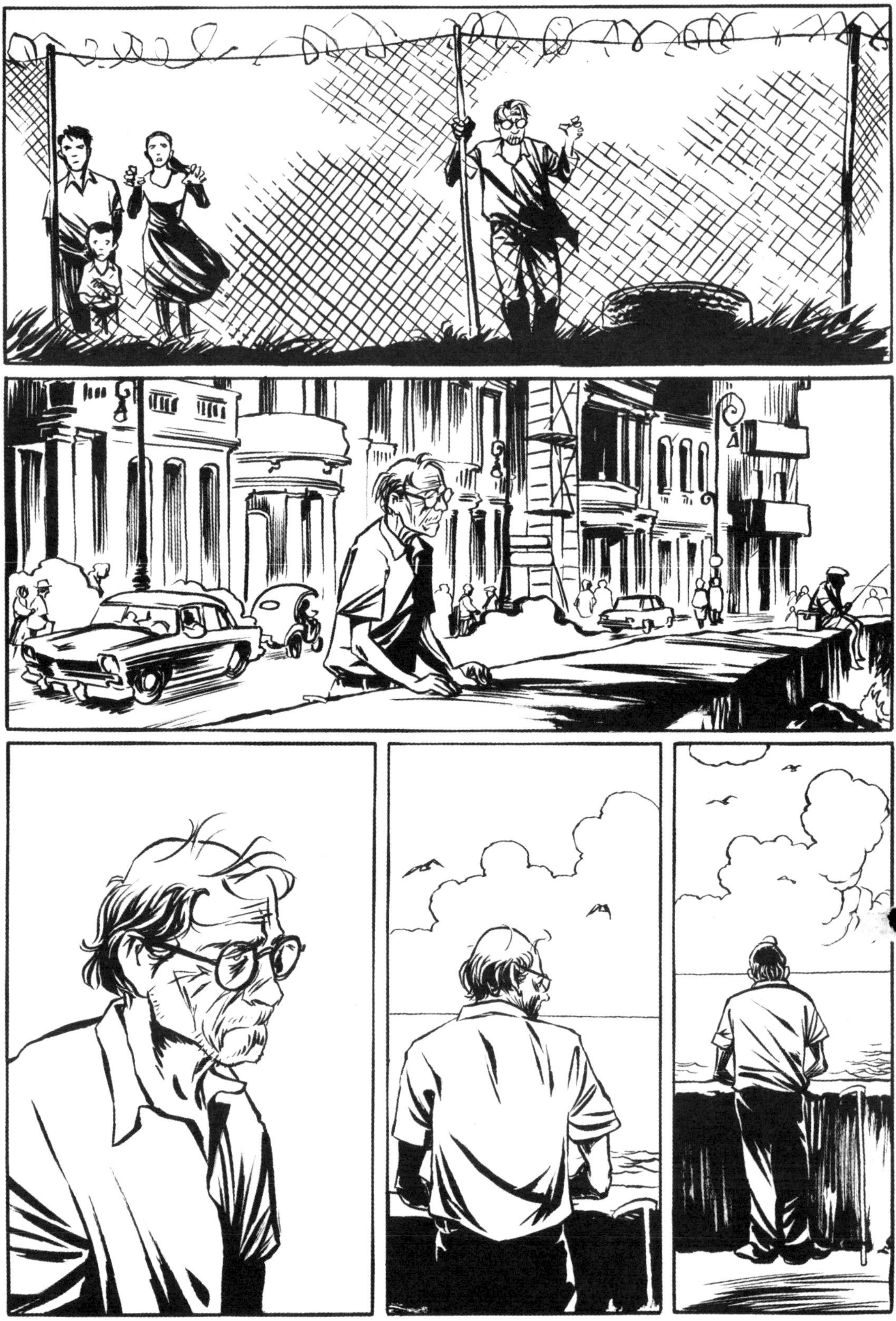

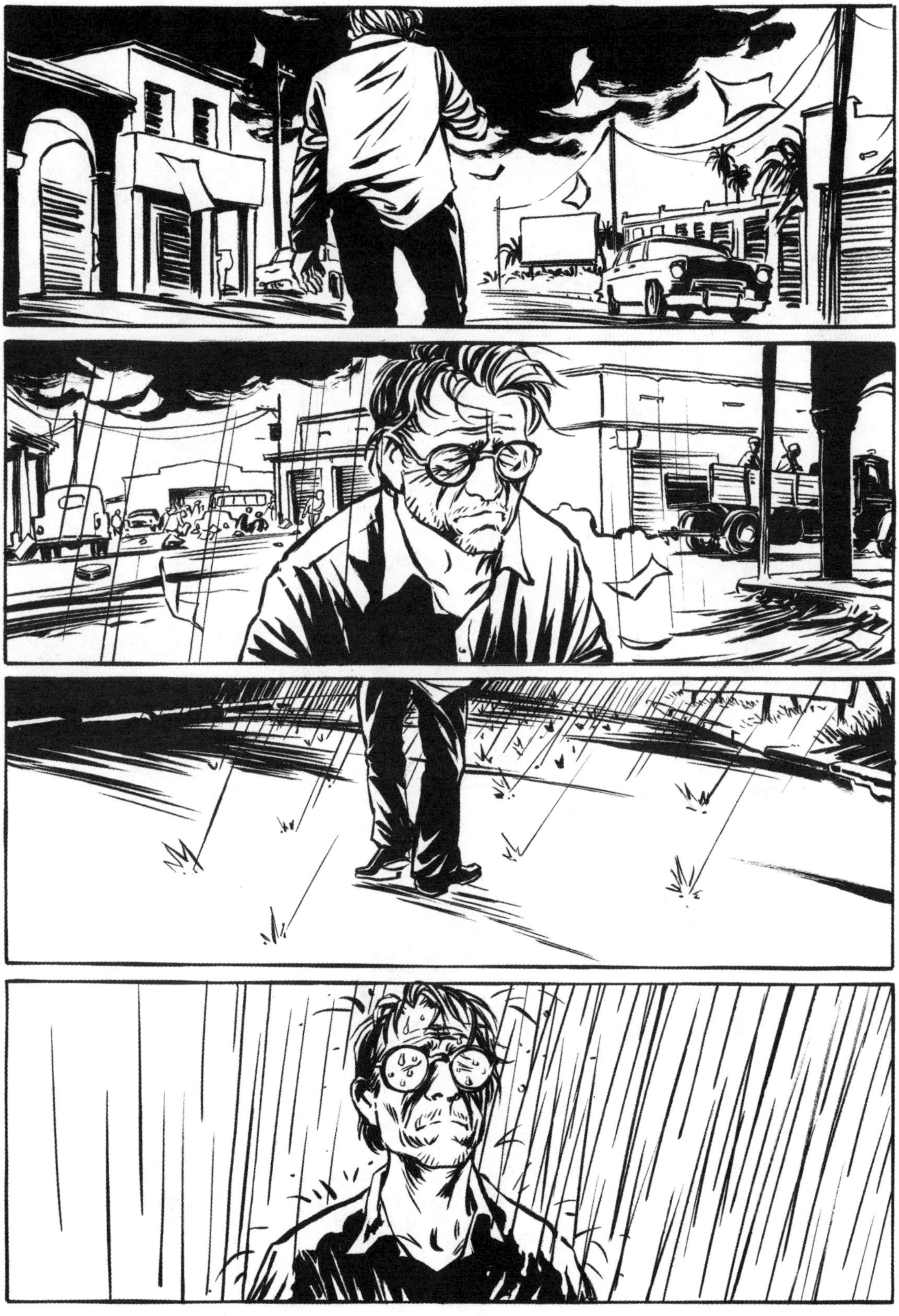

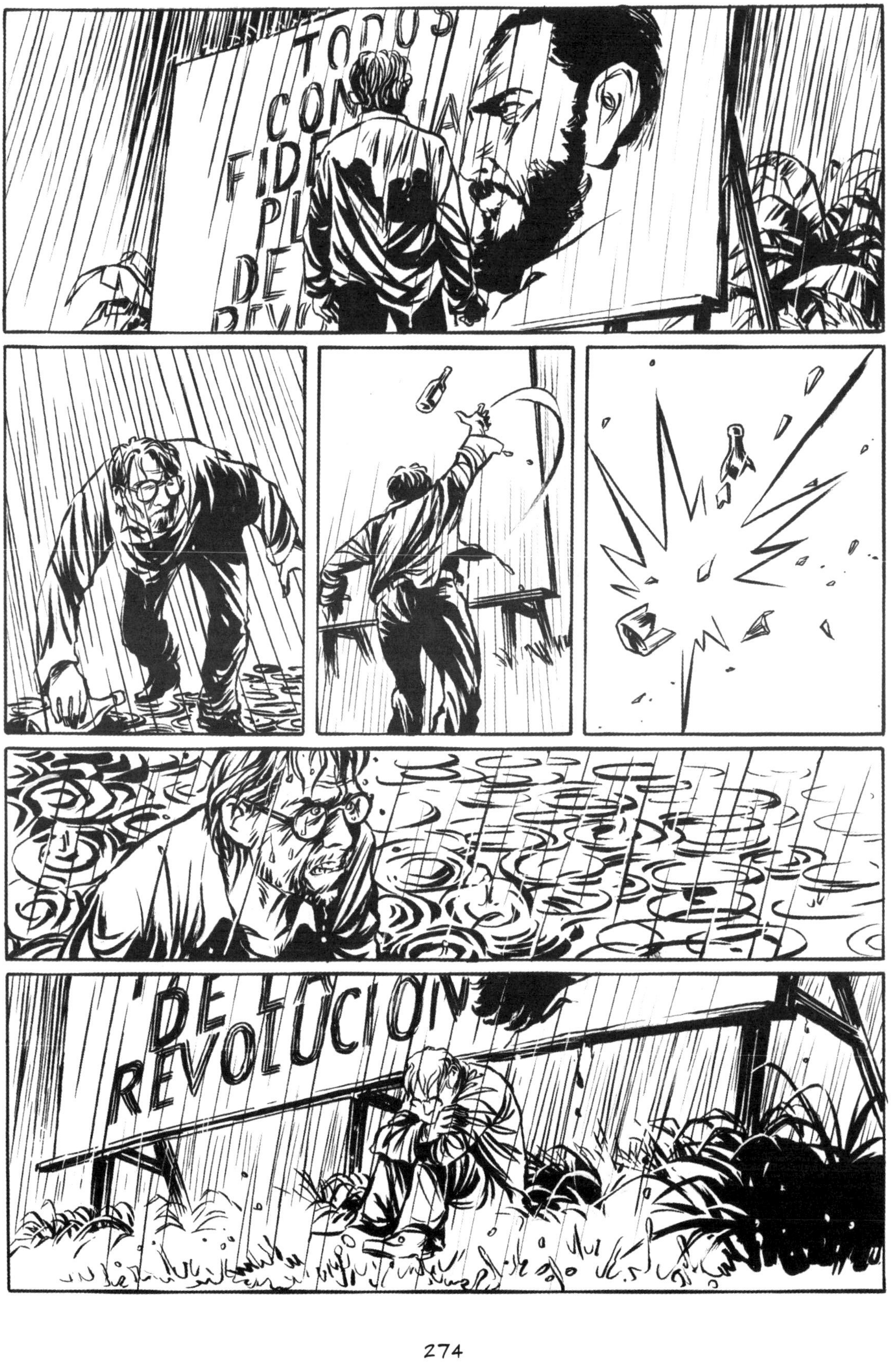
TODOS
REVOLUCION

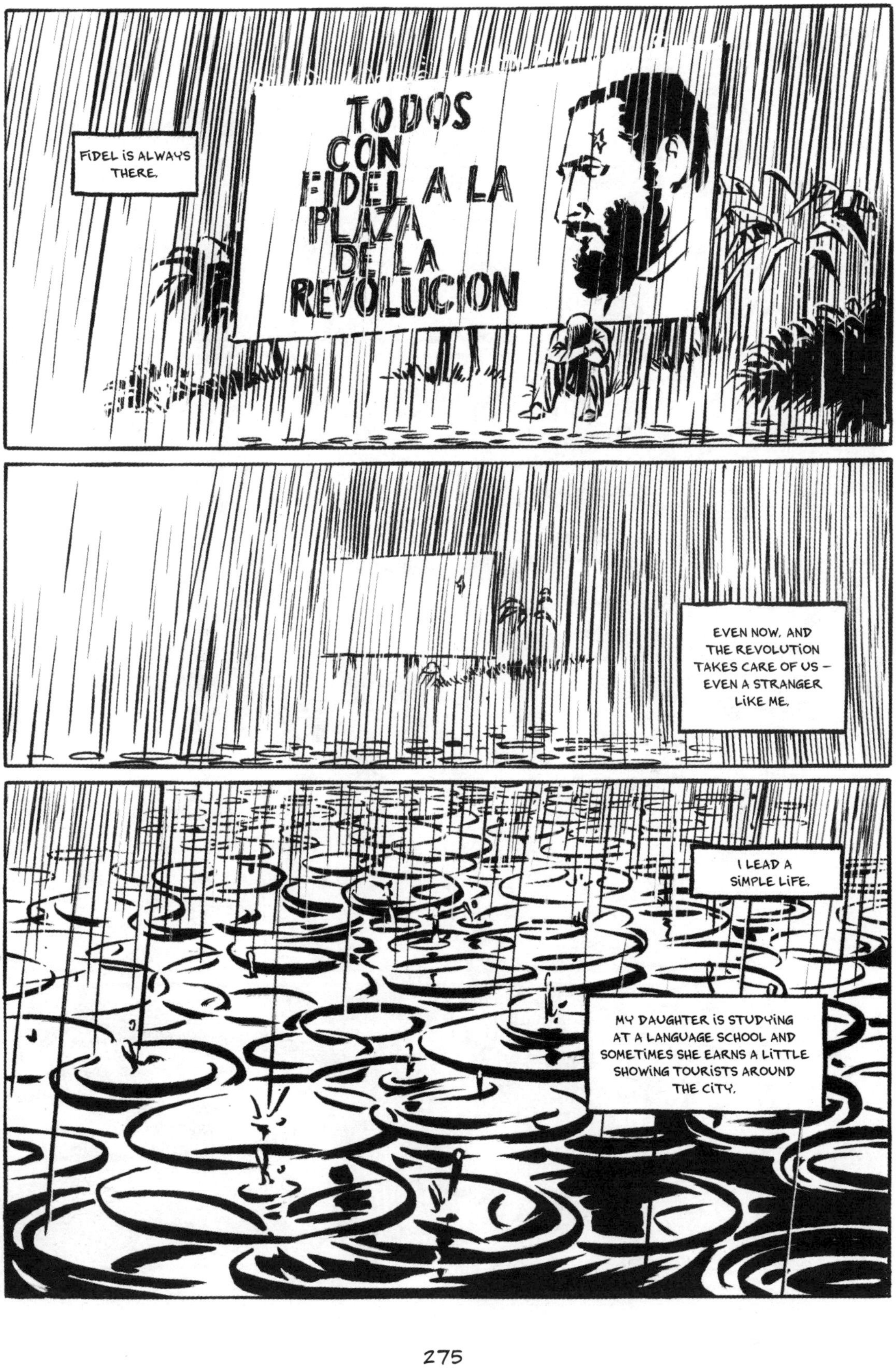
FIDEL IS ALWAYS THERE.
TODOS CON FIDEL A LA PLAZA DE LA REVOLUCION
EVEN NOW. AND THE REVOLUTION TAKES CARE OF US – EVEN A STRANGER LIKE ME.
I LEAD A SIMPLE LIFE.
MY DAUGHTER IS STUDYING AT A LANGUAGE SCHOOL AND SOMETIMES SHE EARNS A LITTLE SHOWING TOURISTS AROUND THE CITY.

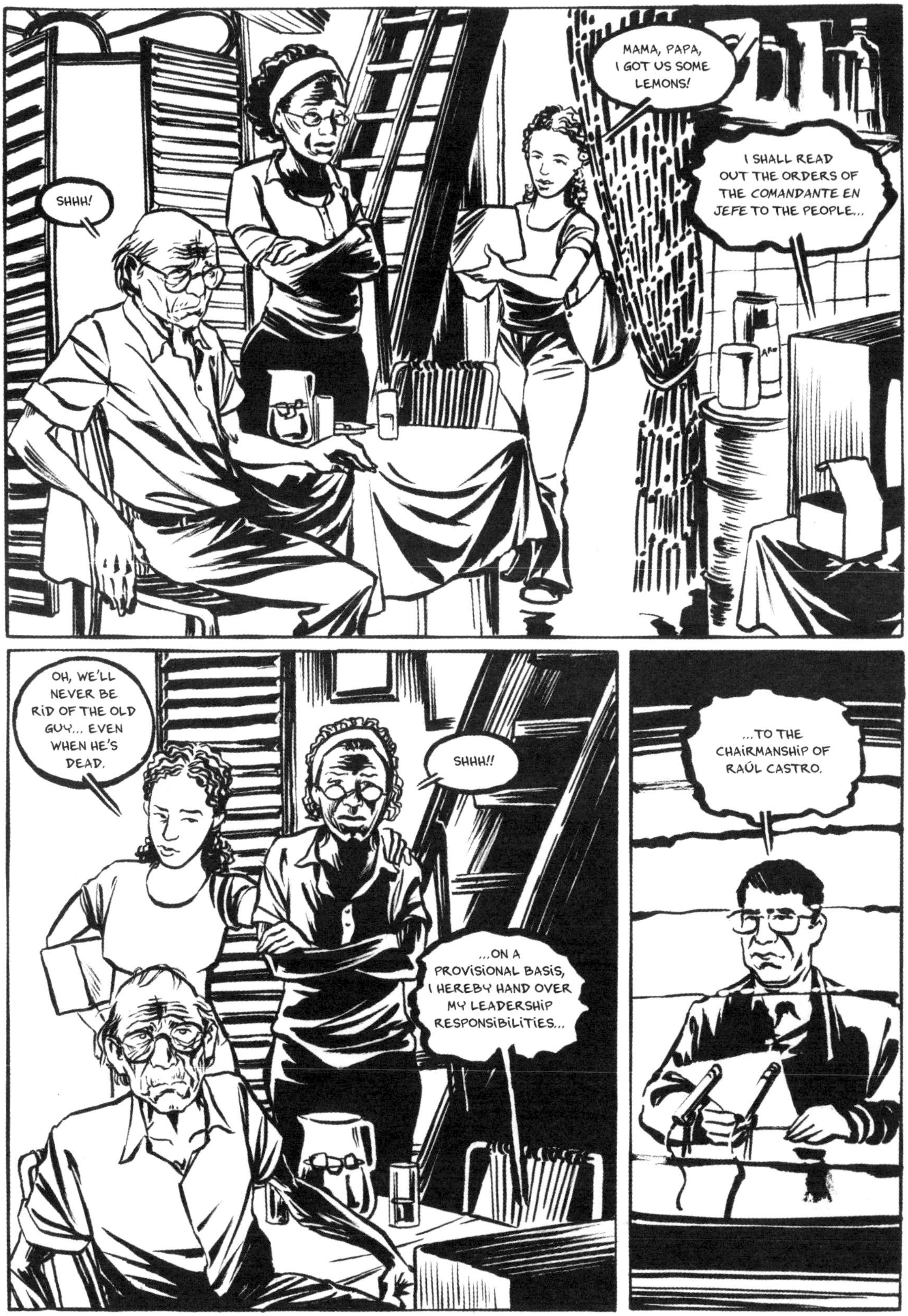
MAMA, PAPA, I GOT US SOME LEMONS!
SHHH!
I SHALL READ OUT THE ORDERS OF THE COMANDANTE EN JEFE TO THE PEOPLE...
OH, WE'LL NEVER BE RID OF THE OLD GUY... EVEN WHEN HE'S DEAD.
SHHH!!
...ON A PROVISIONAL BASIS, I HEREBY HAND OVER MY LEADERSHIP RESPONSIBILITIES...
...TO THE CHAIRMANSHIP OF RAÚL CASTRO.

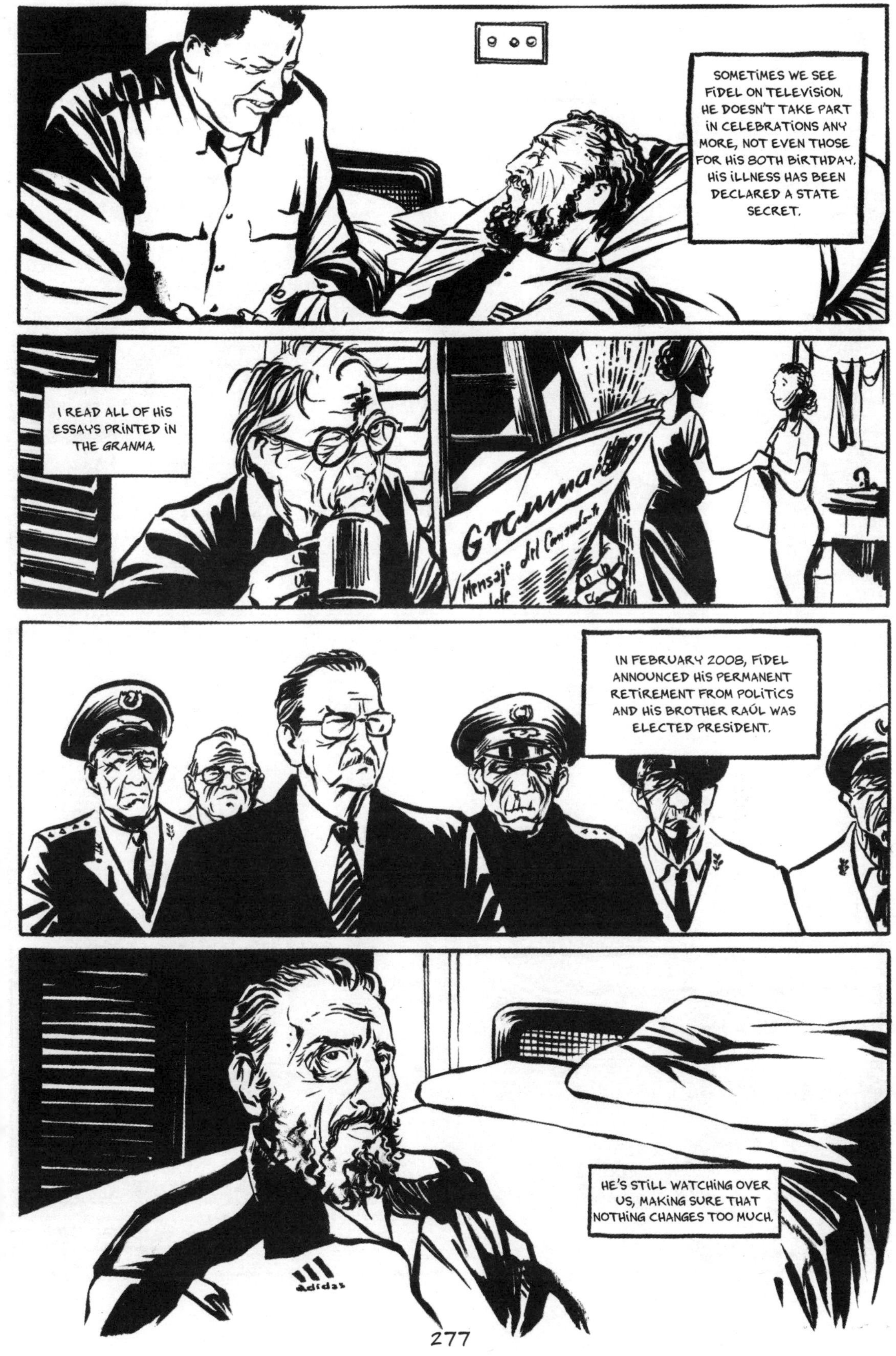
SOMETIMES WE SEE FIDEL ON TELEVISION. HE DOESN'T TAKE PART IN CELEBRATIONS ANY MORE, NOT EVEN THOSE FOR HIS 80TH BIRTHDAY. HIS ILLNESS HAS BEEN DECLARED A STATE SECRET.
I READ ALL OF HIS ESSAYS PRINTED IN THE *GRANMA*.
IN FEBRUARY 2008, FIDEL ANNOUNCED HIS PERMANENT RETIREMENT FROM POLITICS AND HIS BROTHER RAÚL WAS ELECTED PRESIDENT.
HE'S STILL WATCHING OVER US, MAKING SURE THAT NOTHING CHANGES TOO MUCH.
adidas

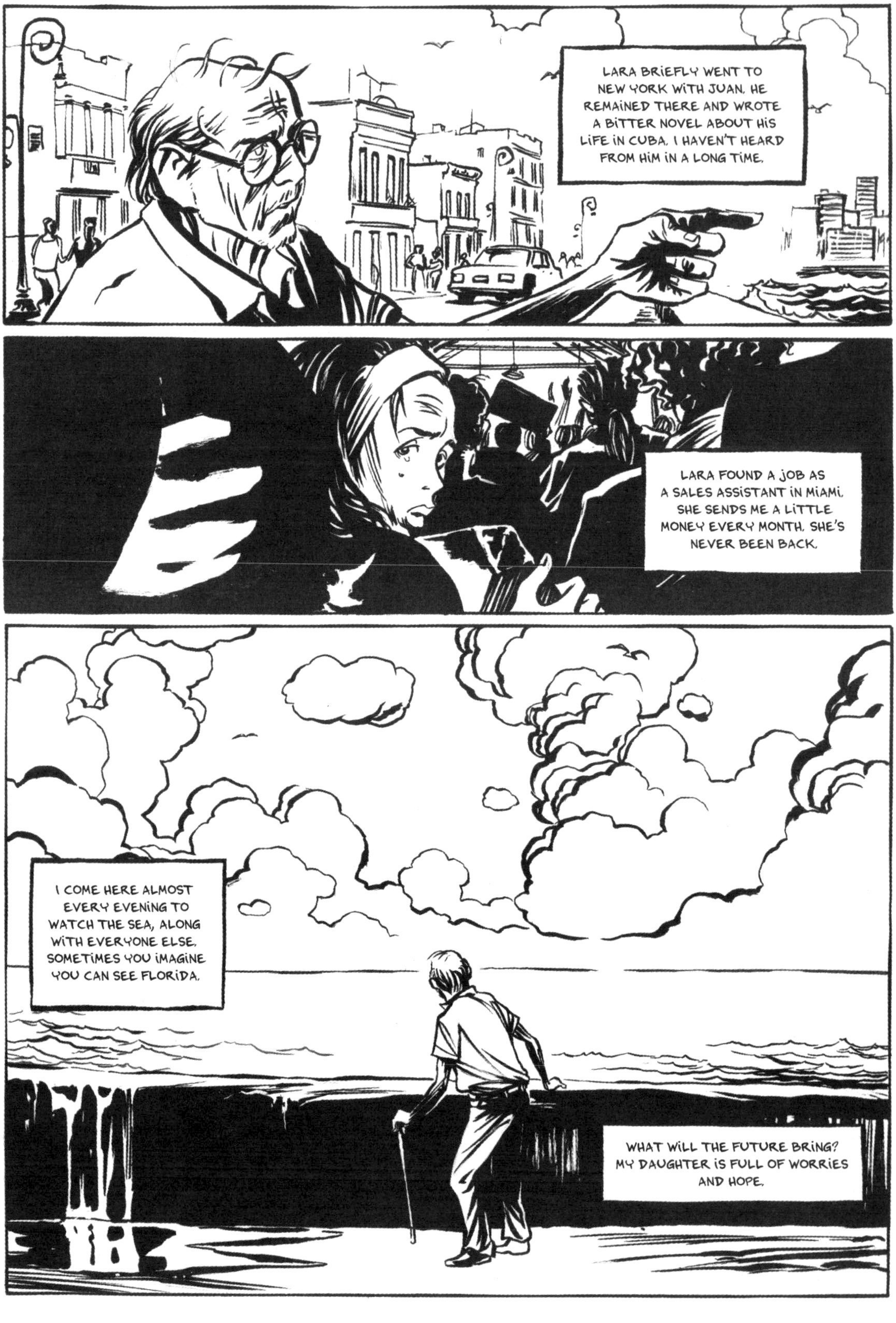
LARA BRIEFLY WENT TO NEW YORK WITH JUAN. HE REMAINED THERE AND WROTE A BITTER NOVEL ABOUT HIS LIFE IN CUBA. I HAVEN'T HEARD FROM HIM IN A LONG TIME.
LARA FOUND A JOB AS A SALES ASSISTANT IN MIAMI. SHE SENDS ME A LITTLE MONEY EVERY MONTH. SHE'S NEVER BEEN BACK.
I COME HERE ALMOST EVERY EVENING TO WATCH THE SEA, ALONG WITH EVERYONE ELSE. SOMETIMES YOU IMAGINE YOU CAN SEE FLORIDA.
WHAT WILL THE FUTURE BRING? MY DAUGHTER IS FULL OF WORRIES AND HOPE.

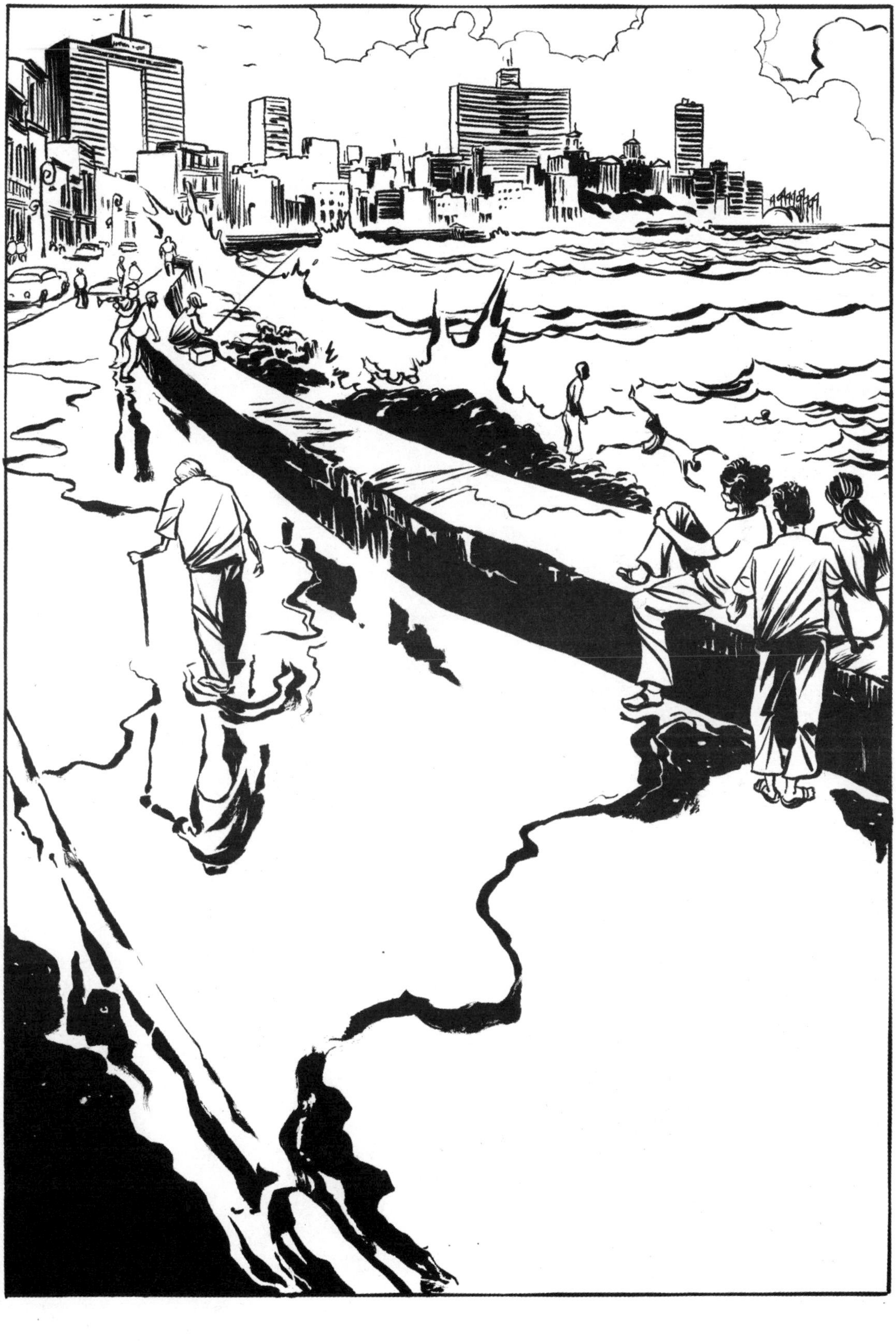

EPILOGUE

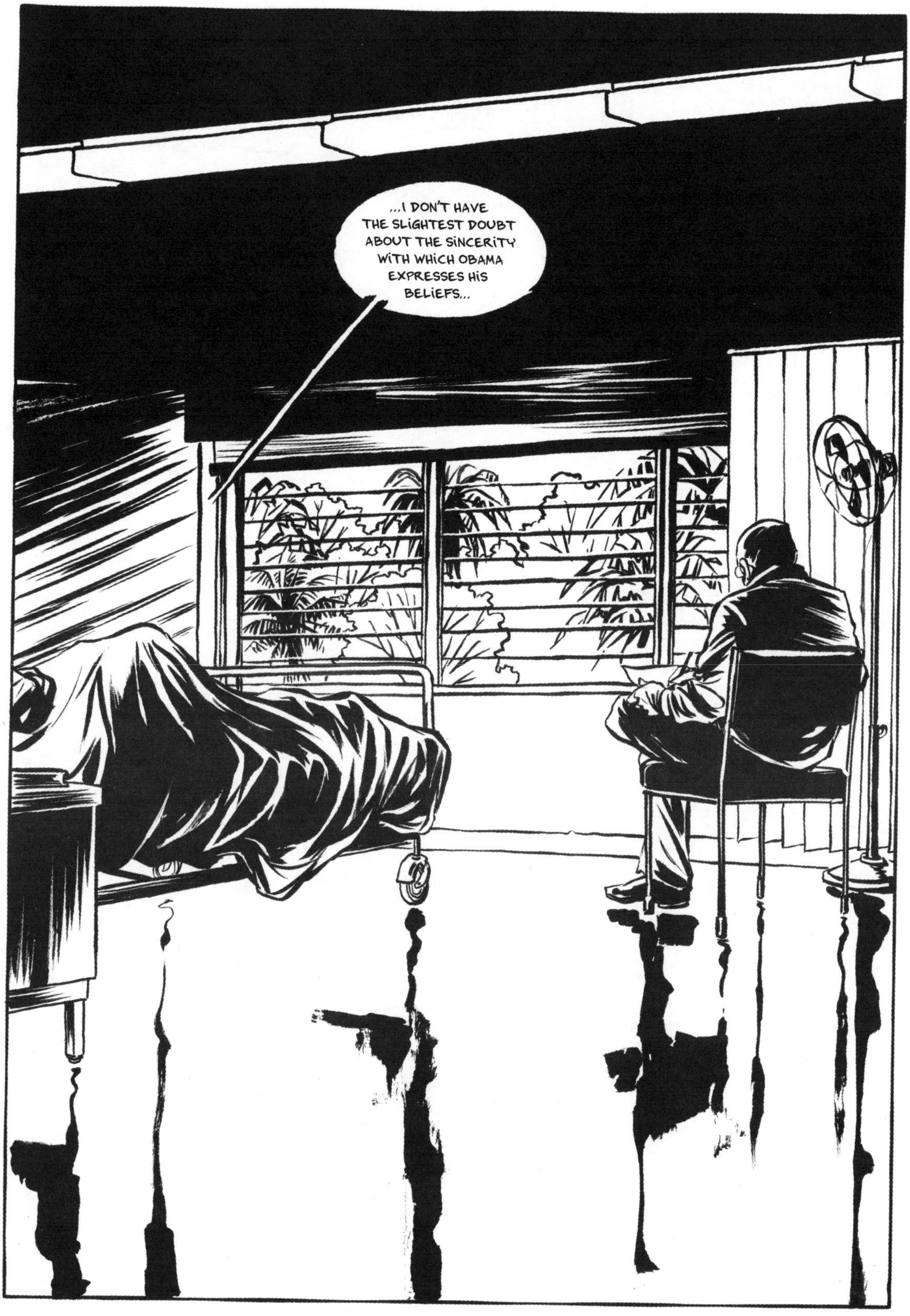
...I DON'T HAVE THE SLIGHTEST DOUBT ABOUT THE SINCERITY WITH WHICH OBAMA EXPRESSES HIS BELIEFS...

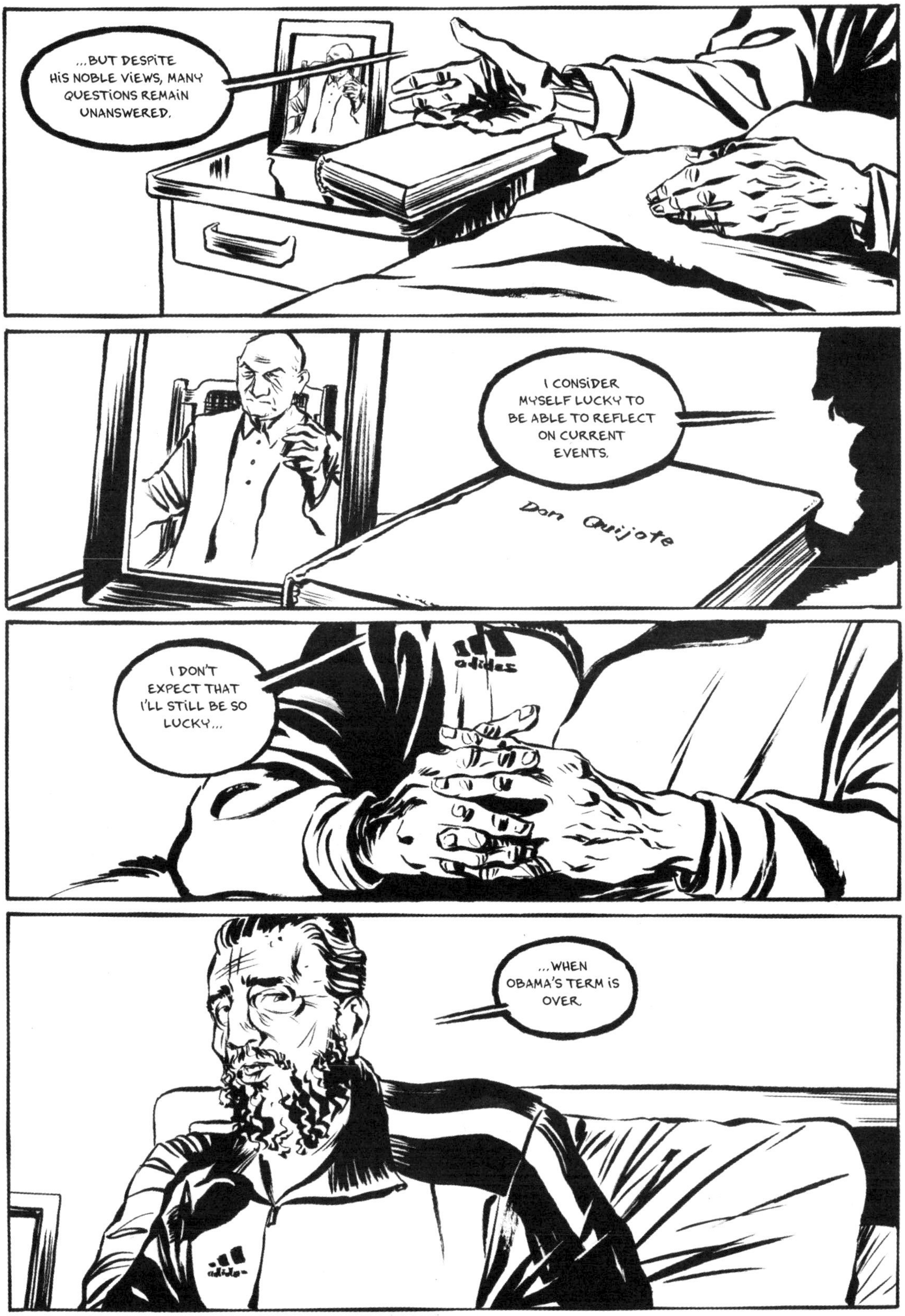
...BUT DESPITE HIS NOBLE VIEWS, MANY QUESTIONS REMAIN UNANSWERED.
I CONSIDER MYSELF LUCKY TO BE ABLE TO REFLECT ON CURRENT EVENTS.
Don Quijote
adidas
I DON'T EXPECT THAT I'LL STILL BE SO LUCKY...
...WHEN OBAMA'S TERM IS OVER.
adidas

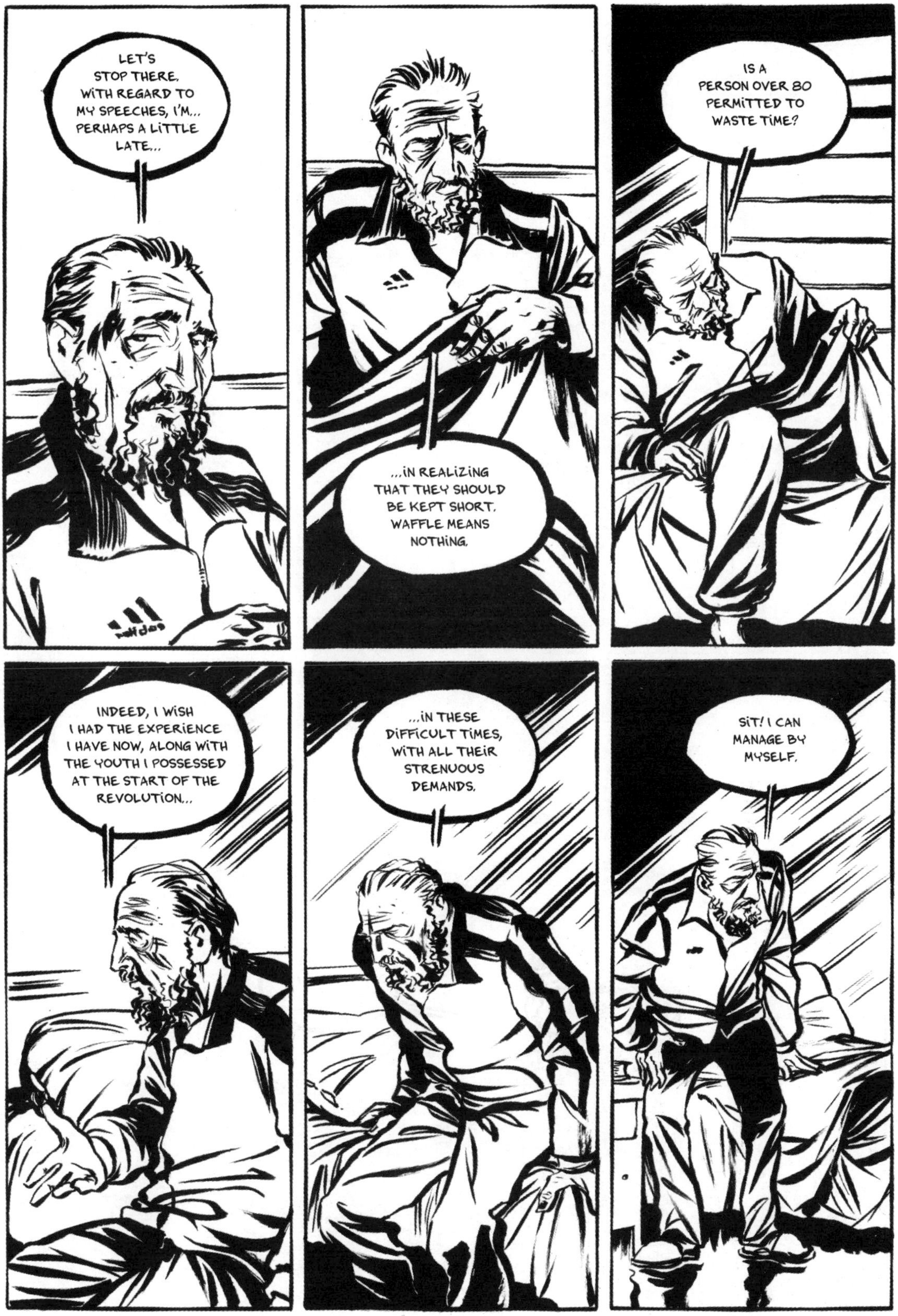
LET'S STOP THERE. WITH REGARD TO MY SPEECHES, I'M... PERHAPS A LITTLE LATE...
...IN REALIZING THAT THEY SHOULD BE KEPT SHORT. WAFFLE MEANS NOTHING.
IS A PERSON OVER 80 PERMITTED TO WASTE TIME?
INDEED, I WISH I HAD THE EXPERIENCE I HAVE NOW, ALONG WITH THE YOUTH I POSSESSED AT THE START OF THE REVOLUTION...
...IN THESE DIFFICULT TIMES, WITH ALL THEIR STRENUOUS DEMANDS.
SIT! I CAN MANAGE BY MYSELF.

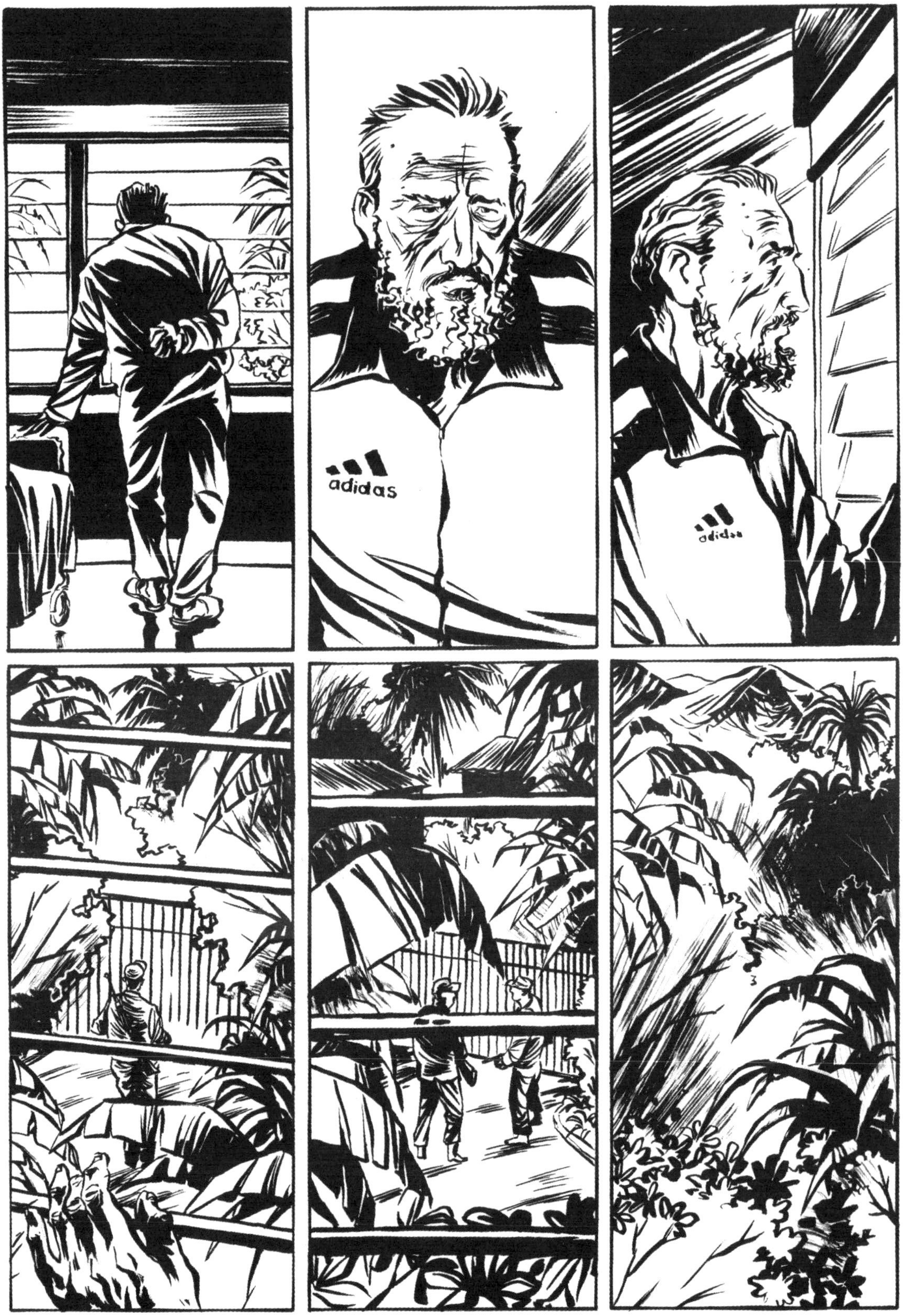
adidas
adidas

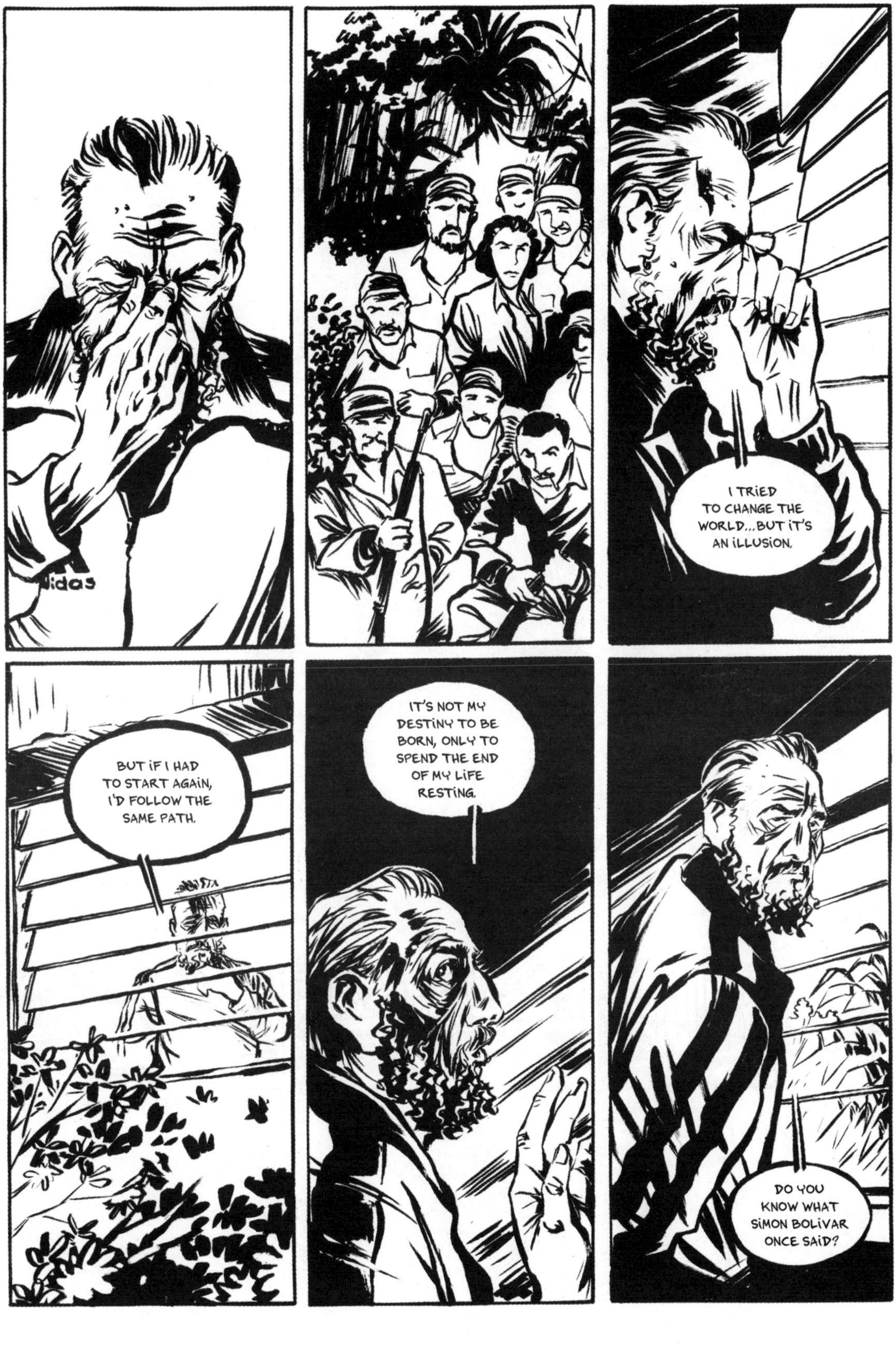
Nidas
I TRIED TO CHANGE THE WORLD... BUT IT'S AN ILLUSION.
BUT IF I HAD TO START AGAIN, I'D FOLLOW THE SAME PATH.
IT'S NOT MY DESTINY TO BE BORN, ONLY TO SPEND THE END OF MY LIFE RESTING.
DO YOU KNOW WHAT SIMON BOLIVAR ONCE SAID?

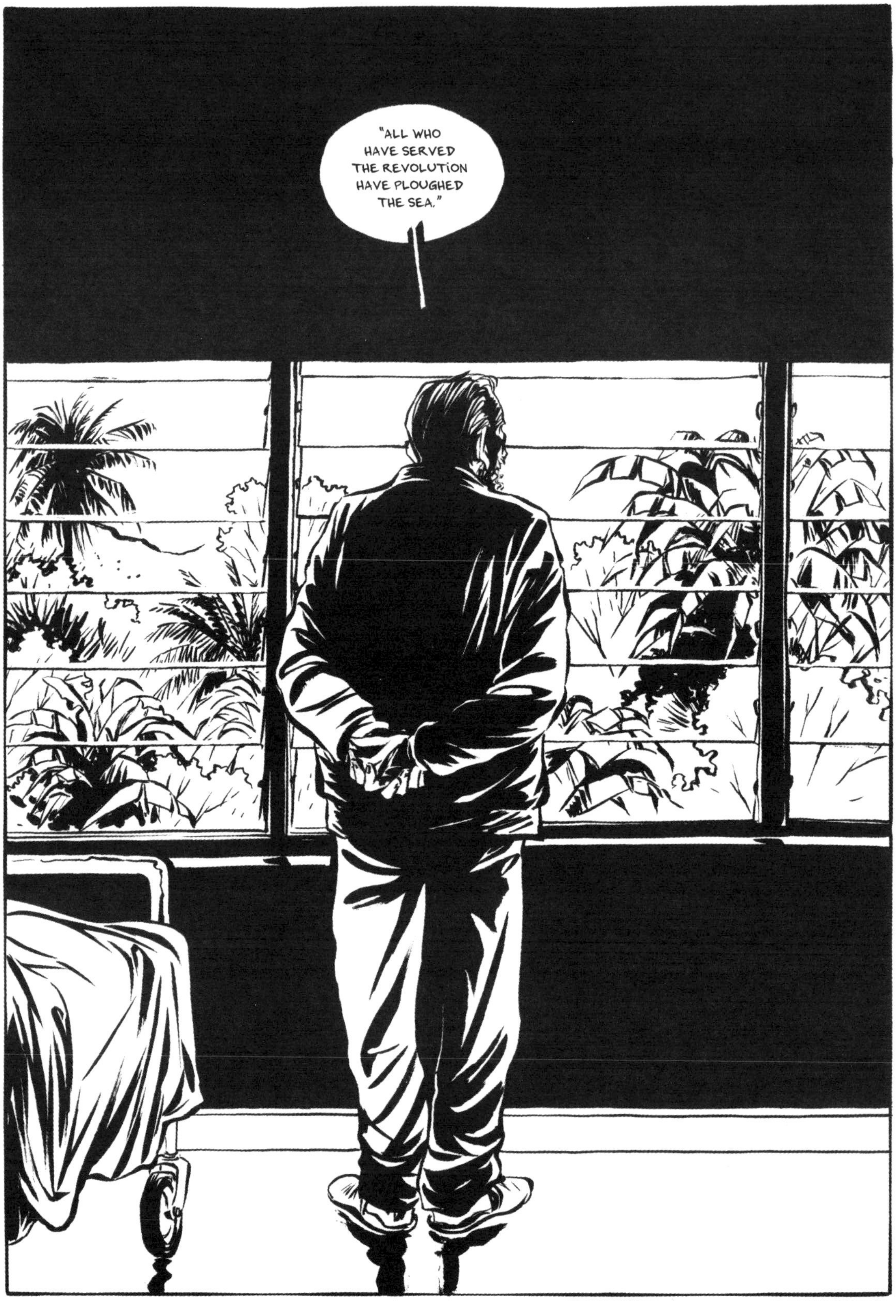
"ALL WHO HAVE SERVED THE REVOLUTiON HAVE PLOUGHED THE SEA."

Thanks to:

Volker Skierka

Michael, Claudia, and Paul Jerusalem-Groenewald

Bettina Oguamanam, Sylvia Schuster, and everyone at Carlsen Verlag

Joachim Werth

Susanne Hellweg

Isabel Kreitz

My parents

My studio: Naomi Fearn, Mawil, Fil

K77

Nebojsa Tabacki

REINHARD KLEIST was born near Cologne in 1970. After studying Graphic Design at Münster University of Applied Sciences, he relocated to Berlin in 1996. There he works in a studio that he shares with the comic artists Naomi Fearn, Fil, and Mawil.

In 1994, while still at university, Reinhard Kleist published the graphic novel *Lovecraft*. Since then, he has followed this with numerous titles. In 1996, *Lovecraft* was awarded the most important comics award in Germany, the Max und Moritz prize at the Internationaler Comic-Salon, Erlangen. His graphic novel on the life of the country musician Johnny Cash saw Kleist also achieve his international breakthrough. *Johnny Cash: I See a Darkness* has been translated into nine languages and repeatedly awarded prizes, including the Sondermann at the Frankfurt Book Fair in 2007, the Max und Moritz prize in 2008, and the Prix des Ados at the literary festival in Deauville, France, in 2009. In 2010 he received nominations for the renowned Eisner Award in America as well as the prestigious Harvey Awards. In 2004 and 2008, Reinhard also received the ICOM prize for his books *Scherbenmund* and *The Secrets of Coney Island*.

As well as being a graphic novelist, Reinhard Kleist is also an illustrator for book publishers, record companies, advertising agencies, magazine editors, and a series of film and TV projects. In 2010, he designed, among other things, an issue of the *Süddeutsche Zeitung Magazin* on the theme of genocide.

As part of preparing for *Castro*, Reinhard Kleist spent four weeks in Cuba in 2008. His impressions and experiences were captured in the graphic non-fiction book *Havanna: Eine kubanische Reise*.

OTHER GRAPHIC NOVELS BY REINHARD KLEIST:

(English)

Johnny Cash: I See a Darkness (Abrams, 2009)

(German)

Lovecraft, with Roland Hueve (Ehapa, 1994)
Dorian, with Roland Hueve (Ehapa, 1996)

Amerika (Jochen Enterprises, 1998)

Fucked (Reprodukt, 2001)
Steeplechase (Reprodukt, 2001)

Das Grauen im Gemäuer (Edition 52, 2002)
Geschichten aus dem Comicgarten, with Fil, Andreas Michalke, Mawil and Oliver Naatz (Berlin Comix, 2002)

Scherbenmund – Berlinoir 1, with Tobias O. Meissner (Edition 52, 2003)
Mord! – Berlinoir 2, with Tobias O. Meissner (Edition 52, 2004)
Narbenstadt – Berlinoir 3, with Tobias O. Meissner (Edition 52, 2008)

Elvis. Eine illustrierte Biografie, with Titus Ackermann u.a. (Ehapa, 2007)
The Secrets of Coney Island (Edition 52, 2007)

Havanna. Eine kubanische Reise (Carlsen, 2008)

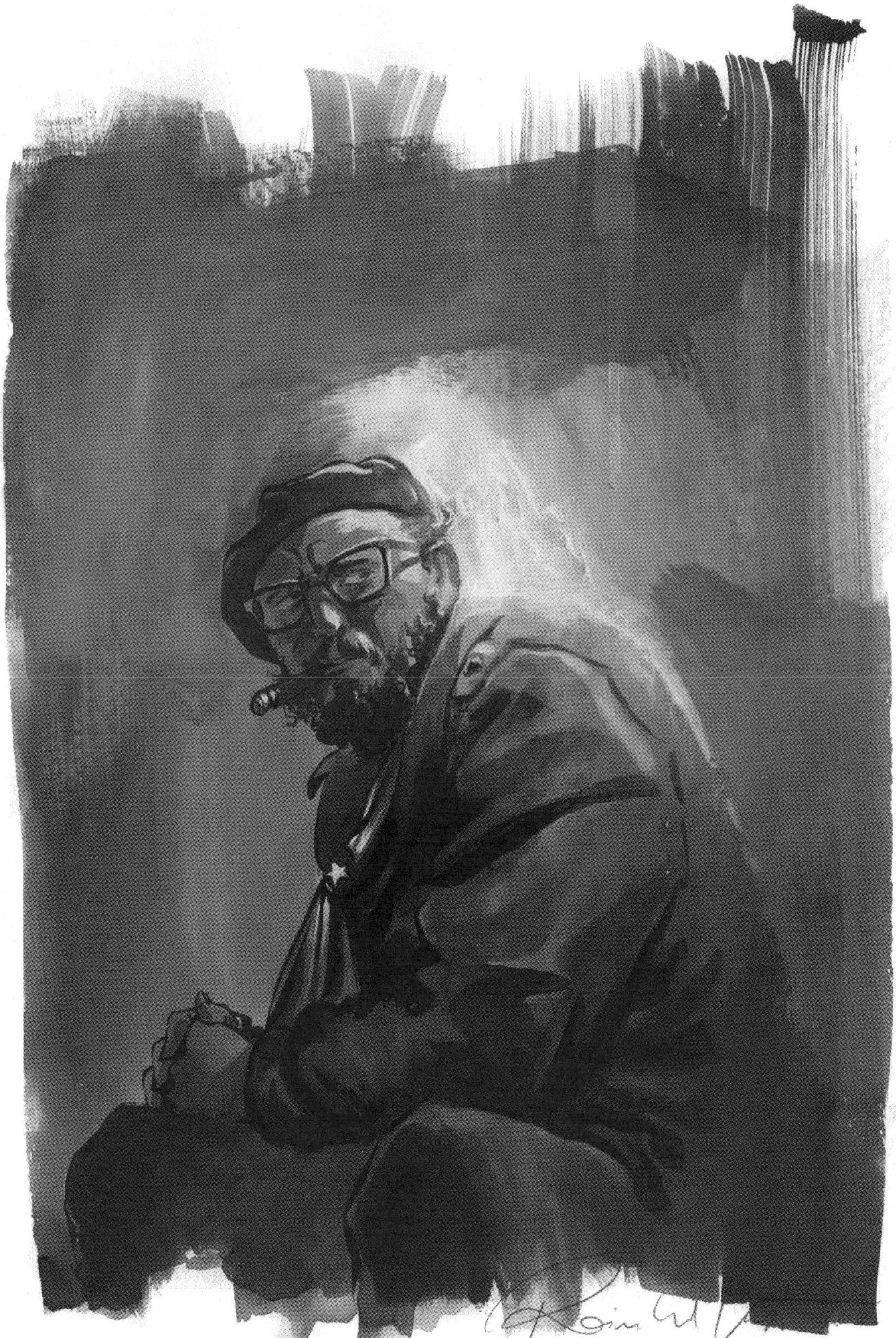

THIS BOOK IS BASED PRIMARILY ON THE FOLLOWING SOURCES:

Documentary and feature films
La Revolución Cubana en Imágenes
Documentary by Adolfo Marino, 2002

El Mérito es Estar Vivo
Documentary by Otto Miguel Guzmán and Ernesto Miró
Orozco, 2006

Fidel Castro. Ewiger Revolutionär
Documentary by Volker Skierka and Stephan Lamby, 2004

Mythos Che Guevara
Documentary by Candida Pinto, 2005

Fidel Castro. Ende einer Ära
Documentary by Adriana Bosch, 2009

Wege der Revolution. Augenblicke mit Fidel
Documentary by Rebeca Chávez, 2004

Memorias del Subdesarrollo
Feature film by Tomás Gutiérrez Alea, 1968

Fidel & Che
Feature film by David Attwood, 2002

Literature
Fidel Castro. Eine Biographie
by Volker Skierka, Munich: Kindler, 2001 /
Reinbek, Hamburg: Rowohlt, 2002
(in English: Fidel Castro: A Biography; Patrick Camiller, trans.,
Malden, MA: Polity, 2004)

Die letzten Diktatoren
by Erich Follath, Hamburg: Rasch & Röhring, 1993

Fidel Castro
by Luciano Garibaldi, Wiesbaden: White Star Verlag, 2007

Unterwegs mit Fidel
by Antonio Núñez Jiménez, Berlin: Dietz Verlag, 1986

Das Leben war ein Pfeifen. Kubanische Fluchten
by Michael Saur and Thomas Schuler, Vienna:
Picus Verlag, 2000

Fidel Castro. Beschreibung einer Revolution
by Enrique Meneses, Esslingen: Bechtle Verlag, 1968
(in English: Fidel Castro, New York: Taplinger, 1968)

Korda sieht Kuba
by Christophe Loviny (ed.), Munich: Kunstmann, 2003
(in English: Cuba: by Korda, Melbourne: Ocean Press, 2006)

Kuba. Bilder einer Revolution
by Harald Falckenberg (ed.), Hamburg: Philo Fine Arts,
2008

Lieber Fidel. Mein Leben, meine Liebe, mein Verrat
by Marita Lorenz and Wilfried Huismann, Munich: List, 2001

Ich, Alina. Mein Leben als Fidel Castros Tochter
by Alina Fernández Revuelta,
Reinbek, Hamburg: Rowohlt, 1999
(in English: Castro's Daughter, An Exile's Memoir of Cuba,
New York: St. Martin's Press, 1997)

Fidel Castro. »Máximo Líder« der kubanischen Revolution
by Peter G. Bourne, Munich: Heyne, 1990
(in English: Fidel: A Biography of Fidel Castro, New York:
Dodd Mead, 1986)

Fidel Castro
by Frank Niess, Reinbek, Hamburg: Rowohlt, 2008

Das tägliche Nichts
by Zoé Valdéz. Munich: btb Verlag, 1998

Der General in seinem Labyrinth
by Gabriel García Márquez,
Cologne: Kiepenheuer & Witsch, 1989
(in English: The General in His Labyrinth; Edith Grossman,
trans., New York: Knopf, 1990)

Che Guevara
by Stephan Lahrem, Frankfurt a. M.: Suhrkamp, 2005

Fidel. Ein privater Blick auf den Máximo Líder
by Jeanette Erazo Heufelder, Frankfurt a. M.: Eichborn,
2004

Cien Imágenes de la Revolución Cubana: 1953 – 1996
by Pedro Alvarez Tabío (ed.),
Havana: Instituto Cubano del Libro, 2004

La Plaza en la Revolución
by Juan Carlos Rodríguez and Marilyn Rodríguez,
Havana: Editorial Capitán San Luis, 2006

Che. Die Biographie
by John Lee Anderson, Munich: List, 1997
(in English: Che Guevara: a Revolutionary Life, New York:
Grove Press, 1997)

Kubanisches Tagebuch
by Ernesto Guevara, Bonn: Pahl-Rugenstein, 1990

Fidel Castro. Mein Leben
by Fidel Castro with Ignacio Ramonet, Berlin: Rotbuch,
2008
(in English: Fidel Castro: My Life: A Spoken Autobiography,
Andrew Hurley, trans., New York: Scribner, 2009)

Fidel Castro. Vaterland oder Tod
by Thomas Mießgang, Cologne: Fackelträger, 2007

Fidel Castro
by Albrecht Hagemann, Munich: Deutscher Taschenbuch
Verlag, 2002

Selbstportrait Che Guevara
by Víctor Casaus (ed.), Cologne: Kiepenheuer & Witsch,
2005
(in English: Self-Portrait: Che Guevara, Melbourne: Ocean
Press, 2004)

Materialien zur Revolution in Reden, Aufsätzen, Briefen
by Fidel Castro, Che Guevara, Regis Debray
Darmstadt: Melzer, 1968